PATIENTS WITH PASSPORTS

Patients with Passports

MEDICAL TOURISM, LAW, AND ETHICS

I. Glenn Cohen

OXFORD

UNIVERSITY PRESS

OXFORD
UNIVERSITY PRESS

Oxford University Press is a department of the University of Oxford. It furthers the University's objective of excellence in research, scholarship, and education by publishing worldwide.

Oxford   New York
Auckland   Cape Town   Dar es Salaam   Hong Kong   Karachi   Kuala Lumpur   Madrid
Melbourne   Mexico City   Nairobi   New Delhi   Shanghai   Taipei   Toronto

With offices in
Argentina   Austria   Brazil   Chile   Czech Republic   France   Greece   Guatemala   Hungary
Italy   Japan   Poland   Portugal   Singapore   South Korea   Switzerland   Thailand
Turkey   Ukraine   Vietnam

Oxford is a registered trademark of Oxford University Press in the UK and certain other countries.

Published in the United States of America by
Oxford University Press
198 Madison Avenue, New York, NY 10016

Library of Congress Cataloging-in-Publication Data
Cohen, I. Glenn, author.
  Patients with passports : medical tourism, law, and ethics / I. Glenn Cohen.
    pages cm
  Includes bibliographical references and index.
  ISBN 978-0-19-997509-9 ((hardback) : alk. paper)—ISBN 978-0-19-021818-8 ((pbk.) : alk. paper)
1. Medical tourism—Law and legislation. 2. Medical tourism—Moral and ethical aspects. I. Title.
  K3607.C64 2014
  362.1—dc23
                                                                                            2014011125

9 8 7 6 5 4 3 2 1

Printed in the United States of America on acid-free paper

Note to Readers
This publication is designed to provide accurate and authoritative information in regard to the subject matter covered. It is based upon sources believed to be accurate and reliable and is intended to be current as of the time it was written. It is sold with the understanding that the publisher is not engaged in rendering legal, accounting, or other professional services. If legal advice or other expert assistance is required, the services of a competent professional person should be sought. Also, to confirm that the information has not been affected or changed by recent developments, traditional legal research techniques should be used, including checking primary sources where appropriate.

(Based on the Declaration of Principles jointly adopted by a Committee of the American Bar Association and a Committee of Publishers and Associations.)

**You may order this or any other Oxford University Press publication
by visiting the Oxford University Press website at www.oup.com**

For J.R., S.S., H.A., and B.M.
...who all mattered to me, perhaps more than you knew.

Contents

Preface

IT HAS BECOME a cliché that the world is getting smaller every day. The people we know, the television we watch, the food we consume, the drugs we take, the clothing we wear is likely, in whole or in part, to come from places outside of our home countries. Up until recently, though, the health care world remained flat. In a prior book I examined the effects of this kind of globalization for health care quite generally, everything from research and development, to brain drain, to telemedicine.[1] This book is about a specific part of that globalization and the patients, doctors, and companies who are its pioneers and in some cases its victims. I will call these patients "medical tourists." I use the term because it is the most common one employed in this nascent literature, though some view it as pejorative. Others call them "medical travelers" or "cross-border health care patients," but I will stick to the more common term without any desire to debase or trivialize them or the reasons they are traveling. I will define them as individuals who travel abroad for the primary purpose of getting health care (as opposed to expatriates who receive care while living abroad, or individuals who get sick on vacation). The first chapter of this book gives a detailed overview of what is known about this industry.

---

[1] THE GLOBALIZATION OF HEALTH CARE: LEGAL AND ETHICAL ISSUES (I. Glenn Cohen ed., 2013).

To introduce medical tourism and get a sense of the varied form of this phenomenon, I begin with the stories (some real, some composites) of people who have used medical tourism and the legal and ethical issues it raises:

I. THE VOICES OF MEDICAL TOURISTS

A. Carl

Carl is one of the estimated 47 million Americans without health insurance. After experiencing the symptoms of angina, he reluctantly sees a cardiologist in his hometown of Milwaukee, whom he pays out-of-pocket. A battery of tests reveals significant atherosclerotic narrowing in several arteries, and the cardiologist recommends bypass surgery. In Milwaukee, bypass surgery purchased out-of-pocket costs somewhere between $48,350 and $73,300 depending on the hospital.[2] Carl can get the same surgery for $10,000 at Bumrungrad Hospital in Bangkok, Thailand, and decides to do so. Unfortunately, he suffers an ischemic stroke (the cutting off of blood supply to the brain) during the procedure. As a result, he experiences partial paralysis in his right arm, moderate speech problems, pain, and depression.

Should the United States have taken steps to discourage Carl from going on his trip? Should it have to have evaluated or pre-cleared the hospital? If Carl believes the stroke to be the result of medical error, he may want to sue the foreign hospital and his doctors in a U.S. court for medical malpractice. Are there barriers in the U.S. legal system that will prevent him from successfully bringing suit? If so, knowing about these difficulties, should (and could) the government have prevented him from getting treated abroad or placed other requirements on foreign providers as a condition of treating him? Would the answers to these questions change if Carl was an EU and not a U.S. citizen? These are questions to do with quality and liability, the topics of Chapters 2 and 3 of this book.

B. Joy and Gary

Joy Guion, thirty-nine years old, was a utility worker in the town of Hickory in the U.S. state of North Carolina. Weighing 238 pounds at 5-foot-9 she was diagnosed with "severe chronic obesity" and has a family history of diabetes and heart disease. She needs gastric sleeve surgery.[3] She worked for HSM, a furniture and auto parts manufacturer in western North Carolina. Gary Harwell, sixty-five, was a retired manager at the same

---

[2] This case is hypothetical but the data I use comes from Guy Boulton, *States Push for Hospital Price Lists, Initiatives Aim to Clarify Billing for Consumers*, MILWAUKEE J. SENTINEL, Oct. 15, 2007, at 1A.

[3] This account is drawn from Byron Pitts & Nikki Battiste, *As More Americans Have Surgeries Overseas, US Companies Consider "Medical Tourism" a Health Care Option*, ABC NEWS/NIGHTLINE (Sept 30, 2013), http://abcnews.go.com/Health/americans-surgeries-overseas-us-companies-medical-tourism-health/story?id=20423011.

plant at which Joy worked. He needed his knee replaced. What they have in common is that both were induced by HSM to leave North Carolina and travel to Costa Rica for their treatment at the same private hospital, the Hospital Clinica Biblica. As reported by ABC news,

> Even with their insurance, both Harwell and Guion said each would have paid $3,000 out of pocket in the U.S.—an amount Guion said she wouldn't have been able to afford. But in Costa Rica, they both pay nothing—their company picks up the bill.

Indeed HSM will not only charge the two nothing, but each will get a "bonus check for at least $2500" from HSM, a "percentage of the corporate savings in insurance costs." HSM can afford to be "generous" in this regard because it stands to save money from this practice. "Outsourcing medical care has saved it nearly $10 million in health care costs over the past five years, according to the company. Close to 250 of its employees have traveled abroad so far for medical care, and more are scheduled to go." HSM takes advantage of the price differential between the U.S. and Costa Rica.

> In the United States, Harwell's knee replacement would have cost more than $50,000. In Costa Rica, it costs half that amount at $23,531. In North Carolina, Guion's gastric sleeve surgery would have cost about $30,000, but in Costa Rice, it comes to $17,386. Both were placed in pristine rooms in state-of-the-art hospitals.

I call this "private insurer prompted" medical tourism. It, too, raises a series of legal and ethical questions I tackle in Chapter 4 of this book: What obligations do home country insurance companies have to insure the quality of the foreign facilities to which they send patients? What kinds of legal liability do they bear when something goes wrong? Does the law regulate what kinds of "deals" they can offer patients as incentives to go abroad, or whether they can even penalize patients who refuse to use medical tourism? Should it? What kind of insurance regulation would be most appropriate?

Chapter 5 examines a different kind of insurance market that interfaces with medical tourism—that of public insurance programs. Most of that chapter examines the ongoing controversies about the circumstances under which home countries must cover care received in another EU Member State, tracing the jurisprudence of the European Court of Justice and a new directive that is currently being transposed into national law. This chapter also examines the potential for medical tourism to become an important part of public financing of retirement. For example, in the United States, can and should Medicare benefits be portable such that an older American can retire in Mexico and use these benefits there?

C. Mr. Steeles

Chapter 6 examines what effects medical tourism of the kind undertaken by Carl, Joy, Gary, and others has on the lives of those in the countries to which they travel, especially in the developed world.

Consider, for example, the case of Mr. Steeles, a "60-year-old car dealer from Daphne, Ala., [who] had flown halfway around the world last month to save his heart [through a mitral valve repair] at a price he could pay" and sought treatment at India's Wockhardt hospital. A *New York Times* article on his care describes in great detail the dietician who selects Mr. Steeles's meals, the dermatologist who comes as soon as he mentions an itch, and his "Royal Suite" with "cable TV, a computer, [and] a mini-refrigerator, where an attendant that afternoon stashed some ice cream, for when he felt hungry later." This treatment contrasts with the care given to a group of "day laborers who laid bricks and mixed cement for Bangalore's construction boom," many of whom "fell ill after drinking illegally brewed whisky; 150 died that day." "Not for them [was] the care of India's best private hospitals," writes the article's author; "[t]hey had been wheeled in by wives and brothers to the overstretched government-run Bowring Hospital, on the other side of town," a hospital with "no intensive care unit, no ventilators, no dialysis machine," where "[d]inner was a stack of white bread, on which a healthy cockroach crawled."[4]

Are such disparities, standing alone, enough to establish a moral problem with medical tourism, or does it matter what effects medical tourism has on care for those in the destination country? Is medical tourism likely to have a positive effect on the economies and health care access for those in the destination country, enabling them to fight physician brain drain and have faster technology diffusion, or is medical tourism sapping doctors away from the public system and causing governments to redirect resources away from public health to support facilities aiming to attract wealthier foreign patients? What, if any, moral responsibility do medical tourists, insurers, and home and destination country governments have for the ill effects that might occur? Chapter 6 tackles these and other tough questions.

All these stories are about medical tourism for services that are legal in the patient's home country and in the country to where they are going. There is a very different side of the industry, which is the focus of Part Two of the book, where patients are traveling abroad to get services that are illegal or unavailable for regulatory reasons at home.

---

[4] Somini Sengupta, *Royal Care for Some of India's Patients, Neglect for Others*, N.Y. TIMES, June 1, 2008, at K3.

D. Akash[5]

Akash is a twenty-four-year-old man living in Dhaka, the capital of Bangladesh. He sees an advertisement run in the *Daily Ittefaq*, the local newspaper, which reads:

Request for Kidney Donation

Both kidneys of a USA resident, Kulsum Begum, are damaged. Kidney specialists advise her to transplant a kidney immediately. A heartfelt request is made to the good persons who can donate a kidney with the following criteria.

1. The interested donor's blood group and the tissue must be matched with those of Kulsum Begum. Blood group O +.

2. The donor (male or female) must travel to the donation. The transplant will be performed at [a U.S. university] medical center.

3. The donor must be in good health and between 19 and 40 years of age.

All the relevant expenses will be covered by Kulsum Begum. To discuss details, contact urgently the following address.

Md Iman Ali, House B-12/7, Agargoan Taltala Government Quarter

Sher-E-Bangla Nagar, Dhaka—1207, Telephone: 8125959.

Akash contacts that number and meets a broker who tells him he wants him to participate in the noble act of kidney donation and promises to cover all expenses and compensate him as well. He tells Akash that the operation is completely safe and that he will be in the hands of a world-renowned specialist. He also tells him the story of "the sleeping kidney," where selling a kidney is presented as a win-win situation in which, by removing one of a person's kidneys, the transplant surgeon "awakens" the other "sleeping kidney" through medication, and the seller is portrayed as living perfectly well with only the one remaining kidney. The broker tells Akash he might even get a job or a visa out of the kidney transplant. The broker also tells Akash that going abroad for transplantation to India will be fun and that he can eat out, shop, and watch Indian movies. He offers Akash 100,000 Taka (US$1,400), but tells him he will not receive the entire amount until just before entering the operating room, for fear the seller might renege.

The broker arranges a fake passport and forged legal documents for Akash that indicate he is donating a kidney to a relative, and advises Akash to hide his identity so the Indian health care personnel do not reject the case. After Akash crosses the Indian border, the broker seizes his passport to ensure that he cannot return to Bangladesh before the kidney is removed. He is housed in poor accommodations, rooming with as many as

---

[5] Akash is a composite of the sellers interviewed in Monir Moniruzzaman, *"Living Cadavers" in Bangladesh: Bioviolence in the Human Organ Bazaar*, 26 MED. ANTHROP. Q. 69 (2012).

ten other sellers in a bachelor apartment rented by the broker. Medical tests are redone because the Indian doctors do not trust the Bangladeshi results.

The day before the operation Akash asks for his promised money, but is now told that he will not be paid until after returning to Bangladesh. After the surgery, Akash notices a twenty-inch scar along his side, which the surgeon could have avoided by using a laparoscopic surgery resulting in a small four-inch incision (but costing an additional US$200). Akash is released from the hospital after five days to a less-than-hygienic apartment. He is returned to Bangladesh within a few days despite the doctors' orders to rest in India. Along the train route his wounds bleed a little.

Upon return, Akash experiences a decline in his health, including psychological suffering, and begins to refer to himself as "handicapped." He experiences pain, weakness, weight loss, and frequent illness. He also has to confront the stigma of a twenty-inch scar. People who see it refer to him as a "kidney man," so he tries to hide it or makes up stories about an accident. The scar also interferes with his eligibility for marriage. He refers to the day of the transplant as his "death day."

Although selling a kidney is typically illegal in the destination country, those laws are often not fully enforced, opening up a black market. Should home countries seek to criminalize the activities of their citizens who go abroad to buy kidneys? Should those patients be denied reimbursement for immunosuppressive drugs as a deterrent, or is that too draconian? Would a regulated kidney market be better than prohibition? What kinds of international and domestic, hard and soft law, would best effectuate a ban? Chapter 7 deals with these and other issues regarding Transplant Tourism.

E. Daniel James[6]

Daniel played rugby for England Youth teams until he suffered a tragic injury during a training session in March 2007: spinal compression leading to dislocation of two vertebrae producing tetraplegia (paralysis from the chest down) and an inability to move his hand or fingers. Although he was determined to prove that the diagnosis was incorrect and to make a substantial recovery, he failed to do so, became suicidal, and began to express the wish that he had died in the accident. He attempted suicide several times, and in February 2008—after his third failed attempt—he contacted the Swiss Clinic, Dignitas, for assistance in dying.

In May 2008, Dignitas accepted his application and arranged for a Swiss doctor to write a barbiturate prescription for Daniel's suicide. After repeated attempts to persuade him to change his mind, Daniel's parents eventually accepted that their son was resigned

---

[6] This account is drawn from Alexandra Mullock, *Commentary: Prosecutors Making (Bad) Law?*, 17 MED. L. REV. 290 (2009); Suzanne Ost, *The De-Medicalisation of Assisted Dying: Is a Less Medicalised Model the Way Forward?*, 18 MED. L. REV. 497 (2010); Richard Huxtable, *The Suicide Tourist Trap: Compromise across Boundaries*, 6 BIOETHICAL INQUIRY 327 (2009).

to ending his life and began assisting him in arranging the suicide abroad. An unnamed family friend who had originally offered to arrange travel abroad to let Daniel see specialists who might assist in his recovery ultimately assisted Daniel's parents in arranging a flight to Zurich for his suicide, although the friend also arranged a return flight to the United Kingdom in case Daniel changed his mind. With the flights booked, Daniel signed a declaration on August 27, 2008, witnessed by his doctor, stating his wish to travel to Switzerland for assisted suicide and his desire that his body be returned to England after he ended his life. On September 12, 2008, accompanied by his parents, Daniel traveled to Zurich. As required by Swiss law, Daniel was evaluated several times for competency to consent and lack of coercion. In the presence of his parents, a doctor assisted him in ending his life—apparently, according to postmortem blood samples, using a fatal dose of a barbiturate.

In the wake of this case, the Director of Public Prosecutions in the United Kingdom declined to prosecute Daniel's parents or the unnamed friend in assisting his suicide, despite a potential legal hook for doing so in English law. Was the prosecutor right to decline to prosecute? If assisting suicide is illegal in a patient's home country, can the home country prosecute someone who assists a patient to end his life in Switzerland, where the practice is legal? As a doctrinal matter? What about as a normative matter? Should the answers be any different if it was a woman leaving Poland or Portugal for the Netherlands to secure an abortion rather than traveling for assisted suicide? These questions are the focus of Chapter 8.

F. Samuel Ghilain[7]

Samuel Ghilain was born in Ukraine to a surrogate commissioned by his intended parents, Laurent Ghilain and Peter Meurrens. The men were married in Belgium, which permits same-sex couples to adopt, but faced administrative difficulties that led them to surrogacy. They hired a gestational surrogate in Ukraine to carry a child created from Ghilain's sperm and the egg of an anonymous egg provider.

Upon the birth of their son in November 2008, Samuel's parents went to the Belgian embassy in Kiev, Ukraine, which refused to recognize the child as a citizen of Belgium. Because Belgian law was silent on the legality of surrogacy, the Belgian government denied Samuel citizenship, reasoning that it had no legal basis to recognize the Ukrainian birth certificate, despite the fact that the child's genetic father was a Belgian citizen. Samuel also could not be a Ukrainian citizen because Ukrainian law recognizes the intended parents as the child's legal parents, so Samuel was neither a Ukrainian nor a Belgian citizen. Without citizenship Samuel could not get a passport and thus could not leave Ukraine.

---

[7] This account is taken from Tina Lin, Note, *Born Lost: Stateless Children in International Surrogacy Arrangements*, 21 Cardozo J. Int'l & Comp. L. 545, 546–48 (2013).

It took two years and three months to resolve the issue, with Samuel placed first with a foster family and then a Ukrainian orphanage until a Belgian court ruled in favor of Samuel's parents, and the Belgian Foreign Ministry finally agreed to give him a passport. At that point, after a long odyssey, Samuel was finally brought back to Belgium. At the same time, his case did not set a precedent for the future: following the resolution of Samuel's citizenship, the Belgian Foreign Ministry issued a press release advising against the hiring of foreign nationals as surrogates because of the difficulties in recognizing the citizenship of the children abroad, and, as of this writing, Belgium has still not passed a law on surrogacy.

How should home countries treat children born through surrogacy or egg or sperm donation abroad when their citizens are the intended parents? If the home country prohibits the form of reproductive technology at use, for example, commercial surrogacy, is it appropriate for it to refuse to grant citizenship to the resulting child to try to deter its citizens from engaging in fertility tourism? Or does that approach unfairly penalize the child? Should the home country at least criminalize the activities of the parents who circumvent domestic law prohibiting certain kinds of reproductive technology by going abroad to a place where it is legal? These and other questions are answered in Chapter 9.

G. C and His Parents [8]

C, eighteen months old, was born with septo-optic dysplasia. The disease is characterized by underdevelopment (hypoplasia) of the optic nerve, and abnormal formation of structures along the midline of the brain and pituitary gland. It is associated with reduced vision in one or both eyes, unusual side-to-side eye movements (nystagmus) and other eye abnormalities, abnormal brain development that can lead to intellectual disability and other neurological problems, and slow growth and unusually short stature, among other symptoms.[9] C's parents took him to China for an experimental stem cell therapy. As they describe their motivations:

> C was only 18 months old, his health was deteriorating, we had been told numerous times when C was admitted to the hospital, "All we can do for C is to try to stabalize [sic] him and try to level out his blood sugars because there is no treatments available for his disorders." For us as a family the reality was do we continually risk C dieing [sic] in a hospital in the United States where there is no treatment or do we risk an unproven, experimental treatment in China that may give him a

---

[8] This account comes from Haidan Chen & Herbert Gottweis, *Stem Cell Treatments in China: Rethinking the Patient Role in the Global Bio-Economy*, 27 BIOETHICS 194 (2013).

[9] NIH, NATIONAL LIBRARY OF MEDICINE, GENETICS HOME REFERENCE, *What Is Septo-optic Dysplasia, available at* http://ghr.nlm.nih.gov/condition/septo-optic-dysplasia (last visited May 3, 2014).

better Quality of Life! We are extremely thankful that C was accepted for umbilical stem cell treatments in China.

If, as we will see is true of most stem cell therapies, there is no scientific evidence that these therapies work and some evidence that they pose risks, what attitude should the home country take to these therapies? Should adults who believe this is in their best interests be allowed to go abroad and get these therapies? Should the companies be allowed to advertise these therapies and recruit patients in the home country? In the case of parents taking their children, should social services become involved if they feel these therapies are potentially harmful to the children? What are the reporting responsibilities of doctors treating these children in the home country? Are there ways of incentivizing these foreign clinics to conduct rigorous clinical trials and share their data, rather than continuing on in an unproven and largely clandestine way? These and other topics are covered in Chapter 10.

II. ACKNOWLEDGMENTS

Writing this book took me around the world to legal and medical cultures as distant as Korea and Barbados. I met with government, industry leaders, doctors, lawyers, and public health experts too numerous to mention, to try to get a sense of this industry. This book is the culmination of those conversations and experiences.

I have three groups of people to thank.

The first are those who gave me comments on chapters in this book or the law review, bioethics, and medical journal articles that are its precursors; some of this book is adapted from work I did in *Protecting Patients with Passports: Medical Tourism, Medical Tourism and the Patient-Protective Argument*, 95 IOWA L. REV. 1467 (2010); *Medical Tourism: The View from Ten Thousand Feet*, 40 HASTINGS CENTER REPORT, Mar.–Apr. 2010, at 11–12; *Medical Tourism, Access to Health Care, and Global Justice*, 52 VA J. INT'L L. 1 (2011); *Circumvention Tourism*, 97 CORNELL L. REV. 1309 (2012); *How to Regulate Medical Tourism (and Why Bioethicists Should Care?)*, 12 J. DEVELOPING WORLD BIOETHICS 9 (2012); *Transplant Tourism: The Ethics and Regulation of International Markets for Organs*, 41 J. L. MED. & ETHICS 269 (2013); *Ethical and Legal Implications of the Risks of Medical Tourism for Patients: A Qualitative Study of Canadian Health and Safety Representatives' Perspectives*, 3 BRITISH MED. J. OPEN e002302 (2013) (coauthored with several others).

In this category I thank the following people:

Bill Alford, Anne Alstott, Susan Appleton, Ronen Avraham, Hans Baade, Miriam Baer, Betsy Bartholet, Gabriella Blum, John Blum, David Boucher, Rachel Brewster, Michael Cahill, Cansu Cana, Hector Carillo, Tim Caulfield,

YY Chen, Brietta Clark, Anthony Colangelo, Grainne De Burca, John Deigh, Einer Elhauge, Nita Farahany, Lilian Faulhaber, Marcelo Rodriguez Ferrere, Kim Ferzan, Chad Flanders, Colleen Flood, Dov Fox, Michael Frakes, Ann Freedman, Charles Fried, Jesse Fried, Stavros Gadinis, John Goldberg, Bryna Goodman, Michele Goodwin, Larry Gostin, Tim Greaney, Jim Greiner, Janet Halley, Adil Haque, Jill Hasday, Tamara Hervey, Allison Hoffman, Bert Huang, Kyron Huigens, Insoo Hyun, Rory Johnston, Jonathan Kahn, Joshua Kleinfeld, Adriaan Lanni, Trudo Lemmens, Katerina Linos, Pablo de Lora, Holly Fernandez Lynch, Kristin Madison, Anup Malani, Dan Markel, John O. McGinnis, Lisa McGirr, Michelle Meyer, Frank Michelman, Martha Minow, Abigail Moncrieff, Kelly Mullholand, Andrea Mulligan, Kim Mutcherson, Gerald Neuman, Kevin Outterson, Vijay Padmanabhan, Thad Pope, Katherine Pratt, Mike Raavin, Naveen Rao, Morris Ratner, Mathias Risse, Chris Robertson, John Robertson, Ben Roin, Rand Rosenblatt, Bill Rubenstein, Ben Sachs, Bill Sage, Brendan Salonger, Jed Shugerman, Charles Silver, Aaron Simowitz, Joseph Singer, Robert Sitkoff, Jeff Skopek, Jeremy Snyder, Rayman Solomon, Larry Solum, Carol Steiker, Allan Stein, Paul Steinhardt, Matthew Stephenson, Richard Storrow, Jeannie Suk, Talha Syed, Nick Terry, Leigh Turner, Detlev Vagts, Judith Vichniac, Carlos Vasquez, Alec Walen, Rebecca Walkowitz, Stephen M. Weiner, Doug Williams, Mark Wu, and Jonathan Zittrain for comments on earlier drafts. I also want to give particular thanks to Nathan Cortez, who gave me comments on almost everything I have written in this book and whose own work has influenced and inspired me.

This work also benefitted from many public presentations. I thank participants at the Petrie–Flom Health Law Policy, Biotechnology, & Bioethics Workshop at Harvard Law School on November 6, 2008; at the Annual Conference of the American Society for Law, Medicine & Ethics on June 6, 2009; at the Faculty Workshop at Loyola Law School on September 3, 2009; at the Health Law Scholars Workshop of the American Society for Law, Medicine & Ethics at the St. Louis University School of Law Center for Health Law Studies on September 12, 2009; at the Harvard Law School Faculty Workshop on November 30, 2009; at the International Conference on Ethical Issues in Medical Tourism at Simon Fraser University on June 25, 2010; at the Harvard Law School Program on Ethics and Health Population-Level Bioethics Reading Group on January 6, 2011; at the Harvard Law School Petrie-Flom Center Health Law Workshop on April 18, 2011; at the Harvard Law School Petrie-Flom Center Globalization of Health Care Conference on May 21, 2011; at the ASLME Health Law Professors Conference on June 11, 2011; at the NYU/Brooklyn Law School Criminal Law Theory Workshop on September 15, 2011; at the University of Texas at Austin Faculty Workshop on October 28, 2011; at the Rutgers Law School Faculty Workshop on February 28, 2012; at the 2012 National Health Conference in Toronto, Canada, on May 4 and 5, 2012; at the Tel Aviv University Law School Faculty Workshop on June 6, 2012; at the Hamline University

School of Law Health Law Institute Colloquium Series on October 11, 2012; at the Northwestern Law, Philosophy, and Legal Theory Colloquium on October 15, 2013; at the University of Minnesota Public Law Workshop on October 17, 2013; and at the St. Louis University Law School Faculty Workshop on March 1, 2014.

Second, I need to thank my remarkable research assistants: Mollie Bracewell, Joseph Brothers, Annaleigh Curtis, Cormac Early, Erik Graham-Smith, Mischa Feldstein, Irene Sobrino Guijarro, Roxanna Haghihat, Katherine Hicks, Russell Kornblith, Katherine Kraschel, Shengxi Li, Teel Lidow, Rebecca Livengood, Justin McAdams, Keely O'Malley, Patrick McKeown, Sophia Chua-Rubenfeld, Yoni Schenker, Lisa Sullivan, and Desta Tedros. Two of them read almost every word of this book and deserve particular thanks: Gabrielle Hodgson and Adam Johnson. I also give great thanks to my assistant Kaitlin Burroughs.

Third, I am extremely grateful to the organizations that funded me. Much of this book was written while I was a fellow at the Radcliffe Institute from 2012 to 2013. I also received significant funding to carry out this work from the Greenwall Foundation, which named me a faculty scholar in bioethics from 2012 to 2015. I thank the Women's College Hospital Institute for Health System Solutions and Virtual Care for supporting me for the month of August 2013. Finally, I have to thank Harvard Law School, which has supported me as I have written this work.

In the interests of full disclosure I also should mention that I attended some events with funding from stakeholders—the government of Korea, through its KHIDI program, invited me to lecture at the Medical Korea conference in Seoul on April 13, 2011, and paid me an honorarium; the government of Malaysia through the Malaysia Health Care Travel Council paid my travel expenses to attend their 2013 medical tourism conference in Kuala Lumpur and to tour hospitals in other regions; and *Scientific American* paid me an honorarium to participate in an event in New York City on medical tourism in co-sponsorship with the Malaysia Health Care Travel Council. Although I have endeavored to avoid having any of this influence my judgments in this book, sunlight is the best disinfectant.

* * *

Medical tourism is a fast-evolving area. On June 26, 2014, after this book was typeset but before it went to print, the European Court of Human Rights issued a Chamber Judgment (not final) in two cases *Mennesson v. France* (application no. 65192/11) and *Labassee v. France* (no. 65941/11), the first of which I discuss in Chapter 9 of this book.[10] While it was too late to update that Chapter, the Press has generously allowed me to add a few words on the case here:

The Mennessons are a French couple who, due to infertility and the fact that France banned surrogacy on its own soil, employed a surrogate mother in California, USA. The

---

[10] I am drawing here from Registrar of the Court, European Court of Human Rights, *Press Release, Totally prohibiting the establishment of a relationship between a father and his biological children born following surrogacy arrangements abroad was in breach of the Convention* (June 26, 2014).

couple implanted an embryo (fertilized by the French father's sperm) into the paid surrogate, leading to the birth of twins. While the Mennessons were recognized by the US government as the parents, the French authorities sought to block recognition of them as French citizens and the paternity and maternity of the French would-be parents in France.

After significant litigation, the case made its way up to the European Court of Human Rights. The Court found that Article 8 of the European Convention on Human Rights, the right to respect for private and family life, had been violated at least in the case of a French biological father. To quote from the press release on the decision:

> [W]ith regard to the twins' right to respect for their private life, the Court noted that they were in a state of legal uncertainty: the French authorities, although aware that the twins had been identified in another country as the children of Mr and Mrs Mennesson, had nevertheless denied them that status under French law. The Court considered that this contradiction undermined the children's identity within French society. Moreover, although their biological father was French, they faced worrying uncertainty as to the possibility of obtaining French nationality, a situation that was liable to have negative repercussions on the definition of their own identity.... In thus preventing the recognition and establishment of the children's legal relationship with their biological father, the French State had overstepped the permissible margin of appreciation. The Court held that the children's right to respect for their private life had been infringed, in breach of Article 8.

This decision, if it becomes final, will likely force the hand of many countries in Europe described in Chapter 9 who refuse to recognize the citizenship of the children born in these circumstances. While I have no strong view as to whether this result was the correct one at a doctrinal level of interpreting the Convention, for the reasons I offer in Chapter 9 I disagree with some of the conclusions from a bioethical and political philosophical perspective. By framing the question as one of the best interests of children and playing on our repulsion at children suffering from parental misdeeds, the Court makes a very rhetorically powerful case for its position. However, as I explain in Chapter 9, it is unclear if that rhetoric withstands scrutiny. In particular, I think that in some circumstances where home countries criminalize commercial surrogacy at home and extraterritorially it may be appropriate to also deny citizenship to children formed through commercial surrogacy done abroad.

1

An Introduction to the Medical Tourism Industry

BEFORE WE CAN wrestle with the many legal and ethical issues raised by medical tourism, we need a better understanding of the industry, its scope, and its components. This chapter aims to put flesh on the bone. I begin by offering a taxonomy of kinds of medical tourism. I then discuss the major components of the industry: traveling patients, destination country hospitals and health care workers, destination country governments with a hand in medical tourism, facilitators (also called "intermediaries" in some parts of the literature), insurers covering the practice, accreditors, and home country hospitals that partner with destination country hospitals. This is a lot of ground to cover, and merely mapping the industry in this way could fill up a book on its own. For that reason, I will focus my discussion on the pieces that are most relevant to the legal and ethical discussions that follow, in many cases taking a 10,000-foot view.

One general caution that I will repeat throughout this book is worth emphasizing upfront: throughout this chapter and this book, I will mention the best available numbers on patient flow, costs, etc. These numbers should be taken with a heavy grain of salt. Much of the data is based on self-reporting by destination country governments or hospitals that have reasons to want to inflate their numbers when it comes to patient flow and lowball them when it comes to costs. Few of these numbers are audited. To make matters worse, in many instances, estimates are based on extrapolations from small pools of existing data. As with all modeling, the bodies are buried deep in modeling assumptions that may not be apparent.

I. KINDS OF MEDICAL TOURISM

John Berger once wrote that "[n]ever again will a single story be told as though it's the only one," and I take that advice to heart when I try to divvy up various forms of medical tourism.[1] Perhaps more iconically, Wallace Stevens titled a famous poem "Thirteen Ways of Looking at a Blackbird";[2] although I will not propose a full thirteen ways of viewing the industry, I want to offer three different ways of dividing the industry as a way of introducing it: by the legal status of the treatment, by the payer type, and by the direction of patient flow.

A. Dividing the Industry by Legal Status of Treatment

The first division, which mirrors the way I have divided this book, is by the legal status of the treatment. There are treatments for services that are legal in the patient's home country *and* destination country, such as hip replacements, cardiac bypass, cosmetic surgery, etc. This is the subject of Part One of this book. Then there is medical tourism for services that are illegal in *both* the patient's home and destination country, but where travel abroad may facilitate receiving the treatment due to laxer destination country enforcement. Transplant tourism, the subject of Chapter 7, is one of the best examples of this part of the industry. Finally, there is medical tourism for services illegal (or unavailable due to regulatory restrictions) in the patient's home country but legal in the destination country, what I call "circumvention tourism." Most of Part Two of this book is about this kind of travel, with chapters on travel for abortion, assisted suicide, some forms of reproductive technology usage, and stem cell therapies.

B. Dividing the Industry by Payer Type

We can also analyze medical tourism based on who pays for the procedure. Doing so generates a tripartite division.

i. Patients Paying Out-of-Pocket

First, we have patients paying out-of-pocket.

Medical tourism for services illegal in the patient's home country will almost always involve patients who are paying their own costs. Thus, the services described in Part Two of this book are almost always paid for by patients directly out-of-pocket. But the same may also be true of some patients who purchase services that are legal in their home country, the topic of Part One of the book.

---

[1] JOHN BERGER, G. 129 (1972).

[2] Wallace Stevens, *Thirteen Ways of Looking at a Blackbird* (1917), *available at* http://www.poetryfoundation. org/poem/174503.

In the United States, the uninsured represent one large group who may find medical tourism an attractive way of covering health care they cannot afford or choose not to consume at the high domestic rates. The most recent U.S. census estimated that approximately fifty million U.S. residents were uninsured at some point in 2010.[3] Since the Affordable Care Act, sometimes referred to as "ObamaCare," was passed, that number dipped to approximately 48.6 million in 2011, and it is now projected that by 2016 there will be approximately 30 million uninsured individuals in the United States, although many will be undocumented immigrants.[4]

These individuals may consider medical tourism for non-emergency care, in part because of cost savings. To illustrate, let me offer a pricing chart based on one set of estimates from the National Center for Policy Analysis in 2007 and another from data compiled by Neil Lunt in March 2011—I emphasize here once again that these numbers, like most others you see bandied about in the industry, should be taken with a heavy grain of salt, but they can hopefully give a sense of magnitude, if not precise points:

TABLE 1.1-A

NATIONAL CENTER FOR POLICY ANALYSIS ESTIMATES OF COSTS FOR COMMON PROCEDURES FOR U.S. PATIENTS AT HOME AND ABROAD[5]

Procedure	U.S. Retail Price	U.S Insurers' Cost	India	Thailand	Singapore
Angioplasty	$98,618	$44,268	$11,000	$13,000	$13,000
Heart bypass	$210,842	$94,277	$10,000	$12,000	$20,000
Heart-valve replacement (single)	$274,395	$122,969	$9,500	$10,500	$13,000
Hip replacement	$75,399	$31,485	$9,000	$12,000	$12,000
Knee replacement	$69,991	$30,358	$8,500	$10,000	$13,000
Gastric bypass	$82,646	$47,735	$11,000	$15,000	$15,000
Spinal fusion	$108,127	$43,576	$5,500	$7,000	$9,000
Mastectomy	$40,832	$16,833	$7,500	$9,000	$12,400

[3] CARMEN DENAVAS-WALT ET AL., U.S. CENSUS BUREAU, INCOME, POVERTY, AND HEALTH INSURANCE COVERAGE IN THE UNITED STATES: 2011, at 21 (2012).

[4] *Id.*; Rachel Nardin et al., *The Uninsured after Implementation of the Affordable Care Act: A Demographic and Geographic Analysis*, HEALTH AFFAIRS BLOG (June 6, 2013), http://healthaffairs.org/blog/2013/06/06/the-uninsured-after-implementation-of-the-affordable-care-act-a-demographic-and-geographic-analysis/.

[5] Devon M. Herrick, Nat'l Ctr. for Policy Analysis, *Medical Tourism: Global Competition in Health Care*, at 11 Table 1 (2007), *available at* http://www.ncpa.org/pdfs/st304.pdf (relying on data from Unmesh Kher, *Outsourcing Your Heart*, TIME.COM, at 44 (May 21, 2006), *available at* http://www.time.com/time/magazine/article/0,9171,1196429,00.html).

TABLE 1.1-B

LUNT ET AL. ESTIMATES OF COSTS FOR COMMON PROCEDURES FOR U.S. PATIENTS AT HOME AND ABROAD[6]

Procedure	US	India	Thailand	Singapore	Malaysia	Mexico	Cuba	Poland	Hungary	UK
Heart bypass (CABG)	113 000	10 000	13 000	20 000	9 000	3 250		7 140		13 921
Heart Valve replacement	150 000	9 500	11 000	13 000	9 000	18 000		9 520		
Angioplasty	47 000	11 000	10 000	13 000	11 000	15 000		7 300		8 000
Hip replacement	47 000	9 000	12 000	11 000	10 000	17 300		6 120	7 500	12 000
Knee replacement	48 000	8 500	10 000	13 000	8 000	14 650		6 375		10 162
Gastric bypass	35 000	11 000	15 000	20 000	13 000	8 000		11 069		
Hip resurfacing	47 000	8 250	10 000	12 000	12 500	12 500		7 905		
Spinal fusion	43 000	5 500	7 000	9 000		15 000				
Mastectomy	17 000	7 500	9 000	12 400		7 500				
Rhinoplasty	4 500	2 000	2 500	4 375	2 083	3 200	1 535	1 700	2 858	3 500
Tummy tuck	6 400	2 900	3 500	6 250	3 903	3 000	1 831	3 500	3 136	4 810
Breast reduction	5 200	2 500	3 750	8 000	3 343	3 000	1 668	3 146	3 490	5 075
Breast implants	6 000	2 200	2 600	8 000	3 308	2 500	1 248	5 243	3 871	4 350
Crown	385	180	243	400	250	300		246	322	330
Tooth whitening	289	100	100		400	350		174	350	500
Dental implants	1 188	1 100	1 429	1 500	2 636	950		953	650	1 600

[6] NEIL LUNT et al., Medical Tourism: Treatments, Markets and Health System Implications: A Scoping Review, at 12 Table 1 (Organization for Economic Co-operation and Development 2011), *available at* http://www.oecd.org/els/health-systems/48723982.pdf. (Lunt's US. Prices appear to be the out-of-pocket price and not the insured price, though he is not explicit on this.)

The National Center for Policy Analysis data pertains to the types of surgical procedures that are typically covered by health insurance in the United States. While those without health insurance at all are a significant set of consumers for medical tourism in the United States, there is a second set of potential consumers paying out-of-pocket for medical care abroad who are *functionally uninsured as to a particular service*, many of which are covered in Lunt's data. There are services such as cosmetic surgery (Lunt's data includes rhinoplasty, tummy tuck, breast reduction, and breast implants) that are not covered by typical health insurance plans, as well as dental services (crowns, tooth whitening, and dental implants from Lunt's data) that may be part of a separate dental insurance plan in the United States, for which patients will pay separately.

Beyond the uninsured (whether in general or simply uninsured as to specific procedures) a third set of U.S. out-of-pocket medical tourism consumers are the *under*insured. The work of Cathy Schoen and others shows that underinsurance—health plans with high deductibles, patient cost sharing, and/or a restricted scope of benefits—may be just as significant a problem to accessing good quality care.[7] Schoen and her colleagues found that, in 2003, sixteen million Americans ages nineteen to sixty-four who had health insurance were underinsured, and that these individuals were significantly more likely to go without care because of costs, lack of confidence that high-quality care would be available when needed, and negative experiences with care actually received. They also found that nearly half of underinsured adults had been contacted by a collection agency in that year for medical bills and just more than a third reported they had to change their way of life dramatically to pay for medical bills (including increased credit-card debt, taking out further mortgages against their home, etc.). All of these findings were most acute among sicker adults.

Although we cannot pinpoint exactly how many U.S. users of medical tourism are uninsured or underinsured, there is good evidence that many in this population will be attracted to medical tourism. In 2007, Arnold Milstein and Mark Smith conducted a U.S. nationwide representative sample of 1003 Americans that showed how cost savings might motivate many Americans to use medical tourism.[8] Focusing on a 148-household subsample that had sick family members (and thus most likely to be near-term hospital users) they asked,

> How much savings do you think would cause the sicker person (in your household)
> to agree to obtain major, nonemergency surgery at a very good hospital outside the

---

[7] This information comes from Cathy Schoen et al., *Insured but Not Protected: How Many Adults Are Underinsured?*, W5 HEALTH AFF. 289, 289, 295–96 (2005), *available at* http://content.healthaffairs.org/cgi/content/abstract/hlthaff.w5.289. The U.S. health reform, colloquially referred to as ObamaCare, will alter these numbers somewhat.

[8] This data is taken from Arnold Milstein & Mark Smith, *Will the Surgical World Become Flat?*, 26 HEALTH AFF. 137, 139–40 (2007).

United States (for example, in Thailand, India, or Mexico) by a good surgeon who was trained in the United States, England, or Canada and speaks English or the patient's language?

For respondents who self-identified as uninsured or stressed by spending, at $500–$999 of savings roughly 10 percent would go abroad, at $1000–$2400 roughly 25 percent, and at $5000–$9996 approximately 35 percent. For those who did not self-identify as such, at $500–$999 of savings, roughly 10 percent would go abroad, at $1000–$2400 still roughly only 10 percent, and at $5000–$9996 approximately 20 percent would go abroad. This suggests that there is significant room for the industry to grow in attracting American medical tourists, although there is a ceiling effect in that only about a quarter of all Americans currently have passports.[9]

Outside the United States, where patients tend to have robust universal health care coverage in their home country, waiting times are a major driver for those patients who travel abroad and pay out-of-pocket.[10] Focusing on waiting lists in the United Kingdom, for example, Lunt and coauthors suggest that "[i]f one takes the waiting lists for a selected number of procedures suitable for medical tourism, and compares the cost of sending those patients (plus an accompanying adult) to India, with the costs of getting treatment in the UK, the savings would be of the order of £120 million." This is above and beyond the fact that wait times would be eliminated. The following table reproduces Lunt's calculations, but it is important to note that, for some procedures (angioplasty, hernia, etc.), the researchers conclude that the costs of going abroad are not worth it.

Finally, some individuals may decide to travel abroad and pay out-of-pocket for quality reasons. Ronald Labonté finds that the "[t]he reputation of physicians and quality of the facilities compete with cost for most frequently cited reasons for medical travel,"[11] and notes that "[r]eputation and quality are prominent in web-sites which, whenever possible, reference the Western licensing and training of medical facilities, and their facilities' international accreditation by…Joint Commission International (JCI)." JCI, an accrediting body we will discuss below, "has been responsible for accrediting more

---

[9] *E.g.*, Frederic Charles Schaffer & Tova Andrea Wang, *Is Everyone Else Doing It? Indiana's Voter Identification Law in International Perspective*, 3 Harv. L. & Pol'y Rev. 397, 401 n.25 (2009).

[10] *See, e.g.*, Valorie Crooks et al., *What Is Known about the Patient's Experience of Medical Tourism? A Scoping Review*, 10 BMC Health Serv. Res. 266, 266 (2010), *available at* http://www.biomedcentral.com/content/pdf/1472-6963-10-266.pdf (noting that, in addition to cost, "[t]he other most frequently noted push factor was that of wait-times, with the promise of more timely care in other countries potentially drawing them abroad." *Id.* at 270.); Neil Lunt et al., Medical Tourism: Treatments, Markets and Health System Implications: A Scoping Review, at 15, 31, *available at* http://www.oecd.org/els/health-systems/48723982.pdf

[11] Ronald Labonté, *Overview: Medical Tourism Today: What, Who, Why and Where?, in* 4 Travelling Well: Essays in Medical Tourism, Transdisciplinary Studies in Population Health Series 6, 12 (Ronald Labonté, Vivien Runnels, Corinne Packer & Raywat Deonandan eds., 2013).

TABLE 1.1-C

LUNT ET AL. ESTIMATES OF COSTS FOR PATIENT FOR ONE ACCOMPANYING PERSON TRAVELING AS AGAINST WAITING LISTS AND SAVINGS TO UK[12]

Procedure	Cost UK (£)[a]	Cost procedure India (£)[b]	Cost of flight[c]	Hotel Stay[d]	Total cost India	Cost saved per operation (£)	Waiting list[e]	Total saved (£)
CABG	8,631	3,413	1000	230	4,643	3,988	97	386836
Coronary angioplasty	2,269	2,363	1000	69	3,432	−1,163	25,241	Not worth it
Total hip replacement	8,811	3,413	1000	322	4,735	4,076	28,800	117,388,800
Total knee re lacement	6,377	5,145	1000	161	6,306	71	53,911	3,827,681
Femoral hernia repair	1,595	819	1000	69	1,888	−293	1,686	Not worth it
Inguinal hernia repair	1,595	717	1000	46	1,763	−168	65,064	Not worth it
Total								121,603,317

[a] NHS reference costs 2007–2008

[b] From Fortis Healthcare Mohali (JCI accredited)

[c] From British Airways, two weeks in advance of flying (i.e. 30th of September)

[d] Used exchange rate E-1.89.7 Rp£23/night in Mohall (where Fortis is), luxury accommodation (Imperial Hotel Mohali).

[e] Obtained from Hospital Episode Statistics, Main procedures and operations 2007–2008

than 400 medical facilities in over 50 countries across Asia, Europe, the Middle East, the Caribbean and South America," a number reflecting nearly a fourfold increase in the past decade.[13] In selling their quality, foreign hospitals, facilities, and governments typically tout their JCI accreditation, the fact that many of their staff members are foreign-trained health care providers that have been deemed qualified to practice in the United States, and collaborations with U.S. medical centers of excellence such as the Mayo Clinic and Harvard Partners International.[14]

A related but separate type of "quality" shopping is where a technique is not yet available or has not yet been approved in the home country but is available abroad. The

[12] LUNT ET AL., *supra* note 8, at 31 Table 2.

[13] *Id.*

[14] *See* I. Glenn Cohen, *Protecting Patients with Passports: Medical Tourism and the Patient-Protective Argument*, *95* IOWA L. REV. 1467, 1484–85 (2010); Labonté, *supra* note 9, at 13.

examples are plentiful: before the Food and Drug Administration approved hip resurfacing in 2006, some U.S. citizens went abroad to Canada, Europe, and Asia for the procedure; the Indian Wockhardt Group of hospitals claims to have performed the first COPCAB (conscious, off-pump coronary artery bypass), a heart surgery designed for patients that were poor candidates for surgery using anesthesia; the Cuban Clinic Cira Garcia offers a unique procedure for retinitis pigmentose (night blindness); and Thai hospitals became very adept at gender reassignment surgery during the 1970s.[15]

Much of the out-of-pocket trade is mediated by "facilitators," sometimes called "intermediaries"—for-profit health care middlemen who attract patients for destination country hospitals and manage the patient's selection of a hospital and physician, travel abroad, transmission of records, follow-up care, etc. In the next part of this chapter, I describe these facilitators in much greater depth.

ii. Patients Whose Medical Tourism Is Covered by Private Insurers

Some patients with private health insurance engage in medical tourism that is paid for by their insurer, especially in the United States: the four largest commercial insurers in the United States (UnitedHealth, WellPoint, Aetna, and Humana) have either introduced medical tourism pilot programs or are considering it; BlueCross BlueShield of South Carolina contracted with a hospital in Bangkok, Thailand, to perform certain surgeries; two hundred U.S. employers offer a network of foreign providers through BasicPlus Health Insurance, which sells group plans and contracts with medical tourism facilitator Companion Global Healthcare; and United Group Programs, a third-party insurance administrator, has contracted to outsource surgeries for at least forty U.S. companies.[16]

This kind of medical tourism is the focus of Chapter 4 of the book. For private insurers and their patients, as I will discuss in greater depth in that chapter, cost is once again a major motivator. If we return to the data presented in Table 1.1-A above, we can see that while U.S. health insurers pay less for (for example) a hip replacement than the price paid by uninsured individuals paying out-of-pocket—in part because of insurers' market force in negotiating rates—the insurer would still pay about two-and-a-half times less if the patient went to Thailand. For insurers with large numbers of covered patients, the aggregation of these smaller savings across a large number of patients will result in a dramatic cost savings. Private insurers therefore have an incentive to get their covered populations to use medical tourism. As I will discuss more fully in Chapter 4, this has caused them to experiment with schemes through which they share some of their savings with the covered patients as an incentive to go abroad through deductible waivers, lower copays, and other mechanisms. But, as we will see, existing regulation of the health

---

[15] Cohen, *supra* note 11, at 1483; Labonté, *supra* note 9, at 13.
[16] Nathan Cortez, *Embracing the New Geography of Health Care: A Novel Way to Cover Those Left Out of Health Reform*, *84* S. CAL. L. REV. 859, 882–83 (2011).

insurance market cabins some of their room for experimentation, and this form of medical tourism raises new legal and ethical issues as well.

Even the *threat* of relying on medical tourism can prove to be a potent lever in negotiating prices within the home country. For example, in the United States in 2008, Hannaford Brothers, operator of 160 supermarkets, offered its nine thousand employees the option of traveling to Singapore for surgery, with the incentive that it would "work with insurer Aetna to pay 100% of the patient costs."[17] The *Wall Street Journal*'s reporting on Hannaford's program prompted a U.S. insurer to offer Hannaford coverage "for comparably priced operations in the U.S.," thus enabling employees to travel to "other parts of the U.S." rather than Singapore, while the company realized the same cost savings.[18] In other instances, the threat of medical tourism may be used to get concessions in the local health insurance market.

iii. Patients Whose Medical Tourism Is Covered by Public Insurers (Home Country Governments)

It is not just private insurers that are covering or incentivizing patients to travel abroad for health care. As I will discuss in Chapter 5, European Jurisprudence and now a new European Directive has long instantiated a regime of cross-border care within the European Union. This regime is what I focus on in this portion of the book, in part because it is the largest form of medical tourism involving public insurance. By one estimate, in 2007, 4 percent of Europeans received health care outside of their home country, 53 percent of Europeans said they would be willing to travel abroad for medical treatment,[19] and a study of German patients enrolled in a nationwide insurance plan found that 40 percent of patients had obtained non-urgent care in another EU country in 2008, which was up from 7 percent in 2003.[20] As with those paying out-of-pocket, waiting times and quality were a significant driver. For example, one study of EU citizens

---

[17] Bruce Einhorn, *Hannaford's Medical-Tourism Experiment*, Bus. Wk. (Nov. 9, 2008), http://www.businessweek.com/stories/2008-11-09/hannafords-medical-tourism-experimentbusinessweek-business-news-stock-market-and-financial-advice.

[18] *Id.*

[19] Chantal Blouin, *The Impact of Trade Treaties on Health Tourism, in* Travelling Well, *supra* note 9, at 178, 184 (citing Irene A. Glinos & Rita Baeten, A Literature Review of Cross-Border Patient Mobility in the European Union (Observatoire Social Européen 2006), *available at* http://www.ose.be/files/publication/health/WP12_lit_review_final.pdf; The Gallup Organization, Hungary, Cross-Border Health Services in the EU: Analytical Report (2007), *available at* http://ec.europa.eu/public_opinion/flash/fl_210_en.pdf).

[20] Richard D. Smith et al., *Medical Tourism, the European Way, in* Risks & Challenges in Medical Tourism: Understanding the Global Market for Health Services 37, 40 (Jill R. Hodges, Leigh Turner & Ann Marie Kimball eds., 2012). That said, these authors also caution that for Europe "accurate statistics on patients moving across borders are almost nonexistent," and that "national health systems did not systematically record provision of health care to foreign patients, and that even when foreign patients were documented, the information was sometimes lost or details were missing." *Id.*

from other Member States who traveled to the Netherlands for health care reported that "almost 90% of respondents declared faster access to health care as a reason," while "78% of respondents said that care abroad was more thorough/complete and 72% that treatment was different compared to [t]he Netherlands."[21] This data supports researchers' presumptions that European travellers make choices based on familiarity, affordability, perceived quality, and availability of services.[22]

EU Member States have used medical tourism as a way of reducing their waiting times. For example, in 2001–2002, the UK's National Health Service (NHS) reduced its waiting times by sending 190 patients—153 for orthopedics and 37 for opthamology— to France and Germany for inpatient treatment, focusing on its "long waiters."[23] Eighty percent of those patients reported that they were very satisfied with their experience. As is the case for private insurance in the United States, in Europe even the threat of promoting medical tourism can exert pressure to drive down costs and prices in the domestic services, and some saw the NHS 2001–2002 experiment as aimed primarily at this goal.

Beyond the European Union, which I discuss extensively later in this book, other home countries have also experienced smaller-scale medical tourism of this kind. In Canada, for example, each of the provinces and territories has regulations under which the public payer will authorize and fund medical tourism out of country (primarily to the United States). Although their details vary, in general, authorization depends on a finding that "the treatment or care must be medically required; the medical or hospital service must be demonstrated to be unavailable in the province/territory and/or elsewhere in Canada; . . . the delay in the provision of medical care available in the province/ territory or elsewhere in Canada must be considered to be immediately life threatening or may result in medically significant irreversible tissue damage; the treatment must fall under insured medical, oral surgeries and/or hospital services; and, the applicant must be a resident of the province/territory."[24]

C. Dividing by Direction of Patient Flow

A third way of dividing the phenomenon of medical tourism is by the direction of patient flow. Though doing so masks some additional levels of detail, Labonté and others have suggested that we can usefully divide medical tourism into four quadrants: North-North,

---

[21] GLINOS & BAETEN, *supra* note 16, at 35. This study was from 2006 and the data reported is older still, so it is likely that the picture has changed and will change even more as the EU Directive is transposed, as discussed in Chapter 5.

[22] *See id.* at 6.

[23] For this account I rely on Smith et al., *supra* note 17, at 47–48.

[24] Vivien Runnels & Corinne Packer, *Travelling for Healthcare from Canada: An Overview of Out-of-Country Care Funded by Provincial/Territorial Health Insurance Plans, in* TRAVELLING WELL, *supra* note 9, at 133, 137.

South-South, North-South, and South-North.[25] This is a useful set of terms, but in some instances will prove to be a bit of a misnomer because by "North" what is typically meant is "high income," and by "South," "low or middle income"—and this mapping will not always accurately track hemispheres. Thus, when an Australian travels from the Southern Hemisphere to the United States for health care, technically a South-North travel, in reality, it is high-income to high-income and thus would be more properly grouped with "North-North" travel in this four quadrant mapping.

South-North: This flow involves wealthy patients in low or middle-income countries seeking care in high-income countries, typically because they seek high-quality or state-of-the-art treatment or specialties not available at home. In the twentieth century, this was the dominant direction of patient flow, and much of the modern phenomenon of medical tourism tackled in this book is the story of how this flow became less dominant, the opening up of the other three patient flows discussed below, and the legal and ethical issues that stemmed from that change. Why did this flow decline in dominance? A fully fleshed out answer might take a book in itself (one that would be more historical and less focused on the pressing present legal and ethical needs than this book), but those who write in this field typically identify a few root causes. First, some of the supporting financing for this flow began itself to decline. Labonté, for example, notes that the United Kingdom saw its numbers of in-bound medical tourists, many from the Middle East, peak in the 1970s and 1980s with the rush of money from oil—that number has since declined. Second, 9/11, the tightening of immigration, and increase in anti-Arab sentiment in the United States and the United Kingdom led many Middle Eastern citizens who would have used this method of medical tourism to think again. This also opened up room for entrepreneurial growth within the Middle East to build more regional centers of excellence that would not require leaving for the West to get high-quality care.

To be sure, the patient flow from the Middle East is still high—a 2009 study estimated that London received 130,000 outpatient visits by medical tourists, leading to 7,800 foreign inpatient stays and generating between €280 and €330 million in direct revenue and almost €300 million in additional (touristic) spending[26]—but the forces mentioned above have opened up room for other flows, including the South-South flow within the Middle East, which I discuss below.

The United States has long been a hub for this kind of South-North medical tourism, offering high-quality and cutting edge treatments at brand name institutions (the Mayo Clinic, the Cleveland Clinic) at prices that wealthy foreign patients can afford. The National Coalition on Health Care, for example, estimated that five hundred thousand

---

[25] Much of the material in this section is drawn from Labonté, *supra* note 9, at 15–23. When I have relied on additional sources for data I will so indicate.

[26] *Id.* at 17 (citing TEAM TOURISM CONSULTING, *London and Medical Tourism* (2010)).

foreign patients traveled to the United States for health care in 2005.[27] Other countries have also tried to access this flow. For example, Poland is attempting to position itself as a destination for Russian and Central European patients, with a current focus on dental and cosmetic surgery.[28]

North-North: This form of medical tourism involves patients moving from one high-income country to another, typically within the Northern Hemisphere. The EU cross-border health care patterns discussed above and in more depth in Chapter 5 are a good example of this kind of travel. Another good example is when residents of Toronto, Canada, drive across the border to Buffalo, New York, United States, for a CT scan to avoid a waiting list in their home province of Ontario.

South-South: This flow involves travel from one low-to-middle income country to another for treatment. Again, there is some terminological mismatch with the category because, as Labonté notes, at least three popular destinations for this kind of medical tourism—Singapore, Hong Kong, and the United Arab Emirates—are actually high-income countries, and yet are typically grouped in as South-South flow by most researchers. This flow is characterized by individuals with the ability to pay to leave their home country, who leave because of concerns about the quality of health care, the lack of infrastructure, or the lack of specialized procedures they need, and who travel to "South" countries with better performance on these things. As I suggested above, the growth of this flow is a function both of (1) the improvement in quality, access, and specialty care centers in destination countries in the "South"; and (2) immigration and other post-9/11 complications with travel to the "North"—but it is also a function of the growth of the middle class in these countries. An emerging middle class created a market for patients who could afford to purchase better health care than what was offered in their home country, even when they could not afford the top prices in the United States and other destination countries in the North-North trade.

As Labonté and others have emphasized, the South-South flow tends to be heavily regionalized. Yemenis—with estimates ranging from forty thousand to two hundred thousand medical tourists a year out of a population of 17 million—tend to travel to Jordan and India for treatment for cancer, heart disease, and other serious medical conditions for which there are no good treatments in their home country. Tunisia has also become a regional destination country for this trade, with approximately forty-two thousand medical tourists visiting in 2003, about thirty-four thousand of whom were Libyans.[29] Jordan has been ranked first in the region and fifth globally as a destination

---

[27] Nathan Cortez, *Patients without Borders: The Emerging Global Market for Patients and the Evolution of Modern Health Care*, 83 IND. L.J. 71, 94 (2008) (citing Ann Tatko-Peterson, *Going Abroad for Health Care*, SAN JOSE MERCURY NEWS, Oct. 16, 2006, at A3).

[28] Labonté, *supra* note 9, at 17.

[29] *Id.* at 18 (citing M. Lautier, *Export of Health Services from Developing Countries: The Case of Tunisia*. 67 SOC. SCI. & MED., 101, 101–10 (2008)).

for medical tourism,[30] with data published in 2010 suggesting that 70 percent of its medical tourists come from other Middle Eastern countries.[31] Labonté notes data showing that medical tourists occupy roughly 25 percent of all hospital beds in Jordan, a country that has only 1.9 hospital beds per 1,000 person—below the world average of 3 per 1,000—which gestures toward some of the equity issues I will discuss in Chapter 6.[32]

Moving from the Middle East to the Caribbean and Central America, we see Cuba as a major destination country in South-South flow due to its neighboring countries (that make up approximately 80 percent of its medical tourism). Cuba's government is heavily involved in stimulating this trade through bilateral agreements with neighbor countries and through the establishment of *Servimed*, a company that facilitates foreigners accessing Cuban health services.[33] As mentioned above, the Cubans have a particular niche in treating vision loss, and they promote this in part through charitable outreach to foreigners: by 2008, Cuban health services had performed more than one million free surgeries of this kind to poor persons from thirty-two countries.[34] Other countries in the region are improving their infrastructure for medical tourism in an attempt to compete, at least as to specific therapies. Barbados currently specializes in fertility treatments but is aiming to expand into cardiac care. Panama focuses on dental services, cosmetic surgery, and knee and hip replacements, but also has made forays into cardiovascular work. Costa Rica has been a significant destination country for many types of medical tourism, but most recently has aimed to offer "liberation therapy," a controversial therapy for multiple sclerosis that is unavailable or uncovered in many home countries. Guatemala claims to serve about five hundred foreign patients annually, and Mexico also has a significant portion of the South-South trade in addition to its trade from the United States and other North countries. It has ten hospitals in Cancun, Merida, and the Mayan Riviera that focus on foreign patients, with promises of significant further investment.[35]

---

[30] *Id.* (citing *A Postcard from the Middle East: Jordan: Medical Tourism Uplifts the Economy*, THOMASWHITE.COM (July 17, 2009), http://www.thomaswhite.com/world-markets/jordan-medical-tourism-uplifts-the-economy/).

[31] *Id.* (citing M.J. Alsharif, R. Labonté & Z. Lu, *Patients beyond Borders: A Study of Medical Tourists in Four Countries*, *10* GLOBAL SOC. POL'Y 315, 315–35 (2010)).

[32] *Id.* at 18–19 (citing World Health Organization—Eastern Mediterranean Regional Office, *Trade in Health-Related Services and GATS* (2005); World Health Organization—Eastern Mediterranean Regional Office, *Health Systems Profile—Jordan: Regional Health Systems Observatory* (2007)).

[33] *Id.* at 19.

[34] *Id.* (citing C. Gorry, *Sight for Sore Eyes: Cuba's Vision Restoration Program*, *10* MEDICC REV. (INT'L J. CUBAN HEALTH AND MED.) 49–51 (2008)).

[35] *Id.* at 19–20 (citing PR Newswire, *World-Class Hospital to Open in Barbados to Serve Global Medical Tourism Market*, PRNEWSWIRE.COM (July 6, 2011), http://www.prnewswire.com/news-releases/world-class-hospital-to-open-in-barbados-to-serve-global-medical-tourism-market-125078069.html; Medical Tourism Magazine Newsletter, *Guatemala Innovate* [sic], *in Health Services Export*, CIDNEWSMEDIA.COM (Mar. 21, 2011), http://www.medicaltourismmag.com/newsletter/57/guatemala-innova-en-la-exportaci-n-de-servicios-de-salud.html; Panama Medical Tourism, http://panamamedicaltourism.com).

For Asian medical tourism there is both significant South-South and North-South flow. In 2011, NaRanong and NaRanong estimated that collectively India, Thailand, and Singapore are destination countries for 90 percent of the medical tourism in the region, and much of that trade is interregional South-South flow.[36] India, one of the first innovators in this sector, has long attracted patients from Sri Lanka, Bangladesh, Nepal, Bhutan, and Pakistan, and, in the late 2000s, per year about fifty-thousand neighboring Bangladeshis crossed the border to India for care.[37] Thailand remains the world leader as a destination country for medical tourists, attracting an estimated 1.5 million foreign patients in 2010 (twice the number of India, the next best). However, as with all numbers in the industry, the definitions matter: only about 420,000 to 500,000 individuals traveled to Thailand for the purpose of getting health care, so on some definitions (including the ones I am most supportive of), only those in that smaller population would be treated as "medical tourists."[38] According to some reports, in 2003 alone, Thailand's largest medical tourism center, the Bumrungrad Hospital in Bangkok, admitted close to five hundred thousand patients in 2003 with 2005 numbers suggesting that ninety-three thousand Arab patients alone were treated in that year.[39] Together, Thailand, Singapore, and Malaysia attracted more than 2 million medical tourists in 2006–2007, resulting in 3 billion USD of revenue, with the majority going to Thailand.[40] In 2004, Malaysian hospitals treated 130,000 foreign patients—a 25 percent rise from the previous year—and the most recent figures report that the country treated 578,403 foreign patients in 2011.[41] A large part of Malaysia and Singapore's trade comes from medical tourists from neighboring Indonesia, and for all three destination countries the majority of medical tourists come from Association of Southeast Asian Nations (ASEAN) countries.[42]

North-South: This flow has gained the most attention in the popular media, in what Labonté describes as a "gold rush of primarily private, but also some public, providers in low- and middle-income countries attempting to capitalize on what they perceive to be

---

[36] Labonté, *supra* note 9, at 20 (citing A. NaRanong & V. NaRanong, *The Effects of Medical Tourism: Thailand's Experience*, 89 BULL. WORLD HEALTH ORG. 336, 336–44 (2011)).

[37] *Id.* at 20 (citing A. Whittaker, *Pleasure and Pain: Medical Travel in Asia*, 3 GLOBAL PUB. HEALTH 271, 271–90 (2008)).

[38] *Id.* at 20–21 (citing NaRanong & NaRanong, *supra* note 33).

[39] LUNT ET AL., *supra* note 8, at 14 (citing L. Turner, *"First World Health Care at Third World Prices": Globalization, Bioethics and Medical Tourism*, 2 BIOSOCIETIES 303, 303–25 (2007); K. McClean, *Medical Tourism: Or, for the Politically Correct... Cross Border Health Care*, University of Saskatchewan (2008); N. MacReady, *Developing Countries Court Medical Tourists*, 369 LANCET 1849, 1849–50 (2007)).

[40] Labonté, *supra* note 9, at 20–21 (citing N.S. Pocock & K.H. Phua, *Medical Tourism and Policy Implications for Health Systems: A Conceptual Framework from a Comparative Study of Thailand, Singapore and Malaysia*, 7 GLOBALIZATION & HEALTH (2011)).

[41] MILICA Z. BOOKMAN & KARLA K. BOOKMAN, MEDICAL TOURISM IN DEVELOPING COUNTRIES 3 (2007); Vasantha Ganesan, *Medical Tourism in the Pink of Health*, MEDICALTOURISMMAG.COM (Mar. 6, 2012), *available at* http://www.medicaltourismmag.com/newsletter/73/medical-tourism-in-the-pink-of-health.html.

[42] Labonté, *supra* note 9, at 20–21.

an unfilled demand from the wealthier and demographically aging North."[43] Patients from the United States are a particular focus of destination country facility recruitment because the United States's lack of universal health care produces a large population of individuals without better options. Moreover, the relatively high cost of health care in the United States, even for those with insurance, gives insurers and employers incentives to consider sending patients abroad. The Deloitte Center for Health Solutions concluded that 750,000 U.S. patients traveled abroad in 2007 for both inpatient and outpatient procedures and predicted that the total number would rise to six million by 2010.[44] By contrast, McKinsey & Company calculated in 2008 that only five to ten thousand U.S. patients per year were medical tourists.[45] The difference resulted in part due to undercounting by McKinsey because it excluded patients traveling in "contiguous geographies" such as from Canada to the United States or from the United States to Mexico.[46] Travel to Mexico represents a very significant share of all medical tourism from the United States, and in one year alone 952,000 California residents (roughly half of whom were Mexican immigrants) traveled to Mexico for medical care, dental care, or prescription drugs.[47] In any event, in 2009 Deloitte downgraded its estimate to only 1.6 million U.S. medical tourists traveling per year in the foreseeable future.[48]

Although all destination countries try to reach expatriates and those who share language and cultural affinities in the home country, this strategy has been the most pronounced in Mexico's recruiting of U.S. citizens or residents of Hispanic background. Mexico's largest private hospital chain, Grupo Star Médica, is partly owned by Carlos Slim Helu—recently ranked the world's wealthiest man—and is underway on the construction of fifteen new facilities aimed at attracting patients from the United States.[49] Chrisus Health, a Texas-based Catholic not-for-profit hospital group, is the half owner of the recently established Mexican CHRISTUS MUGUERZA® chain, which operates eight hospitals and is seeking to expand its medical tourism business. In 2010, the

---

[43] *Id.* at 22.

[44] I. Glenn Cohen, *Introduction, in* The Globalization of Health Care: Legal and Ethical Issues xiv (I. Glenn Cohen ed. 2013); Cortez, *supra* note 13, at 878.

[45] Cortez, *supra* note 13, at 878 (citing Tilman Ehrbeck et al., *Mapping the Market for Medical Travel*, McKinsey Q. 2, 3, 6 (May 2008)).

[46] *Id.* at 878 n.119 (citing Ian Youngman, *Medical Tourism Statistics: Why McKinsey Has Got It Wrong*, Int'l Med. Travel J. (2009), http://www.imtjonline.com/articles/2009/mckinsey-wrong-medical-travel/).

[47] *Id.* at 881 (citing Steven P. Wallace, Carolyn Mendez-Luck & Xóchitl Castañeda, *Heading South: Why Mexican Immigrants in California Seek Health Services in Mexico*, 47 Med. Care 662, 662 (2009) (using 2001 data)).

[48] *Id.* at 878 n.119 (citing Tom Murphy, *Health Insurers Explore Savings in Overseas Care*, Associated Press, Aug. 23, 2009).

[49] *See* Thomas Black, *Mexico Builds Hospitals to Lure Medical Tourists from America*, Bloomberg (Mar. 27, 2008), http://www.bloomberg.com/apps/news?pid=newsarchive&sid=audTNhIlsFSg; Grupo Star Médica, *Grupo Star Médica Continues Its Expansion in Mexico*, Hospitales Star Médica (June 13, 2013), http://www.star-medica.com/_en/_HOSPITAL/news-details_Grupo-Star-Médica-continues-its-expansión-in-México_25_22.aspx.

Mexican Minister of Tourism announced its goal of 450,000 medical tourists by 2015 and 650,000 by 2020.[50]

Now that we have an understanding of the basic divisions within the industry, I turn to a focus on its major players.

II. UNDERSTANDING HOW THE INDUSTRY WORKS AND ITS MAJOR PLAYERS

Health care is a profession, but even in places where it is largely government run, it is also inescapably a business. The business side of health care is much closer to the surface when it comes to medical tourism, and in this part I will describe in greater depth how the industry works and its major components. Those components can be seen from this diagram (Figure 1.1).

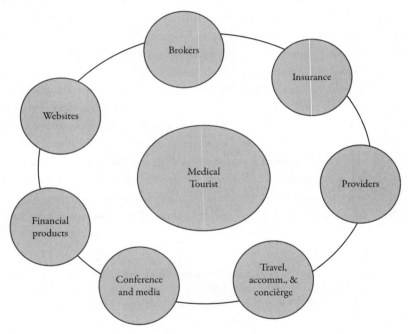

FIGURE 1.1 A Sketch of the Medical Tourism Industry.

A. Destination Country Governments

Medical tourism did not emerge by accident in the destination countries where it thrives. It is the result of the synergy between entrepreneurs in the health care space and governmental support to establish an industry. Why are destination countries so interested in

---

[50] Labonté, *supra* note 9, at 25–26.

becoming a medical tourism hub? The short answer is that there is money in it, and it enables the destination country to further support its health care infrastructure.

Thailand was one of the earliest to seize this opportunity and it remains one model for doing so. In the 1980s, the Thai government prompted a rapid growth in direct investment from foreign sources into private hospitals. These new entities, however, faced a threat of collapse in the late 1990s due to the one-two punch of the 1997 Asian financial crisis and a new health insurance scheme aimed at moving patients from the public to the private sector. To combat this failure, in 2003 the Thai government initiated a campaign to pro- mote the country as the "Medical Hub of Asia," which sold Thailand as a combination of high-tech and high-quality medical treatment, alongside the mysticism of the East and alternative medicine with its reputation for pleasure and relaxation through spas, mas- sage, etc. These efforts paid off by propping up demand for private hospitals and generat- ing about US$2 billion in medical tourism, about 0.4 percent of the country's GDP. In 2006 only one Thai hospital was JCI accredited whereas in 2012 there were four, further illustration of the growth of the Thai medical tourism sector. Medical tourism is *tour- ism*: the goal of destination country governments is not only to attract patients for health care but to create a multiplier effect from their tourism spending while in the country.[51]

For some destination countries, medical tourism is desirable because foreign patients can be charged much more than domestic patients, albeit much less than those patients typically pay at home. By contrast, some destination country governments are inter- ested in medical tourism not because of these price differences, but as a way of building health care infrastructure. In Malaysia, for example, there is a single price charged by Malaysian hospitals to foreign and domestic patients. When I learned about this while touring facilities in Malaysia, I was puzzled. Why was Malaysia expending resources to attract foreign patients if it was getting the same per-patient revenue? The answer I was repeatedly given had to do with infrastructure. The population of Malaysian patients alone is not numerous enough to sustain the level of trauma, transplant, IVF, and other specialty care the government thinks is needed. By adding patients from else- where (particularly from neighboring Indonesia), they can maintain multiple facilities with better geographical coverage and also maintain economies of scale. To this end, the Malaysia Healthcare Travel Council mounts a huge (and quite lavish) conference in Kuala Lumpur, "Fami tours" (familiarity tours involving touring various hospitals in the region, a ubiquitous piece of the industry), and has conducted satellite events in various destination country cities, including one in the United States where it partnered with *Scientific American*.[52] This is becoming a fairly standard "playbook" for destination country governments serious about increasing the patient flow to them, and, like much

---

[51] *Id.* at 23–24 (citing LUNT ET AL., *supra* note 8; NaRanong & NaRanong, *supra* note 33; Pocock & Phua, *supra* note 37).

[52] Full disclosure, I attended one of its conferences and spoke at an event it held with *Scientific American* on the industry more generally, and was paid to do the latter.

in the industry, was pioneered by Thailand. Malaysia has also given significant incentives to its own hospitals to pursue this growth: it has allowed hospitals catering to medical tourists to double deductions for their marketing expenses and to enjoy a 100 percent tax holiday on any revenues earned from treating foreign patients.[53]

Singapore offers another case study of a coordinated governmental attempt to foster an industry along similar lines. It realized that its domestic population was not sufficient to finance a system of high-end medical care and sought to increase the number of fee-paying international patients, with a target of one million medical tourists by 2012.[54] To execute this strategy, as of 2003 the country established "SingaporeMedicine"—a multiagency government-industry partnership led by the Ministry of Health, with the support of the Development Board (in charge of new investments and health care industry capabilities); International Enterprise Singapore (in charge of growth and expansion of Singapore's health care interests overseas); and Singapore Tourism Board (in charge of branding and marketing of its health care services).[55]

Although coming on to the scene a bit later, South Korea is positioning itself to be a large player in this market, taking advantage of large numbers of Korean expatriates and a good existing health care infrastructure. The Korea Health Industry Development Institute (KHIDI) has followed a playbook similar to these other medical tourism hubs—sponsoring a lavish annual conference in Seoul, running Fami tours, and, together with the Korean Ministry of Health and Welfare, establishing a U.S. foothold with an organization based in New York called KHIDI USA.[56] The South Korean government has also tried to foster its industry by, among other things: establishing tax-free special economic zones in which for-profit hospitals can operate; relaxing visa laws for medical tourists; and attempting to build "healthcare cities" in Seoul, Daegu, and Jeju.[57]

India has also developed a concerted strategy to increase its share of medical tourists. The Confederation of Indian Industry lobbied for an official government policy, which the government adopted as part of its national health policy in 2002. As Labonté writes:

> The government subsidizes growth in this sector through tax and land concessions, duty and tax concessions on various imports, income tax holidays for those investing in the industry and special "M" visas for medical tourists. It actively markets the country as a medical tourism destination ("Incredible India—the global healthcare destination"): a case in point being the involvement of many Indian government

---

[53] Labonté, *supra* note 9, at 24 (citing H.L. Chee, *Medical Tourism and the State in Malaysia and Singapore*, 10 GLOBAL SOC. POL'Y, 336–57 (2010)).

[54] *Id.* (citing Pocock & Phua, *supra* note 37).

[55] LUNT ET AL., *supra* note 8, at 22.

[56] Again, full disclosure, I attended one of the KHIDI conferences in Seoul and was a paid speaker on legal and ethical issues in medical tourism there.

[57] *See* Labonté, *supra* note 9, at 24; LUNT ET AL., *supra* note 8, at 23.

departments in a major medical tourism conference in Canada in 2009. The government also offers credit for hospitals with more than 100 beds and subsidizes the training costs of physicians, the majority of whom work in the private healthcare sector. The value of these public training subsidies to the private medical sector is estimated to be US$100 million annually. At least thirteen of India's private hospitals are now JCI accredited, with the sector dominated by three chains. The largest is the Apollo Hospital chain with 43 hospitals and over 10,000 beds, reportedly treating 60,000 foreign patients from 55 countries between 2003 and 2008. It has established partnerships with tourism and insurance businesses, and developed bilateral agreements with the governments of Tanzania and Mauritius to treat their citizens. The Apollo Chain is 12.5 percent owned by Malaysia's sovereign wealth fund.[58]

As we will see in more depth in Chapter 6, although many of the Indian governmental incentives to foster the industry in theory require set-asides by the hospitals to protect access for the destination country poor, many commentators claims that these are routinely denied in practice.

Turning our attention to the Americas, the Mexican Minister of Tourism announced his intent to make the country a major medical tourism destination with a goal of 450,000 medical tourists by 2015, and 650,000 by 2020.[59] In Mexico, as in many Latin American destination countries in recent years, a major strategy has been to partner with the U.S.-based Medical Tourism Association (described below) to fund Fami tours for insurance companies and medical tourism brokers, primarily from the United States, in an attempt to improve the flow of patients.[60]

B. Destination Country Hospitals and Their Staff

Destination country hospitals trying to provide for the medical tourist patient population come in quite varied sizes and organizational forms.

Some of them are stand-alone institutions, such as Bumrungrad International Hospital in Bangkok, Thailand (Figure 1.2). Bumrungrad is one of the industry leaders. It looks more like a four-star conference hotel than what one may imagine a hospital in Thailand would look like. It claims to admit about four hundred thousand foreign

---

[58] Labonté, *supra* note 9, at 25 (citing P.S. Saligram, Trade Aspects of Medical Tourism in India (Aug. 2009) (unpublished master's dissertation, University of Edinburgh); R. Chanda, *Trade in Health Services*, *80* BULL. WORLD HEALTH ORG. 158, 158–62 (2002); V. Runnels & L. Turner, *Bioethics and Transnational Medical Travel: India, "Medical Tourism," and the Globalisation of Healthcare*, *8* INDIAN J. MED. ETHICS 42, 42–44 (2011); A. Sengupta & S. Nundy, *The Private Health Sector in India*, *331* BRIT. MED. J. 1157, 1157–58 (2005); Whittaker, *supra* note 34; Chee, *supra* note 50).

[59] Labonté, *supra* note 9, at 26.

[60] Labonté, *supra* note 9, at 26 (citing R-M STEPHANO & J. EDELHEIT, MEDICAL TOURISM: AN INTERNATIONAL HEALTHCARE GUIDE FOR INSURERS, EMPLOYERS AND GOVERNMENTS (2010).

patients a year, and it claimed in 2007 to have more than 200 U.S.-certified physicians and to have treated fifty-five thousand patients from the United States.[61]

FIGURE I.2 Bumrungrad International Hospital, Bangkok, Thailand

In part because cultural affinities and shared language play a major role in how patients decide where to go for care, Bumrungrad in Bangkok has built a special wing for Middle Eastern patients (staffed by Arabic interpreters and containing halal kitchens and Muslim prayer rugs).[62] Similarly, the International Medical Center in Bangkok has a wing catering to Japanese patients.[63]

As mentioned above, Apollo Hospitals has reportedly treated sixty-thousand foreign patients from fifty-five countries between 2003 and 2008. Although based in India, Apollo has facilities in Sri Lanka, Ghana, Nigeria, Qatar, and Kuwait, with the Malaysian government a part owner of the chain. Apollo Hospitals has also taken on an operations management contract for a 330-bed tertiary care hospital in Dhaka, Bangladesh, with its Bangladeshi partner, STS Holdings.[64]

In Mexico, we also see the formation of larger hospital networks, such as Hospital Angeles. It operates twenty-two hospitals in Mexico, "all equipped with state-of-the-art technology, a total of 1,700 beds and over 11,000 specialists." Included in the list of hospitals is "Hospital Angeles Tijuana, a US$60 million, 122-bed private hospital."[65] The network claims to have treated more than six thousand American and Canadian

---

[61] Labonté, *supra* note 9, at 7, 22 (citing Bumrungrad International Hospital, http://www.bumrungrad.com/en/about-us/overview; R. De Arellano, *Patients without Borders: The Emergence of Medical Tourism*, 37 INT'L. J. HEALTH SERVS. 193, 193–98 (2007)).

[62] Cohen, *supra* note 11, at 1482 (citing BOOKMAN & BOOKMAN, *supra* note 38, at 57).

[63] *Id.*

[64] Labonté, *supra* note 9, at 25 (citing Saligram, *supra* note 55; Whittaker, *supra* note 34; Chee, *supra* note 50); Rupa Chanda, *Medical Value Travel in India: Prospects and Challenges*, *in* TRAVELLING WELL, *supra* note 9, at 62, 69; Cohen, *supra* note 11, at 1479 (quoting Nicolas P. Terry, *Under-Regulated Health Care Phenomena in a Flat World: Medical Tourism and Outsourcing*, 29 W. NEW ENG. L. REV. 421, 426 (2007)).

[65] Mariella Ferreyra Galliani, *Exploring Medical Tourism in Latin America: Two Case Examples*, *in* TRAVELLING WELL, *supra* note 9, at 85, 89.

patients over a three-year period and offers bariatric, spinal, and orthopedic surgery; interventional cardiology; dental care; and organ transplant services.[66]

On the other extreme, we see more local, unaffiliated, and smaller facilities also aimed at trying to attract foreign patients. One good example is the Barbados Fertility Center, (Figure 1.3a–c) founded in 2002 and located in a renovated colonial home on the south side of the island.[67]

(a)

(b)

(c)

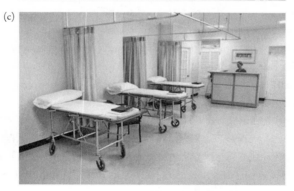

FIGURE 1.3a–c Barbados Fertility Center

---

[66] *Id.*

[67] RORY JOHNSTON ET AL., AN OVERVIEW OF BARBADOS' MEDICAL TOURISM INDUSTRY, Version 2.0 (April 2013), at 23, *available at* http://www.sfu.ca/medicaltourism/An%20Overview%20of%20 Barbados%27%20Medical%20Tourism%20Industry%20-%20Version%202.0.pdf.

The clinic has one gynecologist specializing in fertility services and five nurses. Of these six health workers, all but one nurse was trained in the United States or the United Kingdom.[68]

As Rory Johnston et al. describe the clinic:

The clinic has four outpatient beds in a post-implantation recovery room, an embryology laboratory, offices, and an operating room for fertility procedures. Signage in the facility is in English. Advertising on the clinic grounds is limited to brochures and pamphlets in reception and waiting rooms throughout the building.

There are no advertisements for the facility's services posted in the building or on the grounds. Patient testimonials are also not prominently posted anywhere aside from the pamphlets and brochures, although photos of babies successfully conceived at the facility are posted on a cork board and in a number of photo albums in the main reception area.

The Barbados Fertility Centre employs "in-vitro fertilization nurse coordinators" as care coordinators for both international and local patients. Nurse coordinators are assigned when prospective patients make initial contact with the facility. Three internationally trained nurses are solely used for international patients, with one locally trained nurse assigned to Barbadian and other Caribbean patients. This arrangement is believed to better align cultural attitudes and expectations between care providers and patients and improve the delivery of care. The Barbados Fertility Centre has created satellite clinics in Antigua, St. Maarten, and Trinidad that provide pre-implantation screening for residents in these countries....

Medical tourists comprise the bulk of the Barbados Fertility Centre's patient base, representing roughly 80% of its clientele. Of this 80%, roughly half are from within the Caribbean region and the other half from the United States, Canada, the United Kingdom, and Continental Europe. Most patients come from the Caribbean region, United States, and United Kingdom. Medical tourists represent an increasing share of patients treated at the facility each year, and it is estimated that the clinic received roughly 260 medical tourists in 2011. This is a marked increase over the previous year, estimated at roughly 130% more medical tourists in 2011 than 2010.

While medical tourists are a large portion of the clinic's business, they are not offered any special wards or services that local patients are not. Medical tourists are charged 15% more than local patients if they are from outside of the Caribbean, and 10% more if they are regional patients from outside of Barbados. Recreational and wellness tourism are routinely incorporated into patients' itineraries as the clinic partially attributes their high success rates to the low-stress tourist environment

---

[68] *Id.*

that Barbados provides. The clinic has connections with hotels, complementary and alternative medical providers, and tour operators in Barbados, and the Barbados Fertility Centre regularly refers their patients to them.[69]

The clinic has managed to achieve JCI accreditation, the part of the industry I discuss next, which is no easy feat for a small clinic.

C. Accreditors

Accreditation is a "very particular form of external quality assessment carried out by a third-party assessment body" that involves both a self-assessment and a peer review by an external group of surveyors.[70] There are many regional accreditators, but the most important international accreditation used is JCI accreditation, given by an affiliate of the Joint Commission (formerly called the Joint Commission on Accreditation of Healthcare Organizations (JCAHO)), which accredits most U.S. hospitals for participation in the Medicare and Medicaid programs through a similar process. The Joint Commission is itself governed by the major trade associations, primarily the American Medical Association, the American Hospital Association, the American College of Surgeons, and the American College of Physicians.[71]

To qualify for JCI hospital accreditation, the hospital must achieve the requisite scores on JCI's six patient safety goals and its more than a hundred standards, which are divided into thirteen chapters: seven chapters of Patient-Centered Standards and six of Health Care Organization Management Standards.[72] Each hospital is fully evaluated at the time of initial accreditation and at the time of reaccreditation every three years. When an evaluation shows that one or more conditions for accreditation are not met, the organization is provided a period of time to come into acceptable compliance demonstrated by written proof or by a follow-up visit by one of the JCI evaluators. As of January 2011, for JCI to accredit an organization, it must score a "5" on each of JCI's many standards, "an aggregate score of at least '8' for each chapter of standards," and an overall "aggregate score of at least '9' on all standards."[73]

---

[69] *Id.* at 23–25.

[70] Stephen T. Green & Hannah King, *Independent Health Care Accreditation: Medical Tourism and Other International Aspects, in* Risks & Challenges in Medical Tourism, *supra* note 17, at 230, 231.

[71] Cohen, *supra* note 11, at 1485–86 (citing Mark A. Hall et al., Health Care Law and Ethics 1196–97 (7th ed. 2007)).

[72] Joint Comm'n Int'l Accreditation Standards for Hospitals 4th Ed. (Expanded) (2013), *available at* http://www.jointcommissioninternational.org/News/2012/7/17/JCI-Releases-New-Standards-for-Academic-Medical-Center-Hospitals/ (follow "Download a copy of the Academic Medical Center Hospitals Standards Only Version" hyperlink).

[73] Joint Comm'n Int'l Hospital Accreditation, Survey Process Guide 4th Ed., Accreditation Decision Rules 14–15 (2011), *available at* http://share.pdfonline.com/97ffc79b23fd46bcbb1ea8bbb44f3916/JCI%20Hospital%20Survey%20Process%20Guide,%204th%20Edition.htm#page_18.

Of course, as Nathan Cortez and others have noted, JCI has its own incentives that come into play in its role as accreditor and may give us pause: it has a very high rate of accreditation and low rate of revocation, and its revenues depend on the number of hospitals it accredits.[74] JCI has accredited more than four hundred medical facilities in over fifty countries across Asia, Europe, the Middle East, the Caribbean, and South America.[75]

Becoming JCI-accredited is a very expensive process for an individual hospital,[76] but it is usually a mark of a well-funded and more mature industry in a destination country to have at least one JCI-accredited hospital and to pursue it for a second or more. Beyond its obvious marketing appeal, when done properly accreditation can have significant benefits as Green and King note: it can help guide consumer choice, it can reduce legal liability, it can minimize bad publicity, it can help attract business through third-party payers who may want assurances of quality, and it can facilitate access to overseas markets.[77]

D. Facilitators

Facilitators, also called "intermediaries," are the middlemen that connect patients in the home country with destination country hospitals and physicians. To give one example of how this works, consider the company MedRetreat based in the United States:

Med[R]etreat's website offers an online presentation or podcast about its services, followed by a free online membership application form. It then assigns the patient a "U.S. Program Manager," who has an "extensive conversation" with the patient regarding his or her care needs, and it sends an electronic "Authorization Release Form," which gives the corporation "consent to collect and disseminate [the patient's] personal information." The patient provides digital copies of MRI's, x-rays, photos and other medical records and tests; a description of the expected outcome sought from surgery; possible travel dates; and a three-page medical-history questionnaire. The Manager then provides a price quotation for various possible doctors who could do the surgery sought, a list of possible accommodations, and coordinates communication between the patient and possible surgeon by email or teleconference. If the patient and Manager reach agreement on the details, the patient then deposits 20% of the total estimated cost into MedRetreat's U.S. holding account, at which point all final arrangements are made. After pre-surgical

---

[74] See Cortez, *supra* note 24, at 125–26.

[75] Labonté, *supra* note 9, at 12.

[76] Green and King attempted to get cost estimates for 500-bed hospitals, but based on the information they were able to obtain, they noted that the "results were extremely difficulty to interpret." Nonetheless, Green and King do come up with an estimate range for costs, based on published data for various accreditation schemes: US$46,000 to US$630,000 (a range that mixes various international and national accreditations of various forms). Green & King, *supra* note 67, at 243.

[77] Green & King, *supra* note 67, at 238–39.

consultation and additional testing in the destination country, the surgery is performed. When the doctor is satisfied with the patient's condition, the patient is released from the hospital to recuperate back in the patient's hotel, with the service offering to arrange excursions to "some of the interesting attractions your destination offers." The patient then returns home, where the U.S. Program Manager "will be available to assist [him] with any future requirements."[78]

There is high level of heterogeneity as to the structure, size, business plan, and practices of facilitators. Some deal with hundreds of patients a year and are in corporate forms; others are sole proprietors who deal with fewer than twenty patients a year. Some specialize in a certain subset of the industry, such as fertility or cosmetic, while others will handle multiple forms of procedures. Some see their role as patient advocates coordinating care for patients and also trying to be agents of change for the health care system in the patient's home country, while others see themselves as technical middlemen handling logistics of care abroad but not much more.[79]

In a recent paper, Jeremy Snyder et al. reviewed the existing studies on medical tourism facilitators (primarily through reviews of facilitators' websites, interviews with patients, and interviews with facilitators themselves) to draw together some common facts and descriptions about these entities:[80]

First, there is no commonly accepted training or accreditation process for facilitators. Many come to this role from a tourism background, with experience booking vacations, flights, and other tourist services but without specific training on the medical end. This mismatch is a concern, in part because many facilitators may offer to evaluate for patients which medical procedure, from a range of possible procedures, a patient should consider. Or, facilitators may purport to judge the quality of various potential providers, and might advise on safety and other concerns. Many patients may be unaware of the lack of medical training these individuals have, because many facilitators use the word "medical" in their title, description, or business name.

Second, facilitators operate under situations of significant conflict of interest. Although some patients will pay a facilitator directly for its service, very commonly the facilitator's income derives from referral fees from the hospital where it directs the patient. I discuss legal and ethical issues with such referral fees in greater depth in Chapter 3, but here let me emphasize the various ways in which these financial arrangements can shade facilitator (and thus ultimately patient) decision-making. These arrangements, in theory— empirical evidence is harder to come by—can lead to supplier-induced demand effects

---

[78] Cohen, *supra* note 11, at 1483–84 (citing MedRetreat, Medical Tourism Process, http://www.medretreat.com/index.php?t=medical_tourism/medical_tourism_process).

[79] *See* Jeremy Snyder et al., *Medical Tourism Facilitators: Ethical Concerns about Roles and Responsibilities, in* RISKS & CHALLENGES IN MEDICAL TOURISM, *supra* note 17, at 279–80.

[80] I draw what follows from their study, *id.* at 283–93.

where facilitators convince patients to opt for surgeries they do not "need" or to choose a more extensive rather than a less extensive approach to a problem for which the patient already wants care. Of course, drawing the line between educating/informing patients versus inducing their preferences is very fraught indeed. A different way the conflict can manifest is where the facilitator steers patients to particular facilities for which it will get referral fees rather than other facilities that might have higher quality or lower cost or otherwise more suitable care. As I will emphasize in my discussion later in the book, disclosure to patients of potential conflicts—something that does not regularly occur, or so it would appear from what we know—is an important part of the solution. What is less clear is whether it would be good to police possible referral fee arrangements more stringently.

Third, facilitators have an important role to play in follow-up care, an issue discussed in greater depth in Chapter 2. Coordinating care between health care teams in different countries, using different standards, and communicating through sometimes different languages is no easy feat. The doctor to whose care the patient returns may be unfamiliar with the procedure or reluctant to provide follow-up care for legal liability reasons I discuss in greater depth in this book. Facilitators can bridge this gap by ensuring that medical records are available in a format that home country care professionals can use. They can also ensure a smooth continuity of care by securing follow-up care for the medical tourist patient *before* he or she leaves the country. However, this is another place where the heterogeneity in expertise and motivations of facilitators can work against the interests of patients. Because of a lack of "skill" or "will," some facilitators may not adequately explain to patients the intricacies of coordinating care, or may not choose facilities with international patient coordinators employed by the destination country facility to oversee logistics on-site and off-site.

In an interview study of twelve Canadian medical tourism facilitators, Johnston et al. found a wide range of facilitator approaches to continuity of care: some arranged follow-up care only by patient request, some contacted patients upon return to assist in follow-up care as a matter of course, and some accepted patients as clients only if they were able to secure the follow-up care in advance.[81] Website studies suggest a similar range of approaches: Kali Penney et al.'s content analysis of seventeen Canadian facilitator websites found that some clearly stated that the facilitator had no role in arranging follow-up care, while others offered an extensive range of services without being clear if an extra fee would be charged for that service.[82] Alicia Mason and Kevin B. Wright found in their study that only 4.9 percent of facilitators web pages addressed follow-up

---

[81] *See* Rory Johnston et al., *An Industry Perspective on Canadian Patients' Involvement in Medical Tourism: Implications for Public Health*, *11* BMC Pub. Health 416, 416, 419 (2011).

[82] *See* Kali Penney et al., *Risk Communication and Informed Consent in the Medical Tourism Industry: A Thematic Content Analysis of Canadian Broker Websites*, *12* BMC Med. Ethics 17, 17, 22 (2011).

care on the main page and only 18.2 percent addressed it on other pages.[83] A study by Neil Lunt and Percivil Carrera of fifty English language websites of facilitators found that only 10 percent addressed follow-up care at all.[84]

Fourth, facilitators represent an important channel of information for patients of medical tourism and are the primary way that some potential patients learn about their options. At the same time, the existing empirical work depicts facilitators largely as "cheerleaders" for the industry—overstating benefits and understating risks. Facilitator websites typically use several branding techniques in advertising their services, such as noting that many physicians in the destination country hospitals to which they direct patients have been trained in Europe or North America, discussing JCI accreditation of the facilities they work with and explaining accreditation's connection to quality, and emphasizing the fact that state-of-the-art technologies are available—all in order to counter patients' preconceptions that developing countries, in particular, will offer lower standards of care.

It is very hard to say as a general matter whether this information is truthful or misleading, and whether it usefully corrects unfounded patient preconceptions or instead lulls patients into a sense of false security. Based on a study of facilitators' websites, what is clear from empirical work is that there is a lack of discussion of risk. For example, Penney et al.'s study of Canadian facilitators' websites found that "47.1% made no general or specific mention of risks at all"—and of those that did, the information often came under headings titled "Disclaimer" or "Frequently Asked Questions."[85] Mason and Wright's study of sixty-six U.S. facilitators' websites found that only 4.9 percent addressed postoperative care, 2.2 percent complications, 2.2 percent procedural risks, and 1.1 percent legal recourse.[86] Other studies reach similar conclusions: if facilitator websites address risks at all, they often downplay them and hide them in "terms and conditions" pages to which patients are unlikely to pay much attention.

Moreover, some facilitators use ethically questionable techniques to get patients to endorse the services or facilities they send them to. For example, in one account of a Canadian patient going to Costa Rica, Johnston et al. recount that the

[T]he facilitator made a proposition to Jolene. If she were to help him promote his company's services and medical tourism on a broader scale by agreeing to be interviewed by Canadian media outlets, he would secure her and her husband an upgrade for the recovery portion of their trip by booking them a stay at a 5-star hotel, up from a 3-star, at no extra charge. However, this upgrade was contingent

---

[83] *See* Alicia Mason & Kevin B. Wright, *Framing Medical Tourism: An Examination of Appeal, Risk, Convalescence, Accreditation, and Interactivity in Medical Tourism Web Sites*, *16* J. HEALTH COMM.: INT'L PERSP. 163, 170 (2011).

[84] *See* Neil Lunt & Percivil Carrera, *Systematic Review of Web Sites for Prospective Medical Tourists*, *66* TOURISM REV. 57, 62 (2011).

[85] Penney et al., *supra* note 79, at 21.

[86] Mason & Wright, *supra* note 80, at 170.

on Jolene agreeing to "blame" the Canadian healthcare system for her decision to go elsewhere, insisting she must offer herself and her story up as a symptom of a failing system.[87]

In some sectors of the industry, facilitators play an almost motherly role, providing emotional labor along with this expertise. For example, the facilitators in the cosmetic surgery portion of trade are often themselves previous cosmetic surgery tourists who not only facilitate the trade but offer emotional support and companionship as well.[88]

E. Insurers

As described above, and in much greater depth in Chapter 4, private health care insurers operating in a patient's home country or across borders can decide to cover travel abroad for medical tourism, at what facilities, for what procedures, and under what conditions. Moreover—and we have seen some experimentation on this front—they can offer incentives to patients to travel abroad for care, such as waiving copays or deductibles or sharing in parts of the profit. In the future, we may see plans that charge patients more if they opt for domestic health care or require travel abroad as a precondition for coverage for certain procedures.

Public insurers in universal health care countries are also important players in medical tourism, as I discuss in great depth in Chapter 5. The European Union has long struggled with the rules authorizing and reimbursing patients for travel from their Member State of residency to the Member State of treatment, giving rise to regulation, European Court of Justice jurisprudence, and now a new EU Directive. Canada has also struggled with when it will reimburse its citizens' travel to the United States for care, and there have been some discussions of the portability of retirement health benefits in the United States and elsewhere.

As I will discuss later in this book, both public and private insurers have an important role to play in regulation, not only in regulating the patients *they* send abroad, but because the rules that govern them and the information they solicit in formulating their policies may have positive spillover effects in the much harder to regulate forms of medical tourism involving patients who pay out-of-pocket.

F. Home Country Partners

Frequently, up-and-coming destination country hospitals pair themselves with established "brand name" hospitals in the United States or elsewhere as part of their attempt

---

[87] Rory Johnston et al., *Exceptional Aspects of the Experiences of Canadian Medical Tourists from Patient Narratives*, *in* TRAVELLING WELL, *supra* note 9, at 103, 106.

[88] *See* David Bell et al., *Bikinis and Bandages: An Itinerary for Cosmetic Surgery Tourism*, 11 TOURIST STUD. 139, 146–47 (2011).

to improve their quality and attract patients. These kinds of associations can take very different forms and very little about them is publicly available, including the fee structure or remuneration for the home country hospital, degree of interweaving of services, etc. Among the examples most commonly cited in the literature are: Partners Harvard Medical International and their associated hospitals/facilities in the Dubai Health Care City and in India (the Wockhardt hospital chain); Johns Hopkins in Abu Dhabi and in India (the Apollo Hospital chain); Weill Cornell Medical College in Qatar; the Duke-NUS partnership; and the University of Pittsburgh Medical Center's transplant hospital in Sicily. Other partnerships that are mentioned less often in the literature include: the Partners Harvard Medical International partnership with Acibadem Hospital in Turkey (Flat Medicine); Johns Hopkins International and Anadolu Medical Center in Turkey (Medical Tourism Facilitators); and Hospital CIMA in Costa Rica—affiliated with Tulane Medical Center (Medical Tourism Facilitators).[89]

In what is by far the most comprehensive survey of these kinds of partnerships, Michael G. Merritt, Jr. et al. suggest four stages of development of these kinds of programs:

Stage One: Educational programs and training
Stage Two: Consulting and advisory services
Stage Three: Management services to hospitals, medical schools, or education and research centers
Stage Four: Delivering and/or owning patient care, education, and/or research abroad

Stage One involves the provision of education and training abroad. In Stage Two, those services are extended into advisory and consulting-oriented services that can include support to organizations across the academic missions. Generally, the major programs include some type of affiliation status with the U.S. organization that includes the use of that institution's name. In Stage Three, long-term managed service agreements are established with offshore health care organizations, medical schools, or education centers. A few Stage Four institutions actually own and/or operate programs and facilities abroad, representing the greatest organizational commitment and risk. Although activities across the four stages span the globe, the vast majority of these activities are in emerging and developing

---

[89] For discussions, *see* Lydia L. Gan & James R. Frederick, *Medical Tourism Facilitators: Patterns of Service Differentiation*, *17* J. VACATION MKTG. 165 (2011); Leigh Turner, *"Medical Tourism" and the Global Marketplace in Health Services: U.S. Patients, International Hospitals, and the Search for Affordable Health Care*, *40* INT'L J. HEALTH SERVS. 443 (2010); Michael G. Merritt, Jr. et al., *Involvement Abroad of U.S. Academic Health Centers and Major Teaching Hospitals: The Developing Landscape*, *83* ACAD. MED. 541 (2008); R. Sanders William et al., *A Global Partnership in Medical Education between Duke University and the National University of Singapore*, *83* ACAD. MED. 122 (2008); Robert K. Crone, *Flat Medicine? Exploring Trends in the Globalization of Health Care*, *83* ACAD. MED. 117 (2008).

countries, primarily eastern Asia and the Middle East, where the levels of activity and economic development in the respective countries are significant.[90]

Merritt et al. then provide a survey of the existing partnerships and their characteristics as of 2007:

LEVEL OF INSTITUTIONAL INVOLVEMENT ABROAD OF EACH OF 16 U.S. ACADEMIC HEALTH CENTERS (AHCS) AND MAJOR TEACHING HOSPITALS, BY DEVELOPMENT STAGE, 2007*

Cluster and institution	Development stage			
	Stage One. Educational programs and training	Stage Two. Consulting and advisory services	Stage Three. Management services to hospitals, medical schools, or education and research centers	Stage Four. Delivering/owning patient care, education, andtor research abroad
Cluster A				
Cleveland Clinic	X		X	X
Duke University School of Medicine		X		X
Harvard Medical International	X	X	X	
Johns Hopkins International	X	X	X	X
University of Pittsburgh Medical Center	X	X	X	X
University of Texas—M.D. Anderson Cancer Center	X	X		X
Weill Cornell Medical College	X			X

---

[90] Merritt, Jr. et al, *supra* note 86, at 542–43.

Cluster and institution	Development stage			
	Stage One. Educational programs and training	Stage Two. Consulting and advisory services	Stage Three. Management services to hospitals, medical schools, or education and research centers	Stage Four. Delivering/owning patient care, education, andtor research abroad
Cluster B				
Harvard Medical Faculty Physicians at Beth Israel Deaconess Medical Center		X		
Jackson Memorial Hospital	X			
Mayo Clinic	X			X
Memorial Sloan-Kettering Cancer Center	X	X		
The Methodist Hospital System	X	X		
New York Presbyterian Hospital	X	X		
Partners HealthCare	X			
Cluster C				
Baylor College of Medicine	X			
Hospital for Special Surgery, New York City	X	X		

* The authors classified the 16 institutions studied into the above stages after gathering information from a variety of sources (e.g., telephone interviews with institution leaders, Web sites, annual reports, and literature reviews).

Source: Merritt, Michael G. Jr; Railey, Chris J. MFA; Levin, Steven A. MBA; Crone, Robert K. MD, "Involvement Abroad of U.S. Academic Health Centers and Major Teaching Hospitals: The Developing Landscape," 83 Academic Medicine, 541 (2008).

The authors also interviewed leaders in charge of these partnerships for sixteen major U.S. academic health centers and teaching hospitals to get a sense of *why* they had pursued these partnerships. The major reasons cited were:

(1) *Attract foreign patients.* Especially given the decline in foreign patients post-9/11 and the competition from European, Indian, and Thai facilities for

these patients, these partnerships were thought of as useful for "building bet-ter referral mechanisms abroad and developing infrastructure to help interna-tional patients efficiently access services in the United States."[91]

(2) *Develop/improve an international reputation and branding.* Governments and investors were looking to "partner with recognized leaders to aid in the devel-opment of large-scale 'greenfield' health care developments that often include an academic component and clinical care," and many of the major academic health centers and teaching hospitals saw "the future of health care as global and expect[ed] that 20 years from now, the leaders w[ould] be those who became global."[92] The university-based centers also suggested that these partnerships helped attract talented students from outside the United States as well.

(3) *Advance their own educational and research goals.* Some interviewees suggested that one motivation for partnerships was "the opportunity to collaborate on research, to share research findings, to enroll different types of patients in clin-ical trials, and to enable their faculty to directly participate in research in other countries or collaborate with scientists at affiliates."[93]

(4) Finally, interviewees saw these partnerships as: *A way of providing financial benefits to the home country institution as well.* In particular, the interview-ees expressed that although "the future may see more direct investments abroad...until then, institutions are more interested in ensuring appropriate remuneration for services provided and licensing rights for use of their name to help fund the infrastructure needed to manage and develop international programs and to fund future international business development."[94]

In terms of the organizational structure of the home country facility versus the destina-tion country hospitals, Merritt et al. found that most U.S. academic medical centers and major teaching hospitals that were "involved in providing significant services abroad have established separate entities for their offshore activities" that are owned by the par-ent institution.[95] Among the motivations for this demarcation are: to implement tax and business reasons (including separating out tax-exempt charitable services from taxable services); to minimize comingling of funds or staff that would make it harder to evalu-ate the performance of foreign facilities; to insulate the U.S. core assets from risk; and to serve as a contracting entity with the foreign affiliates.[96]

As the medical tourism industry grows, these collaborations seem to be becoming increasingly important in marketing quality to patients in an increasingly crowded

---

[91] *Id.* at 544–45.
[92] *Id.* at 545.
[93] *Id.*
[94] *Id.*
[95] *Id.* at 546.
[96] *Id.*

marketplace. They also represent an important "soft law" kind of regulatory potential: to the extent the Harvard Partners International, Mayo, and Johns Hopkins of the world can be induced to build in some of the legal and ethical safeguards discussed throughout this book as preconditions to forming partnerships, they may be able to induce positive changes in the industry.

G. Industry Associations

Helping to grease the wheels of commerce in medical tourism are a series of industry associations. The largest and most prominent is the Medical Tourism Association (MTA).

As the MTA describes itself on its own website:

> The Medical Tourism Association is a Global Non-profit association for the Medical Tourism and International Patient Industry. The MTA works with healthcare providers, governments, insurance companies, employers and other buyers of healthcare—in their medical tourism, international patient, and healthcare initiatives—with a focus on providing the highest quality transparent healthcare. The MTA is also committed to raising consumer awareness of international healthcare options, and has specific initiatives designed to educate and increase the number of consumers who travel for healthcare. The MTA is also committed to educating consumers about their options internationally for medical treatment....
>
> [The] Association, is the first membership based international non-profit trade association for the medical tourism and global healthcare industry made up of the top international hospitals, healthcare providers, medical travel facilitators, insurance companies, and other affiliated companies and members with the common goal of promoting the highest level of quality of healthcare to patients in a global environment. Our Association promotes the interests of its healthcare provider and medical tourism facilitator members. The Medical Tourism Association™ has three tenets: Transparency in Quality and Pricing, Communication and Education....
>
> The Medical Tourism Association™ seeks to provide transparency in both quality of care and pricing. Every day we see more and more that the globalization of healthcare has created a very flat world. We exchange technology, information, communication, physicians and patients. In order to ensure patient safety, it is our goal to create a transparency about the quality of healthcare that can be found in each country. With this, it is increasingly important to create a transparency in pricing as well so patients traveling overseas for care can be sure of what they are receiving without hidden costs or unforeseen expenses. The Medical Tourism Association™ is also working on the Quality of Care Project, which will change the way we look at the reporting of global healthcare statistics and the quality of care available at hospitals around the world....

The Members of the Medical Tourism Association™ agree that communication is the key to success, particularly with respect to ensuring positive patient outcomes. The members of the Medical Tourism Association™ have agreed to put competition aside and work together to resolve the issues one by one and to work together to address them as they arise. We have created a forum for communication for all of the actors in the global healthcare environment....

Although we live in a world where information is at our fingertips, there are so many people who lack the information that they [need in order to] receive the highest quality of care outside of their home country. Some patients in countries like the United States, Canada, and the United Kingdom have a lack of access to healthcare due to high cost and high wait times. Patients in some other regions as in some parts of Africa and the Middle East do not have access to high quality of care in their own country and need to look elsewhere. Some patients just would like to travel outside of their country for healthcare to incorporate high quality of care with a holiday and tourism. Regardless of the reason, patients need education and information to understand what they should look for in finding a provider overseas and considerations that should be taken seriously to ensure patients' safety. As insurance companies continue to incorporate global healthcare and medical tourism options into their benefit plans and domestic healthcare providers are required to treat patients for aftercare when patients return to their home country, education is required to accomplish this seamlessly. The Medical Tourism Association™ strives to provide education to anyone with any interest in this industry using various means: the media, conferences, and through the Medical Tourism Magazine and Health Tourism Magazine. The Medical Tourism Magazine and the Health Tourism Magazine are bi-monthly medical tourism and health tourism trade journals aimed at providing a wealth of information for anyone interested in or affected by the globalization of healthcare.[97]

The MTA has also begun to offer its own set of accreditations for hospitals and facilitators including an "International Patient Services Certification™ for Hospitals and Clinics," "International Patient Center Training," and "Certified International Patient Specialist™"certification.[98]

The MTA is also well known for its lavish annual conference. Most recently, the 6th Annual Conference was held in November 2013 in Las Vegas at Caesar's Palace Resort and Casinos. Website promotions for the event advertised:

Up to 2,000 US & International Delegates
More than 10,000 Pre-Arranged Networking Meetings

---

[97] Medical Tourism Association, *About Us*, http://www.medicaltourismassociation.com/en/about-us.html (last visited Sept. 10, 2013).

[98] Medical Tourism Association, *MTA Certification Programs*, http://www.medicaltourismassociation.com/en/certification-programs.html (last visited Sept. 10, 2013).

Up to 400 Buyers of Healthcare Services
Up to 200 Sponsored Buyers through our Buyers VIP Program
Up to 140 Exhibitors and Sponsors
Delegates from over 90 different countries
Cocktail Receptions and Entertainment each Night[99]

Some academics on the outside are more skeptical. For example, Labonté writes that the Association:

> [M]anages MedicalTourism.com, a "free, confidential, independent resource for patients and industry providers," publishes the association's trade journal, the *Medical Tourism Magazine*, and convenes annual conferences bringing together countries developing medical tourism industries, hospitals catering to international patients, broker firms and insurance companies. Its web-site lists close to 50 countries which are described as "the most popular medical tourism destinations around the world." ... The descriptions of many of the countries emphasize tourism over healthcare, suggesting that medical tourists first choose the country based on their interest in tourism (such as the Galapagos Islands in Ecuador), and then check into the medical services available.[100]

He also gives a scathing first person account of visiting one of their conferences— obviously his negative viewpoint shines through:

> The banners proclaim it: over 2,000 attendees, 200 exhibitors, 400 healthcare buyers, 10,000 networking meetings, and "get the most from your investment." The conference halls are filled with suits, ties and briefcases. Everywhere posters and placards are emblazoned with "business." It's the fourth World Medical Tourism and Global Healthcare Congress, bringing together buyers, sellers and purveyors of cross-border healthcare for customers who can afford it. Sessions end with an almost confetti-like exchange of business cards, a celebration of business done and business to come. For an academic health researcher, the event feels surreal and oddly voyeuristic.
>
> Walking into the "great hall" of exhibits, one is immediately struck by three things:
>
> First, it is like any other gathering of health conference delegates. The people at this event look main street international ordinary.

---

[99] Medical Tourism Association, *6th Annual World Medical Tourism & Global Healthcare Congress*, http://www.medicaltourismassociation.com/en/medicaltourismconference.html (last visited Sept. 10, 2013).
[100] Labonté, *supra* note 9, at 26–27.

Second, it is unlike any other gathering of health conference delegates. This is a commercial meeting, marked by an appropriately inflated registration fee, a particularly American in-your-face flavour and a complete lack of public health embarrassment at its broadcasted entrepreneurial core. Countries marketing their medical tourism have booths full of conference swag (pens, bags, calculators, full colour costly brochures) to attract potential buyers (employers and health insurers), with intermediaries (medical tourism brokers) selling their abilities to bridge between the two.

"Our business sends European patients to have surgery abroad. At the World Medical Tourism Congress I established contact with hospital groups and key officials from almost every potential medical tourism destination in the world." (Medical tourism broker)

"Medical tourism is a direct outgrowth of the globalization of healthcare," one of the opening speakers explained in boldface. What he didn't mention is that, apart from the EU and a handful of other contiguous countries, there is little globalization of *public* healthcare, which tends to stop at national borders. It is *private* or commercial healthcare that is able to leap huge territories in a single bound (or two).

Third, despite the private market nature of medical tourism, governments are here in complicit enthusiasm. Private medical brokers share booths with governments' external economic development corporations. Staff working for government tourism departments (and confessing little knowledge of their own countries' healthcare system) push glossy magazines and travel DVDs to show how attractive their locales can be for the accompanying family of the recovering medical tourist. It is hard to discern which word is the more important—the "medical" adjective, or the sun, surf and exotic "tourism." Panama, as one example, is doing a stronger sell on its "get sick or injured in Panama and we'll treat you free for 30 days" than on its cheaper bariatric surgery—a clear case where healthcare is marketing tourism rather than the reverse.[101]

Labonté does later discuss some of the speakers who address health care inequities resulting from medical tourism and potential remedies, but he finds it far too little too late. I am, perhaps, more charitable to the institution, or less expectant than he is. The MTA is focused on the business side of medical tourism, which is its purview, so it is not surprising to me that it has not done much on legal or ethical issues relating to medical tourism. The rest of this book is focused on exactly those discussions missing at the MTA.

* * *

[101] Ronald Labonté, *Let's Make a Deal: The Commerce of Medical Tourism, in* Travelling Well, *supra* note 9, at 190, 190–92.

The medical tourism industry is a complex web of relationships among private and public, the charitable and the desperate, commerce and care. It is growing and evolving at a very rapid rate and much is in flux, but with this sketch of the industry and its major players in hand we are now ready to examine the legal and ethical issues posed by medical tourism.

PART ONE

Medical Tourism for Services Legal in the Patient's Home Country

2

Quality and Information

AS WE SAW in the last chapter, there is significant heterogeneity in terms of the size, sophistication, and accreditation of facilities that cater to medical tourists. The result, unsurprisingly, is vast differentials in terms of quality.

There is no reason to think price and quality will vary in any monotonic way, or even in any predictable way. For example, writing in *Health Affairs*, Aaditya Mattoo and Randeep Rathindran claim that Bumrungrand Hospital in Bangkok, Apollo Hospital in New Delhi, and Crossroads Center in Antigua are "examples of reputable medical facilities in developing countries that are comparable to the best in industrial countries," and note that the Apollo hospital chain has maintained a 99 percent success rate in more than fifty thousand cardiac surgeries performed, which is "on par with surgical success rates of the best U.S. cardiac surgery centers."[1] This is true notwithstanding the fact that these facilities charge only a fraction of the costs charged in the United States for these surgeries, as we saw in the last chapter. On the other hand, there are considerably more expensive hospitals catering to medical tourists that perform less well.

Patients traveling abroad (as well as those who stay in their home countries) are literally putting their lives in a physician's hands. What, if any, information can they ascertain about the quality of foreign physicians and facilities? Are there meaningful proxies for the quality of care in foreign facilities, such as JCI accreditation? Can the regulatory system

---

[1] Aaditya Mattoo & Randeep Rathindran, *How Health Insurance Inhibits Trade in Health Care*, 25 HEALTH AFF. 358, 360 (2006).

push foreign facilities to share more information? Should home country regulators set quality standards and thereby create obstacles for patients choosing high-risk procedures or facilities abroad, or at least facilitate and incentivize travel to higher quality facilities?

I will address these and related questions in this chapter. First, I will review some of the existing literature on the quality of foreign facilities seeking to attract medical tourists, including issues about the spread of infectious diseases and the problem of patients returning and potentially spreading antibiotic-resistant bugs. Second, I will discuss potential regulations aimed at improving information sharing to patients. Third, I will examine what, if any, steps home country governments can and should take to try to limit patient choice in terms of quality concerns. Issues related to quality are also discussed to some extent in the next chapter focused on liability, in that poor quality care can lead to liability, and some forms of liability may put pressure on foreign facilities to improve the quality of care they deliver.

I. WHAT IS KNOWN ABOUT THE QUALITY OF FOREIGN FACILITIES AND PROVIDERS AND THE RISKS FACED BY MEDICAL TOURISTS?

In the United States, there are several interlocking regulatory and tort mechanisms designed to protect patients in the health care setting. These include (the list is illustrative, not exhaustive) the accreditation, certification, and professional self-regulation of physicians and other health care providers; the medical-malpractice system, including the reporting of malpractice suits in the National Malpractice Database; licensure and accreditation of hospitals; medical staff bylaws; hospital privileges regulation; conflict of interest regulation; and anti-kickback statutes.[2] The United Kingdom, Canada, and many other home countries for patients have their own set of laws that play a similar function. Many foreign countries may lack these or have versions that do not neatly correspond to those familiar to home country patients.

But merely because these regulations or systems are not isomorphic to the ones with which we are familiar does not mean a lot on its own in terms of predicting quality. Even within a home country such as the United States, we see vast quality differentials between facilities governed by the same or similar regulatory structures.[3] Moreover, even

---

[2] The tables of contents of leading health care law textbooks give a good bird's eye view of this. *See, e.g.,* MARK A. HALL ET AL., HEALTH CARE LAW AND ETHICS, at xi–xxviii (7th ed. 2007); CLARK C. HAVIGHURST ET AL., HEALTH CARE LAW AND POLICY, at xix–xxxi (2d ed. 1998).

[3] *See, e.g.,* Amitabh Chandra & Jonathan S. Skinner, *Geography and Racial Health Disparities, in* CRITICAL PERSPECTIVES ON RACIAL AND ETHNIC DIFFERENCES IN LATE LIFE 604, 604 (Norman B. Anderson et al. eds., 2004); Victor R. Fuchs et al., *Area Differences in Utilization of Medical Care and Mortality among U.S. Elderly, in* PERSPECTIVES ON THE ECONOMICS OF AGING 367, 367 (David Wise ed., 2004); *see also* CENTER FOR THE EVALUATIVE CLINICAL SCIENCES, DARTMOUTH MEDICAL SCHOOL, THE DARTMOUTH ATLAS OF HEALTH CARE (1998), *available at* http://www.dartmouthatlas.org/downloads/ atlases/98Atlas.pdf (providing detailed information by region of the United States).

in countries with "good" health care systems, we see a significant number of adverse event reports. It has been estimated in the UK National Health Service and in "many other highly developed health systems" that "10 per cent of hospital patients experience an adverse event during their stay."[4]

A third complication in evaluating quality is the question of "better than what?" As discussed in the last chapter, many patients are traveling abroad because for some reason—they are uninsured or underinsured, the service is illegal or unavailable at home—they cannot get the treatment they seek where they live. For these patients, the alternative to getting the care at home will often be not getting this form of care at all.[5] For some patients and for some procedures—especially nonessential procedures, such as some forms of cosmetic surgery—the risks involved in poor quality care may be such that they are better off forgoing medical tourism even if it means forgoing getting the desired treatment at all. For many patients and for many services, though, even if the quality of care they will receive abroad is worse than the comparable service offered at home, the patients may be better off with a poorer quality of care experience that they can actually obtain rather than forgoing or delaying treatment. This is just to say that it is a mistake to view quality in isolation or to think that, when it comes to safety, the maximum is always the optimum. For many patients, their welfare will be improved if they travel abroad even if they get a lower quality of care than other patients may get in their home country.

All of this assumes that medical tourists will receive lower quality care abroad. Is that right? As Neil Lunt et al. recognize, as in many areas of medical tourism, it is hard to give an empirically grounded analysis:

> Evidence of clinical outcomes for medical-tourist treatments is sparse and research reports are difficult to verify. Little is known about the relative clinical effectiveness and outcomes for particular treatments, institutions, clinicians and organisations. There is scant evidence on long- or short-term follow up of patients returning home following treatment abroad. That positive treatment outcomes should result is important not least because the patient's local health-care system [in at least some countries] takes on responsibility and funding for post-operative care including treatment from complications and to remedy any side effects of poor care abroad…. There are also some in-depth case studies of poor outcomes from surgery abroad incurring significant public costs to rectify poor treatments.[6]

---

[4] Neil Lunt et al., *Quality, Safety and Risk in Medical Tourism, in* MEDICAL TOURISM: THE ETHICS, REGULATION, AND MARKETING OF HEALTH MOBILITY 31, 35 (C. Michael Hall ed., 2013).

[5] I discuss quality issues pertaining to private and public insurer–prompted medical tourism, where the analysis is somewhat different, in Chapters 4 and 5.

[6] Lunt et al., *supra* note 4, at 37.

Similarly, bioethicist Leigh Turner observes that "[g]iven the absence of databases tracking movement of patients and documenting clinical outcomes in medical tourism, there is at present no credible basis for making" many types of empirical claims, including "evidence-based assertions about how many medical tourists experience clinical benefits and how many experience surgical complications, infections, and other treatment-related health problems." Rather, Turner asserts that there is "considerable uncertainty concerning whether individuals traveling to particular locations are at greater risk of experiencing complications from treatment when they travel for care instead of visiting domestic medical facilities."[7]

Although I will review below the key existing studies on adverse events and patient safety as to medical tourism, for these reasons we need to be somewhat pessimistic as to how much this data can teach us. In this chapter, I focus on bread-and-butter health care procedures such as cardiac bypass, knee replacement, hip replacement, etc. I review safety information pertaining to stem cell therapies and transplant tourism in more depth in later chapters focused on those phenomena.

Patients traveling abroad for health care face a few different risks for which we have some data: improperly performed procedures (carrying risks of morbidity and mortality), disease transmission (where the risks are not only to themselves but to other home country citizens they may infect when they return), and finally, poor follow-up care. I review what we know about each in turn. Although I sort the material into these boxes, in reality the three phenomena are highly correlated, and in many instances it will be hard to pinpoint which of the phenomena causes a particular patient's problems.

A. Risks due to Complications from Improperly Performed Procedures

Some number of patients who travel abroad for health care die due to complications related to their care. Of course, patients sometimes die in the hospitals of their home countries from complications as well. What would be relevant to evaluating the risks of medical tourism is a comparison of the risks at home versus abroad, in order to understand how much higher the risk is of going abroad for a procedure. Unfortunately, the data to do this kind of comparison are largely unavailable both at the home country and destination country level. Even if it were available, there would be complications in analyzing the data related to selection effects. For example, are the patients who go abroad sicker than patients who get treated at home? Do they wait longer because some of them are trying to save up for the foreign treatment? Are foreign doctors more likely to see sicker patients who have "tried everything" and are trying medical tourism as a last

---

[7] Leigh Turner, *Patient Mortality in Medical Tourism: Examining News Media Reports of Deaths following Travel for Cosmetic Surgery or for Bariatric Surgery, in* THE GLOBALIZATION OF HEALTH CARE: LEGAL AND ETHICAL ISSUES 3, 25 (I. Glenn Cohen ed., 2013).

resort, and thus more likely to die even if the care is better than that in their home country? To which home country hospital or hospitals should performance be compared? After all, within the United States, for example, there are huge disparities in hospital quality.[8] Should comparison be to the best, the worst, the average, or to what we expect a patient might realistically have access to—and how might we figure that out?

In the absence of this kind of data and analysis, we are not totally in the dark about mortality risks from medical tourism, though the existing studies leave huge gaps, as their authors recognize.

What do we know?

In a study published in 2013, bioethicist Leigh Turner sought to work backward from news media accounts to examine cases of deaths relating to medical tourism for cosmetic and bariatric surgery.[9] He searched for death reports in databases including ProQuest Newsstand, Google News, Google News Archive, and Google, using search terms such as "death medical tourism, death medical tourist, medical tourist dead, medical tourist died, medical tourist investigation ... died facelift medical tourist ... death medical tourist bariatric surgery," and many others.[10] He then eliminated news reports that were not in the English language, those involving postoperative complications but not death, "and those that mentioned deaths of medical travelers but provided little information about such details as individuals' ages, their gender, the countries from which they departed, the nations to which they traveled for surgery, and when they died."[11] With the remaining articles, he discarded all those that did not relate to a patient who had died shortly after undergoing cosmetic or bariatric surgery. At that point:

> Once I identified an article that provided an account of someone who had traveled abroad for cosmetic surgery or bariatric surgery and died during or after his or her operation, I then used that person's name as a search phrase. In some instances that step generated additional articles for review. In the case of more recent deaths, some searches revealed Facebook memorial walls and Internet posts by family members and friends. For reasons related both to research methods and research ethics, in this chapter I restrict my analysis to news media reports that are in the public domain and were intended for public consumption.[12]

Using this search method, Turner generated twenty-seven reported cases of deaths of patients who traveled abroad and underwent bariatric surgery or cosmetic surgery at international medical facilities from 1993 to 2011.

---

[8] *See supra* note 3, and sources cited therein.

[9] What follows is taken from Turner, *supra* note 7.

[10] *Id.* at 7.

[11] *Id.* at 4.

[12] *Id.* at 7.

In summarizing the data, he reports that:

Of the twenty-seven reported deaths, twenty-five of the individuals were women. The youngest person reported to have died was twenty-one, and the eldest was sixty-five. Eleven individuals died after receiving health care in Mexico. Of the eleven reported deaths in Mexico, eight occurred in Tijuana. Of the remaining patients, four died after receiving care in the Dominican Republic, two died after having liposuction in Hungary, two died after having duodenal switch surgery in Brazil, and single deaths were reported to have occurred in Colombia, Cyprus, India, Malaysia, Panama, Spain, the United Arab Emirates (Dubai), and the United States. Identified surgical interventions included thirteen liposuction procedures, four tummy tucks, three breast implants/breast lifts, three breast reductions, two facelifts, two injections of fat into buttocks or calves, two lap bands, one gastric bypass, two gastric reduction duodenal switch procedures, one vaginal surgery with the specific type of procedure unspecified, one facial surgery with the specific type of surgery unstated, one plastic surgery with the specific procedure unspecified, and one patient reported as having surgery to her nose, chin, lips, and eyelids. There were more surgical procedures than there were individuals because nine patients underwent more than one surgical procedure.

Law enforcement officials including state pathologists, state attorney generals, local public prosecutors, and local police were reportedly contacted in fourteen of twenty-seven cases. In most of the reported cases it was not possible to locate additional information concerning outcomes of investigations by law enforcement authorities. It is possible that most investigations did not result in meaningful findings concerning how medical complications occurred and whether negligent medical care played a role in causing deaths of patients. Investigations might have generated results that were not reported. It is also possible that results of investigations were reported but were not captured by my repeated efforts to find them. Of reported outcomes, in three cases physicians settled lawsuits, spent time in jail, surrendered their license to practice medicine, and/or paid fines. In one court decision the treating physician was sentenced to jail and fined but left the country prior to sentencing. One investigation is presently under way; the physician is charged with manslaughter and is in a state penitentiary awaiting trial. Though family members requested investigations in nearly half of all cases, I was unable to establish how many of these requests resulted in thorough investigations of how patients died following cosmetic surgery or bariatric surgery.[13]

In trying to analyze the data in order to establish potential regulatory interventions, Turner notes that in many of these cases the use of medical tourism was prompted by

[13] *Id.* at 15, 18.

the desire to save on costs for the procedure. In response, Turner proposes that " if public health officials in various countries are concerned about the quality of care offered by some international medical facilities it might be prudent to place particular emphasis upon targeting to low- and middle-income women public safety messages about risks of cosmetic surgery and bariatric surgery procedures"[14]—though he notes that one case involved Stella Obasanjo, the wife of Olusegun Obasanjo, then president of Nigeria, who traveled to Spain and was clearly a woman of means.[15]

Second, he notes that many of the cases involved surgeries performed outside hospital settings and recommends "mandating that all but minimal-risk cosmetic surgery procedures, and all bariatric surgery procedures, be performed in hospitals and ambulatory medical centers rather than in small clinics and physicians' offices," observing that "[i]mmediate access to intensive care units and other specialized health services combined with better access to appropriately trained health care specialists would increase the likelihood that patients with potential life-threatening medical emergencies have access to optimal medical care."[16]

Turner also expresses concern about information provision:

> Though domestic government agencies lack capacity to unilaterally regulate Web sites and other promotional materials outside their domestic legal jurisdictions, they nonetheless could alert citizens if international medical tourism companies and destination health care facilities are failing to disclose risks and making misleading claims about benefits of surgical procedures, patient safety, and quality of care. In addition, they could work in bilateral fashion with their regulatory counterparts in other countries, share information about particularly egregious instances of misleading advertising, and attempt to improve the quality of information provided to patients by international hospitals, clinics, and medical tourism companies.[17]

In an interview study I participated in with coauthors, we studied the experience of professionals responsible for patient safety in Canada, representing the domains of tissue banking, blood safety, health records, organ transplantation, dental care, clinical ethics, and infection control.[18] What we found was that several participants had particular concerns about complications risk as a result of medical procedures obtained abroad. One participant who had seen many severe complications following medical tourism

---

[14] *Id.* at 19.

[15] *Id.* at 11.

[16] *Id.* at 19.

[17] *Id.* at 22.

[18] Valorie A. Crooks et al., *Ethical and Legal Implications of the Risks of Medical Tourism for Patients: A Qualitative Study of Canadian Health and Safety Representatives' Perspectives,* 3 BRIT. MED. J. OPEN 1, 1 (2013).

explained that "when it goes wrong it really goes wrong."[19] The risk of complications was thought to be dependent on the procedure obtained and the patient's existing health status. For example, several participants discussed the risks particular to patients managing chronic disease with complex medical histories or pharmacological regimes. It was thought that, in these cases, there could be a greater risk of complications "given the demographic…many [medical tourists]…have some chronic disease management that they're dealing with…and it's like oh my God [the risks they could face]."[20]

More anecdotally, a few commentators have claimed that *some* medical tourism facilities have very good morbidity and mortality rates compared to *some* U.S. hospitals. In their 2006 *New England Journal of Medicine* article, Arnold Milstein and Mark Smith express their "doubt" over whether the average U.S. hospital can "offer better outcomes for common complex operations such as coronary-artery bypass grafting, for which several JCI-accredited offshore hospitals report gross mortality rates of less than 1%."[21] Milstein and Smith are not alone in their thinking. As stated in the introduction to this chapter, Aaditya Mattoo and Randeep Rathindran single out Bumrungrand Hospital in Bangkok, Apollo Hospital in New Delhi, and Crossroads Center in Antigua as "examples of reputable medical facilities in developing countries that are comparable to the best in industrial countries," noting that the Apollo hospital chain has maintained a 99 percent success rate in more than fifty thousand cardiac surgeries performed, which is "on par with surgical success rates of the best U.S. cardiac surgery centers."[22] Others have made similar claims and comparisons, though the basis of their evaluations is not always clear.[23] It is hard to know what to make of these more armchair assessments, except to say that they reveal the need for more data and the reality that quality can only be evaluated on a facility-by-facility (indeed, perhaps facility-by-procedure-by-facility-by-procedure) basis.

B. Disease Transmission (Especially Antibiotic-Resistant Bacteria)

Medical tourists are very good targets of opportunities for pathogens. Many are traveling with compromised or suppressed immune systems to destination countries with relatively high infection rates, including the risk of exposure to multi-drug–resistant

---

[19] *Id.* at 3.

[20] *Id.*

[21] Arnold Milstein & Mark Smith, *America's New Refugees—Seeking Affordable Surgery Offshore*, 355 New Eng. J. Med. 1637, 1639 (2006).

[22] Mattoo & Rathindran, *supra* note 1, at 359.

[23] *See, e.g.*, Michael Klaus, *Outsourcing Vital Operations: What if U.S. Health Care Costs Drive Patients Overseas for Surgery?*, 9 Quinnipiac Health L.J. 219, 225 (2006) ("While paying greatly discounted prices for surgery, American patients traveling to Asia do not appear to sacrifice quality or incur greater risks of death or infection."); Thomas R. McLean, *The Global Market for Health Care: Economics and Regulation*, 26 Wis. Int'l L.J. 591, 601 (2008) ("Surgical care provided in a Joint Commission Accredited hospital in India by a member of the Royal College of Surgeons is unlikely to be inferior to the same care provided in an American hospital with Joint Commission Accreditation by a member of the American College of Surgeons.").

pathogens.[24] In medicine, it is common to distinguish commensals—the bugs we normally carry on our skin, mouth, digestive tracts, etc.—from pathogens, the harmful bacteria that cause disease through infection. When traveling for medical care, "one person's commensal bacteria can be another individual's exotic pathogen."[25] Medical tourist patients are transporting their commensals and pathogens to the hospital environments of the destination countries to which they travel, and are exposed to the commensals and pathogens of the health care providers, hospitals, and population at large in the destination country. The tourist patients may then bring the unwanted "hitchhiker" home with them to the destination country. The result is that "at any point in the circular migration of patients traveling for medical care, microbes may travel from one location where they constitute a harmless bacteria, or at least a known and treatable infection, to another where they are unknown, making diagnosis and treatment much more problematic."[26]

The transit involved with medical tourism may also put patients at greater risk of infection. While recognizing that "[f]or the most part, the risk of disease transmission on a commercial aircraft is minimal," infectious disease experts Jill R. Hodges and Ann Marie Kimball also note that the fact that "passengers typically are confined for a period of hours in close quarters, presents opportunities for disease transmission."[27] Air travel entails all four modes of disease transmission: contact (e.g., body-to-body or touching an armrest), common vehicle (e.g., via food or water), vector (e.g., via insects or vermin), and airborne (although more recent planes are equipped with high efficiency particulate air (HEPA) filters reducing transmission risk, older planes are not).[28] The Severe Acute Respiratory Syndrome (SARS) outbreak of 2003 gives a good example of how this might occur, with a three-hour flight from Hong Kong to Beijing carrying one SARS-infected passenger leading to sixteen passengers being subsequently confirmed as cases of SARS, with eight of those passengers sitting in the three rows in front of the passenger.[29]

Although in theory airline or national travel rules can prevent infected patients from boarding planes, detecting these infections in passengers is very difficult for the airline or immigration officials, and concerns about privacy of patients may chill some interventions. A 2007 case of a man who flew from the United States to Europe with extensively resistant tuberculosis and who ultimately circumvented authorities who tried to stop him on return by flying to Montreal, Canada, and renting a car, shows some of the limits on these restrictions.[30] As mentioned above, although most later-model commercial

---

[24] *See, e.g.,* Jill R. Hodges & Ann Marie Kimball, *Unseen Travelers: Medical Tourism and the Spread of Infectious Disease, in* Risks and Challenges in Medical Tourism: Understanding the Global Market for Health Services, 111, 111 (Jill R. Hodges et al. eds., 2012).

[25] *Id.* at 115.

[26] *Id.*

[27] *Id.* at 118.

[28] *Id.*

[29] *Id.*

[30] *Id.* at 119.

airplanes have HEPA filters that can help prevent the circulation of infectious microbes, older planes may not, and, as HEPA filters are only effective when in use, many passengers can sit for hours on flights with the ventilation systems turned off due to delays in takeoff, etc.[31] Kimball and Hodges recount one case study of an influenza patient who sat with co-passengers for three hours without the ventilation system activated; the result was 72 percent of the fifty-four passengers developed influenza symptoms within seventy-two hours of the flight.[32] Even when these filters work, patients can still get infections—for example, the SARS infection on a plane as mentioned above. Travel on buses and trains can also be problematic, where proximity and duration of these trips are large risk factors.[33] Although the rapidity of air travel is usually a plus in terms of infections, air travel may also spread infections farther much faster and the flight may be over before the passengers exhibit symptoms, at which point they may be on to their next destinations.[34]

Many major destination countries for medical tourism, especially Thailand and India, are places where "infectious diseases of global concern such as TB and Malaria are endemic."[35] As I will discuss in greater depth in Chapter 6, destination countries that redirect health care resources away from their general population to build medical tourism industries may actually exacerbate the risks of disease transmission to medical tourists, due to patients' exposure to the general (and disease-ridden) population. Many medical tourist patients will also be exposed to infections by fellow patients in resorts aimed at allowing patients to recover. For example, in their article on infectious disease transmission, Hodges and Kimball refer to the South Korean government's building of Jeju "Health Care Town" outside of Seoul, a center designed for the treatment and convalescence of international patients. This facility, they note, will bring together patients from alternate hemispheres, which in turn may lead to off-season exposure to influenza as patients come into contact with new and virulent strains of the virus before the season has arrived in their home countries and vaccinations have been developed and properly administered.[36]

Then we have "nosocomial" infections, those acquired in hospitals or other health care facilities that were not present when a patient was admitted. Common pathways of transmission for these kinds of infections include contaminated water, contaminated medical devices (e.g., catheters and ventilators), and contact with physicians and nurses who may carry infections from one patient to the next. In high-income countries, urinary

---

[31] *Id.* at 118.

[32] *Id.* at 118 (citing M.R. Moser et al., *An Outbreak of Influenza aboard a Commercial Airliner*, *110* Am. J. Epidemiology 1 (1979)).

[33] *Id.* at 119.

[34] *See id.*

[35] *Id.* at 120.

[36] *Id.* at 121.

tract infections are the most common nosocomial infection, whereas in low-resource settings the more serious risk is surgical-site infection.[37]

High-income countries themselves face significant problems with these infections. A 2002 study estimated that 1.7 million patients (ninety-nine thousand of whom died as a result) developed health care–acquired infections in the United States that year, and in Europe nosocomial infections are estimated to cause thirty-seven thousand deaths a year and add US$9.4 billion in direct costs.[38] Still, the risks are worse in low-income countries: on average, 10–15 percent of all hospitalized patients in low-income countries acquire a nosocomial infection, compared to 7–8 percent in high-income countries. For intensive care units, 30 percent of patients in high-income countries acquire at least one nosocomial infection, while the rate is two to three times that in low- and middle-income countries.[39] Blood transfusions are particularly risky, with 39 of the 164 countries that responded to a 2008 WHO survey on blood safety indicating that they do not follow the WHO recommendation to routinely screen donated blood for HIV, hepatitis B and C, and syphilis.[40] All that said, it is not clear how relevant these kinds of statistics are for the medical tourist facilities that are sought out by out-of-country patients in destination countries. Especially in larger operations, many of the facilities may have state-of-the-art ventilation and isolation technology and well-developed infection control protocols. At the same time—and this cuts against some of the recommendations I make in Chapter 6, which try to ameliorate medical tourism's negative effects on the destination country's patient population—if health care providers see patients in *both* the public and the medical tourist facilities, this may enhance the exposure and spread of bacteria by enabling health care providers to "serve as vectors ferrying bacteria."[41]

The consequences of this "circular migration" of bacteria through medical tourism can be devastating when the bacteria are multi-drug–resistant. We are at a moment in drug development history where bacteria are evolving to resist antibiotics faster than we can construct new antibiotics, where "[a]lmost every bacterial pathogen has developed resistance to at least one antibiotic, and some are resistant to nearly all."[42] Among other things, the increased flow of animal products and human beings around the world has exacerbated this problem. The major causes of drug resistance include overuse of antibiotics when not effective or necessary, underuse of antibiotics when they are needed, failure to complete a full course of antibiotics, counterfeit drugs, and excessive antibiotic use in food

---

[37] *Id.* at 122.

[38] *Id.* (citing World Health Organization, WHO Health Care–Associated Infections Fact Sheet (2011); R.M. Klevens et al., *Estimating Health Care Associated Infections and Deaths in U.S. Hospitals, 2002*, 122 Pub. Health Rep. 160 (2007)).

[39] *Id.* at 122.

[40] *Id.* (citing World Health Organization, WHO Blood Safety Fact Sheet (2011)).

[41] *Id.* at 123.

[42] *Id.* at 115.

animals.[43] In countries where antibiotics are widely available without prescription, many of these risk factors are more likely, but these problems occur even in places with prescription systems such as the United States.[44] Hodges and Kimball, relying on work by Sho-Shin Jean and Po-Ren Hsueh note that Asia—where many major medical tourist hubs are located— is one of the main centers for antibiotic-resistant bacteria, in part because of "limited sanitation, health care, and surveillance infrastructures, as well as misuse of antibiotics."[45]

The risk is not merely theoretical. In January 2008, a new type of enzyme was detected in bacteria found in a fifty-nine-year-old man with a urinary tract infection being treated in Sweden. The man, Swedish but of Indian origin, had in the previous month undergone surgeries at two hospitals in India. The enzyme, which they labeled "New Delhi metallo-beta-lactamase-1 (NDM-1) . . . equips bacteria to disarm a wide range of antibiotics, including the carbapenems, one of the last line of defenses against common respiratory and urinary tract infection."[46]

In 2009, a study found that twenty-nine UK patients had tested positive for the bacteria-carrying NDM-1 and that seventeen of the twenty-nine (60 percent) had traveled to India or Pakistan in the year before. Of those seventeen, fourteen had received medical treatment while abroad in those countries, some for accidents or illness while traveling and others for medical tourism, either for kidney and bone marrow transplants or for cosmetic surgery. The authors of the study claimed that this bacteria was present not just in Indian hospitals but in the general community as well, and suggested that the cost of treating these infections made dubious the claims of those who thought that the United Kingdom's National Health Service could save money by giving patients the option of traveling to India if faced with a long wait list.[47]

Some health systems reacted quite quickly to this report. The United Kingdom's health protection agency warned patients and clinicians that travel to India and Pakistan was a major risk factor in acquiring bacteria with this enzyme, and authorities in Canada, France, and the United States issued their own warnings.[48] The Indian government, unsurprisingly, took issue with these warnings by pointing out that many countries struggle with multi-drug–resistant bacteria, and just because the enzyme was

---

[43] *Id.* at 116.

[44] *Id.*

[45] *Id.* at 117 (citing S-S Jean & P-R Hsueh, *High Burden of Antimicrobial Resistance in Asia*, 37 INT'L J. ANTIMICROBIAL AGENTS 291, 291 (2011)).

[46] *Id.* at 111–12 (citing D. Yong et al., *Characterization of a New Metallo-beta-lactamase gene, bla(NDM-1), and a Novel Erythromycin Esterase Gene Carried on a Unique Genetic Structure in Klebsiella Pneumoniae Sequence Type 14 from India,* 53 ANTIMICROBIAL AGENTS & CHEMOTHERAPY 5054 (2009)).

[47] *Id.* at 112 (citing K.K. Kumarsamy et al., *Emergence of a New Antibiotic Resistance Mechanism in India, Pakistan, and the UK: A Molecular, Biological, and Epidemiological Study,* 10 LANCET: INFECTIOUS DISEASES 597 (2010); N. Lakhani, *NHS "Could Save Millions" by Flying Patients to India—Experts Urge Department of Health to Consider Using Hospitals outside Europe,* INDEPENDENT, Jan. 17, 2010).

[48] *Id.* at 113.

first detected in India did not mean it originated there.[49] At the same time, it acknowledged the need to address drug-resistant agents and convened a task force to enforce and enhance policies pertaining to antibiotic use and to develop an effective surveillance system for drug-resistant bacteria.[50]

The threat has not died down. Since January 2008, NDM-1 has been detected in several different bacteria in hundreds of patients in more than thirty countries (the list includes Australia, Canada, China, France, Israel, Japan, Norway, Turkey, etc.), and most cases have been linked to travel to and treatment in India or the Balkans.[51] Further research has confirmed that the bacteria is not found merely in Indian hospitals but in standing water on the street and tap water as well, suggesting risks to both medical tourists and their traveling companions.[52] Swedish researchers concluded that of 444 Methicillin-resistant Staphylococcus Aureus (MRSA) infections related to international travel, 55 percent were acquired through health care provided abroad.[53] In 2004, the U.S. Centers for Disease Control and Prevention (CDC) and the New York City Department of Health and Mental Hygiene determined that of twenty women who had traveled from the United States to the Dominican Republic for cosmetic surgery and who had subsequently developed *Mycobactereium abscessus* wound infections, eight had visited the same clinic for surgery. The investigators thought that one source of infection may have been water from the tap that at least one patient used to clean her surgical wound on the instruction of her doctor.[54] Ian Cheung and Anthony Wilson reported on a patient who traveled from Australia to India for knee surgery (when her Australian doctor had recommended against surgical intervention) and developed a mycobacterium fortuitum infection that required four subsequent operations to address.[55]

Treating drug-resistant infections that are the product of medical tourism is difficult. In our interview study, our patient care professionals

expressed frustration at the lack of good solutions to these problems at the hospital level and, in particular, their inability to quarantine, test or even identify all medical tourism patients. The solutions they offered focused on infection control measures, such as hand-washing procedures, which are not specific to addressing

---

[49] *Id.*

[50] *Id.*

[51] *Id.*

[52] *Id.* (citing T.R. Walsh et al., *Dissemination of NDM-1 Positive Bacteria in the New Delhi Environment and Its Implications for Human Health: An Environmental Point Prevalence Study*, 11 LANCET: INFECTIOUS DISEASES 355 (2011)).

[53] *Id.* at 123 (citing M. Stenhem et al., *Imported Methicillin-Resistant Staphylococcus Aureus, Sweden*, 16 EMERGING INFECTIOUS DISEASES 189 (2010)).

[54] *Id.* (citing E.Y. Furuya et al., *Outbreak of Mycobacterium Abscessus Wound Infections among "Lipotourists" from the United States Who Underwent Abdominoplasty in the Dominican Republic*, 46 CLINICAL INFECTIOUS DISEASES 1181 (2008)).

[55] *Id.* at 123–24 (citing I.K. Cheung & A. Wilson, *Arthroplasty Tourism*, 187 MED. J. AUSTRALIA 666 (2007)).

the health and safety risks posed by medical tourism in particular. They did, how-ever, hint at system-level reforms such as limiting coverage for unauthorized trans-plant tourism or better regulation of medical tourism facilitators (eg, licensing, standardised training).[56]

Coping with such infections is also very costly. For example, Hodges and Kimball relate the case of a forty-one-year-old patient from Indonesia (which has comparably high rates of tuberculosis (TB)) who showed up in a Singapore emergency room with a cough and fever and was diagnosed with extensively drug-resistant tuberculosis, which ultimately required "five months of intensive multidrug treatment, hospitalization in a special iso-lation facility, and lung surgery at a total cost of more than ... $78,000 USD ... before she could return home."[57]

Even when they do not involve multi-drug–resistant bacteria, the infections that medical tourists and other travelers can bring home with them can be very costly for a domestic health care system.

To be sure, international travel *in general*—for medical tourism or work or vacation—is a major vector. One study showed that the spread of influenza in the United States accelerates as the volume of travel increases, and another found that spring vacation to Mexico was associated with the spread of H1N1 in home countries in that sixteen of the twenty countries with the highest volume of travel of their residents to Mexico in 2008 had confirmed cases of H1N1 imported from Mexico in 2009.[58] Hodges and Kimball note that "[a]s many as half of the more than 100 million people who travel annually from nontropical areas to developing countries develop some kind of health problem during their travels, including infectious diseases ranging from flu to malaria."[59]

But medical tourists are at greater risk. They often have compromised immune sys-tems making them more vulnerable to infection, and thus more likely to bring back TB or malaria than the average traveler.[60]

These tourists put not only themselves at risk but also other home country hospital patients. As we heard in our interview study of Canadian patient-care professionals:

Treating patients with "really interesting bugs" is challenging, wherein health and safety officials need to identify unusual strains of organism that they might not have previously encountered, which can delay treatment.

---

[56] Crooks et al., *supra* note 18, at 6.

[57] Hodges & Kimball, *supra* note 24, at 115–16.

[58] *Id.* at 117 (citing J.S. Brownstein et al., *Empirical Evidence for the Effect of Airline Travel on Inter-regional Influenza Spread in the United States*, 3 PLoS MED. e401 (2006); K. Khan et al., *Spread of a Novel Influenza A (H1N1) Virus via Global Airline Transportation*, 361 NEW. ENG. J. MED. 212 (2009)).

[59] *Id.* (citing J. Torresi & K. Leder, *Defining Infections in International Travellers through the GeoSentinel Surveillance Network*, 7 NATURE REVS. MICROBIOLOGY 895 (2009)).

[60] *See id.*

Participants discussed the challenges of policy formulation to address the risk of the spread of antibiotic-resistant organisms locally from outbound medical tourism. They focused on the costs of screening, isolation and testing for antibiotic-resistant organisms after medical tourists sought treatment upon return home. A participant noted that "if you write a policy that says anybody who's been admitted to a hospital abroad needs to be isolated when they're brought into your hospital, that has huge implications, and/or if you would say 'well I'm going to do a screening swab on every single one of these patients whose been hospitalized abroad before I admit them to my hospital,' huge lab costs." Agreeing that effective policy responses will be difficult to create, participants stressed the important role played by hospital infection control protocols in [the Canadian province of British Columbia], such as hand washing, to limit organism spread.[61]

Transplants abroad, the subject of Chapter 7, pose some of the greatest risk because patients are put into immune-compromised states as part of the transplant procedure, and with transplant tourism the patients may be accepting an organ that has been less rigorously typed for genetic matching than what they would have received as part of a transplant at home, if available. Transplants have been linked to "transmission of hepatitis, HIV, malaria, Creutzfeld-Jakob disease, rabies, and tuberculosis," among other diseases.[62]

When such infections go undiagnosed, they may spread to other patients in the home country. For example, in one reported case, hepatitis B was spread in two hospitals outside London in connection with a patient who traveled to India to get a kidney transplant. The patient did not exhibit symptoms until returning to the United Kingdom and was not diagnosed for more than six months, after he had already infected several members of his household.[63] Although noting that the evidence on cross-border transplantation infection rates is somewhat "mixed" and there have not been enough studies, Kimball and Hodges review several studies in existence on the matter across the world and conclude that "patients who travel internationally for transplants are more likely to contract infectious disease than those who have procedures in their home countries."[64] We heard similar concerns from patient-care professionals in Canada, who told us that they "were particularly concerned about the impacts of organ transplant patients' acquired infections on the BC health system upon return home, and the potential public

---

[61] Crooks et al., *supra* note 18, at 4.

[62] Hodges & Kimball, *supra* note 24, at 124 (citing P. Mártin-Dávila et al., *Transmission of Tropical and Geographically Restricted Infections during Solid-Organ Transplantation*, 21 CLINICAL MICROBIOLOGY REVS. 60 (2008)).

[63] *Id.* at 125 (citing R. Harling et al., *Passage from India: An Outbreak of Hepatitis B Linked to a Patient Who Acquired Infection from Health Care Overseas*, 121 PUB. HEALTH 734 (2007)).

[64] *Id.* at 125.

health implications of infection spread."[65] I discuss some of these and other studies in the chapter on transplant tourism later in this book.

C. Continuity of Medical Documentation and Difficulties in Providing Follow-Up Care

There is also good evidence in the literature that some medical tourists return with poor quality medical documentation that makes it more difficult to provide adequate follow-up care. In our study of Canadian care professionals participants told us that they learned

> from clinicians and other front-line providers that patients returning from medical care abroad often bring back incomplete medical records or no documentation of the care they received. Although some clinicians have requested results and records from international medical providers, destination facilities were often uncooperative. "One letter [about a patient's treatment abroad]…was sent to me blacked out…from a Mexican clinic and they just said 'how dare you ask me for this.'" Participants suggested that limited medical documentation provided to medical tourists could reflect a low standard of care abroad, masking shortcomings.
>
> Participants agreed that patients typically understand it is their right to request records to bring home with them when engaging in medical tourism. However, they indicated that patients rarely do so, even though it would be reasonable for them to insist: "I want to see my chart, I want to see…I'm going back to wherever I live, I want to take my stuff with me in case something goes wrong." Participants also did not believe patients had enough health literacy to question why a destination facility would not take their medical histories, something they reported was common. Meanwhile, failure by clinicians to obtain this information can result in complications or other negative outcomes. In effect, "the procedure [becomes] compromised…because they [were not asked for] a health history…So it kind of goes back to that health literacy point."[66]

A different issue with continuity of care stems from the unwillingness of some *home country* physicians to treat patients who have undergone medical tourism when they have returned from being treated through medical tourism. I discuss in greater depth in Chapter 3 whether home country physicians can make these refusals. However, even if/when the law forbids this practice, many patients will encounter reluctant or refusing physicians, and such gaps in continuity of care further compromise these patients' health.

* * *

---

[65] Crooks et al., *supra* note 18, at 4.

[66] *Id.*

When it comes to quality, we are still missing much of the data needed to make deep comparisons about the complication rates for health care provided domestically versus by medical tourism. What data we do have paints an unsurprisingly complex picture—when it comes to morbidity and mortality, for example, some foreign facilities are better than the very best U.S. facilities, while some are far worse when it comes to avoidable deaths and injury per procedure. This heterogeneity is unsurprising—we see similar variance *within* a health care system—but when combined with the fact that it is not always clear what the right point of comparison should be for an individual patient (the best facility at home? The best facility the person could reasonably access? The facility the person would be most likely to access?) and the fact that these comparisons can only be made on a procedure-by-procedure and hospital-by-hospital basis, it makes it hard to concretely compare "medical tourism" with "domestic healthcare" in terms of complication rates, etc. There is better evidence that medical tourism carries unique risks relating to disease transmission (especially multi-drug–resistant bacteria), gaps in documentation, and poorer continuity of care—risks that negatively impact the quality of care it can deliver. Although it would be desirable to be more definitive than this, I think that this tentative assessment is all that the current empirical literature can rigorously support. In the rest of this chapter, I consider what steps we might take to get more information for policymakers and patients to empower better decision-making, and also what steps we might take to try to push for higher-quality care experiences for patients.

II. WHAT MIGHT BE DONE TO ENSURE THAT PATIENTS ARE PROTECTED?

Improving the quality of patient care is—along with cost and access—one of the three sides of the "golden triangle" of health policy. If it were very easy to ensure high quality of care for patients, we would not see the extreme heterogeneity in measures of care quality in developed countries such as the United States, health care academics and advocates would not spill oceans of ink on measuring and innovating in this area, and this chapter could be fairly straightforward. Unfortunately, that is just not the case. Although we have made extreme jumps forward in the last fifty years in infection control, checklists, care coordination, etc., we still have a long way to go.

This book is primarily about the law and ethics of medical tourism, not the medicine involved. As such, my goal in this part of the chapter is not to try to summarize all the myriad of attempts to improve care quality that might be put into place as part of medical tourism—a topic worth several books in itself—but instead to examine what role the law might play and what limits or obligations ethics might dictate.

When I think about the role for law and the dictates of ethics in this area, I imagine a spectrum of possible regulations home countries and international bodies (and, to a lesser extent, destination countries) could put into place. These interventions can usefully be placed on a spectrum of paternalism, based on how much they restrict patient choice.

On one end of the continuum are interventions very compatible with libertarian (or, if you prefer, anti-paternalist) conceptions of regulating patient choice: providing patients information about foreign facilities. On the other end of the spectrum are much more intrusive measures, such as making it against the law for a patient to use a particular facility for a particular procedure. In-between are several different kinds of interventions. Some are "libertarian paternalist" nudges that seek to "influence behavior while also respecting freedom of choice" through choice architecture—manipulating the circumstances in which patients make choices in order to nudge them in a certain direction.[67] Others use carrots rather than sticks, trying to give foreign facilities an incentive to comply with certain best practices and also trying to direct patients to these facilities and exclude others.

The kind of interventions I mostly champion in this chapter, and more generally in this book, are of the latter variety. I call these "channeling" interventions. Channeling involves creating a list of criteria that results in a sort of "approved" list and an "unapproved" list of providers and/or services. I put "approval" in air quotes, because although it is easier to understand if done by a home country government or its delegate, such "approval" can also be done by health care accreditors, NGOs, etc. By virtue of being on the "approved" list, a particular provider receives some perquisite—promotion by the home country to its patients, the ability to see insured patients from that home country, qualification for a tax deduction for medical care by home country patients that use it—or, in some versions, those on the unapproved list are deprived of some desired thing or subject to a more searching review by the home country government or limited in some ways in terms of their permitted activities in the home country. This kind of intervention works both by pushing patients to approved medical tourism and by giving providers incentives to become approved, with this latter mechanism amplifying the effect beyond that achieved simply by patient choice.

Channeling is a middle ground between hard law interventions on the one hand and merely providing information on the other. Before I go on to sketch what a channeling regime for quality might look like, let me first explain why I think merely providing information to patients, though desirable, will not be effective on its own. I then explain why I would find an attempt to legally prohibit medical tourism altogether due to quality both unjustified and infeasible. I then return to the channeling regime and explain in more detail how it might operate to improve quality.

---

[67] Cass R. Sunstein & Richard H. Thaler, *Libertarian Paternalism Is Not an Oxymoron*, 70 U. Chi. L. Rev. 1159, 1159 (2003).

A. Why Providing Information Is Desirable but Insufficient

i. What Information Is Currently Available?

Imagine you are a patient trying to decide whether to use medical tourism and what facility to go to. How would you decide? Perhaps you decide not to decide and instead hire a facilitator to help make decisions for you. We described some of these facilitators and how they operate in the last chapter. Such facilitators sometimes have conflicts of interest, a problem I return to in more depth in the next chapter when we discuss referral fees, but let us put that aside and imagine a white knight facilitator free of agency problems who is really simply trying to bring expertise to bear and help patients make the best choice. How would such a facilitator decide whether a particular foreign facility has high quality for the procedure the patient is interested in?

There are three things, which we saw in the last chapter, that foreign facilities point to as an attempt to signal their quality. First, that their hospital has achieved JCI accreditation or another high value form of accreditation. Second, that their staffs are made up of foreign-trained health care providers who have been deemed qualified to practice in the United States;[68] for example, Bumrungrad Hospital in Bangkok states on its website that "[t]he hospital's medical Chairman is board certified in the UK. Its Group Medical Director is board certified in the US. Other top medical officers were trained in the US or UK"[69] and of its "[o]ver 1,200 physicians and dentists, most [have] international training/certification."[70] Third, they point to collaborations they have with U.S. medical centers, of the kind we saw in the last chapter.

Though all three pieces of information are useful and better to know than to not know, none is really sufficient to help patients make good decisions.

JCI accreditation, as we saw in the last chapter, is based on the processes and procedures one's hospital has in place, not its outcomes. Are those procedures aimed at improving quality? Absolutely. But they are insufficient to ensure high quality care. The proof is in the pudding, for as discussed earlier, the JCI accreditation mirrors that done by its parent, formerly known as the Joint Commission on Accreditation of Healthcare Organizations (JCAHO), which accredits most U.S. hospitals for participation in the Medicare and Medicaid programs through a similar process.[71] And yet, we see huge

---

[68] *See, e.g.*, Mattoo & Rathindran, *supra* note 1, at 359.

[69] Bumrungrad International, *Management*, http://www.bumrungrad.com/en/about-us/bumrungrad-management (last visited Feb. 9, 2014).

[70] Bumrungrad International, *Factsheet*, http://www.bumrungrad.com/en/about-us/bumrungrad-factsheet (last visited Feb. 9, 2014). Other work in the field suggests results similar to these unaudited numbers. Milstein and Smith found that Wockhardt had "four cardiac surgeons trained in U.S. or Australian hospitals" and Bumrungrad had three cardiac surgeons trained in the United States, United Kingdom, and Australia—two of which were confirmed as "board certified." Arnold Milstein & Mark Smith, *Will the Surgical World Become Flat?, 26* Health Aff. 137, 139 (Jan.–Feb. 2007).

[71] Hall et al., *supra* note 2, at 1196–97.

disparities in the quality of health care outcomes in the United States among hospitals, all of which are JCAHO accredited. Moreover, JCI may have a design that pushes it to be pro-accreditation. As Nathan Cortez and others have noted, JCI has its own incentives that come into play in its role as accreditor and may give us pause: it has a very high rate of accreditation and low rate of revocation, and its revenues depend on the number of hospitals it accredits.[72]

As we saw in the last chapter, JCI accreditation *is* very expensive to achieve, but that tells us only that a particular foreign facility has the finances and/or support of its home government necessary to achieve that accreditation, not necessarily that its quality is very high. To be sure, when friends and colleagues ask me for advice on foreign hospitals I always ask if they have received JCI or another well-regarded accreditation, and this information is useful, but it is not sufficient as a guide for quality.

Though the fact that many foreign physicians and nurses are U.S. or UK trained or board certified is likely reassuring to Western patients, it is not very probative of high quality. Again, most (if not all) physicians and nurses in U.S. hospitals are U.S. trained or board certified, and yet we see wide disparities in health care quality across U.S. hospitals. Moreover, foreign facilities sometimes use ambiguous language to describe the training of their physicians—we will see a study dissecting this in further detail in the chapter of this book on stem cell therapies—and no one audits these claims, which may be inadvertently inaccurate or beset with puffery or even fraud. There is no study I know of that shows that the number of U.S. or UK (or other highly respected health care system—I do not mean to be parochial) trained physicians is predictive of the outcomes of patients seeking care at a facility.

Finally, we have the collaborations with prestigious Western medical institutions such as the Mayo and Cleveland Clinics, or Harvard. As we saw in the last chapter, there is considerable heterogeneity as to what such affiliations mean—everything from merely a branding innovation, to a referral arrangement, to a true partnership—such that merely knowing that such a partnership exists will not tell a patient very much. There is also no published data of which I am aware suggesting that hospitals *with* such partnerships perform better than those without it. It seems reasonable to think that the reputational interests of these outstanding Western facilities are such that they would be loathe to partner with a medical tourist facility that was engaged in egregious malfeasance or obvious and repeated negligent provision of care. So a patient who goes to one of the affiliated facilities can take at least some solace in that. But beyond such clear-cut cases, it seems to me that many of these partnerships are hands-off enough to question whether the U.S. partner hospital will be exerting enough effective control on

---

[72] *See* Nathan Cortez, *Patients without Borders: The Emerging Global Market for Patients and the Evolution of Modern Health Care, 83* IND. L.J. 71, 125–26 (2008).

the medical tourism facility to make a meaningful difference. At the very least, we have no published studies answering that question.

Beyond those three indicia, which are of limited value, patients and facilitators do not have much to go on.

ii. What Kind of Information Would We Want to Have Available for Patients to Make Rational Choices and How Would We Induce Disclosure?

Imagine you were made international health-policy czar and could get whatever data you wanted to help facilitate patient decision-making about the quality of providers at destination country hospitals—what would you ask for? One model is the "report card" system that provides risk-adjusted mortality and readmission rates for certain procedures by provider, similar to what is in place in Pennsylvania and New York.[73] Another model is the attempt of states such as Massachusetts to make available to patients online information about licensed physicians' education, training, disciplinary, and malpractice records.[74] Because multi-drug–resistant bacteria are such a concern in this domain, we might also want to have further disclosure of the rates of such infections detected in various destination country hospitals.

These U.S. state systems have ready mechanisms for getting the needed information. For example, the Massachusetts Board of Registration in Medicine helped build that state's system, which draws on court judgments, statutorily mandated reporting from courts about malpractice tribunal findings and from malpractice insurers about closed claims, and physician disciplinary action reporting from medical associations, hospitals, and other facilities.[75] Pennsylvania law requires disclosure of the relevant information to its Health Care Cost Containment Council.[76]

By contrast, home country governments lack the direct power to force foreign hospitals to disclose information to them or their patients. Foreign hospitals and governments

---

[73] The Pennsylvania scheme requires hospitals to report various data to the Pennsylvania Health Care Cost Containment Council, which then "publishes annual report cards that present individual hospitals' and physicians' risk-adjusted mortality and readmission rates for cardiac bypass surgery as well as various quality measures for hip and knee replacement." Kristin Madison, *Regulating Health Care Quality in an Information Age*, 40 U.C. DAVIS L. REV. 1577, 1591 (2007). New York's system is similar. *See id.* at 1609 (refering to New York's "report card efforts"); M.R. Chassin et al., *Benefits and Hazards of Reporting Medical Outcomes Publicly*, 334 NEW ENG. J. MED. 394, 394–95 (1996) (describing a model developed by the Department of Health that compares mortality rates among hospitals in New York).

[74] Madison, *supra* note 73, at 1591 & n.39. California, Maryland, and Minnesota, among other states, have attempted similar systems. *Id.* at 1591 n.39.

[75] *Id.* at 1590; Frances H. Miller, *Illuminating Patient Choice Releasing Physician-Specific Data to the Public*, 8 LOY. CONSUMER L. REP. 125, 128 (1995–1996).

[76] 35 PA. STAT. ANN. § 449.5 (2005); *Pennsylvania Health Care Cost Containment Council, About the Council*, http://www.phc4.org/council/mission.htm (last visited July 18, 2010).

seeking to promote their medical tourism business may have an incentive to voluntarily disclose such information so as to signal their quality to consumers. We have seen this, for example, with the Apollo hospital chain's 2010 advertising, boasting of its better than 99.6 percent cardiac bypass success rate in a large number of procedures.[77] But these reports may be prone to selective reporting (e.g., a hospital may tout its cardiac success rates but not its high rate of secondary infection), puffery, or even fraud.

What we really need is for a third-party institution to require, audit, and provide this data in a form accessible to patients. The easiest solution would be JCI or another accreditor to make disclosure of such data a condition of the foreign hospital's continuing accreditation. It would be better still if JCI not only required *disclosure* of that information but also evaluated it and reformed its accreditation standards to adopt an outcome-based measure as well. Although that is, I think, the most desirable intervention of this sort, my own sense is that this would require more of a transformation of JCI and the view of its mandate than seems likely. Perhaps it would be better to have a new third-party organization do this, if JCI is perceived by some as too much "in the pocket" of foreign hospitals. Having a new institution take on this function would also overcome concerns about taking JCI too far out of its comfort and expertise zone. Such a new institution could be a home country government such as the United States itself, with the United States maintaining the list and reporting the outcomes the way the U.S. Centers for Disease Control and Prevention (USCDC) does for fertility clinic success rates.[78] Alternatively, another major patient home country, or the European Union, could take charge. Several home countries with significant medical tourism patient flow could cooperate in this venture, and we could also imagine WHO or another intergovernmental institution taking the lead.

What is essential here is that the organization that will foster disclosure, audit, and publish results have leverage over destination country facilities and their governments, such that it can get the power to audit and be able to effectuate disclosure. In the current medical tourism market, JCI accreditation seems valuable enough that if JCI were to start demanding this disclosure as a precondition of renewal of its accreditation or its accreditation *vel non*, it likely has the market power to make destination country facilities do so. True, some current facilities that are JCI accredited would rather give up their accreditation than disclose—but that may itself be revealing information to patients about quality problems. More worrisome is the fact that many facilities do not currently have or plan to pursue JCI accreditation due to the high cost involved. The fact

---

[77] Apollo Hospitals, *Medical Milestones of the Apollo Hospitals Group*, http://www.apollohospitals.com/milestones-a-accolades/medical-milestones.html (last visited July 18, 2010). For reference to this advertisement in medical tourism websites, *see, e.g.*, Patients beyond Borders, *Apollo Hospitals Group*, http://www.patientsbeyondborders.com/hospital/apollo-hospitals-group (last visited Feb. 9, 2014).

[78] 42 U.S.C. § 263a-5(1)(A) (2012). The data is available at http://www.cdc.gov/art/ARTReports.htm (last visited May 4, 2014).

that these facilities have not provided their data might give patients an unclear signal about the facilities' quality: Are the facilities of poor quality or merely lacking the requisite patient volume for the destination country to support JCI accreditation in the first place—or both? For these reasons, it would be desirable for JCI both to publish audited data for *all* foreign facilities willing to provide it (JCI-accredited or not) and to make that disclosure a prerequisite for JCI accreditation. Although it would be optimal for JCI to adopt both of these functions, even if JCI only took on the publishing and auditing of the facilities it itself accredits, that alone would greatly improve the disclosure of information to patients in regards to the facilities that patients are most likely to visit. This would also pressure non-JCI hospitals to become accredited or otherwise publish audited data.

Although conditioning JCI accreditation on disclosure is a powerful leverage device, there are other options. As I discuss in more depth below, we could pair this disclosure with some of the channeling techniques to derive further leverage. We could also piggyback on the insurer-covered portion of the medical tourism industry discussed in greater depth for private and public insurers in Chapters 4 and 5. We could make it a condition of being approved for insurer-covered medical tourism that the facility disclose the requisite information. If, as I suggest at various points in this book, this portion of the industry is likely to see substantial growth and prove quite lucrative for destination country facilities, this will provide a strong incentive for these facilities to disclose.

It might also be possible to put pressure on medical tourism facilitators to be better conduits of information for patients; however, because their compensation is often paid by destination country facilities rather than the patients, they are in a real sense servants of two masters, and we would likely encounter major agency problems in using them as good informational portals.

iii. Problems with Information Disclosure

Imagine we were successful in getting robust disclosure of the relevant information from medical tourism facilities. We then face a tough intellectual problem of what that information should be compared to. Take the United States as the home country, for example. Although some U.S. states have followed New York and Pennsylvania's lead in producing these report-card measures, many have not, and even those that have done so have used widely different measures, making comparisons between providers in different states quite difficult, let alone comparisons between providers in a particular U.S. state and those abroad.[79] Further, the information is usually limited to specific procedures, such as cardiac bypass.

---

[79] *See* Kristin Madison, *The Law and Policy of Health Care Quality Reporting*, *31* Campbell L. Rev. 215 (2009).

But imagine we were able to get sufficient information disclosure abroad and in the United States and transformed that information into a standard set of metrics. To what should the home country patient compare the foreign hospital? The best facility in the United States? The worst? The average? What seems most probative would be a comparison to the facility he or she would realistically be able to seek care from given cost, travel, etc. But patients paying out-of-pocket in the United States will have great difficulty determining the prices of various treatments at various facilities ahead of time, and thus may find it quite difficult to realistically make these comparisons.

But suppose we could solve even all of these problems. Will patient choice be meaningfully improved? Given the U.S. domestic experience with these kinds of informational interventions, we should have fairly low expectations. There are questions about the quality and utility of the information. As has been suggested with the Massachusetts provider-searchable database, the link between a provider's having been sued for med-mal and their propensity for medical error may be problematic. For example, a 2006 *New England Journal of Medicine* study found that 37 percent of claims paid in med-mal cases by insurers who cover physicians were judged by expert reviewers not to have been the result of medical error, while for 27 percent of cases where they did find error, no payment was issued.[80] Med-mal suits or verdicts against a provider may depend on specialty or practice type, and some doctors may find ways to "game" the reporting system.[81] For report-card systems such as Pennsylvania's and New York's, there are ongoing debates about whether these devices contain accurate measures or whether patient-selection problems skew the data.[82]

Even if we were convinced that the information contained in these types of work was relevant to good patient decision-making, prior work suggests that patients fail to make use of that information because of bounded-rationality problems. In a recent article critiquing the promise of consumer-directed health care more generally, Carl Schneider and Mark Hall collect decades of empirical work on these problems, emphasizing doctors' reluctance to help patients make choices as health care consumers, patients' failure to understand health care delivery and statistics, patients' tendency to avoid making medical decisions, and patients' fixation on cost over quality.[83] A Kaiser Family Foundation

---

[80] David M. Studdert et al., *Claims, Errors, and Compensation Payments in Medical Malpractice Litigation*, 354 NEW ENG. J. MED. 2024 (2006).

[81] *See, e.g.*, Jennifer Arlen, *Contracting over Liability: Medical Malpractice and the Cost of Choice*, 158 U. PA. L. REV. 957, 970 (2010); Michelle M. Mello & David M. Studdert, *Deconstructing Negligence: The Role of Individual and System Factors in Causing Medical Injuries*, 96 GEO. L.J. 599, 600–02 (2008); HALL ET AL., *supra* note 2, at 442; Kathryn Zeiler et al., *Physicians' Insurance Limits and Malpractice Payments: Evidence from Texas Closed Claims, 1990–2003*, 36 J. LEGAL STUD. S9, S18 n.17 (2007).

[82] *See, e.g.*, David M. Cutler et al., *The Role of Information in Medical Markets: An Analysis of Publicly Reported Outcomes in Cardiac Surgery*, 94 AM. ECON. REV. (Papers & Proc.) 342, 342–43 (2004).

[83] Carl E. Schneider & Mark A. Hall, *The Patient Life: Can Consumers Direct Health Care?*, 35 AM. J.L & MED. 7 (2009).

survey from 2000 surveyed 2,014 adult Americans and found that only roughly 10 percent of Americans had used information comparing quality among health plans, hospitals, and doctors, when available, and that in making provider selections respondents
favored recommendations from friends, family, and other doctors over actual data on
health care quality.[84] Empirical studies of the New York and Pennsylvania report-card
systems suggest the same.[85]

How well these bounded-rationality problems translate to medical tourism remains
to be seen. Although overoptimism bias and trust in their U.S. physicians cause many
American patients to fail to use quality information,[86] it is possible that Americans or
other Western patients may have inaccurately negative views of foreign physicians, in
part because of an availability heuristic fueled by negative depictions in film and television of unsanitary, third-world hospitals. Second, those paying for medical tourism
out-of-pocket are already sick and may be more likely to consult report cards than the
average American respondent who is the focus of the aforementioned domestic studies.
As I will emphasize further below, these patients are also not seeking emergency care and
thus have some time to research their options. Third, given the current penetration of
the medical-tourism industry in the U.S. market and other Western markets, at present
these patients are unlikely to have friends, family, or primary-care providers to advise
them on providers abroad once they have decided to use medical tourism. They may pay
more attention to objective information than do their counterparts seeking domestic
care who instead attach a lot of weight to recommendations from those they know. If
the industry expands, though, this point of distinction from the domestic context is
likely to diminish, and it may be less true for certain pockets of the existing market—for
example, Californians of Mexican descent who go to Mexico for medical tourism services may already have such informal informational sources, as do the many Indonesians
who travel to Malaysia to receive care. Moreover, information and referrals made by
medical-tourist intermediaries may also push in the other direction.

To be sure, the extent to which bounded-rationality problems in using state- or
accredit-provided information carry over to the medical-tourism sphere is an empirical
question, and one for which currently we have little direct evidence. But the failures-of-
information provision alone have been so widespread in the domestic sphere that it
seems likely that to meaningfully alter patient behavior in this context will require a

---

[84] The Kaiser Family Found. & Agency for Health Care Research & Quality, National
Survey on Americans as Health Care Consumers: An Update on the Role of Quality
Information (2000), *available at* http://www.ahrq.gov/downloads/pub/kffchartbk00.pdf.
[85] Chassin et al., *supra* note 72, at 394–96; Richard G. Frank, *Behavioral Economics and Health Economics*,
20–21 (Nat'l Bureau of Econ. Research, Working Paper No. 10881, 2004), *available at* http:// www.nber.
org/papers/w10881.
[86] Madison, *supra* note 72, at 1637.

more robust regulatory intervention that restricts patient choice to some extent. I examine the design of these types of interventions in the next subpart.

B. Interventions That Restrict Patient Choice
i. Three Important Considerations

From a political theory point of view, information-forcing interventions are easy to support, but, as the last section shows, we ought to be fairly skeptical of their effectiveness at meaningfully influencing patient choice. The policy question this presents is whether and how far to go in instead *restricting* patient choice in the name of patient protection.

Sound public policy in this area would, I believe, attempt to triangulate between a few different kinds of considerations:

(1) **Efficiency/Administrability**: How costly or easy to administer would the intervention be and how effective in achieving its goals? This in turn depends both on the kinds of levers of control the home country has to implement its program, and on what means the home country has of detecting rule-breaking, as well as the effectiveness and the cost of those detection strategies.

(2) **Overinclusivity**: For how many of the patients whose behavior is affected by the intervention does the intervention actually decrease rather than increase their welfare? This factor will vary from patient home country to patient home country because the counterfactual care a patient can access *without* medical tourism will be better or worse depending on the setup and quality of his or her home country's health care system. In particular, at least some medical tourists (especially in the United States, but in universal health care systems as well where a particular service may not be covered) are traveling for services they cannot afford at home. For this population, the deep cost savings that medical tourism makes possible may mean the difference between getting and not getting certain nonemergency care at all.

Even in the United States, it is true that uninsured Americans are not wholly without domestic care options. The Emergency Medical Treatment and Active Labor Act (EMTALA) indirectly requires hospitals that accept Medicare reimbursement to have an emergency room that provides some care to the uninsured. EMTALA requires such facilities to "screen[]" any patient that presents herself, to determine "whether or not an emergency medical condition [within the meaning of the statute] exists," and, if it does, then the hospital must either stabilize (give "treatment as may be required to stabilize the medical condition") or transfer the patient to another facility, which can be done only if the patient requests the transfer in writing after being informed or if a health care provider certifies that "the medical benefits reasonably expected from the provision of appropriate medical treatment at another medical facility outweigh the increased risks to the individual."[87] But care received through an EMTALA admission is unlikely to overlap to any significant extent with the types of procedures sought by medical tourists, as EMTALA covers only "emergency medical condition[s]," whereas medical tourists are typically scheduling surgeries far in advance when the patient is well enough to travel. I discuss in Chapter 4 how this plays out a little differently for those with health insurance in the United States.

Thus, a ban on medical tourism for those paying out-of-pocket may, in some proportion of cases, result in preventing access to nonemergency health care for the patients we seek to "protect." There will, of course, also be some cases where receiving care in a foreign country (because of quality-of-care or med-mal disparities) would be worse than receiving no care at all. But there is also a risk that an outright ban or too discouraging a regime threatens to not only restrict patient choice and diminish patients' self-assessed welfare, but in fact to diminish some of these patients' actual welfare by blocking access to nonemergency care entirely. The overinclusivity element of the analysis will turn on our estimates of how many cases fall within each of these buckets and also our estimates about how much receiving poor quality of care makes patients worse as compared to no care at all.

Unfortunately, we must make decisions here in a condition of uncertainty, in that the kinds of data we would need to really evaluate these trade-offs are currently unavailable. As a second-best approach to the problem, far coarser to be sure, we might try to divide medical tourism care into different categories and adopt different strengths of interventions for each. All medical tourism care is nonemergency, almost by definition, but some is for medical necessities (cardiac bypass, for example), some for goods on the periphery of health care (cosmetic surgery is on this periphery in many cases), and others lie in between. It may seem reasonable to think a patient's home country ought to have a wider berth in implementing interventions that will block access to medical tourism the less medically essential the service is. This would suggest that interventions that restrict patient choice are more justifiable for things such as cosmetic surgery than for things such as hip replacements for patients for whom this may be their only option.

Although this approach is reasonable, it depends in part on one's view about whether health care is special in this regard. For those who argue that health care is "special" in comparison to other kinds of goods and services people seek out in their daily lives,[88]

---

[87] Emergency Medical Treatment and Labor Act (EMTALA), 42 U.S.C. §§ 1395dd(a)-(d) (2012); *see, e.g.,* Burditt v. U.S. Dep't. of Health & Human Servs., 934 F.2d 1362, 1368–73 (5th Cir. 1991).

[88] *See, e.g.,* NORMAN DANIELS, JUST HEALTH: MEETING HEALTH NEEDS FAIRLY 29–78 (2008). Daniels, a Rawlsian, connects the special importance of health to its importance in ensuring equality of opportunity to ensure access to the "normal opportunity range"—the "array of life plans reasonable persons are likely to develop for themselves." *Id.* at 43; *see id.* at 29–60 (discussing health needs and how they relate to normal functioning and access to opportunities). Martha Nussbaum, writing from a more aretaic perspective (i.e., Aristotelian, focusing on character, virtue, and human flourishing), has also singled out health as having

the State may have a greater obligation to provide care that is at the core of health and not stand in the way of patient choice in securing it elsewhere when the home country fails in this obligation. The contrasting view would treat health care as just one among any number of inputs to an all-purpose view of what matters—call it welfare. On this view, what matters is how much patients will benefit from going abroad to secure the care unavailable at home, not whether that care is at the core of health care or more at its periphery like cosmetic surgery.

(3) **The Scope of Justified Paternalism**: Finally, one has to have a normative position about how important it is to protect individuals from making poor decisions that will have significant negative impacts on their lives, when doing so requires mobilizing the State's more coercive powers.

We can understand attitudes here as a continuum. On one extreme, true libertarians would say that freedom includes the freedom to fail and put oneself at jeopardy, and that the State's role ends with providing or regulating the flow of information. Libertarians are comfortable regulating on the basis of *externalities*, costs that the patient's decision foists on others in the society.[89] On the other pole, those who are true paternalists think it is the State's role, indeed its duty, to protect individuals from bad choices.[90] This will lead to a distinction in terms of when problems stemming from quality of care will justify interventions that restrict patient choice. For the libertarian, choice-limiting interventions in medical tourism will be most justified in cases where patients pose a physical risk of infecting other patients in the home country, such as in that of multi-drug–resistant bacteria discussed above and perhaps also in the case of individuals who will impose large financial costs on other patients paying into a universal health care system. The neonatological costs associated with multiple embryo transfer is one example of this.[91] Paternalists find choice-limiting interventions justified when intervening seeks to protect the patient from risks that do not pose externalities to others. They will feel more justified limiting patients' choice the more serious the risk involved and/or the more unfavorable the risk-to-benefit ratio is for the patient (and thus the more confident they are that the individual is "choosing wrong").

---

particular importance in her capabilities/functioning theory. MARTHA C. NUSSBAUM, FRONTIERS OF JUSTICE: DISABILITY, NATIONALITY, SPECIES MEMBERSHIP 75–76 (2006).

[89] *E.g.*, Richard Epstein, *Surrogacy: The Case for Full Contractual Enforcement, 81* VA. L. REV. 2305, 2315–16 (1995).

[90] For a particularly thorough discussion of this topic, *see* 3 JOEL FEINBERG, THE MORAL LIMITS OF THE CRIMINAL LAW: HARM TO SELF (1986).

[91] One difficulty with this latter reason is that true libertarians tend to disfavor universal health care systems and the collectivization of risk in health care to begin with. But if stuck in such a system, the externalities posed by travel abroad in such a system seem to me to be fair game in terms of what might count for libertarians as a reason to restrict patient choice.

Most of us fall in-between these two poles in terms of our attitude toward when intervention is justified—we will find intervention most justified when it involves *both* externalities and paternalistic concerns, but may also be comfortable acting in some instances that pose a serious enough risk of harm to a patient, especially when unaccompanied by an offsetting chance of benefit.

Now that we can understand these three elements in the analysis, I will apply them in greater depth to the question of choice-restricting interventions pertaining to quality.

ii. Mechanisms for Restricting Patient Choice

First, let us examine the question of the efficiency/administrability of various forms of intervention.

Imagine a home country was motivated to try to discourage its home country patients, who are paying out-of-pocket, from using a particular kind of medical tourism; what levers does the home country have? In theory, it could criminalize the behavior altogether. As we shall see in Chapters 8 and 9, some countries have done this for reproductive technology use or assisted suicide abroad. Such an approach might run into problems with home countries that protect their citizens' right to travel, for example,[92] but the larger problem is that it seems disproportionate to the aim of the State (especially when paternalism rather than externalities is the motivation), and it would be very difficult to administer. It would require the detection of the consumption of medical services abroad in a situation where neither party has an incentive to alert the home country government. Although, as we will see in Chapter 8, some home countries have attempted this kind of detection in the case of travel for abortions, doing so on a widespread basis for large categories of medical tourism would be much more difficult. It would also require prosecutors and courts to distinguish medical care purchased incident to other travel from medical tourism pursued as the primary purpose for a trip—although pre-travel communications and deposits in some cases might serve as good evidence. Still, that evidence would be difficult and expensive to acquire in the case of patients paying out-of-pocket. As we will see when we discuss private and public insured medical tourism later in this book, the levers are much easier to administer within the regime of insurance-covered care.

A different approach might penalize medical tourism indirectly through the forfeiture of benefits in the home country. In the United States, for example, we could treat engaging in medical tourism as rendering an individual ineligible for Medicare/Medicaid coverage, which might dissuade some potential medical tourists. I will discuss in Chapter 7 the possibility of adopting this kind of approach—denying coverage for immunosuppressive drugs—as a way of trying to curb transplant tourism. In the

---

[92] I. Glenn Cohen, *Protecting Patients with Passports: Medical Tourism, Medical Tourism and the Patient-Protective Argument*, 95 IOWA L. REV. 1467, 1513 (2010).

United States, such an approach would depend for its deterrence value on the medical tourists' assessment of the value of and likelihood that they will qualify for or need Medicare and Medicaid, which is hard to determine. Moreover, Medicare/Medicaid ineligibility may just cause the affected patients to instead seek treatment in the ER, which produces expensive externalities for patients in the home country. Of course, we could pair Medicare/Medicaid ineligibility with ineligibility for treatment under EMTALA, an act that, as discussed above, indirectly requires hospitals that accept Medicare reimbursement to have an emergency room that provides some care to the uninsured. However, blocking access to EMTALA services would be quite difficult to administer, as it would require identifying a patient on a no-go list at emergency admission. This might be easier to implement in universal health care systems such as Canada's or the United Kingdom's where an individual who goes abroad could be held to temporarily—or, perhaps, more permanently—forfeit access through his or her national health insurance card.

All this is to say that these approaches to regulating medical tourism are relatively inefficient and hard to administer. They also seem quite overinclusive in that we have every reason to suspect (although, again, empirical evidence is hard to come by to fully answer the question) that many patients whose medical tourism we will deter through such measures actually benefit (or at least perceive themselves to benefit) from medical tourism notwithstanding these risks. But perhaps the strongest argument against this approach is on the question of justified paternalism: a prohibition of medical tourism seems too draconian a response, especially if the motivation is paternalistic rather than stemming from externalities law meant to protect the general population. Although it is true that home countries domestically sometimes use the threat of sanction through their police power to protect their citizens (motorcycle-helmet laws are a good example), I think most home countries probably lack the stomach for these more powerful sanctions, though it will partially depend on how significant the risk of externalities are. For these reasons, in all points of the triangulation it seems plausible to me that this approach to regulating medical tourism for *legal* services is not good public policy. I emphasize *legal* because, as we will see in the second half of this book, things look quite different when the home country is seeking to prevent patients from going abroad to get services it has criminalized at home, especially when those services involve the imposition of serious bodily harm on others.

A more promising alternative in regulating legal medical tourism for those who purchase it out-of-pocket, it seems to me, is to use mechanisms of regulation that involve incentives more than punishments, and focus on civil rather than criminal law. For example, in the United States, we might use the tax system. Section 213 of the Internal Revenue Code allows a taxpayer to deduct her expenses for medical care (for herself, her spouse, or a dependent, including the cost of insurance for that care) not covered by insurance to the extent the expenses exceed 10 percent of the taxpayer's adjusted gross income (AGI). The current section appears to cover the cost of medical care wherever it is received, which would include medical tourism.[93] One could amend the Code to exclude medical expenses incurred through medical tourism just as the tax code section currently carves out cosmetic surgery.[94] For a stronger deterrent, one could provide that anyone who uses medical tourism becomes ineligible for the Section 213 deduction entirely. Indeed, in one sense, this is not penalizing unapproved medical tourism use at all, but instead merely refusing to subsidize it through tax deductions.

This approach has the virtue of requiring individuals to police themselves through statements on their income tax forms, while using an already existing enforcement and detection scheme. Massachusetts's current requirement of stating on one's tax form whether one has health insurance and thus complying with the state health insurance mandate (the precursor for the national version now being put in place in "Obamacare") is a possible model. Nevertheless, the level of deterrence this approach would provide against using medical tourism is debatable. How worried would patients be about getting caught? Only those whose medical expenses exceed the 10 percent threshold become eligible for the deduction, which may exclude some portion of medical tourists. Moreover, the value of the deduction to a taxpayer diminishes with lower incomes, and many uninsured medical tourists will be low income. For some, the cost savings of medical tourism are likely to exceed the value of the Section 213 deduction, such that, if faced with choosing between forgoing medical tourism or forgoing the deduction, most will forgo the deduction. That said, there are ways of amplifying the deterrent within the tax code. One could make medical tourism care ineligible for other health care–related tax benefits, such as health savings accounts (HSAs),[95] or link eligibility for other kinds of tax deductions to not having used medical tourism.

C. Channeling

As compared to the current regime—where individuals can get both the cost savings of medical tourism and claim the medical-expense deduction—such changes would decrease the incentive to use medical tourism, though the decrease is hard to quantify. Still, there are ongoing debates about the appropriateness of using the tax code for enforcing health policy and legitimate concerns about whether the IRS is already overburdened in its enforcement capabilities. Also, to the extent undocumented immigrants in the United States make up part of the population of medical-tourism users,

---

[93] I.R.C. § 213(a), 213(d)(1)(D) (2012); *see also* 26 C.F.R. § 1.213–1(e)(v)(c) (2013) ("It is immaterial for purposes of this subdivision whether the medical care is furnished in a Federal or State institution or in a private institution.").

[94] I.R.C. § 213(d)(9)(A) (2012). For a discussion of whether this analogy works from a tax theory point of view, *see* Cohen, *supra* note 92, at 1513 n.88.

[95] I.R.C. § 223 (2012); *see also* Timothy S. Jost & Mark A. Hall, *The Role of State Regulation in Consumer-Driven Health Care*, *31* Am. J.L. & Med. 395, 395–97 (2005) (discussing HSAs).

as discussed in Chapters 1 and 4, a solution implemented through the income tax code is unlikely to reach them. Moreover, in most universal health care jurisdictions, the personal tax code does not have a major role to play in health care, and it is unclear what other equivalent ways of penalizing individuals exist short of criminal sentences or depriving them of health care in whole or in part. Again, there are many unknowns here, but although it seems more favorable than the first set of interventions on the three axes of policy analysis I set out, I tend to think effectiveness will be the biggest problem with this kind of intervention.

The most promising way forward, I think, is to focus on positive incentives. The idea would be to create an "approved" list and an unapproved list of providers/services, and apply incentives to engage in medical selectively of those providers/services on the approved list. This kind of intervention works both by pushing patients to approved medical tourism and by giving providers incentives to become approved, with this latter mechanism amplifying the effect beyond that achieved simply by patient choice. I call this kind of regime a "channeling" regime and return to it frequently in different forms in this book. Channeling, as a concept, can be used for both positive incentives to use "approved" provider/services and negative "punishments" for "unapproved" ones, though in some cases (such as the revenue code deduction), whether something is a punishment or incentive will depend on one's baseline.

For patients paying out-of-pocket, one important incentive that home countries can offer foreign facilities to become "approved" is access to patients. Although, at the time of this writing, the American Affordable Care Act (colloquially called "Obamacare") web exchange portals have been less than successful at start-up, we could imagine the home country hosting an information pathway/sign-up website that listed only "approved" centers and tried to direct business to them. Although it might be a problem in the United States with robust protection under the First Amendment for commercial speech, other home countries may be able to prohibit the advertising of unapproved medical tourism altogether, for example.

These are attempts to incentivize or punish medical tourism providers for activities directly relating to recruitment of patients who pay out-of-pocket. In fact, however, some of the most successful "carrots" involved in medical tourism would connect those paying out-of-pocket with those seeking to use medical tourism in conjunction with public or private health insurance, the subject of later chapters. This is a kind of "harnessing" approach to channeling. Facilities' incentive to get "approved" by the home country government stems from their desire to have access to private and public insurance dollars, markets in which the home country has much more regulatory control, as we will see in later chapters. In order to access those markets, though, the home country would require medical tourism providers to meet its "approval" standards not only as to patients with public or private insurance but for *all* home country patients, even those who are paying out-of-pocket. I call this "harnessing" because the home country government is using its ability to control and incentivize behavior in a market where it has lots of regulatory power (the insured) to achieve gains for a market where it has much less power (the out-of-pocket market). For this to work, one would need a home country (1) which has carrots in terms of access to insured patients are "delicious" enough to motivate medical tourism facilities to alter their behavior, (2) which has sufficient regulatory control over accessing these patients, (3) which has the willingness to tie the markets together, and (4) which has the legal authorization (or at least absence of legal impediment) to do so.

It would also be helpful, though perhaps not strictly necessary, if the kinds of changes in foreign facility behavior induced by the regulatory pressure are "lumpy" and harder to segment as between the insured and uninsured population. As we will see in the next chapter when we discuss medical malpractice liability, many of the care-enhancing activities that we think are potentially induced by increased liability—increased training for physicians, better checklists and safeguards—may be lumpy, although one could imagine that other kinds of care-enhancing interventions (for example the size of the care team involved, the quality of the machines used) may be easier to segment as between insured and out-of-pocket patients. As a matter of authorization to access the insured market, the home country can insist "as thou does to my insured patients thou shalt do to my out-of-pocket patients as well," but such symmetrical treatment may be hard to monitor. That is why lumpiness is helpful, because it means that in making progress for one category of patients, one will in effect make progress for the other, whether or not one is seeking to merely comply with the legal mandate of the home country.

i. Forms of Channeling

This is the basic idea behind a channeling regime, which directs patients to particular facilities for particular procedures abroad based on positive and negative incentives. In so doing, it not only directs patients to where we think their welfare would be best served, but also gives foreign facilities incentives to improve themselves in order to increase their patient flow. This could be done on several different dimensions, separately or in conjunction. Again, how far to go depends on triangulating the answers to the questions discussed above about overinclusivity, administrabiltiy/efficiency, and paternalism.

1. Channeling by Service

Home countries could channel patients toward medical tourism only for certain services. Motivated by the overinclusivity fear, a home country could only create "blockages" for medical tourism in its channel when the services sought by patients are less essential, such as some forms of cosmetic surgery. It could also instead try to pick out particular services it views as "low-risk" and channel patients toward foreign providers only for those services.

Along this second variant, a home country could adapt an approach taken by Mattoo and Rathindran in their paper attempting to estimate the savings from medical tourism, where they construct a subset of fifteen procedures that met the following criteria:

(1) The surgery constitutes treatment for a nonacute condition; (2) the patient is able to travel without major pain or inconvenience; (3) the surgery is fairly simple and commonly performed with minimal rates of postoperative complications; (4) the surgery requires minimal follow-up treatment on site; (5) the surgery generates minimal laboratory and pathology reports; and (6) the surgery results in minimal postprocedure immobility.[96]

They then applied these criteria to "the 230 most commonly performed procedures ... [as] published by the Agency for Health care Research and Quality." This reduced their list to fifteen procedures to study, including knee surgery, shoulder anthroplasty, tubal ligation, hernia repair, adult tonsillectomy, hysterectomy, cataract extraction, and glaucoma procedures.[97]

Although these authors used this mechanism to construct a list for the purpose of study design, home countries or others involve in channeling could instead apply this list of criteria, or a variation thereof, to construct a list of "approved" procedures for which channeling will be done. The fact that a particular surgery is simple, is commonly performed with minimal rates of postoperative care, and requires minimal on-site follow-up treatment may all be good proxies for types of care for which concerns about quality are at their lowest. This is not to say that Mattoo and Rathindran's own application of their criteria to generate fifteen procedures was perfect or that the criteria could not be usefully refined, but it does suggest that we may be able to sort procedures into high- and low-risk groups and channel patients only to low-risk ones. One could imagine gathering together a broad group of stakeholders and experts and generating a similar list and using positive and negative incentives to try to make these kinds of procedures become the main ones used for medical tourism.

2. Channeling by Experience

Separately or in combination, a home country or other regulator could instead construct a list of "approved" providers based on experience. One way of doing this (which to be sure somewhat mixes channeling by "service" and "provider") would be to take advantage of research that "consistently show[s] an inverse relation between volume of procedures performed per provider (or of patients treated in a single diagnostic category) and adverse outcome rates (as measured by risk-adjusted mortality or complication rates),

---

[96] Mattoo & Rathindran, *supra* note 1, at 361.
[97] *Id.* at 361 exhibit 1.

no matter what procedure is studied, and thus suggest[s] that 'practice makes profi-ciency.'"[98] This approach would channel patients toward facilities that have performed the particular surgery in question a set number of times. It would require some auditing system to determine just how many of a particular procedure the hospital or its physi-cians has performed, a system that has some costs in terms of administrability but is much easier to implement than full-on outcome monitoring.

3. Channeling by Accreditation or Other Signal of Quality

Separately or in combination with either of the two prior approaches, we could also channel patients based on accreditation or other signal of quality. As discussed above and in the prior chapter, hospitals that have received a JCI accreditation have shown their ability to meet a demanding (and expensive) set of process-based requirements. Home countries or other regulators could treat as "approved" only those facilities with JCI or another major accreditation process. Whether this is a good approach depends on how good a proxy such accreditation is for quality. I suggested above some doubts about whether it was a sufficient signal, but if one concludes that most non-JCI accredited hos-pitals are of lower quality, that may be a good enough reason to channel in this regard (given how easy it is to implement), even if one is less confident that all JCI-accredited hospitals are of uniformly high quality. A regulator could also rely on the other signals of quality discussed previously that are sometimes touted by hospitals—the U.S. and UK trained physicians, partnerships with leading medical schools or hospitals in the devel-oping world—as a precondition for channeling. As I have suggested above and in the previous chapter, however, I have serious doubts that these things represent good proxies of quality, and they have some risk of reflecting parochialism instead. So, without fur-ther evidence to that effect, I would disfavor channeling on that basis.

4. Channeling by Outcome and Infection Data

The above three forms of channeling have significant advantages in terms of administra-biltiy because they are relatively easy to put in place and to audit, especially channeling by procedures and by JCI or other accreditation. They, however, use proxies for quality rather than attempt to measure quality directly. The alternative would be for home countries or other regulators using channeling to directly evaluate outcome data such as one-year mor-tality, complication rates, infection rates, completeness of medical documentation, etc. Such a system would demand not only disclosure of these things by destination country physicians and hospitals that wanted to be "approved," but would also arrange to peri-odically audit it, as well as compile data from home country physicians and hospitals to which these medical tourist patients return. Alternatively, as discussed above, it may be possible to induce JCI or another accreditor to take on this function such that channeling

---

[98] *E.g.*, Aaron D. Twerski & Neil B. Cohen, *The Second Revolution in Informed Consent: Comparing Physicians to Each Other*, *94* Nw. U. L. Rev. 1, 13 n.30 (1999) (collecting studies).

by accreditation would be channeling by outcome and procedure (of the kind JCI already monitors) in tandem, though I have my doubts how likely this is given that JCI does not have much motivation to "rock the boat" given its present market dominance.

All things being equal, this form of channeling is, I believe, the most desirable. It is the most likely to guide patients to high-quality facilities and minimize externalities to other home country patients in the form of costs for follow-up and disease transmission, and also gives facilities an incentive to improve themselves on a margin that may benefit not only medical tourist patients but their own citizens (this last point depends on how the domestic and medical tourist parts of the destination country health care sector interact, a topic for Chapter 6). It is, however, the most expensive and difficult to implement. It also raises questions of comparability—how should a "score" be generated across various dimensions such as complications, documentation, and infection control?—and also of where to set baselines; in figuring out what "score" to use as their baseline for treating medical tourism destinations as "approved," how should it set the threshold? That of the worst, median, or best hospital domestically? One option is to individualize it based on what facility the patient would most likely have access to in his/her community, based on geography and cost, but that strikes me as far too complex and also perhaps more politically fraught.

Although we should push for this more robust form of channeling, for these reasons it may be that in the short term the most plausible steps forward are channeling by service, experience, or accreditation.

III. CONCLUSION

Quality of care remains one of the—and probably *the* most—frequently cited concern about medical tourism. Although one can find many anecdotal instances of poor care being delivered as part of medical tourism, the kind of data one would need to make a full-fledged assessment is currently largely absent and, even if present, faces difficult questions (as well as data difficulties) as to what the right baseline is for quality of care being provided to this patient population in the home country. At the same time, the existing often-touted signals of high quality—JCI accreditation, number of Western-trained physicians, partnerships with prestigious facilities in the developed country—seem more about branding and less about rigorous measures of quality. Of these, the fact that a foreign hospital has achieved the JCI process-based accreditation is some signal about resources that hospital has at its disposal, and plausibly one might infer some quality information from the accreditation as well, but again we lack rigorous empirical evaluation of that issue. The place where quality concerns are the best grounded is in the world of disease transmission, and in particular multi-drug–resistant bacteria. Here, based on what we know about the vectors of disease transmission and also the clinical case reports, I think it is fair to see that there is a significant problem posed by medical tourism, and one that has serious consequences not only for the medical tourist patient but for other citizens of the home country who may be exposed to foreign pathogens, as well as a major cost to hospitals that need to deal with these infections.

This book is about the law and ethics of medical tourism, not the medicine of infection control. The question then becomes: What work can the legal and ethical rules do to help deal with quality concerns?

The first strategy I have detailed is one to generate better information for patients. I have discussed how home countries and accreditors can use their leverage, especially as to the insured population, to get foreign facilities to disclose infection, complication, morbidity, and mortality data and how home countries or intergovernmental agencies or private sector partners can attempt to package that data in a way that could be used by patients selecting foreign facilities.

Although I support efforts in this direction, a combination of the difficulty of giving patients meaningful comparisons to the care they can expect in the home country and skepticism stemming from the poor patient use of domestic health care information when available convinces me that information-provision will not be sufficient.

Instead, I have argued for the adoption of "channeling" regimes wherein home countries take the further step of "approving" foreign facilities based on various criteria, and offering carrots for approved facilities and sticks for unapproved ones, with the purpose of both directing patient flow to high-quality facilities and also giving lower-quality facilities an incentive to improve their performance. In particular, I have discussed channeling by service (focusing on low-risk procedures), channeling by experience (the number of procedures performed by the physician/practice group/facility), channeling by accreditation, and channeling by outcome and infection data. Of these, the last would be the most useful regulatory intervention but also the most difficult to implement (both in terms of administrability and political feasibility). Although home country, accreditors, and intergovernmental organizations should continue to try to develop that latter form of channeling, which I view as the best, in the interim they ought to consider adopting some of the other channeling approaches, individually or in tandem. All that said, we should be honest about the fact that the law faces limits in regulating the quality of the services offered as part of medical tourism, especially for medical tourists paying out-of-pocket. In the next chapter, we will examine an area where legal interventions are, unsurprisingly, more promising, because they are very much "in their element": liability.

3

Legal Liability

⌒

IN THE LAST chapter, we saw that there may be significant differences between foreign hospitals in terms of quality of care, and that in the current regulatory environment it is very difficult to determine what quality of care a patient can expect from a particular hospital. I also stressed that the most relevant question for bioethical purposes is not "What is the quality of care?" but rather "How does the quality of care compare to that which the patient would have access to at home given his current health care access?"

But even if the quality of care of a foreign facility were truly excellent—as good or better than in the patient's home country—medical error is inevitable in some proportion of cases. Even if we were to assume comparable rates of medical error in home and destination country facilities, that does not mean the patient receiving care abroad will experience the same likelihood of success and extent of financial recovery should she bring suit as she would if she had been treated at home. Such recovery is, the objection goes,[1] less likely and less extensive in medical-malpractice suits for care administered in the destination country rather than in the home country.

The first part of this chapter explains why that is the case and examines whether it should worry us and what might be done about it, focusing on suits against foreign providers and briefly discussing how matters might be different in suits against medical

---

[1] *See, e.g.*, Nathan Cortez, *Patients without Borders: The Emerging Global Market for Patients and the Evolution of Modern Health Care*, 83 IND. L.J. 71, 74, 91 (2008); Leigh Turner, *Medical Tourism: Family Medicine and International Health-Related Travel*, 53 CAN. FAM. PHYSICIAN 1639, 1640 (2007).

tourism facilitators. In this, I focus on these issues for patients paying out-of-pocket, and revisit these issues in Chapter 4 in regards to insurer-prompted medical tourism. I focus on outbound U.S. medical tourists here in part because the liability issue has been more of a concern for them than for tourists from other countries. This is largely because (as we will see) U.S. medical tourists face the largest differential as to med-mal recovery domestically versus in medical tourism as the damages available in the United States for medical malpractice are much higher than in the rest of the world.

The second part of this chapter then shifts attention to legal liability risks that are faced by *home* country health care providers whose patients use medical tourism, focusing on referral liability, abandonment liability, and liability for follow-up care.

I. MEDICAL-MALPRACTICE LIABILITY FOR INJURIES SUSTAINED DURING TREATMENT[2]

Let us reconsider the case of Carl, our hypothetical medical tourist whose case is based on real facts about the industry, that we discussed in the Preface to this book. Recall that Carl is one of the estimated 47 million Americans without health insurance. After experiencing the symptoms of angina, he reluctantly sees a cardiologist in his home town of Milwaukee, whom he pays out-of-pocket. A battery of tests reveals significant atherosclerotic narrowing in several arteries, and the cardiologist recommends bypass surgery. In Milwaukee, bypass surgery purchased out-of-pocket costs somewhere between $48,350 and $73,300 depending on the hospital.[3] Carl can get the same surgery for $10,000 at Bumrungrad Hospital in Bangkok, Thailand, and decides to do so. Unfortunately, he suffers an ischemic stroke (the cutting off of blood supply to the brain) during the procedure. As a result, he experiences partial paralysis in his right arm, moderate speech problems, pain, and depression. Believing the stroke to be the result of medical error, he wants to sue the foreign hospital and his doctors in a U.S. court for medical malpractice. Are there barriers in the U.S. legal system that will prevent him from successfully bringing suit? If so, knowing about these difficulties, should (and could) the government have prevented him from getting treated abroad or placed other requirements on foreign providers as a condition of treating him?

I will primarily use Carl's case to examine issues with medical malpractice. It is worth noting, though, that not all patients who pay out-of-pocket are doing so because they are uninsured or underinsured. As was discussed in Chapter 1, some patients may be going abroad because the foreign hospital is particularly adept at performing a surgery (such as

---

[2] This part of the chapter is adapted from I. Glenn Cohen, *Protecting Patients with Passports: Medical Tourism and the Patient-Protective Argument*, 95 IOWA L. REV. 1467 (2010), and I gratefully acknowledge the journal's permission for allowing me to do so.

[3] Guy Boulton, *States Push for Hospital Price Lists, Initiatives Aim to Clarify Billing for Consumers*, MILWAUKEE J. SENT., Oct. 15, 2007, at 1A.

going to Thailand for sex reassignment) or because a particular technique is not yet available at home (such as patients who traveled to the Cuban Clinic Cira Garcia for a unique treatment for retinitis pigmentose (night blindness)).[4] These patients may also experience medical error and want to sue for med-mal, but face the same obstacles I will describe below.

In this part of the chapter, I will first briefly discuss the reasons for having medical malpractice liability so that we can evaluate what kind of a threat it would be to lose that liability in medical tourism. I will then explain why U.S. patients face a substantial reduction in the likelihood and/or amount of financial recovery (from now on I will just say "recovery," but, to be clear, I do not mean "medical recovery") when they get treated abroad as opposed to within the United States. I will then discuss whether this fact constitutes a problem that should motivate a regulatory intervention. Finally, I develop possible regulatory interventions that could be used if we decide the lack of recovery is a problem.

A. Why Care about Medical-Malpractice Liability

At the threshold, one might ask, why should we, or our hypothetical patient Carl, care about medical malpractice liability ("med-mal" for short)? The traditional answer from tort law is twofold: medical malpractice liability helps deter doctors from committing medical error (or, to put it more positively, incentivizes them to invest in care-enhancing training, technology, etc.) and compensates those who have been harmed by the medical error, allowing them to be made whole (or at least partially so).

It is an open question how well med-mal serves either function. On compensation, authors have offered numerous critiques such as: the poor connection between the fact and amount of med-mal recovery and whether medical error actually occurred;[5] the effectiveness of alternative systems, most notably enterprise liability, med-mal mediation and arbitration, health courts, and a no-fault compensation system;[6] and the fact that the system is quite costly to maintain.[7] As to the deterrence function, there are disputes about how responsive health care providers are to med-mal liability and whether the liability induces

---

[4] Cohen, *supra* note 2, at 1483.

[5] *See, e.g.*, Richard A. Epstein, *Contractual Principle versus Legislative Fixes: Coming to Closure on the Unending Travails of Medical Malpractice*, 54 DEPAUL L. REV. 503, 512 (2005); David M. Studdert et al., *Claims, Errors, and Compensation Payments in Medical Malpractice Litigation*, 354 NEW ENG. J. MED. 2024 (2006); Paul C. Weiler, *Reforming Medical Malpractice in a Radically Moderate—and Ethical—Fashion*, 54 DEPAUL L. REV. 205, 215 (2005).

[6] *See, e.g.*, Philip G. Peters, Jr., *Health Courts?*, 88 B.U. L. REV. 227 (2008); Elizabeth Rolph et al., *Arbitration Agreements in Health Care: Myths and Realities*, 60 LAW & CONTEMP. PROBS. 153 (Winter 1997); William M. Sage, *Enterprise Liability and the Emerging Managed Health Care System*, 60 LAW & CONTEMP. PROBS. 159 (Spring 1997); David M. Studdert et al., *Can the United States Afford a "No-Fault" System of Compensation for Medical Injury?*, 60 LAW & CONTEMP. PROBS. 1 (Spring 1997).

[7] In the United States, most estimates peg the direct costs of medical-malpractice liability at 2 percent of the total system cost. *See, e.g.*, Patricia M. Danzon, *Liability for Medical Malpractice*, in 1B HANDBOOK OF HEALTH ECONOMICS 1339, 1343 (Anthony J. Culyer & Joseph P. Newhouse eds., 2000).

doctors to practice "defensive medicine," in which time and money are expended on care that does not improve the health outcomes of patients but that staves off threats of liability.[8]

Whether med-mal is desirable is a much larger debate that I will not resolve here. Even if one thought the U.S. med-mal system, for example, was hopelessly deficient, one would need to compare it to each foreign system under which the plaintiff's claim might be judged—lest the perfect become the enemy of the good. Such a country-by-country analysis would be quite difficult and contested, and in any event I do not purport to offer that here. Instead, I will simply assume that having one's claim covered by the home country medical malpractice system is, all things being equal, desirable for the home country patient seeking care where the destination country system will be less remunerative or the patient's claim less likely to succeed in that system.

In some forms of medical tourism, the dynamic will go in the opposite direction. For example, when an Indian patient travels to the United States for heart surgery at the Mayo Clinic, the damages recoverable under U.S. law, as we will see, are likely to be greater than that of Indian law. As a result, medical tourists for whom the United States is the *destination* country will usually receive a windfall in terms of tort actions, and deficient recovery is less of a concern.[9] Because in this chapter I am focused squarely on cases where patients will face reduced likelihood and amount of recovery due to medical tourism, my focus is largely on outbound U.S. medical tourists. However, where possible, I try to work in information on patients from other home countries. My ultimate normative question is whether to allow them to depart from their home countries' protection in return for the benefit of lower-cost health care abroad.[10] Before I reach that

---

[8] *See* MICHAEL D. GREENBERG ET AL., RAND INSTITUTE FOR CIVIL JUSTICE, IS BETTER PATIENT SAFETY ASSOCIATED WITH LESS MALPRACTICE ACTIVITY? EVIDENCE FROM CALIFORNIA (2010), *available at* http://www.rand.org/content/dam/rand/pubs/technical_reports/2010/RAND_TR824. pdf; Janet Currie & W. Bentley MacLeod, *First Do No Harm? Tort Reform and Birth Outcomes*, 123 Q.J. ECON. 795 (2008); Michael Frakes, Does Medical Malpractice Deter? The Impact of Tort Reforms and Malpractice Standard Reforms on Health Care Quality (June 25, 2012) (Cornell Legal Studies Research Paper No. 12-29), *available at* http://papers.ssrn.com/sol3/papers.cfm?abstract_id=2090595.

How much of spending goes to "defensive medicine" in the United States has been quite difficult to ascertain, and most estimates are deeply contested on either definitional or measurement grounds. David M. Studdert et al., *Defensive Medicine among High-Risk Specialist Physicians in a Volatile Malpractice Environment*, 293 JAMA 2609, 2609 (2005).

[9] To be sure, they still may face difficulties in recovery in that they will need to sue in U.S. courts, and it is possible that some elements of substantive med-mal law are less friendly to patients in the United States than in their home country. These potential difficulties would have to be balanced against the amount of recovery conditional on succeeding, a kind of expected value calculation that could only be done on a country-by-country basis. I cannot do that kind of intensive comparative med-mal work here, but suffice it to say for most medical tourists treated in the United States deficient med-mal recovery is unlikely to be a serious legal or ethical concern, so I focus on the outbound U.S. medical tourists.

[10] Because my ultimate argument largely favors allowing this trade to continue, I have actually made the argument *harder* not *easier* for myself. For those who are true med-mal skeptics, losing the protection of this form of tort law is no great loss and may even be thought of as a gain. By contrast, it is those who believe med-mal liability is doing much good for whom losing these protections is a more serious concern.

question, though, let me explain why an outbound U.S. medical tourist is likely to face reduced likelihood/amount of med-mal recovery when traveling abroad.

B. Why Patients Face a Lower Likelihood and Amount of Recovery for Injuries Sustained as Part of Medical Tourism Compared to Health Care Provided at Home

In this section, I will first show why U.S. patients such as Carl will face a substantial reduction in the likelihood and/or amount of recovery when they get treated abroad as opposed to within the United States. I will then much more briefly discuss the situation for patients from non-U.S. home countries who go abroad, where there are difficulties as well but the differences are somewhat less stark.

i. U.S. Patients Traveling Abroad for Care

As far as I know, there have been no medical malpractice lawsuits by U.S. medical-tourist patients treated in Less Developed Countries (LDCs) against their providers that have resulted in published opinions;[11] as such, we can only predict how courts will treat them. But, although the analysis in actual cases will be fact specific, it seems reasonable to conclude that several doctrines of American civil procedure work in conjunction to substantially reduce the likelihood and amount of recovery in med-mal when medical error from care causes injury abroad as opposed to when care is delivered within the United States. In particular, I focus on four obstacles: personal jurisdiction, forum non conveniens, choice of law, and enforcement of judgments.

1. Personal Jurisdiction

To begin with, under U.S. constitutional law, a U.S. court must have personal jurisdiction over the foreign hospital and/or health care provider for the plaintiff to maintain suit. That jurisdiction must also be authorized by statute or rule through what are known as "long-arm" statutes in every state of the country. The long-arm statute of a particular state may not reach foreign health care providers or hospitals because the long-arm has been read as limited to tortious conduct by act or omission committed within the forum state, which would exclude med-mal committed abroad,[12] because the long-arm extends jurisdiction over foreign corporations only if the defendant "regularly does or solicits business, engages in any other persistent course of conduct in the State or derives substantial revenue from services, or things used or consumed in the State," which may not be true of

---

[11] The closest (though still far-off) unpublished case I have seen (with very scant facts set out in the complaint) involved a suit in Pennsylvania federal district court by a man who underwent an allegedly unwanted heart surgery while in police custody in Canada. Romah v. Scully, No. 06-698, 2007 WL 3493943 (W.D. Pa. Nov. 13, 2007). The case was dismissed for lack of personal jurisdiction over the Canadian hospital. *Id.* at *8.

[12] *E.g.*, HAW. REV. STAT. § 634-35 (1993); IDAHO CODE ANN. § 5-514 (2004).

many foreign hospitals and providers;[13] or because the long-arm extends only to corporations or partnerships and not natural persons, which might permit jurisdiction over foreign hospitals but not individual foreign providers.[14]

Even if a long-arm statute purports to reach the injurious medical act committed abroad, the exercise of personal jurisdiction over these defendants may not be permissible under the Due Process Clause of the U.S. Constitution. The Due Process Clause requires that the defendant have minimum contacts with the state where the suit is brought; but establishing that jurisdiction in these cases, either through so-called "general" or "specific" jurisdiction, may be difficult.[15]

Although the inquiry is fact intensive, in most cases we would expect a foreign doctor or even a foreign hospital to lack the systematic and continuous contacts with the plaintiff's home state required to establish general jurisdiction.[16] Plaintiffs will also have difficulty establishing specific personal jurisdiction against foreign doctors, who do not usually purposefully avail themselves of the benefits and protections of the laws of U.S. jurisdictions.[17]

When the foreign hospital is a defendant, the case for specific in personam personal jurisdiction would depend in part on how patients were solicited, and, for online contacts, the nature of the foreign hospital's Web presence. For example, personal jurisdiction would be easier to establish if a foreign hospital solicited a particular patient via a website and/or specifically targeted U.S. patients.[18]

To examine one real example, Wockhardt Hospitals in India advertise "International Patient" services on their website and list two specific toll-free numbers, one for the United Kingdom and one for the United States and Canada.[19] This seems like a pretty

---

[13] DEL. CODE ANN. TIT. 10, § 3104 (1999); GA. CODE ANN. § 9-10-91 (2007).

[14] *See* JACK H. FRIEDENTHAL ET AL., CIVIL PROCEDURE § 3.13 (4th ed. 2005).

[15] Int'l Shoe Co. v. Washington, 326 U.S. 310, 316 (1945); Kerrie S. Howze, Note, *Medical Tourism: Symptom or Cure?*, 41 GA. L. REV. 1013, 1013–21 (2007).

[16] *See, e.g.*, Helicopteros Nacionales de Columbia, S.A. v. Hall, 466 U.S. 408, 415 (1984); Perkins v. Benguet Consol. Mining Co., 342 U.S. 437, 445–46 (1952).

[17] *See, e.g.*, Burger King Corp. v. Rudzewicz, 471 U.S. 462, 475–76 (1985). However, if a particular physician were to enter the forum state, even briefly, then jurisdiction could be asserted over him by serving him with process. *See* Burnham v. Superior Court, 495 U.S. 604, 619 (1990) (Scalia, J.) (plurality opinion); *id.* at 638 n.12 (Brennan, J., concurring in the judgment).

[18] *See, e.g.*, Graduate Mgmt. Admission Council v. Raju, 241 F. Supp. 2d 589, 598–99 (E.D. Va. 2003) (finding personal jurisdiction where Indian defendant's website "targeted" the U.S. market, including through the provision of "specific ordering information for United States customers"); Howze, *supra* note 15, at 1031–32 ("If the plaintiff and Indian physician had Internet contact, however, the plaintiff may be able to establish specific jurisdiction based on email exchanges or perhaps an interactive website."). *See also* Zippo Mfg. Co. v. Zippo Dot Com, Inc., 952 F. Supp. 1119, 1123–26 (W.D. Pa. 1997) (introducing "sliding scale" of Internet personal jurisdiction occupied by "active," "interactive," and "passive" websites). For a more in-depth discussion of the relationship between personal jurisdiction and the Internet, *see generally* Paul Schiff Berman, *The Globalization of Jurisdiction*, 151 U. PA. L. REV. 311 (2002); Allan R. Stein, *Personal Jurisdiction and the Internet: Seeing Due Process through the Lens of Regulatory Precision*, 98 NW. U. L. REV. 411 (2004).

[19] *International Patients*, WOCKHARDT HOSPITALS, http://www.wockhardthospitals.com/international-patients.html (last visited Nov. 3, 2012).

thin reed on which to hang personal jurisdiction. It does not evince the "targeting" of the U.S. market that some courts have deemed necessary to support jurisdiction, but only the "passive advertisement" that courts have found insufficient.[20] Even if courts found this form of Internet contact sufficient, it would be very easy for Wockhardt and others to adjust their Web presence to avoid personal jurisdiction. Plaintiffs might be able to establish personal jurisdiction more easily by showing that the hospital adopted practices to target U.S. consumers, for example, by adjusting billing practices or fostering referral relationships with in-state providers.[21]

The case for personal jurisdiction is somewhat better for medical-tourist intermediaries located abroad. As our discussion of such intermediaries in Chapter 1 suggests, medical-tourist intermediaries are more likely to purposefully avail themselves of the forum state's laws by actually recruiting patients there. Additionally, these intermediaries are more likely to establish a business presence in the markets from which they recruit. The problem is that intermediaries are also likely to be judged under a set of substantive med-mal doctrines that are less plaintiff friendly than those for hospitals or physicians.[22]

2. Forum Non Conveniens

Even when personal jurisdiction is satisfied, a med-mal suit of this kind brought in a U.S. court would still be subject to a challenge under the doctrine of forum non conveniens. That doctrine gives the U.S. courts discretion to dismiss the case when (1) jurisdiction is proper in an alternative forum, and (2) the alternative forum is preferred under a multifactor balancing test that weighs the burdens to plaintiff and defendant against the public interest.[23]

The first requirement will likely be satisfied in many medical tourism cases, as the legal system of the destination country will often entertain a med-mal suit by a U.S. citizen treated in that country, and the U.S. Supreme Court has made clear that the fact that the law of the alternative forum might be "less favorable to the plaintiffs than that of the present forum...should ordinarily not be given conclusive or even substantial weight" in the analysis.[24] Indeed, other courts have rejected an argument against forum non conveniens dismissals premised on the claim that the law of the alternative forum will yield

---

[20] *See* Mink v. AAA Dev. LLC, 190 F.3d 333, 337 (5th Cir. 1999); Thomas R. McLean, *The Global Market for Health Care: Economics and Regulation*, 26 WIS. INT'L L.J. 591, 634 (2008).

[21] *See* Nathan Cortez, *Recalibrating the Legal Risks of Cross-Border Health Care*, 10 YALE J. HEALTH POL'Y L. & ETHICS 1, 10 (2010).

[22] For an in-depth exploration of whether intermediaries are likely to be treated like independent practice association–type health-maintenance organizations (HMOs) and the med-mal doctrines that would apply if they were, *see* Cohen *supra* note 2, at 1497–98.

[23] *See* Piper Aircraft Co. v. Reyno, 454 U.S. 235, 257–61 (1981); Gulf Oil Corp. v. Gilbert, 330 U.S. 501, 508 (1947).

[24] *Piper*, 454 U.S. at 247; *see* Howze, *supra* note 15, at 1037.

much smaller damages such that the lawsuit would not be economically viable as the costs would exceed potential recovery.[25] Things might be different "where the alternative forum does not permit litigation of the subject matter of the dispute."[26] However, as we will see in a moment, these cases are not likely to meet this standard: although many of the destination countries for medical tourism have less capacious remedies for medical malpractice, and there exist significant practical difficulties in bringing these suits, such suits are not formally barred. The exception has proven rare indeed.[27]

If we turn to the second part of the analysis, although fact specific, many of the factors the Supreme Court listed seem to cut in favor of a forum non conveniens dismissal in this context: "the relative ease of access to sources of proof; availability of compulsory process for attendance of unwilling, and the cost of obtaining attendance of willing, witnesses; possibility of view of premises"; whether the plaintiff's "choice of an inconvenient forum, 'vex[es],' 'harass[es],' or 'oppress[es]' the defendant by inflicting upon him expense or trouble not necessary to his own right to pursue his remedy"; the "[a]dministrative difficulties [that] follow for courts when litigation is piled up in congested centers instead of being handled at its origin"; and the "local interest in having localized controversies decided at home."[28]

Thus, forum non conveniens dismissals may pose a serious challenge to recovery in U.S. courts for medical tourists.

3. Choice of Law, the Enforcement of Judgments, and Suing Abroad
If these doctrines prevent a medical tourist such as Carl from suing foreign hospitals and providers for med-mal in U.S. courts, the alternative is to sue in the foreign court system, which in Carl's case would be in India. Beyond the added expense and difficulty of

---

[25] *See, e.g.*, Gonzalez v. Chrysler Corp., 301 F.3d 377, 382 (5th Cir. 2002) (holding that a $2500 cap on damages for the death of one's child under Mexican law did not establish that "the remedy available in the Mexican forum [was] clearly unsatisfactory"); Howze, *supra* note 15, at 1035.

[26] *Piper*, 454 U.S. at 254 n.23 (citing Phoenix Can. Oil Co. v. Texaco, Inc., 78 F.R.D. 445 (D. Del. 1978)).

[27] The Wright and Miller treatise details the "ease with which a defendant can establish that an alternative forum is adequate" and suggests that the federal courts have "categorically reject[ed] generalized accusations of corruption, delay, and other inadequacies in foreign judicial systems, or imposing too high a level of proof" as being sufficient to fall within *Piper's* exception. 14D CHARLES ALAN WRIGHT ET AL., FEDERAL PRACTICE AND PROCEDURE § 3828.3 (2007); *see also* Tuazon v. R.J. Reynolds Tobacco Co., 433 F.3d 1163, 1179–80 (9th Cir. 2006). That said, at least one court of appeals has found extensive delays (in the range of twenty years according to testimony in the district court) in the Calcutta High Court in India to make the alternative forum inadequate and thus to justify denying a motion to dismiss on forum non conveniens grounds. Bhatnagar v. Surrendra Overseas Ltd., 52 F.3d 1220 (3d Cir. 1995). However, the court went to great length to emphasize the truly extraordinary nature of the delay in the case, and the failure of the nonmoving party to put forth adequate evidence to meet its burden on the issue, and that this was not a more general determination as to the adequacy of Indian fora for litigation. *Id.; see also* Cortez, *supra* note 21, at 12.

[28] *Gulf Oil*, 330 U.S. at 508–09. For further discussion of how the analysis here compares to that in the leading U.S. Supreme Court decisions, *see* Cohen, *supra* note 2, at 1501 & n.143.

suing abroad, this poses a further problem: in some cases it will be much more difficult to prevail in a med-mal claim in the destination country's courts under its substantive law than it would be under U.S. law in U.S. courts. Of course, some potential destination countries have a med-mal system closer to the United States', and a full assessment would require detailed comparative med-mal work.

Drawing on excellent work by others in this vein, though, it is safe to say that many of the destination countries to which today's patients are going have much less plaintiff-friendly med-mal systems. For example, in India "medical negligence claims are rare and multimillion dollar awards are nonexistent."[29] One author claims that although medical malpractice relief is "technically available" there, around 95 percent of cases are dismissed, and the substantial backlog of cases means "that the patient may face a lengthy delay before any adjudication."[30] Further, given the minimal amount of damages likely to be recoverable, "the amount of litigation expenses may total more than any potential recovery, making the suit not economically viable."[31] Another author suggests that it is extremely difficult to get Indian physicians to testify against other Indian physicians, although this may be true to a lesser extent in the United States as well.[32]

India is not alone in this regard. Thai laws "limit medical malpractice awards and do not compensate for pain and suffering."[33] Similarly, some criticize Malaysian and Singaporean med-mal law as doctrinally too deferential to physicians "in determining the standard of care and whether that standard was breached in each case," and one author has suggested that "Mexican courts do not provide any real recourse to victims of medical malpractice."[34]

These divergences from U.S. substantive med-mal law will pose an obstacle for robust recovery, not only for the patient who must sue in the foreign system, but also for the one who (notwithstanding the obstacles discussed) manages to maintain suit in a U.S. court; the application of choice-of-law principles will likely mean that the governing law will be

---

[29] Howze, *supra* note 15, at 1030; *see also The Globalization of Health Care: Can Medical Tourism Reduce Health Care Costs?: Hearing Before the S. Spec. Comm. on Aging*, 109th Cong. 43 (2006) [hereinafter The Globalization of Health Care] (statement of Rajesh Rao) ("[T]he awards in any kind of litigation [in India] are proportionately lower [than in the United States].") *available at* http://purl.access.gpo.gov/GPO/LPS78404; Cortez, *supra* note 1, at 91.

[30] Howze, *supra* note 15, at 1034–35.

[31] *Id.* at 1035.

[32] Ganapati Mudur, *Indian Doctors Not Accountable, Says Consumer Report*, 321 BRIT. MED. J. 588 (2000); *see also* W. PAGE KEETON ET AL., PROSSER AND KEETON ON THE LAW OF TORTS § 32 (5th ed. 1984); Truill v. Long, 621 So. 2d 1278, 1280 (Ala. 1993).

[33] Cortez, *supra* note 1, at 106–07 (citing Mark Roth, *A Cheaper Alternative for Those with Minimal Health Insurance, Getting Surgery Abroad May Be a Sound Option*, PITTSBURGH POST-GAZETTE, Sept. 10, 2006, at G1).

[34] Cortez, *supra* note 1, at 106 (citing Kumaralingam Amirthalingam, *Judging Doctors and Diagnosing the Law: Bolam Rules in Singapore and Malaysia*, 2003 SING. J. LEGAL STUD. 125). For a more in-depth examination of the med-mal systems of India, Thailand, Singapore, and Mexico, *see id.* at 5, 18–77 (concluding that in each jurisdiction, "U.S. medical tourists will struggle to obtain adequate compensation").

that of the foreign country where the medical care was provided. To oversimplify somewhat for our purposes, the most common approach is to resolve choice of law through state-interest analysis.[35] Under the interest-based approach of the Restatement (Second) of Conflict of Laws, "[i]n an action for a personal injury, the local law of the state where the injury occurred determines the rights and liabilities of the parties, unless, with respect to the particular issue, some other state has a more significant relationship."[36] Courts are instructed to look at: "(a) the place where the injury occurred, (b) the place where the conduct causing the injury occurred, (c) the domicil, residence, nationality, place of incorporation and place of business of the parties, and (d) the place where the relationship, if any, between the parties is centered."[37]

In the example of someone injured by medical care provided abroad, the default choice of law would be that of the foreign jurisdiction—the place where the injury occurred. The multifactor test is unlikely to lead to a divergence from the default as factors (a), (b), and (d) would likely point to the foreign country's substantive law, and factor (c) seems neutral.

All in all, it seems likely that in med-mal cases that arise out of medical tourism, the law of the place of injury will usually apply. Several courts that have dealt with med-mal choice of law have reached this conclusion in choosing among U.S. state laws and in the very few med-mal cases dealing with choice of law between a U.S. state's law and a foreign country's law.[38]

Even if an American patient such as Carl is allowed to maintain a suit in a U.S. court and wins, any judgment may be very difficult to enforce against a foreign physician or hospital without assets in the United States. Foreign courts are often "reluctant to enforce the decisions of U.S. courts," because "[m]any other countries find some of the grounds for jurisdiction in the United States exorbitant," and because "legal systems that do not include punitive damages may object to large U.S. awards."[39] Pessimism as to whether one will ever be able to enforce the judgment will reduce the incentive to sue in the first place, especially given the other obstacles to recovery discussed above.

---

[35] *See* Kermit Roosevelt III, *The Myth of Choice of Law: Rethinking Conflicts*, 97 Mich. L. Rev. 2448, 2466 (1999).

[36] Restatement (Second) of Conflict of Laws § 146 (1971); *see also id.* § 6.

[37] *Id.* § 145.

[38] *See, e.g.*, Blakesley v. Wolford, 789 F.2d 236 (3d Cir. 1986) (Texas rather than Pennsylvania law applied to a med-mal action where a Pennsylvania dentist in Pennsylvania diagnosed and advised the plaintiff to undergo oral surgery in Texas, where she was allegedly injured, even though she only felt the negative effects upon returning to Pennsylvania); Chadwick v. Arabian Am. Oil Co., 656 F. Supp. 857, 858, 860 (D. Del. 1987) (applying Saudi med-mal law to a suit by a Florida citizen who was allegedly treated negligently in Saudi Arabia by the doctor of a Delaware corporation and its subcontractor); *see also* Jeffrey L. Rensberger, *Choice of Law, Medical Malpractice, and Telemedicine: The Present Diagnosis with a Prescription for the Future*, 55 U. Miami L. Rev. 31, 69–74 (2000) (surveying case law in the somewhat analogous field of telemedicine).

[39] Jenny S. Martinez, *Towards an International Judicial System*, 56 Stan. L. Rev. 429, 511 (2003); *see also* Antonio F. Perez, *The International Recognition of Judgments: The Debate between Private and Public Law*

For all of these reasons, U.S. patients treated abroad who sue for medical malpractice seem considerably less likely to succeed—and their recovery substantially more limited if they do—compared to patients treated domestically.

ii. Patients from Home Countries outside the United States

Although I do not purport to offer an in-depth analysis of whether these difficulties in suing foreign providers persist in all possible home countries, I will briefly discuss some differences in the legal treatment of claims and the likelihood of success for patients from non-U.S. home countries.

First, there is the issue of personal jurisdiction. In surveying the lay of the land(s) for telemedicine and medical tourism, Deth Sao et al. note that in many civil law systems, jurisdiction over the defendant in the home country's legal system will not be a problem:

> some civil law countries have enacted legislation broadening their reach of personal jurisdiction. In France, the French Civil Code grants its courts the power to hear any case involving a French citizen. Similarly, Luxembourg and the Netherlands grant their courts jurisdiction over almost all cases where parties are nationals or residents.[40]

As in the United States, even where when one can establish jurisdiction, the defendant can seek to dismiss the case on the grounds of forum non conveniens. As compared to the situation in the United States, in some of these countries that doctrine is more friendly to the plaintiff who will sue for an injury from medical tourism. For example, in the UK jurisprudence, "the defendant must show the availability of another clearly more appropriate forum, i.e., one 'in which the case could be tried more suitably for the interests of all the parties and for the ends of justice,'" and "if the defendant has made a prima facie case for a *forum non conveniens* dismissal, the plaintiff can [then] show that there are circumstances by reason of which justice [nonetheless] requires that the British court exercise its jurisdiction."[41] Australian courts are even more hostile to dismissals on this ground (and therefore more friendly to patients suing). Unlike the modern UK and U.S. jurisprudence, Australian jurisprudence does not look "to whether there is a 'clearly more appropriate forum' abroad," but instead "focuses on whether the Australian forum

---

Solutions, 19 BERKELEY J. INT'L L. 44, 57 & n.66 (2001). For more on difficulties with enforcing judgments in medical tourism cases, *see* Cary D. Steklof, Note, *Medical Tourism and the Legal Impediments to Recovery in Cases of Medical Malpractice*, 9 WASH. U. GLOBAL STUD. L. REV. 721, 734 (2010).

[40] Deth Sao et al., *Healthcare Disputes across National Boundaries: The Potential for Arbitration*, 42 GEO. WASH. INT'L L. REV. 475, 488–89 (2010).

[41] Martine Stückelberg, *Lis Pendens and Forum Non Conveniens at the Hague Conference*, 26 BROOK. J. INT'L L. 949, 955–56 (2001) (citing Spiliada Maritime Corp. v. Cansulex Ltd., [1987] 1 A.C. 460 (H.L.) (appeal taken from Eng.)).

is 'clearly inappropriate,' *i.e.*, seriously and unfairly burdensome, prejudicial, or damaging to the defendant."[42] As the Australian high court put it: "[i]t is a basic tenet of our jurisprudence that, where jurisdiction exists, access to the courts is a right. It is not a privilege which can be withdrawn otherwise than in clearly defined circumstances."[43]

There can also be commercial or civil agreements to which other non-U.S. countries are party that inflect the analysis. For example, the Brussels Convention on the Jurisdiction of Courts and the Recognition and Enforcement of Judgments in Civil and Commercial Matters (Brussels Convention), which applies to EU Member States only, prohibits a Member State from employing " 'exorbitant' jurisdictional devices" against defendants domiciled in fellow Member States and mandates enforcement of judgments rendered by fellow Member State courts.[44] To simplify significantly, under that Convention, where the patient and the provider are "domiciled in different European Union member states, then the Brussels Convention gives the country where the [foreign provider or hospital] is domiciled jurisdiction over medical tourism transactions," as a general rule, subject to alteration by: "(1) [the provider's] willingness to make a voluntarily appearance in a court where the patient is domiciled; (2) locus of the contract's performance; (3) arbitration and forum-shifting jurisdictional clauses; and (4) a patient's demonstration that he or she is a consumer."[45]

---

[42] *Id.* at 957 (quoting *Oceanic Sun Line Special Shipping Co. v Fay*, (1988) 165 CLR 197, 247 (Austl.) (confirmed and clarified in *Voth v Manildra Flower Mill Pty.*, (1990) 171 CLR 538 (Austl.))).

[43] *Id.* (alteration in original) (quoting *Oceanic Sun Line*, 165 CLR at 252) (internal quotation marks omitted). In fact, at least for tort actions, it seems as though things might depend on which State of Australia the patient is suing in. *See* Dan Jerker B. Svantesson, *From the Airport to the Surgery to the Courtroom—Private International Law and Medical Tourism*, 34 COMMONWEALTH L. BULL. 265, 271 (2008) ("Where an Australian medical tourist suffers damages due to a medical procedure carried out overseas, the tort will not have been committed within Australia. Consequently, it would seem unlikely that medical tourists from Western Australia, the Australian Capital Territory or Tasmania would be able to rely on a tort action to sue an overseas provider of health services in their home jurisdictions. However, depending on how the law defines the place where damage is sustained, Australian medical tourists from Victoria, New South Wales, Northern Territory, Queensland and South Australia may successfully initiate legal proceeding for a tort committed overseas.... [I]t seems that, as far as Victoria, New South Wales, Northern Territory, Queensland and South Australia are concerned, an aggrieved medical tourist with ongoing damages can sue in the courts of her/his home state in relation to a medical procedure carried out overseas."). Svantesson also argues how theories of liability sounding in tort rather than contract may be more promising from the perspective of jurisdictional and other procedural obstacles. *See generally id.* Although I will not review the details here, it is worth noting that forum non conveniens is not an exclusively common law phenomenon in that civil law jurisdictions, such as Quebec and Japan, recognize doctrines akin to forum non conveniens. Stückelberg, *supra* note 41, at 957 n.44.

[44] Brussels Convention on Jurisdiction and the Enforcement of Judgments in Civil and Commercial Matters, Sept. 27, 1968, 29 I.L.M. 1413, *available at* http://curia.europa.eu/common/recdoc/convention/en/c-textes/brux-idx.htm; *see also* European Commission, Fifth Framework Programme, *available at* http://cordis.europa.eu/fp5/src/3rdcountries.htm; Sao et al., *supra* note 40, at 490; Gary B. Born, *Reflections on Judicial Jurisdiction in International Cases*, 17 GA. J. INT'L & COMP. L. 1, 13–14 (1987).

[45] Thomas R. McLean, *Jurisdiction 101 for Medical Tourism Purchases Made in Europe, in* THE GLOBALIZATION OF HEALTH CARE: LEGAL AND ETHICAL CHALLENGES 33, 35 (I. Glenn Cohen ed., 2013).

Patients' home countries may differ substantially on choice-of-law principles as well. For example, Switzerland and Quebec are more apt to apply the *lex loci delicti* rule, in which the law of the place where the medical injury occurs (i.e., the destination country) will govern, while other jurisdictions may adopt rules more favorable to the application of the home country.[46] France and the United Kingdom traditionally follow this rule as well,[47] and this approach is now codified across the European Union in "Regulation (EC) No 864/2007 of the European Parliament and of the Council of 11 July 2007 on the law applicable to non-contractual obligations (Rome II)," which governs choice-of-law rules for tort/delict actions in Member States.[48] This regulation, which went into effect on January 11, 2009, states that: "the law applicable to a non-contractual obligation arising out of a tort/delict shall be the law of the country in which the damage occurs irrespective of the country in which the event giving rise to the damage occurred and irrespective of the country or countries in which the indirect consequences of that event occur."[49]

Finally, the enforceability of judgments will depend on prior existing agreements between the home and destination country apart from the destination country's own domestic law. In addition to setting jurisdictional rules, the Brussels Convention "establishes, for European Union member states, an exequatur procedure for the immediate recognition and enforcement of foreign judgments, with very narrow exceptions that are unlikely to apply even in many cases of default judgments."[50] To give another example, the Inter-American Convention on Extraterritorial Validity of Foreign Judgments and Arbitral Awards signed in Montevideo on May 8, 1979 (often called the "Montevideo Convention") provides (subject to some specific reservations) for the enforcement of "judgments and arbitral awards rendered in civil, commercial or labor proceedings in one of the States Parties," among each of its signatory nations centered in Latin America.[51]

For these reasons, the likelihood and amount of recovery for medical tourist patients from non-U.S. countries injured abroad may be better than for U.S. patients, sometimes

---

[46] Loi fédérale sur le droit international privé [LDIP] [Federal Law on Private International Law], Dec. 18, 1987, RS 291, art. 133 (Switz.); Civil Code of Québec, S.Q. 1991, c. 64, art. 3216 (Can.). For a survey, *see* William Tetley, *New Development in Private International Law:* Tolofson v. Jensen *and* Gagnon v. Lucas, 44 Am. J. Comp. L. 647, 659–65 (1996); Sao et al, *supra* note 40, at 492.

[47] Sao et al., *supra* note 40, at 492.

[48] Regulation (EC) No 864/2007 of the European Parliament and of the Council of 11 July 2007 on the law applicable to non-contractual obligations (Rome II), 2007 O.J. (L 199) 40.

[49] *Id.* For more background, *see* Jan von Hein, *Something Old and Something Borrowed, but Nothing New? Rome II and the European Choice-of-Law Evolution*, 82 Tul. L. Rev. 1663, 1692–702 (2008).

[50] *See* McLean, *supra* note 45, at 35.

[51] Organization of American States, Inter-American Convention on Extraterritorial Validity of Foreign Judgments and Arbitral Awards, May 8, 1979, 1439 U.N.T.S. 91, *available at* http://www.weil.com/wgm/cwgmhomep.nsf/files/montevio/$file/montevio.pdf [hereinafter Montevideo Convention]; *see also* Yoav Oestreicher, *The Rise and Fall of the "Mixed" and "Double" Convention Models regarding Recognition and Enforcement of Foreign Judgments*, 6 Wash. U. Global Stud. L. Rev. 339, 353 (2007).

to a significant extent, but on other occasions only in small part. In what follows, I take the most disturbing case, the radical effect on recovery for U.S. patients such as Carl, as my primary one on the thinking that what I say about this extreme case will apply, to a lesser extent, to the others.

iii. Liability for Facilitators

Now that we understand the difficulties for a patient such as Carl in recovering in med-mal from a foreign doctor or hospital, I will address whether the situation is different if care is arranged via a medical tourism facilitator (also called "intermediary") whom the patient sues. Although some of the procedural obstacles are less likely to be a challenge for suits against facilitators (as compared to providers), differences in the substantive law might make things worse for patients seeking to recover for injuries, at least in the United States.

In terms of the procedural hurdles, facilitators are more likely to have contacts with the patient's home country that are sufficient to sustain personal jurisdiction. For example, one company, Medretreat

offers an online presentation or podcast about its services, followed by a free online membership application form. It then assigns the patient a "U.S. Program Manager," who has an "extensive conversation" with the patient regarding his or her care needs, and it sends an electronic "Authorization Release Form," which gives the corporation "consent to collect and disseminate [the patient's] personal information." The patient provides digital copies of MRI's, x-rays, photos and other medical records and tests; a description of the expected outcome sought from surgery; possible travel dates; and a three-page medical-history questionnaire. The Manager then provides a price quotation for various possible doctors who could do the surgery sought, a list of possible accommodations, and coordinates communication between the patient and possible surgeon by email or teleconference. If the patient and Manager reach agreement on the details, the patient then deposits 20% of the total estimated cost into MedRetreat's U.S. holding account, at which point all final arrangements are made. After pre-surgical consultation and additional testing in the destination country, the surgery is performed. When the doctor is satisfied with the patient's condition, the patient is released from the hospital to recuperate back in the patient's hotel, with the service offering to arrange excursions to "some of the interesting attractions your destination offers." The patient then returns home, where the U.S. Program Manager "will be available to assist [him] with any future requirements."[52]

---

[52] Cohen, *supra* note 2, at 1484.

As this example suggests, facilitators are more likely to reach out to patients' home countries and to purposefully avail themselves of their laws by actually recruiting patients there. Additionally, these intermediaries are more likely to establish a business presence in the markets from which they recruit.[53] Indeed, some of them may have officers or a place of incorporation within the patient's home country.[54] Although some of the other problems discussed above may persist, these contacts will facilitate a finding of personal jurisdiction over the facilitator and will more easily enable the enforcement of judgment against those home country assets.

However, differences in the substantive theories of liability available against facilitators (as opposed to foreign providers) cut in the opposite direction—against the likelihood of robust recovery. In terms of straight-up med-mal liability, facilitators are more likely to be judged under a less plaintiff-friendly standard than foreign hospitals or physicians. In the U.S. context, there is currently no direct case law on the subject, but one plausible analogy would be to treat facilitators like independent practice association–type health-maintenance organizations (HMOs), that is, HMOs with large contractual networks of physicians who see patients with many types of insurance.[55] HMOs have occasionally been subjected to direct liability when their doctors commit medical malpractice, but only when the HMO directly employs the doctor or, under a theory of apparent or implied authority, when the doctor is an independent contractor.[56] Neither seems a good fit for intermediary liability here: foreign doctors are in no way employees of the intermediary, and apparent or implied authority is a considerable stretch. A different HMO-liability theory evaluates HMOs for negligence in reviewing the credentials and competency of the doctors to whom it refers patients—that is, breach of the "duty to select and retain only competent physicians."[57] In "a managed care program the patient has chosen the particular program, but not the physicians who are provided. The patient must use the physicians on the panel.... [Thus, the program's] obligation for the patient's total care [is] more comprehensive than in the hospital setting."[58] Under current law, this standard may not provide much med-mal traction against a facilitator because it can satisfy this duty quite easily. A leading treatise suggests that, in the domestic U.S. context, the kinds of things that would violate this duty are selecting "a panel physician or dentist who has evidenced incompetence in her practice, or has dementia from AIDS."[59] If held to this standard, facilitators might satisfy the duty merely by pointing to the Joint

---

[53] *Id.* at 1497.

[54] *Id.* at 1497 n.120.

[55] *Id.* at 1497; Leigh Turner, *"First World Health Care at Third World Prices": Globalization, Bioethics and Medical Tourism*, 2 BIOSOCIETIES 303, 320 (2007).

[56] Cohen, *supra* note 2, at 1497; Cortez, *supra* note 21, at 15; Philip Mirrer-Singer, *Medical Malpractice Overseas: The Legal Uncertainty Surrounding Medical Tourism*, 70 LAW & CONTEMP. PROBS. 215–16 (2007).

[57] *E.g.*, McClellan v. Health Maint. Org. of Pa., 604 A.2d 1053, 1058 (Pa. Super. Ct. 1992).

[58] BARRY R. FURROW ET AL., HEALTH LAW 404–05 (2d ed. 2000).

[59] *Id.* at 405.

Commission International (JCI) or other widely recognized accreditation of the hospital to which it referred the patient or to the board certifications of the foreign physicians it selected.[60] Moreover, patients may have problems in proving that a facilitator knew or should have known that the foreign provider was unfit or incompetent based on some pattern of misconduct, especially if the standards for credentialing and practice depart from U.S. standards and thus might be argued to be outside the provider's duty of inquiry.[61]

A separate theory of liability relating to the duty to supervise or control staff[62] is also unlikely to apply to these intermediaries, as they have very little direct control over physicians in destination-country facilities. Nor are patients likely to succeed in claims against facilitators asserting vicarious liability for the injuries done by foreign providers or hospitals. Courts generally refuse to impose that kind of liability against HMOs and similar entities unless the physician is an employee or agent of the company (which is not the case with a facilitator), and facilitators can safeguard against even that liability through a contractual disclaimer.[63]

The final theory of liability patients may try against facilitators is failure to obtain informed consent, premised on the idea that the company misrepresented the qualifications or quality of the foreign provider.[64] This cause of action is particularly tempting because facilitators have demonstrated a tendency to boast on their websites about the quality or qualifications of the providers they use. Though recovery is possible, patients will face a large number of obstacles in pursuing this cause of action: they must show that (1) the facilitator had a duty to obtain informed consent, (2) the facilitator failed to do so, (3) the facilitator made a misrepresentation (which would be hard to prove as it would require the court to evaluate the quality and credentialing of foreign hospitals or providers), and (4) the misrepresentation was material in the sense that it caused the patient injuries.[65] Moreover, even in the United States, courts have not shown a willingness to extend informed-consent liability beyond the treating physician.[66]

Thus, although some of the procedural difficulties are less of an obstacle for asserting liability against facilitators rather than foreign providers in the medical tourism context, the substantive law governing the applicable causes of action is very unfriendly to plaintiffs, leading us to expect much lower likelihood of recovery.

---

[60] *See id.* at 383–84 (discussing the role of compliance with Joint Commission regulations in negligence suits against hospitals).

[61] Cortez, *supra* note 21, at 15; Mirrer-Singer, *supra* note 56, at 217–18.

[62] FURROW ET AL., *supra* note 58, at 405–06.

[63] Cortez, *supra* note 21, at 16; Mirrer-Singer, *supra* note 56, at 217–18.

[64] Cortez, *supra* note 21, at 16; Mirrer-Singer, *supra* note 56, at 217–18.

[65] Cortez, *supra* note 21, at 16; Mirrer-Singer, *supra* note 56, at 217–18.

[66] Cortez, *supra* note 21, at 16; Mirrer-Singer, *supra* note 56, at 217–18.

C. Should It Matter?

Based on what I have said thus far, it is safe to assume that U.S. patients such as Carl will experience significant declines in the likelihood and amount of recovery for medical error as compared to what they might recover if the injury had occurred during treatment within the United States. Does this *fact* constitute a *problem*, and if so, is it one that regulation should address?

One easy answer, hinted at above, is that the medical malpractice system is riddled with flaws such that losing access to it is of no great moment. While no one would portray the American med-mal system as anywhere near perfect, there are sharp disagreements about how bad it is and how feasible it would be to implement a better system, lest the Perfect become the enemy of the Good. Few critics of the med-mal system would likely go so far as to suggest that we would be better off if we replaced access to that system with the huge obstacles for recovery faced by medical tourist patients discussed above. For those who *would* go so far, the question is easy: to the extent that medical tourism sharply reduces the amount and likelihood of recovery for med-mal, so much the better. For the rest of us, however, the question becomes more difficult, as I detail below.

i. Thinking about Baselines and Counterfactuals

Imagine we were able to end all medical tourism (as have seen throughout the book, even if we wanted to do so, it would be quite difficult to implement). Would the deficiency in med-mal recovery justify doing so? As I suggested in the last chapter as to quality of care, we must look at counterfactual care available to the medical tourist if choice is restricted and press on the question of whether a ban is really in patients' interests. The patient-protective argument is no doubt correct that a reduction in the likelihood and extent of med-mal recovery is bad for the tourist patient, but the relevant question is: As compared to what? Currently the CBO estimates that about 53 million individuals are uninsured.[67] The Obama administration's major health reform move, the Patient Protection and Affordable Care Act (ACA), will reduce that number but not eliminate it. In the wake of the U.S. Supreme Court's decision on the Act's constitutionality, which restricted some of the Act's Medicaid expansion, the Congressional Budget Office (CBO) now estimates that some 30 million individuals will remain uninsured in the United States in 2022.[68] It is a bit harder to predict the number of *under*insured

---

[67] Robert Pear, *Court Ruling May Blunt Reach of the Health Law*, N.Y. TIMES, July 15, 2012, at A6.

[68] *Id.* To be more precise, according to a prior CBO estimate, about one-third of the non-elderly uninsured would be undocumented immigrants. Letter from Douglas W. Elmendorf, Dir., Cong. Budget Office, to Nancy Pelosi, Speaker, U.S. House of Representatives 9, *available at* http://www.cbo.gov/doc.cfm?index=11379&type=1 (last visited May 4, 2014).

Americans in the wake of the ACA reforms, but it too is likely to remain substantial. For the medical tourists, such as Carl, who are my focus in this chapter (private insurance and medical tourism is discussed in Chapter 4), who travel because of lack of insurance coverage, the deep cost savings that medical tourism makes possible may mean the difference between getting and not getting certain nonemergency care at all.[69]

It is true that uninsured Americans are not wholly without domestic care options. Emergency care received through an EMTALA admission is possible. But it is unlikely to overlap to any significant extent with the types of procedures sought by medical tourists, as EMTALA covers only "emergency medical condition[s],"[70] whereas medical tourists are typically scheduling surgeries far in advance when the patient is well enough to travel.

The uninsured can also theoretically purchase services out-of-pocket in the United States. Although lack of health insurance correlates with low income (over 60 percent of the uninsured earn under 200 percent of the Federal Poverty Level), the U.S. uninsured are a heterogeneous group also made up of self-employed entrepreneurs and young adults who assess their need for health insurance to be too low to justify the expense. Additionally, there is fluidity in this group in that people move in and out of insurance coverage based on changes in their employment status, age, income, marital status, and other factors.[71] That said, it is important not to overstate the point and mythologize the

---

[69] The case for restricting medical tourism is less compelling for patients who have access to some care in the United States for their need but prefer a foreign provider for other reasons, such as my example above of traveling abroad to Thailand because its doctors are particularly adept at sex reassignment surgery. In part because most out-of-pocket U.S. medical tourists are travelling for cost/access reasons, I focus mostly on such cases. It does seem to me that the threshold for regulatory intervention should be lower for those who are traveling for these other reasons, as the costs of over-regulation are less threatening, but it will be very hard to develop regulatory policies that segregate these two populations of medical tourists paying out-of-pocket, such that we may need to take the bitter with the sweet.

[70] The Emergency Medical Treatment and Active Labor Act (EMTALA) requires hospitals that accept Medicare reimbursement to have an emergency room to "screen[]" any patient that presents herself to determine "whether or not an emergency medical condition [within the meaning of the statute] exists." Emergency Medical Treatment and Labor Act (EMTALA), 42 U.S.C. § 1395dd(a) (2006); see, e.g., Burditt v. U.S. Dep't of Health & Human Servs., 934 F.2d 1362, 1368–73 (5th Cir. 1991). If it does, the hospital must either stabilize (give "treatment as may be required to stabilize the medical condition") or transfer the patient to another facility, which can be done only if the patient requests the transfer in writing after being informed or if a health care provider certifies that "the medical benefits reasonably expected from the provision of appropriate medical treatment at another medical facility outweigh the increased risks to the individual." 42 U.S.C. § 1395dd(b)–(d) (2006). The statute defines "emergency medical condition" as "acute symptoms of sufficient severity (including severe pain) such that the absence of immediate medical attention could reasonably be expected to result in...placing the health of the individual" in "serious jeopardy," "serious impairment to bodily functions," or "serious dysfunction of any bodily organ or part." Id. § 1395dd(e)(1) (2006).

[71] THE HENRY J. KAISER FAMILY FOUNDATION, THE UNINSURED: A PRIMER: KEY FACTS ABOUT AMERICANS WITHOUT HEALTH INSURANCE 4–5 (2009); JOHN HOLAHAN ET AL., THE HENRY J. KAISER FAMILY FOUNDATION, CHARACTERISTICS OF THE UNINSURED: WHO IS ELIGIBLE FOR PUBLIC COVERAGE AND WHO NEEDS HELP AFFORDING COVERAGE 1–16 (2007), available at http://

U.S.-uninsured population into a group of risk assessors whose lack of health insurance is strategic rather than driven by lack of resources.[72] Moreover, the extremely high price of purchasing domestic care out-of-pocket means that even among those uninsured who are *not* low income, out-of-pocket purchasing may not be feasible.

Thus, under our current health care system, a ban on medical tourism for uninsured Americans would, in many cases, result in preventing access to nonemergency health care for the patients we seek to "protect." There will, of course, be some cases where receiving care in a foreign country (because of quality-of-care or med-mal disparities) would be *worse* than receiving no care at all. But across the entire class of uninsured patients, medical tourism seems likely to improve the lot of many. That is, an outright ban or even too onerous a regulatory regime for medical tourism threatens not only to restrict patient choice and diminish patients' self-assessed welfare, but also to diminish some of these patients' *actual* welfare by blocking access to nonemergency care entirely. Thus, as to uninsured (and perhaps to a lesser extent underinsured) medical-tourism users who use medical tourism to access services they could otherwise not afford, patients such as Carl, the patient-protective argument must meet a high standard of proof to justify restricting choice, especially wholesale bans. Although there are admittedly empirical questions one would need to answer before making a definitive assessment, it seems reasonable to favor patient choice when judging under conditions of uncertainty. Any attempt to regulate medical tourism for the purpose of protecting patients' med-mal rights has to be calibrated against the real threat of "protecting" them out of any care at all.

Second, one way of thinking about the problem is to view medical tourism against the larger backdrop of foreign consumption of goods or services. We currently impose little or no limits on the purchase of other potentially tortious goods and services abroad. No one thinks the United States ought to intervene in the decision of a college student to go bungee jumping in Costa Rica. This is true notwithstanding the fact that differences in regulation between the United States and other countries may make the good or service consumed abroad less safe than its U.S. equivalent, and the fact that if a tort occurs abroad, many of the obstacles discussed above will make recovery in the United States much more difficult. Indeed, a system wherein we allowed U.S. citizens to carry their tort regimes with them on their back wherever they go might be thought of as an affront to Costa Rican sovereignty—that what happens in Costa Rica should stay in Costa Rica, as far as tort liability is concerned. Indeed, a more pointed comparison would be with the treatment of injuries incurred in traveling to get medical tourism. No one thinks it problematic that our courts will not apply our tort law to injuries from

---

www.kff.org/uninsured/upload/7613.pdf; Nan D. Hunter, *Risk Governance and Deliberative Democracy in Health Care*, 97 GEO. L.J. 1, 58 (2008).

[72] *See* Sara Rosenbaum, *A Dose of Reality: Assessing the Federal Trade Commission/Department of Justice Report in an Uninsured, Underserved, and Vulnerable Population Context*, 31 J. HEALTH POL. POL'Y & L. 657, 665–66 (2006).

food poisoning at the hotel one stays at the night before surgery, to give but one example. Why should the actual health care consumption be treated differently?

My point is that there are competing baselines at work in the discussion, and focusing on one may obscure the others. Below, I will discuss how an unregulated approach to medical tourism might be thought of as exceptional against the baseline of the domestic prohibition on med-mal waivers and licensure requirements; by contrast, preventing individuals from using medical tourism because of protective concerns seems exceptional against the baseline of our laissez-faire approach to the consumption of other services abroad.

Of course, one rejoinder is that health care is special in a number of ways. Philosophers such as Norman Daniels have argued for the "special moral importance of health," such that government has a duty to improve access to health care in a way it does not for other goods that might improve individuals' welfare.[73] Accepting that argument may cause us to endorse universal health care. But, as discussed above, once we are outside of a first-best world with universal health care, it seems that accepting the "special moral importance of health" might in fact suggest that a laissez-faire approach for health goods is more justified than for other goods. That is, if we easily reach a conclusion that intervention is not justified as to bungee jumping, the same justification might apply a fortiori to health care as that which is lost if access is denied is so much greater. An individual who loses the ability to bungee jump faces disappointment, to be sure, but an individual who loses access to nonemergency care loses something much worse—years of life or quality of life.

Health care is also "special" because of the complex health-insurance regime of the United States and the resulting agency problems that surround it. I focus on these differences and where they should lead us in Chapter 4.

A different way in which health care might be "special" is that it is a credence good, a good whose quality cannot be evaluated by the consumer even after consumption,[74] and, as discussed in the last chapter and elsewhere in this book there is a market failure as to the information provision. The former might distinguish health care from bungee jumping (which is an experience good whose value cannot be assessed before use but can be assessed after), but it would not distinguish it from something such as legal services provided abroad, an area where we have adopted a relatively laissez-faire regulatory approach.

These two points of distinction nicely justify the type of information-forcing interventions discussed in the last chapter on quality. We could adopt a similar information-forcing approach to med-mal recovery risk here: the federal government could give country-by-country profiles about how receptive foreign states are to med-mal

---

[73] See NORMAN DANIELS, JUST HEALTH: MEETING HEALTH NEEDS FAIRLY 29–78 (2008).

[74] See Sivaramjani Thambisetty, Patents as Credence Goods, 27 OXFORD J. LEGAL STUD. 707, 726 (2007).

actions, giving both detailed information on things such as standards of care and damages caps, as well as (perhaps more usefully for the medical tourist) placing the different systems into categories. The model here would be the State Department's travel warnings.[75] Although doing so would require developing expertise in comparative med-mal law, the few scholars who have so far attempted that work show that the task is a feasible one. In determining how far beyond those interventions we ought to go in restricting patient choice, this framing point is useful: we should subject health care purchase abroad to a "special" form of regulation compared to the purchase of other services abroad only in proportion to the extent it presents concerns about patient choice (even given informational interventions) that render it "special" as compared to consumption of these other services.

With these framing points in mind, I now turn to assessing whether there is a compelling case for restricting patient choices because of concerns over diminished med-mal recovery.

D. Should Patients Be Permitted to Choose Deficient Med-Mal Recovery through Medical Tourism?

As discussed above, med-mal is thought to serve both a deterrent and a compensatory function for individuals who suffer injury.

How one thinks about opting out from its protection, at least at first glance, may depend on one's more general normative views. For those who have fairly libertarian/anti-paternalist leanings, the idea of preventing individuals from pursuing treatment abroad (with its attendant cost savings) because of insufficient med-mal protection may seem unthinkable. And yet, in the domestic context, one might reply, this is exactly what we *already* do. We largely prevent individuals from trading a reduction in med-mal remedies for better surgical prices.

In the United States, there is a well-established line of cases forbidding individuals from contractually waiving med-mal liability or altering the standard of liability. The leading case in this line is *Tunkl v. Regents of the University of California*, which involved a patient admitted to the UCLA Medical Center who signed a contract releasing the "hospital from any and all liability for the negligent or wrongful acts or omissions of its employees, if the hospital has used due care in selecting its employees." After the patient died during surgery, his estate brought suit, and the California Supreme Court rejected the hospital's claim that the waiver barred liability, finding the contract contrary to public policy. While the *Tunkl* court conceded that "obviously no public policy opposes private, voluntary transactions in which one party, for a consideration, agrees to shoulder

---

[75] *See Current Travel Warnings*, U.S. DEPARTMENT OF STATE, http://travel.state.gov/travel/cis_pa_tw/tw/tw_1764.html (last visited Nov. 4, 2012).

a risk which the law would otherwise have placed upon the other party," it thought the circumstances in this case "pose[d] a different situation." It argued that, in this context, the patient "does not really acquiesce voluntarily in the contractual shifting of the risk, nor can we be reasonably certain that he receives an adequate consideration for the transfer," because the services were a "practical and crucial necessity," because the hospital "holds itself out as willing to perform its services for those members of the public who qualify for its research and training facilities," and because the "would-be patient is in no position to reject the proffered agreement, to bargain with the hospital, or in lieu of agreement to find another hospital." This was a contract of adhesion because "[t]he admission room of a hospital contains no bargaining table where, as in a private business transaction, the parties can debate the terms of their contract."[76]

Later cases have extended the prohibition outside the exceptionally adhesive ER-admission context to attempts to contractually waive med-mal liability more generally.[77]

To be clear, *Tunkl* and its progeny, as a doctrinal matter, do not control in our context because they govern only attempts to *contractually* alter the standard of liability for med-mal. The argument is instead that the same *public policy* reasons relied on by *Tunkl* and its progeny counsel interventions to discourage or prevent medical tourism where they will lead to deficiencies in med-mal recovery. Why allow individuals to relinquish ex ante their ability to recover in med-mal through travel when we prevent them from doing it contractually? On this view, far from being crazy, banning medical tourism seems simply to reflect the principles of the current practice in place domestically.

One approach to this supposed tension would be to concede that the domestic treatment of contractual waivers of med-mal is inconsistent with permitting patients to de facto waive that protection by traveling abroad. In the words of the jazz standard, "Something's Gotta Give," the "something" being the prohibition on med-mal waivers domestically, which should be gutted, as some have argued. Some legal scholars writing outside the medical tourism context have indeed urged embracing contractual waiver of med-mal liability.[78]

---

[76] Tunkl v. Regents of the Univ. of Cal., 383 P.2d 441, 442–49 (Cal. 1963).

[77] *See, e.g.*, Belshaw v. Feinstein, 65 Cal. Rptr. 788, 798 (Ct. App. 1968) (discussing neurosurgery); Emory Univ. v. Porubiansky, 282 S.E.2d 903, 903–05 (Ga. 1981) (discussing dental services); Cudnik v. William Beaumont Hosp., 525 N.W.2d 891, 892–93 (Mich. Ct. App. 1994) (discussing radiation therapy for cancer); Ash v. N.Y. Univ. Dental Ctr., 564 N.Y.S.2d 308, 309 (App. Div. 1990) (discussing dental services); Olson v. Molzen, 558 S.W.2d 429, 429–31 (Tenn. 1977) (discussing abortion); Eelbode v. Chec Med. Ctrs., Inc., 984 P.2d 436, 440–41 (Wash. Ct. App. 1999) (discussing physical therapy).

[78] *See, e.g.*, Richard H. Thaler & Cass R. Sunstein, Nudge 207–14 (2008); Richard Epstein, *Medical Malpractice: The Case for Contract*, 1 Am. B. Found. Res. J. 87, 119 (1976); Glen O. Robinson, *Rethinking the Allocation of Medical Malpractice Risks between Patients and Providers*, 49 Law & Contemp. Probs. 173, 185 (Spring 1986).

But this is not the track I will take. Instead, I seek to make the harder case that even if we maintain fidelity to the policies and principles behind the prohibition on contractual waiver domestically, the medical-tourism case differs in some key ways, suggesting those policies and principles do not justify intervention here.

I will offer four ways to reconcile medical tourism with the contractual-waiver prohibition. The first two try to reconcile medical tourism with the domestic prohibition on waiver, at least to some extent, by suggesting that the prohibition currently exists alongside domestic practices through which patients reduce their med-mal recovery. I will argue that these are practices to which international medical tourism may be analogized. The second two indicate reasons that the policies underlying the waiver prohibition are less apposite to medical tourism.

Intra-national Medical Tourism: One way to resist the applicability of the medical tourism-waiver analogy is to recognize that in the domestic sphere, the doctrine coexists with a toleration of U.S. intra-national medical tourism. Because state law governs med-mal, a med-mal suit by an individual treated and injured in a given state will not be treated in the same way by each state's legal system. Yet we impose no obstacles on traveling to another U.S. state for health care.

The majority rule is that (unlike other potential tortfeasors) the reasonableness of physician conduct is determined by ascertaining a physician's compliance with customary practices. By contrast, twelve states have expressly refused to be bound by medical custom, instead in favor of a reasonable-doctor standard, and nine other states, "while not explicitly rejecting deference to custom, ha[ve] chosen to phrase the duty owed by physicians in terms of reasonability, rather than compliance with medical customs."[79] Even in states that have moved to the reasonableness standard, there is variation as to whether reasonableness is premised on the prevailing standard of care in a given locality, in a similar locality, or nationwide.[80] These variations may be outcome determinative as to how the same claim would fare in different states.

State tort reform also has a major impact on how much an individual suing for med-mal may recover and therefore on whether he brings suit in the first place. Between 1980 and 2005, legislatures and courts have introduced several reforms: (1) limiting the doctrine of joint and several liability for medical malpractice; (2) limiting the collateral source rule (under the usual collateral source rule payments by insurance or other sources to the injured party are not counted against (i.e., they do not reduce) the liability of the party who committed the tort); (3) allowing the defendants to pay some amount of the damages through periodic payments (i.e., allowing defendants to purchase an annuity to make payments and to relieve them of paying if the patient dies before payments are finished); (4) placing caps

---

[79] Philip G. Peters, Jr., *The Quiet Demise of Deference to Custom: Malpractice Law at the Millennium*, 57 WASH. & LEE L. REV. 163, 170 (2000).

[80] *See, e.g.*, Hall v. Hilbun, 466 So. 2d 856 (Miss. 1985); BARRY R. FURROW ET AL., LIABILITY AND QUALITY ISSUES IN HEALTH CARE 147–48 (5th ed. 2004).

on noneconomic damages; (5) placing caps on punitive damages; and (6) changing the evidentiary showing required to receive punitive damages.[81]

The fact that the United States permits unrestricted *intra*-national medical tourism notwithstanding its effects on med-mal recovery is helpful in resisting a ban on *inter*national medical tourism.

To be sure, there are also important dis-analogies. Although the substantive med-mal law governing the action may differ between states, the inconvenience of suing in the "foreign" forum is much less when that foreign forum is another U.S. state (even one on the opposite coast) than when it is another country: the litigation systems are likely to be much more similar, securing a lawyer and being present for trial is less daunting, and there is protection for out-of-state plaintiffs through federal subject matter jurisdiction for cases involving diversity of citizenship.[82] Further, if one can achieve personal jurisdiction over an out-of-state physician-defendant in one's home state, one can rely on the Full Faith and Credit statute or the Full Faith and Credit Clause in the federal Constitution to enforce the judgment against that physician in the state in which she has assets.[83] This protection is unavailable for foreign defendants with assets abroad. In addition, comparably few patients will turn to intra-national medical tourism out of desperation, although in keeping with our concern about "protecting" patients out of nonemergency care, that distinction may cut in favor of the extra-national case. Finally, it is open to the critic to suggest that intra-national medical tourism is itself problematic and should be reexamined.

Nevertheless, the analogy is helpful in reminding us that we do already allow patients, through travel, to reduce their probable med-mal recovery ex ante in a way we do not allow them to do contractually, although the scope of that reduction is certainly much more pronounced in international medical tourism.

Arbitration: Second, one might argue that contractual waiver of liability, as in *Tunkl*, is the wrong analogy. Rather than conferring the provider almost complete immunity, as in that case, in medical tourism the plaintiff's decision to be treated abroad merely reduces the chance or amount of med-mal recovery (albeit significantly).[84] A different and perhaps better analogy is agreements to arbitrate med-mal disputes, which courts have largely upheld.

For example, in *Madden v. Kaiser Foundation Hospitals*, the California Supreme Court (the same court that decided *Tunkl*) found an agreement to undergo binding arbitration of med-mal disputes enforceable as a matter of law despite accepting that

---

[81] Ronen Avraham, *An Empirical Study of the Impact of Tort Reforms on Medical Malpractice Settlement Payments*, 36 J. LEGAL STUD. S183, S191–94 (2007).

[82] 28 U.S.C. § 1332 (2006).

[83] U.S. CONST. art. IV; 28 U.S.C. § 1738 (2012).

[84] *Cf.* Clark C. Havighurst, *Private Reform of Tort-Law Dogma: Market Opportunities and Legal Obstacles*, 49 LAW & CONTEMP. PROBS. 143, 164 (Spring 1986) (arguing that *Tunkl* "should not control the outcome of a case in which something substantially less than complete immunity is sought").

the provision was inserted through negotiation between the state employee's union and Kaiser six years after the plaintiff's employment began, that the plaintiff never signed an individualized agreement to arbitrate, and that, due to work absences, she had received no notice and was not aware of the requirement. It found the agreement was not contrary to public policy and distinguished *Tunkl* by stating that the agreement at issue represented "the product of negotiation between two parties, Kaiser and the board, possessing parity of bargaining strength." The plaintiff did not lack "any realistic opportunity to look elsewhere for a more favorable contract," but instead "enjoyed the opportunity to select from among several medical plans negotiated and offered by the board, some of which did not include arbitration provisions, or to contract individually for medical care," and the provision in question did "not detract from Kaiser's duty to use reasonable care in treating patients, [or] limit its liability for breach of this duty, but merely substitute[d] one forum for another."[85]

Perhaps the same distinctions can be made for this population of medical tourists: as in *Madden*, and unlike *Tunkl* (where waiver occurred during an ER admission!), concerns about adhesion are muted here. There is not an obvious asymmetry in bargaining power, lack of alternative options, or lack of "a realistic opportunity to look elsewhere."[86] Indeed, the default care option the patient faces is treatment in the United States with the particular state's level of med-mal protection, and he must go out of his way to alter that default by arranging care and actually traveling abroad—a strong "altering rule."[87]

Further, as in *Madden*, it can be argued that the patient seeking medical tourism has not waived his or her right to med-mal altogether, but instead "merely substitute[d] one forum for another." In *Madden*, that other forum is an arbitral one; for medical tourism, it may be a foreign court system. Because of the differences from foreign law and choice-of-law principles discussed above, the medical tourist will likely face quite different substantive med-mal law, but that is equally true in arbitration. Arbitrators need not be judges, or even lawyers. They "commonly do not write reasoned opinions attempting to explain and justify their decisions" and are "actively discourage[d] from doing so." In fact, an arbitrator need not "necessarily 'follow the law'—or indeed apply or develop any body of general rules as a guide to his decision." Instead, he may "do justice as he sees it, applying his own sense of law and equity to the facts as he finds them to be and making an award reflecting the spirit rather than the letter of the agreement... [I]n the words of one older case, arbitrators are a law unto themselves."[88] Thus, in some cases adjudication

---

[85] Madden v. Kaiser Found. Hosps., 552 P.2d 1178, 1180–86 (Cal. 1976).

[86] In the arbitration context, courts have thus been more inclined to enforce agreements when they were made in advance rather than at the point of service. *See* MARK A. HALL ET AL., HEALTH CARE LAW AND ETHICS 422 (7th ed. 2007) (citing Broemmer v. Abortion Servs. of Phoenix, 840 P.2d 1013 (Ariz. 1993); Obstetrics & Gynecologists v. Pepper, 693 P.2d 1259 (Nev. 1985); Sosa v. Paulos, 924 P.2d 357 (Utah 1996)).

[87] To use the terminology of Ian Ayres, *Menus Matter*, 73 U. CHI. L. REV. 3, 6 (2006).

[88] ALAN SCOTT RAU ET AL., PROCESSES OF DISPUTE RESOLUTION 612 (4th ed. 2006).

in a foreign judicial system may more closely approximate adjudication in the United States than do some forms of domestic arbitration.

Again, although this argument is helpful, it only goes so far.

First, there is no analog to the personal-jurisdiction difficulty in arbitration cases. Second, a party who succeeds at arbitration under the Federal Arbitration Act may use a federal district court to confirm the award and enforce judgment,[89] whereas enforcing a U.S. judgment against a foreign health care provider or hospital is much more difficult. That said, the enforceability of judgments against foreign defendants is a general problem of international private law, and it has not prompted us to block or restrict activities in other spheres. Third, while the California Supreme Court has upheld these arbitration agreements generally, it has also struck down particular arbitration schemes as applied. For example, courts found Kaiser Permanente's med-mal arbitrations system to be beset with fraud and designed to increase delay so that the patient will die before the decision and thus receive fewer damages.[90] It might be thought that some of the foreign systems, in which individuals will have to litigate, share many of those features. Fourth, as the *Madden* court noted, there are "benefits of the arbitral forum" for the patients as a group by "facilitat[ing] the adjudication of minor malpractice claims which cannot economically be resolved in a judicial forum,"[91] a phenomenon without an analog in the medical tourism context. Finally, any attempt to use the med-mal arbitration jurisprudence as a touchstone will obviously not convince those who think *Madden* and its progeny were wrongly decided.[92]

Search Costs, Timing Concerns, and Collective-Action Problems: Recent scholarship in the law and economics tradition has defended the prohibition on waiving med-mal. Such arguments suggest that even if we think patients would make good choices as to contractual waiver, which is far from clear, there are nonetheless strong reasons not to allow them to make such decisions. In order to get his desired level of protection, a patient offered a nonnegotiable waiver at the point of service must bear search costs associated with seeking a new provider, including the adverse health consequences of delaying health care.[93] For medical tourism, however, the patient is presented with any number of possible providers in the home state offering the standard med-mal

---

[89] 9 U.S.C. § 9 (2006); *see, e.g.*, IDS Life Ins. Co. v. Royal Alliance Assocs., 266 F.3d 645, 653 (7th Cir. 2001). Another distinction is that the Federal Arbitration Act allows federal courts to review decisions by the arbitrator, albeit under extremely narrow standards aimed at fraud or egregious misconduct. 9 U.S.C. § 10 (2006) First Options of Chicago, Inc. v. Kaplan, 514 U.S. 938, 942 (1995).

[90] Engalla v. Permanente Med. Group, 938 P.2d 903, 908, 912 (Cal. 1997).

[91] Madden v. Kaiser Found. Hosps., 552 P.2d 1178, 1185–86 (Cal. 1976).

[92] *E.g.*, Kenneth A. DeVille, *The Jury Is Out: Pre-dispute Binding Arbitration Agreements for Medical Malpractice Claim*, 28 J. LEGAL MED. 333 (2007).

[93] Jennifer Arlen, *Contracting over Liability: Medical Malpractice and the Cost of Choice*, 158 U. PA. L. REV. 957, 1007–08 n.123 (2010).

regime; he only incurs search costs of finding a foreign provider governed by a different med-mal regime when he decides he does not want care at home. Moreover, medical tourists are typically not seeking the kind of emergency care for which delay is detrimental; indeed medical tourism may in fact facilitate access to nonemergency care otherwise unavailable.

Other law and economics scholars argue that med-mal contracting engenders collective-action and timing problems. Following the recent trend of scholars to view the causes of medical error as system-wide rather than pertaining to the care of an individual patient, Professor Jennifer Arlen has suggested that an isolated patient who contracts for med-mal liability cannot get the same benefits as she can if the system imposed it nonnegotiably on all patients, because quality-of-care-enhancing investments are both lumpy (they cannot be doled out to individual patients) and collective to all patients seen by that doctor. Thus, there is a collective-action problem. Doctors make these med mal–induced investments at the system level and cannot turn them on and off as to individual patients, such that rational patients will not purchase the liability condition on an individual-contracting basis, even if it is their preferred condition were it imposed by fiat. There is also a timing problem in that many of the quality-enhancing investments in care that med-mal liability theoretically induces occur before the doctor assumes the care of a particular patient, for example better post–medical school training, equipment, or staffing. Thus, patients cannot use contracting to induce the adoption of those quality-enhancing investments because they occur prior to the point of contracting.[94]

Neither of these problems applies to medical tourism. Instead of individual patients determining their desired level of liability within a system, patients select a system that has a set level of malpractice liability and therefore a set level of inducement for care-enhancing investment. Thus, there is no collective action problem: all patients receive the same level of liability within the system, so there are no free riders. Nor is there a timing problem, because the level of liability has already been set by the domestic medical-malpractice system.

The same answer is available to a related concern. Some argue that making an entitlement (such as minimum wage) waivable allows individuals expanded choice: those who value what is offered for the waiver may waive, and those who do not will not. The classic rejoinder is that this expansion of choice is superficial. For example, in the minimum-wage context, given enough providers of labor, every individual might feel pressure to accept the below-minimum wage offer for fear that everyone else will, such that the system unravels to the point where everyone is below minimum wage. Applied to

---

[94] *Id.* at 963, 966, 992–1000. For a discussion of whether U.S. medical tourists actually face a lower standard of care than the patient from the destination country because the foreign physician is discounting for the reduced likelihood the U.S. patient will sue him at all, and my doubts regarding that argument, *see* Cohen, *supra* note 2, at 1535 n.257.

the medical-tourism context, the analogous argument is that medical tourism pressures doctors offering unwaivable liability to leave the market such that there is no physician available who will offer patients the full liability package. But here there is an important difference: the patient can always choose to use a domestic provider. Thus, the existing rule prohibiting domestic waiver of med-mal liability offers a sort of backstop against complete unraveling; that is, doctors offering the "full" med-mal "benefit" will remain in the market because they cannot offer another option and still practice domestically.

A different, harder to categorize concern with liability waivers in general is that they affront rule-of-law or fairness values by allowing regulated entities to contract out of mandated duties. It would take a lot more space than I can devote here to fully articulate and evaluate that kind of concern. All I will say for our purposes is that this concern also seems much weaker in the context of medical tourism. Foreign providers have not tried to escape a domestic regulatory system by persuading patients in desperation to waive rights. It is the patients who have chosen (admittedly often for lack of better options) the liability and regulatory system of the foreign country by pursuing treatment there.

Self-Insurance: The fact that the medical tourist is making the decision to be treated abroad far in advance also distinguishes medical tourism in a second, perhaps more significant, way: any patient sufficiently concerned with the possibility of diminished med-mal recovery could hypothetically insure against that risk by buying medical malpractice insurance. Given this reality, some would predict that a market for such insurance for medical tourism would spring up, and indeed that market is emerging.

At least one insurance company, AOS, has offered "Patient Medical Malpractice Insurance" that insures against "the risk of suffering Medical Malpractice abroad."[95] The product pays out for "economic damages" such as "wage loss," "cost of repair," "out-of-pocket expenses," and "rehabilitation," as well as "non-economic damages" such as "severe disfigurement," "loss of reproductive capacity," and "death."[96] The company states that it handles "claims in accordance with the customs and standards of the employee's home country and not the country of injury" and that it estimates claims will be settled 80 percent faster through its process "than the traditional litigation environment…(based on US standards)."[97] The patient can select a predetermined maximum amount of damages against which to be insured (up to $1 million) and must pay $1000 to AOS to "start the claim process," which will be refunded to the patient if his claim is approved or forfeited if it is denied.[98] If the patient is "dissatisfied with a claim

---

[95] *Patient Medical Malpractice Insurance (PMMI)*, AOS ASSURANCE COMPANY LIMITED, http://www.aosassurance.bb/readmore.htm (last visited Nov. 5, 2012).

[96] *Patient Medical Malpractice Insurance (PMMI™) Product Sheet*, AOS ASSURANCE COMPANY LIMITED 1, http://www.aosassurance.bb/Documents/PMMI/PMMI%20Product%20Sheet.pdf (last visited Nov. 5, 2012).

[97] *Id.*

[98] *Id.* at 2.

settlement offer under the terms of the policy the patient can elect for third party bind-ing arbitration on both AOS and the patient."[99] AOS insures against med-mal when treatment is done by a predetermined list of physicians abroad, but it indicates in its materials that "[i]f your doctor is US board certified or an internationally equivalent, we will add your doctor to our list."[100] When I first started examining this possibility in 2010, the website listed several dozen procedures and generated quotes based on the level of coverage desired. For example, a policy for $1 million in med-mal damages coverage for coronary bypass and grafting would cost $6816.15. If one reviews the price differen-tials discussed earlier for cardiac bypass at major foreign hospitals, those differentials far exceed $6816.15. This means that an individual can purchase medical malpractice insurance for $1 million worth of damages and still achieve very substantial cost savings by seeking treatment abroad.[101]

This, too, importantly distinguishes medical tourism from the domestic med mal–waiver context, in that the cost of a similar product for patients who had contractually waived med-mal coverage domestically, were it permitted, would likely approach the cost savings offered by physicians in return for waiver.

Of course, there are many important unanswered questions here. How good is an insurer such as AOS about paying out as promised? What are the terms of the arbitra-tion, and do those terms pose a concern? How does the insurer preselect which doctors it will add to its list, and is this process fair? We would need to know more about the answers to these questions, the nature of the competitive marketplace for this kind of insurance, and the possibility of patients suing the insurer if it fails to live up to its obli-gations. But in a sense, this product partially enables the patient to substitute arbitral protection for litigation protection—a move that, as discussed above, we currently allow a person to contract for domestically. Notwithstanding these concerns and questions, the fact that an uninsured patient using medical tourism can protect himself through insurance against diminished med-mal recovery represents a powerful additional reason to resist a prohibitory stance on medical tourism.

Although this kind of product can replace the compensatory function of med-mal liability, how well it can replace its deterrence function is less clear. On the one hand, the health care provider bears neither the burden of the liability nor the cost of this insur-ance. On the other hand, the med-mal insurance provider may refuse to insure patients

---

[99] *Id.*

[100] *Frequently Asked Questions*, AOS ASSURANCE COMPANY LIMITED, http://www.aosassurance.bb/PMMI-FAQ.htm (last visited Nov. 5, 2012).

[101] *See* Cohen, *supra* note 2, at 1537 (citing AOS, Quick Quote for Patient Medical Malpractice Insurance (PMMI), https://www.aosassurance.bb/Reaktor2K7/application/quickquote/quickquote.aspx (last vis-ited July 21, 2010)). This quote was achieved by selecting "Coronary bypass and grafting" in the "Procedure" drop-down and "$1,000,000" from the "Amount of insurance coverage in US$" drop-down on Oct. 20, 2008. *Id.*

who select physicians responsible for prior claims, which may mean significant loss of revenue for those physicians.

* * *

Although none is perfect in itself, these four reasons collectively make a persuasive case for distinguishing the policies and principles behind the domestic-waiver prohibition from the case of medical tourism. Also, whereas the domestic contractual-waiver prohibition sanctions the provider directly by making the contract unenforceable, the hypothetical interventions we would have to use in the case of medical tourism would sanction the patient, the individual in need of care. When combined with (1) problems with the tools available to discourage medical tourism (discussed in Chapter 2, regarding Quality of Care), (2) general framing ideas about the legal treatment of consumption of other services abroad, and (3) the concerns about the potential counterfactual—that certain nonemergency care would be unavailable if medical tourism is blocked—these points of distinction make a clear case for rejecting attempts to ban or discourage medical tourism wholesale on the basis of med mal–recovery concerns for this population.

E. Softer Regulatory Interventions Focused on Channeling?

For the reasons stated, it would be foolish to try to prevent or strongly discourage patients who are under- or uninsured from going abroad because of fears related to diminished likelihood and amount of med-mal recovery. It does not follow, however, that no regulation is worthwhile.

To begin with, wherever one falls on the libertarian-paternalist continuum, it seems sensible to provide information to patients about their likelihood of med-mal recovery at various facilities. From most general to most specific, this information would include (1) an explanation of the kinds of procedural barriers discussed above; (2) a country-by-country breakdown of the way in which the domestic legal system and choice of law might retard their ability to sue; and (3) a facility-by-facility review of the way in which individual facilities have either reduced these risks (for example, through patient-favorable consent to jurisdiction, forum selection, or choice-of-law clauses or agreements to arbitrate), or made them worse (for example, by contractually providing for application of the destination country's law or exclusive jurisdiction of the destination country's courts).[102]

Although a national regulator, such as the U.S. Department of State or Department of Health and Human Services, might initially find it costly to provide this information, it could share the burden by inducing or requiring an accreditor such as JCI to amass, audit, and publish this information as a condition of accreditation. In the United States, individual states or the federal government could also try to use some of the carrots of insurer-prompted medical tourism, discussed in greater depth later in this book, to

---

[102] Cortez, *supra* note 21, at 3, 18.

induce such disclosure by requiring it as a precondition to allowing insurers to direct patients to this facility. Assuming, as seems plausible, that the same facilities angling for insured patients are also catering to the under- and uninsured patient markets, this would induce disclosure that benefits both markets.

The question is whether to go further still. Rather than merely requiring disclosure, we could require that foreign providers adopt some subset of devices aimed at increasing the plaintiff's likelihood and amount of med-mal recovery. This would adapt the "channeling regime" introduced in the last chapter, wherein national or international regulators create conditions for the "approval" of foreign facilities and providers, and attaching preferential benefits to the use of "approved" providers (such as allowing medical tourists to take tax deductions for services of "approved" providers) or applying "penalties" to the use of "unapproved" providers (such as requiring facilitators or insurers to use only "approved" providers and facilities as a condition of licensure or insurance regulation) that do not require restricting individual medical tourism decisions by patients paying out-of-pocket. For instance:

- To solve the problem of the lack of personal jurisdiction over foreign providers, we could treat as "approved" only those providers who have consented to jurisdiction in the patient's state (or at least somewhere in the United States). These could be providers with express consent-to-jurisdiction clauses in their patient agreements or providers that have impliedly consented to jurisdiction (for example, by appointing an in-state agent for service of process or through the foreign-corporation "domestication" statutes of some states, which require registration in the state as a condition of doing business there).[103]
- To solve the forum non conveniens problem, we could require forum-selection clauses as a condition of being on the "approved" list. Most state courts follow the U.S. Supreme Court in enforcing "such clauses provided that they are reasonable and do not deprive a litigant of his day in court." Although some state courts have endorsed a "theoretical[] ... power to use the forum non conveniens doctrine to decline jurisdiction despite the presence of a valid forum selection clause," that power is rarely invoked.[104]

---

[103] *See, e.g.*, JACK H. FRIEDENTHAL ET AL., CIVIL PROCEDURE: CASES AND MATERIALS 187–88 (10th ed. 2009); Mark Schuck, Comment, *Foreign Corporations and the Issue of Consent to Jurisdiction through Registration to Do Business in Texas: Analysis and Proposal*, 40 HOUS. L. REV. 1455, 1456–58 (2004). For some cautionary cases on registration as a basis for personal jurisdiction, *see, e.g.*, Wenche Siemer v. Learjet Acquisition Corp., 966 F.2d 179, 180–83 (5th Cir. 1992); Ratliff v. Cooper Lab., Inc., 444 F.2d 745, 748 (4th Cir. 1971).

[104] Jens Dammann & Henry Hansmann, *Globalizing Commercial Litigation*, 94 CORNELL L. REV. 1, 39–40 (2008).

- For choice-of-law problems, we could require a choice-of-law clause that points to either the home state of the patient or a particular U.S. state's law as a pre-requisite for "approved" status. Choice-of-law rules vary by state, but most follow the Restatement (Second) of Conflict of Laws in applying the contractually selected state's rules, subject to an override that is unlikely to apply to these cases.[105] Alternatively, we could channel toward facilities in countries that have more plaintiff-friendly substantive med-mal law, by treating as "approved" only providers in those countries.

- Even with all this in place, enforcing judgments in still difficult. To correct for this, states could "approve" only foreign providers that are "bonded," that is, foreign facilities that put substantial assets into a fund in the United States, against which judgment could be enforced by medical-tourist plaintiffs in potential med-mal suits. Because of the operation of the Full Faith and Credit Clause, which allows a court in a state where the defendant has assets to enforce the judgment rendered in another state court (provided it has personal jurisdiction), it would be enough that these assets be in place somewhere in the United States.[106]

As an alternative to these interventions, or as an option in addition to it, we could require agreements to arbitrate or engage in other alternative dispute resolution (ADR) mechanisms for medical tourism as a condition for treating facilitators and providers as "approved." ADR attempts to shift the resolution of disputes from formal public adversarial court procedures to more consensual and informal private resolution. In dispute systems design, it is typical to layer several different ADR methods from most informal to most formal, beginning with negotiation, moving toward mediation, and culminating in arbitration, the most litigation-like of the processes. In many transnational commercial contexts, arbitration is used in part because of the existence of the United Nations Convention on Recognition and Enforcement of Foreign Arbitral Awards of 1958 (commonly known as the "New York Convention").[107]

What might an ADR system for such a system look like? Internationally, countries such as Mexico, India, and France have adopted some form of arbitration system to address deficiencies in domestic litigation for medical malpractice claims.[108] While both the Indian and French systems offer some lessons applicable here, in particular, Mexico's system might be a model for a gold-standard ADR system for med-mal in medical

---

[105] RESTATEMENT (SECOND) OF CONFLICT OF LAWS §§ 186–88 (1971).

[106] U.S. CONST. art. IV, § 1; Dammann & Hansmann, *supra* note 104, at 40–41

[107] Gil Siegal, *Enabling Globalization of Health Care in the Information Technology Era: Telemedicine and the Medical World Wide Web*, 17 VA. J.L. & TECH. 1, 20 (2012).

[108] Nathan Cortez, *A Medical Malpractice Model for Developing Countries?*, 4 DREXEL L. REV. 217 (2011); Marc A. Rodwin, *French Medical Malpractice and Policy through American Eyes: What It Reflects about Public and Private Aspects of American Law*, 4 DREXEL L. REV. 109 (2011).

tourism. In the mid-1990s, then president Ernesto Zedillo created a new national arbitration agency within Mexico's Ministry of Health, the "Comisión Nacional de Arbitraje Médico," or "Conamed."[109]

Conamed provides three progressive stages of dispute resolution. The first is an "immediate, somewhat informal intervention" that opens up negotiations between the parties, and sometimes involves a Conamed "specialized consultant."[110] Nathan Cortez reports that between 2001 and 2003, approximately 73 percent of the fifteen thousand cases filed with Conamed were resolved at this juncture, often within two days of the initial submission.[111] The second stage of dispute resolution is called "conciliation."[112] During this process, Conamed distinguishes between medical malpractice claims and other disputes between physicians and patients. According to Cortez, "Conamed will advise the parties on the latter, but will not admit complaints formally unless the dispute involves allegations of malpractice."[113] Once the dispute reaches the second stage, both Conamed's experts and the "treating physician(s)" conduct a medical review of the claim.[114] During conciliation, the parties can agree to a resolution of the claim, opt out of the process and file a traditional lawsuit, or proceed to the final phase, arbitration.[115] Of the 27 percent of cases that proceeded to conciliation between 2001 and 2003, "over half were resolved at this second stage, typically within three to six months."[116] As Cortez describes the third phase of the Conamed process:

> To arbitrate, the parties must sign an agreement that precludes them from taking the case to court. The arbitrators are independent physicians or attorneys trained to handle these cases. Conamed supports the arbitrators by peer-selecting expert consultants based on the medical issues in each case....
>
> If arbitrators conclude that the physician committed malpractice—typically through "negligence or inexperience"—it can award compensation, including damages, medical expenses, or cancelling the patient's debt to the provider. Conamed arbitrators calculate damages based on the same workers' compensation formula used in the Civil Code, though arbitration awards are usually less than those awarded by a court. Conamed may not sanction physicians and cannot award "moral damages" like civil courts can. As a counterbalance, patients avoid the costs of litigation.[117]

---

[109] Cortez, *supra* note 108, at 237 (citations omitted).

[110] *Id.* at 238.

[111] *Id.*

[112] *Id.*

[113] *Id.*

[114] *Id.*

[115] *Id.*

[116] *Id.*

[117] *Id.* at 239.

Between 2001 and 2003, only eighty-one cases (0.05 percent) were resolved at this third phase of the Conamed process. Those cases that made it through the entire Conamed process took an average of fifteen months to resolve. Over 10 percent of all cases filed during that period were not resolved within the three stages. Of those, "Conamed estimates that a third of complainants simply left the process," and "the remaining unresolved cases probably went to court."[118]

To be sure, we should be cautious about treating Conamed as too much of a touchstone. First of all, the providers appear to win about two-thirds of the cases, and even patients who win receive relatively modest compensation—free treatment, costs, and financial compensation that averages only $4841 per patient.[119] Second, it is not clear "whether or to what extent patients and physicians are represented by counsel and if there is any discrepancy between the parties,"[120] which, from a U.S. perspective, may amount to a threat to due process. Finally, one needs to be sensitive to important cultural differences that make a system such as Conamed more likely to thrive than it would in the United States. In Mexico, "there is widespread distrust of courts and an aversion to litigation," most personal injury cases are settled by parties, and "medical providers generally offer to treat whatever harms they might have caused."[121] Similarly, Conamed has built up significant "credibility both with the judicial and medical communities in Mexico—it provides expert opinions for courts and consults with hospitals about medical errors," an element that may be "difficult to replicate for developing countries with weaker pools of medical and legal experts."[122] That said, parties using the Conamed system to resolve disputes report remarkably high levels of satisfaction with the system, with 97 percent of the roughly 5,500 patients and providers surveyed anonymously by Conamed rating it as "good" or "excellent."[123]

In fact, the system developed in India highlights the difficulties of imposing ADR on a system where plaintiffs have difficulty meeting a high burden of proof. India has created a network of Consumer Disputes Redressal Agencies (CDRAs) to provide, as an alternative to the litigation system, "structured as quasi-judicial forums"[124] that offer speedy, but limited relief (compensatory, but not noneconomic damages, and very rarely punitive damages as well). The Indian system is an example of ADR as an alternative where traditional legal relief may be hard to come by, and offers the advantages of a significant reduction in delays and costs—complaints must be resolved within six months. However, these time goals are very rarely met in practice, and plaintiffs in the Indian

---

[118] *Id.*
[119] *Id.* at 240.
[120] *Id.*
[121] *Id.* at 237.
[122] *Id.* at 240.
[123] *Id.*
[124] *Id.* at 231.

system still face significant hurdles to relief because medical experts are frequently unwilling to testify against their colleagues and physicians often refuse to release medical records to malpractice plaintiffs.[125]

There are also domestic med-mal arbitration programs in the United States from which we might pattern a solution. The states of Alabama, Alaska, Illinois, Kansas, Kentucky, North Dakota, Ohio, Utah, Vermont, Virginia, and West Virginia have statutes providing for arbitration of some med-mal cases, with significant variations on things such as which claims will be arbitrated, the size of the arbitral panel, the manner of selection of arbitrators, and the right of revocation.[126] Other states, such as California, facilitate such arbitration through the enforceability of agreements to arbitrate and state and federal laws governing judicial review of that arbitration.[127] A RAND study in California found that these agreements were being used on a routine basis by only 9 percent of hospitals and doctors, which constituted roughly 20 percent of overall hospital admissions. The physicians involved pointed to conformity with the practice group's policies (31 percent) and cost-effectiveness (34 percent) as their reasons for implementing the system, and they reported high rates of satisfaction with these agreements.[128] The United States General Accounting Office also studied the results of arbitrating med-mal claims under a Michigan statute from November 1976 to March 1991, a time period in which 882 claims were made.[129] Of the 882 claims, 222 (25 percent) were withdrawn or administratively closed without a hearing, another 331 (38 percent) settled without a hearing, 272 (31 percent) resulted in panel decisions, and 57 (6 percent) were still open at the time the study concluded.[130] For the 272 claims that led to panel decisions, 72 (26 percent) resulted in payments ranging from $250 to $1,700,000, with it taking an average of twenty-three months to resolve the claim, with a range of 3 to 114 months.[131]

The med-mal ADR systems in the United States are not without their detractors and are often criticized for being too "defendant-friendly."[132] Critics have raised constitutional concerns as to whether arbitration agreements violate the due process rights of

---

[125] *Id.* at 234.

[126] Stanley A. Leasure & Kent P. Ragan, *Arbitration of Medical Malpractice Claims: Patient's Dilemma and Doctor's Delight?*, 28 Miss. C. L. Rev. 51, 56 & n.42 (2008–2009) (citing U.S. Gen. Accounting Office, GAO/HRD-92-28, Medical Malpractice: Alternatives to Litigation (1992); Deville, *supra* note 92).

[127] *Id. See also* 9 U.S.C.A. § 9 *et seq.* (West 2000); Uniform Arbitration Act (2000), 7 U.L.A. 1 (2009); Uniform Arbitration Act (1956), 7 U.L.A. 99 (2009).

[128] Elizabeth Rolph et al., *Arbitration Agreements in Healthcare: Myths and Reality*, 60 Law & Contemp. Probs. 153, 171–74 (1997).

[129] U.S. Gen. Accounting Office, *supra* note 126.

[130] *Id.*

[131] *Id. See* Leasure & Ragan, *supra* note 126, at 64 & n.123.

[132] *See* DeVille, *supra* note 92, at 336.

plaintiffs, although these challenges have thus far not been well-received by the courts.[133] Further, arbitration is often the product of a contractual arrangement before treatment between patient and physician, but such agreements are sometimes challenged as unconscionable or on the ground that the patient was incapable of consent.[134]

Nevertheless, it is possible that a dedicated medical tourism med-mal arbitration process could provide superior relief for plaintiffs, including reduction in delays. Even if the likelihood and amount of recovery is worse for medical tourists as against the baseline of med-mal plaintiffs in their home country, at least for U.S. patients this is clearly the wrong counterfactual comparison. Instead, the question is whether this is a meaningful improvement over the status quo—a de facto waiver of liability because of civil procedural obstacles toward recovery—or against other feasible fixes, such as choice-of-law clauses, consent-to-jurisdiction clauses, requirement that assets be in place in the home country against which judgment can be enforced, etc. Clearly, any relief afforded under med-mal arbitration is significantly better than the de facto waiver of liability under the status quo. Furthermore, the primary criticisms of the med-mal arbitration process in the United States are inapposite in considering a med-mal arbitration process for medical tourism. Voluntary arbitration agreements in the United States are often criticized for being contracts of adhesion, signed in advance of medical treatment without genuine and informed consent, used by defendants to block plaintiffs' access to the legal system. Like most of the policy-based criticisms of med-mal arbitration, this argument primarily focuses on how patients are taken advantage of by physicians seeking to avoid court, whereas in the medical tourism context, plaintiffs are seeking to force defendants *into* their home country legal system. Nor do problems faced in ADR systems internationally counsel against the use of ADR in the medical tourism context. Even if ADR offers lower recovery amounts or takes longer to resolve for medical tourist plaintiffs such as Carl than for run-of-the-mill med-mal plaintiffs, it is still better than the current de facto waiver system they would otherwise face.

This second inquiry, whether ADR is better than other fixes to the litigation system, in turn depends on an assessment of whether through channeling regimes (such as conflict-of-law or consent-to-jurisdiction provisions) home countries can feasibly force medical tourism providers to agree to be channeled into litigation processes, whether they have the political will to do so, and, more generally, one's assessment of the benefits of ADR as opposed to litigation systems for med-mal claims. In part because I generally favor ADR, and in part because I think it is simpler in terms of system design, I tend to

---

[133] *See generally,* Ann H. Nevers, *Medical Malpractice Arbitration in the New Millennium: Much Ado about Nothing?,* 1 PEPP. DISP. RESOL. L.J. 45 (2000); Florence Yee, *Mandatory Mediation: The Extra Dose Needed to Cure the Medical Malpractice Crisis,* 7 CARDOZO J. CONFLICT RESOL. 393 (2006).

[134] *See* Matthew Parrott, *Is Compulsory Court-Annexed Medical Malpractice Arbitration Constituitonal? How the Debate Reflects a Trend towards Compulsion in Alternative Dispute Resolution,* 75 FORDHAM L. REV. 2685 (2007).

think a channeling regime requiring the use of an approved ADR process for med-mal disputes is more plausible and more desirable than the alternatives. For skeptics, another solution would be to require as part of a channeling regime that foreign providers *either* adopt the ADR solution *or* the other fixes, and over time examine how many providers opt for one rather than the other and the effectiveness of these provisions. Because I do not have strong views as to which is *better*, even though I lean toward the ADR approach, and because I am fearful of the Perfect becoming the enemy of the Good, I would be satisfied with any of the three approaches (channeling to require ADR, channeling to require the other fixes, or channeling to require one or the other).

A different but related way forward is to require, via a channeling regime, bundling of something like the AOS med-mal insurance product discussed above with any medical tourism provided to patients in one's home country. Instead of replacing litigation *against the provider* with arbitration *against the provider*, this would now shift recovery as *against the insurer*. As we saw above, AOS already has its own arbitration process in place for patients dissatisfied with how the insurer responds. This approach would once again replace litigation with arbitration, but only if the insurer did not pay out. When patients buy such insurance, as discussed above, it has the potential to provide adequate compensation. However, one potential shortcoming of such a bundling scheme is that when patients buy such insurance, the patient does not capture the potential deterrent value of med-mal liability, as foreign facilities do not internalize the costs of the liability. Any deterrence is indirect, to the extent that the insurers' evaluation of the pricing for the product at various facilities nudges patients toward competitors and/or reveals information about the likelihood of error at a facility (or at least the insurer's estimation thereof). Requiring the foreign facility to bundle that insurance product with its service might have two advantages. First, critics may argue that this solution is no better, as whatever costs the provider incurs will be passed on to patients. However, this regime helps overcome bounded rationality problems that might ordinarily lead patients not to purchase this insurance even if it is in their best interests, and it also helps reduce some of the costs to the home country of follow-up care that patients would otherwise have an incentive to externalize. Second, to the extent that these products appear to be priced according to the insurer's estimation of facility-specific risks for each procedure (or "experience rated," to use the term from insurance), it will make some facilities more expensive than others; patients will be steered toward cheaper facilities, giving facilities an incentive to improve or to reduce their other costs to make up for this element of risk to patients in order to remain competitive. All of these effects would be positive dynamics for patients and would increase provider incentives to reduce the risk of medical error.

Again, in this part that aims for improving the industry, I am trying to be more creative than definitive. It seems to me that this "bundled med-mal insurance" might be added as an *additional* possible way that a foreign facility could qualify for preferential treatment in a channeling regime, in addition to the ADR and other fixes discussed above, and this is an area where experimentation and evaluation is highly desirable.

*F. More Radical (but Less Likely) Interventions: Strict Liability for
Facilitators and Victim's Compensation Funds*

I have championed forms of channeling that I think are both well suited to the magnitude of the problem and within the feasible set of potential interventions. There are,
however, two more radical possible interventions that I want to briefly discuss, even
though I do not think their implementation likely enough to deserve much attention.

First, home countries could create a fund to compensate victims of medical-tourism
med-mal. The model here would be something like the National Vaccine Injury
Compensation Program in the United States (which creates a central fund that pays
for certain vaccine-related injuries in America rather than permitting tort suits), or the
worker's compensation system, or the September 11th Victim Compensation Fund.[135]
A patient such as Carl who is injured as part of medical tourism could apply to the U.S.
Medical Tourism Compensation Fund and be given a set payout based on a schedule of
injuries. This need not be a mandatory system that *replaces* tort law; the system could
permit patients to elect this remedy rather than making it the only remedy available.
Scholars have proposed comparable models for health courts or no-fault compensation systems as a reformation of med-mal litigation against domestic providers.[136] Such
a scheme could be funded by levying a fee on facilities that wished to be part of the
"approved" list in the channeling regime and using that revenue to pay for this system, or by charging facilitators who recruit in the United States. Alternatively, funding could come from charging insurers using medical tourism (the focus of Chapter 4)
a per-patient fee and using that revenue to cross-subsidize the no-fault compensation
system for uninsured patients. This would mirror to some extent the UNITAIDS
scheme: UNITAIDS is an NGO aimed at scaling up access to treatment for HIV/
AIDS, malaria, and tuberculosis, primarily for people in low-income countries. "A large
share of its funding (72%) stems from 29 supporting countries (including France and
Chile) that have voluntarily chosen to impose on airlines departing from their countries
a tax on departing passenger tickets collected by the airlines set by the country—for
example France imposes a 1 and 10 euro tax on domestic economy and business/first
class flights respectively, and a 4 and 40 euro tax on departing international economy
and business/first class respectively."[137]

---

[135] 26 U.S.C. § 9510 (2006); 42 U.S.C. § 300aa-10(a)–(c) (2006); FLA. STAT. § 766.303 (2012); 49 U.S.C.
§ 40101 (2012); *see also* Nadia N. Sawicki, *Patient Protection and Decision-Aid Quality: Regulatory and
Tort Law Approaches*, 54 ARIZ. L. REV. 621, 653 (2012); Gordon Shemin, Comment, *Mercury Rising: The
Omnibus Autism Proceeding and What Families Should Know before Rushing Out of Vaccine Court*, 58 AM.
U. L. REV. 459, 467–78 (2008).

[136] *See, e.g.,* Peters, *supra* note 6, at 230–36; Studdert et al., *supra* note 6, at 10–18.

[137] I. Glenn Cohen, *How to Regulate Medical Tourism (and Why It Matters for Bioethics)*, 12 J. DEV. WORLD
BIOETHICS 9, 13 (2012).

One risk of this approach is that it creates inequity between victims of domestic- and foreign-provider med-mal—only the latter can elect the compensation scheme. One possible rejoinder is that although the medical-tourist patient may "benefit" in this regard, it is only because her chance of succeeding in a regular med-mal civil suit is so greatly diminished as compared to the patient getting care domestically, though this may be an unsatisfying response. A different concern exists with the way in which this decouples the compensatory and deterrent functions of tort law. If foreign hospitals know that medical tourists will be compensated for injuries from a fund they pay into whether or not they cause the injuries, then they have less of an incentive to seek to avoid injuries. If this proved to be a problem, one solution might be to "experience rate" the amount a foreign provider/facility must pay in based on prior claims against it from the compensation fund, a method sometimes used in driver insurance programs.[138] In practice, though, it is not clear how serious a worry the decoupling is. If foreign physicians currently see a mix of local and tourist patients, their standard of liability as to the medical tourists will alter only their incentive to make costly improvements in their technology or skills to avoid liability in proportion to the number of patients they see who are medical tourists. Because, as we saw above, most investments in improving care are lumpy and cannot be segmented as between different patients, the effect of the liability standard for the medical tourists specifically may not be great. Moreover, because of the reasons discussed above, most foreign providers who see medical tourists (either as their entire practice of just a part thereof) currently face very little chance of tort recovery by these patients; it is unclear that a compensation fund would make things much worse from a deterrence perspective than the status quo, although it certainly would improve things from the compensation side.

A second possibility, which Cortez has raised, would be to make facilitators vicariously liable to medical tourism patients for any injury that results from the action of the foreign physician.[139] This would allow the patient to recover against the facilitator, who, for reasons discussed above, is more likely to be amenable to suit in the United States. In the version pressed by Cortez, facilitators would be *strictly liable* for injuries sustained by medical tourists, without the need for the patient to prove that the facilitator or foreign provider was negligent.[140] The advantage to this approach would be to better align the incentives of patients, providers, and facilitators (thus overcoming an agency problem) as it would encourage facilitators to "more carefully[] monitor quality, and perhaps purchase insurance to cover injuries," which is useful because "these companies are also in a better position to regulate, confront, and negotiate with foreign providers."[141] However, as Cortez

---

[138] Nora Freeman Engstrom, *An Alternative Explanation for No-Fault's "Demise,"* 61 DePaul L. Rev. 303, 331 & n.134 (2012).

[139] Cortez, *supra* note 21, at 84.

[140] *Id.*

[141] *Id.*

recognizes, there are also challenges with such an approach: it would require the govern-ment to develop something akin to the no-fault compensation schemes discussed above, and "most governments may be reluctant to devote the time and energy required to do so."[142] Moreover, "such heavy-handed approaches might have the perverse effect of driving medical tourism intermediaries overseas to less regulated jurisdictions."[143]

A different and less drastic variant of this approach that I have discussed elsewhere would retain the possibility of vicarious liability but require a showing of negligence, mak-ing facilitators vicariously liable for the negligent treatment of their providers.[144] There is a parallel debate in domestic U.S. health care law about whether to make insurers vicari-ously liable for the torts of the doctors for whose work they reimburse. At one extreme, scholars such as Bill Sage, Clark Havighurst, Jennifer Arlen, and Bentley Macleod have argued that insurers should be fully liable (and, in Sage's case, exclusively so) for physi-cian negligence; this recommendation is premised on the modern conception of systems as the major source of medical negligence and the assumption that managed-care organi-zations have the power to alter physician behavior.[145] However, these scholars were writ-ing in the domestic insurer context, and it seems facilitators may be less able to influence their foreign providers. The other extreme, represented by Patricia Danzon and Richard Epstein, would wipe out insurer liability entirely; this view is premised on the idea that physicians are already on the line for liability, such that insurer liability merely adds redundant and unnecessary cost.[146] However, this is less true for medical tourism, where, as discussed above, foreign physicians are not likely to be subject to U.S. med-mal liabil-ity. An intermediate view espoused by Gail Agrawal and Mark Hall would support full liability for insurers where doctors are essentially employees of the insurer but not other kinds of insurance designs.[147] This view would suggest *not* expanding vicarious liability to facilitators in the absence of an employment-like level of control of foreign provid-ers or facilities, which seems absent as to most facilitators currently operating in the market. Using the negligence variant of vicarious liability would also introduce a series of complications regarding proving the claim, including (1) whether the U.S. patient would have to prove the negligence of the foreign provider first, and whether he could

---

[142] *Id.* at 85.

[143] *Id.*

[144] *See* Cohen, *supra* note 2, at 1564.

[145] *Id.* (citing Gail B. Agrawal & Mark A. Hall, *What If You Could Sue Your HMO? Managed Care Liability beyond the ERISA Shield*, 47 St. Louis U. L.J. 235, 236 (2003); Jennifer Arlen & W. Bentley MacLeod, *Malpractice Liability for Physicians and Managed Care Organizations*, 78 N.Y.U. L. Rev. 1929, 1987–97 (2003); Clark C. Havighurst, *Vicarious Liability: Relocating Responsibility for the Quality of Medical Care*, 26 Am. J.L. & Med. 7, 9, 16–20 (2000); William M. Sage, *Enterprise Liability and the Emerging Managed Health Care System*, 60 Law & Contemp. Probs. 159, 160–69, 194 (Spring 1997).

[146] *Id.* (citing Agrawal & Hall, *supra* note 145, at 268; Patricia M. Danzon, *Tort Liability: A Minefield for Managed Care?*, 26 J. Legal Stud. 491, 493–94 (1997); Richard A. Epstein, *Vicarious Liability of Health Plans for Medical Injuries*, 34 Val. U. L. Rev. 581, 590–94 (2000)).

[147] *Id. See also* Agrawal & Hall, *supra* note 145, at 269.

do so from a U.S. court given that all the evidence is abroad; (2) whether suit would be adjudged under the U.S. or foreign standard of care; and (3) whether U.S. courts would give preclusive effect to findings of negligence or lack thereof abroad.[148]

My own sense is that the level of control currently exercised by facilitators would make allowing the assertion of vicarious liability against them, through negligence or strict liability, relatively ineffective as a solution to the problems identified. I also think that any talk of expanding liability in this way may prove less politically feasible. For these reasons, I think the softer regulatory interventions are a surer bet, but for those who disagree I have outlined a way forward using compensation funds or expanded vicarious liability as well.

* * *

To sum up this part of the chapter, medical tourism patients (especially those from the United States) such as Carl face dramatic reductions in the likelihood and amount of recovery in medical malpractice for injuries that occur abroad as compared to injuries that occur when treated at home. I have argued that this is *somewhat* problematic, but not nearly as problematic as it first seems, and that this reality of de facto waiver can be distinguished from existing domestic U.S. law whereby ex ante *contractual* waiver of med-mal liability is largely forbidden. When combined with the fear that too much intervention will "protect" patients out of access to nonemergency care at all, I have suggested that a more laissez-faire approach is desirable. We shall see in Chapter 4 that I come to quite different conclusions as to patients engaged in insurer-prompted medical tourism. Still, for those more inclined to paternalistic interventions, there are a series of softer ways of intervening in this market that involve adopting channeling regimes that require foreign facilities to either (1) bundle an approved med-mal insurance product with their services, (2) engage in an agreement to arbitrate with an approved arbitral process, or (3) adopt contractual terms pertaining to consent to jurisdiction, forum selection, and choice of law that are favorable to the patient, as well as putting aside assets against which judgment can be enforced. I also reviewed a few more radical interventions that on balance I do not champion.

II. HOME-COUNTRY PHYSICIAN LIABILITY: REFERRAL LIABILITY, ABANDONMENT LIABILITY, AND LIABILITY FOR FOLLOW-UP CARE

We now have a good idea of the liability of foreign providers and facilitators for injuries acquired that are related to medical tourism. In the second part of this chapter, I want to turn to an examination of the liabilities faced by home-country physicians that arise out of medical tourism.

---

[148] Cohen, *supra* note 2, at 1564.

First, I will discuss liability related to home-country physician activity *before* the medical tourism care takes place, focusing on negligent referral. I will then discuss home-country physician liability for activities *after* the care episode, including liability related to follow-up care for the patient and also for patient abandonment. Finally, I will discuss the practice of foreign providers paying "referral fees" to facilitators to home country providers and whether that practice is or should be illegal.

A. Liability for Actions or Omissions of Home-Country Physicians before the Patient Travels: Referral Liability

A number of authors have raised the possibility that home-country physicians will face liability in advising patients on medical tourism options.[149] In U.S. domestic law, "referral liability" refers to the possibility that one physician will bear some legal liability for injuries to a patient done by a doctor recommended by the first physician. The general background rule is that "a physician who calls in or recommends another physician or surgeon is not liable for the latter's malpractice where there is no agency or concert of action and no negligence in the selection of the other physician or surgeon," that is, "[a] referral of a patient by one physician to another competent physician, absent partnership, employment, or agency, does not impose liability on the referring physician."[150] In most medical tourism contexts, the home-country physician will not be in an employment or agency relationship with the foreign physician, so to avoid liability she must only avoid a negligent referral.

A home-country physician may run into trouble if the physician knew (or if a reasonably prudent physician should have known) that the foreign physician or facility was incompetent; unaccredited; lacking in proper staff, equipment, or facilities; or ineffective.[151] With regard to care in the United States, negligent referral is not a very common cause of action brought against physicians, so the case law is not very developed in this area. Its application to medical tourism is even more nascent, and I am unaware of any case considering such liability of a home-country physician for the actions of a provider or hospital in the destination country. That said, I think it unlikely that this will

---

[149] *See, e.g.*, Brian S Kern, *Medical Tourism Liability May Fall on Domestic Doctors*, MED. ECON., Dec. 4, 2009, at 42; Laura Carabello, *A Medical Tourism Primer for U.S. Physicians*, MED. PRAC. MGMT., March/April 2008, at 291. I discuss a related question, when home-country physicians have an ethical or legal duty to inform patients about the possibility of medical tourism, in Chapter 10, covering a place where the issue is front and center: advising patients on stem cell and other experimental therapies. In this chapter, though, I am interested in the opposite fact pattern: when a physician can be liable for informing (rather than failing to inform) the patient about medical tourism options.

[150] Stovall v. Harms, 522 P.2d 353, 357 (Kan. 1974); Reed v. Bascon, 530 N.E.2d 417, 421 (Ill. 1988); 61 AM. JUR. 2D PHYSICIANS, SURGEONS, ETC. § 272 (2012).

[151] Aaron D. Levine & Leslie E. Wolf, *The Roles and Responsibilities of Physicians in Patients' Decisions about Unproven Stem Cell Therapies*, 40 J.L. MED. & ETHICS 122, 128 (2012).

yield a robust form of liability in the United States in the future for two reasons: first, the "referral" here is much less formal than in the domestic health care system, where health insurers and health systems often use general practitioners as the gatekeeper for access to specialists such that an actual referral is needed to access those services. In the medical tourism context, the home-country physician is more likely merely to provide patients with information on potential foreign providers or possibly a recommendation to use a particular provider. It is unclear to me whether these informal recommendations will be enough to trigger referral liability doctrine to begin with, and in any event I think courts are likely to hold physicians to a lower standard when the "referral" is informal (if not as a doctrinal matter, than at least in practice).

Second, at least in cases where the question is whether the home-country physician "should have known" of the deficiencies of the foreign provider, I suspect courts will expect less of home-country physicians regarding their foreign peers given the well-established opacity of information on foreign hospitals and practices.

It is likely (though we cannot know until tested in litigation) that a home-country physician could point to the fact that a foreign hospital is JCI-accredited, has a certain number of U.S.-trained or -certified specialists, or partners with a leading American health care institution as evidence that he should *not* have known of a potential deficiency abroad. As a result, home-country physicians making recommendations to use foreign facilities will likely be able to avoid referral liability so long as they do not *know* of the deficiency of a foreign provider and limit their referrals to providers who have some of these signals of competence. Of course, as we saw in Chapter 2, it is far from clear that these commonly touted indicia of excellence are actually good reflections of quality, but they are likely to be enough to enable a court to determine that a referral was not negligent.

B. Liability for Follow-Up Care and/or Abandonment

Whether or not medical tourism patients consult them *before* going abroad for treatment, many home-country physicians will face potential liability issues in treating of medical tourism patients on the back end when the patients return and need additional care.

Although hard numbers are sparse, we do have some empirical studies documenting that a substantial number of home-country physicians will treat patients seeking follow-up care.

In a 2011 study, Melendez and Alizadeh emailed a survey to two thousand American Society of Plastic Surgeons (ASPS) members "concerning their experience treating medical tourism patients with complications who returned to the United States for resolution of their issues." They received a total of 368 responses (18.4 percent), and found that the "vast majority of respondents (80.4%; 296) had experience with patients who had traveled abroad for cosmetic procedures; they mostly reported seeing one to three such patients in the past five years." More than half of the respondents suggested they had noticed "an increasing trend in the number of patients presenting with complications from surgical tourism." They also found that "[t]he majority of the patients who were self-referred via the emergency room underwent either breast augmentation or body contouring procedures." In terms of the needs of these tourist patients, more than half of them "required multiple operations, and at least one patient required over a month of hospitalization in a surgical intensive care unit," with complications from infection being the largest reported problem (31 percent) followed by "dehiscence, contour abnormality, and hematoma." A large number of respondents (83.9 percent) also reported treating "patients with complications who had undergone cosmetic procedures by noncore practitioners (ie, non–plastic surgeons)." The study authors also found that the availability of compensation or coverage for follow-up care and corrective surgery varied greatly among patients and that "not all patients/procedures were covered by insurance."[152] An earlier study of British plastic surgeons by Jeremy Birch and coauthors also found that there were significant complications from medical tourism for cosmetic surgery.[153]

In a more general review of the medical, bioethics, and policy literature on medical tourism, Valorie Crooks and her coauthors observed significant concerns among patients and physicians about follow-up care and its availability:

> Patients may not seek advice from their regular doctors, or may go against their doctors' advice, regarding whether or not surgery is needed. Related to this, patients' medical records may become discontinuous, in that there are not presently adequate systems in place for transferring health information between medical tourism hospitals and patients' home doctors This problem may be overcome by patients carrying their records with them overseas and bringing back new files from abroad for inclusion in their permanent records. Some reviewed sources further suggested that there may also be health risks upon return due to a lack of after-care planning or that after-care may be challenging due to informational discontinuity.... [S]ome doctors in home countries may be reluctant to treat medical tourists upon returning home for fear that they will be sued for complications arising from procedures undertaken abroad in countries with limited options for legal redress.[154]

---

[152] Mark M. Melendez & Kaveh Alizadeh, *Complications from International Surgery Tourism*, 31 AESTHETIC SURGERY J. 694, 694–95 (2011).

[153] J. Birch et al., *The Complications of "Cosmetic Tourism": An Avoidable Burden on the NHS*, 60 J. PLASTIC RECONSTRUCTIVE & AESTHETIC SURGERY 1075 (2007).

[154] Valorie Crooks et al., *What Is Known about the Patient's Experience of Medical Tourism, A Scoping Review*, 10 BMC HEALTH SERVS. RES. 1, 7 (2010) (citations omitted).

Given these concerns, there are two related liability questions. First, can home-country physicians be liable for injuries relating to medical tourism if they provide follow-up care? Second, when a patient who has engaged in medical tourism appears for follow-up care, can home-country physicians refuse to provide treatment, or will they face liability if they do so?

As a matter of U.S. medical malpractice doctrine, to prevail on his or her claim, a plaintiff must show (1) the standard of care, (2) breach of the standard of care, (3) proximate causation, and (4) damages.[155] Under this framework, in providing follow-up care to a patient treated abroad as part of medical tourism, the home-country physician had to worry only about his own conduct, in that even if the home-country physician breaches an applicable standard of care, he is the proximate cause *only* of the injury (and thus damages) he produces, and not the proximate cause of whatever damage the prior physician produced.[156]

Although that is the doctrinal rule, in the real world it may provide cold comfort to the home-country physician. An injured patient will often be tempted to sue the home-country physician who treated her, even if that physician was not negligent or his negligence did not cause much (or any) of the injury, because of the difficulties discussed above in suing a destination country provider. Even if, as a doctrinal matter, the plaintiff should lose in a perfect system, she may have a higher probability of victory against the home-country physician than against the foreign one given the difficulties we discussed. Judges or juries may be quite bad at sorting out which physician caused which part of the injury, should the case make it to trial. Moreover, it may be difficult for the home-country physician to achieve access to documentation of the care abroad to defend his claim, and such a physician may not be able to force the destination country provider(s) to appear at trial in the home country. Finally, even if the claim would ultimately fail at trial, the home-country provider and his medical malpractice insurer

---

[155] *E.g.*, Woodard v. Custer, 702 N.W.2d 522, 524–25 (Mich. 2005).

[156] RESTATEMENT (SECOND) OF TORTS § 881 (1979). To be clear, though, under the loss-allocation rule of "joint and several liability" in place in many (but not all) American states, the situation is quite different for the foreign physician who engages in medical malpractice. Although the home-country physician providing follow-up care who behaves negligently, the "subsequent tortfeasor," is liable only for the injury he or she causes and not the injury caused by the foreign physician who initially treated the patient, under joint and several liability, the foreign provider is potentially liable both for the injuries caused by his initial negligence *and* for the injuries caused by the home-country physician who provides follow-up care. *See id.* § 457 ("If the negligent actor is liable for another's bodily injury, he is also subject to liability for any additional bodily harm resulting from normal efforts of third persons in rendering aid which the other's injury reasonably requires, irrespective of whether such acts are done in a proper or a negligent manner."). There is also a separate set of rules for cases where we are uncertain who caused which injury that may also put the home-country physician providing follow-up care at risk. "Where the conduct of two or more actors is tortious, and it is proved that harm has been caused to the plaintiff by *only* one of them, but there is uncertainty as to which one has caused it, the burden is upon each actor to prove that he has not caused the harm." *Id.* § 433B(3) (emphasis added); *see also* BARRY R. FURROW ET AL., HEALTH LAW: CASES, MATERIALS AND PROBLEMS 282 (5th ed. 2001).

may face strong pressure to settle the case to avoid the risk of liability. For all these reasons, even if the law on the books perfectly severed liability based on who caused it, home-country physicians providing follow-up care would nonetheless face significant risk of being sued and having to pay out.

Faced with this reality, the home-country physician has a strong incentive to avoid seeing a patient treated abroad for follow-up care when he or she suspects the patient has undergone medical injury. Does the law permit the home-country physician to do so? In order to answer this question and understand the relevant legal doctrines pertaining to the formation and termination of a treatment relationship and abandonment liability, it is helpful to parse out two separate kinds of cases. In the first, a patient travels abroad for care and seeks treatment from a new home-country physician for follow-up. In the second, a patient travels abroad for care and seeks treatment from a physician who was treating him before he left.

In the first case, the key question is about the *formation* of a new treatment relationship, and whether the home-country physician can refuse to form a treatment relationship with a new patient who underwent medical tourism. The general background legal rule is that outside of an emergency situation, a physician is not obligated to provide care to a particular patient unless the physician has agreed to do so, either by way of an explicit agreement or implicitly agreeing (for example, by examining the patient).[157] This rule generally governs unless there is a basis for wrongful refusal to take on the patient, such as disability or racial discrimination.[158] No such ground appears present in our context, so, as a legal matter, a home-country physician *can* refuse to take on a patient who engaged in medical tourism, for fear of potential liability in providing follow-up care.

More tricky, though, is whether the home-country physician providing follow-up care may, under some circumstances, have unwittingly formed an implicit treatment relationship with the patient. If the home-country physician takes a phone call from a patient who has undergone medical tourism and provides him with medical advice in the course of that phone call, she may be held to have formed a treatment relationship.[159] Similarly, although merely scheduling an appointment with a doctor is not enough to form a treatment relationship, at least one court has held that scheduling an appointment for a particular purpose (in the case in question, the appointment was "for treatment of a vaginal infection") might be sufficient to indicate the formation of a treatment relationship.[160] Further, some courts have held that although informal consultation with a colleague regarding a patient the colleague is seeing will not form a treatment relationship, such a

---

[157] *E.g.*, HALL, *supra* note 86, at 113; Oliver v. Brock, 342 So. 2d 1, 3 (Ala. 1976); FURROW et al., *supra* note 58, at 260–61.

[158] *See* HALL, *supra* note 86, at 132–46.

[159] *See* FURROW, *supra* note 58, at 261 (citing Weave v. Univ. of Mich. Bd. of Regents, 506 N.W.2d 264 (Mich. App. 1993)).

[160] Lyons v. Grether, 239 S.E.2d 103 (Va. 1977).

relationship may be formed if a physician "assumes some responsibility for diagnostic or treatment relationships."[161] Indeed, one treatise suggests that "[c]onducting laboratory tests, reviewing the results of tests performed by others, preparing reports, [or] billing the patient" may be sufficient to create a treatment relationship "even if the physician has never met or examined the patient," and the same is true if the physician merely "evaluates information provided by a nurse and makes a medical decision as to a patient's status."[162]

The upshot of all this is that many home-country physicians treating new medical tourist patients may be held to have formed a treatment relationship with those patients *before* they are even aware that the patient engaged in medical tourism. Thus, it will be quite difficult for a physician seeing a new patient who may be a medical tourist to avoid any potential liability for follow-up care-related complications by not forming the initial treatment relationship. A minority of states try to split the difference; instead of asking whether a full treatment relationship was triggered, they hold physicians to a "duty of care to the extent of his involvement, whatever it is."[163] In these states, physicians have less to fear in treating medical tourism patients.

Let us turn to our second case, where there is a relationship with the patient that is in place before the patient seeks medical tourism, and the patient has now returned to the doctor seeking follow-up care. Even though in common language we might think of this as a continuing treatment relationship, as a legal matter, at least in some cases, courts may treat this as the formation of a *new* treatment relationship with a physician who had seen the patient before, not as another episode in an existing and continuing treatment relationship. One casebook suggests that "once a patient recovers from an illness or stops seeking treatment, a new treatment relationship must be formed in order to invoke a duty of continuing treatment."[164] The actual case law on this subject, though, varies by state, and the decisions seem extremely fact dependent. Because this "continuous treatment" issue arises most often in the context of issues relating to statute of limitations, it is hard to firmly generalize to our context.[165]

Imagine, then, that a new treatment relationship has been inadvertently formed or an existing treatment relationship is held to continue after the patient returns from medical tourism. Can the home-country physician at this stage refuse to continue treating the patient due to fears of liability related to the patient's medical tourism? A physician can face so-called "abandonment liability" for unilaterally terminating a treatment

---

[161] *See* HALL, *supra* note 86, at 155 (collecting cases).

[162] *See* FURROW, *supra* note 58, at 261–62.

[163] HALL, *supra* note 86, at 156 (citing Diggs v. Ariz. Cardiologists, 8 P.3d 286 (Ariz. Ct. App. 2000); Monzingo v. Pitt Cnty. Mem. Hosp., 415 S.E.2d 341 (N.C. 1992)).

[164] HALL, *supra* note 86, at 114.

[165] *See, e.g.,* Castillo v. Emergency Med. Assocs., 372 F.3d 643, 648–49 (4th Cir. 2004).

relationship before meeting the patient's treatment needs for the condition that brought the patient to the physician.[166]

However, physicians are not without recourse. They can terminate the relationship "as long as they give notice to the patient such that the patient has sufficient opportunity to secure care from another physician."[167] For example, in *Payton v. Weaver*, a case involving a personally difficult and allegedly abusive and non-cooperative patient who needed dialysis for chronic end-stage renal disease, the California Court of Appeal held that the treating physician had discharged his duty by warning the patient he would terminate the treatment relationship at a future date and providing her with a list of names and telephone numbers of area dialysis providers.[168] Thus, a home-country physician can avoid both any liability relating to follow-up care *and* abandonment liability by finding another willing provider to take on the patient and providing the patient with his or her contact information. That the doctor is discontinuing the treatment relationship out of self-serving fear of liability seems immaterial as a doctrinal matter; indeed, courts have found unproblematic termination of treatment relationships where patients are unable to pay doctors' bills, perhaps a still more morally questionable motivation.[169]

What if there is no such provider? After all, given the liability risks here, it may be possible that the other doctors will react to the patient like a "hot potato." A leading casebook suggests there is "little guidance" on the issue,[170] but at least some scholars have read the *Payton* case as suggesting that "there might be an obligation on the part of the community as a whole to locate a source of treatment, but not one that binds a particular doctor or institution."[171] Moreover, some states are apt not to find abandonment liability at all where the patient is not in "critical condition," and will excuse the physician from providing adequate notice or finding a substitute physician.[172] Some medical tourists seeking follow-up care will likely fall in this exception.[173]

Thus, home-country physicians face a risk of being sued and held liable for the malpractice of a foreign provider if they treat as part of his follow-up care a patient who engaged in medical tourism. They therefore face a strong incentive to try to avoid providing that care. If they have no continuing treatment relationship with the patient,

---

[166] HALL, *supra* note 86, at 170.

[167] *Id.*

[168] Payton v. Weaver, 182 Cal. Rptr. 225 (Cal. Ct. App. 1982).

[169] Mark A. Hall, *A Theory of Economic Informed Consent*, 31 GA. L. REV. 511, 531 (1997) (collecting cases).

[170] HALL, *supra* note 86, at 170.

[171] Hall, *supra* note 152, at 532 (citing Mathew Gregory, *Hard Choices: Patient Autonomy in an Era of Health Care Cost Containment*, 30 JURIMETRICS J. 483, 499 (1990); Edward B. Hirshfeld, *Should Ethical and Legal Standards for Physicians Be Changed to Accommodate New Models for Rationing Health Care?*, 140 U. PA. L. REV. 1809, 1840 (1992)).

[172] Hall, *supra* note 152.

[173] By contrast, for medical tourists who appear at an emergency room, there may be separate statutory law forcing them to take on the patient, EMTALA, discussed above at note 70.

they can avoid forming one, although, as we have seen, courts are relatively permissive in terms of what they will count as the formation of such a relationship, such that providers will need to be vigilant to avoid this result. If they do have a treatment relationship with the patient, they can discontinue it without incurring abandonment liability by giving the patient sufficient notice and suggesting alternative providers who can help. In the case where no alternative provider is available or willing to take on the patient, the precedents are less clear, but it appears as though (especially for patients not in critical need of care) providing the names and numbers of other physicians will discharge the duty even if those other physicians prove unwilling to help.

The discussion thus far has adopted the perspective of the home-country provider seeking to avoid liability. In the course of attempting to do so, however, many patients may end up without home-country physicians willing to help. Many medical tourism facilities are beginning to pair agreements to provide follow-up care with their initial agreement to provide care, that is, to correct their error. As part of a channeling regime of the kind discussed above, we could also *require* them to do so. However, having recently been injured by the foreign facility, it is easy to see why many patients will be unwilling to return there for more care, and return travel abroad may exacerbate existing injuries. The foreign facility could voluntarily agree to pay for follow-up care, or, by a channeling regime, we could encourage them to do so. Nevertheless, this still assumes a home-country provider willing to see the patient and provide follow-up, which, for the reasons discussed above, may not be the case. Moreover, there may be disputes between the hospital or insurer and the patient as to what constitutes medical error in the initial treatment justifying the follow-up care.

For these reasons, it may be better to consider interventions that improve home-country physicians' willingness to treat medical-tourist patients for follow-up care. Because straightforward immunity for home-country physicians would over-correct matters, it may be that we would be better off altering substantive med-mal in some respects for cases of follow-up care to medical tourists. One possibility would be to introduce a damages cap, although there is little existing evidence suggesting that damages caps significantly affect physician behavior measured in terms of outcome measures such as avoidable hospitalization and inpatient mortality.[174] A more targeted remedy might be to alter the burden of persuasion as to causation for medical tourism cases by requiring the patient to demonstrate that the home-country physician caused his portion of the injury, at a higher standard of proof than in conventional medical malpractice.

Each of these interventions would provide a "carrot" to home-country physicians. The other alternative is the "stick": we could make it unlawful to refuse to enter into a treatment relationship with a patient because he underwent medical tourism and/or increase the duties relating to abandonment liability such that a physician may avoid

---

[174] *See generally* Frakes, *supra* note 8.

liability only if she can actually secure treatment for the patient from another competent home-country physician, rather than merely providing him with some possible names. Whether to favor the carrot or the stick or some combination thereof will depend on orthogonal views on the importance of physician autonomy in selecting patients and the usefulness of medical-malpractice liability to begin with. I tend to favor carrots more than sticks here, in part because I think patients are not helped very much by physicians who are treating them grudgingly under threat of legal sanction, but it is really an empirical question of what would improve the availability of follow-up care at the lowest cost to patients, doctors, and the health care system. Until we begin experimenting with potential policies, we will be unable to make that determination.

C. Referral Fees

Finally, let me consider possible liability for paying referral fees. According to Roy Spece, many medical tourism facilitators are paid thousands of dollars by foreign facilities for the patients they recruit, a fee of which patients are not made aware.[175] As he puts it:

> For example, if a medical tourism company's website lists medical interventions and prices therefor, indicating that the services can be directly contracted for by filling out a form on the website, the consumer might reasonably believe that he is purchasing care from the company, even if the company states that the care will be provided at its "partners" ' facilities. If the medical tourism company clearly advertises that it will put the patient in contact with a foreign medical provider, the company does not advertise a non-profit designation (which might suggest it is funded by donations and, therefore charges no fees to anybody), and there is no fee paid by the consumer to the medical tourism company, the patient might reasonably assume that there is some sort of brokerage payment from the provider to the medical tourism company—which will in turn be reflected in the price of medical services. Logistically, there is no other way the company could survive. However, even if in this particular context the consumer should realize that there is a fee, he or she is unlikely to know the magnitude of the fee.[176]

On the one hand, as economists note, referral fees can play an important positive role in markets such as the medical tourism market where sellers and buyers have incomplete information regarding each other. Facilitators can perform marketing functions for foreign hospitals, realize economies of scope by arranging travel or pre- and post-hospital

---

[175] Roy G. Spece, Jr., *Medical Tourism: Protecting Patients from Conflicts of Interest in Broker's Fees Paid by Foreign Providers*, 6 J. HEALTH & BIOMEDICAL L. 1, 1–2 (2010).

[176] *Id.* at 8.

housing for multiple foreign hospitals, and screen patients for foreign hospitals as to whether they are appropriate for the facilities.[177] It is not feasible to arrange it so that the patients themselves pay for these services because of moral hazard—here, the fear that "medical tourism companies might encourage unqualified applicants to apply and pay fees or might quickly disqualify qualified applicants after receiving fees, thereby avoiding further work."[178]

Thus, referral fees have some benefits. They also have risks in the medical context, of "(1) paying windfalls to referring physicians; (2) encouraging unnecessary care; (3) increasing the cost of care; (4) encouraging referrals to providers who pay the highest referral fees rather than those who can give the best care; (5) encouraging providers who pay referral fees to cut corners in their care to recoup the costs of referral fees; (6) commodifying patients and commercializing and debasing providers; (7) undercutting societal and individual patient trust in providers; and (8) creating poorer patient outcomes because of the attenuation of trust."[179]

For these reasons, U.S. law and ethical codes have taken a strongly negative view toward referral fees. The American Medical Association condemns them as unethical, individual U.S. states often make giving or accepting such fees unprofessional conduct that may merit professional discipline (including the revocation of one's license), some states criminalize the practice, and in a series of laws referred to collectively as "Stark laws," the U.S. government has made it a felony to pay in cash or in kind for the referral of a patient for any service for which payment may be made under Medicare or Medicaid.[180] These Stark laws have engendered a series of creative attempts by lawyers to circumvent them, along with further legislative modifications and complex interpretative questions as to what they cover—details I will put to one side for present purposes. The existing Stark laws apply only to Medicare and Medicaid, and thus do not apply to patients using medical tourism paying out-of-pocket or via private insurers (discussed in Chapter 4), but they would theoretically apply to patients in government-prompted

---

[177] *Id.* at 10.

[178] *Id.* at 13. As Spece notes, in other markets "professionals—notably personal injury lawyers, medical specialists, and private investigators—frequently arrange their business in such a way that initial consultations are free. At the initial consultation, a determination is made as to whether it makes sense to proceed with the services. The professional thus absorbs the cost of the initial consultation—that is to say; in the long run it is folded into the payment for subsequent provision of services. Thus, those customers who pass the initial screening end up bearing the [*sic*] all the screening costs, including costs from those who were rejected in the screening." *Id.*

[179] *Id.* at 14.

[180] *Id.* at 19 (citing American Medical Association, Code of Medical Ethics: Current Opinions with Annotations 6.01–03; CLARK C. HAVIGHURST ET AL., HEALTH CARE LAW AND POLICY 446–50 (2d ed. 1998); N.Y. PUB. HEALTH LAW § 4500–03 (McKinney 2009); CAL. HEALTH & SAFETY CODE § 445 (West 2009); Mark A. Hall, *Institutional Control of Physician Behavior: Legal Barriers to Health Care Cost Containment*, 137 U. PA. L. REV. 431, 488 (1988); 42 U.S.C. § 1320a–7b(b) (2006); 42 U.S.C. §§ 1395–1395hhh (2008)).

medical tourism in the United States if such programs ever took hold (as discussed in Chapter 5). By contrast, some of the state laws, such as California's,[181] appear to apply more broadly and may currently cover medical tourism facilitators doing business in that state and receiving referral fees (sometimes also called "kickbacks") for sending patients to foreign hospitals.

Would it be desirable to expand the reach of these referral fee statutes such that they cover medical tourism, or, by contrast, should we exempt referrals in that situation? Spece has offered an in-depth analysis of this question in his own work, and I will merely review some of the reasons that aspects of the medical tourism market may make referral fees, on balance, something we should permit as compared to the situation in the domestic health care market. While referral fees in the domestic context reward physicians for doing what they are supposed to do—referring to another physician when that physician has needed expertise—such that it may seem like an unfair windfall to the referring physician, home-country doctors are unlikely to make such a "a referral to a foreign provider because they are not knowledgeable about those providers, they have a fear of liability for making a referral to a provider of unproven quality, or are opposed to the prospect of widening the sphere of competition among medical providers to the entire globe."[182] Thus, referral fees may be needed to enable patients to connect with foreign providers in ways that improve the welfare of those patients as against their available domestic supply for health care.

But even if the referral fees are necessary to some extent to compensate for the marketing and matching functions, might they not be disproportionately large relative to the value they create? It is possible, indeed even likely, that this is the case, but as Spece has argued, the best solution is not to ban those fees but to require disclosure of the fee to patients. Such disclosure will foster competition between facilitators—who can now monitor each other's fees—and competition through patients' choices, helping to bring down prices. The model Spece has in mind is something like the way

---

[181] CAL. HEALTH & SAFETY CODE § 445 (West 2009) ("No person, firm, partnership, association or corporation, or agent or employee thereof, shall for profit refer or recommend a person to a physician, hospital, health-related facility, or dispensary for any form of medical care or treatment of any ailment or physical condition. The imposition of a fee or charge for any such referral or recommendation creates a presumption that the referral or recommendation is for profit.... [V]iolation of the provisions of this section shall constitute a misdemeanor and upon conviction thereof may be punished by imprisonment in the county jail for not longer than one year, or a fine of not more than five thousand dollars ($5,000), or by both such fine and imprisonment."). The statute explicitly applies to events outside California, at least within the United States, specifying that "[a] physician, hospital, health-related facility or dispensary shall not enter into a contract or other form of agreement to accept for medical care or treatment any person referred or recommended for such care or treatment by a medical referral service business located in or doing business in another state if the medical referral service business would be prohibited under this part if the business were located in or doing business in this state." Id. Whether "another state" encompasses foreign countries would be a matter of statutory interpretation.

[182] Spece, supra note 175, at 24.

airplane travel sites such as Kayak.com enable individuals to shop between possible carriers and routes, but some individuals continue to use travel agents (who charge referral fees) "to reduce uncertainty and risks, save time, and reduce transaction costs in general."[183]

Moreover, referral fees are less likely to lead to overutilization and the purchase of unnecessary care the way they are in the domestic context. Although the evidence is somewhat murky, in the domestic context physicians sometimes make unnecessary referrals either as a form of "defensive medicine" to avoid liability or (more likely) because they want to satisfy the desires of their patients who "have an attitude in favor of purchasing care that has any possible benefit, even if its costs exceed its marginal benefits, because most care is paid for by public or private insurance."[184] Thus, many managed care organizations and health reform advocates have pressed for what are essentially "anti-referral fees" that reward physicians for being frugal in their tendency to make referrals.[185] By contrast, in the medical tourism context, the patient such as Carl who is using medical tourism to improve his access to care seeks the facilitator or foreign provider typically after a diagnosis but when priced out of the U.S. market, so there is less of a concern about physician-induced demand.[186] There are parts of the trade, including experimental therapies such as stem cell, whose tourism I discuss in Chapter 10, where this concern is more apt, and where I would be inclined—if possible to segregate the market as a regulatory matter—to institute stricter referral fee rules there. But for medical tourism legal in both the home and destination countries, it seems to me that there may be too little (not too much) incentive to refer.

Do referral fees drive up the cost of care? Certainly. But the key question is whether they increase unnecessary care, which for the reasons stated seems unlikely. Moreover, the advent of robust medical tourism opportunities may increase competition with domestic providers, which in some ways produces a ceiling on how much referral fees can be charged—a ceiling that will lower as the two markets come increasingly into competition.[187] Once again, disclosure seems to be the better solution, in that it enables patients to get a sense of how much they are paying for the facilitator's work, and also enables more robust competition between facilitators on the price margin.

If disclosure is desirable for referral fees, one might ask why facilitators or foreign providers do not already disclose those fees. The answer is related to the so-called "market for lemons" problem in health care pricing: "whenever product information is difficult to verify independently...competitive markets tend to suppress rather than generate...information...because it is difficult for producers to convince consumers that

---

[183] *Id.* at 25.
[184] *Id.* at 26.
[185] *Id.*
[186] *Id.*
[187] *See id.* at 29–30.

they provide better value at a higher price."[188] That is, providers who pay referrals may provide better services, which also "require[s] them to charge higher prices, but those prices are presumably justified because of their entire package of services. However, it is hard to verify what others are doing, explain this to consumers, and convince the consumers that their better practices justify different prices."[189] In a similar vein, although medical tourism facilitators who have higher referral fees may in fact provide superior service, it is "difficult to determine what other tourism companies are doing or to convince consumers that the differences in broker's fees and practices, including the disclosure, signal any difference in the quality of services provided."[190] For this reason, without governmental intervention, most facilitators will not be willing to disclose their referral fees even if they would come out ahead if *every* facilitator disclosed its referral fees, a classic collective-action problem.

A home-country government could directly impose a requirement of referral-fee disclosure on U.S.-based facilitators or, potentially, facilitators who have assets in the United States or whose recruitment practices constitute sufficient contact with the United States in the ways discussed above.[191] To further extend the reach of this disclosure requirement, we could require through our channeling regime that all foreign providers that accept patients via facilitators disclose (or require their facilitators to disclose) any referral fees as a condition of "approval." We could also induce JCI or other accreditors to build requirements of disclosure into their accreditation requirements.

How much of a difference would this make in terms of actual patient choice, to have available the referral fees paid by the provider to the facilitator? The answer is not clear. Mark Hall engaged in an experiment in the domestic health care market to assess the impact of such disclosures, followed by a phone call from his team in which "the statement was read aloud and repeated if subjects failed to correctly answer simple comprehension questions immediately after the first reading."[192] Although his team found a "a fifty percent increase in knowledge of incentives," they also found that "one month following the disclosure, the majority of subjects were not able to correctly recall the answers to more than half the comprehension questions, and fourteen percent had no correct responses."[193]

The more promising economic effect of such disclosures, I think, is between competitors, who may start to compete on this dimension. The effect of these disclosures on medical-tourism patient confidence is less clear. On the one hand, patients may feel

---

[188] Mark A. Hall, *The Theory and Practice of Disclosing HMO Physician Incentives*, 65 LAW & CONTEMP. PROBS. 207, 211–12 (2002); *see also* Winand Emons & George Sheldon, *The Market for Used Cars: New Evidence of the Lemons Phenomenon*, 41 APPLIED ECON. 2867 (2009).

[189] Spece, *supra* note 175, at 32.

[190] *Id.* at 32–33.

[191] *See id.* at 36.

[192] Hall, *supra* note 188, at 209–10.

[193] *Id.*

more confidence at being given the "whole story," but on the other hand, some subset of patients may have been unaware of this aspect of the industry and may be turned off by it. If it was actually a practice likely to be against the patient's interest, that latter effect might be all for the better, but given what we said above, there are many ways in which these referral fees are beneficial even if patients have negative reactions to them. How forcefully to push for referral-fee disclosure, then, will be in part a function of how much one values patient autonomy and information even when it will lead to suboptimal choices. In a strange way, the findings that these disclosures have minimal effects on patient behavior in the domestic context, if carried over to the international one, might be comforting in that patients are less likely to react in a negative way to these disclosures, which would lead to suboptimal decisions.

III. CONCLUSION

When I talk to American medical tourism facilitators and foreign providers seeking to tap into the U.S. market for patients, the number one concern they list to me is liability. In this chapter, I have examined what the liability lay of the land looks like and concluded the following: Americans (and to a lesser extent medical tourists from other major Western countries) will have great difficulty recovering damages from medical errors caused by treatments abroad, and, given the economics of litigation, they will have de facto waived their ability to recover in med-mal. For patients paying out-of-pocket without access to comparable care in the home country, it is very hard to argue that this deficient med-mal recovery should motivate restrictive regulation of the medical tourism sector, even if it were feasibly to implement it. Instead, I have suggested that the circumstances justify informational interventions aimed at assuring patients that they are aware of their likely deficient med-mal recovery, as well as channeling regimes that attempt to incentivize more foreign facilities and providers to make themselves subject to litigation or arbitration, or provide bundled patient med-mal insurance products.

Turning to home-country physicians, I have argued that they face little risk of "referral liability" for informing patients about medical tourism options for care. Home-country physicians face a risk of being sued and held liable for the malpractice of a foreign provider if they treat a patient who engaged in medical tourism as part of his follow-up care. They may be able to avoid this liability risk by being careful about the formation of new treatment relationships with patients who engaged in medical tourism or by being careful in the way in which they terminate existing relationships so as to avoid abandonment liability. That home-country physicians may use these doctrines to avoid treating medical tourism patients, however, creates the potential for a substantial public policy problem in that medical tourists may have difficulty securing care in the home country. We have no good empirical data on how big a problem this is, but should it prove concerning,

I have made several recommendations about how regulation and liability rules could be adjusted to try to reduce the problem.

Finally, there is the matter of referral fees. Although the United States has heavily regulated and, in many instances, criminalized the payment of referral fees to physicians domestically, most of the existing regulation of these practices does not reach foreign providers. I have argued that this is for the better, and that we do not need to extend the referral fee prohibition to the medical tourism industry—which frankly would dramatically reduce patient flow. Instead what we need to do is, by regulation, require disclosure of all referral fees to patients, so they can make informed decisions and so as to increase health competition in the market for services provided abroad.

4

Medical Tourism through Private Health Insurance

⌒―――

THE LAST TWO chapters have focused on medical tourists who purchase services out-of-pocket. This chapter and the next one focus on those who engage in medical tourism through insurance programs: private health insurance in this chapter, and public health insurance in the next chapter. Because private health insurance is the dominant form of health insurance in the United States, I focus this chapter on medical tourists whose home country is the United States, with a focus on EU patients in the next chapter.

Consider the following case study:

In an attempt to reduce healthcare costs, White Hill Paper Products, Inc., a self-insuring American company based in Canton, North Carolina, offers its employees a $10,000 bonus, extra sick-leave time, and the cost of airfare, if its employees agree to have nonemergency surgeries done in the New Delhi, India, hospital approved by the company's preferred provider organization (PPO). Should the company be permitted to adopt this policy? If, impressed by the cost savings, the company considers changing the policy for the following year from incentive payments to travel abroad for surgery to penalties for failing to do so (in the form of copays attaching only to surgeries provided domestically), can it do so under existing law? Should it be able to? What steps could regulators take to prevent this practice? What if the company instead decides not to cover nonemergency surgeries altogether unless they are done in India? If Bob, one of White Hill's employees, takes the company up on its offer, gets a hip replacement in Delhi, and is the victim of medical error causing significant complications, should he be able to sue the company? Would any of this change if it was not a self-insured firm taking these steps, but an insurance company that provides plans that an employer offers to its employees?

This hypothetical case study is adapted from a plan Blue Ridge Paper actually attempted to put into place, although its implementation was ultimately blocked by the company's union in 2006.[1] Since that time, however, many more U.S. companies have begun experimenting with medical tourism plans. In the Preface to this book we met two patients who had used this option in 2013, Joy Guion and Gary Harwell, who traveled from North Carolina to Costa Rica for gastric sleeve surgery and a knee replacement respectively. Their company induced them to travel by waiving their copay and deductible and providing them a "bonus check." As Nathan Cortez reports, the four largest commercial insurers in the United States (UnitedHealth, WellPoint, Aetna, and Humana) have either introduced medical tourism pilot programs or are considering it; BlueCross BlueShield of South Carolina contracted with a hospital in Bangkok, Thailand, to perform certain surgeries; two hundred U.S. employers offer a network of foreign providers through BasicPlus Health Insurance, which sells group plans and contracts with medical tourism facilitator Companion Global Healthcare; and United Group Programs, a third-party insurance administrator, had contracted to outsource surgeries for at least forty U.S. companies.[2]

As Cortez and I have argued elsewhere, there is every reason to believe that demand for private insurance plans that cover medical tourism are likely to *increase* in the wake of the U.S. recent health care reform (the Patient Protection and Affordable Care Act sometimes colloquially referred to as "ObamaCare").[3] In nontechnical terms, among many other provisions, that Act introduces the so-called "individual mandate" that will require non-exempt U.S. citizens to purchase health insurance meeting certain regulatory prerequisites of "minimum essential" coverage.[4] This mandate is likely to stimulate the demand for low-cost

---

[1] Arnold Milstein & Mark Smith, *America's New Refugees—Seeking Affordable Surgery Offshore*, 355 NEW ENG. J. MED. 1637, 1638–39 (2006); Jonathan G. Bethely, *Exporting Patients: Money versus Possible Safety Issues*, AM. MED. NEWS, Sept. 18, 2006, *available at* http://www.ama-assn.org/amednews/2006/09/18/bisa0918.htm; Saritha Rai, *Union Disrupts Plan to Send Ailing Workers to India for Cheaper Medical Care*, N.Y. TIMES, Oct. 11, 2006, at C6, *available at* http://www.nytimes.com/2006/10/11/business/worldbusiness/11health.html.

[2] Nathan Cortez, *Embracing the New Geography of Health Care: A Novel Way to Cover Those Left Out of Health Reform*, 84 S. CAL. L. REV. 859, 882–83 (2011).

[3] Patient Protection and Affordable Care Act, Pub. L. No. 111-148 (2010).

[4] For details, *see* 26 U.S.C. § 5000A; Nat'l Fed'n of Indep. Bus. v. Sebelius (NFIB), 132 S. Ct. 2566, 2580 (2012). The penalty is set at $95 dollars for 2014, $350 for 2015, $695 for 2016, (or no more than 1 percent, 2 percent, 2.5 percent of taxable income in each year, respectively) and cost of living adjusted from that point forward. 26 U.S.C. § 5000A(c) (2006). The Act exempts, among others, incarcerated individuals, aliens unlawfully present, and those with income below a set threshold, from complying with the mandate. *Id.* § 5000A(e). It also provides subsidies for others to assist in the purchasing of health insurance, *id.* § 36B, but I do not discuss the very complex details here.

insurance products among those who had previously preferred to remain uninsured but now are pushed toward health insurance because of the penalty associated with the individual mandate.[5] The "large employer mandate," which penalizes companies (with fifty or more employees) that do not provide health insurance, may also stimulate demand for low-cost plans, though its implementation is at the current moment looking less certain.[6] As I will describe in more depth below, insurance plans incorporating medical tourism of some form are an attractive way for individuals and employers to find low-cost plans that satisfy these mandates. The Affordable Care Act devolves significant regulatory authority to the Secretary of the Department of Health and Human Services (and through control of that official the president) to define exactly what kinds of plans satisfy these mandates,[7] but as of this writing the Secretary has not wielded that authority in a way that would rule out insurance plans with some component of medical tourism. I discuss the effects of the Affordable Care Act on the regulation of private insurers using medical tourism in more depth below.

Given this forecasted increase in private insurance plans that incorporate medical tourism, this is the perfect time to seriously examine the legal and ethical issues raised by medical tourism involving private health insurance, the goal of this chapter. I begin this chapter by briefly describing the growing private insurance medical tourism industry and the possible forms various insurance plans that incorporate medical tourism might take. I then revisit the issues related to quality and liability discussed in the last two chapters and how the issues and their regulation are inflected in the private insurance medical tourism context. Finally, I examine questions relating to the ethics and regulation of private insurance plan design.

I. THE PRIVATE HEALTH INSURANCE MEDICAL TOURISM INDUSTRY: WHERE IT IS AND WHERE IT IS GOING

As I mentioned above, major players in the U.S. insurance industry are beginning to experiment with private health insurance plans incorporating some form of medical tourism. The motivation has largely been cost. Just as individuals paying out-of-pocket can save significant costs by using medical tourism as opposed to purchasing health care in the United States, insurers can also reduce their costs by inducing their covered

---

[5] I. Glenn Cohen, *Protecting Patients with Passports: Medical Tourism and the Patient-Protective Argument*, 95 Iowa L. Rev. 1467, 1541–42 (2010); Cortez, *supra* note 2, at 879–80, 889.

[6] *NFIB*, 132 S. Ct. at 2670 ("Employers with at least 50 employees must either provide employees with adequate health benefits or pay a financial exaction if an employee who qualifies for federal subsidies purchases insurance through an exchange.") (citing 26 U.S.C. § 4980H). For a discussion of the way this will stimulate demand for medical tourism, see Cohen, *supra* note 5, at 1541–42.

[7] *E.g.,* 26 U.S.C. § 5000A (2012) (empowering the Secretary of Health and Human Services through notice and comment rulemaking to partially define what constitutes an "essential health benefits package" that satisfies the individual mandate).

populations to do the same. The relative size of the savings for the two groups is hard to estimate. On the one hand, U.S. insurers pay significantly less for procedures *in* the *United States* then do patients paying out-of-pocket, because of their market power with insurers given their patient volume. To illustrate, let us return to the chart we discussed in Table 4.1-A of Chapter 1 based on one set of estimates from the National Center for Policy Analysis in 2007:[8]

Procedure	U.S. Retail Price	U.S Insurers' Cost	India	Thailand	Singapore
Angioplasty	$98,618	$44,268	$11,000	$13,000	$13,000
Heart bypass	$210,842	$94,277	$10,000	$12,000	$20,000
Heart-valve replacement (single)	$274,395	$122,969	$9,500	$10,500	$13,000
Hip replacement	$75,399	$31,485	$9,000	$12,000	$12,000
Knee replacement	$69,991	$30,358	$8,500	$10,000	$13,000
Gastric bypass	$82,646	$47,735	$11,000	$15,000	$15,000
Spinal fusion	$108,127	$43,576	$5,500	$7,000	$9,000
Mastectomy	$40,832	$16,833	$7,500	$9,000	$12,400

For a bypass, for example, the typical U.S. insurer is already paying less than half of what a patient paying out-of-pocket must pay. Having the procedure performed in Thailand, by these estimates, will reduce the cost for the out-of-pocket payer by seventeen times, while it will reduce the cost for the insurer only about eight times. For other surgeries things may be different. For hip replacement, for example, the U.S. insurer still pays less than 50 percent of the price paid by U.S. patients paying out-of-pocket in the United States for the surgery, but the out-of-pocket patient saves only about six times the cost by going to Thailand, and the insurer pays only two-and-a-half times less. On the other hand, for insurers with large numbers of covered patients, the aggregation of even these smaller savings across a large number of patients will result in a dramatic cost savings. Moreover, the prices listed above reflect the cost in destination countries for patients

---

[8] Devon M. Herrick, Nat'l Ctr. for Policy Analysis, *Medical Tourism: Global Competition in Health Care* 11 tbl.1 (2007), *available at* http://www.ncpa.org/pdfs/st304.pdf (relying on data from Unmesh Kher, *Outsourcing Your Heart*, TIME.COM, May 21, 2006, at 44, *available at* http://www.time.com/time/magazine/article/0,9171,1196429,00.html). As I have cautioned elsewhere, one should not treat any particular estimate as apodictic, and indeed others have come to different numbers. *See* Cohen, *supra* note 5, at 1472. Still this chart gives reasonable estimates of the relative costs, such that I find the numbers useful to understand magnitudes if not to pinpoint specific prices.

paying out-of-pocket. Insurers that send a high enough volume of patients abroad can bargain for better prices, much as they do in the United States, and even play destination country hospitals against each other in order to drive prices down. Thus, even though the cost savings are less for insurers on a per-patient basis than for those paying out-of-pocket, medical tourism represents an extremely desirable way of cutting costs, and especially in the post– Affordable Care Act era, an excellent way to get into the market for lower-cost insurance plans.

A. A Taxonomy of Potential Plan Types

If private insurers faced no constraints on the design of plans incorporating medical tourism, what might plans look like in the future?

Bob, our hypothetical patient from the vignette that began this chapter, might face a series of possible options. To give very skeletal and stylized examples he might be offered one of five plans:

First, he might be offered the kind of plan currently available in the United States before the advent of medical tourism, which we can call Plan SQ for "Status Quo." It costs $7000 per year and fully covers a set of procedures in the United States.

Second, he might be offered what I will call Plan TI ("Tourism Incentivized"): It costs $6800 per year and covers all U.S.-based treatment for all medical procedures the same way as Plan SQ, except nonemergency cardiac care, for which the insurance company allows treatment in Apollo Hospital in India and covers all costs including travel and post-procedure lodging. If a patient opts to have the service performed at Apollo, he receives a $1500 rebate of his premium at the end of the year. To the extent we have seen experimentation with medical tourism built into private health insurance plans, this has been the modal form in the United States (indeed perhaps the only one). This was, indeed, the type of plan that the Hannaford Supermarkets in the American Northeast proposed introducing for their employees in 2008,[9] and the kind of plan that was offered to Joy and Gary as discussed in the Preface.[10]

Third, he might be offered what I will call Plan DE (for "Domestic Extra"), which costs $4000 per year and covers U.S.-based treatment for all medical procedures

---

[9] Bruce Einhorn, *Hannaford's Medical-Tourism Experiment*, Bus. Wk., Nov. 9, 2008, http://www.businessweek.com/globalbiz/content/nov2008/gb2008119_505319.htm. As of November 2008, apparently no employee had used the service, likely in part because *The Wall Street Journal* reporting on Hannaford's program prompted a U.S. insurer to offer Hannaford coverage "for comparably priced operations in the U.S.," thus enabling employees to travel to "other parts of the U.S." rather than Singapore, while the company realized the same cost savings. *Id.*

[10] Byron Pitts & Nikki Battiste, *As More Americans Have Surgeries Overseas, US Companies Consider "Medical Tourism" a Health Care Option*, ABC News/Nightline (Sept. 30, 2013), http://abcnews.go.com/Health/americans-surgeries-overseas-us-companies-medical-tourism-health/story?id=20423011.

the same way as Plan SQ, except nonemergency surgical cardiac care, for which the insurance company conditions full coverage on receiving treatment in Apollo Hospital in India and covers all costs including travel and post-procedure lodging. If a patient covered by Plan DE instead elects to have the procedure performed by a U.S. doctor, the patient must pay a $7000 copay.

Fourth, he might be offered Plan TM (for "Tourism Mandatory"), which costs $1500, is similar to Plan DE, but unlike Plan DE the plan requires all nonemergency surgical cardiac care to be performed at Apollo Hospital to be eligible for coverage, and this plan will not cover the procedures *at all* if they are performed domestically. The patient may still elect to seek the procedure domestically rather than at Apollo, but must pay the full costs out-of-pocket.

Finally, he might be offered Plan TC ("Tourism Covered"). This plan costs $7000 per year and covers all U.S.-based treatment for all medical procedures the same way as plan SQ, but also covers nonemergency cardiac care provided at select facilities abroad, yet does nothing to incentivize its use. The primary incentive to use medical tourism in a TC-type plan occurs when a patient believes that the foreign provider is more adept than the one available at home or the service is not available domestically.[11]

DE, TI, TM, and TC are just a few highly stylized possible plans, and it bears emphasizing (as discussions with several people in the industry confirmed) that no company has put a TM-type plan on the U.S. market (and many industry insiders were skeptical that they would). To the extent medical tourism plans are currently being offered, they are primarily of the TI variety. Still, I think understanding the range of possibilities is useful, even if some are less likely to be realized.

Once we depart from SQ, there is in fact an extremely large number of possible plans that will differ (for starters) on four dimensions: (1) Does the insurer use positive incentives (e.g., premium rebates for selecting foreign care or waivers of deductibles) or negative incentives (e.g., higher copays for domestic care) to induce medical tourism or simply refuse to cover treatment domestically, and what are the sizes of the incentives if used? (2) For what services? (3) At which foreign hospitals? (4) If a procedure is covered in more than one foreign hospital, is the patient given a choice among them? Plans can get much more complicated: refusing to cover domestic care at all for some services while requiring a copay for others, setting differential pricing of the copays as between different foreign hospitals from which the patient can choose, etc. Thus, if the market for health insurance products involving medical tourism were truly unregulated, our hypothetical patient Bob might face a quite bewildering array of possible plans.

---

[11] In some jurisdictions with universal health care coverage, such plans may also be desirable to patients *on top of* the publicly funded health care system as a way of avoiding queuing time. In the next chapter, Chapter 5, we will see that because of the regulation of cross-border health care reimbursement, many patients are seeking to turn their domestic public health insurance coverage into a TC-like coverage.

B. Existing Insurance Regulation Governing Medical Tourism

Given the significant potential savings to U.S. private health care insurers from medical tourism, why are more insurers *not* already in the medical tourism game? There are many possible answers to this question, but one important one comes from law: existing U.S. insurance regulations passed during the rise of managed care were not designed with medical tourism in mind. These regulations make it difficult for insurers other than self-insured employers to employ medical tourism.

To understand why this is the case, let me give a brief primer on the regulation of insurance in the United States:

> In the United States, the regulation of health insurance has been historically left to a large extent to the individual U.S. states.[12] Among the ways in which the states have regulated the market is to pass "mandates." In 1999, there were 1260 such mandates imposed by U.S. states, including mandates requiring that insurers cover particular benefits such as in-vitro fertilization (mandated benefit laws), mandates requiring that insurers guarantee renewal of polices or limit preexisting-condition exclusions (mandated-coverage laws), and mandates requiring that insurers reimburse for specified services performed by nonmedical providers such as chiropractors (mandated provider laws).[13]

A different aspect of state insurance regulation relevant for our purposes relates to the design of insurance plans, which has focused on two particular plan configurations: health maintenance organizations (HMOs) and preferred provider organizations (PPOs, also known as preferred provider arrangements, or PPAs).

HMOs come in many flavors, but the "traditional" HMO model limits subscribers to reimbursement only for providers with whom the plan contracts; PPOs by contrast maintain a provider network and apply deductibles and copayments for patients who go out of network.[14] Thus, conceptually, one can think of the TM-type plan as resembling an HMO that contracts only with foreign providers, and the TI and DE plans as a PPO that imposes differential copays or premiums based on whether care is provided domestically or abroad. Existing laws heavily regulate both analogs in ways that are dense and complex, but let me highlight a few aspects that are particularly important for working through the analogy.

HMOs are regulated by both federal and state law. Federal law requires inter alia that a federally qualified HMO "shall within the area served by the health maintenance

---

[12] *E.g.*, BARRY R. FURROW ET AL., HEALTH LAW 467, 479 (2d ed. 2000).

[13] *Id.* at 479–81. States vary tremendously as to how many mandates they have, with some having as few as six and others as many as thirty-three. *Id.*

[14] FURROW ET AL., *supra* note 12, at 501–03.

organization be available and accessible to each of its members … and in a manner which assures continuity"; that it shall provide "[b]asic health services … with reasonable promptness"; that it shall ensure that "medically necessary [services] be available and accessible twenty-four hours a day and seven days a week"; that an HMO subscriber "shall be reimbursed by the [HMO] for his expenses in securing basic and supplemental health services other than through the organization if the services were medically necessary and immediately required because of an unforeseen illness, injury, or condition," and that the HMO shall have a "quality assurance program for its health services which program (A) stresses health outcomes, and (B) provides review by physicians and other health professionals of the process followed in the provision of health services."[15]

The extent of state regulation of HMOs varies a good deal state by state, so I will not be able to review the details for each state, but one good guide is the National Association of Insurance Commissioners (NAIC) Model Act, on which most state legislation is modeled, which requires the HMO to establish ongoing internal quality-assurance programs that include procedures for problem identification, corrective action, and interpretation and analysis of patterns of care rendered to patients by particular physicians.[16]

State PPO authorization statutes generally require the organization to make medical services reasonably accessible to their members (with some definition of the distances that must be traveled to get to a preferred provider in miles or travel times).[17] Some of these statutes require PPOs to admit any willing provider who will accept the terms offered by the plan, but the most common form is to permit PPOs to choose among providers only if the choice is based on reasonable criteria such as cost, quality, and accessibility.[18] Eighteen states have laws requiring the PPOs to credential providers to assure their competence (with great variation as to the depth of the credentialing), and twenty-three states require quality management programs, sometimes requiring that a physician lead them.[19] These statutes also limit the financial incentives and disincentives that may be imposed by the plan for a subscriber using someone other than a preferred provider, by limiting the deductible or copayment amounts imposed for using a non-preferred provider, or by limiting them to a certain percentage of the difference between preferred and non-preferred providers, commonly to 20 or 25 percent.[20]

Some of these HMO and PPO requirements are compatible with some forms of potential private insurance plans involving medical tourism. For example, a plan could

[15] 42 U.S.C. §§ 300e(b)(4), (c)(6) (2006).

[16] FURROW ET AL., *supra* note 12, at 502 (citing Model Health Maintenance Organization Act § 3.A (Nat'l Ass'n Ins. Comm'rs 1990)).

[17] *Id.* at 506.

[18] *Id.* (citing MASS. GEN. LAWS ANN. ch. 176I, § 4).

[19] *Id.* at 507.

[20] *Id.* at 506; Elizabeth Rolph et al., *The Regulation of Preferred Provider Arrangements*, HEALTH AFF. 32, 40 (Fall 1987).

meet the federal HMO statute requirement pertaining to accessibility of services that are "medically necessary and immediately required because of an unforeseen illness, injury, or condition" by either ensuring that services of this type (such as an ER admission) are covered locally as part of the plan or that patients be reimbursed when they cannot access a service from a preferred provider.[21] The requirement of some PPO statutes that the choice of which providers to include must be based on cost and quality could be implemented for medical tourism plans as well. Likewise, the HMO and PPO statute requirements of quality-assurance programs based on health outcomes could be put in place for medical tourism plans, as could the further PPO statute requirement that physicians be involved with that quality-assurance review—although one would want to be careful in specifying which physicians are reviewing if one feared that domestic providers would be tempted to disfavor foreign providers for reasons having nothing to do with quality comparisons and everything to do with protecting their wages.

Other requirements of the PPO and HMO statutes, by contrast, are either in direct conflict or some tension with the introduction of TI-, DE-, and TM-type plans. The federal HMO-statute requirement that care be "available and accessible to each of its members and in a manner which assures continuity…within the area served by" the HMO and the similar requirement of "accessibility" in PPO statutes could be problematic on some interpretations, especially as to a TM-type plan that explicitly trades the local unavailability of nonemergency care for lower premiums.[22] Given the huge disparity in costs between care provided in the United States and that at medical-tourism centers, which as we have seen is largely what makes these plans attractive, limiting the size of the discount (or penalty) to 25 percent to non-preferred providers in TI- and DE-type plans may also screen out medical-tourism use that both the insurer and the patient prefer.

What this means is that without legislative work carving out exemptions from these HMO and PPO statutes for insurers using medical tourism, most medical insurance plans will be unable to incorporate medical tourism into their insurance plan design in anything more than a TC-type model, which is the least desirable in terms of cost savings. As we will see below, two states—California and Texas—have stepped in and passed medical tourism–specific insurance regulation, the former authorizing and enabling the trade, the latter further prohibiting it, but the inaction by most states mean that the existing HMO and PPO statutes govern, and will prevent a robust private insurance medical tourism market.

What, then, is the source of the growth in the private insurance market for medical tourism as discussed at the outset of this chapter? The answer stems from a quirk of a federal law, the Employee Retirement Income Security Act (ERISA) statute relating to preemption: ERISA largely preempts state insurance regulation for employers that

---

[21] 42 U.S.C. §§ 300e(b)(4), (c)(6) (2006).
[22] *Id.*; Furrow et al., *supra* note 12, at 506.

self-insure.[23] This is a significant loophole, as many firms, especially larger ones, self-insure: in 1997, a survey of seven states showed that employers self-insured in 13 percent of all firms, 56 percent of firms with 500 or more employees, 25 percent of firms with 100–499 employees, and 3 percent of all firms with fewer than 100 employees.[24] A more recent study using a different methodology suggests this number has grown significantly in our decade; self-insured plans that escape the mandates now cover an estimated 55 percent of all workers and 77 percent of workers in large companies.[25]

Thus, state level regulation of health insurance, which makes medical tourism difficult to incorporate in insurance plan design, does not apply to a large number of Americans who receive their health insurance through self-insured employer plans. However, it does pose an obstacle to the remainder of Americans with private health insurance.

C. A Tale of Two Regulatory Approaches: California and Texas

While most states have only indirectly regulated the incorporation of medical tourism into private health insurance, two states have directly addressed medical tourism in their insurance regulation, adopting diametrically opposed regimes. Again, I emphasize, that because of ERISA preemption these regulations apply only to plans that are not self-insured.

Texas has attempted to shut down insurance plans involving medical tourism altogether, by passing an insurance code provision stating that a "health benefit plan issuer may not issue or offer for sale in this state a health benefit plan that requires an enrollee to travel to a foreign country to receive a particular healthcare service under the health benefit plan."[26] The exact scope of this provision remains somewhat uncertain, because it does not define "requires." The most natural reading to me is that it prohibits only TM-type plans, not DE- or TI-type plans, but that interpretation has yet to be tested. The legislative history suggests the prohibition was also meant to apply more broadly to plans that offer a "discount on the amount an enrollee is required to pay to receive a particular health care service under the plan" if the enrollee opts for medical tourism.[27]

---

[23] 29 U.S.C. § 1144(b)(2)(B) (2006); Allison Overbay & Mark Hall, *Insurance Regulation of Providers That Bear Risk*, 22 AM. J.L. & MED. 361, 380 (1996). This is a slight simplification, in that the case law interpreting ERISA may require a self-insured firm to be self-insured in particular ways to take advantage of ERISA preemption of state insurance mandates. *See* BARRY FURROW ET AL., HEALTH LAW: CASES, MATERIALS AND PROBLEMS 657–58 (5th ed. 2004) (discussing ways in which employers can evade regulation requirements).

[24] M. Susan Marquis & Stephen H. Long, *Recent Trends in Self-Insured Employer Health Plans: A Look at the Interplay among Market Forces, Regulation, and Employers' Decisions to Self-Insure*, 18 HEALTH AFF. 161, 163 exhibit 1 (May–June 1999).

[25] KAISER FAMILY FOUNDATION & HEALTH RESEARCH AND EDUCATIONAL TRUST, EMPLOYER HEALTH BENEFITS: 2007 ANNUAL SURVEY 148 exhibit 10.3 (2007).

[26] TEX. INS. CODE ANN. § 1215.004 (Vernon 2009).

[27] Texas Bill Analysis, S.B. 1391, (Apr. 11, 2007), 80th Leg., Reg. Sess., (Tex. 2007), *available at* http://www. legis.state.tx.us/tlodocs/76R/analysis/html/SB01391F.htm. For discussion of the best reading of this reg, *see* Cohen, *supra* note 5, at 1563; Cortez, *supra* note 2, at 890–91.

If the matter is litigated the issue will probably turn on whether the courts follow the plain text of the statute or give more weight to legislative history.

California, by contrast, has adopted a limited authorization for health insurers to provide cross-border health insurance plans covering care in Mexico. This has enabled insurers such as HealthNet, Blue Shield, and SIMNSA to sell such plans with lower premiums and deductibles in California with costs of 40–50 percent less than plans that utilize only U.S. providers. These insurers have typically structured their cross-border plans as HMOs that incorporate providers in Mexico into their networks, although the Western Growers Association (WGA) also offers a self-funded ERISA plan.[28]

Starting in 1998, California insurance regulation permitted Mexican-based HMOs to sell insurance plans providing services in Mexico, but only to Mexican nationals living in California (and thus not to U.S. citizens), and permitted U.S.-based HMOS to sell insurance plans providing services in Mexico to either Mexican or U.S. citizens.[29] In 2004, the authorization was expanded to allow Mexican-based HMOs to provide services to non-Mexican citizens, although that expanded authorization appears to have expired in 2008.[30]

If an insurer wishes to offer one of these plans, the statute imposes certain conditions. Among other things, it requires these insurers to consent to personal jurisdiction in the United States (but not the provider themselves), provide a grievance procedure in the United States, continuously review the quality of Mexican providers, and publish an advisory statement on health care in Mexico.[31] However, because the Mexican providers are independent contractors under the California plans they themselves may not be subject to personal jurisdiction in the United States and thus the legal recourse against these providers under med-mal law remains murky, a fact that "California plans often ask patients to acknowledge."[32]

California law further requires that cross-border plans cover emergency and urgent care in California, but that all other care provided by the plan must be provided in Mexico.[33] According to Cortez:

> The cross-border plans in California seem to ignore the latter requirement. Blue Shield's plan offers most services in Mexico but reserves some for California due

[28] Cortez, *supra* note 2, 883–84; Cohen, *supra* note 5, at 1545.

[29] Ly Tran, Note, *Sick and Tired of the Knox-Keene Act: The Equal Protection Right of Non-Mexican Californians to Enroll in Mexico-Based HMO Plans*, 14 Sw. J.L. & Trade Am. 357, 364–65 (2008); Nathan Cortez, *Patients without Borders: The Emerging Global Market for Patients and the Evolution of Modern Health Care*, 83 Ind. L.J. 71, 100 (2008).

[30] *See* S.B. 1347 (Cal. 2004), *available at* http:// www.leginfo.ca.gov/pub/03-04/bill/sen/sb_1301-1350/ sb_1347_bill_20040913_ chaptered.pdf.

[31] Cal. Health & Safety Code §§ 1350, 1352.1 (West 2008); Cortez, *infra* note 36, at 69–70; Cortez, *supra* note 2, at 898; Tran, *supra* note 28, at 365–66.

[32] Cortez, *supra* note 2, at 898.

[33] Cal. Health & Safety Code § 1351.2(a)(2), (4) (West 2008); Cortez, *supra* note 2, at 895.

to "lack of necessary facilities" and other "cultural standards" in Mexico. Health Net's plans allow the insured to choose between receiving services primarily, but not exclusively, in the Los Angeles or Mexico service areas. The WGA also uses a network of primary and specialty providers in both countries. Only SIMNSA provides all but emergency and urgent care in Mexico.[34]

It is unclear exactly how they get away with this.

As I will argue below, states should address medical tourism head-on as Texas and California have done rather than let it be indirectly regulated by domestic health insurance rules not designed for the specific issues raised by medical tourism. I will also explain below why my own preference is for an approach such as California's, which is a form of channeling regime.

D. Will the Affordable Care Act Change Things?

Up until very recently, the story of medical tourism and insurance regulation would have ended there. Since then, though, Congress has passed and the Obama administration

---

[34] Cortez, *supra* note 2, at 895–96. Cortez also provides significantly greater detail regarding the organizational form and relationships with U.S. facilities for these providers:

> Blue Shield relies on General de Salud to manage its provider network in Mexico, which includes three Mexican hospitals. General de Salud contracts directly with physicians and ensures their credentials and the quality of care they provide, and receives a capitated payment from Blue Shield based on the number of customers served, reimbursing Mexican providers directly. The Blue Shield Access Baja plan operates like an HMO, with primary care gatekeepers needed for referrals to specialists....
>
> Salud con Health Net is a "binational partnership between Health Net, Hispanic Physicians, Tenet HealthSystems in LA county, and SIMNSA in Mexico." Health Net contracts with U.S. providers who agree to lower reimbursement rates to be included in the network. Health Net offers a full-network plan with access to Health Net's broad network in California, and a narrow-network plan that limits access to eight hospitals in Mexico (including SIMNSA's network) and seven in Los Angeles county....
>
> The WGA draws members from agricultural businesses in California and Arizona. Beginning in 1972, it began offering optional cross-border care through self-funded ERISA MEWAs, aimed primarily at seasonal migrant workers, utilizing an extensive provider network in Mexico that now includes at least ninety specialist providers and ten hospitals. The WGA contracts directly with doctors, clinics, hospitals, and pharmacies in Mexico, and contracts with several U.S. insurers for care in the United States. The WGA offers traditional indemnity and HMO and PPO plans, to which an additional cross-border "Mexico Panel" rider can be attached. As an ERISA MEWA that does not offer precapitated HMO plans, the WGA plans are regulated primarily by the U.S. Department of Labor rather than the California Department of Managed Health Care....
>
> SIMNSA is a Mexican insurer that operates in California by contracting with U.S. companies. For example, it contracts with two provider networks (HealthSouth and the Community Care Network) to offer emergency and urgent care in the United States; it contracts with International Healthcare Inc. to perform administrative functions; and it reinsures its coverage with AIG to reduce its financial liabilities.

Cortez, *supra* note 2, at 895–82 nn.218–221.

has begun implementing the most significant federal reform to American health care regulation in at least the last half a century, the Affordable Care Act (ACA). Earlier in this chapter, I explained how the ACA will likely stimulate interest in incorporating medical tourism into private insurer plans and that there are currently no firm obstacles in the ACA or its implementing regulations for doing so. Here I want to be a bit more precise and explain the current landscape and how it might change.

The ACA is a massive document, more than 1600 pages in length, but for our purposes we can focus on a few specific pieces of it. Beginning January 1, 2014, the ACA required most U.S. residents to have "minimum essential coverage," as part of what is known as the individual mandate, requiring most Americans to have health insurance or pay a penalty.[35] The ACA itself does not directly define "minimum essential coverage," instead referring to types of insurance plans that qualify, including "Government sponsored programs" (such as Medicare and Medicaid), "eligible employer-sponsored plans" (meaning a government plan) or "any other plan or coverage offered in the small or large group market within a State," "Plans in the individual market" (i.e., "a health plan offered in the individual market within a State"), "Grandfathered health plan[s]," and "Other coverage."[36] None of these statutory requirements themselves pose obstacles for medical tourism to be incorporated in private health insurance, though much of the ACA devolves authority to the Secretary of the Department of Health and Human Services to promulgate new regulations, which in theory could prove more arduous for private insurers as to medical tourism.[37]

The second important piece of the ACA for our purposes is the Health Benefits Exchanges ("Exchanges" for short), which are meant to create a well-defined market state by state in which to purchase individual and small group insurance plans.[38] The Exchanges in place in each state are to be state-run, unless an individual state chooses not to mount its own Exchange, in which case the federal government will run an Exchange for it. Nevertheless all Exchanges must play by a baseline set of rules set by the federal government in the ACA and its promulgating regulation.

To be clear, plans that do not meet some of these regulations can still be sold in an individual state, but because there are significant subsidies encouraging consumers to

---

[35] 26 U.S.C. § 5000A (2012). Those exempted include individuals who do not file federal income tax returns because their income is too low, those whose premium payments would be greater than 8 percent of their household income, members of Native American tribes, people who show that compliance with the requirement would impose a hardship, etc. *Id.* § 5000A(e). For a more thorough discussion of who is exempted from the requirements of the individual mandate, in particular relating to whether they are lawfully or unlawfully present in the United States, *see* Cortez, *supra* note 2, at 871–72.

[36] 26 U.S.C. § 5000A(f) (2012); *see also* Nathan Cortez, *Cross-Border Health Care and the Hydraulics of Health Reform, in* THE GLOBALIZATION OF HEALTH CARE: LEGAL AND ETHICAL ISSUES 65, 78 (I. Glenn Cohen ed. 2013).

[37] *See id.*; Cohen, *supra* note 5, at 1545.

[38] Cortez, *supra* note 36, at 79.

use plans that are part of the Exchange, the possibility of having plans offering medical tourism in the Exchanges represent a significant growth opportunity for the industry.

I will not attempt to offer a full account of the interplay between the statutory and regulatory requirements for the Exchanges and medical tourism through private insurance here[39]—indeed, as we have seen in the last few months in the United States, the rules governing these exchanges are in a significant state of flux responding to the technical difficulties of enrolling insured individuals by various websites and political and judicial attacks—but merely highlight a few salient points: All plans sold in the Exchanges, including any that incorporate medical tourism, have to offer "essential health benefits." The ACA specifies that "the Secretary shall define the essential health benefits, except that such benefits shall include at least the following general categories and the items and services covered within the categories: (A) Ambulatory patient services. (B) Emergency services. (C) Hospitalization. (D) Maternity and newborn care. (E) Mental health and substance use disorder services, including behavioral health treatment. (F) Prescription drugs. (G) Rehabilitative and habilitative services and devices. (H) Laboratory services. (I) Preventive and wellness services and chronic disease management. (J) Pediatric services, including oral and vision care."[40] The statute further specifies that "[t]he Secretary shall ensure that the scope of the essential health benefits . . . is equal to the scope of benefits provided under a typical employer plan, as determined by the Secretary. To inform this determination, the Secretary of Labor shall conduct a survey of employer-sponsored coverage to determine the benefits typically covered by employers, including multiemployer plans, and provide a report on such survey to the Secretary."[41] The statute also states that the Secretary must ensure that the benefits reflect "an appropriate balance" among these types of services, and "do not discriminate against individuals because of age, disability, or life expectancy, and cover the full 'health needs of diverse segments of the population, including women, children, persons with disabilities, and other groups.' "[42]

Some types of plans have been explicitly exempted from the "essential health benefit" requirements such that they can be sold as part of the Exchange without meeting these rules, most important, "multiple employer welfare arrangements" (MEWAs), a subset of ERISA plans that are self-funded and offered by groups of employers in a bona fide trade, industrial, or professional organization.[43] For other types of plans, though, I agree that nothing in these statutory requirements creates a clear problem for medical tourism,[44] in that a plan could refrain from offering medical tourism in one of these essential benefit categories altogether or the Secretary could determine that a plan incorporating some

---

[39] For a more comprehensive look, *see id.* at 79–82.

[40] 42 U.S.C. §§ 300gg-6, 18022(b)(1) (West 2003 & Supp. 2011).

[41] *Id.* § 18022(b)(2)(A) (2012).

[42] *Id.* § 18022(b)(4) (2012).

[43] 29 U.S.C. §1002(40)(A) (2006); Cortez, *supra* note 36, at 80.

[44] Cortez, *supra* note 36, at 79.

medical tourism was roughly equal to the scope of benefits provided under a typical employer plan. And indeed, since its passage, the Obama administration has given states even more flexibility in determining a "benchmark" plan against which plans wishing to enter the individual exchanges would be judged.[45]

Still, as Cortez has noted, there are many potential obstacles to offering a plan using some forms of medical tourism on a state Exchange, which may be cured or made worse by the Secretary as she promulgates further regulation and guidance on the Exchange. To list a few:

> First, HHS must define through regulation what additional requirements to impose on plans as a condition of certifying them for the exchanges. For example, would cross-border plans that heavily incentivized beneficiaries to seek certain care overseas "have the effect of discouraging the enrollment in such plan[s] by individuals with significant health needs"? Would a cross-border plan be able to offer a "sufficient choice of providers" if it contracts with only one foreign hospital for certain expensive procedures? Would cross-border plans targeted at low-income populations that are not eligible for Medicaid be able to include "essential community providers . . . that serve predominately low-income, medically-underserved individuals"? Would cross-border plans have trouble gaining accreditation for clinical quality, consumer access, provider credentialing, and network adequacy and access? Provider credentialing might be a problem for foreign providers, and network adequacy and access might be viewed with skepticism in a cross-border network. . . .
>
> A second potential barrier for cross-border plans is that the Affordable Care Act requires that exchange plans contract with hospitals and providers that meet patient safety and quality standards prescribed by HHS. For example, the Act allows qualified health plans to contract with hospitals with more than fifty beds only if the hospital uses patient safety evaluation systems under the Public Health Service Act and follows other discharge rules. Providers contracting with qualified health plans in the exchanges must also implement quality improvement requirements issued by HHS. Thus, cross-border exchange plans that integrated foreign hospitals and providers into their networks would have to ensure that the foreign facilities and practitioners could satisfy these potentially large and evolving quality requirements—something that might be difficult to do, and something that might dissuade foreign providers from participating. Again, provisions like this were not written with the idea of excluding foreign providers but might have the practical effect of doing so.[46]

---

[45] *See* Center for Consumer Information and Insurance Oversight, Essential Health Benefits Bulletin (Dec. 16, 2011), *available at* http://cciio.cms.gov/resources/files/Files2/12162011/essential_health_benefits_ bulletin.pdf.

[46] Cortez, *supra* note 36, at 80–81 (quoting 42 U.S.C. § 18031(c)–(h)).

To be sure, these problems may not be insurmountable, and indeed within the ACA statutory requirements there may be opportunities as well. As Cortez notes, the ACA enables individual states to create "subsidiary exchanges" for "geographically distinct area[s]," which might allow states to experiment with health insurance plans that involve some medical tourism components for border areas of states such as California and Texas.[47] Further, plans that seek to expand care for underserved communities, such as some Spanish-speakers along the border who may prefer a Mexican provider, "reduce health and health care disparities." These plans may qualify for some market-based incentives the ACA empowers states to use in rewarding plans that make headway in this area.[48] Third, the ACA has provisions enabling states to design alternatives to the Exchanges for individuals who earn too much to qualify for Medicaid but are below 200 percent of the federal poverty level.[49] These alternatives focus on differences in local access to care, which might be used for programs incorporating some amount of medical tourism.[50] Finally, and most important, beginning in 2017, states can apply to the Secretary to waive Exchange requirements altogether.[51] The state can craft an alternative system that provides coverage and protection for state residents comparable to that provided in the ACA.[52]

In sum, nothing in the new ACA general regulations precludes the incorporation of medical tourism into private health insurance plans that might satisfy the individual mandate and other general requirements. Getting such a plan on to individual state Exchanges, which would be highly desirable for those seeking to increase U.S. medical tourism, is trickier. Some plan types (such as MEWAs) have been explicitly exempted from meeting the statutory requirements for the Exchanges. For those plan types that *are* covered by the statutory requirements, these requirements may create some difficulties for plans incorporating medical tourism, but there are also some possible workarounds I have discussed. All this is tentative, especially as the Secretary is empowered by regulation to add to, clarify, or waive so many of the ACA's requirements. It is worth emphasizing that it appears that all these statutory requirements and regulation have been written in a way that is largely "blissfully ignorant" of medical tourism, seeking neither to regulate not promote it. To the extent these requirements create problems or opportunities for the industry, it appears largely to be accidental rather than as part of a highly reticulated regulatory scheme. This suggests, among other things, that by more directly engaging lawmakers on medical tourism private insurance regulation, friends

---

[47] 42 U.S.C. § 18031(f) (2012); Cortez, *supra* note 36, at 81.

[48] 42 U.S.C. § 18031(g) (2012); Cortez, *supra* note 36, at 81

[49] 42 U.S.C. § 18031(c)–(e) (2012); Cortez, *supra* note 36, at 83.

[50] Cortez, *supra* note 36.

[51] 42 U.S.C. § 18052(2012); Cortez, *supra* note 36, at 82.

[52] Cortez, *supra* note 36.

and foes of the industry may be better able to press for medical tourism–specific forms of regulation.

Now that we understand the existing set of private insurance options incorporating medical tourism and the existing regulation thereof, I want to examine legal and ethical issues with medical tourism in this setting. First, I want to revisit the matters of quality and liability discussed in the previous two chapters, but now examine how they differ when medical tourism is part of a private insurance plan. Second, I want to examine whether governments should regulate the actual design of private insurance plans incorporating medical tourism.

II. QUALITY AND LIABILITY REVISITED

A. How Is Medical Tourism through Private Health Insurance Different?

The same concerns regarding quality and liability we saw in Chapters 2 and 3 can be raised as to medical tourism that is incorporated into private health insurance.

However, I shall argue that our response ought to be somewhat different for several reasons: on the one hand, in favor of *less* regulation of this market as compared to patients paying out-of-pocket is the fact that some of the concerns are less pressing when a private insurer, a repeat and sophisticated player in shopping for providers, is doing the choosing. On the other hand, there are several facts in favor of *more* regulation of this market as compared to patients paying out-of-pocket. As I will explain below, patient choice of providers is mediated by their insurer and employer such that we can be less sure patient autonomy and welfare is being maximized, the risk of overregulating preventing access to nonemergency care altogether is less, patient bounded rationality is high, and the available regulatory tools for implementing protections for patients are much easier to implement.

Risks of Overregulation and Access to Care: In the last Chapter I suggested that one argument against too heavy a regulation of medical tourism for patients paying out-of-pocket was the risk that we would "protect them" out of the only health care they could afford. Interventions discouraging uninsured patients from medical tourism thus face a high bar to be justified as patient protective. The relationship of insurer-prompted medical tourism to that frame is more complex, but in general also suggests a lower threshold for justifying intervention.

On the one hand, there exists a portion of this population, call them "the marginally uninsured," who may become insured as a result of the availability of insurer-prompted medical tourism plans. A patient such as Bob may be willing or able to purchase a plan such as Domestic Extra (DE) at $4000 or Tourism Mandated (TM) at $1500, but not Status Quo (SQ) at $7000; if so, the availability of Plans DE and TM would cause or enable him to become insured. Prohibiting these plans would protect him out of health insurance.

On the other hand, there exists a portion of this population currently insured under a SQ plan who would switch to the other plan types if they became available. Their potential benefit from the availability of these other plans is different. Each new plan offers cost savings in return for required or incentivized travel abroad for coverage and thus a reduced likelihood and amount of med-mal recovery as well as potential quality effects. If a patient values the cost savings more than those drawbacks, the argument goes, why should the government stop her from making that bargain, choosing a plan that balances cost and med-mal protection in the way that is optimal to her? This positive argument for access to robust insurer-prompted medical tourism plans for this portion of the population is a species of what are sometimes called "consumer sovereignty" arguments, that "citizens, assuming they have reasonable access to relevant information are…the best judges of what will promote their own welfare."[53]

I draw this distinction because it seems plausible to me that the threshold risk level for which government intervention, as against private choice, is justified varies substantially between the two frames. On many views, allowing patients to bear the risks associated with medical tourism is more justifiable when one risks "protecting" them out of access to nonemergency health care entirely than when intervention would merely "protect" patients out of potential cost savings.[54] While medical tourism by uninsured Americans falls squarely in the first frame, insurer-prompted medical tourism represents a mix of the two (though tilting toward the second), such that the threshold of risk that justifies government intervention would seem lower here.

Information and Agency Problems Relating to Quality: One of the preconditions to the consumer-sovereignty-type argument is access to relevant information, and the absence of that access is a serious threat to a permissive approach. In discussing medical tourists paying out-of-pocket in the last chapter, I noted the problems caused by serious information deficits especially as to quality. At first blush, this might be an area where we have fewer qualms about insurer-prompted medical tourism. Because insurers can aggregate and evaluate data from the experience of multiple patients using medical-tourist providers, over time they may be better able to overcome information deficits as to care quality in a way that individual shoppers cannot.

There is, however, a divergence of incentives to use that information. One might think that insurers would have a great incentive to select high-quality foreign providers because they will bear the cost of continuity of care that results from medical error: to the extent that the expected costs of this continuing care (i.e., the increased chance that medical error will result through treatment abroad rather than domestically multiplied

---

[53] Christine Jolls et al., *A Behavioral Approach to Law and Economics*, 50 STAN. L. REV. 1471, 1541 (1998).

[54] This is true for views that attach a special importance to health, but not necessarily for purely welfarist views that might treat health and cost savings as commensurable. For a further discussion, *see* Cohen, *supra* note 5, at 1547 n.292.

by the cost of this care) exceed the expected cost savings from using medical tourism as opposed to a U.S. provider, the insurer has an incentive not to use the foreign provider.

However, this incentive is distorted by the fact that U.S. patients switch insurers relatively frequently. Recent empirical work suggests that 16.6 percent of privately insured adults changed their insurer within a twelve-month period, most frequently (38.5 percent of the time) due to a change in the insured's own or spouse's employer.[55] As a result, insurers have suboptimal incentives to invest in the future health of their covered populations, which in our setting provides reason to worry that insurers' incentives to select high-quality care diverge from patients' incentives.[56] While patients care about the costs imposed by poor quality of care throughout their lifetime, insurers care about the costs for the first year completely and then only at a reduced rate (because of expected switching) beyond that. This is what lawyers and economists refer to as an "agency problem" or the "principal-agent tension" wherein the decision-making agent (the insurer) may not have its incentives perfectly aligned with the principal (here the patient), and due to information deficits, monitoring costs, etc., the gap will persist to some extent.

Agency Problems and Difficulties in Suing for Med-Mal: For medical tourism, the agency problem is compounded by the fact that insurers do not completely internalize the negative effects on med-mal recovery either. Whether the patient can recover against his or her provider is not a matter of complete indifference for the insurer because successful med-mal recovery against the provider may diminish the risk that patients will go after the insurer as defendant, and in some cases perhaps the insurer may also seek indemnification from the provider. However, because current substantive med-mal law is relatively insurer friendly in these suits, a divergence should persist between the patient's and insurer's interests. Although an insurer is more likely to be subject to personal jurisdiction and less likely to get a case dismissed on forum non conveniens grounds in the United States, a plaintiff suing his or her insurer for medical malpractice of a foreign provider faces many of the same problems I outlined in the last chapter relating to facilitators. Foreign facilities and providers will typically not be employees of the insurer, nor do implied authority theories seem likely as a way of asserting direct med-mal liability. And negligent credentialing claims are also likely to fail for the reasons suggested in Chapter 3.

Indeed, plaintiffs are likely to face more difficulties in suing an insurer than a facilitator because there are additional obstacles: some states have made HMOs immune from negligent-treatment suits.[57] Further, for those whose health insurance is employer

---

[55] Bradley Herring, *Suboptimal Provision of Preventive Healthcare due to Expected Enrollee Turnover among Private Insurers*, 19 HEALTH ECON. 438, 442 (2010). It is possible that those who have experienced medical injury switch insurers less than the general population, somewhat mitigating the situation here; I am unaware of empirical research on the issue.

[56] *Id.* at 447.

[57] MARK A. HALL ET AL., HEALTH CARE LAW AND ETHICS 480 (7th ed. 2007).

sponsored, some courts have found that, in some cases, liability based on negligent selection of physicians "relates to" an ERISA plan and is therefore preempted by ERISA, although the exact preemptive scope is still very much in flux.[58]

The flip side of ERISA preemption is that the insurer is now open to liability for breach of fiduciary duty under ERISA. Health plans covered by ERISA must act "solely in the interest" of plan beneficiaries and must at minimum avoid making any material misrepresentations about the plan. But the remedies available through that statute pale in comparison to common law med-mal. It is not clear whether an insurer's use of medical tourism would actually violate its fiduciary duty under ERISA, such that it is unclear that this means meaningfully more liability risk for insurers using medical tourism.[59]

It is because of these kinds of difficulties in suing that a 2003 confidential interview study of experienced health care lawyers by Gail Agrawal and Mark Hall found "very little evidence...that health plans are motivated by the threat of liability to improve the quality of medical care delivered by their providers" in the domestic sphere, in part because of low estimates of the chance of success of such litigation.[60]

In sum, while theories of liability such as negligent credentialing and ERISA breach of fiduciary duty may act at the margins to prevent insurers from choosing particularly low quality providers and being completely indifferent as to patients' potential to recover in med-mal should medical error occur, there is also a significant agency problem between patient and insurer in medical tourism incorporated into private health insurance.

Rationality in Choosing Health Insurance Plans: One possible rejoinder to these problems more generally, the kind of answer often offered by champions of "consumer-directed health care," is that a patient could factor in these concerns when determining whether to opt for a plan such as TM or DE and that insurers would adjust their offerings and/or premiums accordingly. Further, as to problems relating to recovering in med-mal, insured patients could once again purchase med-mal insurance protection of the kind discussed in the previous chapter.

However, the same information deficits and bounded-rationality limitations we encountered at the level of choosing a provider, discussed in the last chapter, reappear at the level of choosing a health insurance plan and med-mal insurance, albeit in different forms. Indeed, as the research that Hall and Schneider have recently collected shows, in the domestic sphere, patients are particularly bad at choosing among health plans: they become overwhelmed at the large number of plans on the market, they are

---

[58] *Id.* at 492–93.

[59] For a discussion of the ERISA issue in medical tourism, *see generally* Christopher J. Brady, Note, *Offshore Gambling: Medical Outsourcing versus ERISA's Fiduciary Duty Requirement*, 64 WASH. & LEE L. REV. 1073, 1081–87, 1106–12 (2007). *See also* Nathan Cortez, *Recalibrating the Legal Risks of Cross-Border Health Care*, 10 YALE J. HEALTH POL'Y, L. & ETHICS 1, 16–17 (2010).

[60] Gail B. Agrawal & Mark A. Hall, *What If You Could Sue Your HMO? Managed Care Liability beyond the ERISA Shield*, 47 ST. LOUIS U. L.J. 235, 236 (2003).

highly susceptible to framing effects, and they have trouble understanding even a single plan.[61]

Further, these problems seem to stubbornly resist attempts at education. To give but one example, in a pilot study New York State engaged in heroic efforts to educate patients on plan choice (including individual enrollment meetings, brochures, videotapes, question-and-answer sessions, and required educational seminars), yet when tested less than 30 percent of Brooklyn, New York, respondents understood that their plans covered out-of-area emergency care, and less than 42 percent of all New Yorkers understood that their plans limited hospital choice.[62] The introduction of plans such as TI, DE, and TM into the market will only exacerbate these problems by adding multiplicative layers of complexity—for every service the patient now has to evaluate the quality of physicians selected by the insurer, the effect on med-mal recovery, the size of the reward/punishment for foreign/domestic provider choice, etc.

Mediation of Plan Choice by Employers: All that I have said so far establishes why insurer-prompted medical tourism is of great concern as to those who purchase health insurance in the individual market. But only a small portion of Americans—5 percent of the population, or nearly 15 million people according to 2011 estimates—actually get health-insurance coverage that way.[63] Instead, most insurance choice by individuals is mediated through the employer.[64] Employer-sponsored health care in the United States is popular in part because employers can take advantage of economies of scale in negotiating for and administering health insurance and because of the favorable tax treatment—the employer can deduct the cost of health insurance it provides from its own income-tax base and payroll-tax obligations, and the benefits of the health insurance are excluded from the income of employees as well as from the employee's payroll-tax obligations for Social Security and Medicare contributions.[65]

---

[61] Carl E. Schneider & Mark A. Hall, *The Patient Life: Can Consumers Direct Health Care?*, 35 Am. J.L & Med. 36–59 (2009).

[62] *Id.* at 43–44 (citing Deborah W. Garnick et al., *How Well Do Americans Understand Their Health Coverage?*, 12 Health Aff. 204, 206–09 (Fall 1993). Perhaps unsurprisingly, Manhattanites performed better. *Id.*

[63] KCMU/Urban Institute analysis of 2012 ASEC Supplement to the CPS, *available at* http://facts.kff.org/chart.aspx?ch=477 (May 4, 2013).

[64] Elizabeth A. Pendo, *The Health Care Choice Act: The Individual Insurance Market and the Politics of "Choice,"* 29 W. New Eng. L. Rev. 473, 474 (2007) (citing U.S. Census Bureau, Historical Health Insurance Tables, Table HI-1: Health Insurance Coverage Status and Type of Coverage by Sex, Race and Hispanic Origin: 1987 to 2005, *available at* http:// www.census.gov/hhes/www/hlthins/data/historical/orghihistr1.html); *see also* The Henry J. Kaiser Family Foundation, Health Insurance Coverage in America 2007, *available at* http://facts.kff.org/chartbook.aspx?cb=55 (May 4, 2013) (discussing a more recent study of the entire non-elderly population finding that 61 percent had employer-sponsored health insurance compared to 6 percent in the individual market).

[65] I.R.C. §§ 106(a), 162(a)(1), 3101(a)–(b), 3111(a)–(b), 3121(a)(2) (2006); *see, e.g.,* Richard L. Kaplan, *Who's Afraid of Personal Responsibility? Health Savings Accounts and the Future of American Health Care*, 36 McGeorge L. Rev. 535, 541–44 (2005).

But employer-sponsored health insurance also puts the employer in control of many critical decisions, including whether to offer a plan at all, the scope of the plan's coverage, the health care provider networks to use, the level of premiums to be paid by employees, and the deductibles and copayments that the plan will have.[66] In our context, the decision as to whether plans of the SQ, DE, TI, or TM type are made available to the employees in the first place are predetermined by the employer. Thus, many patients such as Bob may not be choosing a plan they would choose on their own (subject to all the information and bounded rationality constraints discussed above). Even more so than as to health insurance purchased in the individual market, the consumer-sovereignty argument against choice-restricting regulation cannot be satisfied because its precondition that the consumer be the one choosing is not met. This would suggest that in the realm of insurer-prompted medical tourism, more stringent regulation of the employer-sponsored health-insurance market as compared to the individual market is in order.

Against that conclusion, one might offer two objections. First, the employee-employer agency relationship might somewhat *mitigate* the concerns discussed earlier about the insurer-insured agency problem and information overload from plan complexity. Employers are better positioned to evaluate these very complex plans in selecting what to offer their employees. Moreover, if employees stick with an employer longer than they do an insurer (only 38.5 percent of the 16.6 percent of yearly switching, or 6.3 percent of all insurance switching, also involves a change in employer),[67] the employer may have an incentive to pick high-quality providers because employers bear the cost of poor treatment choices in the form of prolonged absences or reduced productivity, although that conclusion is not certain. Further, even if employers do internalize to some extent the costs of poor care for their employees in this way, they will internalize the costs of poor care for the employee's family who is often covered by the same plan in a more attenuated fashion, if at all.

This response to the problem would be more persuasive if, as health care economists such as Patricia Danzon have suggested, "economic theory and evidence indicate that, at least as a first approximation, employees ultimately bear the costs of employer-sponsored plans—including the costs of liability—through lower wages or higher premium contributions" such that "[t]he implication is that the level and structure of health benefits reflect employee preferences" making employers "largely intermediaries."[68] That is, given certain assumptions about competition in the labor market, employees will receive higher wages from employers with less desirable plans as compensation.

A second, related rejoinder draws on the wide latitude offered to employers to predetermine which plans to offer in our status-quo system; that is, why worry about this

---

[66] *E.g.*, Kaplan, *supra* note 65, at 42.
[67] Herring, *supra* note 55, at 443 tbl.1.
[68] Patricia M. Danzon, *Tort Liability: A Minefield for Managed Care?*, 26 J. LEGAL STUD. 491, 493–94 (1997).

comparably small decision (where services are provided) given the large number of decisions the employer is empowered under current law to make in selecting the insurance it will provide? Employers not covered by the employer mandate of the new Obama health care reform or "pay or play" legislation in force in some states can refuse to provide health insurance altogether, and even those covered by these laws can instead choose to pay the penalty.[69] Further, except for the particular services covered by the mandated-benefit state laws discussed above, employers also retain the power to determine whether to offer plans that cover particular services or not. Given the greater power the law provides employers not to provide any health insurance or cover particular services, why should it not provide them the lesser power to determine where services will be offered?

These are powerful points, and there is something there, but they are not completely persuasive. One might respond that these broad employer powers are not justified and thus form a poor touchstone as normative guides, or that they are the result of historical contingencies behind our health care system, or point out that the kind of de facto waiver of liability achieved through medical tourism is one currently not in the power of employers to choose in the domestic context. All this may be right, but for present purposes I want to emphasize a different response that unites the two rejoinders: although it is plausible that employees can adequately detect and assess the failure to provide coverage *altogether* (or perhaps even the failure to cover particular services) when assessing employers and the wages offered in a competitive market, it seems less plausible that they can adequately assess the benefits and costs of the medical-tourism piece of these plans, especially given the bounded-rationality problems discussed above. This may be particularly true as to plans incorporating medical tourism, in that, for the reasons discussed in Chapter 2, patients will have a hard time judging the quality of foreign facilities, and the calculus becomes even more opaque when mediated by employer choices that are invisible to the patient. Another response, this time from analogy, is that notwithstanding the broad leeway given to employers on these scores, many states do heavily regulate insurer-plan design as to which providers will be covered, where they are located, and at what rate, in the ways discussed above. Below I will discuss the ways in which this regulation might serve as a possible model for regulating insurer-prompted medical tourism.

Administrability: Finally, as we saw in the prior chapters, attempts to discourage or curb medical tourism for patients paying out-of-pocket requires some novel regulatory moves that face considerable difficulties in implementation, detection, and enforcement. By contrast, as I hinted at above, discouraging insurer-prompted medical tourism can be done through more straightforward application of existing state powers over health insurance. States have robust power to impose requirements on health insurers doing

---

[69] I.R.C. § 4980H (2012); *see, e.g.,* Elizabeth A. Weeks, *Loopholes: Opportunity, Responsibility, or Liability?,* 35 J.L. Med. & Ethics 320, 323 (2007).

business in that state. Texas and California are examples of the way such power could be used to regulate or prohibit medical tourism by patients of that state. As we saw above, the ERISA preemption of state insurance regulation blunts the effectiveness of this tool for the regulation of self-insured plans. However, the U.S. federal government could amend ERISA to get rid of this preemption as to medical tourism–related insurance requirements or pass its own statute implementing requirements as to medical tourism. Indeed, the brand new health reform legislation seems to provide an even easier way for the federal government to regulate insurer-prompted medical tourism, by specifying that certain kinds of insurer-prompted medical tourism plans do not qualify as satisfying the individual or large employer mandates discussed above.

* * *

To be sure there are differences between medical tourism involving patients paying out-of-pocket and medical tourism for patients with private insurance as to liability and quality-of-care concerns that cut in both directions. Overall, though, I think some combination of the agency problems involved, the reduced negative consequences of over-regulation, and the richness and feasibility of the regulatory tools should lead us to be *more* concerned about these issues as to medical tourism that is part of private insurance and more apt to regulate this market. If I am right that with the advent of President Obama's health care reform medical tourism through private insurance is likely to become a bigger piece of the total pie, then there may also be a way in which regulation of the private insurer market has desirable spillovers into the out-of-pocket medical tourism market. To the extent quality-of-care enhancements are lumpy and cannot be doled out patient-by-patient, and to the extent legal protections offered to patients who are insured become habitual and benchmarks, it may be that the rules we introduce for private insurer-prompted medical tourism become the "new normal," or at least defaults from which providers have to consciously depart. This is another, albeit indirect reason, to be more open to regulation of this market—a market that in the domestic context is already highly regulated via state and federal insurance law.

B. What Should Be Done?

Now that I have made the case for regulating to address quality and liability concerns in the private insurer–prompted medical tourism market, what form should that regulation take?

The regulatory intervention I again most favor is channeling in forms akin to those discussed in the last two chapters as to patients paying out-of-pocket. Indeed, these interventions are actually much easier to implement in this context than that of out-of-pocket patients in that they could more easily be built directly into health-insurance regulation in the form of selective prohibitions on what insurers can do rather than indirectly through fines, tax consequences, etc.

Once again we could channel by a list of approved services that we think pose the smallest risk to the patient, or based on whether the facility has done a fixed number of a particular service in the last calendar year.

A different variation suggested by other elements of state insurance law would be to prohibit medical tourism for any mandated benefit—that is, for any benefit for which insurers are required to provide the service. Requiring domestic provision of emergency services makes obvious sense, and one most insurers will be inclined to adopt without regulation, but I would also argue for statutes that allow insurers to require/incentivize medical tourism only in cases where the patient will be able to travel without significant pain or negative health effects, perhaps requiring a U.S. doctor to certify that fact. Whether to mandate an exception for cases where the patient can travel but it is inconvenient for the patient to do so, for example, because of child or elder care, is a harder question. Administering a form of insurance regulation that also requires this kind of exception might be too hard or costly to administer as compared to medical exemptions given the difficulty of setting a standard and detecting those who are faking their need. But, perhaps insurance companies could administer such a rule more easily than I anticipate.

Given that some foreign countries will not have the same protections for women, same sex–couples, individuals with disabilities, etc., that the patient's home country does, it would also be sensible to build in exceptions for patients falling in these categories. This could be done either by specifically prohibiting insurers from applying any penalty to a patient who makes a bona fide claim that he or she is not traveling because of fear of this kind of discrimination, or by prohibiting insurers from contracting with facilities in countries that lack these protections altogether. Whether the latter and more forceful form of action is desirable might turn on how committed the home country is to these values, its analysis of the expressive value of taking this stance, and its assessment of how likely doing so is to nudge the destination country to introduce such protections.

The question of whether to include other kinds of mandated benefits (such as IVF in some states) is more complex, and the reason the benefit has been mandated will determine whether it makes sense to mandate its provision domestically. If the mandate represents a social judgment that immediate access to that service is particularly important, then mandating domestic provision may be justified. By contrast, if the mandate is justified on distributive-justice grounds in order to spread the cost of some services more fully across the entire pool or to combat adverse-selection problems, it is not clear how strongly this justification supports mandating that the services be provided domestically. Indeed, because medical tourism allows the service to be provided much more cheaply, it may prove an alternative to mandating benefits. If the mandate is meant as a subsidy to certain service providers, whether mandating domestic provision is justified depends in part on one's normative views about that subsidy. In particular, for those who think that certain mandated benefits are the problematic result of lobbying by providers in a state to force insurers to cover their care, a push to mandate that the service be provided in state appears to exacerbate the problem by insulating these providers from competition from abroad.

A different sensible intervention might require insurers to cover domestically all follow-up care from surgeries provided abroad, as an attempt to try and mitigate some of the concerns that I and others have raised about continuity of care.[70]

We could also channel by provider in analogy to the previous discussion in Chapter 3 (among other places in this book) for medical tourists paying out-of-pocket. We could prohibit insurers from incentivizing or requiring tourism with providers unless they are JCI accredited, meet a threshold requirement of U.S. trained or certified doctors, or are partnered with high-quality U.S. institutions. Again, states could go further and construct their own "approval" criteria based on required disclosures with periodic auditing and review, although that would introduce greater costs and complexity. An intermediate approach might be based on some PPO statutes that require quality-management programs, sometimes requiring that a physician lead them. We could go further and actually require a governmental member or (in analogy to requirements for institutional review boards that approve research protocols) a preset number of institutionally unaffiliated community members to be part of the review.[71]

Similarly, taking some inspiration from California's model but going further, we could institute measures aimed at dampening the med mal–recovery-disparity problems by prohibiting insurers from using providers who did not enter consent-to-jurisdiction agreements (or otherwise subject themselves to jurisdiction in the state), forum-selection agreements, or choice-of-law agreements, and/or do not maintain assets in the state. A different way of achieving some of this benefit would be to require insurers to contract with a third-party insurer for medical-tourist medical-malpractice insurance of the kind discussed in the previous chapter. Instead of seeking compensation for the medical error from the foreign provider, the patient would now be able to achieve compensation from this third-party insurer with whom his health insurer would be contractually obligated to have a policy.[72] Finally, as discussed in the prior chapter, we could require insurers to only work with provider who enter into agreements to arbitrate. These protections could be treated as independently or jointly sufficient to satisfy the insurance rules, or some combination thereof.

As with those paying out-of-pocket we could also create a victim's compensation fund modeled on the September 11 compensation fund or worker's compensation, this time funded by a per patient tax on insurers who send patients abroad to use medical tourism. Moreover, as discussed in the last chapter in the context of facilitators, we could also expand vicarious liability as to insurers for the med-mal of the foreign providers or hospitals to

---

[70] For my discussion, *see* Chapter 3. *See also* Cortez, *supra* note 29, at 74, 122.

[71] 45 C.F.R. § 46.107 (2009).

[72] How good a solution this would be would depend in part on what we thought of the process, solvency, etc. of these third-party insurers.

whom they send patients. As I described there, this would make sense if we thought that insurers have enough control over these foreign providers and facilitators such that imposing liability would cause major changes in the behavior of foreign providers—that they were effective levers for inducing optimal behavior rather than merely doubling potential liability. I think the case for vicarious liability is stronger for insurers than it was for facilitators in part because they more plausibly have control of the behavior of foreign providers to whom they direct patients, but I still find the case somewhat strained.

I ultimately think it is more sensible to try to expand direct liability for foreign providers through the regulation of U.S. insurers, and in the mold of California. I think this would be better both in terms of regulatory design and also what is politically feasible. Still, I do not mean any one recommendation I make here to be definitive, and would be open to further developments of a vicarious liability or compensation fund schemes to insurers if they seemed more promising to regulators and/or the regulated industry. The same impact could be partially achieved by making health insurers strictly liable for any med-mal that results from treatment abroad, although this might result in a less predictable expenditure by insurers.

III. REGULATING PLAN DESIGN

Quite apart from the liability and quality concerns shared by medical tourism by patients paying out-of-pocket and those who are using medical tourism through private health insurance, the latter also raises distinct issues relating to the ethics and legality of certain kinds of plan design. As we saw above, one limitation on the robust use of medical tourism among non–self-insured firms is the existing PPO and HMO regulation, which in the domestic context has the effect of permitting only certain kinds of health insurance plans and prohibiting others.

One rationale for limiting PPOs and HMOs in the domestic context has to do with heightened concerns relating to precommitment concerns, which seem just as present here in some types of private insurance medical tourism plans. Precommitment problems are familiar in bioethics and contracts in settings such as surrogacy agreements, slavery contracts, etc.[73] Such problems are characterized by an agent having to commit at Time 1 to an outcome at Time 2, which, when Time 2 rolls around, may no longer comport with his or her current preferences. With a TM- or DE-type plan, individuals have committed at Time 1 to seek medical tourism (or pay a penalty if they do not) for specified procedures when they did not know which services they would need.

Notice that this problem is specific to medical tourism through private insurance. Our hypothetical medical tourist paying out-of-pocket from a prior chapter, Carl, has

---

[73] *See, e.g.,* I. Glenn Cohen, *The Right Not to Be a Genetic Parent?*, 81 S. CAL. L. REV. 1115, 1161–87 (2008); Anthony T. Kronman, *Paternalism and the Law of Contracts*, 92 YALE L.J. 763, 766 (1983).

not precommitted to using medical tourism because at the time he needs services he can purchase care out-of-pocket domestically or abroad (at least theoretically—as discussed cost may pose a practical constraint). However, not all medical tourism insurance plans have these precommitment problem features, or at least not forms of this feature that should cause us concern. If our hypothetical patient Bob choses a TI plan at Time 1, he has just left himself open to a further choice down the road at Time 2 whether to take or refuse an incentive payment to opt for care via medical tourism rather than via domestic provision.[74] In a TC-type plan there is no incentive in either direction relating to medical tourism, and the choice remains the patient's at Time 2. By contrast, a patient who opts for a DE- or TM-type plan has lost something if at Time 2 the person chooses *not* to use medical tourism.

This initially seems like a promising ground for distinction that would lead us to more restrictive regulation of TM or DE plans but not TI or TC plans. Upon further reflection, however, the precommitment argument seems unable to do the work. Private health insurance as it currently exists is awash in precommitment problems. The individual who fails to buy health insurance at Time 1 and becomes ill at Time 2 may no longer be able to purchase it.[75] Conversely, the person who purchases health insurance at Time 1 and pays the premium for the year, but experiences a year of perfect health cannot get the premium back. Given that we allow individuals the freedom to make what are, in some cases, more serious precommitments as to health insurance—whether to be covered at all, whether to choose a plan that covers service X or not—why not allow them to precommit as to medical tourism? To put the point even more forcefully, as a number of authors have pointed out insurance depends on uncertainty, such that the precommitments are central to health insurance;[76] paying the cost of care if and when the need materializes is what those without insurance do. That is not to say any distinction between

---

[74] To be precise, TI plans are not entirely free of precommitment problems in that the individual who subscribes to such a plan as opposed to SQ has precommited himself to being offered the medical-tourism option at the time of consumption of the service. The analogy is to someone who subscribes to a "dessert of the week club," which offers a discounted high-calorie confection by mail every Thursday, which the individual can purchase or refuse but not avoid being offered. If one decided, months after subscription, to try and lose weight, perhaps the precommitment to be offered dessert every week would cause the individual distress in the form of temptation. That said, this kind of precommitment problem seems far enough afield from the ones that really concern us about TM- and DE-type plans that I put it to one side.

[75] The individual who fails to purchase health insurance at Time 1 may also at Time 2 no longer be able to have his or her illness covered due to preexisting condition exclusions. The Obama health-reform legislation fixes that problem by mandating guaranteed issue and renewal for adults, but only beginning in 2014 for adults (for children, the changes go into effect September 23, 2010). 42 U.S.C. § 300gg (2012)..

[76] *See* Clark C. Havighurst & Barak D. Richman, *Distributive Injustice(s) in American Health Care*, 69 LAW & CONTEMP. PROBS. 7, 80 (Autumn 2006) ("It would be seriously destructive of insurance markets, after all, if consumers knew too well what their future health needs would be."); Russell Korobkin, *Determining Health Care Rights from behind a Veil of Ignorance*, 1998 U. ILL. L. REV. 801, 826 ("If individuals operating behind the veil of ignorance would desire health insurance, they have no moral claim to change their mind once they learn that good fortune has rendered them healthy.").

TI or DE and TM plans should not carry any weight, just that precommitment problems seem insufficient to carry the force of the argument for a different regulatory regime.

What then is the argument for regulating plan types? I think it is best thought of as an instance of justified paternalism, that sometimes individuals need to be protected from making *bad* choices they will later regret, especially in areas where they appear to be particularly adept at making poor choices even by their own self-assessed goals. As the empirical evidence mentioned above suggests, choosing health insurance plans is an area where individuals have great difficulty making good choices even based on what plans satisfy their self-assessed goals. In trying to select a health insurance plan that has only domestic options, individuals become overwhelmed at the large number of plans on the market, they are highly susceptible to framing effects, and they have trouble understanding even a single plan.[77]

This critique lends itself to three different types of responses:

The first, and most extreme, would be to suggest that individuals are so bad at making choices in this domain that we should heavily restrict their choice set and the number of plans available to them and/or use a third party intermediary (a kind of agent) to choose for them. This approach would be justified if either (or in combination) there was evidence of profound bounded rationality, we had confidence we could choose better than patients could, and/or as a political philosophical matter, we put low value on consumer sovereignty. My own view is that the existing empirical evidence of bounded rationality is not clear enough, and my confidence is low enough in our ability to make better choices (directly or through agents) for the individual that, when combined with my own modestly libertarian impulses, make this too strong a response.

The second, and least interventionist approach would be to adopt measures that are "libertarian paternalist"—measures that "influence behavior while also respecting freedom of choice," namely "choice architecture" innovations such as setting default rules, presenting options in certain ways, etc.[78] For example, if we think most patients will make bad decisions when choosing health insurance plans involving some amount of medical tourism, we could use the stickiness of defaults in favor of SQ plans by requiring that, when offering patients the choice, the SQ plan is treated as the default option by insurers. That proposal, however, assumes insurers always offer SQ plans. States could mandate that insurers do so by requiring that they offer other plans only in addition to a full SQ plan rather than exclusive of it. The rationale is that "no one is being deprived of local care; rather we are merely expanding the option set and allowing those dissatisfied with their current plan to try something else."

---

[77] Carl E. Schneider & Mark A. Hall, *The Patient Life: Can Consumers Direct Health Care?*, 35 Am. J.L. & Med. 36–59 (2009).

[78] Cass R. Sunstein & Richard H. Thaler, *Libertarian Paternalism Is Not an Oxymoron*, 70 U. Chi. L. Rev. 1159, 1159–60 (2003); *see generally* Richard Thaler & Cass Sunstein, Nudge: Improving Decisions about Health, Wealth and Happiness (2008).

That seems quite unobjectionable and straightforward, but actually would require further regulation to make effective: we might worry that insurers could simply offer SQ
plans but raise their premiums dramatically—making the requirement a paper tiger—or
that even if insurers had to offer such a plan, employers would not be obligated to offer
it to employees. We could, however, introduce further regulation ensuring that such SQ
plans are always offered by every employer and requiring some price controls based on
actuarial data.

My own view is that this specific intervention—mandating that an SQ option be
offered to all patients and be the default option unless and until a patient explicitly
opts for a plan involving some amount of medical tourism—makes eminent sense given
what we know about insurance choice by consumers. Unless they are offered an SQ-type
plan, patients who want some domestic coverage of certain services will have to shop
for supplemental insurance. Empirical evidence suggests that patients are particularly
boundedly rational when they must put together more than one plan. For example, Eric
Johnson and colleagues found that when consumers were offered two sets of hospitalization policies (one covering only diseases and one covering only accidents), respondents
were willing to pay twice as much than for a single more inclusive policy covering both
categories (covering hospitalization for "any reason").[79]

Although I fully endorse this libertarian paternalist approach, it seems unlikely to go
far enough. I say "unlikely" rather than being more definitive, because as I have repeatedly emphasized in this book the proper regulatory approach depends heavily on the
data as to how individuals actually behave when presented with certain choices and how
those decisions affect their welfare. As medical tourism through private health insurance is so new, we lack even rudimentary publicly available data on these issues. Still,
from the literature demonstrating bounded rationality with *domestic* private health
insurance choice as well as research on other non–health insurance choices, I think there
is strong reason to believe that these modest libertarian paternalist interventions are
unlikely to suffice.

Thus, I ultimately would endorse a third approach that falls somewhere between the
poles of the first two: interventions that go beyond true libertarian paternalism—they
will take certain options off the table altogether—but offer only modest restrictions on
plan type, leaving much room for consumer choice. The category of such possible interventions is vast, and I will not even attempt to map even its outer bounds here. Which
specific interventions to support will again turn on political philosophical priors (how
much choice versus how much paternalism can be justified), and in my view how much

---

[79] Eric Johnson et al., *Framing, Probability Distortions, and Insurance Decisions*, 7 J. RISK & UNCERTAINTY
35, 39–40 (1993).

specific evidence we have of bounded rationality in the decision-making. Instead I will merely give a few illustrative examples of where I think this approach might take us.

From a classical economics point of view DE and TI plans might be thought of as relatively equivalent in that they attach one price to domestic use of a service and another (lower price) to medical tourism use, and merely alter the frame of incentive versus penalty. However, behavior law and economics work on loss aversion and framing effects[80] might suggest that individuals will be biased toward choosing medical tourism if they have a DE- as compared to a TI-type plan, because refusing to do so causes a loss in the former but only the foregoing of a gain in the latter. If this is true, this might justify more robust regulation of DE plan types but not other types of plans. This is not to say that TI plans are themselves not worrisome in terms of bounded rationality. There is research in the auto insurance area suggesting that consumers are irrationally attracted to rebate plans and opt for them, even when other available plans are clearly better for the consumer but are not framed in rebate terms.[81] If this research result carried over to the medical tourism arena, it might lead us to impose some additional restrictions on TI plans as well.

What would more robust regulation of some plan types, say for example DE plans, look like? I think it would have two distinct features:

First, it might mean more forceful use of the channeling interventions discussed above relating to quality and liability for DE-type plans rather than other kinds of plans. For example, we might allow DE plans to incorporate medical tourism only for procedures that are determined to be low risk, or send patients only to facilities that have done a fixed number of that service in the last calendar year, or have documented mortality and morbidity rates meeting a certain standard. It bears emphasizing that channeling is not an either/or but instead admits of degrees. So we might, for example, allow the penalty feature of DE plans to apply to a smaller number of procedures than we would the incentive feature of a TI plan. We might also take inspiration from the PPO statutes discussed above that require quality-management programs, sometimes requiring that a physician lead them. For some plan types but not others we could go further and actually require a governmental member or (in analogy to requirements for institutional review boards that approve research protocols) a preset number of institutionally unaffiliated community members to be part of the review process, and specify various indicia of quality to be used as part of the review process. We could also apply differential amounts of channeling as to legal liability. For example, we could require agreements to arbitrate in DE plans as a mandatory feature, but permit TI plans to either use agreements to arbitrate or

---

[80] *See, e.g.*, Christine Jolls & Cass R. Sunstein, *Debiasing through Law*, 35 J. LEGAL STUD. 199, 205–06 (2006); Daniel Kahneman & Amos Tversky, *Prospect Theory: An Analysis of Decision under Risk*, 47 ECONOMETRICA 263 (1979).

[81] Johnson et al., *supra* note 79, at 43–44.

consent to jurisdiction and forum selection clauses. Again, I do not intend to be definitive about these matters here but merely to show the way in which bounded rationality concerns about certain plan types might lead to graduated level of channeling.

Second, we might want to take inspiration from the HMO and PPO statutes discussed above and try to regulate the size of the incentives offered by various plan types, and also put in place additional levels of state or delegated review. In theory the state insurance system could directly regulate the copays (or other incentive/cost) insurers are allowed to charge for each procedure in both its domestic and medical-tourism variety. This would be quite a tall undertaking for the state as it would be hard to get it right ab initio, and costs for procedures change often, requiring the state to constantly update. More administrable variants could either be modeled on some PPO statutes discussed above that establish maximum fixed disparities in copays (20–25 percent in some PPO statutes), require that the disparity be cost justified, or a hybrid one that sets a presumption that no copay or rebate disparity will exceed a set percent but allows the insurer to justify greater disparities on the ground that they are cost justified. Once again, we might tailor the amount of regulation to the level of concern we have regarding certain plan design types. If we concluded that because of bounded rationality DE plans were more of a concern than TI plans, we might, for example, tolerate a higher amount of cost disparity for the insured patient as between the domestic and medical tourism option in a TI plan than for a DE plan.

In this part of the chapter I have tried to explain the various plan designs, varied bounded rationality problems in insurance choice by consumers, and numerous forms of regulatory interventions we could interpose to manage them. The result is a very complex regulatory design project, highly dependent both on information and political philosophical views. My goal here is not to resolve very much on this front, but instead to show how rich and varied our choices are here and to begin a conversation as to how regulators should approach the regulation of plan design for private health insurance products involving medical tourism.

IV. CONCLUSION

With President Obama's major health care reform, the Affordable Care Act, now being implemented in the United States, albeit with significant political and technical hurdles, there is every reason to think that medical tourism through private health insurance will represent a substantial growth market for medical tourism in the next decade. Indeed it seems likely that this market may overtake the market for U.S. patients paying out-of-pocket in terms of market share. Therefore, all parties involved in medical tourism—patients, providers, accreditors, insurers, home country governments, destination country governments, etc.—need to understand the legal and ethical issues raised by this side of the trade and the way different regulatory structures can shape the market.

As it currently stands, the Affordable Care Act does not pose insurmountable barriers to private insurance plans robustly incorporating medical tourism, though much will depend on the regulations implementing the Act. As I show in this chapter, more problematic for widespread incorporation of medical tourism into private insurance is *state*-level insurance regulation, particularly for non–self-insured-plans, though I have explored California's attempts to enable a regulated market permitting private insurance using medical tourism as a possible starting point. In particular, I have discussed the way in which quality and liability concerns raised in the prior two chapters as to patients paying out-of-pocket raise new concerns but also new regulatory possibilities for medical tourism through private health insurance. Medical tourism through private health insurance also raises the question of whether we need to regulate permissible plan design, with rough analogies to the regulation of HMOs and PPOs in the U.S. domestic health insurance system. I have sketched some possible interventions of this sort and explained why I think the potential for bounded rationality in consumer plan design justifies experimenting with these interventions, graduated based on certain types of plans.

In light of the vast complexity of insurance regulation in the United States, the discussion here—both of problems and solutions—only scratches the surface of potential issues that robust incorporation of medical tourism into private health insurance will raise. I have not, for example, discussed the complex issues relating to payment, third-party administrators, review of denials of benefits, etc. Instead I have focused on more basic legal and ethical issues relating to medical tourism through private health insurance, issues that have thus far not been discussed in any depth in the academic literature on the subject. It is my hope that I and others can build on this discussion to analyze the myriad of new issues that will emerge as medical tourism through private health insurance becomes increasingly common.

5

Medical Tourism through Public Health Insurance: The EU Model and Beyond

IN THE LAST chapter, we saw the challenges and opportunities when private insurers begin to incorporate medical tourism into their plans, focusing on the United States as a laboratory for this experimentation. In this chapter, we move from primarily private systems to primarily public ones and examine what happens when public health care systems deal with medical tourism.[1] I will focus on the European Union (EU), which, for the last three decades, has struggled in setting the rules that dictate when Member States should reimburse their citizens for health care services obtained in another Member State: for example, when a citizen of Luxembourg seeks dental surgery in Germany.

The first part of this chapter gives a brief overview of the different health care systems in the European Union and the primary legal documents enabling cross-border access to care. The second part examines the tangled European Court of Justice (ECJ, now renamed the Court of Justice of the European Union, but I will stick with the more traditional abbreviation) case law interpreting these documents and setting ground rules for reimbursement for cross-border health care. I then examine the new European Directive that has been issued and the numerous legal and ethical issues it leaves open. A final section of this chapter briefly considers possible implementation of medical tourism

---

[1] To be clear, it would be wrong to suggest that the EU systems are completely public, just as it would be wrong to claim that the U.S. system is completely private; both are mixtures, but at very different points on the public-private continuum.

programs in non-EU public health insurance programs, such as Medicaid and Medicare in the United States, taking some of the lessons learned in the EU context as inspiration.

Before delving into that analysis, let me say a word on nomenclature. Instead of "home" and "destination" countries, the terms I have used elsewhere in this book to describe the place where a patient is coming from and going to seek care, I will use the terms "Member State of Affiliation" (which also includes those who reside in a Member State and contribute to its social security system even if they are from a different Member State) and "Member State of Treatment" in the EU context as it reflects the way the courts and legislation in the European Union describe these countries.[2]

I. A BRIEF PRIMER ON CROSS-BORDER HEALTH CARE IN THE EUROPEAN UNION

A. The EU System

Many readers will be unfamiliar with the organization of the European Union and its various forms of legislation, regulation, and judicial bodies. A full exposition is far beyond the scope of this chapter, but in understanding the governance of medical tourism in the system, it is useful to begin with a very general overview.

The European Union has a number of EU level institutions, of which the Commission, the Council, the Parliament, and the European Court of Justice are the most important for our purposes.[3] The Commission is responsible for promoting the general interests of the European Union, and can take appropriate initiatives to do so.[4] It also oversees the application of the Treaties and the application of EU law under the control of the ECJ, and proposes the legislative acts of the EU.[5] The Council and the Parliament are bodies that jointly adopt (or decline to adopt) legislation proposed by the Commission.[6]

---

[2] "Member State of Affiliation" has a technical definition given in the Directive discussed below, though I will also use the term a little more loosely. Still, as a technical matter, the Directive defines the term to mean "the Member State that is competent to grant to the insured person a prior authorisation to receive appropriate treatment in another Member State according to Regulation (EC) No 859/2003 or Regulation (EU) No 1231/2010. If no Member State is competent according to those Regulations, the Member State of affiliation shall be the Member State where the person is insured or has the rights to sickness benefits according to the legislation of that Member State." Directive 2011/24/EU of the European Parliament and of the Council of 9 March 2011 on the Application of Patients' Rights in Cross-Border Healthcare 2011 O.J. (L 88) 45 [hereinafter Directive 2011/24], Art 3(c).

[3] For further information on the institutions of the European Union and their respective roles, see DAMIAN CHALMERS ET AL., EUROPEAN UNION LAW 52–89 (2d ed. 2010); PAUL CRAIG & GRÁINNE DE BÚRCA, E.U. LAW: TEXT, CASES, AND MATERIALS 38–80 (2008); GEORGE BERMANN ET AL., CASES AND MATERIALS ON EUROPEAN UNION LAW 31–72 (3d ed. 2011).

[4] Consolidated Version of the Treaty on European Union, May 9, 2008, 2008 O.J. (C 115) 13 [hereinafter TEU], art. 17(1) & (2).

[5] Id.

[6] Id. art. 14(1) & 16(1).

The EU Treaties are the primary law of the European Union, but the EU institutions have been granted certain competencies to enact secondary legislation. There are three main types of "secondary legislation" that the Council and Parliament can enact: Regulations, Directives, and Decisions.[7] *Regulations* have general application and are immediately binding in their entirety upon all Member States of the European Union.[8] *Directives*, by contrast, are only binding as to the result to be achieved, and leave to the Member States' discretion as to how the Directives' objectives are to be achieved. In practice, Directives are an extremely common form of secondary legislation.[9] In other words, Member States must adopt appropriate domestic legislation to give effect to these Directives within a specific time frame provided by the Directive in question, but the particular legislation they adopt will not be uniform.[10] *Decisions* are immediately binding in their entirety upon Member States to whom they have been addressed.[11]

The ECJ has the duty and jurisdiction to ensure "that in the interpretation and application of the Treaties the law is observed."[12] The ECJ is also responsible for the issuance of preliminary rulings on the interpretation of EU law and the validity of EU legislative acts.[13] Among the key features of the ECJ system are a noncompliance procedure that authorizes the European Commission to challenge national policies that conflict with community rules, and a preliminary reference mechanism that sometimes permits or requires national courts to suspend legal proceedings and send questions of interpretation of community law to the ECJ.[14]

B. EU Health Care Systems

The European Union has no single health care system. Instead, the Member States that make up the European Union retain competency in this area, and each provides health

---

[7] Consolidated Version of the Treaty on the Functioning of the European Union, May 9, 2008, 2008 O.J. (C 115) 47 [hereinafter TFEU], art. 288.

[8] *Id.*

[9] *Id.*

[10] Otherwise put, Directives reflect the "principle of subsidiarity" in EU law, under which "decisions are taken as closely as possible to the citizen and that constant checks are made to verify that action at Union level is justified in light of the possibilities available at national, regional or local level," and the Union does not take action (except in the areas that fall within its exclusive competence) unless it is more effective than action taken at national, regional or local level. Europa, Summaries of EU Legislation, Glossary, Subsidiarity, http://europa.eu/legislation_summaries/glossary/subsidiarity_en.htm (last visited Dec., 2013) . *See also* TEU, Art. 5(3); CHALMERS ET AL., *supra* note 3, at 363–67; CRAIG & DE BÚRCA, *supra* note 3, at 100–05; BERMANN ET AL., *supra* note 3, at 117.

[11] CRAIG & DE BÚRCA, *supra* note 3, at 100–05.

[12] TEU, *supra* note 4, art. 19(1).

[13] TEU, *supra* note 4, art. 19(3)(b).

[14] *See, e.g.,* Karen J. Alter et al., *Transplanting the European Court of Justice: The Experience of the Andean Tribunal of Justice*, 60 AM. J. COMP. L. 629, 632 (2012).

care to its nationals. There are two major types of EU health care systems, but these are best thought of as "ideal types" as in fact every system is to some extent hybridized: In a "Beveridge" system, such as the National Health Service in the United Kingdom, health care is funded by general taxation, and services are directly available to patients, generally at no charge, at the point of service.[15] Ireland, Spain, Italy, Portugal, Greece, Denmark, Finland, and Sweden also use this kind of system.[16] By contrast, in a "Bismarck" system, such as that in place in Germany, health care is funded through social insurance funds that are financed through mandatory wage-based premiums and used to pay health care providers for services provided to citizens.[17]

Bismark systems can further be divided into two types. First, there are benefits-in-kind or restitution schemes, such as those in Germany, Austria, and the Netherlands, wherein the citizen pays into a sickness insurance fund that contracts with providers of health care and pays those providers directly in the event of an insured person requiring health care at one of the institutions with which the fund has contracted.[18] Second, there are reimbursement schemes (for example, those in place in France, Belgium, and Luxembourg) where insured persons choose their own health care provider and must pay any fees incurred themselves before those costs are subsequently reimbursed by the insurance scheme.[19]

These differences between EU health care systems in part explains the popularity of cross-border care: Providers can and do offer a vastly different array of services and technologies from one Member State to another, much more so than between U.S. states, for example. Because patients can move from one kind of system to another in seeking cross-border care, the interactions between these systems for EU medical tourism are potentially quite complex.

It is important to emphasize that nationals of Member States are free to obtain health care in another Member State if paid for privately.[20] Therefore, the key question I will

---

[15] Timothy Stoltzfus Jost, *Managed Care Regulation: Can We Learn from Others? The Chilean Experience*, 32 U. MICH. J.L. REF. 863, 863–64 (1999) (citing JUDITH ALLSOP, HEALTH POLICY AND THE NHS, TOWARDS 2000, at 24–25 (2d ed. 1995)).

[16] Mark Flear, *Developing Euro-Biocitizens through Migration for Healthcare Services*, 14(3) M.J. 239, 244 & n.27 (2007).

[17] Jost, *supra* note 15, at 864 (citing Deborah J. Chollet & Maureen Lewis, *Private Health Insurance: Principles and Practice, in* INNOVATIONS IN HEALTH CARE FINANCING: PROCEEDINGS OF A WORLD BANK CONFERENCE 79 (Mar. 10–11, 1997).

[18] Flear, *supra* note 16, at 244 & n.25.

[19] *Id.* at n.26. Although these two systems continue to exist as broad categories, most modern European health care systems are to some extent hybridized. *See, e.g.*, Jouke van der Zee & Madelon W. Kroneman, *Bismarck or Beveridge: A Beauty Contest between Dinosaurs*, 7 BMC HEALTH SERV. RES. 94 (2007).

[20] Joined Cases 286/82 & 26/83, Luisi & Carbone v. Ministero Del Tesoro, 1984 E.C.R. 00377. *See* Tamara K. Hervey, *The Current Legal Framework on the Right to Seek Health Care, in* THE CAMBRIDGE YEARBOOK OF EUROPEAN LEGAL STUDIES 261, 262 (2007).

focus on in this chapter is when a patient's Member State of Affiliation is required to provide reimbursement for medical tourism to another Member State.

At the highest level, the problem medical tourism presses on the EU system is one of mediating between the sovereignty of Member States to organize their own social security systems—and in particular their conceptions of a right to health care access—with the EU's commitment to the free movement of persons, goods, and capital between the Member States and the freedom to provide and receive services.[21] Understanding how the EU's case law has mediated this tension is relevant not only for understanding one of the largest potential markets for medical tourism, but in thinking about the challenges posed by medical tourism to publicly financed health insurance systems more generally.

II. EU MEDICAL TOURISM BEFORE 2011

This section explains the relevant legislation and case law pertaining to medical tourism prior to the new Directive that was introduced in 2011.

A. Treaty Provisions and Secondary Legislation Relevant to Medical Tourism

The central aim of the EU project was and continues to be economic integration, achieved primarily through the breaking down of barriers, hindrances, or restrictions, to the four fundamental freedoms of the EU internal market[22]—goods, services, persons, and capital.[23] Although the free movement between the Member States of goods, persons, and capital is important in relation to the provision of health care throughout the European Union and for the relevant secondary legislation, it is the freedom to provide and receive services that has been central to the development of the law pertaining to cross-border health care. Specifically, Article 56 of the Treaty on the Functioning of the European Union (TFEU)[24]

---

[21] *See, e.g.*, Robert F. Rich & Kelly R. Merrick, *Cross Border Health Care in the European Union: Challenges and Opportunities*, 23 J. CONTEMP. HEALTH L. & POL'Y 64, 73 (2006).

[22] *See* TEU, *supra* note 4, art. 2 & 3; *see also* CATHERINE BARNARD, THE SUBSTANTIVE LAW OF THE E.U.: THE FOUR FREEDOMS (2010); CHALMERS ET AL., *supra* note 3, at 674–711; CRAIG & DE BÚRCA, *supra* note 3, at 604–873; GEORGE BERMANN ET AL., *supra* note 3, at 419–801.

[23] *See* TFEU, *supra* note 7, art. 26(2) ("The internal market shall comprise an area without internal frontiers in which the free movement of goods, persons, services and capital is ensured in accordance with the provisions of the Treaties.").

[24] The Treaty on the Functioning of the European Union (TFEU) is the most recent in a line of Treaties that have governed the internal market of what was initially the European Economic Community, then the European Community, and what is now the European Union. The Treaty article numbering for the provisions concerning the internal market has changed from Treaty to Treaty. Much of the case law that is referred to in this chapter references the numbering of the earlier Maastricht Treaty, and as amended by the Treaty of Amsterdam. For the sake of consistency, because the provisions are virtually identical in every respect, and as it is the current law, I will adopt the numbering of the TFEU. Also for the sake of consistency, I will use "EU" even when referring to what was previously the European Community. For information on the historical

prohibits restrictions on the freedom to provide cross-border services. The ECJ held that, as a natural corollary, this prohibition was also applicable to restrictions on the freedom to receive services.[25] The ECJ has primarily relied on Article 56 to limit restrictions on cross-border health care, in part because early on in its case law the ECJ held that because health care services are provided for remuneration, even when indirect, health care services are considered services under the TFEU.[26]

According to settled ECJ jurisprudence, EU law is supreme over national legislation, and, therefore, domestic legislation must conform to EU law.[27] At the same time however, under Article 168 of the TFEU "the organization and delivery of health care is considered to fall under the purview of the Member States," such that national rather than EU law deals with the internal management of health care systems and patient's claims of entitlement to particular therapies.[28] Between these two principles lies the chief tension that the EU legislation and ECJ case law on medical tourism seeks to mediate.[29]

The relevant secondary legislation on medical tourism was originally aimed at ensuring the free movement of workers and self-employed persons, along with family members who accompany them.[30] Specifically, Regulation 1408/71 was adopted to facilitate the free movement of these persons within what was then the European Community (now the European Union) by coordinating aspects of national social security systems.[31] Those provisions were later superseded in 2004 by Regulation 883/2004, which expanded the coverage of these laws such that it covered all persons lawfully resident in a Member State of Affiliation, and which went into effect in 2010.[32]

---

development of the European Union and its various Treaties, *see* CHALMERS ET AL., *supra* note 3, at 1–50; CRAIG & DE BÚRCA, *supra* note 3, at 1–34; GEORGE BERMANN ET AL., *supra* note 3, at 3–72.

[25] Cases 286/82 & 26/83, Luisi & Carbone v. Ministero Del Tesoro, 1984 E.C.R. 00377.

[26] Case 352/85, Bond van Adverteerders v. The Netherlands, 1998 E.C.R. 02085.

[27] Case 6/64, Costa v. ENEL, 1964 E.C.R. 585, 586; Case 26/62, N.V. Algemene Transport-en Expeditie Onderneming van Gend & Loos v. Nederlandse Administratie der Belastingen, 1963 E.C.R. 1, 2.

[28] Johan W. Van de Gronden, *Cross-Border Health Care in the EU and the Organization of the National Health Care Systems of the Member States: The Dynamics Resulting from the European Court of Justice's Decisions on Free Movement and Competition Law*, 26(3) WIS. INT. LAW J. 705, 707 (2009).

[29] *See, e.g.*, Case C-158/96, Kohll v. Union des Caisses de Maladie, 1998 E.C.R. I-01931, at I-1942–43, ¶¶ 17–21; Case C-157/99, Geraets-Smits & Peerbooms v. Stichting Ziekenfonds V.G.Z. & Stichting C.Z. Groep Zorgverzekeringen, 2001 ECR I–5509, at I-5526–27, ¶¶ 44–46; Case C-372/04, Watts v. Bedford Primary Care Trust, E.C.R. I–4391, at I-4409, ¶ 92. To put it slightly differently, this might be thought of as an instantiation of a more general tension between economic and social integration in Europe as well as a characterization question: Is health care a market good subject to free movement and competition law and other market-centered law (including ECJ opinions), or a public good existing beyond the EU common market? For this framing, *see* Nathan Cortez, *The Elusive Ideal of Market Competition in U.S. Health Care, in* HEALTH CARE AND EU LAW (J.W. van de Gronden et al. eds., 2011).

[30] *See* Regulation 1408/71 of the Council of 14 June 1971 on the Application of Social Security Schemes to Employed Persons and Their Families Moving within the Community 1971 O.J. (L 149) 2 [hereinafter Regulation 1408/71], art. 2 & 3.

[31] Hervey, *supra* note 20, at 262–63.

[32] Regulation 883/2004, of the European Parliament and of the Council of 29 April 2004 on the Co-ordination of Social Security Systems 2004 O.J. (L 200) 1 [hereinafter Regulation 883/2004].

Prior to the new Directive, there were two parallel frameworks for patients to obtain and be reimbursed for cross-border health care.[33] First, there was the ECJ case law on health care in relation to the freedom to provide and receive services under what is now the TFEU. The second route was through 1408/71 (and the later Regulation 883/2004), the operation of which has been tweaked by the ECJ, which relied on the treaties to further the freedom to provide and receive services throughout the European Union's internal market. Regulation 1408/71 provided for reimbursement for medical tourism to another Member State in two circumstances: for emergency care during a temporary visit to another Member State, and for nonemergency care that I will refer to as "scheduled care." My focus will be on scheduled care, which has engendered a complex case law, but I will much more briefly first discuss the other type of care.

B. Emergency Care during a Temporary Visit to Another Member State

One part of the system set up by Regulation 1408/71 provides for reimbursement for emergency treatment while on a temporary visit to another Member State.[34] This system was originally administered through the E111 system and then later the European health insurance card system.[35]

One might think that cases of medical services needed for emergency care during a temporary visit to another Member State are not truly cases of medical tourism in the sense used in this book as they are incidental to other reasons for travel. However, in light of the European Union's primary law, the ECJ has interpreted this secondary law to give a much broader right, holding that, under the regulation for emergency care, treatment is not limited to the onset of a sudden illness, but also encompasses cases where the patient has a chronic illness or existing pathology known in advance.[36] Although the Court also highlighted the distinction between emergency and planned care,[37] and

---

[33] *See, e.g.,* Case C-56/01, Inizan v. Caisse Primaire d'Assurance Maladie des Hauts-de-Seine, 2003 E.C.R. I-12423, at I-12442, ¶¶ 52–53 ("[N]ational provisions whose purpose is to make reimbursement by the competent institutions of the Member State of residence subject to the conditions applied by them, in respect of health treatment received in another Member State, do not fall within the scope of Article 22 of Regulation No 1408/71…On the other hand, such national provisions, which…may in certain circumstances constitute a barrier to freedom to provide medical services, must be examined…in the light of their consistency with Articles [56] and [57 [TFEU]].").

[34] Regulation 1408/71, *supra* note 30, art. 22(1)(a); Hervey, *supra* note 20, at 263–64.

[35] Hervey, *supra* note 20, at 264.

[36] *See* Case C-326/00, Idryma Koinonikon Asfaliseon v. Vasileios Ioannidis, 2003 E.C.R. I-1725, at I-1747, ¶¶ 40–43. This case concerned the rights of pensioners to obtain emergency treatment in reliance on that legislation, but in keeping with the internal market free-movement agenda of breaking down hindrances and restrictions, this holding was later applied to all those entitled to emergency treatment. *See* DECISION No S3 of 12 June 2009 defining the benefits covered by Articles 19(1) and 27(1) of Regulation (EC) No 883/2004 of the European Parliament and of the Council and Article 25(A)(3) of Regulation (EC) No 987/2009 of the European Parliament and of the Council 2010 (C 106) 10, Recital (3) & art. 1.

[37] Case C-326/00 Ioannidis, *supra* note 36, at I-1742–43, ¶ 26.

subsequent legislation emphasized that emergency coverage is not provided for those who deliberately travel to another Member State with the intention of receiving treatment there,[38] this nevertheless arguably leaves open at least the possibility of "gaming the system" by traveling abroad during an episode of ill health and getting treated while in another Member State.[39]

The ECJ has tried in its case law to dampen the incentive for this kind of travel. In *Commission v. Spain*, a Spanish national required emergency care while in France, and then sought reimbursement from the Spanish government for costs that exceeded what would have been paid in Spain had the treatment occurred there.[40] The ECJ held that the patient could not claim reimbursement from his home state to make up the difference; that is, if the Member State to which he travels charges more than his home state, he cannot ask his home state to pay the difference in the amount payable in the host state and the amount he would have been entitled to in the home state.[41]

The Court was careful to contrast the emergency care sought in this case with scheduled care due to the inadequacy or unavailability of treatment in the home state (that I discuss next), noting that unlike in that category, "the rules of the Treaty on freedom of movement offer no guarantee that all hospital treatment services which may have to be provided to him unexpectedly in the Member State of stay will be neutral in terms of cost," and that "given the disparities between one Member State and another in matters of social security cover and the fact that the objective of Regulation No 1408/71 is to coordinate the national laws but not to harmonise them, the conditions attached to a hospital stay in another Member State may, according to the circumstances, be to the insured person's advantage or disadvantage."[42] Although it recognized that in some cases this reimbursement gap would induce a Spanish national to return "early to Spain in order to receive hospital treatment there which has been made necessary by a deterioration in their health during a temporary stay in another Member State, or to cancel a trip to another Member State—for tourism or study, for example," the ECJ found that effect "too uncertain and indirect" to amount to a restriction on the rights protected by the Regulation and the Treaty.[43] Moreover, it worried that a contrary rule of making the Member State of Affiliation pay the full amount in all cases would ultimately undermine the system,[44] especially given the increasing numbers of persons temporarily

---

[38] *See* Decision No S3, *supra* note 36, art. 2.

[39] The European Observatory on Health Systems and Policies, Cross-Border Health Care in the European Union, 78 (Matthias Wismar et al. eds., 2011), *available at* http://www.euro.who.int/__data/assets/pdf_file/0004/135994/e94875.pdf.

[40] *See* Case C-211/08, Comm'n v. Spain, 2010 E.C.R. I-05267, *available at* http://eur-lex.europa.eu/LexUriServ/LexUriServ.do?uri=CELEX:62008CJ0211:EN:HTML.

[41] *See id.* ¶¶ 72–75.

[42] *Id.* ¶ 61.

[43] *Id.* ¶ 72.

[44] *Id.* ¶¶ 76 & 79.

staying in other Member States for a variety of purposes, such as for pleasure tourism or study.[45]

C. Scheduled Care in Another Member State

Regulation 1408/71 also introduced a regime governing reimbursement for nonemergency care, calling it "scheduled" care received in a Member State other than the patient's home country.[46] Under that Regulation, Member States of Affiliation may not refuse the grant of prior authorization "where the treatment in question is among the benefits provided for by the legislation of the Member State on whose territory the person concerned resided and where he cannot be given such treatment within the time normally necessary for obtaining the treatment in question in the Member State of residence taking account of his current state of health and the probable course of the disease."[47] As we will see, the ECJ relied on the treaties to further limit the circumstances in which Member States could refuse to grant prior authorization. Member States also provided for cross-border health care in certain circumstances according to their relevant legislation, and much of the ECJ's jurisprudence grapples with whether these provisions are compatible with the Treaty.

Individuals seeking scheduled care in another Member State raised a series of questions that the ECJ ultimately tried to answer: Was prior authorization by one's Member State of Affiliation a prerequisite for later reimbursement for medical tourism for services sought in another state? To what services would this apply? At what level would the Member State of Affiliation be required to reimburse—its own level or the level of the Member State of Treatment where treatment was provided? This section will explain how it has answered each of those questions.

I will begin my discussion of the ECJ's medical tourism case law for scheduled care in 1998 with the *Kohll* case, though there are certainly earlier ones as well. In *Kohll v. Union des Caisses de Maladie,* a Luxembourg national had requested that his daughter receive treatment from a German orthodontist, but his request was denied prior authorization by Luxembourg on the ground that her treatment could be provided in Luxembourg and was not of an urgent nature.[48] The key question faced by the ECJ was whether the

---

[45] *Id.* ¶ 76.

[46] Regulation 1408/71, *supra* note 30, art. 22(1)(c).

[47] *Id.* art 22(2). *See also* Regulation 883/2004, art. 20(2) ("[A]uthorisation shall be accorded where the treatment in question is among the benefits provided for by the legislation in the Member State where the person concerned resides and where he/she cannot be given such treatment within a time which is medically justifiable, taking into account his/her current state of health and the probable course of his/her illness.").

[48] Case C-158/96, Kohll v. Union des Caisses de Maladie, 1998 E.C.R. I-01931. In another early case, *Decker v. Caisse de Maladies des Employes Prives,* a Luxembourg citizen sought reimbursement for glasses purchased in Belgium based on the prescription of a Luxembourg opthamologist, and made the purchase without prior authorization for the purchase from Luxembourg. Case C-120/95, Decker v. Caisse de Maladie des Employés

pre-authorization requirements of Member State health care systems for care abroad were subject to the freedom of movement provisions of the Treaty.[49]

The ECJ stressed that each Member State had the freedom to regulate and organize its own social security system, but to the extent the organization of one's health care system impacts the freedom of movement within the European Union, the discretion accorded to the Member State must bend to the right to freedom of movement unless justified by a derogation permitted by the Treaty or an overriding reason in the general interest, as is the ECJ approach in all cases where Member State legislation conflicts with the treaties.[50] Speaking specifically to the question of prior authorization, the ECJ found that requiring prior authorization discouraged patients from seeking care outside of the Member State, that this constituted a barrier to the free movement of patients, and that this barrier could not be justified on the basis of either a Treaty derogation on grounds of public health concerns or an "overriding reason" relating to the financial stability of the Member State of Affiliation's social welfare system.[51] It found that Luxembourg had not established that prior authorization was needed to provide a balanced medical and hospital service accessible to all or that it was "indispensable for the maintenance of an essential treatment facility or medical service on national territory."[52]

The court further held that Regulation 1408/71, which ordinarily provides for reimbursement according to the tariffs in the state where care was provided, does not prevent reimbursement at the tariff of the Member State of Affiliation in the absence of prior authorization.[53]

While *Kohll* established the general principles about freedom of movement's encroachment on the freedom to control authorization of reimbursement for medical tourism, it left a series of questions open, namely: (1) Did the holding of *Kohll* apply to both the benefit-in-kind and reimbursement type health care systems in place in some EU Member States; (2) Did its holding apply only to outpatient services, or to hospitalization services as well; and (3) Does the patient's Member State of Affiliation have to reimburse only what it would have paid had the procedure taken place at home, or does it have to pay the Member State of Treatment's reimbursement rate?[54] Subsequent cases answered each of these questions.

Privés, 1998 E.C.R. I-1871. The ECJ's holding in *Decker* is largely in line with *Kohll*, but because it is the rare case in this jurisprudence that involves the provision of health care goods, not services, I will focus on *Kohll*.

[49] Rich & Merrick, *supra* note 21, at 80.

[50] Case C-158/96, Kohll, *supra* note 48, at I-1942–43, ¶¶ 17–19 & I-1946–50, ¶¶ 37–53; Rich & Merrick, *supra* note 21, at 80. *See also* THE EUROPEAN OBSERVATORY ON HEALTH SYSTEMS AND POLICIES, *supra* note 39, at 25.

[51] C-158/96, Kohll, *supra* note 48, I-1945–50, ¶¶ 29–54; Rich & Merrick, *supra* note 21, at 81.

[52] C-158/96, Kohll, *supra* note 48, at I-1950, ¶ 52; Panos Koutrakos, *Healthcare as an Economic Service under EC Law, in* SOCIAL WELFARE AND EU LAW 105, 107 (Michael Dougan & Eleanor Spaventa eds., 2005).

[53] C-158/96, Kohll, *supra* note 48, at I-1944, ¶ 27; Rich & Merrick, *supra* note 21, at 81.

[54] Rich & Merrick, *supra* note 21, at 81.

In 2001, the ECJ decided the combined cases of *Geraets-Smits v. Stichting Ziekenfonds* and *Peerbooms v. Stichting CZ Groep Zorgverzekeringen.*[55] Smits, a Netherlands national, without prior authorization received treatment for Parkinson's disease from a German clinic that specialized in the treatment, paid the clinic directly, and then sought reimbursement from the Netherlands Sickness fund.[56] Peerbooms, also a Netherlands national, received without prior authorization neurological treatment in Austria that was available in the Netherlands only on a restricted experimental basis, also paid directly, and sought reimbursement from the sickness fund.[57] In both cases the sickness fund refused to reimburse the patients.

The ECJ followed the approach of *Kohll* and found that even though the Netherlands had a benefit-in-kind health system—which meant that patients were entitled to receive health services only from providers with which their sickness fund had contracted with in advance—that the requirement of prior authorization remained a barrier on the freedom to provide services under the Treaty, so that the principles behind *Kohll* applied to benefit-in-kind systems as well.[58]

Although this element of the holding favored medical tourists, the court did recognize some differences between the inpatient hospital services that were at issue in these cases (as opposed to the outpatient services at issue in *Kohll*). The ECJ noted that compared to "medical services provided by practitioners in their surgeries or at the patient's home, medical services provided in a hospital take place within an infrastructure with ... certain very distinct characteristics ... for which planning must be possible."[59] It acknowledged the serious risk of undermining the Member States' social security systems' financial balance if no prior authorization requirement were permitted for inpatient care, and viewed this as a plausible "overriding reason in the general interest capable of justifying a barrier to the principle of freedom to provide services."[60] The Court also recognized that the objective of maintaining a balanced medical and hospital service open to all could "fall within the derogations on grounds of public health" under Article 62 of the TFEU.[61] Under the Treaty derogation, Member States could also be permitted "to restrict the freedom to provide medical and hospital services in so far as the maintenance of treatment capacity or medical competence on national territory is essential for the public health."[62] In particular, the Court was worried that "if insured persons were at

---

[55] Case C-157/99, B.S.M. Geraets-Smits v. Stichting Ziekenfonds VGZ & H.T.M. Peerbooms v. Stichting CZ Groep Zorgverzekeringen, 2001 E.C.R. I-5509.

[56] *Id.* at I-5520, ¶ 25.

[57] *Id.* at I-5522, ¶¶ 31–33.

[58] Case C-157/99, B.S.M. Geraets-Smits, at I-5524–43, ¶¶ 40–108; Rich & Merrick, *supra* note 21, at 82; van der Gronden, *supra* note 29, at 711.

[59] Case C-157/99, B.S.M. Geraets-Smits, at I-5534, ¶ 76.

[60] *Id.* at I-5533, ¶ 72.

[61] *Id.* at I-5533, ¶ 73.

[62] *Id.* at I-5533, ¶ 74.

liberty, regardless of the circumstances, to use the services of hospitals with which their sickness insurance fund had no contractual arrangements, whether they were situated in the Netherlands or in another Member State, all the planning which goes into the contractual system in an effort to guarantee a rationalized, stable, balanced and accessible supply of hospital services would be jeopardized at a stroke."[63] That is, if Member States started to lose or gain a substantial number of medical tourists, they have claimed and the ECJ has feared that it would disrupt their ability to allocate scarce health care resources as these fluctuations cannot be well forecasted in advance.

Nevertheless, the ECJ re-emphasized that any restriction on the freedom to provide services must be justifiable and proportionate.[64] As Robert F. Rich and Kelly R. Merrick put it, the ECJ suggested that the freedom to provide services could only be trumped by "(1)...overriding reasons relating to the general interest and are applied to all persons or undertakings pursuing those activities in the territory of the State in question, in so far as that interest is not safeguarded by the provisions to which the Community national is subject in the Member State where he is established; (2) are necessary to ensure that the objective they pursue is attained; and (3) do not go beyond what is necessary to attain that objective."[65] For a prior authorization scheme to be justified, the ECJ said, it must "be based on objective, non-discriminatory criteria which are known in advance, in such a way as to circumscribe the exercise of the national authorities' discretion, so that it is not used arbitrarily."[66] It also pointed out that such a scheme must "be based on a procedural system which is easily accessible and capable of ensuring that a request for authorisation will be dealt with objectively and impartially within a reasonable time and refusals to grant authorisation must also be capable of being challenged in judicial or quasi-judicial proceedings."[67] For a scheme to be proportionate, the Court emphasized that such restrictions on the freedom to provide services must "not exceed what is objectively necessary...and that the same result cannot be achieved by less restrictive rules."[68] The Netherlands's scheme had a prior authorization requirement that the treatment sought had to be normal in professional circles, but in determining what was normal treatment, the Court refused to look only at national mores but instead said the right benchmark was what was "sufficiently tried and tested by international medical science."[69] Such an approach would be more proportionate in accommodating the interest in maintaining "an adequate, balanced and permanent supply of hospital care

---

[63] Id. at I-5535, ¶ 81; Rich & Merrick, supra note 21, at 83.

[64] Case C-157/99, B.S.M. Geraets-Smits, at I-5534, ¶ 75 & at I-5535, ¶ 82.

[65] Rich & Merrick, supra note 21, at 82–83.

[66] Case C-157/99, B.S.M. Geraets-Smits, at I–5537, ¶ 90.

[67] Id.

[68] Id. at I-5534, ¶ 75.

[69] Id. at I–5539, ¶ 94.

on national territory and [] ensur[ing] the financial stability of the sickness insurance system."[70]

In understanding when medical tourism was necessary, the ECJ held that authorization could only be refused where "the same or equally effective treatment can be obtained without undue delay from an establishment with which the insured person's sickness insurance fund has contractual arrangements."[71] Further, to determine whether treatment could be provided in the Netherlands without undue delay, it was necessary "to have regard to all the circumstances of each specific case and to take due account not only of the patient's medical condition at the time when authorisation is sought but also of his past record."[72] This approach was subsequently followed in later cases.[73] Despite the *Kohll* holding that prior authorization for non-hospital care could not be justifiable, in a later case, *Commission v. France*, the ECJ tempered this by recognizing that prior authorization may be justified for non-hospital care that utilized "major medical equipment."[74]

Geraets-Smits answered the question of whether the patient's Member State of Affiliation was required to reimburse the patient for hospital care in another Member State without pre-authorization at all. In *Vanbraekel v. Alliance Nationale des Mutualités Chrétiennes*, the ECJ turned to the question of which country's reimbursement rate should govern, that of the Member State of Affiliation or of Treatment?[75] In that case, Jeanne Descamps, a Belgian national, was denied prior authorization from her sickness fund to get orthopedic surgery in France.[76] She went ahead and got the surgery anyway, and after a legal battle in the national courts brought by her heirs, it was determined that the treatment could be better performed in France than in Belgium, but that left open the question of which Member State's reimbursement rate governed—Belgium or France's?[77] The ECJ noted that, *under Regulation 1408/71*, the reimbursement rate of the

---

[70] *Id.* at I–5539, ¶ 97.

[71] *Id.* at I–5541, ¶ 103.

[72] *Id.* at I–5541, ¶ 104.

[73] *See* Case C-385/99, Muller-Fauré & Van Riet v. Onderlinge Waarborgmaatschappij O.Z. Zorgverzekeringen, 2003 E.C.R. I–4539, at I-4569, ¶¶ 84–85 & I-4571, ¶ 90. That said, the ECJ has not always adhered to the same specific language for what can be considered to be without undue delay. In *Inizan,* another case in which its findings regarding prior authorization for medical tourism for hospital care were upheld, the Court stated that the patient's Member State of Affiliation is to "have regard to all the circumstances of each specific case and to take due account not only of the patient's medical condition at the time when authorisation is sought and, where appropriate, of the degree of pain or the nature of the patient's disability which might, for example, make it impossible or extremely difficult for him to carry out a professional activity, but also of his medical history." Case C-56/01, Inizan v. Caisse Primaire d'Assurance Maladie des Hauts-de-Seine, 2003 E.C.R. I–12439.

[74] Case C-512/08, Comm'n v. France, 2010 E.C.R. 00000, *available at* http://eur-lex.europa.eu/LexUriServ/LexUriServ.do?uri=CELEX:62008CJ0512:EN:HTML.

[75] Case C-368/98, Abdon Vanbraekel and Others v. Alliance Nationale des Mutualités Chrétiennes, 2001-7 E.C.R. I-5382.

[76] *Id.* at I-5391, ¶¶ 11–13.

[77] *Id.* at I-5391–93, ¶¶ 14–19.

Member State of Treatment applies.[78] What if the patient's Member State of Affiliation (Belgium) had a higher level of reimbursement than the Member State where the procedure was performed (France)? The court held that, *under the Treaty*, "if the reimbursement of costs incurred on hospital services provided in a Member State of stay, calculated under the rules in force in that State, is less than the amount which application of the legislation in force in the Member State of registration would afford to a person receiving hospital treatment in that State, additional reimbursement covering that difference must be granted to the insured person by the competent institution."[79]

Thus, the reimbursement rule that emerges out of the case is "heads I win, tails you lose" for the patient: up to the level of costs incurred,[80] the patient is entitled to whichever reimbursement rate is higher, the home or Member State of Treatment's. Put another way, *Vanbraekel* established that "the EU regime on free movement not only entitled EU

---

[78] *Id.* at 5397, ¶ 32; *see also* Gareth Davies, *The Effect of Mrs. Watts' Trip to France on the National Health Service*, 18 K.C.L.J. 158, 164 (2007).

[79] Case C-368/98, Abdon Vanbraekel and Others at 5403, ¶ 53.

[80] There appears to be some disagreement between EU law scholars on how this aspect of the *Vanbraekel* case should be interpreted. Rich, Merrick, and Koutrakos adopt a broad reading and hold the view that where the Member State of Affiliation reimbursement rate is higher than that of the Member State of Treatment, the patient should be reimbursed at the Member State of Affiliation rate even where this exceeds the actual costs incurred. *See* Rich & Merrick, *supra* note 21, at 84 ("Hypothetically, if Ms. Z, a resident of the United Kingdom, travels to Spain for medically necessary surgery, she would be entitled to reimbursement at the UK rates of reimbursement, even if the cost of her surgery in Spain was lower than the UK rates of reimbursement."). *See* Koutrakos, *supra* note 52, at 112 ("[T]he [Member State of Affiliation] should provide additional reimbursement to patients who receive medical services in another Member State where the cost of the services in question is lower than that in the [Member State of Affiliation]."). However, Rich, Merrick, and Koutrakos may be confusing reimbursement with actual costs here. The case did not address costs, but only reimbursement rates. Although the patient would not have incurred any costs at home in Belgium, the patient was left with an amount to pay after receiving treatment in France. The Court held that where the reimbursement rate of the Member State of Treatment rate is lower than that of the Member State of Affiliation, the patient should be entitled to the rate of the Member State of Affiliation. It did not, however, say that this should be above the level of actual costs incurred. There is no mention of actual costs being lower in France, only that the reimbursement rate was lower. Thus, the case is also susceptible to the more narrow reading that this "complimentary reimbursement" is applicable only up to the level of costs actually incurred. *See* CHALMERS ET AL., *supra* note 3, at 817 ("[T]he Court has noted that Member States are free to define the scope of healthcare for which their system will pay, and the rates that they will pay. Provided they do this in a non discriminatory, transparent and rational way, the existence of a defined health package will not in itself contravene Article 56 [TFEU]. These limits then apply equally to treatment abroad, so that the cost risk is avoided. If states determined that a hip operation costs €3,000 in their domestic system, they may, for example, rule that they will pay a maximum of €3,000 for the same operation abroad. They must not have a lower reimbursement tariff for foreign treatment, but it need not be higher."); *see also* Paul Quinn & Paul de Hert, *The European Patients' Rights Directive: A Clarification and Codification of Individual Rights Relating to Cross Border Healthcare and Novel Initiatives Aimed at Improve Pan-European Healthcare Cooperation*, 12(1) MED. L. INT'L 1, 37 (2012) (suggesting that the rule of *Vanbraekel* is that "[t]he Member State of Residence does not…have to reimburse more than the cost of the treatment"). It seems that the narrow interpretation is more likely correct, and that reimbursement is only up to the level of costs actually incurred, as the broader interpretation would mean that patients would end up with extra cash in their back pockets, which does not seem plausibly to be what the ECJ intended.

nationals to receive medical treatment in other Member States, but it was also capable of interfering with the national rules on the financing of health care treatment."[81]

One final case completes the core of this jurisprudence: *Watts v. Bedford Primary Care Trust*.[82] In *Watts*, a British patient associated with the United Kingdom's National Health Service (NHS) sought hospital treatment in France for a hip replacement to avoid a local British waiting list.[83] She sought prior authorization, but was denied that authorization because she would be able to have her surgery in the United Kingdom within one year's time, which was not considered an "undue delay" under the NHS target waiting time.[84] After her health further deteriorated, she was moved up in priority in the United Kingdom to three to four months of waiting time, but she still traveled to France to have surgery more imminently.[85] She subsequently sought and was denied reimbursement for her surgery in France.[86]

The ECJ held that Watts's case fell under the freedom to provide services and that a Member State cannot deny prior authorization merely because the patient would receive treatment there within a government-mandated waiting period.[87] Instead, the Court held that "[a] refusal to grant prior authorisation cannot be based merely on the existence of waiting lists intended to enable the supply of hospital care to be planned and managed on the basis of predetermined general clinical priorities, without carrying out an objective medical assessment of the patient's medical condition, the history and probable course of his illness, the degree of pain he is in and/or the nature of his disability at the time when the request for authorisation was made or renewed."[88]

When it came to reimbursement, the ECJ held that, under the Treaty, even if the treatment was available free of cost in her Member State of Affiliation under the NHS, Watts was entitled to reimbursement at the rate provided in the Member State of Affiliation, such that the State "must reimburse that patient the difference (if any) between the cost, objectively quantified, of equivalent treatment in a hospital covered by [that State] up to the total amount invoiced for the treatment received in the [Member State of Treatment]."[89] Does this mean that, under the Treaty framework, the Member State of Affiliation is always obliged to reimburse the full costs of treatment incurred in a Member State of Treatment? Here, the ECJ held that the difference does not have to

[81] Van de Gronden, *supra* note 28, at 719.

[82] Case C-372/04, Watts v. Bedford Primary Care Trust, 2006 E.C.R. I-4376.

[83] *Id.* at I-4387–89, ¶¶ 24–32.

[84] *Id.*

[85] *Id.*

[86] *Id.*

[87] *Id.* at I-4415, ¶119.

[88] *Id.*

[89] *Id.* at I-4423, ¶ 143.

be reimbursed where "the cost of that treatment is greater than the cost of equivalent treatment" in the Member State of Affiliation.[90]

As for the reimbursement for any related travel and accommodation costs, the Court held that the right conferred on patients is to have access to treatment "in another Member State on conditions...as favourable as those enjoyed by patients covered by the legislation of that other State."[91] This meant that, for hospital treatment, the Member State of Affiliation should reimburse the "inextricably linked costs relating to the patient's stay in the hospital for the purposes of his treatment" as would be covered by an insured person in that state.[92] As for "ancillary costs, such as the cost of travel and any accommodation other than in the hospital itself," where such costs are covered for persons within the Member State of Affiliation, then they should be covered for persons traveling to another Member State for treatment.[93]

Therefore, at the end of this sequence of cases, the ECJ had established the following principles for medical tourism for scheduled care:

- Prior authorization requirements constitute a restriction on the freedom to provide and receive services—freedoms protected by the Treaty—and thus must be examined for conformity with that freedom.
- Prior authorization requirements are not justified in the context of non-hospital (outpatient) treatments, excepting care involving the use of major medical equipment.
- Where the same or equally effective treatment is available without undue delay in the Member State of Affiliation, prior authorization requirements may be justified for hospital (inpatient) treatments, because requiring the Member State of Affiliation to pay for these services without prior authorization constitutes a much greater threat to its ability to fund and organize its internal health care system.
- Where prior authorization schemes are acceptable, they must be done in an objective and transparent manner. As the ECJ put it, they must be based on "objective, non discriminatory criteria which are known in advance, in such a way so as to circumscribe the exercise of the national authorities' discretion so that it is not used arbitrarily....Such a prior administrative authorisation scheme must likewise be...dealt with objectively and impartially within a

---

[90] *Id.* at I-4421, ¶ 132. In fact, as I explain in the main text, the rule varies depending on whether a reimbursement is sought under the Regulation or the Treaty. For a useful discussion of this complicated issue, *see generally* Davies, *supra* note 78.

[91] Case C-372/04, Watts, at I-4421, ¶ 135.

[92] *Id.* at I-4421, ¶ 136.

[93] *Id.* at I-4422–23, ¶¶ 137– 42; *see also* Case C-8/02, Leichtle v. Bundesanstalt für Arbeit, 2004 E.C.R. I-2641, *available at* http://eur-lex.europa.eu/LexUriServ/LexUriServ.do?uri=CELEX:62002CJ0008:EN :HTML.

reasonable time and refusals to grant authorisation must also be capable of being challenged in a judicial or quasi-judicial environment."[94]

- Under the Regulations, as interpreted in light of the Treaty, where these two conditions are met (where the treatment in question is among the benefits provided for by the legislation of the Member State of Affiliation and where he/she cannot be given such treatment within a time which is medically justifiable) and the patient has been granted prior authorization or was unlawfully refused such authorization, he or she is entitled to reimbursement at the level of the Member State of Treatment. Where that level of reimbursement is lower than he or she would be entitled to from the Member State of Affiliation, he or she is additionally entitled to the difference in reimbursement up to the level of actual costs incurred.
- Under the Treaty provisions for the freedom to provide and receive services, as interpreted by the ECJ, the patient is entitled to be reimbursed to the level that her Member State of Affiliation would have reimbursed up to the level of costs actually incurred had the patient been treated at home. This means that, unlike under the Regulations, where the costs of treatment are higher in the Member State of Treatment, the patient will be left to contribute the difference.

Despite the systematic way in which the ECJ constructed this jurisprudence and these rules, it nevertheless left open a series of ambiguities that made the case law difficult to apply in some contexts. Let me single out two of them:

First, there was the line between hospital and non-hospital services that, although clear in theory, was obscure in practice. For example, what to do about an outpatient who, while "not 'staying in a hospital,' may be undergoing complicated and expensive procedures"?[95] Was prior authorization only applicable to those involving treatments that used major medical equipment? When would the equipment be considered to be sufficiently "major" to justifiably permit a prior authorization requirement? There was a sense in which the hospital/non-hospital line was an imperfect proxy for the matter the ECJ was really getting at: the risk of putting too much financial strain or interference on the patient's Member State of Affiliation with an obligation to reimburse without prior authorization for these treatments. Although hospital settings tend to be more expensive, the fit is imperfect. Though the ECJ made several attempts to add more nuance here in its cases, the case law still engendered significant confusion. Second, under what circumstances could the Member State of Affiliation impose pretreatment procedures as a condition of reimbursement for medical tourism, such as prior assessment by a health professional?[96] At a more practical level, as Vassilis Hatzopoulos and Tamara Hervey

---

[94] Case C-157/99, Geraets-Smits, at I-5537, ¶ 90; *see also* Quinn & de Hert, *supra* note 80, at 37.

[95] Quinn & de Hert, *supra* note 80, at 36.

[96] *Id.* at 13.

noted, many Southern European countries resisted the ECJ case law while others, such as France, did so "until recently."[97]

III. THE POST-2011 LANDSCAPE: THE NEW EU DIRECTIVE

The new EU Directive 2011/24 (hereinafter "The Directive") purports to facilitate cross-border health care in the European Union, primarily in regard to the "scheduled care" case rather than the "emergency care" one. Indeed, the Directive makes explicit that the Regulation 883/2004 regime discussed remains in place and is not displaced by the Directive.[98] As we shall see, how much the Directive really achieves its purported aim versus protected national interests and concerns, is very much an open question.

The Directive recognizes that Member States have exclusive responsibility for the organization and delivery of health care, and on the definition of social security benefits.[99] The Directive takes into consideration the "operating principles" that are shared by health systems throughout the Union, and are necessary to ensure patients' trust in cross-border health care and to achieving patient mobility.[100]

Member States are required to "transpose" (i.e., put into effect) the Directive by October 25, 2013,[101] such that it will be some time before we can fully evaluate the scheme.

The Directive is applicable to the provision of health care "regardless of how it is organized, delivered and financed."[102] Health care is defined as "health services provided by health professionals to patients to assess, maintain or restore their state of health, including the prescription, dispensation and provision of medicinal products and medical devices."[103] The Directive is inapplicable to long-term care services that are aimed at supporting people in need of assistance in carrying out everyday tasks, as well as the allocation of and access to organs for the purpose of organs transplant.[104]

The Directive focuses on four topics. The first three are familiar from the EU case law: Prior Authorization, Reimbursement, and Patient Rights. It also provides a number of new initiatives that I group under the heading "Cooperation." I discuss these one by one. The cooperation measures, along with some of the patient rights measures (which

---

[97] Vassilis Hatzopoulos & Tamara Hervey, *Coming into Line: The EU's Court Softens on Cross-Border Health Care*, 10 HEALTH ECON. 1, 2 (2012).

[98] Directive 2011/24, *supra* note 2, Art. 7(1). *See also* Quinn & de Hert, *supra* note 80, at 20.

[99] Directive 2011/24, *supra* note 2, Recitals (10), (33), (35) & (64).

[100] *Id*. Recital (5).

[101] *Id*. art. 21.

[102] *Id*. art. 1(2).

[103] *Id*. art. 3(a).

[104] *Id*. art. 1(3)(a) & (b). That said, the actual reimbursement for the surgical costs of the transplant appear to be within the Directive's ambit, just not the actual availability of organs and their allocation.

extend beyond what the ECJ has done) hold the potential to reshape cross-border care in Europe and force more cooperative structures,[105] but much will depend on interpretation and how it is implemented.

A. Prior Authorization

At the threshold, the Directive answers one of the questions left open by the ECJ case law regarding the ability to impose pretreatment requirements, such as assessment by a health professional or health care administrator. The Member State of Affiliation is permitted to impose a pretreatment requirement as a condition of reimbursement for medical tourism if it would require the same pretreatment procedure to reimburse the same patient within its territory.[106]

Apart from the question of pretreatment requirements, Article 8 of the Directive regulates the conditions in which the process of prior authorization may take place. The Directive largely codifies the criteria that the ECJ had developed in this regard.

The Directive recognizes that the Member State "of Affiliation may provide for a system of prior authorization,"[107] but in accord with the ECJ case law we discussed, also recognizes that such a prior authorization system can serve as a barrier to the freedom to provide medical services. Therefore, following the ECJ case law, the Directive requires that prior authorization must be justified and restricted to what is necessary and proportionate to the objective to be achieved (e.g., financial balance of social security budget, needs for planning, etc.), and may not constitute a means of arbitrary discrimination or unjustified obstacle to the free movement of patients.[108]

The Directive specifies the type of conditions that may justify the establishment of a system of prior authorization,[109] as well as the criteria that have to be met in order to make a refusal of the authorization lawful.[110]

In terms of the conditions justifying prior authorization, the Directive provides that prior authorization is limited to health care that:

(a)   is made subject to planning requirements relating to the object of ensuring sufficient and permanent access to a balanced range of high-quality treatment

---

[105] *See, e.g.*, Miek Peeters, *Free Movement of Patients: Directive 2011/24 on the Application of Patients' Rights in Cross-Border Healthcare*, 19 Eur. J. Health L. 29, 51 (2012).

[106] Directive 2011/24, *supra* note 2, art. 7(7); Quinn & De Hert, *supra* note 80, at 48. There is also a special regime set.

[107] Directive 2011/24, *supra* note 2, art. 8(1).

[108] *Id.* art. 8(1).

[109] *Id.* art. 8(2).

[110] *Id.* art. 8(6).

in the Member State concerned or to the wish to control costs and avoid, as far as possible, any waste of financial, technical and human resources and:
  (i) involves overnight hospital accommodation of the patient in question for at least one night; or
  (ii) requires use of highly specialised and cost-intensive medical infrastructure or medical equipment;
(b) involves treatments presenting a particular risk for the patient or the population; or
(c) is provided by a healthcare provider that, on a case-by-case basis, could give rise to serious and specific concerns relating to the quality or safety of the care, with the exception of healthcare which is subject to Union legislation ensuring a minimum level of safety and quality throughout the Union.[111]

One major advantage of the Directive over the ECJ case law is in answering the question I raised above about what to do regarding an outpatient who, although "not 'staying in a hospital,' may be undergoing complicated and expensive procedures." The Directive embraces the concern raised by the Member States as to the effect on their budget and health policy planning by providing that prior authorization requirements may be put in place for non-hospital overnight care that nonetheless requires highly specialized equipment.

Additionally, under the Directive, Member States will have to provide the Commission with a listing of the categories of health care they determine are subject to these planning requirements.[112] The European Commission, in its proposal for a Directive, had indicated that it would assume the task of elaborating and updating such a list. Member States opposed this approach, suggesting that it would be a breach of the subsidiarity principle. The view of the Member States (represented in the Council of the European Union) prevailed in the final text of the Directive, and the final version provides that the Member States will be the ones to make these lists, but will have to notify the European Commission. One of the results of the adoption of this version of the Directive is it means that it will only be possible to assess whether the Directive has achieved its goal of generating objective and stable criteria for prior authorization of medical tourism once the Member States have constructed and shared their lists.[113]

As constructed by the Directive, these categories for which prior authorization is allowed leave Member States with considerable room to maneuver. For example, it gives Member States latitude in deciding what constitutes major medical equipment in a way that reflects the budgetary constraints of individual Member States.[114] The language regarding "particular risk for the patient or the population" allows Member States of

---

[111] *Id.* art. 8(2).
[112] *Id.*
[113] *See* Peeters, *supra* note 105, at 37.
[114] Quinn & Hert, *supra* note 80, at 56.

Affiliation to require authorization for those with drug-resistant TB or other highly infectious diseases to travel, as well as for those whose unstable condition makes medical tourism a risk to their own health.[115] The language regarding "quality or safety of care" may prove the most malleable, as it enables the Member State of Affiliation to apply prior authorization requirements whenever it is "concerned" that the foreign care is less safe or efficacious, except in cases where the service in question "is subject to Union legislation ensuring a minimum level of safety and quality throughout the Union."[116] To be sure, this requirement is in some senses laudable, in that it reflects the kind of pre-screening for quality and safety I have urged U.S. regulators to incorporate as part of the "channeling" regimes I have discussed in Chapter 3 and elsewhere. It remains to be seen, however, whether Member State of Affiliations use this element of the Directive for that purpose rather than to dampen medical tourism within the European Union.

In cases where *prior* authorization is used, Article 8(6) of the Directive provides that the Member State of Affiliation may refuse to grant its prior authorization if:

(a) the patient will, according to a clinical evaluation, be exposed with reasonable certainty to a patient-safety risk that cannot be regarded as acceptable, taking into account the potential benefit for the patient of the sought cross- border healthcare;

(b) the general public will be exposed with reasonable certainty to a substantial safety hazard as a result of the cross-border healthcare in question;

(c) this healthcare is to be provided by a healthcare provider that raises serious and specific concerns relating to the respect of standards and guidelines on quality of care and patient safety, including provisions on supervision, whether these standards and guidelines are laid down by laws and regulations or through accreditation systems established by the Member State of treatment;

(d) this healthcare can be provided on its territory within a time limit which is medically justifiable, taking into account the current state of health and the probable course of the illness of each patient concerned.[117]

The first three exemptions give the home state latitude to deny authorization for tourism for experimental treatments, or in cases where there are quality-of–health care risks associated with travel. The last exemption reflects the kind of situation faced by the ECJ in *Watts*. Two points of interpretation, which may very well arise in the future, are worth highlighting. Clause (c)'s statement that standards or guidelines could be laid "down by

---

[115] *Id.*

[116] As Peeters observes, it is unclear what the Directive's mention of "Union legislation ensuring a minimum level of safety and quality throughout the Union" refers to, and suggests it most likely is meant to capture "possible future European legislation, providing a minimum harmonisation of quality and safety criteria of medical services." Peeters, *supra* note 105, at 38.

[117] Directive 2011/24, *supra* note 2, art. 8(6).

laws and regulations or through accreditation systems established by the Member State of treatment" would seem by an *expressio uno* type reading to exclude something such as the JCI accreditation system we discussed earlier in this book, as it is not an accreditation system actually "established by the Member State of treatment." Further, the relationship of this language to experimental therapies, such as the stem cell treatments I discuss in Chapter 10, may, perhaps unintentionally, constrain Member States more than was intended: clauses (a), (b), and (c) seem to require "reasonable certainty" regarding patient safety or other forms of risk and/or "raises serious and specific concerns relating to the respect of standards and guidelines on quality of care and patient safety," but that kind of grounded data may not be available for therapies that are brand new.

Paul Quinn and Paul de Hert argue that this part of the Directive has been drafted so "widely" that it actually represents a divergence from the ECJ case law and threatens to undermine the Directive's goal of more free movement for health care altogether.[118] More specifically, because it is "likely that the vast majority of procedures available in another Member State will also be available in the Member State of Affiliation within a suitable timeframe," the fourth exemption means that "unless there are administrative issues unjustifiably delaying an individual's treatment," it is very likely that the Member State of Affiliation can deny authorization.[119] Further, the exemption presents patients with a kind of "catch-22," in that if a treatment is *not* normally available in the Member State of Affiliation, under the Directive, the Member State of Affiliation does *not* have to grant authorization for it to be provided in another Member State.[120] Thus, the Directive basically allows the Member State of Affiliation to deny authorization unless the desired treatment is *both* available in the Member State of Affiliation *and* unreasonably delayed, which is likely true only in "a small minority of cases," and thus "represents a severe dilution of the main principle of the [Directive]: that an individual should be allowed reimbursement for treatment in another Member State if that treatment is supported in the Member State of Affiliation."[121] Quinn and de Hert surmise that this fourth exemption is a "misreading" of the ECJ's holding in *Smits and Peerbooms*, and "seems inconsistent with the case law of the ECJ, which did not include any reference to such blanket grounds for the refusal of prior authorisation."[122] Because that case law was based on treaty interpretation, they go so far as to suggest that this problem "may call into question the validity of the" Directive, and that the exemption is likely to "give rise to future legal challenges, especially in instances where the national health insurance body concerned does not have pre-existing contractual arrangements with national healthcare providers."[123]

---

[118] Quinn & de Hert, *supra* note 80, at 30.

[119] *Id.* at 30–31.

[120] *Id.* at 31.

[121] *Id.*

[122] *Id.* at 32.

[123] *Id.*

Although their account of the effect of the wording of the Directive is correct, it is far less clear if they are correct in claiming that this wording represents a significant change from the pre-Directive case law. In particular, language from the ECJ's decision in *Inizian* seems largely in agreement with this aspect of the Directive, casting some doubt on their claim of a divergence.[124]

What happens when a patient applies for authorization, is wrongfully denied it, goes ahead and receives treatment anyway, and then seeks reimbursement from his or her Member State of Affiliation? Under the Regulation, the ECJ has made clear that patients should be placed in the same position that they would have been in had they been lawfully granted authorization to begin with—the reimbursement rate of the Member State of Treatment will apply.[125] Under the Directive, the situation is not clear. Recital (46) of the Directive indicates that where the conditions of the Regulation have been fulfilled, even if authorization could have been granted under the Directive also, then the Directive Articles concerning prior authorization and reimbursement should not apply. Rather, the Regulation framework would then apply as per the ECJ holding mentioned above. Where the Regulation conditions have not been fulfilled but prior authorization should have nevertheless been granted under the Directive, it is likely that the ECJ will rule that the Member State of Affiliation rate will apply, as this would be in accordance with the Directive framework and would put the patient in the same position as she would have been in had she been lawfully granted authorization under the Directive in the first place. However, we will have to await an ECJ judgment on the issue to be sure that this is how it will go.[126]

B. Reimbursement

On the question of reimbursement (Article 7 of the Directive), the Directive again mostly accepts and reflects the ECJ case law discussed above.

The costs of the service provided in the Member State of Treatment will be reimbursed or paid directly by the home Member States of Affiliation "up to the level of costs that would have been assumed by the [home] state, had this healthcare been provided in its territory."[127] As was seen above, this falls in line with the case law and is a notable

---

[124] Case C-56/01, *Inizan*, at I—12444, ¶60. "Articles [56 and 57 TFEU] must be interpreted as not precluding legislation of a Member State…which, first, makes reimbursement of the cost of hospital care provided in [another] Member State…conditional upon prior authorisation…and, secondly, makes the grant of that authorisation subject to the condition that it be established that the insured person could not receive within the [Member State of Affiliation] the treatment appropriate to his condition. However, authorisation may be refused on that ground only if treatment which is the same or equally effective for the patient can be obtained without undue delay in the territory of the Member State in which he resides."

[125] *See* Case C-368/98, Abdon Vanbraekel and Others v. Alliance Nationale des Mutualités Chrétiennes, 2001-7 E.C.R. I-5382.

[126] For a contrary view, *see* Quinn & de Hert, *supra* note 80, at 27–28.

[127] Directive 2011/24, *supra* note 2, rt. 7(4).

difference between the regime governing treatment under the Regulation, in that the applicable reimbursement tariff under the Directive is that of the patient's Member State of Affiliation, whereas, under the Regulation, the patient was entitled to reimbursement at the level provided by the Member State of Treatment. Under the Regulation, for emergency care, the Member State of Affiliation is not obliged to contribute additional, or "complimentary," reimbursement where its rate is higher than that of the Member State of Treatment, but for planned care it is. Under the Directive, in cases "[w]here the full cost of cross-border healthcare exceeds the level of costs that would have been assumed had the healthcare been provided in its territory," the Member State of Affiliation retains discretion to "top up" its reimbursement to make up the difference, but is not required to do so.[128] Similarly, it is permitted, but not required, to decide to "reimburse other related costs, such as accommodation and travel costs, or extra costs which persons with disabilities might incur due to one or more disabilities when receiving" care in the destination country,[129] although, as the ECJ noted in *Watts*, such costs should be reimbursed where those costs are normally covered as part of treatment in the Member State of Affiliation of the patient.

The Directive also requires that the Member State develop "objective, non-discriminatory criteria known in advance and applied at the relevant (local, regional or national) administrative level" for calculating the amount of reimbursement the Member State of Affiliation will provide.[130]

In fact, the Directive applies its non-discrimination provisions asymmetrically on the Member States of Affiliation and Treatment. The Directive "encourages but does not oblige Member States to adopt legislation ensuring that patients who have availed themselves of the opportunities under the [Directive] for cross-border treatment are entitled to the same rights as if they had opted for treatment in" the Member State of Affiliation.[131] However, as Quinn and de Hert observe, it may be illegal for the Member State of Affiliation to discriminate at home against individuals who had previously used medical tourism in another Member State.[132]

By contrast, the Directive explicitly prohibits discrimination by the Member State of Treatment.[133] In particular, although, to the extent permitted by their national health

---

[128] *Id.*

[129] *Id.*

[130] *Id.* art. 7(6).

[131] Quinn & de Hert, *supra* note 80, at 49; Directive 2011/24, *supra* note 2, art. 7(5).

[132] *See* Quinn & de Hert, *supra* note 80, at 50 ("This is because if a Member State were to allow measures that discriminate at home against individuals who had previously opted for treatment in another Member State, it would surely constitute a barrier to the freedom to provide and obtain services as described under the TFEU. This would probably be illegal, and therefore the EU would probably be able to legislate to prevent such matters. It appears, therefore, that if the main substantive measures of the PRD can be justified by reference to the freedom to provide services found in the TEU then one would also be able to justify measures.").

[133] *Id.*

care system, providers in the Member State of Treatment are free to set their own fees, they are prohibited from charging differential rates to medical tourists.[134] The motivation for this rule was apparently the fear that "if such a requirement were not in place, there would be little to stop providers setting lower prices for residents of other Member States in order to attract non-resident patients ... 'crowding out'" the market for resident patients.[135]

The negotiations regarding the Directive were stalled for a long time due to Spain's (and other countries') fears regarding the movement of expatriate pensioners.[136] In particular, Spain (for example) worried that expatriate pensioners residing in Spain would go home to their Member State of origin for treatment en masse, requiring the Spanish government to foot the bill without the money being used as investment into Spain's health care system.[137] The solution the drafters ultimately settled on was to allow Member States to add themselves to a "list of ... Member States that have declared themselves to be responsible for providing benefits to individuals on their territory if those individuals would be entitled to receive a pension from that Member State even if they are no longer resident there."[138] Currently, the countries on the list are Belgium, Germany, Greece, Spain, France, Italy, Luxembourg, Austria, and Sweden.[139] Under this provision, if a French expatriate living in Spain returns to France for treatment, then France would be responsible for the costs, because France has put itself on the list.[140] Importantly, these rules apply only when a pensioner is "going home" for treatment. If instead he is treated in a third state (i.e., neither his state of expatriate residence nor his state of origin), then the exception I have just mentioned does not apply.[141] Moreover, "if an individual returns to his original Member State for treatment and it is only in that Member State that his entitlement to a pension arises, then," under the Directive, "it is that State that must bear the costs of treatment."[142] And, of course, where Member States do not put themselves on this list, the special rule does not apply. Still, this was enough to apparently resolve the logjam and pave the way for the Directive.

---

[134] Directive 2011/24, *supra* note 2, art. 4(4); Quinn & de Hert, *supra* note 80, at 51.

[135] Quinn & de Hert, *supra* note 80, at 51 (citing Consultation concernant une action communautaire dans le domaine des service de sante'—Communication de la Commission du 26 September 2006—Réponse de la Belgique (p. 9)).

[136] *Id.* at 51–52.

[137] *Id.*

[138] *Id.* at 25; Directive 2011/24, *supra* note 2, art. 7(2).

[139] Quinn & de Hert, *supra* note 80, at 52, n.118 (citing Annex IV of Regulation 883/2004).

[140] *See id.*

[141] *See id.* at 53.

[142] *See id.*

C. New Rights for Patients

The Directive quite self-consciously purports to take what has been called a patient-centered and needs-based approach, which the ECJ, as well as the European Commission, has consistently supported. Specifically, the Directive provides patients a number of new rights. Among these, it requires "healthcare providers [to] provide relevant information to help individual patients to make an informed choice, including on treatment options, on the availability, quality and safety of the healthcare they provide in the Member State of treatment," as well as "provide clear invoices and clear information on prices, as well as on their authorisation or registration status, their insurance cover or other means of personal or collective protection with regard to professional liability."[143] However, it cautions that, to the extent "that healthcare providers already provide patients resident in the Member State of treatment with relevant information on these subjects, this Directive does not oblige healthcare providers to provide more extensive information to patients from other Member States."[144] These rights are important because one must be able to "calculate costs accurately in order to enable migration, to enable rational decisions by patients, and for fair competition."[145] However, the Directive does not appear to require that this information be provided in the various languages of the European Union, such that some patients may find this information unusable.

Second, it requires that Member States of Treatment provide "transparent complaints procedures and mechanisms in place for patients, in order for them to seek remedies in accordance with the legislation of the Member State of Treatment if they suffer harm arising from the healthcare they receive."[146] Although the Directive did not adopt the calls for a separate European dispute resolution system pressed by some constituencies, this requirement of a transparent complaint procedure is likely to help Europeans avoid some of the difficulties regarding the adjudication of medical malpractice disputes faced by Americans, as discussed in Chapter 3. In particular, this may represent fertile soil for the development of robust alternative dispute resolution (ADR) systems that could serve as a model for medical tourism outside of Europe as well, either on a mandatory or contractualized basis.

Third, it requires that Member States of Treatment provide that "[s]ystems of professional liability insurance, or a guarantee or similar arrangement that is equivalent or essentially comparable as regards its purpose and which is appropriate to the nature and the extent of the risk, are in place for treatment provided on its territory."[147]

---

[143] Directive 2011/24, *supra* note 2, art. 4(2)(b).

[144] *Id.*

[145] *See* Gareth Davies, *The Community's Internal Market-Based Competence to Regulate Healthcare: Scope, Strategies and Consequences*, 4 MAASTRICHT J. EUR. & COMP. L. 215, 233 (2007).

[146] Directive 2011/24, *supra* note 2, art. 4(2)(c).

[147] *Id.* art. 4(2)(d).

Fourth, it guarantees some amount of data privacy, indicating that "the fundamental right to privacy with respect to the processing of personal data is protected in conformity with national measures implementing Union provisions on the protection of personal data."[148]

Fifth, the Member State of Affiliation has a responsibility to ensure that, for individuals who seek treatment in another Member State, if "medical follow-up [care] proves necessary, the same medical follow-up is available as would have been if that healthcare had been provided on its territory," such that they will not be disadvantaged in that follow-up care as compared to those who were not medical tourists.[149] Also, "in order to ensure continuity of care," it gives patients who have received treatment an "entitle[ment] to a written or electronic medical record of such treatment, and access to at least a copy of this record in conformity with and subject to national measures implementing Union provisions on the protection of personal data."[150] These provisions were important to address the concern that there was "inadequate communication between doctors in different states" and/or that "doctors are reluctant to complete treatment begun by another," although there was until this point only "anecdotal evidence of patients returning from surgery abroad to find domestic surgeons reluctant to accept them as patients purely for aftercare."[151]

In theory, these rights could mean a lot for patients. They could require changes in patient safety requirements, transparency on morbidity and mortality outcome data as well as pricing, alternative dispute or other means of settling malpractice and other disputes, and ways of facilitating the interoperability of health records and follow-up care. Some authors have suggested that these elements of the Directive provide a major step forward for patients seeking health care across the borders, and even those citizens receiving care in their own destination countries.[152] In practice, however, such gains may prove illusory depending on how the Directive is actually implemented in various Member States.

D. Cooperation

Finally, the Directive initiates a number of additional initiatives to foster cooperative links between Member States on cross-border health care. These include the following:

The Member States must render mutual assistance, as it is necessary for the implementation of the Directive (including standards and guideline formation);[153] Member

---

[148] *Id.* art. 4(2)(e).

[149] *Id.* art 5(c).

[150] *Id.* art. 4(2)(f).

[151] Davies, *supra* note 145, 231.

[152] Peeters, *supra* note 105, at 56–57; Quinn & de Hert, *supra* note 80, at 23–24, 41.

[153] Directive 2011/24, *supra* note 2, art. 10.

States are obliged to recognize prescriptions issued in another Member State for medicinal products when their products are authorized to be marketed in their territory;[154] the Directive enables the voluntary development of European reference networks between health care providers and centers of expertise in the Member States;[155] the Commission will support Member States in cooperating in the development of diagnosis and treatment capacity of rare diseases;[156] the European Union will support cooperation and exchange of information among Member States working within a voluntary network connecting national authorities responsible for "eHealth."[157]

E. Assessing the Directive

Like many EU Directives, and legislation more generally, this Directive bears the mark of compromise. Similar to the ECJ case law from which it sprung, drafting the Directive presented the quite difficult task of balancing respect for and the continued smooth and autonomous operation of distinct Member State national health care systems, including their territorial solidarity and financial sustainability, with principles of free movement and facilitation of medical tourism between EU Member States. In several instances, dilution of the second goal appears to be the price paid in order to get sufficient agreement among Member States to push the Directive forward.[158]

Some of these compromises, such as the special treatment given to pensioners in the reimbursement scheme, seem like understandable "adjustments" that leaves the scheme envisioned largely intact. One of the apparent compromises, regarding the fourth exemption for granting authorization that seems to restrict wrongful denials of authorization to a very small category of cases where services are available at home but unduly delayed, seems more in tension with the goals of the Directive. To be sure, Member States would never have agreed to a system of fully open cross-border health care, but one might have hoped that the Directive could have expanded patients' rights more in this particular area.

Because Member States are only beginning to implement the Directive, and thus it will be several years before we have a real sense of how it is working on the ground, it is too soon to tell if the Directive will be a success in achieving its goal. But, there is much that is very promising in the Directive, not only as to Europe's own needs for medical tourism, but in several areas (liability insurance, ADR, eHealth), as potential models for voluntary adoption by the industry or legislative fiat elsewhere in the world. The Directive has gone a long way in clarifying a very tangled ECJ jurisprudence, and it is

---

[154] *Id.* art. 11.

[155] *Id.* art. 12.

[156] *Id.* art. 13.

[157] *Id.* art. 14; for a discussion of these cooperation elements, *see also* Quinn & de Hert, *supra* note 80, at 59–66.

[158] Quinn & de Hert, *supra* note 80, at 66–68.

worth emphasizing the way other elements of the EU legal system will play a role in the development of the Directive's approach: the Commission will continue to oversee things, and can bring misbehaving Member States before the ECJ, and the ECJ will no doubt be confronted with more preliminary rulings cases where the details and specific balances envisioned by the Directive will be thrashed out.

Although we are still in the early days, it is also worth mentioning the way in which the existence of the Directive may *influence* the ECJ's development of its own jurisprudence, albeit indirectly. Hatzopoulos and Hervey claim that, in the wake of the Proposed Directive, the ECJ "has backtracked on its former 'revolutionary' stance" to some extent, and that the Directive has allowed the ECJ "to change its position *de facto* without departing from the *de jure* consistency that the law values most highly and on which the rule of law and the role of Courts is based."[159] Among other things, they suggest that, in the wake of the proposed Directive, the ECJ made clear that its case law allowing restrictions on the free movement of services due to "objective public interest justification"—most notably the Member States' prerogative to engage in health care planning aimed at balancing access to high-quality treatment with controlling costs and avoiding waste—was not limited to hospital care, but extends to prior authorization rules for major medical equipment outside the hospital infrastructure, such as PET and MRI scanners, hyperbaric chambers, etc.[160] Further they point to "more recent case law" where the ECJ stresses "the wide margin of discretion left to member states in defining their health policies, in the absence of common or harmonised policies, provided they act in a coherent and systematic way."[161] At the moment, it is hard to know whether this represents a new distinct trajectory for the ECJ or merely the usual variance in case-by-case decision-making. It is clear that the relationship between the Directive and the ECJ case law is dynamic and very symbiotic; as Hatzopoulos and Hervey put it, the story I have told of cross-border health care can be seen as the ECJ stepping into the role of "broker," in that its early case law "arous[ed]" the EU legislature and Member States through curbing their discretion on cross-border health care, this arousal prompted the EU political institutions to promulgate the Directive, and now that they have done so the ECJ will "readily step[] down from its proactive stance and align[] its own position with that of the political institutions," such that the "revolution is over."[162] Although I agree with their assessment of the first two stages of this dance, I think it is too soon to count the ECJ's "revolutionary" impulses out yet, and much will depend on what it thinks of the Member States' actual implementation of the Directive.

---

[159] Hatzopoulos & Hervey, *supra* note 97, at 2–3.

[160] *Id.* at 3 (citing Case C-512/08, Comm'n v. France, 2010 E.C.R. 00000, *available at* http://eur-lex.europa.eu/LexUriServ/LexUriServ.do?uri=CELEX:62008CJ0512:EN:HTML).

[161] *Id.* at 4 (citing Case C-169/07 *Hartlauer* [2009] ECR I-1721); Case C-490/09 *Commission v. Luxembourg* (*Laboratory Analyses and Tests* [2011] ECR not yet reported).

[162] *Id.* at 5.

IV. THE POSSIBILITY OF PUBLICLY FINANCED MEDICAL TOURISM IN
THE UNITED STATES (AND ELSEWHERE)

For more than thirty years, the European Union has wrestled with how public health care payers should handle reimbursement for cross-border health care. In the United States, we are seeing only the very beginnings of this possibility. In 2006, West Virginia considered a bill (it ultimately did not pass) that would have incentivized state employees to participate in medical tourism at JCI-accredited facilities by giving employees round-trip airplane tickets for the patient and a companion, payment for lodging for the length of the treatment and an additional seven days thereafter, paid sick leave for the employee for one week upon the employee's return home, a waiver of all deductible and copayments, and a "rebate" to the employee of up to 20 percent of the cost savings as a result of undergoing treatment in the foreign facility.[163] Nathan Cortez has discussed the possibility of using the Affordable Care Act's authorization for states to create alternative programs for low-income individuals not eligible for Medicare or Medicaid, instead of offering such coverage through an exchange, as a further place to incorporate publicly insured medical tourism in the United States.[164] Finally, there have also been proposals to incorporate medical tourism into the U.S. Medicare (which covers health care for those over sixty-five) and Medicaid (which primarily covers low-income Americans). For example, Dean Baker and Hye Rho have proposed offering Medicare and Medicaid patients a voucher they could use if the individual relocates to buy into foreign health care systems with longer life expectancies.[165] They propose taking the incentive payments given to individuals out of the cost savings to Medicare or Medicaid, and forecast that with only 10 percent of Medicare and Medicaid beneficiaries adopting this option in 2020, these federal programs would save $18 billion dollars *per year*.[166]

Because Baker and Rho's plan envisions individuals actually moving to foreign countries full-time, the proposal may be unrealistic in the near term for many Americans, but one could also imagine creating incentive programs within Medicaid or Medicare to

---

[163] *See* H.B. 4359, 77th Leg., 2d Sess. (W. Va. 2006), *available at* http://www.legis.state.wv. us/Bill_Text_HTML/2006_SESSIONS/RS/Bills/hb4359%20intr.htm; *see also* Mark Roth, *Surgery Abroad an Option for Those with Minimal Health Coverage*, POST-GAZETTE.COM, Sept. 10, 2006, http://www.post-gazette.com/pg/06253/719928-37.stm.

[164] Nathan Cortez, *Embracing the New Geography of Health Care: A Novel Way to Cover Those Left Out of Health Reform*, 84 S. CAL. L. REV. 859, 892 (2011) (citing Patient Protection and Affordable Care Act, Pub. L. No. 111-148, § 1331, 124 Stat. 119,199–203 (2010)).

[165] DEAN BAKER & HYE JIN RHO, CENTER FOR ECONOMIC POLICY & RESEARCH, FREE TRADE IN HEALTH CARE: THE GAINS FROM GLOBALIZED MEDICARE AND MEDICAID 3–4 (2009), *available at* http://www.cepr.net/documents/publications/free-trade-hc-2009-09.pdf.

[166] *Id.* at 9, 14.

use medical tourism for high price tag surgical needs that would operate similarly to the insurer-prompted medical tourism plans we discussed in Chapter 4.

Incorporating medical tourism into public health insurance systems in the United States would raise a number of the same concerns discussed in prior chapters: medical malpractice recovery for those injured abroad, disclosure of quality and other information, selection of high quality providers, the effects on health care access to the destination country poor, etc. Many of the same solutions I have proposed on the private insurance side—consent to jurisdiction agreements, ADR mechanisms, medical malpractice insurance, report card systems, follow-up care commitments, requirement that destination country facilities make tangible commitments to ensuring access to their poor, etc.—could also be applied in this context, with one difference: it would be much easier to implement, because here the payer and the regulator are one in the same. For example, Medicare reimburses hospitals domestically only if they meet various Conditions of Participation governing quality control, staff requirements, and a number of other areas.[167] Medicaid similarly attaches conditions to contracts with hospitals and managed care organizations, and both programs induce compliance by threatening not to reimburse hospitals that do not comply.[168]

Medicare and/or Medicaid could similarly simply require as a prerequisite for reimbursement that foreign hospitals have in place some or all of these "solutions." Doing so would not only deal with these concerns as to Medicare/Medicaid patients, but would end up likely having significant regulatory "spillover" onto those who purchase out-of-pocket or through private insurer-prompted medical tourism. Not only do care-enhancing investments tend to be lumpy and hard to divide as between patient groups, but once private insurers know that the hospitals are already generating outcome data and the like for these public programs, they may find it easier to demand it be shared with them as well. When public insurers begin demanding these protections, it is plausible that they will establish a "new normal," a norm to which the rest of the market will also begin to coalesce. The Medicare/Medicaid business is sizable enough that many foreign facilities will find it worth their while to meet these demands, even when costly. Thus, public regulation will have significant positive regulatory externalities for the rest of the market in medical tourism.

That said, if Medicare or Medicaid merely *covered* care provided by approved facilities abroad, it would be unlikely to find many American patients in these populations (who tend to be older and poorer) taking them up on the offer. Instead, to really get this going, some type of incentive scheme would be required, such as enhanced benefits,

---

[167] 42 C.F.R. pt. 482 (2010); *see* Cortez, *supra* note 164, at 911. Medicare, in fact, allows hospitals to satisfy most of the Conditions of Participation by achieving accreditation by the Joint Commission, 42 C.F.R § 488.5; *see* Cortez, *supra* note 164, at 911. If JCI were to beef up its accreditation processes, one possibility would be for JCI accreditation to play a similar role for reimbursement to foreign hospitals.

[168] *See* Cortez, *supra* note 164 (citing James W. Fossett, *Managed Care and Devolution, in* MEDICAID AND DEVOLUTION 106, 122–23 (Frank J. Thompson & John J. DiIulio Jr. eds., 1998)).

lower copays, or higher deductible ceilings for those who elect to use medical tourism facilities abroad. This raises the specter of coercion, in that many of these individuals rely on these programs and have few good options outside of them. I have three responses to this argument. First, if adequate safeguards are in place, there is no reason to think that travel to a foreign facility will result in worse care than that which is currently available to that patient. Of course, rules would have to be put in place to determine who is eligible, in that we do not want to induce those who are too ill to travel to fly halfway across the world in an attempt to gain better benefits than the public system, and, of course, designing such rules will not be easy. Second, as has been hammered home in the latest financial crisis, our current spending on these programs is at an unsustainable level. Reductions in benefits for everyone, including the loss of some covered care, is what is on the horizon. Even if incentivizing individuals to go abroad is not what we would want in a "first best" world, it may be a much better alternative than across-the-board cuts as a way of reducing spending in these programs. Third, even the threat of incorporating medical tourism into these programs may prove a powerful inducement for U.S. hospitals to try to become more efficient and provide cost savings to Medicare/Medicaid rather than losing their business. There is some evidence that a similar phenomenon has happened in the European Union, in that, in the wake of expanded opportunities for cross-border care, local hospitals improved standards to keep patients living in that country who might otherwise have gone abroad.[169]

This last point, though, raises a concern. Could Medicare/Medicaid incorporating medical tourism undercut the U.S. medical system by driving price competition too intensely such that corners are cut substantially?[170] Admittedly, the incentive scheme would have to be carefully reticulated such that the U.S. hospital infrastructure feels pressure, but not *too* much pressure. There will always be a U.S. health care industry because much of the care we consume is needed on a more urgent basis, or is not well-suited to medical tourism for other reasons. Still, as to a portion of the trade—high price surgeries planned well in advance where high quality care at much lower prices is available abroad—for which increased medical tourism might make a significant dent, we must recall the trade theory of comparative advantage: if a foreign country can produce a good more efficiently than we can, it is in our interest to let them produce it and purchase it from them, such that we both benefit. Until the advent of medical tourism, it was not conceivable that health care could also be subject to this rule. With the dawn of medical tourism, for some subsets of health care we can see this possibility for the first time, and should press upon the health care industry why it needs more protectionism than many of our other industries.

All that said, although I think incorporating medical tourism into Medicaid and Medicare is an excellent salve to the already unsustainable costs of those programs, I am

---

[169] *See* TAMARA K. HERVEY & JEAN V. MCHALE, HEALTH LAW AND THE EUROPEAN UNION 142 (2004).

[170] *See, e.g.,* Stuart H. Altman et al., *Could U.S. Hospitals Go the Way of U.S. Airlines?*, 25 HEALTH AFF. 11, 11, 20–21 n.1 (2006).

keenly aware and thus skeptical of the politics involved. In an era where protectionism and patriotism are often treated interchangeably, neither political party will be apt to endorse "offshoring" medical jobs through these proposals. Although I hope it does not come to this, it may be that we are in a Leninist "the worse, the better" moment: the political parties will begin seriously considering incorporating medical tourism into public insurance programs only when their costs become not only unsustainable (as they already are), but when the system teeters on the edge of collapse. Some may say we are already there, given that even after the ACA gets implemented there will be 20 to 30 million people left uninsured in America.[171] Even if we are not there yet, unless something drastic changes, we are on our way to such a moment.

V. MEDICAL RETIREMENT

Most of this chapter has dealt with individuals traveling abroad for health care and using publicly financed health care to pay for it. The one exception was our discussion of concerns over the costs of health care consumption by expatriates in the European Union, and how the Directive adopts some political compromises to satisfy countries such as Spain for whom this was a significant issue.

What of people who retire abroad from the United States and need health care there? Although not strictly speaking "medical tourism," as I have defined it, the issues are close enough that it is worth briefly discussing here.

According to 2001 estimates, there were somewhere between 225,000 and 300,000 American permanent residents who had retired to Mexico. Of these, roughly one-third were middle income and above retirees of non-Mexican origin, about a third were lower-middle to lower income retirees of Mexican origin, and a third were Mexican-origin U.S. retirees entitled to Social Security and Medicare in the United States.[172] Those within the industry suggest that number has increased significantly in subsequent years.[173] As David C. Warner and Lauren R. Jahnke noted in 2001, despite paying into the system many of these medical retirees are unable to use public U.S. health care:

Except in very limited circumstances on the Mexican and Canadian borders and en route to Alaska, Medicare does not pay for services received outside the United

---

[171] *See* CONGRESSIONAL BUDGET OFFICE, ESTIMATES FOR THE INSURANCE COVERAGE PROVISIONS OF THE AFFORDABLE CARE ACT UPDATED FOR THE RECENT SUPREME COURT DECISION 12–13 (July 2012), *available at* http://www.cbo.gov/sites/default/files/cbofiles/attachments/43472-07-24-2012-CoverageEstimates.pdf.

[172] David C. Warner & Lauren R. Jahnke, *Toward Better Access to Health Insurance Coverage for U.S. Retirees in Mexico*, 43 SALUD PUBLICA MEX 59, 61 (2001), *available at* http://www.insp.mx/salud/index.html.

[173] *See* MEDICARE IN MEXICO: INNOVATING FOR FAIRNESS AND COST SAVINGS 9–10 (David C. Warner ed., 2007).

States. Medigap insurance is limited to covering emergency services used during travel or a temporary stay of less than 60 days abroad. Private health insurance in Mexico is very difficult to obtain for persons older than 65. This lack of coverage serves as a disincentive to retire to Mexico. Many who do retire in Mexico return to the U.S.A. sooner than they had planned, often with advanced health problems. Although they receive no coverage in Mexico, Medicare beneficiaries must continue to contribute $45.50 a month (1999 amount) to retain their Part B coverage. For every year they fail to contribute these funds after age 65, their annual premium increases by 10 percent should they choose to join later.... Many who would prefer to retire to Mexico or to remain there are precluded from doing so because of their concern that they might become ill and not be able to afford the illness.[174]

One solution would be Medicare portability, in which individuals could use their Medicare benefits for hospital and other care in Mexico. Again, we could build in some of the safeguards discussed above relating to quality, medical malpractice recovery, etc., and make them conditions of participation in the program. The more interesting and also more difficult question is what effect this would have on the cost of the Medicare program (and, therefore, the U.S. taxpayer), as well as the dynamic effects on the ability of U.S. citizens to retire to Mexico (or another destination country, for that matter).

While admitting that some of the calculation is back of the envelope, Warner and Jahnke suggest the following analysis of how this might go: suppose the average Medicare beneficiary can get treatment for US$1,000 in Mexico that would cost her US$2,000 in the United States. For every one hundred thousand Americans who retire to Mexico, there is a net gain of US$100 million of export income for Mexico and an equivalent net loss for the United States, but there is also a US$100 million savings for U.S. taxpayers in the cost of running the Medicare program. Of course, those who medically retire to Mexico also spend on other goods and services while living there. If we estimate they spend US$10,000 each on goods and services, then an increase of one hundred thousand U.S. retirees a year would amount to an additional $1 billion in foreign exchange. Although it might be tempting to view that as a net loss to the United States, this would also have the effect of increasing Mexico's ability to purchase other goods and services from the United States and elsewhere. Further complicating matters, Warner and Jahnke suggest that "many of the services purchased in Mexico could replace lower-wage workers in the U.S.A. and might create jobs in Mexico for those who might otherwise be likely to relocate to the U.S.A. to find employment."[175] That is all based on a cost savings

---

[174] Warner & Jahnke, *supra* note 172, at 59–60.

[175] *Id.* at 63; *see also* MEDICARE IN MEXICO, *supra* note 173, at 62, 64 (discussing other possible assumptions in the model); Michelle L. Lalonde, *Navigating Medicare, in* MEDICARE IN MEXICO, *supra* note 173, at 89

of 50 percent to Medicare for allowing the consumption of services in Mexico. The data discussed earlier suggest health care expenditures would be closer to 20 percent of the cost in the United States, which would make this analysis more favorable in that the savings to the taxpayer would be considerably greater.

Still, the dynamic effects—on spending in the United States, on immigration to the United States, and on U.S. health care providers who lose a chunk of their Medicare population—are fuzzy enough that it seems premature to champion full Medicare portability for Mexican retirees. Instead, as Warner and Jahnke urge, I think it is worthwhile to experiment with something more limited. They suggest several possibilities, of which I will list three that seem the most sensible to me: seek a waiver from the U.S. government that would allow a demonstration project on Medicare portability; that would waive certain conditions of participation in Medicare, such as requirements for physicians to be licensed to practice in the United States or for hospitals to be certified by the Joint Commission on Accreditation of Health Organizations (JCAHO), in favor of something more along the lines of what I have suggested above as possible safeguards; allow Medicare beneficiaries to redirect a portion of their Medicare Part B benefits toward private insurance policies in Mexico that cover some of the same services; or allow retired Americans to use money put into a Medical Savings Account for purchases of health care needs in Mexico.[176]

To be sure, even in running these smaller scale experiments, there would be a number of serious challenges to overcome. Medicare fraud has proved difficult to curb in the United States, and one might worry that a direct billing agreement between Medicare and Mexican providers would worsen these problems significantly. The problem is real, but Mexican insurers have made some progress toward solutions as well: several Mexican institutions require *facturas*—an official record of that transaction for tax purposes—for each service rendered by the physician. Some have claimed that the *factura* has proven a useful deterrent of fraud within the Mexican system,[177] and, if that is true, it could be incorporated into Medicare Conditions of Participation.

Although the notion of Medicare coverage for those abroad may seem very new, in fact there is a sector of the U.S. population for which a similar program already exists: those in the armed services. TRICARE for Life Overseas (also called TOP TFL), began in 2001 and is funded by the DOD Medicare Eligible Retiree Health Care Fund, which is funded by annual appropriation contributions and general revenues from the U.S. Treasury, and covers retirees living overseas from the U.S. Army, Air Force, Navy, Marine Corps, Coast Guard, Public Health Service, and the National and Oceanic

---

("Although the population of U.S. retirees in Mexico has not yet grown to its full potential, saving on the emergency costs of .05 percent of Medicare enrollees [by allowing coverage in Mexico] would save Medicare between $39.6 million and $129.4 million.").

[176] Warner & Jahnke, *supra* note 172, at 64.

[177] *See also* Lalonde, *supra* note 173, at 89.

and Atmospheric Administration.[178] More specifically, it is available to all covered Dual-eligible (i.e., Medicare and Medicaid) uniformed service retirees (including retired guard members and reservists), their family members, their widows/widowers (with the exception of dependent parents and parents-in-law); Dual-eligible Medal of Honor recipients and their family members; and Dual-eligible un-remarried former spouses, *if* they provide proof of purchase of Medicare Part B (Medicare Card), as well as a valid Uniformed Services identification card.[179] Based on the 2006 formula, TRICARE would ultimately pay the foreign provider 75 percent of the cost of the care, with the individual responsible for the remaining 25 percent.[180]

More specifically, TOP TFL is structured as a fee-for-service plan, wherein the patient has to pay for her care upfront (usually in local currency) and seek reimbursement from the TRICARE Overseas Claims Processor, unless the provider is willing to submit a claim on behalf of the patient.[181] Disputes between the doctors and beneficiaries are adjudicated by the local law and court systems, and TRICARE does not get involved, though it will request more information from a provider when it needs to determine if the procedure was medically necessary or not.[182]

TRICARE has a significant footprint in Mexico. In 2004, TRICARE received a total of 502 claims from retirees and their dependents in Mexico, paying $715,701, with the retirees paying $17,876.[183] Survey work suggested some doctors were reluctant to accept TRICARE reimbursement because its delay was lengthy, but one imagines that a more full-scale experiment with Medicare could overcome this problem.[184]

VI. CONCLUSION

In this period of economic recession, the United States and many other countries are looking for ways to trim the costs of their social welfare programs, and, given demographic trends, publicly subsidized health insurance plans present a clear target of opportunity. In the United States, this possibility is still at a very nascent stage. I have discussed ways in which some of the principles I have proposed in Chapter 4 for medical

---

[178] Marina M. Zolezzi, *Health Benefits Abroad: TRICARE and the Foreign Medical Program, in* Medicare in Mexico, *supra* note 173, at 167, 168.

[179] *Id.* at 168–69.

[180] *Id.*

[181] *Id.* at 170.

[182] *Id.*

[183] *Id.* at 172.

[184] *Id.* at 173. Beyond TRICARE, the Veterans Administration (VA) also has a separate Foreign Medical Program that reimburses beneficiaries for accepted medical procedures approved by the VA and the U.S. medical communities. *Id.* at 174. Because this system requires beneficiaries to get a letter of prior authorization from the program, *id.*, it seems less apt as a model for organizing medical retirement, but may be useful in thinking about true publicly financed medical tourism of the kind discussed earlier in this chapter.

tourism through private insurance–funded care might be adapted for public insurance programs, and how and why the United States and other highly developed nations might want to incentivize publicly subsidized patients to use care that can be provided more cheaply in other countries. Beyond the use of incentives, there is also a separate question of whether public insurance should become more portable and used to cover individuals who have retired in the destination country, and not merely travel there more episodically for the purpose of receiving health care, as in true medical tourism. There are significant communities of U.S. retired individuals currently living in Mexico, and I have examined ways in which it may be beneficial to both these retirees and the U.S. taxpayers to allow Medicare to be used abroad in these instances, proposing some possible demonstration projects.

Although publicly insured medical tourism in its very nascent stages in the United States, Europe has had more than three decades of experience with patients traveling from one EU Member State to another for health care. In this chapter, I also examined the very complex Treaty, Regulatory, and European Court of Justice jurisprudential framework that the European Union has developed as to cross-border care. The key issues raised, which other countries seeking to develop their own publicly insured cross-border care plans will have to wrestle with, surround when prior authorization may be required, when such authorization may be denied (including regarding time to treatment at home), and reimbursement rates. The European Union's new Directive has made significant headway in clarifying the state of play on these issues for patients seeking cross-border health care, as well as adding new initiatives regarding information for patients, dispute resolution systems, recognition of foreign prescriptions, and eHealth initiatives. Still, as so much will depend on how individual Member States implement the Directive (the deadline was October 2013), it is very hard at this juncture to know whether the promise of the Directive in rationalizing the legal framework and facilitating the provision of cross-border care will be fulfilled.

6

Medical Tourism's Effects on the Destination Country: An Empirical and Ethical Examination

THE LAST SEVERAL chapters have focused on legal and ethical issues raised by medical tourism from the perspective of home country citizens and regulators. In this chapter, we shift focus to consider things from the destination country perspective.

From the vantage point of destination country citizens, medical tourism threatens to present a host of cruel ironies. Vast medico-industrial complexes, replete with the newest expensive technologies to provide comparatively wealthy medical tourists hip replacements and facelifts, coexist with large swaths of the population dying from malaria, AIDS, and lack of basic sanitation and clean water. Let us return to someone we met in this book's preface, Mr. Steels, who was described in a recent *New York Times* article entitled "Royal Care for Some of India's Patients, Neglect for Others." The article begins by describing the care given at Wockhardt Hospital in India to "Mr. Steeles, 60, a car dealer from Daphne, Ala., [who] had flown halfway around the world last month to save his heart [through a mitral valve repair] at a price he could pay." The article describes in great detail the dietician who selects Mr. Steele's meals, the dermatologist who comes as soon as he mentions an itch, and Mr. Steeles's "Royal Suite" with "cable TV, a computer, [and] a mini-refrigerator, where an attendant that afternoon stashed some ice cream, for when he felt hungry later." This treatment contrasts with the care given to a group of "day laborers who laid bricks and mixed cement for Bangalore's construction boom," many of whom "fell ill after drinking illegally brewed whisky; 150 died that day." "Not for them [was] the care of India's best private hospitals," writes the article's author;

"[t]hey had been wheeled in by wives and brothers to the overstretched government-run Bowring Hospital, on the other side of town," a hospital with "no intensive care unit, no ventilators, no dialysis machine," where "[d]inner was a stack of white bread, on which a healthy cockroach crawled."[1]

Discomfort with such disparities is not only the stuff of narrative and journalism; one finds it also in the academic and policy literatures. For example, David Benavides, a Senior Economic Affairs Officer working on trade for the United Nations, has noted that developed and developing countries' attempts at exporting health services sometimes come "at the expense of the national health system, and the local population has suffered instead of benefiting from those exports."[2] Rupa Chanda, an Indian professor of business, writes in the *World Health Organization Bulletin* that medical tourism threatens to "result in a dual market structure, by creating a higher-quality, expensive segment that caters to wealthy nationals and foreigners, and a much lower-quality, resource-constrained segment catering to the poor."[3] Although the "[a]vailability of services, including physicians and other trained personnel, as well as the availability of beds may rise in the higher-standard centres," it may come "at the expense of the public sector, resulting in a crowding out of the local population."[4] Similarly, Professor Leigh Turner suggests that "the greatest risk for inhabitants of destination countries is that increased volume of international patients will have adverse effects upon local patients, health care facilities and economies."[5] He explains that the kinds of investments destination country governments must make to compete are in "specialized medical centres and advanced biotechnologies" unlikely to be accessed by "most citizens of a country [who] lack access to basic health care and social services."[6] Furthermore, higher wages for health care professionals resulting from medical tourism may crowd out access by the domestic poor.[7] Thus, "[i]nstead of contributing to broad social and economic development, the provision of care to patients from other countries might exacerbate existing inequalities and further polarize the richest and poorest members" of the destination country.[8] Milica and Karla Bookman, writing about the economics and law of development via medical tourism, worry that the trade "can create a dual market structure in which one segment is of higher quality and caters to the wealthy foreigners (and local high-income patients)

---

[1] Somini Sengupta, *Royal Care for Some of India's Patients, Neglect for Others*, N.Y. TIMES, June 1, 2008, at K3.

[2] David D. Benavides, *Trade Policies and Export of Health Services: A Development Perspective, in* TRADE IN HEALTH SERVICES: GLOBAL, REGIONAL, AND COUNTRY PERSPECTIVES 53, 55 (Nick Drager & Cesar Vieira eds., 2002), *available at* http://tinyurl.com/3crozzd.

[3] Rupa Chanda, *Trade in Health Services*, 80 BULL. WORLD HEALTH ORG. 158, 160 (2002).

[4] *Id.*

[5] Leigh Turner, *"First World Health Care at Third World Prices": Globalization, Bioethics and Medical Tourism*, 2 BIOSOCIETIES 303, 320 (2007).

[6] *Id.*

[7] *Id.*

[8] *Id.* at 321.

while a lower quality segment caters to the poor… [such that] health for the local population is crowded out as the best doctors, machines, beds, and hospitals are lured away from the local poor."[9]

The same point has also been made as to specific procedures or segments of the market. For example, in regards to fertility tourism (of the kind I will discuss in Chapter 9), Andrea Whittaker writes that "a primary concern is that the development of the foreign patient trade in health services will have a detrimental effect upon the public health systems of these countries, by encouraging the further development of inequitable, two-tiered health systems, where elite, technologically sophisticated hospitals, catering to wealthy foreign clients, stand beside poorly resourced public hospitals."[10]

These concerns have also been raised in several more regional discussions: Watatana S. Janjaroen and Siripen Supakankuti argue that, in Thailand, medical tourism threatens to both disrupt the ratio of health personnel to the domestic population and "create a two-tier system with the better quality services reserved for foreign clients with a higher ability to pay."[11] Similarly, the Bookmans' claim that, in Cuba, "only one-fourth of the beds in CIREN (the international Center for Neurological Restoration in Havana) are filled by Cubans, and… so-called dollar pharmacies provide a broader range of medicines to Westerners who pay in foreign currency."[12] They describe a medical system so distorted by the effects of medical tourism as "medical apartheid, because it makes health care available to foreigners that is not available to locals."[13] Numerous authors have made similar claims about medical tourism in India.[14] Similar concerns have even been raised as to medical tourism in developed countries. For example, an investigation by the Israeli newspaper *Haaretz* concluded "medical tourists enjoy conditions Israelis can only dream of, including very short waiting times for procedures, the right to choose their own doctor and private rooms… [a]nd these benefits may well be coming at the expense of Israeli patients' care," and suggested that allowing medical tourists to move to the front of the line on waiting lists for services meant that "waiting times for ordinary Israelis will inevitably lengthen—especially in the departments most frequented by medical tourists, which include the cancer, cardiac and in vitro fertilization units."[15]

---

[9] Milica Z. Bookman & Karla K. Bookman, Medical Tourism in Developing Countries 176 (2007).

[10] Andrea Whittaker, *Cross-Border Assisted Reproduction Care in Asia: Implications for Access, Equity and Regulations*, 19 Reprod. Health Matters 107, 110 (2011).

[11] Watatana S. Janjaroen & Siripen Supakankunti, *International Trade in Health Services in the Millenium: The Case of Thailand, in* Trade in Health Services, *supra* note 2, at 87, 98.

[12] Bookman & Bookman, *supra* note 9, at 177.

[13] *Id.*

[14] *See, e.g.*, Ami Sen Gupta, *Medical Tourism in India: Winners and Losers*, 5 Indian J. Med. Ethics 4–5 (2008); Laura Hopkins et al., *Medical Tourism Today: What Is the State of Existing Knowledge?*, 31 J. Pub. Health Pol'y 185, 194 (2010); Rory Johnston et al., *What Is Known about the Effects of Medical Tourism in Destination and Departure Countries? A Scoping Review*, 9 Int'l J. Equity Health 1 (2010).

[15] Dan Even & Maya Zinshtein, *Haaretz Probe: Israel Gives Medical Tourists Perks Denied to Citizens*, Haaretz.com (last updated Nov. 18, 2010, 12:53 AM), http://tinyurl.com/3auupjc.

Behind all of these claims—scholarly and popular—are some significant and interesting fundamental questions that are the subject of this chapter. I divided them into three: First, under what conditions is medical tourism likely to produce negative consequences on health care access in Less Developed destination Countries (LDCs), and is there good evidence it is having that effect?[16] Second, as a moral matter of global justice, what responsibility do home countries and others bear for health care access disparities related to medical tourism? And finally, what kinds of regulations might best ameliorate such potential negative consequences? I answer these questions in this chapter.

I. THE EMPIRICAL QUESTION: WHAT EFFECT DOES MEDICAL TOURISM HAVE ON HEALTH CARE ACCESS IN THE DESTINATION COUNTRY?

A. Framing the Right Empirical Question

Although concerns about effects on health care access abroad are raised by academics and policymakers discussing medical tourism, they have thus far been undertheorized. The first step in searching for answers is to look for the right question(s). It is useful to consider upfront three distinct versions of the empirical question that will tie into various potential approaches to global justice: (1) Are there disparities in access to health care for the general population between destination countries in the developing world and home countries in the developed world? (call this the *equity* question); (2) Do we have evidence that medical tourism causes deficits or worsens inequities, or, at the very least, is it associated with deficits or worsening inequities in access by home country citizens to health care? (call this the *causation* question); (3) Irrespective of what caused the deficits, would regulation of medical tourism reduce these deficits or inequities? (call this the *redressability* question).

In their thoughtful paper in the *Journal of Law, Medicine, and Ethics*, commenting on my own prior work on this subject, Y.Y. Brandon Chen and Colleen Flood suggest I have been wrong in the questions that I focus on:

> [W]e argue that there is an *a priori* bias embedded in how Cohen (and other commentators) has framed the problématique of medical tourism. [In Cohen and other commentators' writing,] the burden appears to rest on opponents of medical tourism

---

[16] Of course, as a growing literature emphasizes, it is a mistake to fetishize *health care* in normative analysis instead of *health*, which may depend more on sanitation, housing, and social determinants than on medical services. *See, e.g.,* NORMAN DANIELS, JUST HEALTH 79–102 (2008); Michael Marmot et al., *Contributions of Psychosocial Factors to Socioeconomic Differences in Health*, 76 MILBANK Q. 403, 434 (1998). Although conscious of this issue, I will for the most part focus on health care access because this is the main margin in which medical tourism has been predicted to have negative effects, while acknowledging that it is the negative effects on health stemming from these diminutions in health care access that motivate the concern.

to prove its negative consequences on LMICs' (low- and middle-income countries') health care access before regulatory actions may be considered. In contrast, we argue in this paper that the evidentiary burden should be reversed. We contend that even when access to health care in LMICs is not adversely affected by medical tourism, there are still equity-related concerns that in and of themselves render medical tourism normatively problematic. As we discuss further below, this inequity can (and often does) arise, for example, when access to primary and preventive health services for the general LMIC populations maintains the inadequate *status quo* while medical tourists from well-resourced developed countries are afforded cutting-edge secondary and tertiary care. If equity is considered a relevant goal for health care systems and one accepts our conclusion that medical tourism in LMICs will likely have deleterious equity impacts, then the burden should be borne by medical tourism's proponents to demonstrate its benefits on health care access and to justify why some degree of government regulation is inappropriate.[17]

The paragraph is a bit ambiguous. On the one hand, Chen and Flood assert that "even when access to health care in LMICs is not adversely affected by medical tourism, there are still equity-related concerns that in and of themselves render medical tourism normatively problematic," suggesting a focus on only the equity question. But later they say: "[i]f equity is considered a relevant goal for health care systems and one accepts our conclusion that medical tourism in LMICs *will likely have deleterious equity impacts....*" Those last words suggest that the causation question, or at least the redressability question, is what matters to them after all.

In any event, whatever inquiry Chen and Flood mean to answer, let me be upfront as to what work I think the empirical evidence that they and others have produced can and cannot do. The equity question, as such, is not my concern in this chapter. The empirical answer to that question is easy: it is beyond cavil that there are deep disparities in health care access between developed and developing countries, as there are to access to many good things that make a life go well. For those for whom the existence of that disparity, whatever its cause and whether or not regulating medical tourism will ameliorate matters, is enough to motivate an obligation to render aid, further empirical evidence is largely beside the point.

By contrast, I am interested in the causation question. To the extent medical tourism causes (or at least is associated with) these diminutions in health care access and thus worsens inequities, then it is easier to build a moral case for intervention.[18] And, even if medical tourism does not *cause* the negative effects, for some theories of global justice, it may still be important that regulations of the industry can *redress* health inequities.

---

[17] Y.Y. Brandon Chen & Colleen M. Flood, *Medical Tourism's Impact on Health Care Equity and Access in Low- and Middle-Income Countries: Making the Case for Regulation*, 41 J. LAW, MED. & ETHICS 286, 287–88 (2013).

[18] What if medical tourism did not worsen the health care for the destination country poor, or in fact improved it, but also increased disparities as the wealthy benefitted even more? That is, both the worse- and best-off are made better off, but not equivalently. For true pure egalitarians, who believe inequality is bad,

Thus, in the next section of this chapter, I review empirical data suggesting that medical tourism causes (or is at least associated with) diminutions in health care access, as well as data suggesting regulation of the sector might ameliorate health inequities. I do not focus on the existence of general health inequities that are unconnected to medical tourism. In part II of this chapter, I will use global justice theory to press a little bit more on the line between cause and redress and its implications for what we owe one another.

B. Six Ways in Which Medical Tourism May Affect Health Care Access in the Destination Country: An Evaluation of the Existing Evidence

Although, as discussed, there have been a number of anecdotal statements and analyses offered in favor of the empirical claim (that medical tourism causes deficits in health care access and/or that regulation of the field would redress inequities), there is very little in the way of evidence supporting the empirical claim. As such, this is an area where more developmental economic work would be very helpful. That said, I think it useful to identify six vectors by which medical tourism could have a negative effect on health care access in the destination country. Chen and Flood themselves have adopted my six vector approach, finding it "very helpful in teasing out the key points of contention in the current debate over medical tourism's implications" for developing countries, even where they adopt a "different approach to the burden of proof as described."[19] In reviewing these triggering conditions, I will also borrow from their excellent work and the work of others who have attempted to muster evidence for these factors being operative in various destination countries.

(1) *The health care services consumed by medical tourists come from those that would otherwise have been available to the destination country poor.*

When medical tourists seek travel abroad for cardiac care, hip replacements, and other forms of surgery used by the destination country poor, the siphoning effect is straight-forward. By contrast, the destination country poor are already unlikely to be able to access some boutique forms of treatment, such as cosmetic surgery and stem cell and fertility therapies. Thus, although medical tourism by American patients for these services would diminish access by, for example, Indian patients, it would not necessarily

---

that would be a problem, but of course that view has some well-accepted problems relating to leveling down. For Prioritarians, the pertinent question is whether the worse-off are made better-off, and whether they are made as better-off as they might be compared to other feasible regulatory rearrangements. I am more drawn to the latter view, and so I focus on whether medical tourism "causes deficits" or "fails to improve" the health care of the destination country poor, not on whether it worsens inequality per se. For those who are more attracted to purer egalitarian views, much of what I say in this chapter can be reanalyzed under that standard.

[19] Chen & Flood, *supra* note 17, at 288.

diminish access for *poor* Indian patients (which would remain steady at virtually none). Instead, it would cut into access by upper-class patients. Thus, one triggering condition focuses on whether medical tourism is for services currently accessed by destination country poor.

That said, as discussed below, over time, the salience of the distinction is likely to break down, and even medical tourism for services currently inaccessible to destination country poor may siphon resources away from the poor because increased demand for services such as cosmetic surgery may redirect the professional choices of graduating or practicing physicians who currently provide health care to India's poor into these niche markets. Whether that dynamic obtains would depend in part on the extent to which the destination country regulates specialty choice versus the extent to which health care workers can pursue the specialties most desirable to them.

Chen and Flood provide some evidence for this dynamic in Thailand. They note World Health Organization (WHO) data showing that there were 3 physicians per 10,000 people in Thailand in 2010 (the international average is 14 per 10,000) and that based on 2009 data the country produced approximately 1300 new doctors per year, which in their estimation "was just sufficient to meet the annual increase in health care demand due to population growth and the influx of foreign patients."[20] This data is very suggestive—although it is possible the 2009 numbers already incorporated a certain amount of medical tourism coverage, the growth of the industry in Thailand since then suggests 1300 doctors will be insufficient. Moreover, as Chen and Flood also recognize, in order to compete for foreign patients "hospitals in destination countries commonly offer perquisites that go beyond the requirements of the usual standard of care, such as personalized nursing services, ready access to medical specialists, and hotel-style room accommodation," and cite an estimate that in Thailand "the amount of resources used to treat one foreign patient... is roughly the same as what is generally needed to care for four to five local residents." Chen and Flood thus conclude that the "presence of even a small number of medical tourists could nevertheless make a notable dent in health care resources" for the destination country citizens.[21]

Chen and Flood also offer some evidence supporting the concern that a mismatch between the services sought by medical tourists versus those needed by the destination country's own populations—particularly because some medical tourists travel for elective surgeries and/or surgeries not covered by their insurance plans at home—will result

---

[20] *Id.* at 288 (citing WHO Statistical Information System (WHOSIS), World Health Statistics 2011, *available at* http://www.who.int/whosis/whostat/2011/en/index.html; Churnrurtai Kanchanachitra et al., *Human Resources for Health in Southeast Asia: Shortages, Distributional Challenges, and International Trade in Health Services*, 377 LANCET 769, 771 (2011); NaRanong & V. NaRanong, *The Effects of Medical Tourism: Thailand's Experience*, 89 BULL. WORLD HEALTH ORG. 336, 341 (2011)).

[21] Chen & Flood, *supra* note 17, at 288 (citing Turner, *supra* note 5, at 311; Johnston, *supra* note 14, at 8; S. Wibulpolprasert et al., *International Service Trade and Its Implications for Human Resources for Health: A Case Study of Thailand*, 2 HUM. RESOURCES HEALTH 1, 5 (2004)).

in the siphoning of doctors from the pool available for destination country patients. For example, discussing Thailand and India, Chen and Flood note that the "treatments most commonly obtained by medical tourists in Thailand include heart operations, cosmetic surgery, dental work, cataract removal and bone-related procedures, whereas foreign patients to India frequently undergo, *inter alia,* hip and knee replacement, bone marrow transplant, coronary bypasses, cataract surgery, *in vitro* fertilization and plastic surgery." This procedure-specialization leads to the worry that health care providers and private investors will be "[e]nticed by a higher profit margin associated with caring for foreign patients" to "redirect their attention to these medical (sub)specialties, thus further depriving other essential fields of medicine" of resources in the destination country.[22] As evidence, Chen and Flood point to reports of high concentrations of "Gamma Knife machines, CT scanners and mammography equipment" in Bangkok, a medical tourism center, and note one report that estimates that the number of these machines available "in Bangkok alone is greater than that available in all of England."[23] They interpret this "high concentration of medical technologies within the private sector in one city [as] rais[ing] serious doubts about health resources being spent in a manner that is aligned with priorities of Thailand's general population."[24] In a similar vein, Jeremy Snyder and coauthors note a worry in their case study of Barbados that if "there is no reason to assume that expansion of the private health sector and increased specialization of health services [aimed at capturing medical tourist dollars] will benefit all Bajans," and suggest that focusing on areas such as fertility care may improve access to these specialized services but reduce access to more general health care for Barbado residents.[25]

(2) *Health care providers and resources are "captured" by the medical tourist patient population, rather than serving some tourist clientele and some of the existing population.*

---

[22] Chen & Flood, *supra* note 17, at 288–89 (citing N. Cortez, *Patients without Borders: The Emerging Global Market for Patients and the Evolution of Modern Health Care,* 83 IND. L.J. 71, 93 (2008); G. Tattara, *Medical Tourism and Domestic Population Health* 8, (University Ca' Foscari of Venice, Dept. of Econ., Working Paper No. 02, 2010), *available at* http://ssrn.com/abstract=1544224; C.H. Leng & A. Whittaker, *Guest Editors' Introduction to the Special Issue: Why Is Medical Travel of Concern to Global Social Policy?,* 10 GLOBAL SOC. POL'Y 287, 288 (2010); A. Whittaker, *Pleasure and Pain: Medical Travel in Asia,* 3 GLOBAL PUB. HEALTH 271, 285 (2008); I.G. Cohen, *Medical Tourism, Access to Health Care and Global Justice,* 52 VA J. INT'L L. 1, 9–10 (2011)).

[23] Chen & Flood, *supra* note 17, at 288–89 (citing Ramírez de Arellano, *Patients without Borders: The Emergence of Medical Tourism,* 37 INT'L J. HEALTH SERVS. 193, 196 (2007)).

[24] Chen & Flood, *supra* note 17, at 288–89. That conclusion is, of course, not inevitable, and requires some more data digging as to the proportion of the Thai population living in Bangkok, their comparative health state, etc.

[25] Jeremy Snyder et al., *Caring for Non-residents in Barbados: Examining the Implications of Inbound Transnational Medical Care for Public and Private Health Care, in* MEDICAL TOURISM AND TRANSNATIONAL HEALTH CARE 51, 57 (David Boterrill et al. eds., 2013).

Absent regulation, the introduction of a higher-paying market will likely cause health care providers to shift away from treating patients in the lower-paying market.[26] Thus, for example, Laura Hopkins and her coauthors argue that this dynamic has taken place in Thailand, where "[a]lmost 6000 positions for medical practitioners in Thailand's public system remained unfilled in 2005, as an increasing number of physicians followed the higher wages and more attractive settings available in private care," and that, due to medical tourism, "the addition of internal 'brain drain' from public to private health care may be especially damaging" for "countries such as Ghana, Pakistan, and South Africa, which lose approximately half of their medical graduates every year to external migration."[27] Chen and Flood note that Thai doctors in private hospitals receive salaries that "are reportedly between six and eleven times greater than what are offered by public institutions," and argue that because the "privatization of health care in countries like Thailand, Malaysia and India is predominantly occurring in urban areas, the problem of internal brain drain may be accentuated by an uneven geographical distribution of health care human resources, leaving patients who rely on public facilities in rural regions most severely disadvantaged."[28] They also point to data from Thailand's Ministry of Public Health showing that "since 2000 there has been an accelerated attrition of public sector physicians relative to almost constant medical school output," and mention a "news report" claiming that, in 2005, "despite the government having managed to boost the number of newly trained doctors to 1,300, the public system also saw the outflow of physicians rising to almost 700 in that year." Chen and Flood also point to "[o]ther sources," which present "figures that are more modest…, indicating that over 350 doctors resigned from their public sector posts in the fiscal year of 2004/2005, followed by another 300-plus doctors in the next year," with many of these being the top specialists at medical school–affiliated hospitals. This implies that what is being lost to the private sector are some of the best doctors.[29] This is particularly worrisome because

---

[26] *See* Johnston et al., *supra* note 14, at 11.

[27] Hopkins et al., *supra* note 14, at 194; *see also* Rupa Chinai & Rahul Goswani, *Medical Visas Mark Growth of Indian Medical Tourism*, 85 BULL. WORLD HEALTH ORG. 164, 165 (2007) (quoting Dr. Manuel Dayrit, Director, WHO's Human Resources for Health Department, as saying, "Although there are no ready figures that can be cited from studies, initial observations suggest that medical tourism dampens external migration but worsens internal migration").

[28] Chen & Flood, *supra* note 17, at 290 (citing S. Wibulpolprasert & C.A. Pachanee, *Addressing the Internal Brain Drain of Medical Doctors in Thailand: The Story and Lesson Learned*, 8 GLOBAL SOC. POL'Y 12, 12 (2008)); other sources estimate the salary of doctors in private clinics to be about eight to ten times greater than that of doctors in state hospitals, as seen in A. Chambers, *Thai Embrace of Medical Tourism Divides Professionals*, GUARDIAN (London), Apr. 26, 2011, *available at* http://www.guardian.co.uk/global-development/poverty-matters/2011/apr/26/thailand-medical-tourism-divides-professionals; S. Wibulpolprasert & P. Pengpaibon, *Integrated Strategies to Tackle the Inequitable Distribution of Doctors in Thailand: Four Decades of Experience*, 1 HUM. RESOURCES HEALTH 1, 5 (2003); R. Rasiah et al., *Privatising Healthcare in Malaysia: Power, Policy and Profits*, 39 J. CONTEMP. ASIA 50, 60 (2009); Tattara, *supra* note 22, at 10).

[29] Chen & Flood, *supra* note 17, at 290 (citing Wibulpolprasert & Pengpaibon, *supra* note 28, at 6, 12; Chambers, *supra* note 28; Kanchanachitra et al., *supra* note 20, at 775.) There are news reports that something similar is

these doctors often serve as the teaching staff at medical schools in Thailand; their absence would adversely affect these schools' ability to create new doctors of high quality,[30] which contributes to inelasticity, as discussed below. Drilling down into still more granular Thai data, Chen and Flood note:

[a] report by Bangkok's Chulalongkorn Hospital documented that 70 of the institution's medical specialists left between 2005 and 2010 to work at private hospitals that serve foreign patients. In addition, private sector competition reportedly caused nearly 6,000 vacancies for medical practitioners across Thailand's public health care system to go unfilled in 2005.... In contrast to these staffing challenges in the public sector, the number of medical doctors working in Thailand's private hospitals grew by 29.6% from 3,325 to 4,309 between 1997 and 2006.[31]

Chen and Flood also note that Malaysia has experienced a similar downward trend in the number of professionals in the public health sector, along with an overall public-to-private flow of health professionals.[32] In addition, Chen and Flood point to data suggesting that, in major medical tourism hubs, there have been significant increases in costs for health care. In India, they note government data showing that the inflation-adjusted cost of each hospitalization in urban India increased by 9 percent for public facilities and 36.5 percent for private institutions between 1995 and 2004.[33] They note, too, a study tracking the average costs of five surgical procedures performed in Thai private hospitals, which shows a "continual price escalation between 2003 and 2008, with the annual price increase as high as 10–25% in most hospitals between 2006 and 2008," while, in Singapore, "rising health care charges have led the government to actively encourage citizens to seek more affordable services in neighbouring Malaysia."[34]

---

afoot in Israel and that many medical tourists are attracted to the Israeli system because they can select the best doctors. Chen & Flood, *supra* note 17, at 290 (citing D. Even & M. Zinshtein, *Haaretz Probe: Israel Gives Medical Tourists Perks Denied to Citizens*, HAARETZ (Israel) Nov. 18, 2010, *available at* http://www.haaretz.com/print-edition/news/haaretz-probe-israel-gives-medical-tourists-perks-denied-to-citizens-1.325275).

[30] Chen & Flood, *supra* note 17, at 290–91 (citing Kanchanachitra et al., *supra* note 20, at 775; *NHC Joins Opposition to Medical Hub Plan*, BANGKOK POST, Nov. 4, 2010).

[31] Chen & Flood, *supra* note 17, at 290 (citing *NHC Joins Opposition to Medical Hub Plan, supra* note 30; Hopkins et al., *supra* note 14, at 194; NaRanong & NaRanong, *supra* note 20, at 340).

[32] Chen & Flood, *supra* note 17, at 290 (citing C.H. Leng, *Medical Tourism and the State in Malaysia and Singapore*, 10 GLOBAL SOC. POL'Y 336, 348 (2010); C.H. Leng, *Medical Tourism in Malaysia: International Movement of Healthcare Consumers and the Commodification of Healthcare* 8 (Asia Res. Inst., Working Paper No. 83, 2007), *available at* http://papers.ssrn.com/sol3/papers.cfm?abstract_id=1317163).

[33] Chen & Flood, *supra* note 17, at 291 (citing S. Selvaraj & A. Karan, *Deepening Health Insecurity in India: Evidence from National Sample Surveys since 1980s*, 44 ECON. & POL. WKLY. 55, 58 (2009)).

[34] Chen & Flood, *supra* note 17, at 291 (citing NaRanong & NaRanong, *supra* note 20, at 341; Leng, *Medical Tourism and the State in Malaysia and Singapore, supra* note 32, at 349).

Again, we should be cautious about our inferences from this data, especially as to the causation question but also as to the redressability one. At most, this data shows a *correlation* between being a medical tourism hub and having price increases, not causation, and even as to correlation, it would strengthen the case to compare the data of "control" countries—in the same region but without large volumes of medical tourism—to see if (and by how much) the rate of growth in the costs of medical services in medical tourism hubs exceeds the rate of growth in non-hubs. We are unlikely, though, to have the results of this kind of careful analysis any time soon. We must make decisions in conditions of uncertainty, and, *as a whole*, the evidence amassed is suggestive of a negative effect of medical tourism through this vector, even if no single piece of evidence is entirely convincing.

It is worth emphasizing here that losing physicians and other resources from the public to the private sector is not something unique to medical tourism or even to developing countries. This has also been the dynamic when private options are introduced into public systems, even in the developed world, although a number of jurisdictions, such as Canada and France, have tried to prevent flight to the private system by regulation.[35] Regulations that require providers to spend time in both systems are also more likely to produce positive externalities from the private to public health care systems; for example, a physician who receives extra training as part of her duties in the medical tourism sector may be able to carry that training over to her time spent treating poor patients, if regulation forces her facility to treat poor patients. I discuss such possible regulation more in depth below, but it is worth noting that in medical tourism havens such as India, even when such regulations are in place, many observers have been skeptical that they have been or will be enforced.[36]

(3) *The supply of health care professionals, facilities, and technologies in the destination country is inelastic.*

Theoretically, if medical tourism causes increased demand for health care providers and facilities in the destination country, the country could meet such demand by increasing the supply

---

[35] *See* Colleen M. Flood, *Chaoulli's Legacy for the Future of Canadian Health Care Policy*, 44 OSGOODE HALL L.J. 273, 289 (2006) (discussing evidence that "to the extent that prices are higher in the private sector and where specialists are free to do so, they will devote an increasing proportion of their time to private patients who are likely to have less acute or serious needs than those patients left behind in the public system"); Colleen M. Flood & Amanda Haugan, *Is Canada Odd? A Comparison of European and Canadian Approaches to Choice and Regulation of the Public/Private Divide in Health Care*, 5 HEALTH ECON., POL'Y & L. 319, 320 (2010).

[36] *See, e.g.*, Gupta, *supra* note 14, at 4–5 ("The government would have us believe that revenues earned by the industry will strengthen health care in the country. But we do not see any mechanism by which this can happen. On the contrary, corporate hospitals have repeatedly dishonoured the conditions for receiving government subsidies by refusing to treat poor patients free of cost—and they have got away without punishment. Moreover, reserving a few beds for the poor in elite institutions does not address the necessity to increase public investment in health to three to five times the present level."); Johnston et al., *supra* note 14, at 5.

of these things. Indeed, some "proponents of medical tourism argue that the success of the industry itself could enlarge the pool of health resources available to destination countries by stimulating fresh investment, both domestic and foreign, in the health sector,"[37] potentially freeing resources for the users of the public system in the destination country.[38]

In reality, however, even developed countries have had difficulty increasing this supply when necessary.[39] The evidence of reinvestment of health care resources into the private sector in various medical tourism hubs is, if anything, more dour. As Chen and Flood note, despite heavy increases in the amount of private investment in the health sector in India, "health-related spending as a proportion of overall government expenditure has declined since the mid-1980s from 3.29% to 2.77% in 2005," and "the amount allocated to public health initiatives (e.g., trachoma and blindness control, infectious diseases prevention, etc.) has decreased" to an even larger extent.[40] Although there have been proposals in Thailand and Israel to incentivize doctors to work overtime to meet the additional needs of medical tourists,[41] Chen and Flood express reasonable concern over whether it is "possible to create excess capacity through stretching an already over-extended health system," and, in particular, worry that developing countries lack "a sophisticated regulatory and monitoring system that ensures health practitioners who treat medical tourists also fulfill their duties to public sector patients."[42]

To be sure, there is some elasticity here as well. Thailand, for example, has plans to add 10,678 extra spots in its medical schools between 2005 and 2014.[43] But this is a costly investment that may not be available to all destination countries. 2002 data suggests a cost to the Thai government of roughly US$45,000 to produce one physician, which would mean (putting aside possible fixed costs and economies of scale altering the price)

---

[37] Chen & Flood, *supra* note 17, at 291–92 (quoting Johnston et al., *supra* note 14, at 7).

[38] *See* Chen & Flood, *supra* note 17, at 292 (citing UNITED NATIONS CONFERENCE ON TRADE AND DEVELOPMENT: REPORT OF THE EXPERT MEETING ON UNIVERSAL ACCESS TO SERVICES (2006), at 13, *available at* http://www.unctad.org/en/Docs/c1em3od3_en.pdf).

[39] *See* Greg L. Stoddart & Morris L. Barer, *Will Increasing Medical School Enrollment Solve Canada's Physician Supply Problems?*, 161 CAN. MED. ASSOC. J. 983 (1999); Abhaya Kamalakanthan & Sukhan Jackson, *The Supply of Doctors in Australia: Is There a Shortage?* (Univ. Queensland, Discussion Paper No. 341, 2006), *available at* http://tinyurl.com/3fz7r94.

[40] Chen & Flood, *supra* note 17, at 292 (citing S. Spinaci et al., *Tough Choices: Investing in Health for Development*, WORLD HEALTH ORG. (2006), at 7, *available at* http://www.who.int/macrohealth/documents/report_and_cover.pdf; R. Duggal, *Poverty & Health: Criticality of Public Financing*, 126 INDIAN J. MED. RES. 309, 313 (2007); *Government Health Expenditure in India: A Benchmark Study*, NEW DELHI: ECONOMICS RESEARCH FOUNDATION 15 (2006).

[41] *See* Chen & Flood, *supra* note 17, at 292 (citing Kanchanachitra et al., *supra* note 20, at 775; R. Linder-Ganz & D. Even, *Panel Recommends Using Money from Medical Tourism to Fund Israelis' Healthcare*, HAARETZ (Israel), May 29, 2011, *available at* http://www.haaretz.com/print-edition/news/panel-recommends-using-money-from-medical-tourism-to-fund-israelis-healthcare-1.364638).

[42] Chen & Flood, *supra* note 17, at 292.

[43] *Id.* (citing C.A. Pachanee & S. Wibulpolprasert, *Incoherent Policies on Universal Coverage of Health Insurance and Promotion of International Trade in Health Services in Thailand*, 21 HEALTH POL'Y & PLAN. 310, 316 (2006)).

a total expenditure of US$480 million to add these physicians in Thailand.[44] Many destination countries may not be able to afford such investments, and although, in theory, the investments could be financed through the additional revenue from medical tourism, that assumes a willingness and enough regulatory coordination to do so, which may be absent in some destination countries. Moreover, Chen and Flood point to data showing that a "country's effort to increase medical school enrolments tends to have limited effects on actually improving health care access in areas where human resource shortages are the most severe,"[45] and worry that enlarging the supply of health care providers in developing destination countries "may simply feed ever-expanding demand from foreign patients rather than reducing human resource deficits faced by local residents."[46] As discussed above, the need to match increased demand for the right specialties poses additional problems.

Finally, investments in building capacity always entail an adjustment period. Thus, even countries that are unusually successful in increasing the size of their health care workforce to meet the demands of medical tourism will face interim shortages. Thus, there is good evidence that existing medical tourism hubs will face problems in increasing their supply of health care providers in order to meet increased demand for those resources by medical tourists, at least in the middle term.

(4) *The positive effects of medical tourism in counteracting the external "brain drain" of health care practitioners to foreign countries are outweighed by the negative effects of medical tourism on the availability of health care resources.*

External[47] medical migration, or "brain drain," represents a significant threat to health care access abroad. For example, 61 percent of all graduates from the Ghana Medical School between 1986 and 1995 left Ghana for employment (of those, 54.9 percent worked in the United Kingdom and 35.4 percent worked in the United States), and a 2005 study found that 25 percent of doctors in the United States are graduates of foreign medical schools.[48] According to one estimate, Thailand lost approximately 25 percent of its

---

[44] Chen & Flood, *supra* note 17, at 292 (citing Wibulpolprasert & Pengpaibon, *supra* note 28, at 10).

[45] Chen & Flood, *supra* note 17, at 292 (citing G. Stoddart & M. Barer, *Will Increasing Medical School Enrolment Solve Canada's Physician Supply Problems?*, 161 Can. Med. Ass'n J. 983 (1999); J. Frenk et al., *Patterns of Medical Employment: A Survey of Imbalances in Urban Mexico*, 81 Am. J. Pub. Health 23 (1991); Kamalakanthan & Jackson, *supra* note 39).

[46] Chen & Flood, *supra* note 17, at 292.

[47] "External" brain drain refers to providers who leave one country for another, while "internal" brain drain refers to those who stay put but move from public to private sectors or rural to urban service locations. There are also other distinctions one can draw; for example, external brain drain may be within a region ("interregional") or outside of it.

[48] *See* Fitzhugh Mullan, *The Metrics of the Physician Brain Drain*, 353 New Eng. J. Med. 1810, 1811 (2005); David Sanders et al., *Public Health in Africa, in* Global Public Health: A New Era 46 (Robert Beaglehole ed., 2003).

physicians to the United States alone between 1960 and 1975, while "an estimate in 2006 suggested that there were nearly 60,000 Indian physicians practicing in the U.S., U.K., Canada and Australia, a number equivalent to 10% of doctors registered in India."[49] As Larry Gostin has put it, in the ordinary course of globalization, "[h]ealth care workers are 'pushed' from developing countries by the impoverished conditions: low remuneration, lack of equipment and drugs, and poor infrastructure and management," and "[t]hey are 'pulled' to developed countries by the allure of a brighter future: better wages, working conditions, training, and career opportunities, as well as safer and more stable social and political environments."[50] The cost to less developed countries and the benefit to the United States and other countries caused by the brain drain is staggering. A recent report suggested that it would have cost, on average, $184,000 to train each of the three million health care professionals who had migrated, such that richer nations saved $552 billion, whereas poor nations lost $500 million in training costs.[51]

It is possible that for health care professionals tempted to leave their country of origin to practice in other markets, the availability of higher-paying jobs with better technology and more time with patients in the medical tourist sector of their country of origin will counteract this incentive.[52] As Snyder and coauthors put it: "by creating, in the health sector, well-paid jobs that use the latest medical techniques and technologies, the out-migration of the best trained health professionals from LMICs can be lessened."[53] Medical tourism may also enable the destination country to "recapture" some health care providers who left years earlier, or to change "brain drain" into "brain circulation," wherein home country providers leave for training abroad and return home ready to use and impart their skills to other providers in the home country.[54]

There is some preliminary data that supports this vector. For example, a report by the UN Economic and Social Commission for Asia and the Pacific done in 2007 notes that the majority of the six hundred health care professionals then employed at Bumrungrad International Hospital in Bangkok were Thais who had returned from the United States; in India, the Apollo Hospital Group has claimed to have hired 138 expatriate doctors by 2008, and the Wockhardt hospital chain has claimed to have attracted

---

[49] Chen & Flood, *supra* note 17, at 293 (citing Wibulpolprasert & Pengpaibon, *supra* note 27, at 3; F. Mullan, *Doctors for the World: Indian Physician Emigration*, 25 HEALTH AFF. 380, 381 (2006)).

[50] Lawrence O. Gostin, *The International Migration and Recruitment of Nurses: Human Rights and Global Justice*, 299 JAMA 1827, 1828 (2008).

[51] BOOKMAN & BOOKMAN, *supra* note 9, at 106.

[52] *See* Matthias Helble, *The Movements of Patients across Borders: Challenges and Opportunities for Public Health*, 89 BULL. WORLD HEALTH ORG. 68, 70 (2011) (discussing as-yet-unpublished data supporting this claim in Thailand).

[53] Jeremy Snyder et al., *Beyond Sun, Sand, and Stitches: Assigning Responsibility for the Harms of Medical Tourism*, 27 BIOETHICS 233, 234 (2013).

[54] For discussions of these possibilities in other contexts, *see, e.g.*, Ayelet Shachar, *The Race for Talent: Highly Skilled Migrants and Competitive Immigration Regimes*, 81 N.Y.U. L. REV. 148, 168 (2006).

twenty-four professionals from the United States and the United Kingdom.[55] Chen and Flood caution that these are small amounts given the needs involved of these countries, writing that:

> In Thailand, an injection of 600 new doctors from abroad, while important, would represent an increase of less than 0.1 physician per 10,000 population, and hardly closes the gap between the existing physician density of 3 per 10,000 population and the world average of 14 per 10,000. Likewise, the number of expatriate doctors working in Apollo and Wockhardt hospitals [in India] falls far short of the 600,000 more physicians that India requires, and it equates only to 10% of the amount of Indian-trained physicians that enter the licensing process in the U.S. annually.[56]

They are no doubt correct, but this answers the equity question, not the causation or redressability questions that I think are relevant. The issue is not whether medical migration represents a serious problem leading to health care inequity between the developed and developing world. That is clearly the case, and this problem stems from the recruitment of doctors and pull and push factors, and raises global justice and regulatory issues (as well as complex issues such as the flow of remittances) that I and others have written about elsewhere.[57] But on either the causation or redressability approaches I outlined above, the mere fact of this inequity is not itself a problem of medical tourism, and is instead a problem with migration. In other words, if medical tourism is not causing the problem, and/or changes to medical tourism regulation will not redress the problem, then this is not an issue about medical tourism at all. If, by contrast, medical tourism is having a positive impact on reducing the problem, as Chen and Flood seem to recognize, the question then becomes whether it could have a *more* positive effect if the industry

---

[55] Chen & Flood, *supra* note 17, at 293 (citing S. Tata et al., *Medical Travel in Asia and the Pacific: Challenges and Opportunities*, UN Econ. Soc. Commission for Asia and Pac.: 2009, at 24; Cortez, *supra* note 22, at 110; C. Madden, *Medical Tourism Causes Complications*, Asia Times, Nov. 7, 2008, *available at* http://www.atimes.com/atimes/Asian_Economy/JK07Dk01.html).

[56] Chen & Flood, *supra* note 17, at 293 (citing Kanchanachitra et al., *supra* note 20, at 771 (Table 2); I. Hazarika, *Medical Tourism: Its Potential Impact on the Health Workforce and Health Systems in India*, 25 Health Pol'y & Plan. 248, 249 (2010); L. Hopkins et al., *Medical Tourism Today: What Is the State of Existing Knowledge?*, 31 J. Pub. Health Pol'y 185, 192 (2010)).

[57] *See, e.g.*, Cohen, *supra* note 22, at 52–56; Vivien Runnels et al., *Global Policies and Local Practice in the Ethical Recruitment of Internationally Trained Health Human Resources*, in The Globalization of Health Care: Legal and Ethical Issues 203 (I. Glenn Cohen ed., 2013); Nir Eyal & Till Bärnighausen, *Conditioning Medical Scholarships on Long, Future Service: A Defense*, in The Globalization of Health Care: Legal and Ethical Issues 220 (I. Glenn Cohen ed., 2013); Allyn L. Taylor & Ibadat S. Dhillon, *A Global Legal Architecture to Address the Challenges of International Health Worker Migration: A Case Study of the Role of Non-binding Instruments in Global Health Governance*, in The Globalization of Health Care: Legal and Ethical Issues 233 (I. Glenn Cohen ed., 2013).

was regulated differently (on the redressability view), and whether whatever positive effect it is having counterbalances the negative effects medical tourism is otherwise having on health care access (on the causation and redressability views).

All that said, Chen and Flood are correct to note that the amount of positive migration due to medical tourism is small, and it is unclear whether retained doctors will benefit the worst-off in these societies, or instead primarily serve the best-off. These questions can only be answered country-by-country after in-depth and difficult to conduct empirical research.[58] In any event, only a few of the countries that experience significant medical brain drain are also developing strong medical tourism industries; many are *only* sources of medical brain drain and not destinations for medical tourism, which means that they are being drained of their medical resources without the positive regeneration due to medical tourism. Of course, an influx of medical tourism into these regions is not necessarily a good solution, not only because it may be infeasible for some of these countries, but also because the creation of medical tourism hubs may actually exacerbate *intra*-regional medical migration.

(5) *Medical tourism prompts destination country governments to redirect resources away from basic health care services in a way that outweighs positive health care spillovers.*

In order to compete for patients on quality and price against both the patient's home country and other medical tourism hubs, destination countries will need to invest in their nascent medical tourism industry through, for example, direct funding, tax subsidies, and land grants.[59] Unfortunately, such funding often comes from money devoted to other health programs, including basic health care and social services,[60] and those effects are likely to be felt most strongly by the destination country poor. In other words, we need some sense of whether governments actually invest in health care services accessible by the poor (or at least do not take them away) in a counterfactual world where medical tourism is restricted. We also need to examine this dynamic as against a potential countervailing dynamic wherein medical tourism leads to a diffusion of better foreign

---

[58] *See, e.g.*, Snyder et al., *supra* note 25, at 58 (noting that "at present there is no indication of mass movement of health-care professionals from Barbados' publicly funded health system to the private, for-profit health sector" but that this was a concern on the minds of many stakeholders and an issue on which the Barbados government was actively at work to prevent).

[59] BOOKMAN & BOOKMAN, *supra* note 9, at 105–09; Turner, *supra* note 5, at 314–15, 320.

[60] *See* Benavides, *supra* note 2, at 55; Johnston et al., *supra* note 14, at 5–6 ("[T]he hiring of physicians trained in public education systems by private medical tourism facilities is another example of a potentially inequitable use of public resources. Furthermore, physicians in [low and middle income countries] who might normally practice in resource-poor environments can instead treat high-paying international patients, thereby gaining access to advanced technologies and superior facilities while receiving a higher wage."); Turner, *supra* note 5, at 320.

medical technology or standards of practice or other health care spillovers that are beneficial to the entire patient population.[61] Which dynamic wins out can only be answered on a country-by-country basis, but in India, for example, some commentators have suggested that the product of these countervailing forces has ultimately been a net negative for the destination country poor.[62]

In their own analysis of these competing dynamics, Chen and Flood note that "during the course of our research, we did not uncover empirical data that clearly demonstrates such constructive competition between the public and private health sectors," finding instead that "the overemphasis on medical technologies and the pressure to vie for skilled health practitioners appear to have distorted health care supply and demand, and pushed up the prices of treatments in some medical tourist destinations." From this, they conclude that such "medical tourism-induced inter-sectoral competition may well increase health care outlays without necessarily upgrading health service quality."[63] These authors do concede that there have been some instances of positive spillovers, noting that "Bumrungrad and Apollo hospitals offer charitable cardiac treatments to low-income children, and the Wockhardt hospital group operates a mobile eye clinic and deworming camps for underprivileged Indians."[64] But they caution that "since these initiatives are never formally evaluated, little is known about their cost-effectiveness," that "these programs are philanthropic in nature, [so] their scope and length are solely determined by private donors, sometimes based on considerations that are independent of the programs' efficacy," and, finally, that the programs may not represent the best resource allocation "since they may selectively target patients whose circumstances have a higher profile or are media-friendly."[65]

Again, in theory, governments can mandate that tourism facilities be operated to maximize the chance of spillover, and indeed in India the law and regulation of hospitals frequently has resulted in such obligations on the part of tourism facilities. In reality, though, several authors allege that these promises have not been kept. For example, Chen and Flood write:

> In 1988, the municipal government of Delhi, India entered into an agreement with the Apollo hospital group to jointly develop a multispecialty medical centre. While the government provided land and portions of the start-up capital

---

[61] Nathan Cortez, *International Health Care Convergence: The Benefits and Burdens of Market-Driven Standardization*, 26 Wis. Int'l L.J. 646 (2009).

[62] *See, e.g.*, Hopkins et al., *supra* note 14, at 194 ("In India, medical professionals are trained in highly subsidized public facilities. The annual value of these public training subsidies to the private sector where many physicians eventually work is estimated at more than $100 million, at least some of which accrues to the medical tourism industry. This diverts public funds that might otherwise have gone into improving public health care for the poor—to private care for more affluent individuals.").

[63] Chen & Flood, *supra* note 17, at 294.

[64] *Id.* at 294 (citing J. Connell, Medical Tourism 152–53 (2011)).

[65] *Id.* at 294.

amounting to nearly US$8 million, it tasked Apollo with operating the medical centre and ensuring that one-third of the inpatient and 40% of the outpatient capacity would be available at no cost to low-income patients referred from public hospitals. Nevertheless, in 2003, a committee assembled by High Court of Delhi revealed that Apollo's undertakings were mostly honored in the breach:

- less than 19% of the hospital's beds (and only 10% of the beds in the intensive care unit) were allocated to public patients;
- of all outpatient services provided in 2002/2003, a meager 0.0015% was to public patients;
- instead of free care, public patients were billed for costs relating to diagnostic imaging, medical consumables and pharmaceuticals; and,
- facilities designated for public patients were qualitatively inferior to those enjoyed by private patients.

Although Apollo's disregard for its contractual obligations was ultimately condemned by the High Court of Delhi as having violated indigent patients' right to health, similar practices are apparently common within India's private health sector and often occur with legal and political impunity. A study in early 1990s found that among 27 private health facilities that had agreed to offer free services to low-income patients in exchange for government subsidies, a majority failed to fulfill their promises. Another study by India's Public Accounts Committee in 2005 reached similar conclusions. Commentators observe that public officials generally turn a blind eye on these contractual breaches as they are frequently offered free treatments at these public-private partnership hospitals. Thus, as described by the Public Accounts Committee, "what... started [as] a grand idea of benefiting the poor turned out to be a hunting ground for the rich in the garb of public charitable institutions."[66]

In theory, destination country governments could blunt some of the negative impact of the industry by a tax-and-transfer regime wherein the medical tourism industry is taxed, and the revenue is transferred to reinvest into health care infrastructure to serve the destination country poor.[67] However, Chen and Flood claim that "there is no indication to date that any destination countries have adopted this type of resource transfer

---

[66] Id. at 294–95 (citing All India Lawyers Union (Delhi Unit) v. Government of N.C.T. of Delhi & Others, (2009) 5410 WP(C) 1997 (Delhi H.C.), at para. 20, 30, available at http://www.indiankanoon.org/doc/1508125/; Tattara, supra note 22, at 10; P. Shetty, Medical Tourism Booms in India, but at What Cost?, 376 LANCET 671, 672 (2010);. G. Thomas & S. Krishnan, Editorial, Effective Public-Private Partnership in Health Care: Apollo as a Cautionary Tale, 7 INDIAN J. MED. ETHICS 2, 2–3 (2010); CONNELL, supra note 64, at 266).

[67] E.g., I. Glenn Cohen, How to Regulate Medical Tourism (and Why It Matters for Bioethics), 12 J. DEVELOPING WORLD BIOETHICS 9 (2012).

mechanisms."[68] Such approaches to the problem also require mechanisms to enforce inter-sectoral cooperation as well as anticorruption mechanisms that may be in short supply in some destination countries. If anything, the current tendency is for transfers to run *to* the medical tourism sector in order to make it competitive as against other destination countries, as Chen and Flood detail: corporate tax breaks for hospitals aimed at medical tourists and reduced tariffs on imported medical equipment in India; a proposed tax exemption on the revenues from hospitals serving medical tourists in Malaysia; and the United Arab Emirates plans to form a tax-free health care zone.[69]

Thus, although such spillovers remain possible, there is neither as yet any good evidence they are taking place nor have destination country governments taken major steps to try to regulate in order to ensure spillovers.

(6) *Profits from the medical tourism industry are unlikely to "trickle down."*

Although spillovers of technology or health care services are one way that medical tourism may benefit the general public of a destination country, it is far from the only way. Successful medical tourism industries promise an infusion of wealth into the destination country and the possibility that all boats will rise.[70] It is quite clear that medical tourism generates significant revenue for destination countries. For example, 2007 data showed that Thailand made up to US$1.35 billion in profits from medical tourism, of which approximately 84 percent were from health service provision and the rest coming from tourism, and in the same year Singapore was estimated to have made US$1.2 billion and Malaysia US$78 million from medical tourism (as with all the figures I quote in this book, we should take them with a grain of salt as definitions and estimates vary significantly).[71] Yet there is to date not much evidence these gains have trickled down.

What might get in the way of this trickle-down effect? The reason might be something insidious such as rampant corruption, or it may be something more benign, such as a tax system that is not particularly redistributive, or a largely foreign-owned medical

---

[68] Chen & Flood, *supra* note 17, at 295 (citing C. Blouin, *Trade in Health Services: Can It Improve Access to Health Care for Poor People?*, 10 GLOBAL SOC. POL'Y 10, 293, 294 (2010)).

[69] Chen & Flood, *supra* note 17, at 295 (citing Johnston et al., *supra* note 14, at 5; Gov't of India, Ministry of Tourism, Press Release, *Medical Tourism Included under the Marketing Development Assistance (MDA) Scheme* (Nov. 15, 2010), *available at* http://www.pib.nic.in/newsite/erelease.aspx?relid=67035; Leng, *Medical Tourism in Malaysia: International Movement of Healthcare Consumers and the Commodification of Healthcare, supra* note 32, at 13; M. Alsharif et al., *Patients beyond Borders: A Study of Medical Tourists in Four Countries*, 10 GLOBAL SOC. POL'Y 315, 329 (2010)).

[70] Cortez, *supra* note 61, at 693–94 (citing Alain Enthoven, *On the Ideal Market Structure for Third-Party Purchasing of Health Care*, 39 SOC. SCI. & MED. 1413, 1420 (1994)).

[71] I take these numbers from Chen and Flood, *supra* note 17, at 296 (NaRanong & NaRanong, *supra* note 20, at 338, N. Pocock & K.H. Phua, *Medical Tourism and Policy Implications for Health Systems: A Conceptual Framework from a Comparative Study of Thailand, Singapore and Malaysia*, 7 GLOBALIZATION & HEALTH 1, 2 (2011)).

sector.[72] This last factor is not uncommon in the general tourism world, with the UN Conference on Trade and Development estimating that, on average, almost half of all tourism revenues in developed countries accrue to stakeholders overseas, and in medical tourism specifically there has been significant foreign investment.[73] Still, others are critical of the theory of "trickle down" economics more generally.[74]

In sum, the fact that a destination country gains economically from medical tourism (for example, in GDP terms) does not necessarily mean that those gains are shared in a way that promotes health care access (or health) among the destination poor. Although one cannot reach a conclusive judgment on the subject, there is thus far no good evidence that there have been major trickle-down benefits from medical tourism.

* * *

Notice, as it will become relevant in the normative analysis, that many of these triggering conditions are themselves in the control of the destination country government to some extent.

As I have said before, data on the effects of medical tourism on health care access in the destination country are scarce—in many cases, they rest on anecdote and speculation—and the analysis can only be done on a country-by-country basis, which is hard to do given the current paucity of data. In countries where the triggering conditions all obtain, one would expect medical tourism to cause some diminution in access to health care for the destination country's poorest, due to medical tourism; as fewer factors obtain, this becomes less likely. The same is true as to redressability: the more of these factors that obtain, the more likely it is that regulation of medical tourism can redress any ill factors.

This list of factors is certainly not exhaustive, and there may be additional ones in particular countries that push in the other direction.

Although I cannot prove that medical tourism causes diminutions in health care in any particular destination country, it seems to me that there is sufficient evidence supporting many of these triggering factors in many destination countries, such that the claim is plausible enough to merit a normative analysis.

---

[72] *See* Helble, *supra* note 52, at 70.

[73] Chen & Flood, *supra* note 17, at 296 (citing R. Scheyvens, *Exploring the Tourism-Poverty Nexus*, 10 CURRENT ISSUES TOURISM 231, 239 (2007); J. Akama, *The Efficacy of Tourism as a Tool for Economic Development in Kenya*, DEV. POL'Y MGMT. F., Bull. 7 (2000), *available at* http://www.dpmf.org/images/tourism-economic-devt-john.html; Z. Meghani, *A Robust, Particularist Ethical Assessment of Medical Tourism*, 11 DEVELOPING WORLD BIOETHICS 16, 28 (2011)).

[74] *See, e.g.*, Chen & Flood, *supra* note 17, at 296.

II. WHAT DUTIES ARE OWED BY HOME COUNTRIES AND OTHER INTERNATIONAL INSTITUTIONS?

Suppose that medical tourism from a particular home country, the United States, has the effect of reducing health care access in a destination country, say India, for its poorest residents (or, at least, that preventing that medical tourism will redress inequities even if the medical tourism is not the cause, though from now on I will merely use the first formulation for parsimony). Does the United States (or an international body) have an obligation to do something about it? In this section, I try to determine how much of an overlapping consensus there is among rival comprehensive moral theories. In the following section, I consider in more depth obligations of individual medical tourists.

A. Obligations of Home Countries and Intergovernmental Bodies

Broadly speaking, one can imagine three different families of theories about what would justify placing obligations on home countries to do something about the negative effects of medical tourism on destination country health care. One family of theories would merely rely on home country self-interest. The second set is composed of Cosmopolitan theories, for which the mere presence of inequity—divorced from home country causation—would be enough to justify home country aid. The final set of theories is, in some respect, composed of causation theories that I have elsewhere called "intermediate" theories of global justice. They require an institutional nexus between the deficits and the home country to justify duties of action. I will examine the families of theories one by one. The treatment here is by necessity brief, but I have explored these theories in more depth elsewhere.[75] I myself favor the intermediate theories, but my main goal here is to map what these different approaches would say about medical tourism and how much of an overlapping consensus they foster as to what should be done, rather than to thoroughly evaluate their pros and cons.

i. Self-Interest

The easiest argument for home country obligations in this sphere argues for restricting or regulating medical tourism based on the interests of the *home* country. As such, one might think of this as not a moral theory at all, or at least not an other-regarding one. In particular, one might press four claims: (1) medical tourism threatens home country patients with poorer care or poorer malpractice recovery, and results in negative externalities in meeting the needs of iatrogenically injured patients when they return home. Even assuming *arguendo* that the factual elements of this claim are true—something I have discussed

---

[75] *See generally* Cohen, *supra* note 22.

in greater depth in Chapter 3—the cases where this particular self-interest argument might push us to curb medical tourism will map on only by coincidence, if at all, to cases posing concerns about the destination country poor's health care access. That is, there can be cases where this particular self-interest concern would urge action but there are no health care access concerns, and cases where there are health care access concerns but this particular self-interest argument is not operative. The same response applies regarding concerns about the importation of diseases (especially antibiotic-resistant strains or "super-bugs") back to developed countries due to medical tourism, as has been reported in a few case studies and discussed in greater depth in Chapter 2.[76]

There are three other arguments one might make in analogy to those deployed elsewhere in the health care globalization literature: (2) Medical tourism that results in decreased access to treatment for infectious diseases might increase the risk of transmission of those diseases to Americans; (3) Indians are valuable to the United States as producer-exporters of cheap goods and consumer-importers of our goods, therefore, improving Indian citizens' basic health care will improve that country's development and ensure more productive trading partners and affluent markets in which to sell U.S.-made goods; and (4) Improving health care access abroad may reduce immigration pressures to the United States or increase national security by reducing global terrorism.[77]

Unfortunately, these arguments are not very persuasive in this context. For the infection-transmission and consumer arguments, we should arguably be more concerned about the health of the higher-socioeconomic-status strata of Indian society, who are more likely to travel to our shores and be better able to buy our goods. While diminishing health care access to India's poorest, medical tourism services may actually improve the health care of the wealthier strata, at least those who are able to buy into these better facilities or take advantage of the diffusion of knowledge and technology. This is not to say there are no infection concerns—Americans traveling to India for pleasure tourism may bring diseases back with them—but they are less salient than in other contexts.

A more serious and general objection to deploying these self-interest arguments here is that even if it is in the American self-interest to help India's poor access health care for these reasons, it will frequently be even *more* in its self-interest to help its *own* poor citizens in this regard. Medical tourism promises to improve the health care of poor Americans even while it (by hypothesis) reduces health care access to poor Indians, and the former effect might be thought to dominate in terms of U.S. self-interest. This objection is particularly salient for those paying out-of-pocket or for government-prompted

---

[76] *See, e.g.*, Snyder et al., *supra* note 53, at 235.

[77] For arguments of this type as to other global health justice issues such as drug pricing in the developing world, *see, e.g.*, William W. Fisher & Talha Syed, *Global Justice in Health Care: Developing Drugs for the Developing World*, 40 U.C. Davis L. Rev. 581, 588–91 (2007); Lawrence O. Gostin, *Meeting Basic Survival Needs of the World's Least Healthy People: Toward a Framework Convention on Global Health*, 96 Geo. L.J. 331, 352–63 (2008).

medical tourism. It is less forceful an objection with respect to insurer-prompted medical tourism, because if medical tourism were restricted, many of the users would continue to have access to health care—they would just pay more for it.[78] For similar reasons, this objection to the self-interest argument may be less forceful for certain subtypes of medical tourism, such as cosmetic surgery.

ii. Cosmopolitan Theories (and Their Statist Critics)

1. Cosmopolitanism in Global Justice

Cosmopolitan theories share a commitment to ignoring geographic boundaries in the application of moral theory. For them, the obligations we bear to each other are the same whether the "other" lives in our nation-state or outside it. As I have detailed elsewhere, they come in many types—for example, Utilitarian, Prioritarian, and the Nussbaum/ Sen Functioning/Capabilities approach (which is in some senses Sufficientarian)—each of which would have somewhat different implications for medical tourism.

Utilitarians are committed to maximizing aggregated social welfare wherever the relevant people reside for nationalist purposes. As William W. Fisher and Talha Syed have suggested in the context of pharmaceutical R & D spending on diseases that predominantly affect the poorest countries, the fact of diminishing marginal utility from health care gives a good prima facie argument on Utilitarian grounds to favor interventions for the worst-off over the better-off, even if each group is a similarly sized population. Increasing health care access is more likely to raise the welfare of the poor than it is that of comparably richer individuals.[79]

Prioritarians do "not give equal weight to equal benefits, whoever receives them," but instead give more weight to "benefits to the worse off."[80] Take, for example, John Rawls's extremely Priortiarian Difference Principle: inequalities in "primary goods" (income, wealth, positions of authority or responsibility, the social bases of self-respect, and, after prompting from Norman Daniels, health) should be allowed to persist only if they work to the greatest benefit of the least-advantaged group.[81] One famous version of Cosmopolitan prioritarianism was put forth by Charles Beitz in his attempt to extend the work of John Rawls to the global sphere[82] (though we shall see that, in later work, Rawls took a quite different approach). Beitz offers a strong and a weak version. The

---

[78] *See* I. Glenn Cohen, *Protecting Patients with Passports: Medical Tourism and the Patient-Protective Argument*, 95 IOWA L. REV. 1467, 1546 (2010).

[79] Fisher & Syed, *supra* note 77, at 602–05.

[80] Derek Parfit, Lindley Lecture at the University of Kansas: Equality or Priority? (Nov. 21, 1999), *reprinted in* 10 RATIO 202, 213 (Dec. 1997).

[81] *See* JOHN RAWLS, A THEORY OF JUSTICE § 46, at 300–01, § 11, at 60–61 (1971); JOHN RAWLS, JUSTICE AS FAIRNESS: A RESTATEMENT § 51.5, at 172 (2001); DANIELS, *supra* note 16, at 44.

[82] *See* CHALES R. BEITZ, POLITICAL THEORY AND INTERNATIONAL RELATIONS (1979); Charles R. Beitz, *Justice and International Relations*, 4 PHIL. & PUB. AFF. 360, 374 (1975).

strong version is that we should apply the Rawlsian redistributive principle internation-ally.[83] This version clearly grounds a normative problem in medical tourism because of the extreme priority given to the worst-off, who are likely to be India's poor in this con-text.[84] By contrast, the weaker version of Beitz's approach instructs us to apply interna-tionally whatever distributive justice policy one adopts domestically.[85] Its implication for medical tourism is less clear and depends on the degree of priority given to the worst-off, although it would seem to more clearly promote interventions restricting medical tour-ism than the Utilitarian approach.

A third Cosmopolitan approach is Sufficientarianism, according to which justice is not concerned with improving the lot of the least well-off (Prioritarianism) or achieving equality per se (Egalitarianism), but instead with ensuring that individuals do not fall below a particular threshold of whatever is the "currency" of distribution.[86] Although emanating from a more Aristotelian starting point, we can understand Amartya Martha Nussbaum's approach (emanating from work she did with Amartya Sen) as roughly fit-ting this category. In a nutshell, this approach is to discern the "functionings" central to a flourishing human life, determine the "capabilities" needed to attain those func-tionings, and then identify and fix natural and social disparities to raise people to the threshold in those capabilities.[87] Nussbaum delineates ten capabilities, two of which are central for our purposes: "Life [—b]eing able to live to the end of the human life of normal length; not dying prematurely, or before one's life is so reduced as to be not worth living" and "Bodily Health [—b]eing able to have good health, including repro-ductive health…."[88] Nussbaum indicates that the responsibility to achieve the threshold on these capabilities falls at all levels: on national governments, on international bodies, and even on corporations, and the failure of one institution to meet its obligations does not reduce the obligation of the others.[89] She also makes clear that the thresholds are

---

[83] Elsewhere I have noted some open questions about whether Rawls's work can be extended beyond the "basic structure" of society, and suggested that this might be better thought of as Rawlsian style extensions and not Rawlsian per se. *See* Cohen, *supra* note 22, at 38–39 n.78.

[84] I say "likely" because it would depend in part on how "worst-off" was defined. Most welfarists would define it in terms of total welfare, but a welfarist focused on health in particular might press for a focus on "sickest" rather than total welfare. Either way, I think it plausible that the poor Indian would qualify.

[85] BEITZ, POLITICAL THEORY AND INTERNATIONAL RELATIONS, *supra* note 82, at 174.

[86] *See* Roger Crisp, *Equality, Priority, and Compassion*, 113 ETHICS 745, 756–63 (2003); Harry G. Frankfurt, *Equality as a Moral Ideal*, 98 ETHICS 21, 21–25 (1987); Alexander Rosenberg, *Equality, Sufficiency, and Opportunity in the Just Society*, 12 SOC. PHIL. & POL'Y 54 (1995).

[87] *See generally* MARTHA NUSSBAUM, FRONTIERS OF JUSTICE 155–216, 273–315 (2006) (setting out the Capabilities approach); MARTHA NUSSBAUM, WOMEN AND HUMAN DEVELOPMENT: THE CAPABILITIES APPROACH 4–14 (2002) (describing the Capabilities approach similarly); AMARTYA SEN, INEQUALITY REEXAMINED 39–53 (1992) (describing the Capabilities approach similarly).

[88] NUSSBAUM, FRONTIERS OF JUSTICE, *supra* note 87, at 76–78.

[89] *Id.* at 171, 313–19.

non-relativistic. For example, the threshold for adequate "life" or "bodily health" is the same if the citizen is American or Indian.[90]

All of these theories would establish significant moral duties on the part of home countries to redistribute resources to destination countries. To simplify: because, at least in North-South trade, the destination country poor whose health care access is diminished by medical tourism are generally worse-off than the home country patients who are seeking the care, each of these theories gives a prima facie reason to oppose medical tourism for this reason. The South-South trade, for example travel by Indonesians to Malaysia for health care, may be more complex on this account when the relative holdings of the two groups is much more closely tied together.

Although focusing on more Prioritarian Cosmopolitan approaches, Beitz has eloquently captured the more general attraction of Cosmopolitan theories as twofold: (1) the desire to avoid moral arbitrariness in the distribution of primary goods—that is, "we should not view national boundaries as having fundamental moral significance"[91]—and (2) that a limitation of redistribution to the domestic sphere is only justifiable on an account of nations as self-sufficient cooperative schemes, a position he views as untenable in today's world of international interdependence, where those regulating trade (World Trade Organization (WTO)) and capital (International Monetary Fund (IMF) and World Bank) "impose[] burdens on poor and economically weak countries that they cannot practically avoid."[92]

Although it is easy to see how Cosmopolitan theories would ground duties on home countries related to medical tourism, there are several related problems with relying on them:

What Cosmopolitan theories offer us is *not* a theory of when we are responsible for harms *stemming from medical tourism*, but when we ought to improve the lives of the badly-off simpliciter. In one sense, causation matters: only if restricting medical tourism causes an improvement in welfare for the worst-off, the raising of health capabilities, etc., are we required to take the action. In another sense, however, causation in the historical and responsibility senses is irrelevant because it is the mere fact of the destination country's citizens' needs that imposes upon us the obligation to help them in whatever way we can, and not anything about medical tourism specifically. Thus, in one direction, the duties may persist even when medical tourism is eliminated or its harms are remedied because the source of the obligation is not anything we have done; it is instead the destitute state of those abroad. In the other direction, once the theories' goals are met (for example, they reach the threshold level on the health capability, to use one variant), we do not bear an obligation (at least under distributive justice principles) to prevent

---

[90] *Id.* at 78–81. For an application of Nussbaum's approach to global health specifically, *see* Gostin, *supra* note 77, at 343–47.

[91] BEITZ, POLITICAL THEORY AND INTERNATIONAL RELATIONS, *supra* note 82, at 151.

[92] Beitz, *Justice and International Relations, supra* note 82, at 374.

medical tourism or remedy its ill effects, even if medical tourism continues to produce significant health care deficits for the destination country poor that would not occur if it were curbed. Moreover, it is possible that other forms of aid or assistance might "cancel out" whatever negative effects medical tourism has in terms of the global Cosmopolitan calculus. To put this point another way, Cosmopolitan theories provide good answers to the equity question and perhaps the redressability question, but not the causation question. If one believes causation is important for moral obligations, then Cosmopolitan theories will not satisfy.

Further, these approaches offer a somewhat unsatisfying resolution to what I have elsewhere called a "self-inflicted wounds problem": that on these views it is not relevant to the scope of the home country's obligation that some of the factors (discussed above) that cause medical tourism to negatively impact health care access in the destination country are within the *destination country's government's control*, that is, that the destination country is partially responsible. The qualification is that, to the extent that we could induce the destination country to alter these facts about its self-governance, such influence would be one tool to meet our obligations under these theories. But to the extent we are unable to prompt these alterations, under the Cosmopolitan approach, our responsibility to improve the welfare and capabilities of the poor in the destination country attaches even for policies for which their own sovereign is actually responsible.

To some, these implications may seem problematic; from others, the reply will be, "It is just not *that* kind of theory." More troubling, though, may be a pragmatic corollary: if we need to rely on these theories to convince public policymakers to take action on medical tourism, they threaten to prove too much. These approaches threaten to become "oppressive in the totality of the claim they make on the moral agent."[93] Addressing the harms caused by medical tourism is a small drop in the bucket in terms of what these theories would call upon us to do to right the balance between developed and developing countries. For starters, they would further demand that we radically increase taxes for all strata in our nation to fund large-scale water purification, housing, and other interventions in LDCs. As Thomas Pogge has stressed, unless a theory of global justice is politically feasible, it is "destined to remain a philosopher's pipe dream."[94] It seems hard to believe that a principle as broad and demanding as the one espoused by Cosmopolitans of this sort would be compelling to U.S. policymakers, even if philosophers ultimately think these theories give the correct account.

In any event, to find common ground with both those who would reject Cosmopolitanism as a *philosophical* matter and those who would reject it as a *pragmatic*

---

[93] CHARLES FRIED, RIGHT AND WRONG 13 (1978).

[94] Thomas W. Pogge, *Human Rights and Global Health: A Research Program*, 36 METAPHILOSOPHY 182, 185 (2005).

matter, it would be desirable to show a normative obligation to correct health care access diminution from medical tourism on less demanding theories as well.

2. Statist Theories

Unlike Cosmopolitans, Statists reach the conclusion that the obligations of distributive justice apply only within the nation-state and not to citizens of other nations; their reasoning is that "[w]hat lets citizens make redistributive claims on each other is not so much the fact that they share a cooperative structure," but that societal rules establishing a sovereign state's basic structure are "coercively imposed."[95] Nagel clarifies that this is because for Rawls (and *contra* the Cosmopolitans), the "moral presumption against arbitrary inequalities is not a principle of universal application"; rather "[w]hat is objectionable is that we should be fellow participants in a *collective* enterprise of *coercively imposed* legal and political institutions that generates such arbitrary inequalities."[96] It is the "complex fact" that in societal rules establishing a sovereign state's basic structure "we are both putative joint authors of the coercively imposed system, and subject to its norms, i.e., expected to accept their authority even when the collective decision diverges from our personal preferences—that creates the special presumption against arbitrary inequalities in our treatment by the system."[97]

Increasing globalization does not change the picture, say Nagel and Rawls, because "mere economic interaction does not trigger the heightened standards of socioeconomic justice."[98] Nor does the existence of international institutions such as the United Nations or WTO trigger those obligations, according to Nagel, because their edicts "are not collectively enacted or coercively imposed in the name of all the individuals whose lives they affect."[99] That is, "[n]o matter how substantive the links of trade, diplomacy, or international agreement, the institutions present at the international level do not engage in the same kinds of coercive practices against individual agents"; it is "[c]oercion, not cooperation, [that] is the sine qua non of distributive justice."[100]

The medical tourism policies of home countries—permitting out-of-pocket purchases, insurer-prompted medical tourism, or government-prompted medical tourism whereby the State creates the incentives to use medical tourism—are not being imposed *in the name of destination country citizens*, nor are those citizens or their governments being forced to open themselves up to medical tourism, and thus cannot ground Statist obligations.[101]

---

[95] Mathias Risse, *What We Owe to the Global Poor*, 9 J. ETHICS 81, 99–100 (2005); *see also* JOHN RAWLS, THE LAW OF PEOPLES 116 (1999); Michael Blake, *Distributive Justice, State Coercion, and Autonomy*, 30 PHIL. & PUB. AFF. 257, 285–89 (2001).

[96] Thomas Nagel, *The Problem of Global Justice*, 33 PHIL. & PUB. AFF. 113, 127, 128 (2005) (emphasis added).

[97] *Id.* at 128–29; *see* Blake, *supra* note 95, at 265, 289.

[98] Nagel, *supra* note 96, at 138; *see also* RAWLS, *supra* note 95, at 115–19 (making a similar point).

[99] Nagel, *supra* note 96, at 138.

[100] Blake, *supra* note 95, at 265, 289.

[101] *Cf.* Nagel, *supra* note 96, at 129 (making a similar point as to immigration).

Nevertheless, I believe that there may exist in Statist theories at least two open avenues for grounding some limited obligations of home countries and international bodies to regulate medical tourism or mitigate its negative effects on health care access in destination countries.

The first avenue stems from Rawls's recognition of a duty (separate from those relating to distributive justice) to assist "burdened societies"—those whose "historical, social, and economic circumstances make their achieving a well-ordered regime, whether liberal or decent, difficult if not impossible"—to "manage their own affairs reasonably and rationally" in order to become "well-ordered societies."[102] These societies "lack the political and cultural traditions, the human capital and know-how, and, often, the material and technological resources needed to be well-ordered" but, with assistance, can over time come to "manage their own affairs reasonably and rationally and eventually to become members of the Society of well-ordered Peoples."[103]

Grounding medical tourism–related obligations in this kind of duty, although possible, faces several challenges and will generate only a much more limited kind of obligation. Many of the destination countries in question may not be burdened societies; India, Mexico, Thailand and Singapore, for example, may have poor populations facing deficits in health care access, but they seem to meet Rawls's more minimal criteria for being well-ordered. Second, there are restrictions on the kind of aid envisioned by this duty. Rawls seems focused on institution building, and Mathias Risse describes the duty's targets as building things such as "stable property rights, rule of law, bureaucratic capacity, appropriate regulatory structures to curtail at least the worst forms of fraud, anti-competitive behavior, and graft, quality and independence of courts, but also cohesiveness of society, existence of trust and social cooperation, and thus overall quality of civil society."[104] Foreign aid by home countries to help the destination countries improve their ability to produce more medical providers, or policy aid in designing health care system regulations designed to control how much time doctors spend in the public or private system—both factors likely to contribute to diminutions in access—seem to fit nicely into this category and are well-supported by this approach. Regulation aimed at trying to prevent or make it more expensive for home country patients to travel for medical tourism fits less well. That kind of regulation may also run afoul of Rawls's caution that "well-ordered societies giving assistance must not act paternalistically."[105] Finally, it is possible that medical tourism may actually help build institutions in the destination country, aiding the burdened State *while* diminishing health care access for the destination country poor.

---

[102] RAWLS, *supra* note 95, at 90, 111.

[103] *Id.* at 106, 111.

[104] Risse, *supra* note 95, at 85.

[105] RAWLS, *supra* note 95, at 111.

For example, the rise in GDP and the need for corporate accountability to support a medical tourism industry attractive to Westerners might carry with it benefits to the destination country in terms of establishing the rule of law or property rights. If so, medical tourism might itself represent aid to burdened states even while it diminishes health care access to the destination country's poor.

Thus, this approach justifies only a much smaller subset of possible interventions regarding medical tourism, but does not rule out a duty of home state action entirely.

A second avenue for grounding a Statist duty is Nagel's separate conception of humanitarian duties of aid. Nagel suggests that "there is some minimal concern we owe to fellow human beings threatened with starvation or severe malnutrition and early death from easily preventable diseases, as all these people in dire poverty are," such that "some form of humane assistance from the well-off to those in extremis is clearly called for quite apart from any demand of justice, if we are not simply ethical egoists."[106] Although he is self-admittedly vague, he thinks that "the normative force of the most basic human rights against violence, enslavement, and coercion, and of the most basic humanitarian duties of rescue from immediate danger, depends only on our capacity to put ourselves in other people's shoes," and speaks of obligations to relieve others, whatever their nation, "from extreme threats and obstacles to [the freedom to pursue their own ends] if we can do so without serious sacrifice of our own ends."[107]

Can this approach ground duties relating to medical tourism? Fisher and Syed suggest that a duty of Western countries to expand access to drugs in LDCs can be grounded in these humanitarian duties because there "is little question that millions of people are suffering and dying from contagious diseases in developing countries and that the residents of developed countries could alleviate that suffering with relative ease."[108]

A parallel argument, however, seems somewhat harder to make in the context of medical tourism interventions. For one thing, the effects of medical tourism seem more marginal. Of course, lack of access to care is as sure a killer as is famine or lack of needed pharmaceuticals, and, over a longer time horizon, its effects may be more significant. Still, we should be cautious when specifying the level of deprivation needed to trigger these humanitarian duties because if we decide a particular kind of deprivation is enough to trigger our duty to intervene here, we will bear a comparable duty to all citizens of that foreign country in comparable conditions. That is, if the health care deficits experienced *due to medical tourism* are enough to ground humanitarian duties regarding medical tourism, should we not also open our immigration doors to those suffering comparable deficits in their home countries? Too expansive a conception would raise the very

---

[106] Nagel, *supra* note 96, at 118.

[107] *Id.* at 131l; *see also* Blake, *supra* note 95, at 271.

[108] Fisher & Syed, *supra* note 77, at 649.

pragmatic and political concerns about the scope of the demands placed upon us that we aimed to avoid by seeking a non-Cosmopolitan approach.

Moreover, to ask whether we "could alleviate that suffering with relative ease" or "without serious sacrifice of our own ends" raises difficulties paralleling those faced by Cosmopolitan theories: at least for medical tourism by those paying out-of-pocket and, to a lesser extent, for some forms of government-prompted medical tourism, trying to satisfy humanitarian duties to the global poor by curbing medical tourism is more likely to come at the expense of our own poor than in the pharmaceutical case. Thus, in the exceptional case, we may face trade-offs not only between satisfying our humanitarian duties to our own poor versus those to the poor abroad, but also between our *distributive* justice duties to our poor and our *humanitarian* duties to the destination country poor. Neglecting our duties to our own poor patients would seem to count as "serious sacrifice of our own ends," suggesting the obligations may more clearly attach to some forms of medical tourism, including insurer-prompted medical tourism, where paying more for health insurance is less clearly such a sacrifice. Similarly, the humanitarian duty approach might more easily justify curbing medical tourism for services such as cosmetic surgeries that are more penumbral to health. This restriction may also limit us to interventions that do not restrict access to health care via medical tourism for our citizens but instead aid the destination country in building capacity. Even that is tricky, though, for dollars spent on foreign aid could always be reallocated to improving Medicaid coverage for America's poor, to give but one example.[109]

Finally, notice that, like the Cosmopolitan theories, the duty toward humanitarian aid is actually somewhat divorced from medical tourism in the causal sense—we have a duty to give humanitarian aid whether or not we caused the need. Thus, if one found this aspect of Cosmopolitan theories undesirable as a ground for duties as to medical tourism, the same problem applies here.

Although, as expected, the Statist theories reject grounding duties as to medical tourism in the distributive justice obligations to those abroad, there may be some room for obligations grounded in duties to aid burdened states or provide humanitarian aid.

---

[109] Is it relevant that the United States has not "cleaned its own house" and adopted universal health care for its citizens, which in part causes the medical tourism need? Here is a place where it seems plausible to me that the philosophical and policy discourse split—it may be that the United States *ought* to deal with medical tourism by cleaning its own house first, but if we concede (as I think we should) that this is not within the political feasibility set, then we are back in a philosophically second-best world where we must ask what steps the United States should take regarding medical tourism directly. In any event, many home countries for medical tourism *have* put in place universal health care coverage, and yet their citizens continue to go abroad to avoid long queues, because their home health care coverage does not encompass a service, because a technique is unavailable, or because they wish to circumvent domestic prohibitions.

B. Intermediate Theories (with a Focus on Causation)

A different set of theories seeks to position itself between the Statist and Cosmopolitan camps such that I have called these theories "intermediate." What ties them together is a focus on causation, either in the direct sense of the harms caused by medical tourism or more indirectly at the role of bridging institutions that intermediate between home and destination countries. I think these are the most fertile grounds for a global justice–based theory of obligations to regulate medical tourism because they generate a *kind* of theory more appropriate for the task: one that focuses on the harms and institutions stemming from particular existing practices, rather than one that focuses on the relative holdings of particular individuals at the current moment and counsels a more general reallocation of primary goods. That said, these theories are not without problems.

I begin by examining one theory I have favored in other work, put forth by Joshua Cohen and Charles Sabel, and applied to health care by Norman Daniels. I then examine a different theory, put forth by Thomas Pogge.[110]

i. Cohen, Sabel, and Daniels

The Cohen, Sabel, and Daniels approach suggests the Statists are too demanding in requiring coercion as the touchstone of distributive justice principles and also too all-or-nothing in the deployment of those principles. Instead, these authors propose lesser duties of "inclusion" internationally, which fall short of full-blown distributive justice but are greater than the minimal humanitarian duties endorsed by Statists: the State should treat those outside of the coercive structure of the nation-state as individuals whose good "counts for something" (not nothing) even if it falls short of the full consideration a State would give its own citizens.[111]

Cohen and Sabel suggest these duties of inclusion may be triggered inter alia by the "coercion-lite" (my term) actions of international bodies such as the WTO; that is, "[e]ven when rule-making and applying bodies lack their own independent power to impose sanctions through coercion," they still shape conduct "by providing incentives and permitting the imposition of sanctions," and "withdrawing from them may be costly to members (if only because of the sometimes considerable loss of benefits)," such that "[i]n an attenuated but significant way, our wills—the wills of all subject to the rule making-authority—have been implicated, sufficiently such that rules of this type can only be imposed with a special justification."[112]

They offer the example of the WTO, suggesting that "[o]pting out is not a real option" because no country in the developed or developing world could really survive without

---

[110] Cohen, *supra* note 22, at 42–46.

[111] *See* Joshua Cohen & Charles Sabel, *Extra Rempublicam Nulla Justitia?*, 34 PHIL. & PUB. AFF. 147, 154–55 (2006); NORMAN DANIELS, JUST HEALTH 351 (2008).

[112] Cohen & Sabel, *supra* note 111, at 165.

participation in the WTO, and that "there is a direct rule-making relationship between the global bodies and the citizens of different states."[113] They argue that for the WTO, duties of inclusion would mean that the rulemakers are "obligated to give some weight to the reasonable concern of the rule takers (who are themselves assumed to have responsibility to show concern for the interests of their own citizens)."[114]

The authors also suggest that consequential rulemaking by international bodies "with distinct responsibilities," such as the International Labor Organization (ILO), might require those bodies to adopt duties of inclusion. They point to a few facets of the ILO that give rise to such an obligation: the ILO has taken on the responsibility for formulating labor standards; the ILO claims that its rulemakings have significant consequences; and the ILO believes that, if it were to disappear, no comparable entity would emerge.[115]

Daniels adds that certain kinds of international independencies may also give rise to duties of inclusion, giving the example of medical migration ("brain drain"). He argues that the International Monetary Fund (IMF)'s historical requirement that countries such as Cameroon make severe cutbacks in their publicly funded health care systems in order to reduce deficits that result in poorer working conditions for medical personnel (a "push" factor), combined with the attempt by the United Kingdom and other Organisation for Economic Co-operation and Development (OECD) countries to recruit medical personnel from developing countries (a "pull" factor), gives rise to a duty on the part of Western countries and the IMF to address the ill effects of this migration.[116] Among the methods to satisfy that obligation, he urges altering "the terms of employment in receiving countries of health workers from vulnerable countries," compensating for "the lost training costs of these workers," "prohibit[ing] recruitment from vulnerable countries," and "giv[ing] aid to contributing countries in order to reduce the push factor."[117]

Can this approach be readily applied to medical tourism? One might be tempted to draw three analogies, but each of them faces problems.

First, one might suggest that, analogously to the ILO, accreditors such as the Joint Commission International (JCI), which we discussed in Chapters 1 and 2, bear some duties to build consideration of the effects of medical tourism to a particular facility on health care access for destination country poor into their accreditation processes. That is, JCI is like the ILO in that it has taken on responsibility for formulating standards, it claims its rules have significant consequences (determining who gets accredited, causing

---

[113] *Id.* at 168.

[114] *Id.* at 172.

[115] *Id.* at 170–71.

[116] *See* DANIELS, *supra* note 16, at 337–39.

[117] *Id.*

facilities to alter their procedures), and perhaps if it disappeared no other institution would take its place.[118]

On reflection, though, the analogy is problematic. The JCI's role is to accredit foreign hospitals, specifically to examine their procedures and determine whether those procedures meet relevant standards of practice.[119] Although this might be loosely thought of as a kind of "rulemaking," the JCI does not purport to regulate the medical tourism market, let alone to weigh the advantages or disadvantages of a particular country or particular hospital opening itself up to medical tourism. The same points apply even more strongly to facilitators who are largely for-profit entities.

Second, we might analogize to the medical migration example and say that, for patients paying out-of-pocket, the lack of affordable health insurance in a system such as the United States', and the system's failure to prevent insurer-prompted medical tourism, drive medical tourism, much like the United Kingdom's recruitment of foreign nurses drives migration. In medical tourism by patients paying out-of-pocket, we do not have the U.S. government or international bodies directly creating push and pull factors. True, the U.S. government has not taken steps to *prevent* travel to India for medical procedures. But if merely not acting and following a background norm of permitting travel to consume goods and services abroad is sufficient under Daniels's intermediate theory, the theory loses much of its attraction as a middle ground between the Cosmopolitan and Statist poles because so much of the day-to-day workings of international trade will trigger obligations under the theory.

That said, it seems that government-sponsored medical tourism initiatives might create home country obligations to destination countries, at least insofar as tourism is incentivized and not merely covered in a way that is cost-neutral from the point of view of the patient. Medical tourism in universal health care countries prompted by long wait times, such as those discussed in Chapter 5, might also better fit the analogy—the failure to produce sufficient medical practitioners in the patient's home country might prompt attempts either to recruit foreign providers (brain drain) *or* to incentivize medical tourism. However, it is unclear where the stopping point is from that analogy to the (problematic) conclusion that the fundamental organization of one's domestic health care system might trigger duties of inclusion *internationally* based on home country patients' reactions to it.[120]

---

[118] This last point of comparison seems dubious. Even with the JCI in place, it faces competition in accreditation, including from the International Organization for Standardization (ISO). The ISO has a less popular certification program that has been used to certify some hospitals in Mexico, India, Thailand, Lebanon, and Pakistan. *See* Arnold Milstein & Mark Smith, *America's New Refugees—Seeking Affordable Surgery Offshore*, 355 NEW ENG. J. MED. 1637, 1639 (2006). Thus, if the JCI were to disappear, there is every reason to believe that others would take its place. That said, while Daniels describes the ILO as having these three characteristics, it may be that meeting the first two is sufficient to ground the duties he has in mind.

[119] *See* Chapter 1, introducing the industry, and Chapter 2, discussing quality of care.

[120] Otherwise, the underlying principle would be something like "for any domestic policy choice our country makes, be it health, education, transportation, etc., we are responsible for remediating any effects that

Third, one might focus on the obligations some destination countries have undertaken to open up their health care sectors to medical tourism under the General Agreement on Trade in Services[121] (GATS) and argue that it plays a "coercion-lite" role analogous to the obligations of WTO membership discussed by these authors. I will say a bit more about this analogy because it gives me an opportunity to discuss the role of trade law in medical tourism and to examine a recurring issue related to self-inflicted wounds.

While GATS imposes general obligations that apply to all WTO members, it imposes obligations relating to "market access"[122] and "national treatment"[123] on countries that have explicitly elected to be bound by them. These obligations—called "specific commitments"—are made as to particular service sectors and particular modes of service (consumption abroad, cross-border supply, etc).[124] Violations of these obligations are subject to trade sanctions. Medical tourism might be implicated by a country's specific commitment to open up its "Hospital Services" sector, which includes inter alia surgical, medical, ob-gyn, nursing, laboratory, radiological, anesthesiological, and rehabilitation services.[125]

To be sure, the analogy (and thus, duties of inclusion) will apply only to countries that have undertaken obligations under GATS to open up their health care system. Even as to these countries, though, the theory faces the self-inflicted wounds problem. The decision to become a signatory of GATS and open up one's medical system to medical tourism is *itself* within the control of the destination country, so how could it give rise to duties of inclusion on the part of the other signatories? In responding to a similar objection to their WTO example, Cohen and Sable suggest that the point "seems almost facetious" because "[o]pting out is not a real option (the WTO is a 'take it or leave it' arrangement, without even the formal option of picking and choosing the parts to comply with), and given that it is not, and that everyone knows it is not, there is a direct rule-making relationship between the global bodies and the citizens of different states."[126] This same response, however, is much less persuasive in the GATS/medical tourism context because unlike the all-or-nothing WTO agreements, the GATS specific

---

follow, whether the conduit is changes in trade, consumption, or travel by our populace." If this is the principle that underlies the intermediate approach, it ceases to be a distinctive middle ground between the Cosmopolitan and Statist theories that can focus on particular institutional arrangements, coercion, and interdependency. Further, such a broad principle reintroduces the pragmatic policy-oriented worry I discussed above that the intermediate approach advantageously seemed poised to avoid.

[121] General Agreement on Trade in Services, Apr. 15, 1994, 33 I.L.M. 1167 (1994) [hereinafter GATS].

[122] *Id.* art. XVI.

[123] *Id.* art. XVII.

[124] *Id.*

[125] *Id.* art. III; *see also* Patricia J. Arnold & Terrie C. Reeves, *International Trade and Health Policy: Implications of the GATS for US Healthcare Reform*, 63 J. Bus. Ethics Reform 313, 316–18 (2006) (discussing the relationship between GATS and trade in health services); Cohen, *supra* note 78, at 1521 n.213 (discussing the relationship between GATS and medical tourism).

[126] Cohen & Sabel, *supra* note 111, at 168.

commitment obligations are incredibly versatile, with individual States making individual commitments as to individual modes for individual sectors.[127] The proof is, to some extent, in the pudding: As WTO officials Rudolf Adlung and Antonia Carzaniga earlier observed, across the board there is a "generally shallow level of [GATS-specific] commitments on health services" with "no service sector[s] other than that of education [having] drawn fewer bindings among WTO Members than the health sector."[128] Thus, the take-it-or-leave-it, offer-you-can't-refuse type of argument relied on by Cohen, Sable, and Daniels in their discussion seems to have less traction here.

This difficulty may not be fatal, and one way out might be to borrow two ideas from the philosophical work done by Gopal Sreenivasan on the effect of GATS rules on national choices and how those rules restrict efforts to expand public health care. In responding to a similar self-inflicted wounds problem, Sreenivasan first suggests (though he does not fully embrace the idea) that although "[v]olunteering for treaty obligations is an exercise of sovereign authority... sovereignty and democratic legitimacy are not the same thing"; rather, the issue of democratic legitimacy turns on the "kind of popular mandate [that] existed for various decisions taken in relation to the GATS."[129]

This would obviously rule out the validity of GATS restrictions for dictator states, but it would also, he suggests, call into question the validity of other less-than-democratic forms of mandate: he contrasts the way GATS was subject to the possibility of a popular referendum in Switzerland before approval with the way the U.S. Congress ratified the agreement not as a treaty, but as ordinary legislation, and did so via approval of the Uruguay Round, in which all the terms of the agreement had to be accepted or rejected at once.[130] By analogy, one could argue that because some of the destination countries also ratified GATS in these less-than-democratic ways, the fact that they chose to enter GATS should not stand in the way of establishing obligations to these countries on Daniels's intermediate theory (i.e., compliance with GATS should not be considered a "self-inflicted wound"). Sreenivasan himself seems understandably ambivalent about how far to take this response, and wonders whether we should instead presume a popular mandate as to ordinary legislation.[131]

Second, and I think more confidently, Sreenivasan argues that because GATS imposes obligations in an intergenerational sense and the penalties for exiting GATS are so large, GATS should be thought of as more akin to constitutional obligations, like a Bill of Rights, than ordinary legislation. Sreenivasan's conclusion is not that "nothing

---

[127] *Id.*

[128] Rudolf Adlung & Antonia Carzaniga, *Health Services under the General Agreement on Trade in Services,* 79 Bull. World Health Org. 352, 356–58 (2001).

[129] Gopal Sreenivasan, *Does the GATS Undermine Democratic Control over Health?,* 9 J. Ethics 269, 274–75 (2005).

[130] *Id.* at 275.

[131] *Id.* at 275–76.

can confer democratic legitimacy on effectively compulsory obligations that span generations"; such obligations "would certainly be going too far." Instead, his claim is that these kinds of obligations "require special measures of democratic scrutiny in order to gain legitimacy," such as the supermajority and dedicated referendums that are commonly required for constitutional amendments.[132]

I do not attempt to fully assess the merits of Sreenivasan's argument here. Instead, my more limited goal is to show that, although Sreenivasan's work is on democratic legitimacy and not international justice obligations, it is possible that Cohen, Sable, and Daniels might graft his approach (or a variant of it) onto their own theory to offer a different kind of response to the self-inflicted wounds problem in the medical tourism context; indeed, this solution, suggested by the application to this case, may be a more generalized direction in which their theory might be extended. Doing so might mean that duties of inclusion arise as to medical tourism, but *only* as to the subset of destination countries who have made GATS commitments impinging on their ability to resist medical tourism, that (1) are dictatorships (or perhaps without a popular mandate), or (2) have ratified GATS in ways that do not meet specified requirements for democratic legitimacy of "effectively compulsory obligations that span generations."[133]

Although this may adequately deal with the "self-inflicted" wounds problem relating to GATS, several of the triggering conditions for medical tourism's negative effects on health care access in the destination country—the supply of health care professionals, whether the system is regulated in such a way that requires professionals to spend time in both the public and private systems—are, as I stressed above, also at least partially within the control of the destination country governments. These decisions represent ordinary legislation, not the extraordinary kind relating to GATS and, in most cases, will enjoy a popular mandate of some sort.[134]

Does this blunt the claim that home country governments or international bodies bear responsibility for deficits associated with medical tourism? Yes and no. As Daniels has argued, even countries with similar domestic policies experience significant differences in population health, such that "[e]ven if primary responsibility for population

---

[132] *Id.* at 277–79.

[133] I say "might" because one might counter that the self-inflicted wounds problem is "turtles, turtles all the way down." If these features of the destination country's political system led to deficits in ratifying GATS, one might counter that those features are themselves "self-inflicted wounds" within the control of the destination country. On such an argument, it would not only be the GATS-ratifying decision itself, but also the constitutional or other political structure that sets up this mechanism for ratifying treaties that would itself have to contain the features Sreenivasan suggests are necessary for democratic legitimacy.

[134] Again, it remains open to press the stronger version of the argument about which Sreenivasan is ambivalent—that even ordinary legislation requires a form of direct democratic or supermajoritarian check to "count" as the will of the people for international justice purposes and create a self-inflicted wound. I feel ambivalent enough about this claim (as I think Sreenivasan does) that I would not want to press this as a way of avoiding the self-inflicted wounds problem, but others may find it a more appealing approach to the issue.

health rests with each state, this does not mean that the state has [the] sole responsibility."[135] In order to clarify home countries' obligations, we ought to try to factor out the elements of destination countries' population health deficits caused by medical tourism that are a result of the domestic policy decisions[136] and then apply the Cohen, Sable, and Daniels duties of inclusion only to the remaining deficits that meet the theories' requirements.

This ability to apportion responsibility between the destination and home countries seems like a major theoretical advantage of this approach as against the prior ones discussed. Of course, although conceptually simple to state, actually doing such apportioning would be extremely difficult in practice, and the absolute best we can practicably hope for is a rough approximation. Thus, only in instances of medical tourism where a plausible case of "coercion-lite" or other pressure can be said to give rise to a duty of inclusion will such duties attach, and only then as to the proportion of the deficits caused by medical tourism to health care access by the destination country poor that is outside the control of the destination country.

Even if one of these routes validly triggers a duty of inclusion on some home countries or international bodies for some sets of medical tourism, there is the further question of what that duty entails. The authors are self-admittedly somewhat vague about the contours of these kinds of duties, telling us on the one hand that it is not a duty of "equal concern" or redistributive justice, but on the other that it requires more than mere humanitarian duties; that is, it necessitates treating individuals abroad as individuals whose good "counts for something" (not nothing), while making decisions that will impact their lives.[137]

That leaves a fair amount of room to maneuver. One could imagine the duties mandating something like "notice and comment rulemaking" in administrative law—which would merely require acknowledging that these interests were considered, but found to be outweighed—to something approaching a weighting formula in which the welfare of those abroad is counted as 0.8 while those in the nation-state are counted as 1 (to use purely fictional discounting factors).

In discussing the brain drain example, Daniels seems to suggest duties of inclusion should have significant bite, arguing that they might prohibit recruitment from vulnerable countries, force recruiting countries to restrict the terms they offer foreign health workers, compensate for losses suffered when health care workers are lost, or give aid to help reduce push factors.[138] By analogy, in the context of medical tourism, such duties could require a home country to take on a number of obligations: channeling its patients

---

[135] DANIELS, *supra* note 16, at 345.

[136] *See id.* at 341–45.

[137] Cohen & Sabel, *supra* note 111, at 154–55; *see also* DANIELS, *supra* note 16, at 351 (making a similar point in the health context).

[138] DANIELS, *supra* note 16, at 353–54.

to medical tourism facilities or countries with programs to ameliorate health care deficits that result; taxing medical tourists, intermediaries, or insurers, and using that revenue as aid aimed at amelioration; and providing more general aid that would either help to build institutional health care capacity in the destination country or would allow the destination country to more appropriately regulate its health care sector. I discuss these and other possible interventions in the next part of this chapter.

ii. Pogge

A quite different intermediate theory, to which it will be difficult to give justice in this short space, is suggested by Thomas Pogge. Pogge begins with the idea that all people have rights to a "minimally worthwhile life," and therefore require a share of minimum levels of basic goods, including health care, that are essential to a decent life—he terms such goods "human rights."[139] According to Pogge's theory, citizens of one State have an obligation to avoid "harming" citizens of another State by imposing "deficits" on their access to these human rights; that is, he argues that "[w]e are harming the global poor if and insofar as we collaborate in imposing" a "global institutional order . . . [that] foreseeably perpetuates large-scale human rights deficits that would be reasonably avoided through foreseeable institutional modifications."[140]

Pogge applies his approach to many examples, but the closest to ours is his claim that wealthy countries have an obligation to loosen their enforcement of the intellectual property rights of pharmaceutical companies to drugs that LDCs desperately need. In this application of his approach, Pogge suggests that "[m]illions would be saved from disease and death if generic producers could freely manufacture and market life-saving drugs" in those countries.[141] Part of his ire is focused on the Trade-Related Aspects of Intellectual Property Rights (TRIPS) Agreement, membership in which was made conditional upon joining the WTO, and which requires members to grant twenty-year product patents on new medicines. Pogge suggests that the TRIPS Agreement, which he claims was disastrous for LDCs, "foreseeably excludes the global poor from access to vital medicines for the sake of enhancing the incentives to develop new medicines for the sake of the affluent," and asks, "How can the imposition of such a regime be justified to the global poor?"[142] Pogge instead proposes a tax-based fund that operates as a prize system, rewarding drug companies for their products' contribution to reductions in the global burden of disease.[143]

---

[139] THOMAS POGGE, WORLD POVERTY AND HUMAN RIGHTS 48–49 (2002); *see also* Fisher & Syed, *supra* note 77, at 644–45 (discussing Pogge's account).

[140] Thomas Pogge, *World Poverty and Human Rights*, 19 ETHICS & INT'L AFFAIRS 1, 5 (2005); *see also* DANIELS, *supra* note 16, at 337–39 (discussing Pogge's account).

[141] Pogge, *supra* note 140, at 6; POGGE, *supra* note 139, at 74.

[142] Thomas Pogge, *Access to Medicines*, 1 PUB. HEALTH ETHICS 73, 75 (2008).

[143] *Id*. at 76–78.

In a second example, paralleling one used by Cohen, Sable, and Daniels, he claims that many WTO policies cause human rights deficits because they permit the affluent countries' "continued and asymmetrical protections of their markets through tariffs, quotas, anti-dumping duties, export credits and huge subsidies to domestic producers," and thereby "greatly impair[] export opportunities for the very poorest."[144] In response, Pogge suggests that the rich countries have an obligation to "scrap[] their protectionist barriers against imports from poor countries," which he claims would lower unemployment and increase wage levels in those countries.[145]

Might the same claims hold as to medical tourism? One might say medical tourism also "foreseeably excludes the global poor from access to" health care "for the sake of enhancing" the health care access and cost savings in the West. Further, like Pogge's own examples, one could say that medical tourism is supported by the existing institutional order insofar as that order facilitates things such as international travel, standard setting, the accreditation of foreign hospitals, the training and credentialing of foreign doctors in the United States and other developed countries, etc.[146]

Snyder and his coauthors, in a recent article in *Bioethics*, have critically examined the suitability of the Poggean model of global justice to medical tourism.

As they write, one major advantage of Pogge's approach is its recognition that "in these cases, multiple agents are causally responsible for harms to numerous others," that the "mechanisms by which these harms take place are typically non-proximate, spanning global institutions and realized through multiple chains of causation," and that "these harms are actually the aggregation of multiple, smaller harms, some of which may be the result of actions taken in the distant past."[147] They have also emphasized, against some of Pogge's critics, that the theory is really an intermediate theory and not a Cosmopolitan one in its approach, noting:

> Critics of Pogge observe that, even if international institutions are not entirely fair, [destination countries] still benefit from their existence. Given the enormous increase in technological and economic development in the past century, it is difficult to argue that [destination countries] would have been better off on their own, completely disconnected from the venues for trade and assistance made possible

---

[144] Pogge, *supra* note 140, at 6.

[145] *Id.* As a descriptive matter, Pogge's account of the negative effects of TRIPS is not without a dissenting view. *See, e.g.*, Rachel Brewster, *The Surprising Benefits to Developing Countries of Linking International Trade and Intellectual Property*, 11 CHI. J. INT'L L. 1 (2011).

[146] *See generally* Cortez, *supra* note 22 (discussing the way these things facilitate medical tourism); Aaditya Mattoo & Randeep Rathindran, *How Health Insurance Inhibits Trade in Health Care*, 25 HEALTH AFF. 358 (2006) (presenting a similar discussion); Graham T. McMahon, *Coming to America—International Medical Graduates in the United States*, 350 N. ENG. J. MED 2435 (2004) (discussing the reliance on foreign doctors in the U.S. health care system).

[147] *See, e.g.*, Snyder et al., *supra* note 53, at 236.

by globalization and increased development of international institutions. Pogge, however, is clear that his argument is not based on a comparison of the welfare of the global poor under the current global order to their welfare in a world lacking international institutions. This comparison rests on a false dichotomy, where the global order must exist as it now stands or be cast aside completely. Pogge's point, rather, is that the present global order harms the global poor when we compare their present welfare to that under a more just international order. Pogge is vague on what a more just global order against which harm would be measured looks like. This vagueness is in part strategic as he seeks to set a minimal baseline for justice with which as many people as possible can agree. This baseline "merely requires that any institutional order imposed on human beings must be designed so that human rights are fulfilled under it insofar as this is reasonably possible." The current institutional order, Pogge argues, does not meet this minimal condition and is, therefore, unjust by any reasonable measure. As this unjust order was created and is maintained by rich countries, their leaders are causally responsible for harming the average citizens of [destination countries] compared to a baseline of their welfare under a minimally just global order.[148]

At the same time, Snyder and coauthors have offered criticisms of the suitability of Pogge's approach as applied to medical tourism, in addition to questions and concerns I have lodged in prior writings.

They write:

Pogge's approach faces significant limitations when identifying responsibilities for global injustice. First, it is limited to those agents that have strong and clear causal roles in establishing the terms on which international institutions are established. As we have seen, this causal focus in not problematic when placing responsibility in the hands of entire Western governments and, specifically, very powerful agents within them. However, it is not clear what should be said of the causal responsibility of the leaders and citizens of [developing countries] and less influential citizens in powerful countries. Second, Pogge's approach focuses on identifying blame for the effects of individual choices rather than on steps that can reduce injustice. In this way, the liability model of responsibility is primarily backward looking, focusing on the harms caused by discrete, past actions. The concern with this focus is that it fails to capture the ways by which structural injustice creates systematic and *ongoing* disadvantages for some groups. In the case of disadvantage caused by

---

[148] *Id.* at 236–37 (citing M. Risse, *Do We Owe the Global Poor Assistance or Rectification?*, 19 ETHICS INT'L AFF. 9 (2005); and quoting Thomas Pogge, *Severe Poverty as a Violation of Negative Duties*, 19 ETHICS INT'L AFF. 55, 56 (2005)).

the structure of the WTO, concern should not only be with the harms that have been caused by the negotiators for rich nations. We should also be concerned, in a forward looking manner, with what actions should be taken to reform the WTO and other unjust international institutions.[149]

My own questions and concerns push on the theory from the other side and note some problems (or at least open questions) that become manifest through this application to medical tourism. First, what is the content of a human right to health? Or, to put it otherwise, how much health care must one have before one's human rights are being violated?[150] In answering this question, the theory faces a problem that parallels ones I have raised elsewhere as to Nussbaum's approach[151]—if the threshold is set too low, the negative effects of medical tourism may not cause a "deficit" to the human right; if the threshold is set too high, then it will cause a deficit, but so will not allowing that tourism to go forward (given the needs of the American patients using medical tourism). Pogge has offered a response to a somewhat similar criticism by suggesting the proviso to his theory that "these human rights deficits must be *reasonably avoidable* in the sense that a feasible alternative design of the relevant institutional order would not produce comparable human rights deficits or other ills of comparable magnitude."[152] But, as in our discussion of a somewhat similar proviso by Nagel, one might wonder what "reasonably avoidable" really means and how much of the institutional order we should feel free to redesign in a given moment. Once again, this problem seems least acute for insurer-prompted medical tourism and medical tourism for services such as cosmetic surgery.

Second, Pogge has tried to avoid some of the pragmatic and political feasibility problems of the Cosmopolitan theories by trying to use a kind of act-omission distinction, with the ideas of "harm" and "imposing… deficits." But, as Daniels has remarked, "[i]nternational harming is complex in several ways. The harms are often not deliberate; sometimes benefits were arguably intended." Daniels has also argued that "harms are often mixed with benefits," such that "great care must be taken to describe the baseline in measuring harm," and the "complex story about motivations, intentions, and effects might seem to weaken the straightforward appeal of" Pogge's theory.[153] To illustrate: as in Pogge's examples, it can be argued that the existence of the phenomenon of medical tourism leads to a "deficit" in one human right for the destination country poor—health care—and one might say that medical tourism is supported by the existing institutional

---

149 *Id.* at 237 (citing Iris Young, *Responsibility and Global Justice: A Social Connection Model*, 23 SOC. PHIL. POL'Y 102 (2006)).

150 *Cf.* DANIELS, *supra* note 16, at 337 (asking whether Pogge's human right to health is frustrated "[w]henever a country fails to meet the levels of health provided, say, by Japan, which has the highest life expectancy").

151 Cohen, *supra* note 22, at 12–13.

152 THOMAS POGGE, WORLD POVERTY AND HUMAN RIGHTS: COSMOPOLITAN RESPONSIBILITIES AND REFORMS 26 (2008).

153 DANIELS, *supra* note 16, at 340.

order insofar as that order facilitates things such as international travel, standard setting, and accreditation of foreign hospitals.

But do these institutional elements "harm" the human right to health care of destination country citizens through medical tourism?[154] In Pogge's examples, we have identifiable state and international actors, chief culprits if you will, at whom he can point the finger as actors who caused the deficit in question: the WTO, the TRIPS Agreement, and those who support them.[155] For medical tourism, by contrast, we have a much more complex web of acts and omissions that together form the system. We have the private decisions of individual citizens in the home country to satisfy health care needs in a foreign country; though satisfying these needs may seem to cause harm, the needs may themselves be caused by a State-level failure to secure universal health care, or even more indirectly by the failure to adopt more redistributive taxation approaches. What about the role played by U.S. health insurance companies in pricing their plans, which in part determines how many Americans are uninsured (which, in turn, is partially a function of the wage demands of health care workers)? We also have the background international law and trade principles allowing for free travel by citizens to foreign states and the consumption of goods and services abroad—but are those causes of deficits?[156] To put the point another way, the baseline against which Pogge's

---

[154] In discussing Pogge's proposal to create a prize system to spur innovation in drugs targeting the global burden of disease, Daniels critiques whether what is going on is really "harming" versus "not optimally helping?" DANIELS, *supra* note 16, at 337. A similar worry seems less apposite as to medical tourism where it is the actions of home country citizens that are setting back the interests of those abroad, assuming *arguendo* that medical tourism makes the Indian poor worse-off than they would otherwise be.

[155] Others writing in much the same vein as Pogge on access to essential pharmaceuticals in LDCs have emphasized similar facts about this context that strain the analogy to medical tourism and suggest the case that global justice obligations may be much stronger in the pharmaceutical context. For example, Outterson and Light, working on an analogy to duties to engage in easy rescue when there are special relationships, suggest several specific reasons that this analogy is applicable in the drug context: the fact that "the patent-based drug companies created the global intellectual property system and are actively preventing rescue by others" with the explicit goal of prohibiting "free trade of low-priced generics from the emerging pharmaceutical industries in developing countries" thereby having created the danger, the fact that the drug companies receive public monies and are able to block development through the patent system, and (according to these authors) the fact that innovation rewards could be set up in such a way to make this a case of "easy rescue" wherein pharmaceutical companies would not lose much if anything from their bottom line. Kevin Outterson & David W. Light, *Global Pharmaceutical Markets, in* A COMPANION TO BIOETHICS 417, 417–29 (Helga Kuhse & Peter Singer eds., 2d ed. 2010). None of these points seems true as to the United States' or other home countries' involvement in medical tourism by those individuals paying out-of-pocket. That said, some elements (such as the use of public funds) are more analogous to government-prompted medical tourism, and some of these points (pursuit of profit-maximizing strategies that may run counter to destination-country health care access) may, in appropriate cases, provide reasons for subjecting medical tourism intermediaries to the same approbation these authors foist on drug companies. This latter point on corporate social responsibility raises questions beyond the scope of this work, which is focused on governmental and intergovernmental obligations.

[156] Larry Gostin has made a similar point as to these kinds of theories more generally: "National policies and globalization have benefited the rich and contributed to global health disparities, but so have many other factors. Blame for harms in the Third World, however, is hard to assess. States usually do not intend to cause harm to poor countries, and political leaders may believe they are doing good. International policies,

concept of harm is drawn is extremely slippery as to medical tourism—a problem that legal realism has emphasized in legal discourse.

All that said, I do not want to overstate the point. The subset of government-sponsored medical tourism, of the kind discussed in Chapter 5, seems to nicely parallel Pogge's own examples: This form of medical tourism has both a clear causal pathway of "harm" and easy-to-specify institutional rearrangements, such that, under Pogge's view, it should give rise to obligations on home countries.[157]

C. From Global Justice Theory to Real World Regulation

Taking a step back, what can we say about the larger landscape of global justice theories, access to health care, and medical tourism? Although I think a true overlapping consensus or incompletely theorized agreement between these different theories eludes us in this area, I do think it is fair to say we can identify two "central tendencies" among the group of theories: insurer-prompted medical tourism and government-prompted medical tourism are the areas where the argument that states and international bodies have a moral obligation to intervene is the strongest, for two different (but on some theories also overlapping) reasons. The case for curbing insurer-prompted medical tourism is stronger because preventing these services is *less* likely to expose the State's own citizens to deficits in health care access,[158] which would be in tension with the same concerns regarding those abroad. Similar reasoning suggests that there is a greater obligation to restrict medical tourism for inessential services or services that are more penumbral to the concept of health (such as cosmetic surgery and, on some accounts, fertility tourism).

The case for intervening in government-prompted medical tourism is stronger because there is a fairly direct causal tie between the State's action and the deficits caused by

---

moreover, often have mixed benefits and harms that defy any simple assignment of blame. Finally, countries themselves may have contributed to the harms due to inadequate attention to population health, excessive militarization, or simple incompetence or corruption. At bottom, reasonable people disagree as to who bears the responsibility for health inequalities and who owes a duty to right the perceived wrongs." Gostin, *supra* note 77, at 345–46.

[157] Snyder et al. reach a somewhat similar conclusion in their application of the Pogge model to medical tourism, as inflected by the "political responsibility" theory of Iris Murdoch, which they also champion in their work. *See* Snyder et al., *supra* note 53, at 237–38 (citing Young, *supra* note 149). They write:

> Insofar as MT [medical tourism] can be promoted in a manner that develops a sustainable model of health care for both host and home countries, these [home country, destination country, and intergovernmental organization] officials are liable for not doing so. When and if MT is empirically demonstrated to be inferior to models of health care that do not rely on international travel for care, these officials are liable for promoting MT at the expense of models that promote better access to care.

Id. at 238.

[158] To be sure, as I cautioned above, even restricting insurer-prompted medical tourism poses some risk of diminution in access domestically; it is just that it appears to pose *less* of that risk such that the case for intervention is concomitantly stronger.

medical tourism (which matter on the intermediate theories). Claims of an obligation on the part of the home country government or international bodies to do something about medical tourism by those purchasing essential services out-of-pocket seem concomitantly weaker.

Beyond these central tendencies, however, there is a fair amount of divergence among the theories in picking out which circumstances give rise to obligations (e.g., only medical tourism to "burdened states"? Only medical tourism to states whose method of ratifying GATS seems suspect?) and whether there are limits on the means by which those obligations can be met (only foreign aid, targeted or otherwise, or more paternalistic attempts to control the flow of home countries' patients as well?). The Nagelian conception of humanitarian aid might be thought of as a floor on which these other theories can build, but, as I have shown above, its demands are somewhat independent of medical tourism and instead stem from the existence of desperate need, regardless of its causal relation to medical tourism.

In any event, my ambition here has been to lay out the terrain of global justice theories, their application to medical tourism, and the problems that arise from that application.[159] Going further and deciding the exact content of those obligations requires choosing among these rival theories and filling many of the lacunae I have identified in their application. Although I have made some tentative suggestions here and there, I have not attempted that task in this chapter. Instead, my goal has been to open a dialogue between moral and political theorists and those making on-the-ground policy prescriptions relating to medical tourism's negative effects on the health of the poor in the destination country.

My own tentative conclusion is that there is a more persuasive case for restricting insurer- and government-prompted medical tourism, and medical tourism for services that are inessential or more in the penumbra of "health." By contrast, due to concerns about health care access in the home country, I find less convincing the case for restricting medical tourism for those purchasing essential health services out-of-pocket, especially when this represents these individuals' best way of getting these services.[160]

---

[159] Although my own theoretical preferences lean toward the Cohen, Sable, and Daniels approach as the most useful one in this area, I have tried to maintain a relatively catholic attitude toward the different contenders so as to pave the way for those more drawn to one of the rival accounts.

[160] One lingering concern with that conclusion is that it seems to "reward" the "bad" countries that have not secured universal health care in their home state, and thus have given more of their domestic poor the incentive to go abroad. Of course, it is beyond cavil that countries such as the United States that have failed to secure truly universal health care have not failed to do so *in order to* be able to send their uninsured abroad for medical tourism without acting unjustly, but that does not seem an adequate response. Here are two that may be more (if not entirely) satisfying. First of all, to repeat something I said earlier, (*supra* note 109), in a world of ideal justice, in my view the United States would have achieved universal health care, but we are faced with a very different world and are asking what obligations we can realistically impose upon it under the circumstances. Second, although we may be "rewarding" the "bad" states, we also want to avoid "punishing" their citizens who lack better options than medical tourism.

Interestingly, that ordering mirrors my conclusions on the policy side as to the ease by which home states can implement policies to curb medical tourism of different varieties, as I have discussed throughout the chapters of this book.[161]

For public insurer–prompted medical tourism, home countries could, by regulation or legislation, restrict the facilities and countries to which they send patients to only those facilities and countries with health care access guarantees or amelioration plans. They could do so in much the same way I have discussed in Chapters 2 and 3 channeling based on quality or medical malpractice risks. Home countries could also leave the market unregulated but dedicate foreign aid to destination countries based on volumes of medical tourism to particular regions. Of course, in so doing, they would have to rely on foreign sovereigns to spend aid appropriately or devise a system whereby nongovernmental organizations (NGOs) are given the aid or monitor its spending. As long as such policies did not result in significantly longer waiting times or fewer procedures covered, the effect on health care access for the home country poor would be small.

Similarly for private insurer–prompted medical tourism, the United States (or another home country) could, by state or federal insurance regulation, prevent sending patients to facilities or countries without health access amelioration plans.[162]

The home country could also (in addition or separately) tax insurers by their volume of medical tourism and redistribute those sums toward health care access amelioration in the destination country. This would mirror to some extent the UNITAID scheme: UNITAID is an NGO aimed at scaling up access to treatment for HIV/AIDS, malaria, and tuberculosis, primarily for people in low-income countries. A large share of its funding (72 percent) stems from twenty-nine supporting countries (including France and Chile) that have voluntarily chosen to impose on airlines departing from their countries a tax on departing passenger tickets collected by the airlines set by the country—for example, France imposes a 1 and 10 Euro tax on domestic economy and business/first class flights respectively, and a 4 and 40 Euro tax on departing international economy and business/first class respectively.[163] One might also think about this in analogy to the use of taxes on tobacco products to offset some of the costs those products impose on the health care system.

As we have seen in several of the prior chapters of this book, it is much harder to regulate the behavior of medical tourists paying out-of-pocket. Even here, though, we do have some options. The United States or another home country could hypothetically render illegal some forms of medical tourism—we will discuss this in greater depth as to circumvention tourism in the second half of this book—or render less attractive

---

[161] *See also* Cohen, *supra* note 67.

[162] *Cf.* Cohen, *supra* note 78, at 1544–46. *But see, supra* notes 36–42 and sources cited therein for skepticism as to how well such regulation is actually enforced in a destination country such as India.

[163] For more information on this program, *see* UNITAID, http://www.unitaid.eu (last visited Dec. 1, 2013).

some forms of medical tourism (for example, by exempting them from the tax deduction available for qualifying medical expenses). These regulatory interventions, however, risk being either too draconian or not terribly effective.[164] More plausibly, home countries could also tax intermediaries and use the revenue to support health care access in LDCs (in a way similar to that discussed above).

Putting pressure on accreditors represents another fruitful way forward. It would be useful for home countries to induce JCI (or another accreditor) to build an evaluation of what work a destination country hospital has done to ameliorate negative effects of medical tourism on local populations *into* its accreditation process. If pressure is needed, major home countries for patients could refuse to rely on JCI accreditation as a bell-wether for authorizing patients' travel (or allowing them tax deductions, etc.) unless and until JCI makes that move.

Home countries or international bodies could also create a separate third-party label-ing or accreditation standard that audits facilities and informs tourists of how attentive a facility is to health care access concerns regarding the local population, as Nir Eyal has proposed under the moniker "Global Health Impact Labels" in analogy to Fairtrade Coffee.[165] I have some doubts about how effective these labels are likely to be, as medical tourism patients are likely to choose facilities based on quite different and much more important priorities (for example, location of service, quality of doctor, and price) than coffee drinkers, though, to be fair, this is an empirical question.

III. OBLIGATIONS OF DESTINATION COUNTRY GOVERNMENTS, MEDICAL TOURISTS, AND OTHERS

My focus in this chapter has been to examine the obligation of home country govern-ments and international organizations to ameliorate diminutions in health care access for the destination country poor that are associated with medical tourism. I do not, how-ever, want to give the impression that these are the only entities that have that kind of responsibility. I share with others the view that this responsibility is widely shared with other entities,[166] and in the remainder of this chapter will much more briefly discuss the responsibility of destination countries and individual medical tourists for these health care deficits.

---

[164] *See* Cohen, *supra* note 78, at 1511–15.

[165] Nir Eyal, *Global Health Impact Labels, in* GLOBAL JUSTICE IN BIOETHICS 241 (Ezekiel Emanuel & Joseph Millum eds., 2012).

[166] *E.g.*, Snyder et al., *supra* note 53, at 242; Chen & Flood, *supra* note 17, at 297.

A. Destination Countries

i. Moral Obligations

The moral obligations of home countries for diminution of health care access in the destination country associated with medical tourism is a philosophically complex question that requires untangling a web of institutional interrelationships and contested ground in global justice theory. The moral case for holding destination country governments responsible for these deficits, by contrast, is quite straightforward. It is well established across a range of political theories that governments owe a duty to promote and protect the health of their populations.[167] To the extent that fostering medical tourism frustrates that objective—what the discussion of part I is aimed as ascertaining—where there are no counterbalancing welfare benefits to the destination country's citizens, medical tourism becomes morally problematic.

That conclusion has to be qualified slightly in two ways.

First of all, the proviso that "there are no counter-balancing welfare benefits to the destination country's citizens" will matter on some moral theories but not others. For Welfarist consequentialist theories, what matters is promoting the welfare of individuals, and all benefits and deficits are translated into that same "currency," such that deficits in health can, in some instances, be made up for in improvements in other positive things such as pleasure, housing, etc. By contrast, other moral theories adopt a "separate spheres" approach, wherein health is not fungible with other good things in this way.[168] Norman Daniels has, for example, argued for a special importance for health connected to equality of opportunity and believes that individuals can make claims relating to— and that governments can properly concern themselves with—the health of citizens in a way that they cannot with a more global conception of well-being or welfare. That is, I may have a good rights claim against the government to provide me health care but not a Magritte painting, even if the Magritte in fact improves my welfare more and costs the same price.[169]

In a related vein, Martha Nussbaum has argued that government's obligation to improve the health (which is part of two of her ten "capabilities" discussed above) of its people cannot be traded off as against other benefits. She makes clear that "all ten of these plural and diverse ends are minimum requirements of justice, at least up to the threshold level"; in other words, "the capabilities are radically non-fungible: deficiencies

---

[167] This is an area where there is deep overlapping consensus. *See, e.g.,* DANIELS, *supra* note 16, at 29–140 (Rawlsian argument); NUSSBAUM, FRONTIERS OF JUSTICE, *supra* note 87, at 76–78 (Capabilities approach argument); MARK S. STEIN, DISTRIBUTIVE JUSTICE AND DISABILITY: UTILITARIANISM AGAINST EGALITARIANISM 33–54 (2006) (Utilitarian argument).

[168] For a more in-depth discussion of this debate, *see, e.g.,* I. Glenn Cohen, *Rationing Legal Services,* 5 J. LEGAL ANALYSIS 221, 248–50 (2013); Dan W. Brock, *Separate Spheres and Indirect Benefits,* 1 COST EFFECTIVENESS & RESOURCE ALLOCATION 4 (2003), *available at* http://www.resource-allocation.com/content/1/1/4.

[169] DANIELS, *supra* note 16, at 33–34, 51–78.

in one area cannot be made up simply by giving people a larger amount of another capability."[170] Her "theory does not countenance intuitionistic balancing or tradeoffs among [the capabilities]," but instead "demands that they *all* be secured to each and every citizen, up to some appropriate threshold level."[171] She recognizes that "[i]n desperate circumstances, it may not be possible for a nation to secure them all up to the threshold level, but then it becomes a purely practical question what to do next, not a question of justice," because "[t]he question of justice is already answered: justice has not been fully done here."[172]

For such theories, counterbalancing gains for the welfare of the destination country population—should there be any through trickle-down or other means—would not justify promoting medical tourism. For Welfarist consequentialist theories they might. There is also a related concern as to who receives these benefits. For Prioritarian, Sufficientarian theories, it matters that those who benefit are those who are particularly badly off, while for Utilitarians, the just distribution matters only indirectly in terms of "bang for your buck" based on diminishing marginal utility from health and other resources. For these reasons, one has to take positions on some significant debates in moral theory to decide whether and in what circumstances the proviso related to counterbalancing benefits will diminish the destination country's responsibility for any negative health effects of medical tourism.

The second qualification is not so much philosophical as practical. As Snyder et al. have argued, destination country governments may be in a tough spot when it comes to the globalization of health care:

> Although it may be satisfying to pin the blame for the harms of [medical tourism] on specific government officials, even at this level the liability model shows its limits. The [Iris Young "Political Responsibility"] model of responsibility [which Snyder et al. endorse] stresses that socioeconomic structures limit individuals' options. For government officials in LMICs, their choice to participate in international health services trade may be predetermined by a global economic system that impoverishes countries that do not participate in free trade arrangements such as the WTO. These countries may also face heavy pressure to build their hard currency reserves and reduce deficits based on International Monetary Fund structural adjustment programs. For these officials, engaging in MT may be the best of a range of bad options constrained by the global economic system. If so, the liability model will do a poor job of assigning responsibility for the effects of these officials' choices, even when they are the most powerful members of their communities.[173]

---

[170] Nussbaum, Frontiers of Justice, *supra* note 87, at 166–67, 175.

[171] *Id.* at 175.

[172] *Id.*

[173] Snyder et al., *supra* note 53, at 238.

Although the "coercion" argument is less powerful for medical tourism—because participation in the GATS regime as to trade in services is less all-or-nothing than the WTO regime—I think these authors get matters right in broad strokes. The responsibility of destination country governments has to be evaluated as against their "degrees of freedom" and the pressures they face from the international system. In my above discussion of "self-inflicted wounds," I have tried to do just that.

ii. Regulatory Interventions

As my discussion of the six triggering conditions in part I suggests, destination countries, in theory, have significant opportunities to regulate medical tourism in a way that will blunt its ill effects on health care access for their populations.

Destination country governments can tax medical tourism providers and redistribute the proceeds to pay for health care access to the poor by investing in health care or public health infrastructure. They can attempt to ramp up the production of physicians and nurses, and use techniques such as conditional scholarships to retain them.[174] They can also regulate the behavior of their physicians and other health care workers and impose requirements that they spend certain amounts of their time serving domestic rather than foreign patients (who may pay higher prices).[175] They can require a uniform reimbursement rate to blunt the incentives of local hospitals to take on foreign patients instead of domestic ones as a way of improving revenue stream, etc.[176] For destination countries where certificates or other licensure are required in order to build a new hospital or expand an existing one, the government can limit the number of entrants into the medical tourism market that exists or extract commitments (such as those pertaining to providing care for indigents) from the facilities.[177] These are just a smattering of the ways in which destination countries can regulate medical tourism from their end, with the exact details varying country-by-country depending on existing domestic health care regulation.

However, as Yogi Berra once quipped when asked for the difference between theory and practice, "in theory there is no difference, but in practice there is." Because medical tourism offers an influx of foreign capital to the destination country and its costs occur mostly to the destination country poor (many of whom may be somewhat disenfranchised in the political system), there is a possibility that many of these regulatory opportunities will never be used, due to a conflict of interest between those who regulate and those who are burdened by medical tourism. Even when these regulations are formally put in place, there is no guarantee that destination country governments will enforce

---

[174] *See* Eyal & Bärnighausen, *supra* note 57.
[175] Cohen, *supra* note 67, at 17–18.
[176] *Id.*
[177] *Id.*

them, and in part I of this chapter, I reviewed some evidence to that effect centered on the Indian experience.

Even where there is a political will and an adequate governance regime to enforce and monitor these kinds of programs in the destination country, in some instances, existing trade commitments under the GATS agreement may create obstacles to implementation. In particular, some of the destination countries have made a "Mode 2" (consumption abroad) commitment to the "Hospital Services" sector that would cover a large swath of medical-tourism services—it includes inter alia surgical, medical, ob-gyn, nursing, laboratory, radiological, anesthesiological, and rehabilitation services.[178] Because GATS specific commitments apply to "measures," which are understood broadly to include regulations, rules, procedures, decisions, or administrative actions, whether adopted by federal, state, or local bodies, for countries that have made such commitments, regulation of the medical tourism sector of the type discussed above may be challenged through the WTO dispute-resolution system as illegal "barriers to trade," and give rise to significant trade sanctions.[179]

Again, the GATS obstacle to regulating medical tourism applies only to those countries that have made the relevant specific commitments—as of 2013, fewer than fifty WTO members (the European Community counting as one) have undertaken commitments in one of the four health services sub-sectors, making health services one of the least-committed sectors in GATS.[180] Further, even for those countries that have become signatories, exactly which forms of destination country regulation would run afoul of GATS is a matter I leave for other work by international trade specialists, but it seems clear that not every such regulation would count. For example, it is hard to see how preventing access to a service by *both* a country's own citizens and those who come to the country from abroad is a trade violation. Still, GATS may partially tie the hands of some destination country governments as to some forms of regulation. This and the realities of destination country conflicts of interest may make robust destination country regulation less likely, however morally desirable.

B. Individual Medical Tourists

What about individual medical tourists, particularly those from well-developed countries traveling to less-developed ones for health care? What are their moral obligations?

As Snyder et al. note, on the one hand "[m]edical tourists as a group can be found to be liable for some of the harms associated with MT." In particular, by "creating a market for MT, they encourage health workers and government officials in host countries to

---

[178] Arnold & Reeves, *supra* note 125, at 316–18.

[179] GATS, *supra* note 121, arts. I, XXVIII; Arnold & Reeves, *supra* note 125, at 317–18.

[180] *Health and Social Services: Current Commitments and Exceptions*, WORLD TRADE ORG., http://www.wto.org/english/tratop_e/serv_e/health_social_e/health_social_e.htm (last visited Dec. 1, 2013).

develop infrastructure for the industry, potentially at a cost to domestic access to health care," and they also "relieve some pressure for health reform in their own countries by seeking care abroad."[181] On the other hand, there are difficulties in assigning liability to medical tourists, as "the lines of causation are unclear and attributions of liability feel unnatural." Moreover, medical tourists may "face unjust constraints on their decisions, [because] patients who decline to participate in MT may be left with lengthy waiting times or unaffordable costs, for essential medical treatment, thus unjustly constraining the range of options available to them."[182]

As I suggested above, not all forms of medical tourism are equal in this regard. Patients traveling abroad for essential services they cannot afford at home, for which they pay out-of-pocket, deserve the most sympathy, while those who seek inessential services such as cosmetic surgery or travel as part of private insurer–prompted medical tourism—where their alternative is simply paying slightly more—bear more responsibility for the ill effects of their consumption.

Snyder et al. helpfully offer a multi-step decision-making tool for medical tourists as to their moral obligations.[183]

First, the potential medical tourist asks herself: "Does going abroad for care entail my participation in an unjust structure that is harmful to the destination country, my community, or others?" If "no," then she may ethically proceed with medical tourism.

If "yes," she should then ask herself: "Is the treatment essential for my physical and/ or mental health?" If "no," Snyder et al. say she should "not proceed with going abroad for [the] procedure." I, however, would instead say she should "not proceed abroad *or if she does she has moral obligations to choose a provider who minimizes the ill effects of her travel and/or to help remedy some of the ill effects.*" This comports with my claim above that there are stronger duties regarding medical tourism for less essential services such as cosmetic surgery, but I part ways with Snyder et al.'s apparent suggestion that travel abroad is always immoral in these circumstances.

If the tourist answers "yes," the procedure is "essential for my physical and/or mental health," they propose that she then ask herself: "Have I established a process for discharging my political responsibility to minimize harm to others and develop more just structures?" If "no," they say that she should not proceed with the medical tourism. If "yes," they say that she should go ahead and travel, but also "[w]ork toward making identified structural change(s)." What they have in mind is that:

Any patient traveling from a democratic high-income country will have a responsibility to lobby for changes in how that government participates in MT, including

---

[181] Snyder et al., *supra* note 53, at 238.

[182] *Id.* at 238–39.

[183] The tool that I reproduce in text can be found at *id.* at 240 fig. 1.

lobbying for the development of ethical bilateral health services trade agreements and reforming the domestic health care system to lessen the need for travel for care. The power of the average citizen to influence government policy is limited, and so individual medical tourists should look to their collective ability to initiate change. Where lobbying groups already exist, all things equal, the medical tourist should join these efforts. Where these groups do not exist, the medical tourist has a responsibility to help organize the efforts of others. As MT for essential health care confers an enormous benefit on patients and their interest in receiving timely and affordable essential medical care is great as well, the [political responsibility] to organize for policy changes may be sizable. The strength of the [political responsibility] will be mitigated by the degree to which the patient was able to seek medical care that was minimally harmful to other persons and the degree to which the patient is otherwise connected to the communities she has affected.[184]

This schema, with the proviso I mentioned above, seems largely correct to me. I would perhaps put matters a little less strongly than Snyder et al. do, but that is a difference in degree not kind. My reservation here has more to do with fears of "medical tourism exceptionalism." Medical tourism is but one of a large number of ways in which consumption behaviors—relating to everything from clothing, to coffee, to financial institutions and customer service—impact the welfare of individuals living abroad, including their health. In part because health care is a focus for bioethicists, it is unsurprising that medical tourism has received more sustained attention on this score from myself and others than have many other activities. Still, at the end of the day, I do not want us to be the proverbial drunk looking for his keys under the lamppost. Instead, the obligations we impose on medical tourists should be commensurate with those we would demand of other consumption behaviors. This means that we should demand of these patients an obligation to organize lobbies commensurate with those we would impose on citizens in other consumption opportunities that have ill effects abroad.

In particular, as Snyder et al. acknowledge, that first step in their logic tree is a very demanding inquiry to place on patients given the current state of the industry, but, like me, they look forward to a day when a labeling system similar to "Fair Trade coffee" is put in place and/or accreditors build these considerations into their accreditation systems.[185] In the interim, I think this moral obligation may only be realistically satisfiable in part, and the depth of the duty of inquiry we place on patients needs to be responsive to the availability of information. To return to an idea I have pressed repeatedly in this book, what we want is a channeling regime. We do not want to adopt a rule that says "any time you cannot completely assure yourself that there will be no ill effects on destination countries, do not use medical tourism." Given the current state of data about these effects, discussed in part I, that rule would end up ruling out medical tourism altogether. What we want instead is to channel patients toward providers and destination countries that are making efforts in this direction, even if imperfect, to reward and reinforce those efforts and deprive the "bad apples" of business, so as to drive them out of the market.

Snyder et al. also rightly acknowledge that in helping medical tourists make these kinds of determinations, we must invest significantly in patient education, both in terms of what patients' moral obligations are and in terms of the range of options they have.[186] As I stress at various points in this book, home country physicians and other health care workers are often patients' first line of information about medical travel. While these workers have self-interested reasons to discourage the practice in many cases, we must work hard to enlist them as agents of good and to provide *them* with the tools to counsel patients on their moral obligations and choices should they pursue that option.

IV. CONCLUSION

A number of authors in both the popular and academic literature have expressed concern about the effects of medical tourism on access to health care for the poor of the destination country, and have claimed that this is a normative problem calling for regulatory intervention. In this chapter, I have broken down this claim into its empirical and normative components and examined both.

On the empirical side, I have specified six triggering conditions for medical tourism having a negative effect on the health care opportunities for the destination country poor and reviewed existing empirical evidence, to the extent it exists, showing that these negative effects are plausible.

Assuming *arguendo* that such negative effects occur, I then examined the normative question of destination country governments and international bodies' obligations as to medical tourism having such effect. I canvassed Cosmopolitan, Statist, and intermediate theories and suggested ways in which application of these theories to medical tourism highlights gaps and indeterminacies as well as reasons some of these theories may not be good fits for this kind of applied ethics inquiry, while building on existing discussions of pharmaceutical pricing and medical migration. I have tried to map divergences and convergences among these theories, and I tentatively conclude that the claim for global justice obligations stemming from medical tourism is strongest (but not without problems) for insurer- and government-prompted medical tourism and for tourism for inessential services, such as cosmetic surgeries, while it is quite weak for medical tourism on the part of those paying out-of-pocket for essential services. I then examined the regulatory options available to home countries to regulate this trade.

---

[186] *See id.* at 242.

Finally, I turned to two other actors in the system. First, I examined the moral obligations of destination countries and their regulatory options. I showed that these countries have significant normative obligations to help blunt the negative impact of medical tourism on their populations and have many potential tools to do so, but also expressed skepticism as to whether these countries are adequately motivated to do this given the realities of the cash flow in the medical tourism industry. Finally, I examined the obligations of medical tourists from developed countries themselves. I conclude that they too have significant moral obligations to remedy health care deficits associated with medical tourism in the destination country, and have adapted a decision-metric proposed by others to help medical tourists evaluate their course of action and potential remedial steps.

Given where we are in terms of this field, more so than the other chapters in this book, this chapter is somewhat aspirational. Currently, the existing empirical evidence on health care deficits associated with medical tourism is woefully incomplete. Regulatory interventions aimed at blunting negative effects are even further behind. It may feel strange, given that reality, to be engaged in a wholesale normative evaluation. I am sensitive to that concern and have tried throughout to temper the aspirations of global justice with realism of program development. Although I am under no illusion that we will see a full-scale mobilization in this direction in the short or middle term, I am hopeful that discussions such as this one will help mobilize the various stakeholders—home and destination country governments, intermediaries, insurers, accreditors, and tourists themselves—to begin inching in the right direction.

PART TWO

Medical Tourism for Services Illegal in the Patient's Home Country

7

Transplant Tourism

⌒—————————————————————————————————————

MEDICAL TOURISM FOR reproductive technology, assisted suicide, and stem cell treatments—the topics of the next few chapters of this book—allows patients to use regulatory differences between the home and destination country to access what is illegal at home but legal in the destination country. Organ sale, by contrast, is currently illegal in every country except Iran.[1] However, many destination countries have thriving black markets due to their willful failure to police the practice or good faith lack of resources devoted to it. This trade in bodies and capital overcomes many religious and social taboos to bring together buyers and sellers from across the world. Israeli patients receive kidneys from Palestinian sellers; Moldovan and Romanian Orthodox peasant patients come to Turkey to sell smuggled cigarettes but end up selling their kidneys to brokers in Istanbul's Askary flea market.[2] And so it goes.

---

[1] As I discuss below, even Iran significantly regulates who can sell and buy organs.

[2] *See* Nancy Scheper-Hughes, *Rotten Trade: Millennial Capitalism, Human Values, and Global Justice in Organ Trafficking*, 2 J. HUM. RTS. 197, 200–03 (2003). Scheper-Hughes, along with Lawrence Cohen, is the cofounder of Organs Watch, which describes itself as a UC Berkeley documentation center designed to "investigate reports and rumors of human rights abuses surrounding organ trafficking, identify hot spots where abuse may be occurring and begin to define the line between ethical transplant surgery and practices that are exploitative or corrupt." http://berkeley.edu/news/media/releases/99legacy/11-03-1999b.html (last visited May 4, 2014). *See also* Scheper-Hughes, *supra*, at 207–11 (describing the formation of Organs Watch). The fact that Scheper-Hughes and Cohen clearly have taken strong advocacy roles on these issues does not disqualify their work; in this debate it is almost impossible to find someone who has invested their time in research *without* strong priors. Still, as some readers may be sensitive to the line between research and advocacy, I mention this upfront and also rely on data and accounts of others that have not adopted advocacy

This chapter examines medical tourism for the sale of organs, what I will call "transplant tourism," its ethics, and its regulation. Although many have no doubt heard the urban legend of someone who wakes up in a bathtub with ice in a particular developing country after a night of heavy drinking with his or her kidney missing, there is little documentation of such kidney thefts actually happening. Much more common and in some ways more tragic is an organized black market where poor sellers sell their kidneys to brokers who in turn resell them at higher rates to potential buyers. The first part of this chapter focuses on describing the existing trade and the problems it engenders. The second part discusses and evaluates the bioethical arguments for prohibiting or regulating the trade in light of this description. Here I examine a series of arguments commonly deployed for prohibiting domestic organ sale: corruption, crowding out, coercion, exploitation, and paternalistic concern for prohibiting individuals from making choices they will later regret. It is this last argument, rather than the more frequently deployed other arguments, that I will contend gives the strongest argument for prohibiting or otherwise regulating transplant tourism. The third part of this chapter considers the regulatory interventions that have dealt with or could be tried to deal with the problems. Throughout this chapter I focus on the sale of kidneys, the most common subject of transplant tourism, though much of what I say could be applied to other organs as well.

I. UNDERSTANDING TRANSPLANT TOURISM MARKETS:
OF SELLERS, RECIPIENTS, AND BROKERS

To understand the international market for organs, one has to understand the three most important players: the sellers, the recipients, and the brokers. Although organ sale tourism is a global phenomenon, its manifestation differs market-by-market. Without trying to be exhaustive, I will provide a sense of how the market currently operates by focusing on a few key locales for the trade: the Philippines, Pakistan, Bangladesh, and India, while giving some attention to Egypt and Iran. I then discuss some data on recipients of commercial kidney transplant tourism, focusing on the small data available from U.S. and Canadian transplant centers and the more qualitative data on brokers.

Before I begin describing this trade, I want to make two points. First, on nomenclature: I will call those who sell their kidneys "sellers" not "donors." Although the term "donor" is sometimes used, the term connotes a certain amount of altruism that, as we will see, is seldom the only motivation of those who provide kidneys in this market.

Second, before delving into these thick descriptions of the local trades, it is helpful to take a step back and try to understand why we have seen a growth in transplant

---

roles as publicly as Scheper-Hughes and Cohen have. Sallie Yea, *Trafficking in Parts: The Commercial Kidney Market in a Manila Slum, Philippines*, 10 GLOBAL SOC. POL'Y 358, 362 (2010); Nancy Scheper-Hughes, *Bodies for Sale: Whole or Parts, in* COMMODIFYING BODIES 1, 53 (Nancy Scheper-Hughes & Loïc J.D. Wacquant eds., 2002); Lawrence Cohen, *The Other Kidney: Biopolitics beyond Recognition*, 7 BODY & SOC. 9, 11 (2001).

tourism in the last decades. The first and most important reason is the scientific advances enabling the widespread availability of the immune-suppressive drug cyclosporine, which has broadened the community of potential kidney donors.[3] Second, the growth of aging populations in the developed world and the rise of diseases of affluence have increased demand for organs.[4] Third, the developing world has seen a growth of relatively high-quality medical personnel who face low employment opportunities and/or salary, making them more vulnerable to corruption and enabling the growth of the black market.[5] Finally, for legal, religious, or cultural reasons, many countries have not developed robust cadaveric organ procurement systems, such that there is unmet demand for organs from live donors.[6] This last reason is more controversial, in that some commentators would dispute the idea of "scarcity" here—contending that the scarcity is artificial and results in donor preferences for transplant over dialysis, preferences for live instead of cadaveric kidneys that tend to lead to longer post-transplant survival, and expansions of those eligible for transplants to those over age seventy or with HIV and other immune-compromised disorders.[7] Moreover, although improved cadaveric organ recovery would decrease demand for transplant tourism, in and of itself it will not eliminate that demand—for example, from U.S. patients.

With that macro-level picture in mind, let us now to turn to locality-based descriptions of who sells their kidneys as part of transplant tourism, the reasons they give, and their outcomes. To put this data into perspective, it is worth emphasizing that a study of more than eighty thousand live kidney donors in the United States found no difference in their long-term mortality rates (the median follow-up was 6.3 years post-surgery) as compared to healthy matched controls, suggesting that legal kidney donation in the United States is very safe.[8]

A. The Sellers

i. The Philippines

In July 2009, Sallie Yea interviewed fifteen kidney sellers in the slum of Manila, Philippines, known as "Baseco" (an acronym for the Bataan Shipping and Engineering

---

[3] Yea, *supra* note 2, at 362; Scheper-Hughes, *supra* note 2, at 53.

[4] *E.g.*, Yea, *supra* note 2, at 362.

[5] *E.g., id.*

[6] *See, e.g.*, Rashad S. Barsoum, *Trends in Unrelated-Donor Kidney Transplantation in the Developing World*, 21 PEDIATRIC NEPHROLOGY 1925, 1927 (2008).

[7] *See* Scheper-Hughes, *supra* note 2, at 198, 206–07, 213. There are also a series of additional reasons for this growth, such as the increase in international travel by those in developed countries and the way in which the Internet has facilitated the exchange of information as to the trade, that seem plausible, if without any direct supporting evidence.

[8] *See* D.L. Segev *Perioperative Mortality and Long-Term Survival following Live Kidney Donation*, 303 JAMA 959 (2010).

Company).[9] Baseco is one of the most densely populated areas of the world, and it has been estimated that three thousand of its hundred thousand residents have sold a kidney. Yae's interviewees suggested that kidney sales became attractive to Baseco's residents in part because of a 2004 fire that destroyed the houses of twenty thousand residents, coupled with government-sponsored rebuilding efforts that produced houses many residents could not afford.

The sellers Yae interviewed were men twenty-nine to forty-seven years old at the time of interview, with most clustered in their early thirties, likely in part a function of the fact that only those older than age thirty can legally donate (not sell) a kidney in the country. Only two of the fifteen sellers had education that extended beyond primary school—those two had dropped out during the second year of high school for financial reasons—and some had received only three or four years of formal education altogether. The majority of the men were the primary breadwinners for their families, and even those who were unmarried and without children supported elderly parents. The men held relatively low paying jobs as construction workers, pedicab drivers, and *kargadors* (who carry goods from the port or nearby railroads). Their average salaries were PP 300 (one Philippine Peso currently equals two U.S. cents, so roughly US$7 per day, which is low even by Filipino standards. As one seller put it "I earn PP 250 a day and I need to support five people, including myself. One meal is PP 100 so if we want to eat three times a day the money is not enough."

Kidney sellers were paid between PP 45,000 and PP 200,000, with a median price of PP 120,000 (US$2,804). At least two of Yea's sellers reported receiving less than they were promised (one PP 60,000 less and one PP 25,000 less) from the broker, and complained that they did not have any recourse as the organ sale was itself illegal. Sellers generally did not know whom their organs would go to or how much they were sold for. Most had contact only with the broker and doctor, although some met the ultimate transplant recipients.

Recruitment in Baseco did not appear to involve physical force, though other kinds of pressure were sometimes applied. Recruiters in Baseco tended to be neighbors and friends who sometimes used guilt and shame to induce selling. Often the broker pressed the seller by telling him that the recipient was seriously ill and would die without the transplant. One seller reported that his broker went from person-to-person in Baseco promising instant cash, and persisting until he reached a quota of sellers. Even more pressure was used against individuals who had agreed to sell kidneys but then thought about reneging, with the brokers emphasizing they had already laid out money to pay for the medical tests and the declining health of the recipients. To be sure, not all brokers sought out donors. One of the sellers reported seeking out a broker himself to locate a

---

[9] The descriptive material in this section is drawn from Yea, *supra* note 2, at 358–72.

potential buyer, and another mentioned merely contacting a relative who had previously sold a kidney in order to connect with the doctor who had performed that operation.

How did the Baseco sellers fare post-transplant? Although most of the men were promised no-cost post-operative and longer-term health care, only a few actually received it, and even they reported that the care was of poor quality. One of the recipients of these promises was not examined by the doctor but instead just given medications, while another was not even provided medication when he checked out of the hospital post-transplant. All but one of the sellers complained that they had become "weaker, tired more easily and often experienced bouts of depression or angry bursts which they had not previously experienced." Half of the men reported a decline of 50 percent in their physical strength, which was important because all but one of the men (who worked as a hairdresser) had jobs that required physical strength and stamina. Some reported having to lie to their construction and shipyard employers about having sold a kidney, because they would not have been hired had they reported having done so.

And yet, as Nancy Scheper-Hughes documents in her more narrative work on kidney sales in the Phillipines, there are many who are clamoring to become kidney donors.[10] She describes throngs of "angry and 'disrespected' kidney sellers who had been 'neglected' and 'overlooked' by the medical doctors at Manila's most prestigious private hospital, St. Luke's Episcopal Medical Center," who chafed that "they had been judged less valuable kidney vendors than some of their lucky neighbors who now owned new VCRs, karaoke machines, and expensive tricyles."[11] Indeed, she describes the willing kidney donors who wait outside transplant units in Manila hoping to have their chance, and others who "check themselves into special wards of surgical units that resemble 'kidney motels' where they lie on mats or in hospital beds for days, even weeks, watching color television, eating chips and waiting for the 'lucky number' that will make them into the day's winner of the kidney transplant lottery" such that they can sell their kidney.[12]

ii. Pakistan[13]

Pakistan is one of the "largest host centres for transplant tourism" in the world, with over two thousand organs sold for transplant per year, about two-thirds of which go to foreigners (primarily from the Middle East, South Asia, Europe, and North America). Syed Naqvi and his coauthors attribute Pakistan's prominence in the transplant tourism trade to several factors: the absence of a deceased donor program, a shortage of unrelated commercial transplants in private sector hospitals, India's cracking down on kidney sales to foreigners, and a well-established living donor transplant program in Pakistan.

---

[10] Scheper-Hughes, *supra* note 2, at 202.

[11] *Id.*

[12] *Id.*

[13] The descriptive material from this section is drawn from Syed Ali Anwar Naqvi et al., *A Socioeconomic Survey of Kidney Vendors in Pakistan*, 20 TRANSPLANT INTERN'L 934 (2007).

In February 2006, Syed Naqvi and his team interviewed 239 kidney sellers (186 male, 53 female) in District Sargodha, a province of Punjab in Eastern Pakistan, an area that is overpopulated with low socioeconomic development and has 34 percent of the population living below the poverty line. They were able to verify nephrectomy scars proving that surgery had taken place in all but 2 percent of the sample. The unverified 2 percent were all female, and examination was not possible because the interview occurred in a public place or because their husbands refused to allow examination.

The mean age of sellers was 33.6 years, with 52 percent being ages 31–40 and 29 percent being ages 21–30. Sixty-six percent of those studied were bonded laborers working as domestic servants, housemaids, and farm workers. Of the fifty-three women in the sample, twenty were housewives and thirty-three were maids who worked for landlords. Most had worked since childhood, with a mean duration of around nineteen years of employment. Ninety percent of the sellers were illiterate.

All sellers were quite poor. Of the 192 sellers who agreed to answer questions on monthly incomes, 62 percent earned US$10–$30 a month, with a mean income of US$15.4, while 32 percent earned less than US$10, and 6 percent earned more than US$20. Despite this poverty, many had dependents. Of the 219 sellers who responded to questions on this issue, all had between two and eleven dependents with a mean of 5.5 dependents. They were also saddled with debt: 176 of the sellers answered questions on the subject, but many of the non-responders indicated they did not know the actual amount they owed because they had no documentation, or answered "too much." Of the responders, 77 percent owed between US$1,000 and $2,500 with a mean debt of US$1,311.40. Nineteen percent were still paying off the debt of their fathers, uncles, or grandfathers.

Almost all sellers identified debt repayment as a significant reason for the sale, with the following breakdowns given: debt repayment (72 percent), debt repayment and business (5 percent), business venture (5 percent), debt repayment and marriage (7 percent), debt repayment and housing construction (4 percent), debt repayment and illness in the family (5 percent), and illness in the family (2 percent).

The sellers came to kidney transplant in a variety of different ways. Forty percent were recruited by the staff of a transplant center, 24 percent were "motivated by family," 19 percent went directly to a transplant center themselves, 15 percent went through agents of a hospital, and 5 percent were coerced by their landlord to sell a kidney in order to repay a debt.

In terms of the recipients, 29.7 percent of sellers indicated they had met or knew the recipient, and 31 percent of this group indicated a local recipient while 69 percent indicated a foreign one. So, to be precise, only a portion of those in this study can be verified to be participating in bona fide transplant tourism.

Sellers were promised between US$1,146 and $2,950 (mean US$1,737) for their kidney, but no seller in the sample was actually paid that price. The mean amount received was instead US$1,377 with a range of US$819 to $1,803, largely because deductions were taken for the costs of the nephrectomy, hospital stay, and travel to and from home.

Importantly, the team tried to determine if the sellers viewed themselves as better off because of the transplant and sale. The sellers were interviewed at a mean of 4.8 years after the surgery.

In terms of health, all sellers indicated that their health was good before the transplant, but only 1.2 percent said their health was as good after it. Sixty-two percent said they felt physically weak and were unable to work the long hours they did before the transplant, and 36.8 percent said their health was poor and they felt ill, suggesting that they had to stop working for periods of time.

When it came to finances, 85 percent said there was no improvement in their lives and they were either still in debt or had not achieved their objectives. Only 4 percent indicated they had paid off their debt, although some had used the money to buy rickshaws, set up shops, construct a house, or pay marriage expenses. When asked if "they would encourage sale of kidney in the family?" 35 percent (eighty-three sellers) said they would encourage a family member to do so, with seventy-five of those eighty-three sellers being bonded laborers (almost half of all bonded laborers who had sold kidneys), two being non-bonded laborers, three being unemployed, and three being housewives.

When discussing this finding, the study authors note that "in our study population where [the] majority were illiterate and many in bonded labour, [the available] opportunities were far less…. Therefore, despite their bad experience, they still preferred to [sell kidneys] in desperation to pay off debts, and/or to save another son or daughter from bondage."

iii. Bangladesh

Although it has been illegal to sell body parts in Bangladesh since 1999 (with fines and jail time as the penalty), there is a growing organ trade in the country where 78 percent of the country's inhabitants live on less than US$2 a day.[14]

As part of his ethnography of kidney sellers in Bangladesh, Monir Moniruzzaman recently interviewed thirty-three kidney sellers (thirty male, three female) in Dhaka, the country's capital, largely by gaining the trust of Dalal, an organ broker working in the market who became his informant and intermediary.

Kidney sellers were often initially recruited by advertising in local newspapers. For example, this ad ran in the *Daily Ittefaq* on January 4, 2000:

Request for Kidney Donation
Both kidneys of a USA resident, Kulsum Begum, are damaged. Kidney specialists advise her to transplant a kidney immediately. A heartfelt request is made to the good persons who can donate a kidney with the following criteria.

---

[14] The descriptive material from this section is drawn from Monir Moniruzzaman, *"Living Cadavers" in Bangladesh: Bioviolence in the Human Organ Bazaar*, 26 MED. ANTHROP. Q. 69 (2012).

1. *The interested donor's blood group and the tissue must be matched with those of Kulsum Begum. Blood group O +.*
2. *The donor (male or female) must travel to the donation. The transplant will be performed at [a U.S. university] medical center.*
3. *The donor must be in good health and between 19 and 40 years of age.*

All the relevant expenses will be covered by Kulsum Begum. To discuss details, contact urgently the following address.
Md Iman Ali, House B-12/7, Agargoan Taltala Government Quarter
Sher-E-Bangla Nagar, Dhaka—1207, Telephone: 8125959.

A poor Bangladeshi seeing the ad and contacting the number it provides ordinarily ends up in contact with either a recipient or a broker. That person emphasizes what is being sought is a "kidney donation," which is a "noble act." The broker (or recipient) promises to cover all expenses and compensate the seller as well. He or she will also tell the seller that the operation is completely safe and that the seller will be in the hands of a world-renowned specialist. Sellers were often told a story about "the sleeping kidney," where selling a kidney is presented as a win-win situation in which in removing one of their kidneys the transplant surgeon "awakens" the other "sleeping kidney" through medication, and the seller is portrayed as living perfectly well with only the one remaining kidney. Moniruzziman's interviewees also told him about other assurances given by brokers: the broker offers the seller land, a job, or a visa and foreign citizenship. The broker tells the seller that going abroad for transplantation, particularly India where most of these transplants occur, will be fun and the seller can eat out, shop, and watch Indian movies.

If the seller is persuaded to participate, the broker then tissue-types the seller and tries to find a match. The seller is typically then offered only 80,000 Taka (US$1,150) for the kidney, and told that the number is low because the seller's particular blood type is in ready supply in the market. After further negotiation, on average the seller is offered 100,000 Taka (US$1,400), but told he or she will not receive the entire amount until just before entering the operating room, for fear the seller might renege.

The broker arranges a fake passport and forged legal documents for the seller that indicates that the seller is donating a kidney to a relative, and advises the seller to hide his or her identity so the Indian health care personnel do not reject the case. In at least one instance, Moniruzziman reports that a thirty-eight-year old Hindu kidney seller underwent circumcision in order to pass as a relative of his Muslim recipient.

Once the seller crosses the Indian border, the broker often seizes the seller's passport to ensure that he or she cannot return to Bangladesh before the kidney is removed. The sellers are housed in poor accommodations, rooming with as many as ten other sellers in a bachelor apartment rented by the broker. Medical tests are redone because the Indian doctors do not trust the Bangladeshi results.

At this point, the seller sometimes discovers that the broker is making a profit of around 400,000 Taka (US$5,500), at which point he or she demands more compensation. The broker offers murky explanations about the huge expense and risk of the venture, in order to resist paying more. One of Moniruzzizam's interviewees, a twenty-two-year-old college student, at this point reported deciding not to donate and asking for his passport back to return to Bangladesh, leading the broker to hire local *mustans* (essentially thugs) to beat him up and threaten him into the operation.

The day before the operation, the seller asks for his or her promised money, but is now told that the seller will not be paid until after returning to Bangladesh. After the surgery, Moniruzziman reports that sellers notice a twenty-inch scar along their bodies, which the surgeon could have avoided by using a laparoscopic surgery resulting in a small four-inch incision (but costing an additional US$200). Sellers are typically released from the hospital after five days into what Moniruzziman describes as the "broker's unhygienic apartment." Sellers typically return to Bangladesh within a few days despite the doctors' orders to rest in India. Some sellers experience bleeding from their wound on the train ride back to Dhaka.

Upon return to Bangladesh and resumption of their old identities, the sellers faced several problems. Twenty-seven out of the thirty-three sellers did not receive the full amount of money they had been promised. Though they repeatedly called the buyer to receive what they were owed, the buyer offered them little sums of money each time and claimed the need to deduct numerous hidden expenses. In at least one case, a seller and his wife were physically abused and threatened with jail when they disputed the charges. Sellers typically used the money they received to pay off debts, start a business, pay bribes to get a job, or arrange a dowry. Some sellers spent the money on material goods, such as televisions, cell phones, and gold chains.

Moniruzziman claims that only "two sellers, Abul (32) and Rahmat (28), benefited economically, opening a livestock farm and buying land with the payment," while the "others have not escaped poverty and are actually living in worse conditions than they were before their operations." Seventy-eight percent of the sellers reported that their economic condition deteriorated after the surgery, with many sellers losing jobs or having to work fewer hours due to physical deterioration.

Moniruzziman also reported that "the sellers' health profoundly deteriorate in the postvending phase," and that they experienced "numerous physical problems and went through severe psychological suffering," referring to themselves as "handicapped." The symptoms included pain, weakness, weight loss, and frequent illness after selling their kidneys. Moniruzziman also notes that none of the sellers he interviewed could afford the biannual post-operative health checkup, which costs only 1,500 Taka (US $22).

Finally, sellers had to confront stigma due to their twenty-inch scar. Male sellers with a scar are referred to as a "kidney man," and sellers try to hide them, make up stories about an accident, and sometimes decide not to get married as a result. Seventy-nine percent of his sellers had become "socially isolated." Many referred to the day of their operation as their "death day." In his sample of thirty-three sellers, 85 percent spoke against the organ market, with many (he does not give an exact number) saying that if they had a second chance, they would not sell their kidneys.

Moniruzziman reports that the ultimate organ recipients in his study were divided between local and foreign citizens (though the latter tend to be Bangladeshi-born foreign nationals) who purchase organs from Bangladeshis but get the transplant surgery performed primarily in India, though sometimes in Bangladesh, Thailand, and Singapore. In contrast to most of the bioethics literature where organ buyers are themselves portrayed as desperate because they are unable to secure a tissue match from a family member, Moniruzziman claims that "many Bangladeshi recipients who can afford to do so purchase organs from the poor, rather than seeking organ donation from their family members." He documents a Bangladeshi fashion designer who arranged a charitable art exhibition and musical concert and used the funds raised to purchase an organ from a poor villager, as well as a seventy-two-year-old politician, a member of a party whose platform is for banning organ sales, who tried to buy a kidney from a twenty-two-year-old slum dweller.

Nephrologists that he interviewed appeared to be in denial about the organ purchase trade, disclaimed that doctors' role was not to police the sellers, and claimed that whatever organ sale transplants were occurring happened outside the country.

iv. India

In 2001, Madhav Goyal led a team of researchers examining the lives of 305 kidney sellers in Chennai, India.[15] Although the study itself did not try to determine how many of these kidney sellers sold organs to foreigners, enabling true transplant tourism, there is good reason to think that many of these kidneys ultimately went to foreign recipients, such that the data is a good approximation of transplant tourism in India. A 1994 Indian law bans the sale of kidneys and requires that all transplant centers have an authorization committee reviewing all potential living unrelated donors to determine that donations were made for altruistic and not commercial reasons. Nevertheless, as the interviews of these sellers show, a significant trade in selling kidneys persists in India.

Of the 305 sellers Goyal and the team interviewed, 71 percent were female and 29 percent male. The mean age was thirty-five years, with a range of twenty to fifty-five years of age. Sixty-five percent of the female sellers and 95 percent of the males worked as laborers or street vendors. They were promised between US$450 and $6,280 for their kidney with a mean of US$1,410, but actually received between US$450 and $2,660 with a mean of US$1,070. Both middlemen and clinics promised on average about one-third more than they actually paid.

---

[15] The descriptive material from this section is drawn from Madhav Goyal et al., *Economic and Health Consequences of Selling a Kidney in India*, 288 JAMA 1589 (2002).

In terms of their motivations for participating, 96 percent indicated it was to pay off debts—more specifically, of these sellers, 55 percent indicated it was for food or household debt, 24 percent for rent, 22 percent for marriage expenses, 18 percent for medical expenses, 8 percent for funeral expenses, 8 percent for business expenses, and 7 percent for other debts. In addition, 3 percent indicated they sold their kidney for future expenses anticipated for the marriage of a daughter, 1 percent to start a business, 1 percent for extra cash, and 1 percent for other reasons. Fifteen percent of the interviewed subjects indicated that their spouses had also sold a kidney. For the remainder of the sample, when asked why they and not their spouse sold a kidney, there were some gender gaps: 30 percent of the women said it was because their husbands were the breadwinners while 28 percent said it was because their husbands were ill. Among the men, 52 percent said they sold their kidneys voluntarily, while 19 percent pointed to the fact that their wives were ill or pregnant. Two women reported that their husbands forced them to donate, but the study authors note that number may underestimate how prevalent this was because interviews were conducted with other family members present.[16]

Like the other research I have discussed, a major focus of this study was whether these individuals were made worse-off by the sale. The financial effects for the seller were largely negative. On average, sellers experienced a one-third decrease in average annual family income from a mean of US$660 before the surgery to US$440 after it. The percentage of sellers below the poverty line increased from 54 percent before to 71 percent after the surgery. Of the 292 participants who were motivated to sell their kidneys in part by paying off debts, 74 percent still had debts at the time of the study.

Change in health status was measured using a five-point Likert scale (excellent, very good, good, fair, poor, with each category being treated as 1 point away from the next). Thirteen percent of participants reported no decline in their health after the transplant, 38 percent reported a 1 to 2 point decline, and 48 percent reported a 3 to 4 point decline. Of all the participants, 50 percent complained of persistent pain at the site of the nephrectomy and 33 percent complained of long-term back pain.

All sellers were asked whether they would advise someone who was selling a kidney for the same reason they did to do so. Of the 264 sellers who responded to the question, 79 percent recommended against selling a kidney.

The longer the time since the transplant, the larger the decline in economic status in that 56 percent of those who sold more than ten years ago experienced a decline in annual family income while only 29 percent of those who sold more recently experienced that decline (P<.001). However, we cannot tell from the study data whether this reflects a deterioration of individual patients' conditions over time, or rather reflects cohort

---

[16] The authors noted that it was unlikely that these declines represented a secular trend since per capita income has increased by 10 percent (or 37 percent adjusted for inflation) in the region in the ten years preceding the study, and between 1988 and 2001 there was a 50 percent decrease in the proportion of the population living below the poverty line. *Id.* at 1592.

effects based on changes in the kidney donation trade over time. Except for the price paid for kidneys (which was a mean of US$1,603 for those who sold more than ten years before the study versus US$873 for those who had sold in the ten years before the study), there were no other statistically significant relationships reported between time of the transplant and other variables.

In 2003, Lawrence Cohen reported more narratively on kidney sellers in Chennai, India.[17] Many of the stories he tells mirror the data from Goyal's study, but he raises a few additional points worth emphasizing: many of the kidney sellers are women who feel they need to contribute to the household and that their husbands cannot risk the negative effects associated with transplant; many of the women subscribed to a gendered mythology that the loss of a kidney affects men more than women; many of the women reported shame at their scar from the transplant, which served as a constant reminder of where they had been.[18] Cohen has also noted that kidney selling has become more prominent as a way to generate a dowry to ensure a comfortable marriage for an "extra" daughter.[19]

v. Other Data on Sellers

Beyond these four in-depth studies, there are also data on Egyptian and Iranian kidney sellers that are suggestive if somewhat less exhaustive.

The Egyptian data collected by Deborah Budiana-Saberi and Frank Delmonico is more sparse and reported on in published work without being published itself, so the data quality is harder to evaluate.[20] Of fifty kidney sellers in the sample, they report that 78 percent reported deterioration in their health conditions. They also reported that 81 percent had spent the money they made within five months of the transplant "mostly to pay off financial debts rather than investing in quality of life enhancements." Moreover, they report that 91 percent expressed social isolation related to donation,

---

[17] Lawrence Cohen, *Where It Hurts: Indian Material for an Ethics of Organ Transplantation*, 38 ZYGON 663 (2003); Patricia McBroom, *An "Organs Watch to Track Global Traffic in Human Organs Opens Mon., Nov. 8, at UC Berkeley* (Nov. 3, 1999), http://berkeley.edu/news/media/releases/99legacy/11-03-1999b.html. In her work on Brazillian kidney sellers, Scheper-Hughes also notes increased pressure on "lower-status, poor, or female" relatives to sell their organ as a way of contributing to their families. Nancy Scheper-Hughes, *The Global Traffic in Human Organs*, 41 CURRENT ANTHROPOLOGY 191, 209 (2000). That said, "lower-status, poor, or female" relatives are not only pressured to sell but also pressured to donate, which also results in stigma, social isolation, etc. *See* FARHAT MOAZAM, BIOETHICS AND ORGAN TRANSPLANTATION IN A MUSLIM SOCIETY (2006).

[18] Scheper-Hughes makes a similar point about Moldovan kidney sellers, reporting that sellers are often excommunicated from the Orthodox church, rendered un-marriable, or called "prostitutes," and thus hide their scar or try to claim the scars were the result of an accident. Nancy Scheper-Hughes, *Keeping an Eye on the Global Traffic in Human Organs*, 361 LANCET 1645, 1646 (2003).

[19] Scheper-Hughes, *supra* note 17, at 194.

[20] These results are briefly described in Deborah Budiani-Saberi & Francis Delmonico, *Organ Trafficking and Transplant Tourism: A Commentary on the Global Realities*, 8 AM. J. TRANSPLANTATION 925 (2008).

85 percent were unwilling to be known publicly as organ sellers, and 94 percent regretted their donations.

The Iranian scholar Jarvaad Zargooshi has published two studies of three hundred kidney sellers in Iran, using a comparison control sample of one hundred patients who had received nephrectomy for benign diseases.[21] Under Iranian law, "[t]o prevent transplant tourism, foreigners are not allowed to undergo renal transplantation from Iranian living-unrelated donors," and are "not permitted to volunteer as kidney donors to Iranian patients." Moreover, although foreigners can receive a transplant in Iran, "the donor and the recipient should be from the same nationality, and authorization for such transplantation should be obtained from the ESRD Office of the Ministry of Health."[22] As with much of Iranian policy, it is hard to determine from outside how well these policies are being adhered to.

Zargooshi's findings on Iranian kidney sellers are largely in line with what the prior studies suggest: sixty-five percent of his sample reported that the transplant had markedly negative effects on their employment and 20 percent reported somewhat negative effects. Seventy percent of vendors became "isolated, irritable, and hated social contacts," with the scar a frequent source of stigma. Many sellers reported depression related to their kidney selling, and five committed suicide, including three who set themselves on fire. Eighty-five percent of the sellers in the sample indicated they would definitely not sell a kidney again had they to do it over again, and 76 percent strongly discouraged potential vendors from doing so. Those who said they would still have sold a kidney if they had it to do all over again reasoned that, despite the risks, it was the only way for them to provide short-term support for urgent financial need.

That said, there is also a study from Iran published in 2009 that reports somewhat different data.[23] In 2005, Alireza Rouchi and her coauthors sent a questionnaire to twenty-five transplant kidney centers in Iran that instructed the head nurse to administer it to patients before discharge, and were able to collect data on 600 living donors of the 721 recorded in the national registry who had donated during a five-month period. The donors were 82.5 percent men, and had a mean age of twenty-eight years (with a range of seventeen to fifty); only thirty-two of the donors were related to their recipients. Of the donors, 96.7 percent were Iranian, 79.9 percent of the donors were married, and 82.6 percent of them did not have any health insurance coverage. In terms of monthly income, the mean was US\$175, with a range of US\$43.5 to \$380.4, and an average monthly income in Iran of US\$225. In terms of employment, 22.5 percent were unemployed or not working (including

---

[21] Javaad Zargooshi, *Quality of Life of Iranian Kidney Donors*, 166 J. UROLOGY 1790 (2001); Javaad Zargooshi, *Iranian Kidney Donors: Motivations and Relations with Recipients*, 165 J. UROLOGY 386 (2000).

[22] Ahad J. Ghods & Shekoufeh Savaj, *Iranian Model of Paid and Regulated Living-Unrelated Kidney Donation*, 1 CLINICAL J. AM. SOC. NEPHROLOGY 1136, 1138 (2008).

[23] Alireza Heidary Rouchi et al., *Compensated Living Kidney Donation in Iran: Donor's Attitude and Short Term Follow-Up*, 3 IRANIAN J. KIDNEY DISEASES 34 (2009).

students and housekeepers), 33 percent had a part-time job, and 27.9 percent had a full-time job, while the general unemployment rate in Iran at the time of the study was 11.2 percent. In terms of education, 4.6 percent were illiterate, 65.2 percent had a secondary school degree, 23.7 percent had finished high school, and 6.5 percent had a university degree.

The authors also sought information on motivation for donation. They found that 37.3 percent of respondents said it was "purely financial," 60.8 percent said both "financial and emotional/altruistic," and 1.9 percent said "purely emotional/altruistic." The financial motivations most often described included paying for medical services for self or family, maintaining family reputation, solving personal problems, paying back a debt, and getting an exemption from military service. The altruistic motivations most commonly emphasized were "God satisfaction, God forgiveness, and emotional relationship with the recipient."

They also attempted to measure "donor's feelings prior to discharge," and the word "prior" is important, as I will explain in a moment. They found that 86.5 percent of respondents reported "complete satisfaction," while 11.5 percent reported "relative satisfaction," 1.5 percent "regret," and .5 percent "indifference." The authors note that "no report of mortality in donors was received," but that "minor complications occurred" in 2.5 percent of donors including "long duration of hospital stay, pain, skin, erythema, and conditions that needs the administration of antibiotics."

Surprisingly, Rouchi and her coauthors do not mention the Zargooshi data or make any attempt to explain the way the studies should be read together, which is surprising, especially given the wide divergence between the satisfaction scores of the two studies. One possibility is that as the data is later in time, the Rouchi data merely reflects a different cohort of patients or a changed regulatory implementation. Though I cannot rule that out, I think there are other reasons to explain the differences found that make the Zargooshi data potentially more useful for our purposes: first, Rouchi and colleagues measure patients before discharge, whereas Zargooshi examines them after discharge when patients have more data on the effects of the transplant on their health, employment, and success at achieving their aims. Second, because they enlisted the head nurse to administer the study, patients in the Rouchi study may have felt some pressure to improve their ratings of their satisfaction while still a patient in the hospital and answering to those same medical professionals.[24]

Nancy Scheper-Hughes has also offered more qualitative accounts of other organ markets, such as sellers from the favelas of Brazil and in South Africa in the years before 2000, suggesting similar patterns.[25]

---

[24] One more cynical explanation is that, unlike Zargooshi's data, this one was published in an *Iranian* medical journal and it is possible that the authors or journal faced pressures regarding the content. I have no evidence for this; it is merely a possibility, but one worth highlighting given how little we know about medical scientific independence in Iran.

[25] Scheper-Hughes, *supra* note 17, at 194–97, 203–10. Although she finds some instances where organs were in fact "stolen," especially from cadavers, she does not document the phenomenon as being widespread and gives a very nuanced account of the way in which such rumors may serve instead as "weapons of the weak" used to "challenge and interrupt the designs of the medicine and the state," and "contribute[] to a growing

B. Studies of Recipients

Far less work has been done on transplant tourists themselves—that is, the recipients of organs purchased abroad. Given that many of these individuals have broken the law and engaged in morally questionable behavior, it is not surprising that few are willing to make themselves the object of rigorous scientific study. Nevertheless, some work on this population has been done, and I report the results of four relatively recent studies of recipients—two from the United States and two from Canada. These studies relate to some of the discussions about risks relating to medical tourism in Chapter 2 of this book; in particular, the prevalence of complications upon return to the patient's home country and the risk of multi-drug–resistant bacteria being brought back with the patient. As I suggested there, because of the immune-suppressed nature of transplant patients, these concerns are particularly worrisome as to them.

i. UCLA, Los Angeles, California, USA

Jagbir Gill and his colleagues studied thirty-three kidney transplant recipients who were U.S. residents who had traveled outside the United States for kidney transplants but returned to UCLA for follow-up care.[26] Twenty-nine of these patients had initially been evaluated at UCLA before transplant, although "very few had expressed their plans to travel abroad for transplantation" to their UCLA providers. Data on when the transplants were performed for the tourist group suggested that transplant tourism had become increasingly common over the study time frame among UCLA's patient population.

The authors compared the tourists to a matched group (on age, race, transplant year, dialysis time, previous transplantation, and donor type) of sixty-six patients who had their transplant done at UCLA. While the study did not code for whether the patient had purchased an organ, it did determine whether the donor was a living related (12 percent), living unrelated (61 percent), or dead donor (12 percent). There is good reason to suspect that many if not most of the living unrelated donors involved a kidney sale. In terms of their destination for transplant, 42 percent went to China, 18 percent Iran, 12 percent the Philippines, 9 percent India, and one recipient each went to Pakistan, Turkey, Peru, Mexico, Egypt, and Thailand. Most patients traveled to their region of ethnicity. The tourists had slightly older mean ages (47.3 percent), were more likely to be Asian, and had spent less time on dialysis than the matched cohort, suggesting that the transplant was sought instead of dialysis.

---

backlash against transplant ethics and to a demoralization among some transplant surgeons themselves." *Id.* at 201–02.

[26] The description is culled from Jagbir Gill et al., *Transplant Tourism in the United States: A Single-Center Experience*, 3 CLINICAL J. AM. SOC. NEPHROLOGY. 1820 (2008).

In terms of results, tourist patients had a higher cumulative incidence of acute rejection in the first year after transplant (30 percent versus 12 percent, P = .02). One-year graft survival was lower for tourists than the matched cohort (89 percent versus 98 percent for tourists), but the result was not statistically significant. There was no overall difference in the incidence of infections in the tourist versus matched cohort, but the infections the tourist patients did have were much more severe. Tourists were much more likely to be hospitalized due to infections (27 percent versus 6 percent), with a range of 1 to 744 days in the hospital (and a mean of 12.5 days).

ii. University of Minnesota Medical Center or Hennepin County Medical Center, Minnesota, USA

Muna Canales and coauthors identified ten patients who traveled abroad for kidney transplantation and returned to their institutions (the University of Minnesota Medical Center or Hennepin County Medical Center) for post-transplant care between September 16, 2002, and June 30, 2006. Sixty percent of the group was male and 40 percent female, the mean age was 36.8 years, and all were born outside the United States (eight were Somali, one was Chinese, and one was Iranian). Only two of the ten patients were not on the hospital's waiting list for kidney transplant before they left the country. Three of the ten patients had disclosed their intent to travel abroad for transplant before they left. Nine of the ten had received kidneys from living donors.

The authors collected significant data on the health of these patients, but most important for our purposes was their conclusion that "[g]raft and patient survival" were "comparable to results obtained for patients transplanted in the United States," while noting that prior studies had conflicting results as to whether transplant tourists had worse results.[27] Nevertheless, they noted several problems that the transplant tourism caused these patients. There was inadequate communication between the transplant site and their institution relating to "vital information" on induction therapy, and immunosuppressive and post-transplant courses of treatment. In three of the cases, the patients were sent back to the United States in the midst of a crisis relating to wound infection, seizure, and acute rejection, where such documentation would have been very helpful. This finding mirrors those in other studies of transplant tourism, though many are from much earlier periods.[28]

---

[27] M.T. Canales et al., *Transplant Tourism: Outcomes of United States Residents Who Undergo Kidney Transplantation Overseas*, 82 TRANSPLANTATION 1658, 1660 (2006) (citing S. Kennedy et al., *Outcome of Overseas Kidney Transplantation: An Australian Perspective*, 182 MED. J. AUSTRALIA. 224 (2005); M.S. Sever et al., *Outcome of Living Unrelated (Commercial) Renal Transplantation*, 60 KIDNEY INT'L 1477 (2001)).

[28] Canales et al., *supra* note 27, at 1660 (citing N. Invanoski et al., *Renal Transplantation from Paid Unrelated Donors—It Is Not Only Unethical, It Is Medically Unsafe*, 12 NEPHROLOGY DIALYSIS TRANSPLANTATION 28 (1997); Z. Morad & T.O. Lim, *Outcome of Overseas Kidney Transplantation in Malaysia*, 32

iii. St. Michael's Hospital, Toronto, Ontario, Canada

G.V. Prasad and colleagues examined twenty Canadian transplant tourists who sought follow-up care after a kidney transplant at St. Michael's Hospital in Toronto, Canada. Kidney sales are illegal in Canada.[29] All twenty patients were legal permanent residents or citizens of Canada who received chronic kidney disease management in Canada and had gone abroad to receive a live kidney donation from a "non-biologically, non-emotionally related" kidney seller outside of Canada between January 1, 1998, and February 28, 2005. They compared this group to those who received live kidney transplants from biologically related individuals (n=175) and from emotionally but not biologically related individuals (n=75) in Canada.

The mean age of the transplant tourists was 49.6 compared to 43.3 for the biologically related and 44.7 for the biologically unrelated. Transplant tourists were more likely to be born outside Canada (P<0.0001) and to be nonwhite (P<0.0001). All but three of the twenty tourist patients received the transplant in their region of birth, with twelve going to South Asia, four to East Asia, four to the Middle East, and one to Southeast Asia (there were twenty-two transplants for twenty patients). Data on when the transplants took place suggested transplant tourism was becoming more frequent for this patient population.

In terms of outcomes, the authors found that graft survival at thirty-six months was worse in the tourist group compared to the biologically related (P<.0001) and emotionally related (P<.01) transplant groups. They also found that 52 percent of the patients in the transplant tourist group had serious post-transplant infections that were considered opportunistic, and two of these patients died due to fungal infection–related sepsis. While the transplant patients were on the same immunosuppressive drug regimes as the Canadian patients, the higher rate of infection was ascribed to poor immunosuppression monitoring, post-transplant hygiene, or delayed recognition. Surgical complications were also "frequent at initial presentation" including wound infection.[30] Like other studies, the authors found that many of these patients were very ill and required intensive medical treatment when they arrived back in Canada, that medical documentation was sparse and in unfamiliar languages making emergency care difficult, and that many of these patients underwent lengthy travel too soon after the surgery.

Transplant Proceedings 1485 (2000); A. Salahudeen et al., *High Mortality among Recipients of Bought Living-Unrelated Donor Kidneys*, 336 Lancet 725 (1990)).

[29] G.V. Prasad et al., Outcomes of Commercial Renal Transplantation: A Canadian Experience, 82 Transplantation 1130 (2006).

[30] Unfortunately, the authors do not provide equivalent numbers for the two control groups on these measures, which would better enable us to put this into perspective.

iv. British Columbia, Canada

Finally, Jagbir Gill and his team also studied ninety-three residents of British Columbia, Canada, who had registered in the provincial transplant registry from January 1, 2000, to April 30, 2008, who had received kidney graft through transplant tourism.[31] The tourists were only 9.7 percent Caucasian, compared to a 67.3 percent of a comparison set of those who received transplants in the province. More than 90 percent of the tourists were minorities traveling to their country of origin, with China (42 percent), the Philippines (17 percent), India (15 percent), Pakistan (12 percent), and Iran (5 percent), being the most frequent places they traveled to. For 33 percent of the sample, the donor source was unknown. Thirty percent of their tourist sample had obtained their transplant before ever being referred for transplantation at home. Of the remaining 70 percent who were referred for transplant evaluation in the province, more than half never initiated or failed to complete the evaluation. Of those who were fully evaluated at home, they opted for transplant tourism after a median waiting list time of two years. In what the authors note is a surprising statistic, over 60 percent of evaluated tourists had a potential living donor who came forward for evaluation, but 65 percent of those were either medically unsuitable or incompatible, whereas 35 percent did not complete the evaluation. The study did not examine the health status of these transplant tourists post-transplant.

v. Other Data

There are also a few other studies on the transplant tourist population. A 2008 analysis suggested that in August 2007, there were 173 wait-list removals in the United States they ascribed to the patient having received a transplant in a foreign center, as well as an estimate of 200–355 additional patients who had received foreign organs, for a total of 373-408 U.S. transplant tourists in that year. The study also found that the number appeared to be increasing and that more than 40 percent of transplant tourists were residents of New York and California.[32] Another study from 2010 looked at liver transplant outcomes of patients from centers in Egypt and Saudi Arabia who went to China to receive transplants from deceased donors. The study found that, compared to patients who had received transplants in their home country center, this group presented decreased three-year patient and graft survival rates, high rates of complications and hospitalization, and higher rates of infection.[33] Another study looked at ninety-three

---

[31] Jagbir Gill et al., *Opportunities to Deter Transplant Tourism Exist before Referral for Transplantation and during the Workup and Management of Transplant Candidates*, 79 KIDNEY INT'L 1026 (2011).

[32] Thomas D. Schiano & Rosamond Rhodes, *Transplant Tourism, in* MEDICAL TOURISM AND TRANSNATIONAL HEALTH CARE 113, 119 (David Boterrill et al. eds., 2013) (citing R.M. Merion et al., *Transplants in Foreign Countries among Patients Removed from the US Transplant Waiting List*, 8 AM. J. TRANSPLANT 988 (2008)).

[33] *Id.* at 119 (citing N. Allam et al., *Clinical Outcomes for Saudi and Egyptian Patients Receiving Decreased Donor Liver Transplantation in China*, 10 AM. J. TRANSPLANT 1834 (2010)).

Saudi patients who received kidneys outside of Saudi Arabia, mostly in the Philippines and Pakistan, and found higher incidences of acute rejection, infectious complications, and hepatitis C virus transmission in this cohort.[34] A 2011 study of patients at Seoul National University Hospital similarly found that patients who had received a kidney allograft outside of Korea in the same period faced higher rates of acute rejection, infectious complications, hospitalizations, and decreased graft survival rates.[35]

C. The Brokers

Given that much of what they do is illegal, it is unsurprising that we lack comparably rigorous studies of large numbers of brokers in the international kidney market. Nevertheless, beyond the studies discussed above that have offered indirect and partial glimpses into the world of kidney brokers, there has been more investigational journalist style work by Nancy Scheper-Hughes and other anthropologists that can shed some light on these individuals.

Transplant tourism is a complicated business, requiring nephrologists, nursing staff, blood and tissue labs, surgical teams, passports, visas, air travel, surgical equipment, and cooperation from immigration officials.[36] Given this complexity, it is not surprising that the process is managed by what Scheper-Hughes characterizes as "a new international network of body Mafia ranging from the sleazy (and sometimes armed and dangerous) underworld 'kidney hunters' of Istanbul and Cesenau, Moldova to the sophisticated but clandestine 'medical tourism' bureau of Tel Aviv and Manila to the medical intermediaries posing as religious or charitable trusts and 'patient's advocacy organizations' founded in downtown Philadelphia, Brooklyn, and Chinatown New York City."[37]

As Scheper-Hughes indicates, this is a very heterogeneous cast of characters, including an Israeli charitable organization that over time morphed from helping Israeli children get expensive cancer treatments in the United States to facilitating travel to the United States for transplant when the waiting lists at home were too long[38] and "outlaw surgeons" in Tel Aviv with partners in Istanbul whom Scheper-Hughes claims "practice their illicit operations in rented, makeshift clinics, or, when political conditions allow, in the operating rooms of some of the best public or private centers in Israel, Turkey, Romania, Iraq," and Europe.[39] In the United States, she describes the activities of Rabbi Levy-Izhak Rosenbaum, an orthodox rabbi with an office in Borough Park, Brooklyn,

---

[34] *Id.* at 120 (citing S.A. Alghamdi et al., *Transplant Tourism Outcome: A Single Center Experience*, 90 TRANSPLANTATION 184 (2010)).

[35] *Id.* (citing R. Cha et al., *Long-Term Outcomes of Kidney Allografts Obtained by Transplant Tourism: Observations from a Single Center in Korea*, 16 NEPHROLOGY 672 (2011)).

[36] Scheper-Hughes, *supra* note 2, at 214.

[37] *Id.*

[38] *Id.* at 215.

[39] *Id.* at 217.

who ran a very lucrative organ brokerage enterprise that would buy kidneys from vulnerable Israelis and sell them for US$160,000, and became the first man ever convicted under a U.S. statute banning the sale of kidneys.[40] In Brazil, she describes a 1997 police investigation of a " 'body Mafia' with connections to hospital and emergency room staff, ambulance drivers, and local and state morgues that traded in blood, organs, and human tissues from cadavers" and, in one case, falsified death certificates to conceal mutilated corpses in the Rio de Janeiro morgue.[41]

Lower down in the pecking order are the "small-time criminals in the employ of highly sophisticated Mafia involved in all kinds of trafficking in human bodies."[42] Many of these brokers are themselves former prostitutes and kidney sellers who now approach young men in Mingir and Chisenau in Moldova to make money. Scheper-Hughes relates the story of the "the infamous Nina Ungureanu," who boasts to an undercover reporter that "the police are not going to do anything to us and certainly not going do anything to the [big shots] in this trade."[43]

Now that we have a clearer picture of what the transplant tourism trade actually looks like, we are poised to examine the bioethical and regulatory questions that surround it.

II. THE BIOETHICAL QUESTIONS

The basic bioethical question is: Should we prohibit transplant tourism, or at least significantly restrict it through regulation? This can be thought of as a sub-question of the question of whether to prohibit organ sales, which is itself a sub-question of what is sometimes called the "taboo trade" or "anti-commodificationist" debates, which sweep more broadly to topics such as prostitution, commercial surrogacy, etc.

---

[40] Nancy Scheper-Hughes, *The Body of the Terrorist: Blood Libels, Bio-Piracy, and the Spoils of War at the Israeli Forensic Institute*, 3 SOC. RES. 849, 850 (2011); *Guilty Plea to Kidney-Selling Charges*, N.Y. TIMES, Oct. 27, 2011, *available at* http://www.nytimes.com/2011/10/28/nyregion/guilty-plea-to-kidney-selling-charges.html; Matthew Lysiak & Carrie Melago, *Sweeping Federal Probe Nabs Crooked Politicians & Alleged Black-Market Kidney Peddler*, N.Y. DAILY NEWS, July 24, 2009, *available at* http://www.nydailynews.com/new-york/sweeping-federal-probe-nabs-crooked-politicians-alleged-black-market-kidney-peddler-article-1.398289#ixzz1ph5ANDSe. The fact that even poor Israelis, undoubtedly part of the developed and not developing world, are sometimes the sellers of kidneys is a good reminder that the colonial narrative of developed world buyers and poor developing world sellers, though often true, is not always accurate. Michele Goodwin has made a similar argument as to the portrayal of African Americans in discourse on organ markets in the United States—that the literature often portrays them as vulnerable victims in a way she perceives to be infantilizing and fails to recognize that they may be a major beneficiary as organ recipients as well. Michele Goodwin, *Private Ordering and Intimate Spaces: Why the Ability to Negotiate is Non-negotiable*, 105 MICH. L. REV. 1367, 1373–78 (2007).

[41] Scheper Hughes, *supra* note 17, at 208.

[42] *Id.* at 215.

[43] *Id.* at 209.

Those in favor of blocking exchanges tend to rely most often on three types of arguments: (1) corruption, (2) crowding out, and (3) coercion/exploitation/undue inducement. I discuss each of these in turn but it is the last of these concerns, which dominates discussions of transplant tourism, on which I focus. Although the vast majority of academics and policymakers take the desirability of bans on transplant tourism as a given, in this section I will show that the arguments in favor of prohibiting transplant tourism are much more difficult to sustain then this discourse would suggest. That said, I conclude that a different kind of argument, focused on bounded rationality and justified paternalism, is actually the strongest justification for prohibiting transplant tourism.

A. Corruption

The basic idea behind what I have elsewhere called the "corruption" argument is that allowing the practice to go forward will do violence or denigrate our views of how goods are properly valued.[44] We will see these kinds of arguments recur in the next two chapters as well. As to the sale of organs (domestically or through transplant tourism), the American Medical Association among others has voiced this kind of objection in the domestic organ sale context, suggesting paying kidney donors would "dehumanize society by viewing human beings and their parts as mere commodities."[45]

In fact, we can distinguish two subcategories of this objection, that I have elsewhere called "consequentialist" and "intrinsic" corruption. Consequentialist corruption justifies intervention to prevent changes to our attitudes or sensibilities that will occur if the practice is allowed—for example, that we will "regard each other as objects with prices rather than as persons."[46] By contrast, the more "intrinsic" form of the objection focuses on the "inherent incompatibility between an object and a mode of valuation," where the wrongfulness of the action is completed at the moment of purchase irrespective of what follows; the intrinsic version of the objection obtains even if the act remains secret or has zero effect on anyone's attitudes.[47]

Both versions of the object run into problems as reasons to condemn transplant tourism.

---

[44] *See, e.g.,* I. Glenn Cohen, Note, *The Price of Everything, the Value of Nothing: Reframing the Commodification Debate,* 117 HARV. L. REV. 689, 691–92 (2003). *Cf.* Margaret Jane Radin, *What, if Anything, Is Wrong with Baby Selling?, Address at McGeorge School of Law,* 26 PAC. L. J. 135, 143–45 (1995) (discussing similar arguments regarding reproduction); ELIZABETH ANDERSON, VALUE IN ETHICS AND ECONOMICS 144, 172 (1993) (similar).

[45] Council on Ethical and Judicial Affairs of the American Medical Association, *Financial Incentives for Organ Procurement: Ethical Aspects of Future Contracts for Cadaveric Donors,* 155 ARCHIVES INTERNAL MED. 581, 581 (1995).

[46] Cohen, *supra* note 44, at 692 n.13; Scott Altman, *(Com)modifying Experience,* 65 S. CAL. L. REV. 293, 294–97 (1991).

[47] Cohen, *supra* note 44, at 692 n.13.

First, at the more metaphysical level, the view has trouble explaining why it does violence to the way kidneys are properly valued to treat them as goods with a market price. One might be tempted to follow Immanuel Kant and suggest that the nature of humans as free and rational beings is such that to treat them simply as means (use goods) rather than ends in themselves (non-use goods) is to do violence to the way human beings ought to be valued.[48] However, it is not clear why we ought to strongly identify my personhood with an organ of mine that can be removed while leaving that personhood intact, and this objection to transplant tourism would seem to prove too much in condemning the selling of blood or human hair and potentially all labor as well.

Second, as I have examined in depth elsewhere, the view seems to prove too much in that if some goods have unique value such that selling them constitutes value denigration, it is unclear why giving them away is not also value denigrating, in that the giver is exchanging them for nothing or other incommensurable goods such as the joy of helping others.[49] As Leon Kass put it, "it is difficult to understand why someone who sees absolutely no difficulty at all with transplantation and donation should have such trouble sanctioning sale" of organs.[50]

Third, as Julia Mahoney has emphasized in her discussion of domestic organ sales, the argument typically presents a false dichotomy between commodification of the organs or non-commodification. In fact, altruistic kidney donation does not result in non-commodification of the organ even if "[m]aterials distributed to prospective donors of transplantable organs, in fact, appear to be designed to further" the "mistaken belief that the absence of a market for particular kinds of tissue at one stage means there is no market at any later point."[51] Instead, Mahoney shows how "Organ Procurement Organizations, the institutions that procure organs from donors and deliver them to transplant programs pursuant to the system established and administered by UNOS, receive payments from transplanting hospitals" and also that transplant programs and the surgeons who staff them often make money from the transplant process.[52] Indeed, a study from the year 2000 in the United States found that 70 percent of the organ procurement agencies regulated by the federal government sell body parts directly to for-profit firms, generating huge profits.[53] One such firm, "Regeneration Technologies

---

[48] *See id.* at 696–700 (citing IMMANUEL KANT, GROUNDING FOR THE METAPHYSICS OF MORALS 434 (James W. Ellington trans., 1981) (1785)).

[49] *Id.* at 700–10; Leon R. Kass, *Organs for Sale? Propriety, Property, and the Price of Progress,* 107 PUB. INT., 65, 77 (Spring 1992).

[50] Kass, *supra* note 49, at 65, 77. To be clear, Kass actually arrives at a different conclusion than I do on this score.

[51] Julia D. Mahoney, *The Market for Human Tissue,* 68 VA. L. REV. 163, 195 (2000).

[52] *Id.* at 179–80. Indeed, there is a way in which the corruption argument proves too much in that even altruistically donated organs are commodified in this way, such that, to be consistent, those pressing this argument should also condemn organ donation.

[53] Michele Goodwin, *Altruism's Limits: Law, Capacity, and Organ Commodification,* 56 RUTGERS L. REV. 305, 383 (2004) (citing William Heisel & Mark Katches, *Organ Agencies Aid For-Profit Suppliers,* ORANGE

Inc., RTI, generated $73 million in revenues in 1999 by processing a third of the human tissue donated in the United States, turning body parts into products for surgery and other medical procedures."[54] Thus, even with organ sale bans in place, it is inevitable that these organs are commodified, and the only question is whether the kidney source will receive the fruits of that commodification or not. Can one argue, contrary to Mahoney's claim, that there is a categorical difference between paying for the initial "donation" versus paying for these later steps?

One might argue that these latter payments are necessary to offset the cost of storage, transportation, etc. Even if this was factually true, which is far from clear, it is unclear how effective a rejoinder that is, in that these payments do not merely offset fixed costs but also go toward providing payment to those who "work" as intermediaries in the industry, including administrators and surgeons. One could instead ask these individuals to "volunteer" their time, and use their special talents to contribute to the "gift of life," and demand that they forgo the payment they desire to avoid corrupting that gift. Why do we not make that demand from them as well? Because we know that without that payment they are very unlikely to participate in the numbers needed, but that is potentially true of organ providers as well. I think the stronger argument for distinguishing these payments is to return to the consequentialist corruption variant, and remember that it is concerned with what actually *will* happen as to an individual's attitudes if sale is allowed and the negative consequences that flow from that. Thus, one might claim that the "incomplete commodification" of the current system, which allows these payments to procurers, has different effects in terms of negative consequences than does the proposal to pay for organs as well. Fair enough, that is a real potential distinction, but it relies on an empirical claim for which those who would make this kind of argument would need to adduce some evidence.

Finally, as I will discuss in more depth in the next chapter relating to travel for abortion and end-of-life organ sale, the medical tourism context may produce special difficulties for the consequentialist corruption argument in terms of the propriety of the home country's prerogative to legislate: sales of kidneys from the developing world may have less effects on home country mores than sales domestically, in which case the home country's justification for regulation is reduced.[55] Indeed, in some States of the world, transplant tourism may act as a "safety valve" that relieves pressure to change the law and permit domestic organ purchase, which all things considered may be worse for the

COUNTY REG., June 25, 2000, *available at* http:// www.ocregister.com/features/body/organ00625cci.shtm).

[54] David E. Winickoff, *Governing Population Genomics: Law, Bioethics, and Biopolitics in Three Case Studies*, 43 JURIMETRICS J. 187, 189 n.9 (2003).

[55] *See* I. Glenn Cohen, *Circumvention Tourism*, 97 CORNELL L. REV. 1309, 1376–81 (2012). To be sure, this point raises a disturbing reality, that the home country may care less about viewing members of the developing world as objects with prices than it does viewing its own citizens that way.

home country on consequentialist corruption grounds.[56] I will elaborate on these points in greater depth in the next chapter and the one that follows.

To be sure, this is not a complete refutation of this kind of argument for banning transplant tourism. There is more that might be said both in favor and against this type of argument, but for present purposes, I am content to leave the matter there with the hope that I have at least shown why I think the corruption argument is not the surest ground for arguing for a prohibition on transplant tourism.

B. Crowding Out

A second objection is that allowing the sale of organs will cause individuals who would have donated organs to instead sell them, thus reducing the number of *donated* organs, or it will even cause individuals to refuse to donate them at all, leading to an *overall* reduction in procured organs.[57] This claim has its roots in behavioral economics work on motivational crowding out, suggesting that (contrary to the classical economic model) allowing payment for goods may change its social meaning in a way that discourages altruistic giving and ultimately decreases supply.[58] The most famous use of the argument in the taboo trades literature is Richard Titmuss's claim that allowing the sale of blood would crowd out altruistic donation of non-diseased blood.[59]

Unfortunately, as Julia Mahoney has noted in her 2009 review of the available literature relevant to motivational crowding out in domestic organ sale, "[t]he chief problem with the 'crowding out' line of argument is that—as even its proponents admit—it is highly speculative"; that is, whether "a particular reward will 'crowd out,' 'crowd in,'

---

[56] *See id.*

[57] *See, e.g.*, Institute of Medicine of the National Academies, Organ Donation: Opportunities for Action 243 (2006); Gabriel M. Danovitch & Alan B. Leichtman, *Kidney Vending: The "Trojan Horse" of Organ Transplantation*, 1 Clin. J. Am. Soc. Nephrology 1133–34 (2006). In fact, one can set out more specific subtypes of crowding out arguments as I do in I. Glenn Cohen, *Regulating the Organ Market: Normative Foundations for Market Regulation*, 77 Law & Contemp. Probs. _, _ (forthcoming 2014). For present purposes, though, we need not get into too many sub-distinctions.

[58] *E.g.*, Bruno S. Frey, Not Just for the Money: An Economic Theory of Personal Motivation (1997).

[59] *See* Richard Titmuss, The Gift Relationship: From Human Blood to Social Policy (1970). There is also a variant of the argument focused on loss of opportunities for altruism. To the extent, as in Titmuss's formulation, that the concern is driving out non-diseased versions of the good in question, there are reasons to question both the original argument and its extension here. Titmuss's claim was premised on a lack of technology to appropriately determine whether blood provided by individuals was diseased or not, something we now have for blood and certainly for organs. Michele Goodwin, Black Markets: The Supply and Demand of Body Parts 158 (2006). Further, Titmuss seemed to assume that it was commercially supplied blood but not altruistically donated blood that provided the contamination risk; in fact, as Michele Goodwin has pointed out, a good deal of the blood contamination of the 1980s was due to altruistic donation by gay men in an era before the HIV virus was widely known to be transmitted through blood transfusion. *Id.*

or have a 'crowding neutral' effect on internal motivation is hard to predict," and "[a] lthough we cannot dismiss it out of hand, in no way does the available evidence for 'crowding out' point to the conclusion that sweeping bans on donor compensation are sensible policy" for organ procurement.[60]

When it comes to transplant tourism, the evidence of motivational crowding out is even sparser. From the armchair there is certainly an intuitive argument that any crowding out will be less than in the domestic context, in that currently there are few if any examples of *altruistic* donation to help unrelated or unknown individuals in foreign countries, such that there is not much altruism to potentially crowd out. At the same time, it is also possible that a robust transplant tourism market will influence the willingness to altruistically donate organs *domestically*. Perhaps individuals will be less likely to give to their fellow citizens if they know that the citizen could instead travel abroad to purchase an organ? It is very hard to know which of our best guesses from the armchair will be confirmed by empirical investigation as occurring in the real world, and even harder to try to estimate the likely effect size. That said, given that motivational crowding out has received only very mixed support as to domestic organ markets, I am hesitant to put too much stock in this argument as a reason to prohibit transplant tourism.

C. Coercion, Exploitation, Undue Inducement, and Justified Paternalism

The argument most commonly raised against transplant tourism relates to coercion, exploitation of the seller, undue inducement, and paternalistic concerns about negative effects of the transplant on the seller's well-being.[61] Although the four aspects are commonly run together, in fact there are four distinct strains of arguments here that I take on one by one. Those in the media and medical literatures often use terms such as "exploitation" and "coercion" and "undue inducement" loosely.

Although I hate to be didactic about nomenclature, in what follows I try to use more philosophically precise definitions of each of those terms, but what matters to me is not so much that we call them by the right names, but instead that we recognize that these are distinct arguments whatever name they travel under. Importantly, they each support a different first-best intervention: coercion should lead to a prohibition on transplant tourism, exploitation to improving the terms for sellers, undue inducement to price

---

[60] Julia D. Mahoney, *Altruism, Markets, and Organ Procurement*, 72 Law & Contemp. Probs. 17, 24–26 (2009).

[61] *See, e.g.*, Goodwin, *supra* note 59, at 12; Francis L. Delmonico, *The Development of the Declaration of Istanbul on Organ Trafficking and Transplant*, 23 Nephrology Dialysis Transplantation 3381, 3382 (2008); Gabriel Danovitch & Alan B. Leichtman, *Kidney Vending: The "Trojan Horse" of Organ Transplantation*, 1 Clin. J. Am. Soc. Nephrology, 1133–34 (2006); Scheper-Hughes, *supra* note 18, at 1647; Naqvi et al., *supra* note 13, at 937; Goyal et al., *supra* note 15, at 1592.

ceilings, and paternalism to information provision and "speedbumps" to try and correct bounded rationality problems.

i. Is Transplant Tourism Coercive?

"Coercion" should be understood to refer to a deep lack of voluntariness on the part of at least one participant in the transaction. The mugger demanding "your money or your life" is the classic example, but coercion can also be subtler. In what is probably the leading bioethical account of the idea, Alan Wertheimer suggests that only threats (as opposed to offers) can be coercive, but not all threats are coercive. To use a stylized framing imagine that A proposes to B:[62]

1. If you do X, I will bring about or allow to happen S.
2. If you do not do X, I will bring about or allow to happen another state of affairs, T.[63]

Has A coerced B? Wertheimer provides a two-pronged test for whether a proposal constitutes a coercive threat. The first part, which Wertheimer names the "choice prong," determines whether "A's proposal creates a choice situation for B such that B has no reasonable alternative but to do X."[64] Importantly, this prong does not ask whether B has *some* alternative to doing X, but rather whether the alternatives available to B are *acceptable* ones.[65] Indeed, even in "your money or your life" the victim has *some* choice. The problem is that surrendering one's life is not an acceptable alternative to turning over one's money; it is too costly an alternative to complying with A's demand.[66] Rather than calling for an empirical determination that B has "no choice" but to do what A proposes, the choice prong requires a judgment as to whether the costs to B of not doing what A proposes are too high.[67] What is an acceptable choice is an inherently normative determination.[68]

Given the data discussed above on the dire straits, indebtedness, and other difficulties faced by of the sellers of kidneys used in transplant tourism, the choice prong seems clearly met: the sellers have no acceptable choice but to sell a kidney.

---

[62] *See, e.g.*, Mitchell N. Berman, *The Normative Functions of Coercion Claims*, 8 LEG. THEORY 45, 56 (2002); ALAN WERTHEIMER, COERCION 204 (1987); JOEL FEINBERG, HARM TO SELF 222 (1986).

[63] *See* WERTHEIMER, *supra* note 62, at 204.

[64] *Id.* at 172.

[65] *Id.* at 267; *see also id.* at 272–74.

[66] *See, e.g.*, Benjamin Sachs, *Unions, Corporations, and Political Opt-Out Rights after "Citizens United,"* 112 COLUMBIA L. REV. 800, 830 n.161 (2012); RICHARD POSNER, ECONOMIC ANALYSIS OF LAW 143 (8th ed. 2011).

[67] Sachs, *supra* note 66.

[68] *E.g., id.*; CHARLES FRIED, CONTRACT AS PROMISE: A THEORY OF CONTRACTUAL OBLIGATION 104 (1981).

However, finding that the person receiving the proposal has no acceptable choice is a *necessary* but not *sufficient* condition for finding coercion. Wertheimer gives the example of a surgeon who refuses to amputate a patient's leg unless the patient pays a a fair price: although the patient had no acceptable choice, we do not think the act morally problematic nor if the patient were to agree to that price for the amputation would we allow him to renege on the contractual obligation after the fact.[69] This points us to the need for a second prong to find coercion, what Wertheimer calls the "proposal prong," which asks whether the proposal is one that A has or does not have a right to make.[70] To illustrate, Wertheimer offers the following paired cases:

> *The Private Physician Case.* B asks A, a private physician, to treat his illness. A says that he will treat B's illness if and only if B gives him $100 (a fair price).
>
>   *The Public Physician Case.* B asks A, a physician, to treat his illness. A is employed by the National Health Plan, and is legally required to treat all patients without cost. A says that he will treat B's illness if and only if B gives him $100.[71]

Although in both cases B has no acceptable alternative but to pursue treatment from the surgeon, the first case (unlike the second) seems unproblematic; the reason is that only in the second case does B make a proposal he does not have *the right* to make. Therefore, only the second case is coercive on Wertheimer's framework.

Of course, what kind of proposals one does or does not have the right to make is itself an inherently normative inquiry. Wertheimer would incorporate a "moral" test to distinguish the two types of proposals,[72] whereas legal scholars have suggested the existing law could also define what we do and do not have the right to propose.[73]

How does transplant tourism fare on the proposal prong? I believe it is problematic to conclude that the proposal prong is met in much of transplant tourism, and indeed I think the case for coercion is actually *weaker* in transplant tourism than in the domestic organ sale context, and here is why: to find the proposal prong met, one would have to show that the seller has a right to the money offered by the broker/recipient or equivalently that the broker/recipient has a duty to provide him that money, such that it is wrongful to condition the payment of that money on the seller providing his kidney. That is a hard claim to make out.

---

[69] Alan Wertheimer, *Exploitation in Clinical Research, in* Exploitation in Developing Countries: The Ethics of Clinical Research 63, 71 (Jennifer S. Hawkins & Ezekiel J. Emanuel eds., 2008); *see also* Wertheimer, *supra* note 62, at 192–201.

[70] *See, e.g.,* Wertheimer, *supra* note 61, at 173; Fried, *supra* note 68, at 104.

[71] Wertheimer, *supra* note 62, at 208.

[72] *Id.* at 207.

[73] Mitchell N. Berman, *Coercion without Baselines: Unconstitutional Conditions in Three Dimensions*, 90 Geo. L.J. 1, 16 (2001).

As Wertheimer emphasizes in discussing the private physician case, in determining whether the proposal prong is met, one must "distinguish B's rights against other individuals and B's rights against the *society* or the state."[74] If one subscribes to a political theory in which everyone has a right to health, "B's moral baseline with respect to the society includes his right to medical care, but his moral baseline with respect to a *private physician* does not," such that a physician who says he will treat the patient only if paid is not engaging in coercion.[75] Similarly, although the organ seller in the real life contexts discussed above may (on some political theories) have a claim against his or her *nation-state* to end bonded labor, to provide food, employment, health care, etc., that is not a claim against the *organ recipient or broker.*

Transplant tourism is an even harder case for coercion than domestic organ sale, because the foreigner's connection to the nation-state of the seller is more attenuated: the foreigner is less causally connected to creating the circumstances giving rise to the seller's need to sell the kidney.[76] As discussed in Chapter 6, on some theories of global justice, any obligation to redistribute primary goods is more limited against those outside the nation-state.[77]

I was careful to say that the proposal prong may not be met "in much of" transplant tourism, because although the general offer to sell a kidney does not seem coercive, some of the particular episodes revealed in the ethnographic work above stand out. In particular, threatening sellers with violence if they do not comply and ensuring compliance by withholding their passports once they have crossed the border seem like the kinds of things that remain coercive on this account. This is reminiscent of Robert Nozick's famous example of the person who makes an offer to his slave to not beat him as usual if he will do a particular task.[78] This violates the proposal prong because the slave has a right not to be beaten at all.[79] The same is true of the sellers of organs, who have rights

---

[74] WERTHEIMER, *supra* note 62, at 218.

[75] *Id.*

[76] As Wertheimer notes, his approach leaves open the possibility of distinguishing "between B's background conditions for which A is not responsible and rights-violating threats to B's welfare which are specifically attributable to A," *id.* at 219—for example, the difference between demanding a "rescue fee" of a drowning person you stumble upon versus one you yourself pushed in the water.

[77] *See also generally* I. Glenn Cohen, *Medical Tourism, Access to Health Care, and Global Justice*, 52 VIRGINIA J. INT'L L. 1 (2011). One tricky aspect of the coercion analysis is whether the existing legal regime can form part of the moralized baseline. *See, e.g.*, Berman, *supra* note 73, at 16. If the question is *whether* to ban transplant tourism, the question I am focusing on in this part of the chapter, then there is no legal prohibition that could form part of the baseline to establish coercion. By contrast, if there is an existing prohibition in place, it seems as though it is coercive to offer the option of selling the kidney when it requires breaking the law.

[78] Robert Nozick, *Coercion, in* PHILOSOPHY, SCIENCE AND METHOD 440, 450 (Sidney Morgenbesser et al. eds., 1969).

[79] WERTHEIMER, *supra* note 62, at 208–09.

not to be subjected to violence or to have their passports taken away. There is a strong case under the coercion argument for intervening to prevent those acts.

If one could not prevent those specific violations without banning the practice of transplant tourism altogether, then that might justify such a ban on the coercion view. However, one would need to show that those particular practices are sufficiently widespread and/or harmful (or some combination of the two) to justify a blanket prohibition, which in my view would be too strong a read of the existing empirical literature. Moreover, one would have to be convinced that a blanket prohibition would effectively clamp down on these particular abuses, which may be unlikely. Recall that organ sale is currently prohibited in all jurisdictions except Iran, and yet these abuses continue to take place. It is at least possible that with a legally regulated market in organs the number of these abuses would be reduced compared to their existing levels.

In sum, the argument to ban transplant tourism outright because it is coercive does not seem very strong.

ii. Is Transplant Tourism Exploitative in a Way That Should Prompt Legal Intervention?

Of course, the fact that transplant tourism is not *coercive* does not mean it is not wrongful or worthy of prohibition, in that coercion does not exhaust all things that may be wrong with the trade. One might instead claim that the problem with the trade is that it is *exploitative*. Coercive transactions may be non-exploitative (as when A forces B to do something that is in B's own interest and does not benefit A)[80] and exploitative transactions may be non-coercive. Therefore, we need to look at exploitation as a separate objection to transplant tourism.

In determining whether transplant tourism involves exploitation of the kind that justifies legal intervention, we should ask three questions: (1) Is it exploitation?; (2) If so, is it harmful or mutually advantageous exploitation, which will turn on whether "both parties (the alleged exploiter and the alleged exploitee) reasonably expect to gain from the transaction as contrasted with the pre-transaction status quo" (mutually advantageous) or not (harmful)?[81]; and (3) Is it consensual or non-consensual exploitation, which will turn on whether the "exploited party has given voluntary and appropriately informed consent" (consensual) or not (non-consensual)?[82]

In this section, I want to momentarily assume that transplant tourism is consensual, because I will consider that question and its implication in much greater depth in the next section. Thus, for now I focus on the first two of these questions and try to determine (1) whether transplant tourism involves exploitation; (2) if so, whether it

---

[80] *Id.* at 226.
[81] Wertheimer, *supra* note 69, at 68.
[82] *Id.*

is mutually advantageous or harmful exploitation; and (3) what the answers to those questions should imply for legal regulation. To answer these questions, we need to be both somewhat philosophically abstract—to understand what the concept of exploitation means and what its conditions are—but also extremely specific, to understand the choice being offered to this particular set of individuals as against their other possible choices, which, sadly enough, may all be bad ones.

To determine that A has wrongfully exploited B, philosophers usually stipulate two requirements that must be met: (1) A benefits from the transaction, and (2) the outcome of the transaction is harmful (in the case of harmful exploitation) or at least unfair (in the case of mutually advantageous exploitation) to B, and A is able to induce B to agree to the transaction by taking advantage of a feature of B or his situation without which B would not ordinarily be willing to agree.[83]

In transplant tourism, it seems relatively uncontroversial that the first requirement is met. Although the Gill, Canales, and Prasad studies on *recipients* discussed above suggest that some transplant tourists die or end up with serious infections or complications after the transplant, we do not have a baseline for their individual health in the absence of the transplant such that we can say they have *not* benefitted. Moreover, they have certainly gained in improving their chance of improving their health from an ex ante perspective.

On a philosophical level, Cécile Fabre has argued that where transplants are ultimately unsuccessful, this first requirement of exploitation is not met.[84] I am much more attracted to the notion that the individual has gained a chance at extending his or her life; just as we will examine the world from the seller's ex ante perspective as to the value of giving up the organ, we ought also to consider this element of exploitation from the organ recipient's ex ante perspective. If we instead focus on the broker, where there is one, as the potentially exploiting party, it is even easier to conclude that this first requirement is met—the broker will benefit from the profits he or she makes from the trade.

Is the second requirement met—is the seller harmed or treated unfairly, and is the buyer unfairly taking advantage? As Wertheimer stresses in his account, the correct frame for answering this question is to consider whether ex ante the seller is, *all things considered*, better off.[85]

Why all things considered? Almost all transactions make us better off in some respects and worse in others. A father who decides to work in a low-paying job rather than spend time at home raising his young daughter is in some ways better off (he makes money and enjoys professional achievement) and in some ways worse-off (he has lost time spent with his child). The mere fact that he has lost something, or that he would not work absent

---

[83] *E.g.*, Cécile Fabre, Whose Body Is It Anyways?: Justice and the Integrity of the Person 142 (2006). Fabre breaks the second condition into two, *id.*, but I find it more useful to treat it as one.

[84] Fabre disagrees. *See id.* at 142–43.

[85] Wertheimer, *supra* note 69, at 71.

the benefits, is not enough to make his relationship with his employer exploitative or to say that he has been harmed. If he finds the work humiliating or a blow to his self-worth, that too is not enough to make us conclude that he has been harmed. If he does the work out of desperation, in that he has a daughter to support and is unable to find better work in this tough economy, that too does not make him harmed by the job offer. Instead, the right frame is to consider whether, all things considered, his gains outweigh his losses.

The same is true in the much more extreme case of the kidney seller who, as we have seen above, may experience health, social, and economic deficits for the sale but also may receive benefits such as reduction of debt, payment of a daughter's dowry, etc. Naqvi's study suggests that many kidney sellers viewed their kidney sales in exactly this way, noting that: "in our study population where [the] majority were illiterate and many in bonded labour, [the available] opportunities were far less....Therefore, despite their bad experience, they still preferred to [sell kidneys] in desperation to pay off debts, and/or to save another son or daughter from bondage."[86]

Further, the right perspective to evaluate the harm or unfairness to the seller is ex ante not ex post. If A sells land to B on which B hopes to find oil, it should not be the case that the transaction is exploitative in a possible world where B does not find oil but not exploitative in a possible world where B does find oil.[87] What should matter is whether there was harm or unfairness from the ex ante perspective, which mirrors contract doctrines on unconscionability.[88] The correct frame to determine if something morally wrong was afoot was the price A charged B based on B's expectations *at the time of* transaction, not how things ultimately turned out. Now things might be different if A deceived B about the chances that there would be oil there, but that is an information deficit that goes to the consensual versus non-consensual nature of the transaction, which I turn to below.

The ex ante versus ex post distinction is important for our purposes; although the ethnographic and statistical studies discussed above suggest that ex post many of the kidney sellers have been harmed and in fact, all things considered, a large percentage (but not all of them) would rather they had not donated, that is the wrong question to ask for the exploitation analysis. The right question is whether ex ante the transaction harmed them or benefitted them. That they agreed to do it (subject to a discussion on information and bounded rationality below) is strong evidence that they ex ante believed themselves to be, all things considered, benefitted rather than harmed by the transaction. If that is right, then transplant tourism appears to be a case of mutually advantageous exploitation, where from the ex ante, all things considered perspective, both seller and recipient benefit.

---

[86] Naqvi et al., *supra* note 13, at 937.

[87] Wertheimer, *supra* note 69, at 71.

[88] RESTATEMENT (SECOND) OF CONTRACTS §208 (1981).

Labeling a transaction as mutually beneficial exploitation does not render it per se unproblematic, although it makes matters more complicated as it will require us to determine if the seller is nonetheless treated unfairly. For reasons similar to the ones we saw in the coercion analysis, the mere fact that a buyer takes advantage of a seller's unfortunate or unjust background situation is not enough to render the transaction unfair: if it were enough to make the situation unfair, the surgeon who demands a fee for amputation (to use a prior example) would be automatically acting in an unjust way, which we do not think he is.[89]

One might be tempted to instead judge the fairness of the transaction by the utility actually derived by both parties as against the baseline where no transaction took place to look to see whether the benefit is unequal.[90] That, however, threatens to prove far too much: in some cases, it seems as though one party will gain much more than the other and yet we do not consider the transaction improper or exploitative. Again, even if the surgeon charges a very high price, the patient whose life is saved (or at least hopes his life will be saved) by the doctor certainly comes out ahead, all things considered. Yet the inequality in a patient's welfare gain as compared to a baseline of no transaction does not make us think the patient is exploiting *the doctor*![91] For the same reason, whether brokers/recipients are benefitting much more from the transaction than sellers, or vice versa, cannot tell us if exploitation has taken place.

Instead what we need is a kind of moralized baseline, a sense of how much the person *ought* to receive to which we can compare what she actually is promised in the transaction. This is not an easy problem to resolve. Wertheimer has suggested that we can sometimes use a hypothetical market approach to establish the relevant baseline, wherein we imagine what price would obtain in an unpressurized market.[92] If the price paid by the purchaser for a kidney to the seller is lower than the price the seller would get in a hypothetical market where the seller is not pressured to transact, then the buyer has exploited the seller. If the price is higher than that which would obtain in the unpressurized market, then the seller has exploited *the buyer*. If the price is the same, there is no exploitation.[93]

This approach runs into problems as to transplant tourism, however, for reasons that Fabre indicates in her discussion of domestic organ markets: unlike the market for shovels in the middle of a snowstorm where we have an unpressurized market to compare to (the price of shovels on sunny days), there is no unpressurized market for organs in that "those who want to sell their organs would not do so if they could raise money by other means; those who want to buy organs are (usually) in desperate need of them."[94] Perhaps

[89] Wertheimer, *supra* note 69, at 71.

[90] *Id.* at 73.

[91] *Id.*

[92] WERTHEIMER, *supra* note 62, at 230–36; FABRE, *supra* note 83, at 144.

[93] *See* FABRE, *supra* note 83, at 144.

[94] *Id.*

the best we could do, suggests Fabre, is to examine whether individuals are willing to take similar risks for similar prices in similar unpressurized markets.[95]

As to transplant tourism, it is not clear exactly where this would lead us. As the accounts discussed above suggest, compared to what the typical organ seller makes in the labor market, the sum being paid by the broker (even when only two-thirds is actually paid) is huge, and it is unclear if it is disproportionate in its risk-to-benefit ratio as compared to being a day laborer, for example, on relatively unsafe job sites. On the other hand, those comparison markets are often *themselves* somewhat pressurized, in that many individuals would not accept day laborship if not required to support their families or pay off debts related to bonded labor. Then again, that is true of employment in general; many would not work (or at least not work in their current job or as much) but for the need to make money to support themselves. Although I cannot prove that the terms being offered to kidney sellers are "fair" in the sense that this analysis uses the term, I also do not think that those in favor of banning transplant tourism can clearly show that it is "unfair."

Thus, I remain in doubt as to whether transplant tourism is exploitative of sellers because it is unclear that kidney sellers have been harmed if we adopt the ex ante all things considered perspective, and because it is unclear that they have been treated unfairly.

Suppose, though, that you remain convinced that I am wrong on these two facets, and think that transplant tourism involves a problematic form of exploitation. That conclusion would not justify an outright ban on transplant tourism for two reasons.

First, if the seller is harmed or treated unfairly, the natural solution is to improve the size of his or her benefit—doing so makes it less likely that he or she is, all things considered, harmed, and also makes it more likely that he or she is given a fair price such that he or she is not treated unfairly by the buyer. Thus, stated as such, the exploitation argument, even if it succeeds, justifies only price floors or other price regulations of the transplant tourism market, not an outright ban.[96]

To see why, understand the way in which a ban that is established to protect exploited parties might problematically make them worse off. Peggy Radin's work on surrogacy and baby selling nicely captures the threatened hypocrisy here, for as she puts it: "[i]f poverty can make some things nonsalable because we must prophylactically presume such sales are coerced, we would add insult to injury if we then do not provide the would-be seller with the goods she needs or the money she would have received"; that is,

---

[95] *Id.*

[96] *Cf. id.* at 148–52. As I have observed elsewhere, notice how this particular intervention of increasing the price paid may make worse the corruption problem on some accounts because it now seems more true that the money being paid is in "value equilibrium" with what has been given up by the seller. *See* Cohen, *supra* note 44, at 703–10. For a more thorough discussion of all the possible ways in which a regulated market for organs could operate, focused on the domestic case, see Cohen, *supra* note 57, at _ - _.

"[i]f we think respect for persons warrants prohibiting a mother from selling something personal to obtain food for her starving children, we do not respect her personhood more by forcing her to let them starve instead" such that "this aspect of liberal prophylactic pluralism is hypocritical without a large-scale redistribution of wealth and power that seems highly improbable."[97] Let us call this the "hypocrisy argument" for short.

It is worthwhile to emphasize the way the cross-border nature of transplant tourism exacerbates this worry: if the United States took further steps to block its patients from buying kidneys from Pakistan's poor, its tools for effectuating that kind of redistribution of resources to Pakistan's poor who are now denied access to the revenue from sale are very few indeed as compared to kidney sales *within the* United States. Even if it provides foreign aid to Pakistan, it must rely on the Pakistani government to distribute that aid appropriately, and it has no way of ensuring the aid will flow specifically to the poor individuals who have lost this particular opportunity to sell a kidney. Moreover, it seems as though the United States is also much less likely to have the will to improve the plight of Pakistan's poor as compared to its own poor, for reasons I have discussed in greater depth elsewhere.[98]

Second, according to a line of thinking that Wertheimer calls the "strategic intervention" argument, price floors might be a more appropriate remedy to exploitation than a complete prohibition.[99] Suppose a kidney buyer proposes to purchase a kidney from the seller at a price term we consider to be unfair. Prohibiting the transaction altogether may make the seller still worse not better off, because even an unfair offer is better for him or her than no offer. What we really want to do is move the seller toward a fair offer, which is even better for the "victim" seller. This can sometimes be achieved by regulation that makes some terms (e.g., some prices) in an offer prohibited, but does not render all transactions for sale of that good or service per se forbidden.[100]

Take, for example, the bilateral monopoly "Rescue case" as a skeletal example: imagine that B is in desperate need of being rescued and A, who happens to be passing by but did not cause the misfortune, demands an exorbitant price to do the rescue. "If we prohibit A from charging an exorbitant price for his services, then A might offer his services for a reasonable price rather than walk away."[101] Labor unions often offer this argument as a way of overcoming collective action problems in that although "it may be perfectly rational for each individual employee to accept a low wage rather than no wage at all, [] it is better for all (or most) if none are allowed to accept a low wage, for they may then be

---

[97] Margaret Jane Radin, *Market-Inalienability*, 100 HARV. L. REV. 1849, 1910–11 (1997). For a more ambivalent version of this argument in the organ sale context, *see* Eduardo Rivera-Lopez, *Organ Sales and Moral Distress*, 23 J. APPLIED PHIL. 41, 44–48 (2006).

[98] *See* Cohen, *supra* note 2, at 14–17, 25–27.

[99] Wertheimer, *supra* note 69, at 81.

[100] Cohen, *supra* note 57, at _ -

[101] Wertheimer, *supra* note 69, at 81.

offered a high wage."[102] Price floors in kidney transplant tourism markets are superior to outright prohibitions as a curb against exploitation because they may enable exactly this kind of strategic intervention.

For these two reasons, even if one were convinced that the basic requirements of the exploitation argument were met as to transplant tourism, in theory the right corrective is price floors or other improvement of terms rather than outright prohibition. I say "in theory," because in a second-best world one might still prefer the complete ban on either epistemic or regulatory grounds or both. The epistemic ground suggests that where we cannot adequately determine or are uncertain whether a particular transaction within a category is mutually beneficial or harmful, "it may make sense to prohibit all such transactions because the expected harms associated with the 'bad' transactions outweigh the expected benefits of the 'good' transactions."[103] The regulatory analog suggests that even if price floors or other policing of deals would be first best, where we cannot adequately do that, a ban may be better than an alternative of no effective regulatory intervention at all.

How well does the existing empirical evidence on transplant tourism discussed above justify either form of this second-best argument? Consider first the regulatory version of the argument: on the one hand, as most of the existing trade takes place against laws rendering kidney sales illegal, there is some reason to believe that gentler legal interventions such as price floors may also be circumvented. On the other hand, if we created a legal "safe harbor" for transplant tourism given certain transactional terms, it might produce a "new normal" and push out the organized crime rings and other unsavory elements that currently dominate the market. If anyone could legally sell a kidney given certain terms, we might see more law compliance (i.e., adherence to those terms) than under the status quo. On the epistemic version of the argument, when we take the ex ante all things considered perspective, it seems that most of these transactions are mutually advantageous and the expected benefits exceed the expected harms, suggesting that we are not really in so much doubt after all on this score. Finally, we ought to be sensitive to the hypocrisy arguments concerns discussed above and the difficulties in ensuring redistribution in the transplant tourism setting.

Although the matter is close, I do not think an outright ban can be strongly defended even on this second-best version of the exploitation argument.

There is another argument lurking in the background that comes to the fore in my discussion of price floors: undue inducement. Although often labeled "exploitation," in fact this argument is the opposite. Exploitation is the claim the seller is getting offered too little, while undue inducement is the claim that they are being paid *too much*, the "offer too good to refuse," which naturally suggests a price *ceiling* not floor. Although

---

[102] *Id.*

[103] *Id.* at 82. The same may be true for doubts about consent, which I discuss in the next section.

there may be some social practices with other logics where the undue inducement argument has merit—such as research ethics with its whiffs of fiduciary relationships and social benefit, although even here I have my doubts—in the context of selling one's body, I must confess that the logical basis for this argument escapes me. In this context, price ceilings seem infantilizing of the poor and seem to retard rather than promote these individuals' self-interest, including by reducing the chance that they will get out of debt and also impairing their ability to self-insure against possible negative health or psychological outcomes. Once again, the hypocrisy argument looms large and we should be wary of interfering with these transactions unless we are committed to redistribution that makes these individuals just as well off without selling their kidney.

iii. Consent, Bounded Rationality, and Justified Paternalism

My discussion of exploitation has proceeded under the assumption that the transplant tourist transaction is consensual rather than non-consensual. Is it? One can think of this in one of two argument flows: as an argument that this is non-consensual exploitation or as an argument for justified paternalism in this market. I am not sure much turns on the framing. Both categorizations of the argument have as a necessary (but not sufficient) condition the fact that the sellers are, all things, considered ex post worse off than they were had they not sold. It is worth emphasizing that this fact is essential for these kinds of arguments but not for other forms of arguments I have mentioned above but found unpersuasive (for example, crowding out and corruption arguments), which can provide reasons for legal intervention in these markets even if no harm is done to the seller.

Like its legal equivalent, "consent" as used by bioethicists is something of a weasel-word. We can at the very least divide it into three constituent parts: whether an individual's agreement to a transaction is (1) voluntary, (2) informed, and (3) competent.[104]

Is consent to selling one's kidney for transplant tourism *voluntary*? In the basest sense of "not done under threat of force," usually, yes, though the empirical evidence discussed above suggested occasional cases where threats of force are used to induce initial compliance, and more often coercive techniques such as threats of force or withholding of passports are used to ensure that individuals do not back out. Still, given our conclusion above that the trade is in general not coercive, it seems the defect in consent, if there is one, does not lie with voluntariness per se but with one of the other elements of consent.

Is the consent given by the kidney seller *informed*? The existing studies suggest frequent problems with the accuracy of the information provided to sellers. Sellers were misinformed about safety, the quality of the doctor performing their surgery, and the needs of the transplant recipient; falsely assured with the myth of the "sleeping kidney," the promises of citizenship or a job, and the pleasantness of the conditions in India where the transplant would take place; and not informed about the possible physical consequences

---

[104] *Id.* at 76–77.

of the surgery. In at least three of the studies—Naqvi's in Pakistan, Moniruzzaman's in Bangladesh, and Goyal's in India—sellers were misled into thinking they would be paid substantially more than they were actually paid. Thus, there does seem to be significant doubts about whether consent is sufficiently informed.

Even when individuals are presented all relevant information, they may lack the *competence or capacity* to effectively process that information. Without education, many individuals will find it difficult to understand and evaluate risks, and indeed psychological research finds even quite educated individuals are poor at understanding risk and susceptible to significant framing effects, especially in health care settings.[105] In many of the studies, the sellers were very poorly educated and illiterate: only two of the fifteen sellers in Yae's study had education that extended beyond primary school, and some had received only three or four years of formal education altogether; in Naqvi's study of sellers in Pakistan, 90 percent were illiterate, and most had been in the work force since childhood; in Zargooshi's study of Iranian sellers, only 5 percent of sellers had high school degrees or more education, and 35 percent were illiterate.

It is easy from within the ivory tower to equate being uneducated with being unable to make complex and difficult decisions. Such a claim has quite an elitist air, and also would seem to problematically imply that the "incapacity" of these individuals should extend to many other important life decisions, and thus support paternalistic intervention in those domains as well. Moreover, Goodwin has cautioned that there is a deep, if unintentional, racial tinge to many of these paternalistic arguments, that originates in Titmuss's own work that "essentialize[s] and infantilize[s] African Americans, in much the way that Titmuss cautioned that 'negro' blood sellers were a menace to themselves and would contaminate the blood supply with insalubrious blood."[106]

In the transplant tourism debate, we should be wary of engaging in a similar infantilization of developing world citizens with its unmistakable whiff of colonialism. Moreover, we should again be wary of the "hypocrisy argument" and the worry that preventing kidney sales may force sellers to *remain* uneducated, rather than using the money gained to improve their lots in life. I am sensitive to this concern that goes with such blanket conclusions, and I instead think that the best approach to considering the issue is data-sensitive.

---

[105] *See, e.g.*, Russell Korobkin, *Bounded Rationality, Standard Form Contracts, and Unconscionability*, 70 U. CHI. L. REV. 1203, 1229–36 (2003) (reviewing evidence for one of "the most robust findings of social science research on judgment and decisionmaking is that individuals are quite bad at taking into account probability estimates when making decisions."); I. Glenn Cohen, *Protecting Patients with Passports: Medical Tourism and the Patient-Protective Argument*, 95 IOWA L. REV. 1467, 1493, 1509–11, 1550–54 (discussing bounded rationality problems in patient interpretation of health care data); Carl E. Schneider & Mark A. Hall, *The Patient Life: Can Consumers Direct Health Care?*, 35 AM. J.L & MED. 7 (2009); *see also* Wertheimer, *supra* note 69, at 77 (philosophical discussion of competency).

[106] Goodwin, *supra* note 40, at 1375.

One major problem with fairly evaluating this argument is that we do not have a good sense of *why* sellers seem to be making this mistake in their estimation of how a kidney sale will change their welfare. Is the problem misleading information? Poor education? Overoptimism bias or other forms of bounded rationality?[107] We simply do not know.

What we do note with some confidence is that the evidence shows that there *is* a problem. In Naqvi's study, based on their own experience only 35 percent of Pakistani kidney donors recommended that a family member or friend sell a kidney; in Moniruzziman's work on Bangladeshi sellers, 85 percent spoke against the organ market, with many (he does not give an exact number) saying if they had a second chance they would not sell their kidneys; in Goyal's study of Indian sellers, of the 264 who answered the question, 79 percent reported that they would recommend against selling a kidney for the same reason that they did and only 21 percent would recommend doing so; Budiana-Saberi reports that 94 percent of her sample of Egyptian kidney sellers regretted their donation; Zargooshi finds that 85 percent of his Iranian kidney sellers in the sample would definitely not sell their kidneys again, and 76 percent strongly discouraged potential vendors from doing so.[108]

The fact that a very high number of kidney sellers later regret their choices for reasons that likely involve informational deficits, bounded rationality, etc., is, to me, the strongest argument in favor of legal intervention. Although I think that this version of the argument is the best one for banning transplant tourism, it is far from unproblematic, and I think that there are three main reasons those opposed to transplant tourism or kidney sales more generally have preferred not to frame their arguments in this form:

First, regret is a slippery concept, both conceptually and in terms of data.[109] As I have said, we lack good information on exactly what is causing the sellers to have so much regret, which seems important in determining whether an outright ban is necessary. There are lots of open questions here. For example, take the Iranian data that I suggested above has significant variance between the two studies on the amount of ex post regret. One way of squaring the data from the Rouchi and Zargooshi studies is to note that one reports high satisfaction pre-discharge (Rouchi) while the other suggests low satisfaction at a point post-discharge. One read of this comparison is that there is not just a

---

[107] *See, e.g.*, Korobkin, *supra* note 105, at 1229–36; Christine Jolls et al., *A Behavior Approach to Law and Economics*, 50 STAN. L. REV. 1471 (2008); Cohen, *supra* note 105, at 1467, 1493, 1509–11, 1550–54; Schneider & Hall, *supra* note 105.

[108] Given well-known findings about the way in which those who become disabled or ill adapt their estimations of their health states in a way that makes them more positive, on some views of whether to use adapted or unadapted states, there may be reason to think that these studies actually *underestimate* the level of ex post regret. *See, e.g.*, Paul Menzel et al., *The Role of Adaptation to Disability and Disease in Health State Valuation: A Preliminary Normative Analysis*, 55 SOC. SCI. & MED. 214 (2002).

[109] For discussions of the use and misuse of regret narratives in the reproductive law area, *see, e.g.*, Jeannie Suk, *The Trajectory of Trauma: Bodies and Minds of Abortion Discourse*, 110 COLUM. L. REV. 1193 (2010); Susan Frelich Appleton, *Reproduction and Regret*, 23 YALE J.L. & FEMINISM 255, 333 (2011).

question of *whether* donors face regret but *when*. This raises a data question (what are we measuring) but also a normative question (if there are differences in satisfaction with a kidney sale over time, which measurement is the one that should matter to us in setting policy) and a regulatory one (could we help potential sellers better understand what their future feelings might be?).

Moreover, as discussed above, many sellers do not get paid what they are promised and instead receive closer to two-thirds of the promised amount. If a regulatory intervention was capable of eliminating that problem, would the high amounts of ex post regret remain?

Further, as I mentioned above, the literature on altruistic kidney donation in the United States suggests that kidney donors have health outcomes as good as non-donors, while the data on transplant tourism suggests significant (self-reported) health deficits. How seriously should we take these self-reports? Are they reliable evidence that the health of those making them really is poorer due to the transplant, or a "sour grapes" phenomenon wherein their dissatisfaction at not having met their financial goals by the sale are being fed back into health evaluations? But imagine that the mechanism causing the regret is real objective negative health outcomes flowing from poor screening of seller health care, surgical, or post-surgical health care. In principle, there may be more targeted regulatory interventions that can improve the situation, such as mandating standards for health assessment, care, and the like.

Second, from a political theory point of view (as we discussed in Chapter 2) the usual regulatory remedy for this kind of problem is not an outright ban on a practice but improvement in information-provision and the use of "libertarian paternalist" interventions—such as altering default rules in ways that "influence behavior while also respecting freedom of choice"—or "debiasing" strategies—that "help people either to reduce or to eliminate" overoptimism, framing effects, or other forms of bounded rationality in their decision-making.[110] In the transplant tourism context, this would lead us to implement regulations designed to ensure that sellers were provided accurate information on the needs of kidney recipients, on the sellers' likely health outcomes post-transplant, on the likelihood that the money received would be successfully used for their goal (e.g., debt elimination), and on the likelihood of post-transplant regret. Moreover, all of this must be presented in an informed consent process that makes it comprehensible to someone with little formal education, and that uses framing and other debiasing strategies to try to quell bounded rationality difficulties. It would also lead us to regulation to make sure that sellers received what they were promised in terms of remuneration.

---

[110] Cass R. Sunstein & Richard H. Thaler, *Libertarian Paternalism Is Not an Oxymoron*, 70 U. CHI. L. REV. 1159, 1160 (2003); Christine Jolls & Cass R. Sunstein, *Debiasing through Law*, 35 J. LEGAL STUD. 199, 200 (2006); *see* Cohen, *supra* note 105, at 1506.

If that list of needed correctives seems quite long, one should take that as a warning: the kind of regulation needed for this would be expensive, extensive, difficult to implement, and difficult to audit. This would be true if it were just a matter of putting in place regulation at the domestic level,[111] but the problems are likely to be worse with transplant tourism where three countries are typically involved (the buyer's, the seller's, and the location of the transplant) and there is a real fear of a regulatory race to the bottom where the countries least willing to take action will be the ones that become the go-to destinations for recruiting sellers or engaging in transplants. Moreover, because there are so many stigmas attached to kidney sales in these societies, it will be difficult for word of the ex post regret of prior sellers to circulate widely. Thus, although in a first-best world of perfect regulatory implementation, the consent deficits identified would lead to targeted correctives, in the real world we are unlikely to avoid the problems identified with anything short of an outright prohibition.

As some (though admittedly imperfect) evidence for this claim, one might look at the data from Iran. As described by Ghods and Savaj in 2006, in Iran, all renal transplantation teams belong to the university, the costs of the transplant are paid by the government, and renal transplant teams receive no incentives from the recipient or the government to procure organs; sellers are provided an award from the government (US$1,200) and health insurance, and most are also provided a "rewarding gift" arranged before the agreement to provide one's kidney "from the recipient or, if the recipient is poor, from one of the charitable organizations"; and foreigners are not allowed to receive transplant organs from Iranians (an element that would obviously be a problem for transplant tourism); the Iranian Society for Organ Transplantation carefully monitors all transplants for ethical violations.[112] Yet even with all these regulatory systems in place, Zargooshi's data suggests that 85 percent of his Iranian kidney sellers in the sample would definitely not sell their kidneys again, and 76 percent strongly discouraged potential vendors from doing so. To be fair, Zargooshi's data comes from an earlier period than Ghods and Savaj's article, such that it is possible that the Iranian system was not as well-regulated at the time his sellers sold their kidneys. Moreover, as discussed, the more recent Rouchi study found donors were much more satisfied with their donation, although I have noted several reasons that data might be less probative because it measures *pre*-discharge regret. Finally, by almost any measure, Iran as a country has some unique facets independent of its organ donation system that should give us pause in generalizing this data.

Still, if in the one heavily regulated legal kidney sale market many of the concerns we have raised do not go away, that should cause us to have some skepticism as to the superiority of regulation here to outright prohibition. Even so, the case is not ironclad, and some have argued from a criminological perspective that criminal prohibition of organ

---

[111] For a more thorough discussion of regulatory interventions, see Cohen, *supra* note 57, at_ -

[112] Ghods & Savaj, *supra* note 22, at 1136.

sales leads to an increase in their value and, therefore, an increase in trafficking as organized crime groups find a lucrative market; accordingly, we ought to instead favor "harm
reduction" strategies that would regulate the market rather than seek to eliminate it.[113]

Third, and more philosophically, paternalism arguments for outright bans are controversial at a political theoretical level, in that libertarians reject them almost as a matter
of first principle.[114] As Tony Kronman astutely observed almost three decades ago, "by
acknowledging that it is ever morally permissible to prevent a person from acting solely
because he himself will be harmed by the action, one embraces paternalism (in however
limited a form) and has an obligation to explain why such interference is permissible
in some instances but not in others," such that "[o]ne who believes, as [John Stuart]
Mill did and I do, that some paternalistic restrictions on contractual freedom are not
only permissible but morally required, must supply a standard or principle for evaluating
paternalistic arguments in particular cases; only in this way can the legitimacy of paternalism be established and its limits defined."[115]

What might such a limiting principle look like in this case? Perhaps something like
this: "where many sellers of a good are being given false information, are poor, desperate,
and uneducated, where their ex post regret is quite high (routinely above 70 percent),
where the practice has significant negative effects on their health and economic fortunes,
and where information-providing and other gentler correctives will not be effective, we
should prohibit a practice outright."

To be sure, there are losers in such a move—not only the recipients who desperately
need organs and are willing to buy them, but also the home country public or private
insurer who must pay for the high cost of dialysis for many patients who do not get transplants, the brokers who make a living mediating the trade, and the proportion of sellers
(likely between 15 percent and 30 percent based on the studies) who sell their kidneys as
part of transplant tourism and are, by their ex post assessment, glad that they did. This
last group, in particular, can legitimately press the hypocrisy argument on us and lament
that we have "protected them" out of their ability to get out of bonded labor and improve
their lot in life. We can respond that we remain committed to making their lives better, to ending bonded labor and lifting people out of poverty, but the cynics among us
will note that the headway we make on those lofty projects will be slow in coming, if it
ever does.

---

[113] F. Ambagtsheer & W. Weimar, *A Criminological Perspective: Why Prohibition of Organ Trade Is Not Effective and How the Declaration of Istanbul Can Move Forward*, 12 Am. J. Transplant. 571, 574 (2012). For a more thorough discussion of these problems in other contexts (including prostitution, drugs, etc.), *see generally* David Michael Jaros, *Perfecting Criminal Markets*, 112 Columbia L. Rev. 1294 (2012).

[114] *See, e.g.*, David Boaz, Libertarianism: A Primer 16–19 (1997); Sunstein & Thaler, *supra* note 110, at 1160.

[115] Anthony T. Kronman, *Paternalism and the Law of Contracts*, 92 Yale L.J. 763, 765 (1983).

Perhaps it will be better to look them in the eye and say "if we had another way that would work, we would use it, but we don't, and while we recognize that you feel you have benefitted from this trade, a clear majority of your neighbors find themselves worse off after selling their kidneys and deeply regret what they have done. Sometimes regulatory prohibitions to protect the many will burden the few, and that is the price of living in a just society." Will *they* be satisfied? Perhaps not. But *we* should be.[116]

Although the advocates of banning transplant tourism portray the issue as easy, in these last few pages I have shown why the bioethical issues are hard indeed. The typical arguments made for prohibitions—corruption, crowding out, coercion, and exploitation—do not carry the day. Instead, the strongest argument for prohibiting this trade—and the one I ultimately subscribe to—is admittedly paternalistic, but I think it is a case of justified paternalism. Let us not lose sight of the fact, though, that this argument foists upon us a tragic choice—to leave people in dire straits who want to better their lives and will actually succeed in doing so by their own estimation if they sell their kidneys in order to protect a larger swath of their neighbors who will be ruined by it.

The argument for prohibition is thus rightly understood as an argument from second-best. First-best, on my view, would be to regulate an international organ market that would avoid or mitigate many of these problems. In the U.S. context, with a well-established infrastructure of hospital, insurer, and government monitoring, I have some hope that such a regulated market *may* work, and have tried to set out the kinds of regulations that would be necessary to make it do so.[117] In the context of transplant tourism, I have much less confidence in whether such implementation is feasible. The major sites of transplant tourism all have criminal prohibitions in place, and yet significant volumes of the trade continue to occur; the body mafia that has grown wealthy on this trade will be difficult to dislodge; the difficulties of regulating individuals in the seller, broker, and recipients' countries and cooperating across borders are formidable. Thus, I think an outright ban may be more justifiable in the transplant tourism case, even if it is second-best from a regulatory perspective to a regulated market.

III. REGULATION

If transplant tourism should be prohibited for these reasons—either because we want to end international organ sales altogether or because we want to root out the "bad" forms of the practice alongside introducing the kind of potential regulated market discussed

---

[116] A prohibition on transplant tourism might also be justified on the ground that it seems unfair for us to prohibit our citizens from buying organs from our citizens but allow them to buy from poor Indians or Pakistanis, increasing their exploitation. I discuss a similar argument as to surrogacy in Chapter 8, and will press on whether a home country's obligation to prevent exploitation by its citizens of its own citizens is the same as the exploitation by its citizens of foreign individuals. *See also* Cohen, *supra* note 55, at 1381–86.

[117] *See generally* Cohen, *supra* note 5⁷, at __ - __

above—we then face the regulatory design question of the best way to do so. Here, I argue for a multimodal strategy, and briefly outline its elements.

A. Destination Country Enforcement

The most obvious solution would be to allow individual countries to ban kidney sales in their territories and prosecute medical tourists who purchase kidneys there or the brokers who facilitate the transactions. As every country but Iran currently criminalizes kidney sale, our legislative work would be done! There have been a few organ trafficking prosecutions of international organ rings, many with substantial ties to Israel, in the last few years initiated in Brazil, South Africa, Kosovo, Turkey, and the United States.[118] Overall, however, as the case studies above suggest, transplant tourism often persists in spite of official legal sanctions on the books. Writing in the *American Journal of Transplantation* in 2011, Frederike Ambagtsheer and Willem Weimar observe that "[o]nly in very few cases have crime control efforts led to accusations by victims and prosecutions of the accused," in part because "organ trafficking may be one of the most difficult crimes to detect" and because "its enforcement is not a priority of local, national and international law enforcement institutions," and the "universal response to the crime is characterized by punitive condemnation through legislation but awareness and expertise on how to detect and enforce the crime is practically nonexistent."[119]

Thus, although domestic destination country criminal prosecutions should be continued, on their own they are unlikely to be effective in ending transplant tourism. The rest of this part considers other interventions that have been or might be tried.

B. Professional Self-Policing and International Documents

In 2008, the Transplantation Society and the International Society of Nephrology convened an international meeting in Turkey that resulted in the "Declaration of

---

[118] *See* Michael Smith et al., *Organ Gangs Force Poor to Sell Kidneys for Desperate Israelis*, BLOOMBERG MARKETS MAG., Nov 1, 2011, http://www.bloomberg.com/news/2011-11-01/organ-gangs-force-poor-to-sell-kidneys-for-desperate-israelis.html; Jean Allain, *Trafficking of Persons for the Removal of Organs and the Admission of Guilt of a South African Hospital*, 19 MED. L. REV. 117 (2011); Sandile Khoza, *The Human Organ Trade: The South African Tragedy*, 2 S. AFR. J. BIOETHICS 47 (2009); *Turkish Authorities Arrest Two Suspected Organ Traffickers*, HURRIYET DAILY NEWS, Jan. 21, 2011, http://www.hurriyetdailynews.com/default.aspx?pageid=438&n=two-people-related-with-organ-mafia-were-arrested-2011-01-21; Nebi Qina, *Organ Recipient Testifies at Trial in Kosovo*, BOSTON GLOBE, Mar. 23, 2012, http://articles.boston.com/2012-03-23/news/31230790_1_organ-transplants-pristina-kosovo; Scheper-Hughes, *supra* note 40, at 850; Lysiak & Melago, *supra* note 39.

[119] Ambagtsheer & Weimar, *supra* note 113, at 572; *see also* Working Group on Incentives for Living Donation, *Incentives for Organ Donation: Proposed Standards for an Internationally Acceptable System*, 12 AM. J. TRANSPLANTATION 306, 310 (2012) (noting that "today, most unregulated markets occur in countries that prohibit incentives for donation, but lack the appropriate control or willingness to enforce the prohibition").

Istanbul."[120] The Declaration defines its key term, "organ trafficking," as "the recruitment, transport, transfer, harbouring or receipt of living or deceased persons or their organs by means of the threat or use of force or other forms of coercion, of abduction, of fraud, of deception, of the abuse of power or of a position of vulnerability, or of the giving to, or the receiving by, a third party of payments or benefits to achieve the transfer of control over the potential donor, for the purpose of exploitation by the removal of organs for transplantation."[121] The act distinguishes the term from "transplant commercialism," which it defines as "a policy or practice in which an organ is treated as a commodity, including by being bought or sold or used for material gain," and suggests that "[t]ravel for transplantation becomes *transplant tourism* if it involves organ trafficking and/or transplant commercialism or if the resources (organs, professionals and transplant centres) devoted to providing transplants to patients from outside a country undermine the country's ability to provide transplant services for its own population."[122]

The Declaration has many principles and proposals aimed at improving organ procurement for cadaveric and live noncommercial donors, the care of donors who have been victimized, etc. For our purposes, though, the key principle is principle 6, which reads:

> Organ trafficking and transplant tourism violate the principles of equity, justice and respect for human dignity and should be prohibited. Because transplant commercialism targets impoverished and otherwise vulnerable donors, it leads inexorably to inequity and injustice and should be prohibited. In Resolution 44.25, the World Health Assembly called on countries to prevent the purchase and sale of human organs for transplantation.
>
> a. Prohibitions on these practices should include a ban on all types of advertising (including electronic and print media), soliciting or brokering for the purpose of transplant commercialism, organ trafficking or transplant tourism;
>
> b. such prohibitions should also include penalties for acts—such as medically screening donors or organs, or transplanting organs—that aid, encourage or use the products of organ trafficking or transplant tourism;
>
> c. practices that induce vulnerable individuals or groups (such as illiterate and impoverished persons, undocumented immigrants, prisoners, and political or economic refugees) to become living donors are incompatible with the aim of combating organ trafficking, transplant tourism and transplant commercialism.[123]

---

[120] Leslie P. France & John G. Francis, *Stateless Crimes, Legitimacy, and International Criminal Law: The Case of Organ Trafficking*, 4 CRIM. LAW & PHIL. 283, 287 (2010); *The Declaration of Istanbul on Organ Trafficking and Transplant Tourism*, 23 NEPHROLOGY DIALYSIS TRANSPLANTATION 3375 (2008) [hereinafter "Declaration of Istanbul"].

[121] Declaration of Istanbul, *supra* note 120, at 3375–76.

[122] *Id.* at 3376.

[123] *Id.*

Among the Declaration's proposals, two are worth highlighting. First, its statement that "[t]he determination of the medical and psychosocial suitability of the living donor should be guided by the recommendations of the Amsterdam and Vancouver Forums," including informed consent, assessment of psychological impact, and psychosocial evaluation by mental health professionals as part of screening.[124] Second, the Declaration makes clear that "[c]omprehensive reimbursement of the actual, documented costs of donating an organ does not constitute a payment for an organ, but is rather part of the legitimate costs of treating the recipient," if costs are calculated using a "transparent methodology, consistent with national norms." These costs may include "lost income and out-of-pocket expenses," including "medical expenses incurred for post-discharge care of the donor, [and] lost income in relation to donation (consistent with national norms)," so long as reimbursement is done by "the agency handling the transplant rather than paid directly from the recipient to the donor."[125]

The Declaration is meant to complement a few earlier international documents that address transplant tourism. The first is the World Health Assembly (WHA) approval of the WHO guiding principles on organ transplantation in 1991, and as amended in 2004. The 2004 version encouraged the use of living kidney donors where possible and the harmonization of global transplant practices, and most important for our purposes, it "requested the Director-General of WHO to provide support for member states to prevent organ trafficking and to draw up guidelines to protect vulnerable groups from the practice" and "urged member states to act against transplant tourism and international organ trafficking."[126] The second is the 2000 "United Nations Protocol to prevent, suppress and punish trafficking in persons, especially women and children, supplementing the United Nations convention against transnational organized crime," which explicitly includes in its definition of trafficking the removal of organs and rejects consent as a relevant defense.[127] As of February 2010, there were 117 signatories, including some (Egypt and India) but not others (Bangladesh, Pakistan, and Iran) of the countries discussed above that are hotbeds for transplant tourism.[128]

---

[124] *Id.* at 3377.

[125] *Id.*

[126] Francis & Francis, *supra* note 120, at 286–87 (citing World Health Organization, *Guiding Principles on Human Organ Transplantation*, 337 LANCET 1470–71 (1991); World Health Assembly, WHA 57.18 (2004), http://apps.who.int/gb/ebwha/pdf_files/WHA57/A57_R18-en.pdf.).

[127] Francis & Francis, *supra* note 120, at 287; United Nations, *Protocol to Prevent, Suppress and Punish Trafficking in Persons, Especially Women and Children, Supplementing the United Nations Convention against Transnational Organized Crime* (2000), *available at* http://treaties.un.org/Pages/ViewDetails.aspx?src=TREATY&mtdsg.

[128] Francis & Francis, *supra* note 120, at 287; United Nations Office on Drugs and Crime, Protocol status as of 26/09/2008, http://www.unodc.org/unodc/en/treaties/CTOC/countrylist-traffickingprotocol.html.

Have these measures been successful in dampening transplant tourism? A precise answer is impossible, but at least one set of informed academic observers, Leslie and James Francis, have claimed that these measures "have been met with limited implementation success at both the domestic and international levels," which they ascribe to the lack of "direct enforcement mechanisms" making these statements "hortatory at best."[129] In some ways, they suggest, these interventions that "lack the imprimatur of an international judicial body" have failed because although they may have stimulated the "[s]tates with vulnerable populations [to take] action to protect their citizens from groups that prey on the poor to secure organs," the "better off states" continue to face "chronic and serious imbalances between seriously insufficient local supplies and expanding demands from an aging population" and their "failure to monitor, develop, or enforce trafficking restrictions—except the sale of organs between their own residents—threatens to undermine nascent efforts in donor nations to restrict trafficking."[130]

To be sure, one should not read the type of criticism leveled by Francis and Francis as a claim that these interventions lack any utility. Supporters of the Declaration of Istanbul suggest that it has played an important role in shifting the mindset of transplant surgeons. In particular, Frank Delmonico, a leading transplant surgeon at Harvard Medical School and a force behind the Declaration of Istanbul, has done a yeoman's effort cataloging other countries' compliance with the Declaration and other law reforms.[131] These documents likely played a role in some important domestic attempts to curb organ tourism—for example, a recent ban on organ sale in Egypt and the Philippines, a Japanese investigation into alleged transplant tourism of its citizens to China, and strengthening of laws in Israel and Pakistan, although some observers have doubted the efficacy of some of these initiatives (such as Pakistan's ban on foreign patients purchasing organs).[132] Instead, I think the lesson is that these documents on their own are unlikely to sufficiently address the problem of organ tourism.[133]

---

[129] Francis & Francis, *supra* note 120, at 287.

[130] *Id.* at 291.

[131] Francis L. Delmonico, *The Implications of Istanbul Declaration on Organ Trafficking and Transplant Tourism*, 14 CURRENT OPINION ORGAN TRANSPLANT 116 (2009).

[132] *See* Francis & Francis, *supra* note 120, at 289; Ambagtsheer & Weimar, *supra* note 113, at 571, 573; Luc Noël & Dominique Martin, *Progress towards Self-Sufficiency in Organ Transplants*, 87 BULLETIN WORLD HEALTH ORG. 647, 647 (2009).

[133] Francis and Francis have argued that the International Criminal Court or a specialized international tribunal should be given jurisdiction to pursue organ trafficking specifically. Francis & Francis, *supra* note 120, at 291. They reach this suggestion because they conclude that "domestic legal regimes have proved ineffective and there is little reason to believe enforcement is likely to improve," and because "the presence of a credible international enforcement regime could prove both a spur and a complement to the strengthening of domestic enforcement regimes." *Id.* at 292. However, as they admit, this would require a significant expansion of the existing scope of international criminal liability and cannot fit within the definitions of genocide and crimes against humanity set forth in the Statute of Rome. *Id.* at 292–93. I think that international criminal liability is worth pursuing, but I am both more skeptical that it is politically feasible in the middle term future than the Francises, and less skeptical of the possibility for effective home country enforcement mechanisms of the kind I set out below.

C. Home Country Measures

Although few academics or policymakers have focused on this kind of regulation, home countries can make significant progress in deterring transplant tourism by adopting their own measures that govern their citizens who receive organs purchased from abroad.

Transplant tourism involves a complex and expensive medical process. One significant way in which home countries can discourage their citizens from engaging in transplant tourism is by making these patients ineligible for insurance coverage relating to a kidney transplant involving transplant tourism. In the U.S. system, regulators may have inadvertently already given the Centers for Medicaid & Medicare Services (CMS), which promulgates rules relating to the payment of those eligible for the Medicaid and Medicare public assistance programs, the power to do so. As part of the informed-consent process for patients seeking transplantation, patients must be informed that "if a transplant is not provided in a Medicare-approved transplant center it could affect the transplant recipient's ability to have his or her immunosuppressive drugs paid for under Medicare Part B."[134] These drugs, which are required to avoid tissue rejection, are expensive and cost a kidney transplant patient about US$15,000 to $20,000 annually.[135] I have found no data on how often this power has been used to deny or threaten to deny coverage for those who have engaged in transplant tourism, but CMS could certainly alter the regulation to put in place a flat bar on covering such drugs or other expenses for those who have undergone transplant tourism.

However, these assistance programs cover only a portion of the American population (around 90 million people),[136] and many transplant tourists are unlikely to be among this group. In order to deter those who are privately insured in the United States, individual U.S. states could use their powers regulating health insurance to forbid insurers from reimbursing for immunosuppressive drugs or other costs related to transplant tourism.[137] Blocking public or private health insurance reimbursement for extremely

---

[134] 42 C.F.R. § 482.102(b)(9) (2009).

[135] John S. Gill & Marcello Tonelli, *Penny Wise, Pound Foolish? Coverage Limits on Immunosuppression after Kidney Transplantation*, 366 N. ENGL. J. MED. 588 (2012).

[136] *See, e.g.*, Allison K. Hoffman, *Three Models of Health Insurance: The Conceptual Pluralism of the Patient Protection and Affordable Care Act*, 159 U. PA. L. REV. 1873, 1904 (2011).

[137] For a discussion of how states can use this power of health insurance to regulate medical tourism, *see* Cohen, *supra* note 105, at 1544–47. This would be somewhat unusual in that most state coverage is aimed at expanding, not restricting, the number of covered procedures, but it is not unheard of. We would also likely have to alter the Emergency Medical Treatment and Active Labor Act (EMTALA), 42 U.S.C. §§ 1395dd(a)–(d) (2006), which requires hospitals to either stabilize (give "treatment as may be required to stabilize the medical condition") or transfer patients that show up in emergency rooms to prevent patients repeatedly showing up at the ER to get immunosuppressive drugs they are not entitled to receive. As to U.S. prison populations, the Supreme Court has recognized a right to health care under the Eighth Amendment to the U.S. Constitution, Estelle v. Gamble, 429 U.S. 97, 104, 106 (1976), which may introduce some complications that mean that the state must supply immunosuppressive drugs during the length of incarceration. That said, because they cannot seek transplant tourism *while* incarcerated and still face the deterrent effects of my proposal *after release*, and because future prisoners are likely to be a small segment of all potential transplant tourists, the effect of this exemption is likely to be small.

costly follow-up care would dramatically reduce the amount of transplant tourism, leaving it as a viable option only for those who can self-finance not only the organ purchase itself but also all follow-up care.

Is such a response too draconian? I am told by those in the tissue transplant community that the most likely result of tissue rejection from failing to receive immunosuppressive drugs will be the need to remove the newly transplanted organ, but there is some chance of additional health complications including possibly death. Transplant and other physicians will no doubt find it difficult to watch patients undergoing tissue rejection they could prevent, especially in cases of serious complications where there is a threat that in some percent of cases this intervention will transform transplant tourism into an offense with a de facto death penalty.

Although I do not intend to try to fully resolve the matter here, I think there are a few responses to this kind of objection. First, if the rule is clearly publicized and applied only prospectively, the home country is likely to significantly deter transplant tourism—especially for those who are opting for it as an alternative to dialysis—such that there will be few (if any) on whom the "penalty" is actually imposed.

Second, unlike in capital punishment, one is not imposing death on an individual. Indeed, one is not even prohibiting access to immunosuppressive drugs or other therapies when purchased out-of-pocket. All the proposal does is set the terms of an entitlement to a particular kind of insurance coverage in the public or private sector. In the U.S. Medicare/Medicaid context and in universal health care systems where the question is one of rationing—we cannot cover all individuals for everything that will improve their health, and indeed in the United States immunosuppressive drugs are currently covered for only three years post-transplant by Medicare[138]—it merely gives those who have achieved their transplant by a criminal violation less priority.

The nexus is quite tight. The proposal does not give those who committed a crime a general diminution in priority for health care as a punishment, but instead treats their criminal acquisition of an organ as a specific forfeiture of their priority over other deserving claimants for state-funded health care related to that act. If transplant tourism is understood as a crime that victimizes the recipient, then we can understand paying for immunosuppressive drugs as allowing individuals to profit from their crimes. The law often provides tools to deprive those who commit crimes of their ill-gotten gains,[139] and although depriving someone who broke the law through transplant tourism of the *kidney itself* would be a kind of corporal punishment that takes matters too far, barring their insurer from covering their post-operative needs seems much more defensible.

---

[138] *See* Gill & Tonelli, *supra* note 135, at 588.

[139] *E.g.*, U.S. Sentencing Guidelines Manual §§ 5E1.1, 1.4 (orders of restitution and forfeiture for individuals) (2013).

Israel has already adopted a form of this approach by limiting insurer reimbursement for transplant tourism.[140]

In the private insurance market the matter is closer. Because the costs of dialysis are considerably larger over a patient's expected life than the cost of kidney transplant and immunosuppressive drugs,[141] insurers on their own are likely to prefer to cover transplant tourism rather than the alternative, unless mandated to do otherwise. Still, I think such an intervention has some merit. In the United States at least, the government's power to regulate what is covered by private health insurance is relatively unquestioned, and symmetry on the private and public system is desirable to avoid unfairness to those using the public system.

As an alternative or in addition, home countries could alter their existing prohibitions on organ sale and purchase such that they apply to extraterritorial activities of their citizens. In the United States for example, the National Organ Transplant Act of 1984, which prohibits the sale of kidneys and other organs, does not apply extraterritorially.[142] Therefore, if a U.S. citizen travels abroad to buy a kidney, his act is not prohibited by NOTA, and it is generally accepted that more general U.S. laws prohibiting trafficking do not apply to organ sales.[143] However, consistent with international and domestic law the United States could make NOTA's prohibition on organ sales applicable to those who purchase kidneys outside the United States as well, for reasons I have discussed in earlier chapters and other work.[144]

As we will see again in our discussion of travel for abortion, assisted suicide, and reproductive technologies in the next few chapters, detecting violations of domestic law that occur abroad is no easy feat, and it is important to design context-specific ways of implementing the prohibition. As prescriptions are required for immunosuppressive drugs, it is possible that doctors could be induced to monitor and report patients who have engaged in transplant tourism. As we will discuss in greater depth in Chapter 10, involving doctors in such reporting situations would constitute a not insignificant incursion into the doctor-patient relationship. However, doing so seems in keeping with other reporting duties already imposed upon physicians, including the abuse of children or the elderly.[145] Although one might try to distinguish those provisions by suggesting

---

[140] Francis L. Delmonico, *The Hazards of Transplant Tourism*, Clin. J. Am. Soc. Nephrology 249, 249 (2009).

[141] *See* Gill & Tonelli, *supra* note 135, at 588; Lara Rosen et al., *Addressing the Shortage of Kidneys for Transplantation: Purchase and Allocation through Chain Auctions*, 36 J. Health Pol. Pol'y & L. 717, 718 (2011).

[142] 42 U.S.C. § 274e (2007); *see* I. Glenn Cohen, *Can the Government Ban Organ Sale? Recent Court Challenges and Future of U.S. Law on Selling Human Organs and Other Tissue*, 12 Am. J. Transplantation 1983, 1984 (2012).

[143] *See* Francis & Francis, *supra* note 120, at 288.

[144] *See* Chapters 8 and 9 of this book; Cohen, *supra* note 55, at 1328–36.

[145] Furrow et al., Health Law 155 (2d ed. 2000) (collecting statutes).

that they are aimed at preventing future abuses by the patient of particular individuals, it is not clear why deterring such abuses before they happen is not an equally worthy goal. In any event, other reporting requirements, such as the requirement to report gunshot or other violent wounds to the authorities, are primarily about crimes that have already occurred,[146] and reporting suspected cases of transplant tourism would fit quite well with such obligations. Still a recent study of transplant physicians in the Netherlands suggests significant resistance by doctors there in reporting patients and the need for clearer legal and ethical rules authorizing such reporting in the specific case of transplant tourism.[147]

There are benefits and drawbacks to each of these methods of home country regulation. One the one hand, the fine and jail time associated with violating a version of NOTA with extraterritorial application avoids the "death penalty" objection of the insurance reform entirely. On the other hand, the insurance approach may offload some of the professional responsibility concerns of doctors onto insurers instead and may enable easier detection of malfeasance due to the existing requirements for submitting claims to private and public insurers. My main point here is that we should be pushing home countries to adopt one or both of these measures as a way of deterring transplant tourism.

D. Improving the Supply and Allocation of Organs Locally

Although the prior regulatory interventions I have discussed focus on deterring transplant tourism by punishing or otherwise dissuading buyers and brokers, it is essential to couple these approaches with measures aimed at increasing the supply of organs locally in patients' home countries, thereby diminishing demand for transplant tourism. This is a theme that has been recognized in the Declaration of Istanbul's principle that "jurisdictions, countries, and regions should strive to achieve self-sufficiency in organ donation by providing a sufficient number of organs for residents in need from within the country or region," and its proposals to "remove obstacles and disincentives to deceased organ donation," including by using national legislation to facilitate the organ recovery and the sharing of technologies and expertise between nations on the matter.[148] The

---

[146] *E.g.*, IND. CODE ANN. § 35-47-7-1 (West 1998) (requiring reporting of injuries caused by firearms).

[147] Ambagthseer and her colleagues interviewed seventeen Dutch "transplant physicians, transplant coordinators, and policy-makers," and found that some resisted reporting suspected organ sale due to their "professional secrecy oath," and said "they do not register cases of alleged transplant tourism because they are legally withheld from bringing out information about patients," with one nephrologist stating "[i]t's not my responsibility anyway" when asked if he had inquired about his patient's experience abroad. Frederike Ambagtsheer et al., *Cross-Border Quest: The Reality and Legality of Transplant Tourism*, 2012 J. TRANSPLANTATION Article ID 391936 (2012).

[148] *See* Declaration of Istanbul, *supra* note 111, at 3376–77.

relationship of transplant tourism and deficits in procurement has also been well recognized by those in the medical and policy communities.[149]

Improving rates of organ procurement is desirable in its own right quite apart from its effects on transplant tourism, and a full review of the feasibility and difficulties faced by such programs is beyond the scope of this book. For present purposes, I will just list the kinds of interventions that have been tried and deserve further support: changing the law as to the definition of death to make cadaveric donation easier by expanding the donor criteria to encompass donation after cardiac death (DCD) donors; moving from opt-in to opt-out ("presumed consent") regimes for cadaveric donation; improving organ yield and quality through better organ preservation and clinical management; encouraging donation through public messaging and education (in particular, focused on secondary school students); improving willingness to donate by creating organ chains and preferential receipt programs for those who have themselves been donors.[150] Developed and developing countries keen on reducing transplant tourism should adopt and encourage others to adopt these kinds of measures. However, to make progress on reducing organ tourism, such measures cannot stand alone.

IV. CONCLUSION

Transplant tourism is a tragic and increasingly common response to worldwide shortages of organs. The outlook one gets from the empirical data on these markets is bleak indeed: extremely poor men and women in the developing world are selling their kidneys to get out of bonded labor or secure a better future for their children. The brokers who manage the trade are often affiliated with organized crime and rely on misinformation, pressure, and sometimes threats to recruit sellers. Most but not all sellers regret their donation, in part because of the health and social effects that the transplantation brings to their lives and because they fail to achieve their objective of getting out of debt.

Confronted with this grim picture, it is understandable that many feel anger and a desire to intervene. However, I have shown that many of the bioethical arguments offered in favor of prohibiting transplant tourism—corruption, crowding out, coercion, and exploitation—are not up for the task. Luckily, there is a strong argument to justify prohibiting these practices that relates to deficits in information provided to sellers and their bounded rationality. The argument is not without its difficulties, but I think it is the soundest argument for moving forward.

---

[149] *See, e.g.*, Noël & Martin, *supra* note 132, at 647; Danovitch & Leichtman, *supra* note 61, at 1134; Jacob Lavee et al., *A New Law for Allocation of Donor Organs in Israel*, 375 LANCET 1131 (2009).

[150] For a good recent review of these kinds of measures, *see* Leo Roels & Axel Rahmel, *The European Experience*, 23 EUR. SOC. ORGAN TRANSPLANT. 350 (2011); Symposium, *Organs and Inducements*, 77 LAW & CONTEMP. PROBS. _ _ (forthcoming 2014).

Attempting to prohibit transplant tourism also raises a series of difficult regulatory design choices. Although I think that destination country domestic criminal enforcement ought to be continued, it has proven insignificant on its own. In this chapter, I have pressed in particular for increasing home country attempts to deter transplant tourism, along with the work of international societies and institutions and increased attempts to increase the supply of organs in tourists' home countries, and thus dampen the incentives for transplant tourism.

8

Medical Tourism and Ending Life: Travel for Assisted Suicide and Abortion

⌒ ——————————————————————————————————————

FOR SOME TRAVEL is a matter of life and death, while for others it is only a matter of death. Consider the story of Daniel James, whom we met in this book's preface.

Daniel played rugby for England Youth teams until he suffered a tragic injury during a training session in March 2007: spinal compression leading to dislocation of two vertebrae producing tetraplegia (paralysis from the chest down) and an inability to move his hand or fingers. Bringing some of the fortitude he had shown on the rugby pitch, Daniel was determined to prove that the diagnosis was incorrect and to make a substantial recovery. When he accepted the view of his doctors that such improvement was unlikely, he became suicidal, and began to express the wish that he had died in the accident. As his psychiatrist put it, as a "dynamic, active, sporty young man who loved travel and being independent, he could not envisage a worthwhile future for himself now." He attempted suicide several times, and in February 2008—after his third failed attempt—he contacted the Swiss clinic, Dignitas, for assistance in dying.[1]

Dignitas is a Swiss clinic founded in 1998 that, in a 2010 publication, claims to have "helped a total of 1,062 people to end their lives gently, safely, without risk and usually in the presence

---

[1] Except where otherwise noted, this description of Daniel James's case is adapted from Alexandra Mullock, *Commentary: Prosecutors Making (Bad) Law?*, 17 MED. L. REV. 290, 291–93 (2009).

of family members and/or friends."[2] As one academic has summarized the process by which Dignitas assists with suicide:[3]

(i) The individual requesting an assisted suicide must become a member of the organisation.

(ii) S/he must send a letter to Dignitas stating the reason for requesting an assisted suicide, accompanied by a medical file/report regarding diagnosis, prognosis, etc.

(iii) There is an initial assessment of whether Dignitas' guidelines are satisfied (the individual must be suffering from a fatal disease or have an unacceptable disability).

(iv) Dignitas finds one of their collaborating Swiss physicians who will state an initial willingness to write a prescription (usually about two and a half months after the initial request).

(v) An appointment with this physician is made and the physician conducts a detailed medical assessment of the individual. A period of around two months is usual between this and the next step.

(vi) A volunteer from Dignitas is present and assists during the final part of the assisted suicide process. Before the final act, the individual is asked again whether s/he still wishes to die and a declaration of suicide is signed.

(vii) The individual takes anti-vomiting medication, followed by Pentobarbital about half an hour later.

(viii) A representative of Dignitas informs the police that an assisted suicide has occurred.[4]

As of 2011 at least 107 British citizens (and as of 2007 more than eight hundred non-U.S. citizens altogether) have used the services of the Swiss group Dignitas to end their lives, with many more having become members.[5] Why did James and so many others turn to Dignitas and Switzerland as the place to end their lifes? There are several places in the world where assisted suicide is legally permitted, including Belgium,

---

[2] *DIGNITAS, How DIGNITAS Works, On What Philosophical Principles Are the Activities of This Organization Based?*, DIGNITAS 2 (June 2010), http://www.dignitas.ch/images/stories/pdf/so-funktioni-ert-dignitas-e.pdf.

[3] It is sometimes called "aid-in-dying," though I will use the more familiar term "assisted suicide," also used by Dignitas itself, while recognizing that for some proponents and opponents the choice of term is significant, even if not for me.

[4] Suzanne Ost, *The De-medicalisation of Assisted Dying: Is a Less Medicalised Model the Way Forward?*, 18 MED. L. REV. 497, 521–22 (2010) (footnotes omitted).

[5] *See* George P. Smith, II, *Refractory Pain, Existential Suffering, and Palliative Care: Releasing an Unbearable Lightness of Being*, 20 CORNELL J.L. & PUB. POL'Y 469, 514 n.332 (2011); Richard Huxtable, *The Suicide Tourist Trap: Compromise across Boundaries*, 6 BIOETHICAL INQUIRY 327, 329 (2009).

Colombia, the Netherlands, Switzerland, and the U.S. states of Montana, Oregon, and Washington.[6] What makes Switzerland unique is that certain Swiss cantons allow *non-Swiss residents* to use the assisted suicide services of organizations such as Dignitas.[7]

But back to Daniel. In May 2008 Dignitas accepted his application and arranged for a Swiss doctor to write a barbiturate prescription for Daniel's suicide. As required by Swiss law, prior to making that prescription, prior to the assisted suicide (planned for September 12, 2008) Daniel arranged to meet the doctor for an evaluation, despite his parents' attempt to dissuade him from going forward. In a July 2, 2008, report Daniel's psychiatrist wrote that Daniel "clearly understood that no other parties, be they professionals or family members wished him to pursue this course of action and was clearly aware that he could reverse his decision at any point. He remained firmly of the opinion that support from any agency would not be helpful for him or change his decision."[8] Further, the psychiatrist concurred with an earlier report from March 11, 2008, by a consultant psychiatrist that Daniel "has full capacity.... He is fully aware of the reality and potential finality of his decision, displays clear, coherent, logical thinking processes in order to arrive at his decision and had clearly weighed alternatives in the balance."[9] After repeated attempts to convince him to change his mind, Daniel's parents eventually accepted that their son was resigned to ending his life and began assisting him in arranging the suicide abroad. An unnamed family friend who had originally offered to arrange travel abroad to let Daniel see specialists who might assist in his recovery ultimately assisted Daniel's parents in arranging a flight to Zurich for suicide, although the friend also arranged a return flight to the United Kingdom in case Daniel changed his mind. With the flights booked, Daniel signed a declaration on August 27, 2008, witnessed by his doctor, stating his wish to travel to Switzerland for assisted suicide and his desire that his body be returned to England after he ended his life. On September 12, 2008, accompanied by his parents, Daniel traveled to Zurich, where (in the presence of his parents) a doctor assisted him in ending his life—apparently, according to postmortem blood samples, using a fatal dose of a barbiturate.

In the wake of this case, the Director of Public Prosecutions in the United Kingdom declined to prosecute Daniel's parents or the unnamed friend in assisting his suicide, despite a potential legal hook for doing so in English law. Was the Direction of Public Prosecutions right to decline to prosecute? If assisting suicide is illegal in a patient's

---

[6] *E.g.*, Winsor C. Schmidt, *Medicalization of Aging: The Upside and the Downside*, 13 MARQ. ELDER'S ADVISOR 55, 71 (2011).

[7] I. Glenn Cohen, *Circumvention Tourism*, 97 CORNELL L. REV. 1309, 1326 n.80 (2012); Alexandra Mullock, *Overlooking the Criminally Compassionate: What Are the Implications of Prosecutorial Policy on Encouraging or Assisting Suicide?*, 18 MED. L. REV. 442, 450 (2010).

[8] Mullock, *supra* note 1, at 292 (quoting *Decision on Prosecution—The Death by Suicide of Daniel James*, THE CROWN PROSECUTION SERVICE (Dec. 12, 2008), www.cps.gov.uk/news/nationalnews/death_by_suicide_of_daniel_james.html).

[9] Mullock, *supra* note 1, at 292 (quoting *Decision on Prosecution, supra* note 8).

home country can the home country prosecute someone who assists a patient to end his life in Switzerland, where the practice is legal? As a doctrinal matter? What about as a normative matter?

From the other end of the life cycle, consider this case.

Andrea, a twenty-one-year-old Irish woman, experiences an unwanted pregnancy. Abortion is illegal in Ireland. She therefore travels by boat to "Women on Waves," a floating abortion clinic anchored in international waters off the coast of Ireland. Ships in international waters are governed by the law of the country whose flag they fly, and this ship flies the flag of the Netherlands, where abortion is legal. Nevertheless, on Andrea's return to Dublin, the Irish government initiates a criminal process against her.[10] Can Ireland do so? As a doctrinal matter? What about as a normative matter?

This chapter is aimed at answering these questions. Each of these activities is a form of what I have elsewhere called "Circumvention Tourism"—traveling abroad for the express purpose of doing something illegal in the home country but not the destination country, a kind of regulatory arbitrage.[11] In the first part of this chapter I describe the existing practice and case law of travel for assisted suicide and abortion more fully. The second part of this chapter argues that home countries clearly have the power to apply their domestic prohibitions on abortion and assisted suicide to patients who travel abroad for these services even to places where it is legal. The third part argues that in the case of abortion there is a strong moral argument for applying their criminal prohibition abroad, but that the case is somewhat weaker for assisted suicide. A final part of this chapter briefly examines other ways that home countries might attempt to control their citizens who travel abroad for abortion and assisted suicide—the regulation of home country physician speech.

I. THE HISTORY AND CURRENT PRACTICE OF TRAVELING ABROAD FOR ABORTION AND ASSISTED SUICIDE

A. Abortion

Women currently travel abroad to circumvent domestic criminal prohibitions on abortion in countries such as Ireland, Portugal, and Poland, and have been doing so for a long time, though we lack good numbers on exactly how many, in part due to the clandestine nature of the travel and the social stigma of the activities in their home countries.[12]

---

[10] The facts of this hypothetical are stylized from a description of Women on Waves in Allison M. Clifford, Comment, *Abortion in International Waters off the Coast of Ireland: Avoiding a Collision between Irish Moral Sovereignty and the European Community*, 14 PACE INT'L L. REV. 385, 387–89 (2002).

[11] *See* Cohen, *supra* note 7.

[12] *E.g.*, Rosalind Dixon & Eric A. Posner, *The Limits of Constitutional Convergence*, 11 CHI. J. INT'L L. 399, 419 (2011).

For almost as long as this form of circumvention tourism has taken place, these women's home countries have struggled as to how and whether to regulate those abortions. Consider, for example, the case of West Germany before reunification. West German law, codified in 1976, made abortion a criminal offense unless the mother's health was in danger or in cases involving "(1) pregnancies which result from criminal activity, (2) an 'incurable defect' in the unborn child [or] (3) overall poor social conditions which would adversely affect pregnancy."[13] This criminal law extended to citizens' abortions performed abroad (i.e., "extraterritorially" in legal parlance), with penalties resulting in up to three years of imprisonment unless the woman previously received a "Beratungsschein," a certificate from a West German doctor.[14] Merely having such a prohibition on the books will deter some individuals from engaging in circumvention tourism, but the deterrence value is amplified when there is a real chance of detection and prosecution. For that reason, the West Germany customs officials performed gynecological examinations on women reentering West Germany; for example, one such examination was prompted when an official spotted a nightgown and a brochure for a Dutch abortion clinic in a woman's car.[15]

Ireland also has a long and complex history relating to its citizens traveling abroad for abortion. This development harkens back to September 1983, when Ireland adopted the Eighth Amendment to the Irish Constitution, now codified in Article 40.3.3, which provides that "[t]he State acknowledges the right to life of the unborn and, with due regard to the equal right to life of the mother, guarantees in its laws to respect, and, as far as practicable, by its laws to defend and vindicate that right."[16]

The Irish courts' most important confrontation with the impact of this constitutional amendment on travel abroad occurred in 1992 in the case of *Attorney General v. X* (the "X case").[17] The case's dramatic facts involved a fourteen-year-old rape victim who sought to travel to England to obtain an abortion but, when the victim's family contacted the Irish police to ask about collecting DNA evidence during the procedure to assist with the rape prosecution, the Attorney General petitioned for an injunction to prevent the travel.[18] The patient argued that her life was at stake because the prospect

---

[13] Karen Y. Crabbs, Note, *The German Abortion Debate: Stumbling Block to Unity*, 6 FLA. J. INT'L L. 213, 220 (1991).

[14] *Id.* at 222–23.

[15] *See id.* at 222–23 & n.106; *see also* Tamara Jones, *Wall Still Divides Germany on the Abortion Question*, L.A. TIMES, Oct. 19, 1991, at A3, *available at* http://articles.latimes.com/1991-10-19/news/mn-515_1_legal-abortions (reporting that a woman was taken into custody when sanitary napkins and a brochure from a Dutch clinic were found in her car as she was returning to West Germany from the Netherlands). Since reunification, more expansive judicial interpretations of abortion law, combined with State insurance covering the procedure for low-income women, have likely reduced the need for German women to engage in travel abroad for abortion. *See* Martha F. Davis, *Abortion Access in the Global Marketplace*, 88 N.C. L. REV. 1657, 1682–83 (2010).

[16] IR. CONST., 1937, art. 40.3.3.

[17] [1992] 1 I.R. 1 (H. Ct.) (Ir.).

[18] *Id.* at 6–7.

of giving birth under the circumstances made her suicidal, and thus abortion was permissible under Article 40.3.3's provision for "due regard to the equal right to life of the mother";[19] however, the Irish High Court found that the prospect of suicide did not qualify as a threat to the mother's life and enjoined the trip.[20] The Supreme Court ultimately reversed on the grounds that suicide was a threat to the mother's life, but the Court did not indicate whether the trip would have been permissible in the absence of a life-threatening condition.[21]

In response to the *X Case* and the fear that the European Court of Justice or the European Court of Human Rights would rule against the Irish abortion law, the Irish people passed the Thirteenth Amendment (often called the "Travel Amendment"), which provides that Article 40.3.3 "shall not limit freedom to travel between the State and another state."[22] Subsequent case law suggests that Irish women seeking abortion may travel abroad even in cases not involving threats to the mother's life.[23]

In the United States, the 1973 *Roe v. Wade* decision secured a constitutional right for American women to access abortions under certain circumstances and during certain periods of pregnancy.[24] Prior to *Roe*, though, when abortion remained banned in several states, individual U.S. states faced the question of whether to criminalize abortions sought outside of the state. Most of the cases and the commentary on them (and the possible future should *Roe* be curtailed) have focused on *intra*-national travel for abortion in the United States to more permissive U.S. states.[25] My focus in this chapter is on travel *abroad* for abortion and assisted suicide rather than travel to more permissive parts of the same country, though, especially in the normative discussion, we will see that some of the issues are similar in the two contexts.[26] But even as to *inter*national medical tourism, in the period prior to *Roe* at least one U.S. case considered the application of domestic criminal prohibitions on

---

[19] IR. CONST., 1937, art. 40.3.3.

[20] X, [1992] 1 I.R. at 12.

[21] Att'y Gen. v. X, [1992] 1 I.R. 16, 53–54 (S.C.) (Ir.).

[22] IR. CONST., 1937, art. 40.3.3; *see* Clifford, *supra* note 10, at 412.

[23] *See* D (A Minor) v. District Judge Brennan, the Health Services Executive, Ireland and the Attorney General, unreported judgment of the High Court, 9 May 2007 (holding that Ireland could not constitutionally prohibit a seventeen-year-old girl with anencephalic fetus from traveling to Britain for an abortion); *see also* Lisa Smyth, *From Rights to Compassion: The D Case and Contemporary Abortion Politics*, *in* THE UNBORN CHILD, ARTICLE 40.3.3 AND ABORTION IN IRELAND: TWENTY FIVE YEARS OF PROTECTION? (Jennifer Schweppe ed., 2008) (discussing case). Ireland also has tried to control counselor and physician speech regarding the possibility of abortion outside of the country, giving rise to a separate line of cases I discuss below.

[24] 410 U.S. 113, 166 (1973).

[25] *See* Edge v. State, 99 S.W. 1098, 1098 (Tenn. 1907) (involving intra-national travel for abortion from Tennessee to North Carolina); C. Steven Bradford, *What Happens if* Roe *Is Overruled? Extraterritorial Regulation of Abortion by the States*, 35 ARIZ. L. REV. 87, 100 (1993).

[26] For good discussions of travel for abortion and assisted suicide *within* the United States, *see, e.g.*, Brian H. Bix, *Physician-Assisted Suicide and Federalism*, 17 NOTRE DAME J.L. ETHICS & PUB. POL'Y 53–69

abortions performed outside of the United States. In *People v. Buffum* a California doctor arranged for an associate to transport pregnant women to Tijuana, Mexico, where another doctor performed abortions.[27] The court ultimately reversed a conviction under California criminal law because the "statute makes no reference to the place of performance of an abortion, and we must assume that the Legislature did not intend to regulate conduct taking place outside the borders of the state"; the court further noted that the prosecution had not charged the defendant with a conspiracy to violate Mexican abortion law.[28] Therefore, the court was able to resolve the question as a matter of statutory interpretation and prosecutorial charging decisions and not wade into the power of the California legislature to criminalize its citizens' going abroad for abortions or the propriety of criminal charges for conspiracy in California to procure an abortion abroad.

B. Assisted Suicide

Daniel James was just one of many non-Swiss citizens who have gone to Switzerland for assisted suicide; by one estimate from the United Kingdom alone there have been 107 UK citizens that have used Dignitas's services to end their lives.[29] The majority of the case law on the subject has emanated from the United Kingdom.

In one well-known European Court of Human Rights (ECHR) case, Dianne Pretty suffered from motor neuron disease, a degenerative illness that rendered her increasingly debilitated, and she sought confirmation from the Director of Public Prosecution (DPP) that her husband would not face prosecution were he to assist her in committing suicide by accompanying her to a Swiss suicide clinic.[30] The relevant criminal offense fell under the English Suicide Act of 1961, which stated that "[a] person who aids, abets, counsels or procures the suicide of another, or an attempt by another to commit suicide, shall be liable on conviction on indictment to imprisonment for a term not exceeding fourteen years."[31] When the DPP refused the confirmation, Pretty argued before the

---

(2003); Lea Brilmayer, *Interstate Preemption: The Right to Travel, the Right to Life, and the Right to Die*, 91 MICH. L. REV. 873, 898 (1993); Gerald L. Neuman, *Conflict of Constitutions? No Thanks: A Response to Professors Brilmayer and Kreimer*, 91 MICH. L. REV. 939, 944 (1993); Seth F. Kreimer, *"But Whoever Treasures Freedom…": The Right to Travel and Extraterritorial Abortions*, 91 MICH. L. REV. 907, 923 (1993).

[27] 256 P.2d 317, 319 (Cal. 1953).

[28] *Id.* at 320–22.

[29] *See* Smith, *supra* note 5, at 514 n.332. *See also* Hazel Biggs & Caroline Jones, *Tourism: A Matter of Life and Death in the United Kingdom*, *in* THE GLOBALIZATION OF HEALTH CARE: LEGAL AND ETHICAL ISSUES (I. Glenn Cohen ed., 2013) 164, 167 & n.10 (noting that it "is believed that upward of two hundred British citizens have travelled to Switzerland for an assisted suicide, and more than 650 British citizens have joined Dignitas" but also recognizing that "accurate figures are difficult to obtain because these acts give rise to potential criminal liability in the United Kingdom and there is no mechanism for reporting them.").

[30] Pretty v. United Kingdom, 2002-III Eur. Ct. H.R. 155, 161; *see also* Mullock, *supra* note 7, at 443–45 (discussing *Pretty* and the resulting guidelines from the DPP).

[31] Suicide Act, 1961, 10 Eliz. 2, c. 60, § 2 (Eng.).

House of Lords and then before the ECHR that the DPP's refusal infringed her rights under Article 8 of the European Convention of respect for private and family life.[32] Both courts rejected Pretty's claim: the Lords held that Article 8 did not include the right to control one's own death, while the ECHR found that any infringement of Article 8 could be justified as necessary to protect the interests of the State in preventing terminally ill people from being taken advantage of by those with an interest in encouraging their suicide.[33] The ECHR also found that a blanket ban was not disproportionate to the aim of public protection because past attempts to carve out exceptions had created the potential for abuse of the exception, particularly in cases with vulnerable individuals.[34]

A more recent English case involved Deborah Purdy, a multiple sclerosis sufferer who anticipated a time when she would want to end her life and applied to the High Court seeking an order that the DPP issue guidance clarifying that her husband would not face charges under the Suicide Act if he assisted her travel to Switzerland to die.[35] The High Court, noting the prior decision in *Pretty*, refused to issue the order, at which point Purdy took her case to the House of Lords.[36] The Lords upheld the criminal prohibition on assisted suicide but found a problem under Article 8 of the European Convention of fair warning and consistency of application regarding the Code for Crown Prosecutors, which outlines the principles under which prosecutors exercise their discretion.[37] They specifically found a failing in the fact that an individual assisting a loved one with suicide could not adequately determine from the Code before acting whether prosecutorial discretion would be exercised in favor or against the individual's prosecution.[38]

In response to the decision, in 2010, the DPP issued final guidelines listing sixteen factors in favor of and six against prosecution. Namely:

Public interest factors tending in favour of prosecution:
(1) The victim was under 18 years of age;
(2) The victim did not have the capacity (as defined by the Mental Capacity Act 2005) to reach an informed decision to commit suicide;
(3) The victim had not reached a voluntary, clear, settled, and informed decision to commit suicide;

---

[32] *See* R (Pretty) v. Dir. of Pub. Prosecutions, [2001] UKHL 61, [2002] 1 A.C. 800 (H.L.) (appeal taken from Eng.); Pretty, 2002-III Eur. Ct. H.R. at 174–76.

[33] R (Pretty), [2001] UKHL 61; Pretty, 2002-III Eur. Ct. H.R. at 174–76.

[34] *See* Pretty, 2002-III Eur. Ct. H.R. at 176.

[35] R (Purdy) v. Dir. of Pub. Prosecutions, [2009] EWCA (Civ) 92, [4]–[6] (Eng.).

[36] *See id.* at [61]; Kate Greasley, *R(Purdy) v DPP and the Case for Wilful Blindness*, 30 OXFORD J. LEGAL STUD. 301, 305 (2010).

[37] *See* R (Purdy) v. Dir. of Pub. Prosecutions, [2009] UKHL 45, [2010] 1 A.C. 345 (H.L.) [73]–[74] (appeal taken from Eng.); Greasley, *supra* note 36, at 305.

[38] *See* R (Purdy), [2009] UKHL 45, [2010] 1 A.C. [73]–[74].

(4) The victim had not clearly and unequivocally communicated his or her decision to commit suicide to the suspect;

(5) The victim did not seek the encouragement or assistance of the suspect personally or on his or her own initiative;

(6) The suspect was not wholly motivated by compassion; for example, the suspect was motivated by the prospect that he or she or a person closely connected to him or her stood to gain in some way from the death of the victim;

(7) The suspect pressured the victim to commit suicide;

(8) The suspect did not take reasonable steps to ensure that any other person had not pressured the victim to commit suicide;

(9) The suspect had a history of violence or abuse against the victim;

(10) The victim was physically able to undertake the act that constituted the assistance him or herself;

(11) The suspect was unknown to the victim and encouraged or assisted the victim to commit suicide by providing specific information via, for example, a website or publication;

(12) The suspect gave encouragement or assistance to more than one victim who were not known to each other;

(13) The suspect was paid by the victim or those close to the victim for his or her encouragement or assistance;

(14) The suspect was acting in his or her capacity as a medical doctor, nurse, other healthcare professional, a professional carer [whether for payment or not], or as a person in authority, such as a prison officer, and the victim was in his or her care;

(15) The suspect was aware that the victim intended to commit suicide in a public place where it was reasonable to think that members of the public may be present;

(16) The suspect was acting in his or her capacity as a person involved in the management or as an employee (whether for payment or not) of an organisation or group, a purpose of which is to provide a physical environment (whether for payment or not) in which to allow another to commit suicide.

Public interest factors tending against prosecution:

(1) The victim had reached a voluntary, clear, settled, and informed decision to commit suicide;

(2) The suspect was wholly motivated by compassion;

(3) The actions of the suspect, although sufficient to come within the definition of the offence, were of only minor encouragement or assistance;

(4) The suspect had sought to dissuade the victim from taking the course of action which resulted in his or her suicide;

(5) The actions of the suspect may be characterised as reluctant encouragement or assistance in the face of a determined wish on the part of the victim to commit suicide;

(6) The suspect reported the victim's suicide to the police and fully assisted them in their enquiries into the circumstances of the suicide or the attempt and his or her part in providing encouragement or assistance.[39]

It remains to be seen whether further litigation will find this guidance document sufficient under Article 8 of the European Convention.

In the next parts of this chapter I consider whether as to abortion and assisted suicide, home countries have the power under international law to extend criminal law prohibitions in the home country (if they exist) to their citizens' activities in the destination country where the act may be legal under destination country law.

II. CAN HOME COUNTRIES CRIMINALIZE THE ACTS OF THEIR CITIZENS SEEKING ASSISTED SUICIDE OR ABORTION IN DESTINATION COUNTRIES WHERE THOSE ACTS ARE LEGAL?

If a home country prohibits abortion or assisted suicide at home, then, as a matter of international law, is it forbidden, required, or permitted as a matter of discretion to criminalize those activities by its citizens when they occur in a destination country (such as Switzerland for assisted suicide) where the act is legal? In this part I will show that home countries have discretion to do so and are neither forbidden nor required to do so under international law.

Before this showing it is important to be clear what question I am and am not answering. Imagine, like the UK's Suicide Act we saw above, a home country had a statute prohibiting a citizen from assisting in a suicide or seeking an abortion. The question I am asking is whether, under international law, it is permissible for the home country to expand the geographic scope of that statute such that it claims prescriptive jurisdiction over the citizen's doing the same domestically prohibited activity in a destination country where the activity is permitted.

Thus I am focusing on what is called "jurisdiction to prescribe" or "prescriptive jurisdiction."[40] Such jurisdiction consists of the power "to prescribe rules"—for example, to make it a crime in Ireland for an Irish citizen to procure an abortion in the

---

[39] Mullock, *supra* note 7, at 444–45.

[40] *See, e.g.*, Comm. of Ministers, Recommendation of the Committee of Ministers to Members States on the Amended Model Plan for the Classification of Documents Concerning State Practice in the Field of Public International Law, Recommendation No. R (97) 11, 64 (1997) (describing jurisdiction of the state); Vaughan Lowe, *Jurisdiction, in* INTERNATIONAL LAW 335, 337, 340 (Malcolm D. Evans ed., 2d ed. 2006).

Netherlands—where the local territorial law does not make the act illegal.[41] This jurisdiction is in contrast to "enforcement jurisdiction," for example, the ability of Ireland in the same circumstance to violate Dutch sovereignty and march into the Netherlands to arrest the Irish citizen for a crime made illegal by Irish criminal law.[42] Even when a country has and exercises its power to prescribe, it typically does not have jurisdiction to enforce, and instead relies on extradition processes to get the offender back into the country's sovereign territory and custody.[43]

When I am discussing extraterritoriality here I am focusing on prescriptive jurisdiction. It is commonplace under existing international law doctrines for a country to have prescriptive jurisdiction to declare an extraterritorial activity of its citizen a crime under its domestic law but *not* to have jurisdiction to enforce the law by arresting its citizen in the foreign country. Because many patients who travel abroad to have an abortion or to assist a loved one with a suicide intend to return to their home countries after engaging in prohibited activities, prescriptive jurisdiction, even unaccompanied by enforcement jurisdiction, remains a powerful tool for deterring and punishing circumvention tourism. Although detection of and the ability to prove extraterritorial circumvention is imperfect, as the history of State attempts to regulate travel for abortion and assisted suicide discussed above show, many countries have been able to deter, detect, and punish these violations.

With those clarifications in mind, we are now ready to examine under what conditions the home country can assert extraterritorial criminal prescriptive jurisdiction over home country citizens in cases of travel abroad for abortion and assisted suicide.

A. Bases for Prescriptive Jurisdiction

Under customary international law, prescriptive jurisdiction may be premised on several different possible bases. The easiest basis for asserting that jurisdiction over a home country citizen who travels abroad for an abortion or to assist a suicide is the "Nationality Principle"—permitting a State to assert jurisdiction over the acts of its citizens wherever they take place.[44] Citizenship or nationality of a person might be the result of being born in the country, having a parent who is a citizen, or being naturalized.[45] As a leading treatise observes, "[f]or practical purposes,... States remain free to decide who are their

---

[41] *See, e.g.*, Lowe, *supra* note 40, at 338.

[42] *See id.*

[43] *Id.* at 339. Sometimes these two jurisdictions are further contrasted with "jurisdiction to adjudicate," or "curial jurisdiction," which involves the right of courts to receive and try cases referred to them. *Id.*

[44] Lowe, *supra* note 40, at 345. For an in-depth discussion of nationality-based criminal jurisdiction, *see generally* Geoffrey R. Watson, *Offenders Abroad: The Case for Nationality-Based Criminal Jurisdiction*, 17 YALE J. INT'L L. 41 (1992).

[45] Lowe, *supra* note 40, at 346–47.

nationals"; it notes, however, exceptions that prove the rule, such as "[t]he mass imposition of nationality upon unwilling people, or nationality obtained by fraud or corruption."[46]

In the cases of abortion and assisted suicide abroad I have discussed the Nationality Principle would be enough. My focus has been on prescriptive jurisdiction on home country citizen *patients* who travel abroad for abortion or home country citizens who assist a loved one in ending his or her life in the destination country. I am thus not focused on attempts to assert extraterritorial jurisdiction over the *physician* who provides the services. In the rare case where the physician who performs the procedure in question in the destination country happens to be a home country citizen the Nationality Principle will also support prescriptive jurisdiction. In the more common case where the physician is a citizen of the destination country (or a third country) it is much less likely that the assertion of extraterritorial prescriptive jurisdiction would be proper. Moreover, most extradition treaties prohibit a country from allowing the extradition of its own citizens,[47] such that, in cases where the home country criminalizes the actions of the abortion provider or a provider who assists a suicide who is a destination country citizen, extradition will not be possible. Unlike the patients who travel abroad (or their family members), destination country physicians are not that likely to travel to the patients' home countries, in particular if they know criminal charges are pending against them there, such that as a practical matter even if a home country could assert prescriptive jurisdiction over the destination country physician the home country is unlikely to be able to actually punish the foreign provider. [48]

Although for these reasons attempts to assert prescriptive criminal jurisdiction over foreign citizens who participate in performing abortion or assisting in suicide in the destination country are less likely to be fruitful, under international law there are several possible bases for asserting that jurisdiction I will briefly review. Moreover, these theories will also provide additional bases for prescriptive jurisdiction over home country citizens in these cases, though the Nationality Principle will usually be sufficient and the most straightforward theory.

"Subjective territorial jurisdiction" comprehends crimes that are initiated in one's home territory but completed in another territory, such as loading a bomb in the United States onto a plane that will explode in Israel.[49] This basis may apply in our cases when referrals to foreign physicians are involved or when much of the planning and arrangements are done on home soil.

---

[46] *Id.* at 343.

[47] William Magnuson, *The Domestic Politics of International Extradition*, 52 Va. J. Int'l L. 839, 879–80 (2012).

[48] *See also* Rohith Srinivas, *Exploring the Potential for American Death Tourism*, 13 Mich. St. U. J. Med. & L. 91, 117 (2009) (arguing that home country prosecution of Swiss physicians is "implausible" because it "would damage diplomatic relations between interdependent countries").

[49] Lowe, *supra* note 40, at 343; *see also* Restatement (Third) of the Foreign Relations Law of the United States § 402(1)(a) (1987).

"Objective territorial jurisdiction" refers to the opposite case: a crime initiated abroad but completed in one's home territory.[50] Some countries, most notably the United States, have sought to extend this jurisdiction through an "effects doctrine," especially asserting antitrust jurisdiction against foreign companies based on acts done entirely outside the United States that had economic repercussions on the price of a commodity in the United States.[51] Perhaps prescriptive jurisdiction could be premised on this basis in some of our cases as well—one fewer child born in the home country or one fewer adult returning home and thus paying taxes, etc.—although admittedly this seems to be a stretch.

A third additional basis, "passive personality," represents the flip side of the National Principle, stating that a home country has jurisdiction based on the fact that the victim (rather than perpetrator) is a national of that country.[52] The principle is controversial, and a leading treatise suggests that its increased acceptance is category specific: although it is "widely tolerated when used to prosecute terrorists," it is far from clear that it would be found "acceptable if used to prosecute, for example, adulterers and defamers."[53] Passive personality may be used to justify extending extraterritorially sanctions on assisting suicide on the theory that it protects the home country citizen whose life is ended. Relying on passive personality in the abortion case would be more controversial and would depend on treating the fetus as a citizen, a matter on which there is no established precedent. I return to a parallel issue on the normative side below.[54]

---

[50] United States v. Yousef, 327 F.3d 56, 91 n.24 (2d Cir. 2003); RESTATEMENT, *supra* note 49, § 402; Lowe, *supra* note 40, at 343.

[51] United States v. Aluminum Co. of Am., 148 F.2d 416, 443, 447–48 (2d Cir. 1945) ("On the other hand, it is settled law… that any state may impose liabilities, even upon persons not within its allegiance, for conduct outside its borders that has consequences within its borders."). Various foreign courts in other countries have resisted the extension of jurisdiction based on the effects doctrine. *See, e.g.*, Rio Tinto Zinc Corp. v. Westinghouse Elec. Corp. [1978] 1 A.C. 434 (H.L.) 437–38 (appeal taken from Eng.).

[52] Lowe, *supra* note 40, at 351.

[53] *Id.* at 352.

[54] Customary international law also recognizes two other bases for jurisdiction I think are less helpful here. First, it recognizes "universal jurisdiction" over crimes "so heinous as to be universally condemned by all civilized nations." *Yousef*, 327 F.3d at 91 n.24; *see* Lowe, *supra* note 40, at 348. Piracy was the traditional example, though premised less on the heinous nature of the crime than on the idea that activities on the high seas made them likely to evade jurisdiction so any State that could apprehend the pirates could try them. *See* Lowe, *supra* note 40, at 348. To simplify slightly, in recent years this category has been extended to cases more along the "heinous" line, including slave trade, war crimes, and genocide. RESTATEMENT, *supra* note 49, § 404. The use of this basis in our cases seems unlikely. Although the termination of fetuses or those seeking assisted suicide may be seen as bad things, at most they seem more in line with "ordinary" murder than the especially heinous crime of genocide, for which universal jurisdiction has been (controversially) invoked.

Second, the "protective principle" allows the State to assert jurisdiction when "essential interests of the State are at stake" and jurisdiction is necessary for the State to preserve itself. Lowe, *supra* note 40, at 347; *see* RESTATEMENT, *supra* note 49, § 402(3); *Yousef*, 327 F.3d at 91 n.24. Although its exact borders are fuzzy, and the United States has pushed its boundaries, *see* RESTATEMENT, *supra* note 49, § 402 cmt. f; Lowe, *supra* note 40, at 347–48, I do not think the principle can plausibly be used for prescriptive jurisdiction in our cases.

B. Limitations on Jurisdiction to Prescribe

As discussed, home countries will usually have a basis for prescriptive jurisdiction over extraterritorially performed abortions or assisted suicides on their citizens. However, that is not enough, as the Restatement (Third) of the Foreign Relations Law of the United States cautions, "a state may not exercise jurisdiction to prescribe law with respect to a person or activity having connections with another state when the exercise of such jurisdiction is unreasonable."[55] The Restatement then suggests that whether jurisdiction is unreasonable should be determined by "evaluating all relevant factors, including, where appropriate" (thus not exhaustively), a set of eight factors.[56] Although the outcome of any multifactor, highly standard-like test is hard to predict, there is a strong argument in each of my case studies that jurisdiction is reasonable. In the next few paragraphs, I explain factor by factor:

(1) *"[T]he link of the activity to the territory of the regulating state, i.e., the extent to which the activity takes place within the territory, or has substantial, direct, and foreseeable effect upon or in the territory."*[57] Although the health care activity itself takes place extraterritorially, abortions and assisted suicide result in one fewer member of society being born or staying alive.

(2) *"[T]he connections, such as nationality, residence, or economic activity, between the regulating state and the person principally responsible for the activity to be regulated, or between that state and those whom the regulation is designed to protect."*[58] In all of these cases, the "perpetrator" (the person seeking the abortion, assisting the suicide) is a citizen and at least one "victim" is a home country citizen (though the abortion case is more controversial for reasons I discuss below).

(3) *"[T]he character of the activity to be regulated, the importance of regulation to the regulating state, the extent to which other states regulate such activities, and the degree to which the desirability of such regulation is generally accepted."*[59] The end of life, fetal or adult, is extremely important in most countries that have criminalized these acts and also heavily regulated by criminal law and health law regulating health care professionals, facilities, etc. How "desirabl[e]" such regulation would be is, of course, in the eyes of the beholding country, but even regimes that are relatively permissive with regard to abortion or assisted

---

[55] RESTATEMENT, *supra* note 49, § 403(1).

[56] *Id.* § 403(2).

[57] *Id.* § 403(2)(a).

[58] *Id.*, § 403(2)(b).

[59] *Id.*, *supra* note 49, § 403(2)(c).

suicide typically regulate things such as timing, information provision, age of consent, mental competency evaluation, and waiting periods.[60]

(4) *"[T]he existence of justified expectations that might be protected or hurt by the regulation."*[61] Given that the activity is illegal at home, the circumventing patient is unlikely to have justified expectations in accessing the service.[62] Also, unlike cases of medical tourism for legal services such as hip replacements or cardiac bypass (and perhaps services illegal in some home countries such as reproductive technologies), the destination country's provider base is unlikely to plausibly claim that providing abortion or assisted suicide to foreigners is a significant part of the medical system's total business.

(5) *"[T]he importance of the regulation to the international political, legal, or economic system."*[63] It is unclear what this means in our cases.

(6) *"[T]he extent to which the regulation is consistent with the traditions of the international system."*[64] The application of this factor to our cases is also not obvious. There have certainly been other instances in which the international system allowed home countries to criminalize the activities of their citizens in destination countries where the practice is legal.[65] For example, the U.S. PROTECT Act levies either a fine, thirty years in prison, or both for any U.S. citizen or permanent resident "who travels in foreign commerce, and engages in any illicit sexual conduct" including "any commercial sex act... with a person under 18 years of age." [66]

(7) "[T]the extent to which another state may have an interest in regulating the activity; and... [(8)] the likelihood of conflict with regulation by another state." [67] Of the factors, these two seem to provide the most likely basis for arguing against reasonableness, yet the argument does not seem strong. This is especially true when, as is my focus, the extraterritorial criminalization

---

[60] *See, e.g.*, Planned Parenthood v. Casey, 505 U.S. 833, 844–69 (1992) (plurality opinion) (reviewing such regulation of abortion for constitutionality); Alexander R. Safyan, *A Call for International Regulation of the Thriving "Industry" of Death Tourism*, 3 LOY. L.A. INT'L & COMP. L. REV. 287, 301–03 (2011) (reviewing the many regulations in place in Oregon and Washington States' assisted suicide legislation).

[61] RESTATEMENT, *supra* note 49, § 403(2)(d).

[62] This analysis is somewhat formalistic and circular: Until we know whether international travel to circumvent is permitted or prohibited, it is hard to say what patients reasonably expect.

[63] RESTATEMENT, *supra* note 49, § 403(2)(e).

[64] *Id.*, § 403(2)(f).

[65] Jeffrey Meyer has provided an illustrative list of the numerous instances where the United States has criminalized extraterritorial conduct on the basis of its citizens' activity. Jeffrey A. Meyer, *Dual Illegality and Geoambiguous Law: A New Rule for Extraterritorial Application of U.S. Law*, 95 MINN. L. REV. 110, 182–83 (2010). He also provided other lists premised on effects test prescriptive jurisdiction and still others that are "geoambiguous" in their scope. *See id.*

[66] 18 U.S.C. §§ 2423(b), (c), (f)(2) (2006).

[67] RESTATEMENT, *supra* note 49, §§ 403(2)(g), (h).

focuses the conduct of a home country citizen, not of the destination country doctor or other provider, which dilutes the interest of the destination country. Moreover, countries can avoid these conflicts by adopting the solution that all countries other than Switzerland have used regarding assisted suicide: requiring that the person seeking to use the service be a resident of the destination country.[68] Unlike the extraterritorial extension of a country's antitrust or fair labor standards, for example,[69] these cases entail minimal interference with the existing practice in the destination country: one need not remake competition policy or wage and hour regulation in the destination country. The industry can persist as is; it merely becomes inaccessible to foreigners. In any event, given the extent to which the other factors favor reasonableness, even an adverse finding on this factor is unlikely to make a difference.

One useful point of comparison is the PROTECT Act covering child sex tourism, which has been upheld by several U.S. circuit courts as consonant with both U.S. and international law.[70] Thus, I conclude that criminalizing circumvention tourism for abortion or assisted suicide will not run afoul of the balancing approach of the Restatement.[71]

---

[68] *See, e.g.,* Alexander R. Safyan, *A Call for International Regulation of the Thriving "Industry" of Death Tourism,* Loy. L.A. Int'l & Comp. L. Rev. 287, 304 (2010–2011) (discussing the residency requirements in place to use assisted suicide in the U.S. states of Oregon and Washington); *id.* at 307–08 (examining whether safeguards in place that appear to prevent foreigners from using assisted suicide in the Netherlands can be circumvented); *cf.* Brian Bix, *Physician Assisted Suicide and Federalism,* 17 Notre Dame L.J. Ethics & Pub. Pol'y 53, 60 (2003) (noting in the *intra*state context of travel from one U.S. state to another for assisted suicide that a "state might thus create a residency, or duration-of-residency requirement, both to prevent unwanted travel by outsiders merely to take advantage of an in-state benefit, and to lessen concerns and hostility of other states based on the way the state's law and benefits might undermine the policies of other states").

[69] *See* cases cited *supra* note 51.

[70] *See* United States v. Tykarsky, 446 F.3d 458, 470 (3d Cir. 2006); United States v. Clark, 435 F.3d 1100, 1103–04 (9th Cir. 2006); United States v. Bredimus, 352 F.3d 200, 205–07 (5th Cir. 2003); United States v. Han, 230 F.3d 560, 563–64 (2d Cir. 2000).

[71] The same conclusion follows under the U.S. Supreme Court's jurisprudence on the subject. At times, that jurisprudence sounded an even more permissive note than the balancing test. In *Hartford Fire Insurance Co. v. California,* the Court held that the Sherman Act applied extraterritorially to cover conspiracies by British reinsurance companies affecting the U.S. market that were not illegal in the United Kingdom. 509 U.S. 764, 769–70 (1993). The Court's reasoning was that "[n]o conflict exists, for these purposes, 'where a person subject to regulation by two states can comply with the laws of both,'" and the British companies could still comply with U.S. law without putting themselves in violation of British law. *Id.* at 798–99 (quoting Restatement, *supra* note 49, § 403 cmt. e). Similarly, in the medical tourism context, it appears that no law requires destination country providers to provide abortions, female genital cutting, assisted suicide, or reproductive technology services to noncitizens of the destination country. Later cases in this line, however, have clarified that the jurisprudence is meant to match the Restatement balancing test approach. *See, e.g.,* F. Hoffmann-La Roche Ltd. v. Empagran S. A., 542 U.S. 155, 161–62 (2004) (applying the balancing test to analyze the extraterritorial reach of the Sherman Act).

In sum, this analysis shows that existing customary international law will permit, but not require, home countries to criminalize circumvention tourism abortion and assisted suicide. There is also a separate question of whether, independent of international law, domestic (and in the case of the European Union, supranational) law obligates, forbids, or gives the home country discretion to criminalize the circumvention tourism of its home country citizens. This analysis can only be done on a country-by-country basis, but here I will just note my conclusions as to the United States (though I hope to publish that analysis on another occasion): the U.S. government faces no structural constitutional obstacles to criminalizing the circumvention tourism of its citizens. It is far less clear, though, whether an individual U.S. state could attach criminal liability to the activities of its citizens abroad that violate the state's existing criminal prohibitions.[72]

III. THE NORMATIVE QUESTION: SHOULD HOME COUNTRIES CRIMINALIZE THEIR CITIZENS' ABORTION AND ASSISTING SUICIDE WHEN DONE IN DESTINATION COUNTRIES WHERE THE ACT IS LEGAL?

Now that we know that home countries can extend prescriptive jurisdiction over home country citizens who pursue abortions or assist suicide abroad, in this part of the chapter I want to examine whether they *should* do so as a matter of political philosophy and bioethics.

One way into this problem would be to take a stand on whether home countries should criminalize abortion or assisted suicide simpliciter, that is to treat the domestic and extraterritorial criminalization as presenting an identical question and resolving both in tandem. That is not my approach here—huge amounts of ink have been spilled on the question, and I am not sure part of a chapter in a book on medical tourism will convince many readers to change their mind on these matters. Instead, I want to take a different approach in this chapter asking readers to assume (for the sake of argument) that the domestic prohibition in each of these case studies is both legally and normatively well-grounded. My goal is to avoid "re-litigating" the validity of these domestic prohibitions in either a normative or doctrinal sense. Instead, I ask—conditional on the existence, lawfulness, and validity of these prohibitions—whether the home country *should* take the further step of criminalizing the use of these services by its citizens *outside* the home country. Of course, what makes a domestic criminal prohibition on

---

[72] By structural I have in mind the Commerce Clause, Dormant Commerce Clause, Foreign Affairs preemption, etc. I say "structural" because for abortion in particular, other U.S. constitutional law doctrines might be relevant, but those would apply equally to criminalizing the conduct domestically. *See, e.g.,* Planned Parenthood v. Casey, 505 U.S. 833, 860 (1992) (plurality opinion).

something such as abortion either unlawful or immoral is an extremely contested question,[73] but one I purposefully bracket here. For readers with deep investments on this issue, it may require considerable mental effort to try to determine what they would think about extraterritorial application if they believed that something such as the abortion prohibition really is normatively valid and lawful in the United States;[74] nonetheless, I think the payoff is great enough to beg this forbearance.

I will argue that assuming their domestic prohibition is valid and lawful, there is a strong argument that countries with prohibitions on abortion should criminalize abortions by their citizens abroad, even where it would be legal in the destination country, and thus that these home countries ought to alter their laws to incorporate extraterritorial conduct to the extent those domestic laws are to the contrary (as is true in the case of Ireland, discussed above, among other countries). For assisted suicide I also think that those countries that criminalize providing that assistance at home should also criminalize it when done by a home country citizen in a destination country even where it is a destination country where that would be legal. That said, I think the case against extraterritorial criminalization in the assisted suicide case is a little less strong than in the abortion case.[75]

I am one of the few bioethics and law scholars to have written on this issue. One of the others, who will serve as my intellectual interlocutor for this part of this chapter, is Guido Pennings, whose work I always admire and learn from even where we disagree. Professor Pennings has advocated for a notion he calls "external tolerance" that he applies to travel abroad for abortion or assisted suicide; in this concept he argues that "a certain norm is applicable and applied in society as wanted by the majority while simultaneously the members of the minority can still act according to their moral view by going abroad," that "[a]llowing people to look abroad demonstrates the absolute minimum of respect

---

[73] *See, e.g., id.* at 850 ("Men and women of good conscience can disagree, and we suppose some shall always disagree, about the profound moral and spiritual implications of terminating a pregnancy, even in its earliest stage.").

[74] I am, myself, one of the readers for whom such forbearance is in part requested, in that in my published writing I have often defended the abortion right in many circumstances. *See, e.g.,* I. Glenn Cohen & Sadath Sayeed, *Fetal Pain, Abortion, Viability and the Constitution,* 39 J. L. MED. & ETHICS 235 (2011); I. Glenn Cohen, *The Flawed Basis behind Fetal-Pain Abortion Laws,* WASH. POST, Aug. 1, 2012, *available at* http://www.washingtonpost.com/opinions/the-flawed-basis-behind-fetal-pain-abortion-laws/2012/08/01/gJQASow8PX_story.html?hpid=z4.

[75] To be clear, when I say "extend extraterritorially" or "criminalize the extraterritorial conduct of their citizens abroad," I am imagining that the home country legislature will be explicitly extending its domestic prohibition extraterritorially by statute, as the U.S Congress did in the PROTECT Act criminalizing child sex tourism abroad. 18 U.S.C. § 2252(B)(b) (2012). This is a different question about whether to construe an *ambiguous* statute as having extraterritorial scope; for that the Supreme Court appears to require "a clear statement of extraterritorial effect" in order to construe a statute as applying extraterritorially. Morrison v. Nat'l Austl. Bank Ltd., 130 S. Ct. 2869, 2883 (2010). For a discussion of the way in which the same issue is handled in UK law, *see* Michael Hirst, *Suicide in Switzerland: Complicity in England?,* 5 CRIM. L. REV. 335, 336–37 (2009).

for their moral autonomy."[76] For Pennings, circumvention tourism becomes a kind of modus vivendi, which "prevents a frontal clash of opinions which may jeopardise social peace."[77] Although the values of accommodation and social peace are seductive, I will ultimately argue against this approach and show why home countries with prohibitions on abortion and assisted suicide should apply those prohibitions to the same conduct when done in a destination country where the practice is legal.

In prior work, taking inspiration from interest-balancing approaches to civil conflict of laws, I have developed a more general framework for determining when a home country should extend extraterritorially its criminalization of a domestic medical procedure.[78] I have argued a number of factors should be considered in constructing a rule-based approach. Central among them are: (1) What type(s) of criminal law justifications underlie the home country's domestic prohibition? For example, is the prohibition aimed at physical-harm prevention, attitude modification, or distributive justice? (2) Is the "victim" the home country seeks to protect a citizen of the home country, the destination country, a third country, or a stateless person? (3) If the "victim" is a citizen of the destination country, is the victim represented in governance decisions?

In this chapter, though, I am focused only on extraterritorial criminalization as to circumvention tourism for abortion or assisted suicide. I will offer two separate but related arguments—one more directly grounded in political theory and one emanating from a thought experiment—for the following principle:[79] *if* the home country criminalizes territorially (i.e. domestically) an act causing serious bodily harm and the reason for the prohibition is victim-protection, *and* the perpetrator and victim are both citizens, *then* the home country should extend its criminal prohibition extraterritorially to circumvention tourists *even when* the same conduct is permitted under the law of destination

---

[76] Guido Pennings, *Reproductive Tourism as Moral Pluralism in Motion*, 28 J. MED. ETHICS 337, 340 (2008). Richard Huxtable has made a similar argument as to travel for assisted suicide, explicitly relying on Pennings's work, and arguing for non-prosecution in the name of "pluralism." Huxtable, *supra* note 5, at 334 ("If we continue to presume that the originating state is broadly prohibitive, then that must constitute a considerable victory for opponents of the practice. Such a position necessarily excludes the proponents, including those who would themselves wish to take up the option if available. As assisted suicide is indeed available elsewhere (subject to the satisfaction of certain criteria) it seems unduly heavy-handed of the jurisdiction of origin to seek to prevent or penalise those who seek to take up the offer.").

[77] *Id.*

[78] *See generally* Cohen, *supra* note 7.

[79] The motivation for offering the two separate arguments is not just that two arguments are better than one, but also because some are skeptical of thought experiments and intuition pumps as a tool of normative reasoning. Some have suggested that these methods risk giving normative weight to what may be mere artifacts of social norms. *E.g.*, LOUIS KAPLOW & STEVEN SHAVELL, FAIRNESS VERSUS WELFARE 60–81 (2002). Although there is a long tradition of relying on this method in bioethics (and indeed common law reasoning), I recognize that this is a serious concern. I have partially addressed this risk here by not adopting thought experiments that are too outlandish, by testing the principles I derive against real world cases, but also by mixing in a second argument based on top-down political theorizing with the bottom-up casuistic reasoning.

country. I will show that this principle provides a prima facie case for criminalizing circumvention tourism for abortion and assisted suicide.

To be sure, as I have argued elsewhere, this principle may not exhaust the cases where extraterritorial criminalization is normatively justified or mandated, but it does provide a sufficient condition for extraterritorial criminalization in these cases. After offering positive arguments for the principle, I consider some general exceptions to this principle (cases where even on my theory the general principle does not apply), and then consider arguments for exceptions/objections to the principle as applied to abortion and assisted suicide.

I should be very clear as to what I am doing and not doing in this part of the chapter. I am asking whether home countries that criminalize certain medical activities at home should do so abroad as well, and whether turning a blind eye to circumvention tourism is problematic. I am not attempting to offer a grand theory of international relations that answers when home countries should be *permitted* to criminalize these activities abroad. Instead I am taking the current answer offered by the law of international relations discussed above, which would permit prescriptive jurisdictional criminalization over these activities, as given, and asking whether home countries have a moral reason to use that power. The former would be an interesting and worthwhile project, but it is not mine here.

A. A Prima Facie Argument for Extraterritorial Criminalization of Abortion and Assisted Suicide

i. A Thought Experiment: Murder Island

My first argument for the principle emanates from a thought experiment I call "Murder Island":[80]

Imagine there exists a foreign island nation called "Murder Island." Murder Island has laws very similar to those in the United States, with one important exception: by an act of

---

[80] Although "Murder Island" is hypothetical, there is a family resemblance to a real world case: the United States has made certain activities that are criminal in its territory, such as murder by or against a U.S. citizen, also illegal in Antarctica where the United States has no territorial prescriptive jurisdiction. *See* Lowe, *supra* note 40, at 348–49. Apparently, however, the United States has not extended its prohibition against murder in the same way in another legal vacuum—outer space itself as opposed to "territorial space," or on an American shuttle or the International Space Station where there is governing criminal law. *See* James A. Beckman, *Citizens without a Forum: The Lack of an Appropriate and Consistent Remedy for United States Citizens Injured or Killed as the Result of Activity above the Territorial Air Space*, 22 B.C. Int'l & Comp. L. Rev. 249, 253 (1999); R. Thomas Rankin, *Note, Space Tourism: Fanny Packs, Ugly T-Shirts, and the Law in Outer Space*, 36 Suffolk U. L. Rev. 695, 716 (2003). Antarctica, however, is a place without a particular government or law, not a place where the territorial government has passed a law declaring murder is not a criminal offense. Beckman, *supra*, at 253. It is to such a hypothetical jurisdiction that I now turn.

its parliament, Murder Island has decreed that murder is not a crime on Murder Island.[81] Imagine that two U.S. citizens, Benjamin Linus and John Locke, travel together from the United States to Murder Island. After touring some of the ruins, Ben stabs John in the heart, killing him instantly.

Let us stipulate that John's presence on the island was voluntary in at least a shallow sense—he was not transported there at gunpoint. Perhaps he was asleep when the boat docked or was merely unaware that the island's name was rather telling as to its legal system, although he certainly did not consent to being murdered. If you find it helps you to imagine that there was no meaningful consent, you can alter the thought experiment such that John was a very young child whose consent we would not typically count, or in a coma during the journey, etc. When I discuss assisted suicide, below, I will consider relaxing this condition with potentially more robust forms of voluntariness and consent. By contrast, in abortion we will see that there is no prospect for the consent/voluntariness of the victim.

Notwithstanding the fact that the action was lawful by Murder Island's own legal code, I think we would all conclude that it would not be wrong for the United States to seek to extend its criminal law extraterritorially to cover Ben's act in this instance. Indeed, I think our intuitions support the view that the United States should extend its criminal law to Ben's actions. As I show in political theoretical analysis below, this intuition is very strong, in part because of what I will call the "double coincidence of citizenship"—that both the perpetrator and the victim are U.S. citizens.

The double coincidence of citizenship idea has a family resemblance to what Brainerd Currie called in civil conflict of laws a "false conflict" or "false problem" case in which both the plaintiff and defendant were domiciliaries of a common state and he believed

---

[81] I specify that this is the key divergence between the two countries' laws to focus the example, though it is possible there would also have to be attendant differences in conspiracy law, wrongful death law, etc. I do not think anything turns on whether those differences are there too. Although I find that making the thought experiment turn on the divergence on whether murder is criminalized simpliciter produces a crisper thought experiment, some might worry about how such a society would function in the real world. For example, would its population annihilate itself? For those who are bothered by such practical questions, one can easily substitute a more elaborate version of Murder Island: murder is allowed only on December 11 (my birthday), only of children under the age of four, only of persons over the age of fifty-five, or only in the narrow context of the honor killing of young women. For my purposes, any of these variants will do in generating a strong intuition that the United States should criminalize extraterritorially when a murder is committed by one U.S. citizen against another. For this reason, I will stick to the simpler and less elaborate version, but invite readers to substitute one of these variants if they prefer.

I am fully aware that Murder Island is about as easy a case as I could derive for extraterritorial application. My decision to begin by "stacking the deck" is neither accidental nor insidious. I begin with a kind of "pole star" case for two reasons. First, it immediately shows that an extreme pluralist or territorialist view that the home country is *never* justified in extending its prohibition in the face of a contrary rule of the destination country is incorrect. Second, by beginning with a case in which our normative intuitions are fairly certain, we can begin to map the ways in which the harder real world cases diverge from it and critically examine which divergences should matter.

that the state of their common domicile's law should govern as the only state with a true interest.[82] My claim about the importance of the double coincidence of citizenship persists even if we grant an objection made by Currie's critics that the foreign State does have an interest in the availability of these procedures to noncitizens.

The underlying intuition about Murder Island should remain unchanged even if I embellish the thought experiment by imagining that the reason the island has adopted its stance on murder is because of its religious and cultural tradition, which leads the islanders (rather bizarrely from our point of view) to see murder as a way of reaching the island's spirits and honoring the murdered in the afterlife via the murders. That their lack of a prohibition is based on a different, benign, religiously motivated view of murder seems immaterial as to whether the home country should criminalize the murder of its citizen by another one of its citizens abroad. Indeed, it seems that this conclusion persists even if we specify that the Murder Island residents' religious beliefs are such that they actively desire for the U.S. citizens to murder each other on the island and that their theology dictates that the more murders are committed on the island, the more the island gods will bless them with health and good crops. Or perhaps the residents' reasoning is more altruistic: they view Ben and John's home country as denying an important way of worshipping G-d and wish to provide a refuge for U.S. citizens as well. These beliefs strike me as good reasons Murder Island may not want the United States to extend its criminal prohibition extraterritorially, but they seem to fail as sufficient reasons that the United States, from its own perspective, should refrain from extending its criminal prohibition of murder to killings of one of its citizens by another.

Thus, Murder Island presents a strong prima facie case that the home country should criminalize circumvention tourism in the case of murder, subject to some exceptions discussed below.

ii. A Political Theoretical Account

Let me complement the "Murder Island" thought experiment with a political theoretical argument for extraterritorial extension in the case of murder with a more political theoretical account.

At least one justification that underlies the home country's prohibition on murder is that it is wrong for U.S. citizens to murder other citizens. The wrongfulness of that act (to speak

---

[82] *See generally* Brainerd Currie, *Married Women's Contracts: A Study in Conflict-of-Laws Method*, 25 U. CHI. L. REV. 227 (1958) (discussing this concept). A good example of this approach in practice comes from the New York Court of Appeals' decision in *Neumeier v. Kuehner*, which suggests that where the plaintiff and defendant shared a common domicile, its law as to guest-host immunity ought to apply even when the accident occurs in another state with the opposite rule in place. *See* 286 N.E.2d 454, 458 (1972). I prefer to use my term "double coincidence of citizenship" to emphasize that we are talking about criminal law, and that I am not intending to import all of the intellectual baggage of this choice-of-law approach. I also wish to connect this notion more deeply to political theories regarding the power of the State to criminalize conduct in the first place.

retributively) and the desirability of preventing it (to speak in a key of deterrence) seem to attach irrespective of whether the murder takes place on U.S. territorial land, in outer space, or on Murder Island. Ben has done something wrong that deserves punishment, and John has wrongfully suffered injuries that we would have wished to prevent.

Ben benefits from U.S. diplomatic responsibility and U.S. laws that provide for his protection when abroad.[83] Thus, there is nothing unfair about the United States asking him to abide by its law when abroad. Had Ben wanted to avoid the sanction, he had an "Exit" option in that he could have renounced his U.S. citizenship and taken up Murder Island citizenship. That he failed to do so and that he wants to enjoy the advantages of U.S. law in many regards demand that he agree to also be subject—at least prescriptively—to the U.S. criminal prohibition on murder. He must take the bitter with the sweet. One might object of course that although "Exit" is theoretically possible it is not easily doable by many, and I will discuss this issue in greater depth below.

That is the argument in broad strokes. It can be reformulated more precisely in a more communitarian, liberal, or distributive justice version, though the strongest version of the argument would borrow from the various traditions and argue for an overlapping consensus between them.

Communitarian: For the communitarian, the key value is community membership, and it is contextualized community traditions rather than universalist reasoning that form the backbone of political principles and personal identity.[84] For this reason, the propriety of extending law on the basis of citizenship ties seems, if anything, more natural than doing so merely on the basis of territorial presence. As Lea Brilmayer puts it when discussing general jurisdiction in civil procedure in the intra-national context, "[c]ommunitarianism leads naturally to a view that interstate authority should be based on community membership" because "the community would have an interest in regulating the individual regardless of the location in which the individual acts and without concern for the victim's residence," such that "[a]s long as that individual is a member of the community, the communitarian should be satisfied that the state has a legitimate concern with the dispute."[85]

---

[83] *Cf.* Kreimer, *supra* note 26, at 923 ("Unlike the United States' diplomatic responsibility to provide for [a U.S. citizen's] protection when [that citizen] visit[s] Mexico, Pennsylvania has no similar responsibility—or capacity—to ensure [such] protection, whether by direct intervention or by threat of war, when [that citizen] visit[s] California.").

[84] *See, e.g.,* ALASDAIR MACINTYRE, WHOSE JUSTICE? WHICH RATIONALITY? 6–11 (1988) (setting out the communitarian approach); MICHAEL WALZER, SPHERES OF JUSTICE: A DEFENSE OF PLURALISM AND EQUALITY 31–32 (1983) (similar); Lea Brilmayer, *Liberalism, Community, and State Borders,* 41 DUKE L.J. 1, 9–10 (1991) (discussing the view that "[t]he community is both the chief source of political norms and an important source of personal identity").

[85] Brilmayer, *supra* note 84, at 11. Religious law presents a useful analogy in understanding the communitarian conception. In determining whether a person transgressed Jewish law, for example, what matters is that person's membership in that religious community; the territorial location where the person committed the transgression is irrelevant. *See, e.g.,* Yuval Merin, *Anglo-American Choice of Law and the Recognition of Foreign Same-Sex Marriages in Israel—On Religious Norms and Secular Reforms,* 36 BROOK. J. INT'L L. 509, 528 (2011).

Indeed, the legal philosopher Antony Duff has suggested that a form of communitarianism underlies, as a jurisprudential matter, the sovereign's right to punish at all. He argues that "national legislatures should not begin with the idea that they have good reason to criminalise all moral wrongdoing, and then see reasons to limit their jurisdictional ambitions"; rather, they should "begin with the idea that only a certain range of wrongdoings are even in principle their business" and that the key marker is citizenship: we "say that we are responsible as citizens, to our fellow citizens."[86] In other words, "[t]he wrongs that properly concern a political community, as a political community, are those committed within it by its own members."[87] On this account, the territorial coverage of domestic criminal law follows from the citizenship relation and not vice versa. That is, "in the case of crimes against [our] citizens, that the perpetrator is answerable to [our] polity for wrongs against [our] members; and, in the case of crimes [committed by our] citizens, that any member of [our] polity is responsible to [our] polity for any such wrongs that he commits."[88] Indeed, as Duff's statement suggests, the propriety of extraterritorial criminalization is at its zenith on this account when it is crimes by our citizens against our citizens—the double coincidence of citizenship.

Liberal: The more liberal version of the argument for extraterritoriality here might be put in terms of the John Stuart Mill's "Harm Principle,"[89] a more social contractualist form, or some combination of the two.

The Harm Principle account is somewhat analogous to the international law doctrinal "effects test" reasoning (as well as its U.S. civil procedural equivalent).[90] It emphasizes that a murder on Murder Island has negative effects within U.S. territorial boundaries. The victim will typically have friends, family, and an employer at home; at the very least,

---

[86] R.A. Duff, Criminal Responsibility, Municipal and International 12 (2006) (unpublished manuscript) (on file with author).

[87] *Id.* at 13.

[88] *Id.* at 15. One challenge for Duff's view is the protection of noncitizens in U.S. territory. Duff says that "the criminal law of any decent polity also covers visitors to, and temporary residents of, the polity as well as its citizens" and that saying so "is not to revert to a geographical or territorial account of jurisdiction" in that "what makes normative sense of jurisdiction is still the law's character as the law of a particular polity, whose members are its primary addressees"; it is just that "its law can also bind and protect visitors to the polity and its territory." *Id.* at 14–15. I am not sure that I am entirely convinced by this, but, for present purposes, I need not choose between the territorial and citizen conceptions; it is enough to sustain my argument that the citizenship strand standing alone can ground extraterritorial criminalization, even if it supplements rather than replaces the territorial conception. Further, even some proponents of the territorial conception think it might support extraterritorial application of domestic criminal law based on perpetrator or victim citizenship, although the logic is somewhat opaque. *See* Alejandro Chehtman, *Citizenship v. Territory: Explaining the Scope of Criminal Law*, 13 NEW CRIM. L. REV. 427, 442 (2010) (arguing that "universal jurisdiction over international crimes can also be satisfactorily explained on the basis of territorial considerations").

[89] JOHN STUART MILL, ON LIBERTY 13 (Elizabeth Rapaport ed., 1978) (1859) ("That the only purpose for which power can be rightfully exercised over any member of a civilized community, against his will, is to prevent harm to others. His own good, either physical or moral, is not a sufficient warrant.").

[90] Brilmayer, *supra* note 84, at 14–16 (discussing this possibility in relation to extraterritorial application of Title VII, which is the statute that covers employment discrimination in the United States).

the victim will have owed the United States duties relating to citizenship. Although this approach would treat as a sufficient trigger the murder of one citizen by another citizen, the perpetrator's citizenship is not strictly necessary, as the effects on the home country produce the tie.

The second more social contractualist liberal route focuses more clearly on the perpetrator's citizenship. It follows a Lockean social contract theory mode "whereby one assents to cast his lot with others in accepting the burdens as well as the benefits of identification with a particular community" and therefore "cedes to its lawmaking agencies the authority to make judgments... [that] strik[e] the balance between his private substantive interests and competing ones of other members of the community."[91]

This double coincidence of citizenship implies conflicting claims of two U.S. citizens—Ben, who, despite the social contract, wants to be exempted from U.S. law, and John, who would like its protection. As I will discuss below this may be an important divergence from the assisted suicide case where the most direct "victim," the one seeking aid in dying, does *not* want the benefit of the home country's prohibition. Here, Ben can only be excused from the obligations of U.S. law by forcing John to forgo that law's benefit. On the other side of the ledger, Murder Island does have an interest in the matter—it just seems like a relatively weak one. To use Wesley Newcomb Hohfeld's famous terminology, the imposition of a duty by the United States on its citizens not to murder one another clashes with Murder Island's grant of a privilege to those within its territory to murder.[92] Allowing the United States to extraterritorially apply its domestic law subordinates Murder Island's grant of privilege as to American citizens present in its domestic territory who murder.

Indeed, as I suggested above, Murder Island may want to be a haven for those whom it views as refugees from unjust American laws prohibiting the proper worship of G-d through murder,[93] or Murder Island may affirmatively enjoy economic benefits from the murder of U.S. citizens by U.S. citizens—perhaps the Island's knife makers enjoy the extra revenue. But from the perspective of the United States, when the crime is murder, and where there exists a double coincidence of citizenship, the island's claim that the interests behind its privilege ought to trump the duty of the United States seems unlikely to prevail. The United States has not sought to impose this duty on every person irrespective of citizenship. It has not sought to march in to Murder Island and seize its citizens. Instead, it has focused its prescriptive jurisdiction on U.S. citizens who murder other U.S. citizens.

---

[91] Harold L. Korn, *The Choice-of-Law Revolution: A Critique*, 83 COLUM. L. REV. 772, 799 (1983).

[92] *See* Wesley Newcomb Hohfeld, *Some Fundamental Legal Conceptions as Applied in Judicial Reasoning*, 23 YALE L.J. 16, 30 (1913) (describing as "jural opposites" the concepts of privilege and duty).

[93] *Cf.* Brilmayer, *supra* note 26, at 889–92 (arguing that a clash of interests occurs in the intrastate abortion context not only where one State requires and the other State forbids abortion but also where one State wants to promote autonomy by allowing women to choose abortion).

Given the home country's retributive and deterrence interests in punishing the murder, and given its political theoretical bona fides in demanding that Ben subordinate himself to its laws as its citizen, the case for extraterritorial application seems strong. As Gerald Neuman puts it with beautiful flourish, "[I]n the international context, there is a name (even mentioned in the Constitution) for giving the claims of territorial situs absolute priority over the claims of citizenship. The name is 'treason.' "[94]

Distributive Justice: Apart from the liberal and communitarian approaches, there is also an argument for extraterritorial criminalization based on distributive justice concerns. To the extent that freedom from punishment for murder is a kind of "good" that particular individuals find desirable, it seems unfair to allocate it based on the ability to travel abroad to Murder Island.

In the reproductive tourism context, Guido Pennings has responded to this kind of argument by suggesting that "this is a strange argument when it is advanced by those who installed the restrictive legislation in the first place" because "[i]f the prohibitive laws were abolished, neither poor nor rich people would need to go abroad."[95] Richard Huxtable has also relied on Pennings response to deflect similar claim as to assisted suicide.[96]

As the application to Murder Island shows, however, Penning's response somewhat misses the point: it would be desirable from the home country's perspective to end *all* instances of the prohibited activity, and it adds insult to injury that only the rich can circumvent.

Thus, at least as to murder, there is a strong political theoretical argument for extraterritorial criminalization. One might nonetheless object to this argument, especially the social contract elements, by suggesting that the voluntariness of the tacit consent underlying the argument may be questionable. As Seth Kreimer puts this kind of "voluntariness" objection in the *intra*-national context, "[w]hen an impoverished woman in Mississippi declines the opportunity to escape Mississippi citizenship by abandoning her family, friends, community, and job, does she thereby 'voluntarily' consent to application of Mississippi's law, or does she only bow to necessity?"[97] Another way of putting this is that "Exit" is a nice idea, but many individuals who will need to travel for circumvention tourism for abortion or assisted suicide or other things do not have the resources to effectuate Exit nor do they necessarily have another country willing to accept them.

---

[94] Neuman, *supra* note 26, at 944.

[95] Pennings, *supra* note 76, at 122.

[96] Huxtable, *supra* note 5, at 335.

[97] Kreimer, *supra* note 26, at 928. The locus classicus of this argument is Hume, who wrote that "[w]e may as well assert that a man, by remaining in a vessel, freely consents to the dominion of the master, though he was carried on board while asleep, and must leap into the ocean and perish the moment he leaves her." David Hume, *Of the Original Contract, in* HUME'S MORAL AND POLITICAL PHILOSOPHY 356, 363 (Henry D. Aiken ed., 1948); *see also* RONALD DWORKIN, LAW'S EMPIRE 192–93 (1986) (rejecting the argument that "we have in fact agreed to a social contract... by just not emigrating when we reach the age of consent").

As a descriptive matter this claim may in many cases be true, but as an argumentative gambit it fails. This argument seems to prove too much for present purposes, however, in that it gives reason to cast doubt not only on the propriety of criminalizing the murder by one's citizen of another of one's citizens in the extraterritorial case but within the country's territorial borders as well, as the hypothetical Mississippian cannot escape U.S. borders either. That is, if the fact that "Exit" may be difficult or impossible to effectuate stands as an obstacle to justifying extraterritorial criminalization it is just as much an obstacle to justifying domestic criminalization.

Putting that to one side, in response to this "voluntariness" objection to actual consent, one standard political theory move is to shift to an account of hypothetical (or sometimes more accurately labeled "normative") consent of the original contract entered into by the founders of the commonwealth: if a State "meets the terms of such a legitimate original contract, it has a claim to obedience."[98] As Joseph Raz has put it, "[I]f there is a common theme to liberal political theorizing on authority it is that the legitimacy of authority rests on the duty to support and uphold just institutions."[99] If citizens can justly be bound by a hypothetical social contract not to murder fellow citizens at home, why should that social contract not also apply to murders against fellow citizens abroad?

Against this kind of move, in the *intra*-national context, Kreimer has objected that "the obligation to 'support' just institutions does not carry any necessary implications as to the geographical scope of the duty" and thus

> [i]t is entirely consistent with the proposition that, as long as I do not actively seek to undermine the just institutions of my home state—as by committing treason or shooting a cannon into its territory or discharging noxious fumes across its border—my obligation to "support" my home institution is liquidated by my obedience to its laws within its boundaries and my payment of taxes while I reside there.[100]

However, murdering one's fellow citizen on Murder Island much more obviously undermines the hypothetical social contract: members of the society are being killed. Indeed, it seems mysterious why a social contract governing citizen murder of citizens within the territory would not extend to the same acts outside the territory, as our ties to one another as equal citizens seem like a firmer ground for an obligation not to murder than our mere transitory presence in the same territorial space. As I argue below, most of the abortion and assisted suicide circumvention tourism cases share this feature with

---

[98] Kreimer, *supra* note 26, at 929.

[99] Joseph Raz, *Authority and Justification, in* AUTHORITY 115, 138 (Joseph Raz ed., 1990).

[100] Kreimer, *supra* note 26, at 929–30.

Murder Island: the goal of prohibiting acts by citizens causing serious bodily harm to citizens.[101]

Kreimer also has a second reply in the *intra*-national context: "when a woman travels from Mississippi to California, this theory imposes upon her a duty to 'support' California as well" such that "[w]hen California tells her that abortions are a constitutional right, she owes deference to its 'just judgments' as well as those of her home"; in addition, "[t]he theory of just institutions provides no obvious way to decide which judgment is correct." This argument trades on an artifact of the intra-national case that seems largely absent for the international one: that in a federal system, one's allegiance is split between the national and potentially multiple state sovereigns. By contrast, in our case, the U.S. citizen, while on Murder Island, may have actually consented not to violate the destination country's laws but owes no allegiance to Murder Island to commit murder while there.

Still another response to the voluntariness objection focuses on reciprocity:[102] criminalizing our citizens' activities abroad can be justified by "general" reciprocity in the enjoyment of the benefits of one's home country citizenship while abroad, including diplomatic protection. Indeed, the reciprocity claim is stronger still because here it is "specific" and symmetrical—a U.S. citizen may not murder or be murdered by another U.S. citizen while traveling abroad.

In the U.S. case, one could reach quite a different conclusion about the *intra*-national medical tourism case as opposed to the international one for a number of additional reasons. The identification of a citizen of one of a series of coequal states is a much thinner conception for social contract or communitarian purposes than is the identification as a citizen of a nation; however, too strong a notion of state citizenship might undercut national citizenship in an undesirable way for a federalist model of a country such as the United States.[103] The reciprocity-based notion of one's home country protecting one while traveling abroad is also more strained in the intrastate context. Pennsylvania does not have the same responsibility or capacity to protect its citizen while that citizen travels in California that the United States does when its citizen travels to Mexico.[104]

---

[101] *Id.* at 930. From a political theory point of view this may be a reason to limit the scope of extraterritorial criminalization to serious bodily harm, something I examine in greater depth in the next chapter.

[102] *Cf.* Burnham v. Superior Court, 495 U.S. 604, 637–38 (1990) (Brennan, J., concurring) (suggesting that four days of enjoying California's roads and other amenities was sufficient to justify a California court's assertion of personal jurisdiction on a non-Californian plaintiff).

[103] *See* Kreimer, *supra* note 26, at 918, 927. On some contested accounts, the United States has no robust historical tradition regarding criminal activities done in another State, which might also be relevant. *See, e.g., id.* at 925, 935, 936; Mark D. Rosen, *"Hard" or "Soft" Pluralism?: Positive, Normative, and Institutional Considerations of States' Extraterritorial Powers,* 51 St. Louis U. L.J. 713, 738 (2007). The tradition of criminalizing activities done in other countries may be better established.

[104] *See* Kreimer, *supra* note 26, at 923. One colleague usefully suggested to me that the obligations of a citizen to her home country while abroad are like the obligations of individuals who put "away messages" on their e-mail to senders. I like this analogy because I think it nicely captures the notion that the obligations of citizenship fall on a continuum. Although there are some duties that as a professor I could reasonably disclaim through an

Moreover, in the *intra*state U.S. context, it might be thought that an explicit part of the vision of our horizontal federalism is that different states can reach different conclusions about the appropriate scope of criminal prohibition in the absence of a national consensus because it is desirable that states should act as laboratories in the sense that Justice Brandeis famously exposited unless and until the national government reaches a conclusion as to the "right" answer.[105] Such a view may be rooted in the importance of providing opportunities to participate in subfederal democratic lawmaking in areas important to the people or in its ability to make more room for diverse political commitments.[106] By contrast, in the international context, no higher authority can tally the local experiments and decide when to step in to end them, and, given that the home country has already reached its own consensus domestically across its territory, it is not clear that the other points transfer.[107] To be fair, however, there is also something cutting in the other direction: the costs of Exit are lower in the intrastate context, where one can relocate to another state and still maintain all the perquisites of national citizenship.

Still, both top-down political theoretical reasoning and bottom-up thought experiment reasoning seem to converge on the claim that the United States has very good reasons to extend its murder prohibition to murders by U.S. citizens of U.S. citizens taking place on Murder Island.

iii. When Extraterritorial Criminalization Is Inappropriate

I have offered a prima facie case for extraterritorial criminalization of the crime of murder in my Murder Island hypothetical. Nevertheless in some instances, even as to this example, I think a home country should not criminalize the conduct of someone such as Ben. In particular, in other work in greater depth I have suggested three types of cases where extraterritorial criminalization would be a bad idea: (1) retaliation, (2) safety valve, and (3) peripheral divergence.[108] Here I will just briefly summarize these exceptions.

"away message" in my absence (e.g., meeting with groups of students for lunch or moderating a panel of outside speakers), there are other duties that I could not disclaim whether or not I am out of the office (e.g., entering grades for students in a timely fashion). The same is true when a citizen is out of the *country*; although there are some obligations of citizenship that the State might not reasonably demand its citizens comply with while abroad, the obligation not to impose serious physical harm on a fellow citizen seems to be one a State might reasonably demand, which is why extraterritorial application of these kinds of prohibitions is most justified.

[105] New State Ice Co. v. Liebmann, 285 U.S. 262, 311 (1932) (Brandeis, J., dissenting) ("It is one of the happy incidents of the federal system that a single courageous State may, if its citizens choose, serve as a laboratory.").

[106] *See* Rosen, *supra* note 103, at 749 (listing these "three distinct considerations that have been well rehearsed by federalism scholars").

[107] Although these distinctions are quite sharp when applied to the United States, they are less clear when applied to a home and destination country that are themselves part of a supranational governance structure, such as medical tourism from one European Union (EU) Member State to another. As supranational governance ties between home and destination countries thicken, the distinction between the intra- and international cases seems less sharp.

[108] Cohen, *supra* note 7, at 1349–56.

Retaliation: If an extraterritorial prohibition were in place and enforced in our hypothetical case, it is at least possible that prosecuting Ben upon his return to the home country would ruffle some feathers with the island's government and cause diplomatic tension. If the threat of retaliation were large enough, perhaps we might think differently. Imagine that Murder Island had nuclear weapons aimed at our capital and that the island credibly threatened to launch if we prosecuted Ben. For the most extreme deontologists who would view us as duty-bound to punish Ben for what he has done, the fact may be immaterial. For those who have at least some consequentialist leanings for which the goods of retribution and deterrence have to be traded off against other goods, I suspect that we would think the home country should back down in such a case.

Our reactions to intermediate cases—the loss of cooperation with Murder Island's authorities on hunting down wanted terrorists, significant trade sanctions on goods, the threat that the destination country will apply a reciprocal rule on their citizens' activities in our country, etc.—are presumably also intermediate. The best we can say is that the more serious the crime involved, the more serious a threat of retaliation would need to be to sway us *not* to extend the law extraterritorially.

To the extent that actual prosecution rather than the extraterritorial assertion of prescriptive jurisdiction would prompt retaliation, the home country might in theory assert prescriptive jurisdiction but reign it in through prosecutorial discretion rules keyed to the threat of retaliation. Doing so would achieve some of the deterrence value even if the discretion were not frequently used, especially if an "acoustic separation" were maintained where potential offenders would not know how much fear of retaliation would diminish actual prosecution.[109]

Safety Valve: Second, imagine that the following (admittedly fanciful) state of the world is true: although we as the home country legislature are convinced that murder should be prohibited, our populace's support of that prohibition is more fickle. It turns out that our well-heeled elites, who are able to spend on elections and lobbying, view murder much more favorably. Were the elites to face an outright prohibition on murder at home and abroad that stood inexorably together, they would direct their resources toward successfully reversing the domestic prohibition as well. However, because they are able to perform murders on Murder Island, they are willing to let the domestic prohibition remain in place and satisfy their desire by travel to Murder Island for the occasional murder.

I call this problem the "safety valve" effect because the existence of circumvention medical tourism acts as a safety valve that releases pressure to eliminate the domestic prohibition. Indeed, this is the exact kind of modus vivendi that Pennings and others discussed above advocate for some forms of circumvention tourism.

---

[109] *See* Meir Dan-Cohen, *Decision Rules and Conduct Rules: On Acoustic Separation in Criminal Law*, 97 HARV. L. REV. 625, 630 (1984) (describing a model of acoustic separation whereby the law sets "conduct rules" for the general public and "decision rules" for public officials).

Again, for consequentialists the case is relatively straightforward: imagine that, in a world in which the United States criminally prohibits murder but does not extraterritorially extend the prohibition to Murder Island, one hundred American citizens are murdered each year. By contrast, if we eliminate the circumvention tourism loophole, the elites would abolish the domestic prohibition as well, and a thousand (or ten thousand or a hundred thousand) Americans would now be murdered. On standard consequentialist views, the numbers matter, and if our goal is to minimize the number of murders, we should oppose criminalizing circumvention tourism. On deontological views, as I have discussed in greater depth in other work, things are murkier. Further, on some political process theories, the fact that the domestic prohibition would itself be repealed if we forced its extension extraterritorially is not a good reason to oppose that extension.

Of course, it is hard to know when (if ever) a safety valve effect will obtain. The transaction costs of lobbying the domestic government to change its position would have to be lower than the cost of simply changing one's citizenship to a country that does not prohibit the act; one has to know and be able to coordinate one's desire to change the law with other like-minded members of the elite far enough in advance of one's desire to actually do the activity (which, in the cases of abortion and assisted suicide tourism seem less likely to obtain). Moreover, it is conceivable that allowing the procedures extraterritoriality might increase pressure rather than release it—if enough citizens are traveling to permissive regimes and becoming familiar with the way they function, this might undermine domestic home country support for the prohibition.[110]

Peripheral Divergences: The version of Murder Island I presented has a "core" or "central" conflict between the home country and the island's murder rule: whether murder will be criminalized *vel non*. We can imagine more "peripheral" differences too. Suppose that Murder Island's rule on murder is just like the United States' but with one exception: to succeed on a self-defense defense, the United States requires an individual seeking to use the defense to take an opportunity to retreat before the use of deadly force, while the island has carved out an exception to that rule when the setting is the physical home, such that one is under no obligation to escape one's home.

Suppose that U.S. citizen Ana Lucia Cortez—despite having an opportunity to retreat—fatally wounds U.S. citizen Shannon Rutherford after Shannon attacks Ana Lucia in her vacation home on the island. Although the act would be criminal in the United States, it is explicitly excluded from criminal liability on Murder Island. Should the United States seek to prescriptively extend its criminal prohibition on murder to

---

[110] *See, e.g.*, Kimberly M. Mutcherson, *Open Fertility Borders: Defending Access to Cross-Border Fertility Care in the United States, in* The Globalization of Health Care: Legal and Ethical Issues 148, 161 (I. Glenn Cohen ed., 2013) ("If it is right that countries feel less constrained to liberalize their laws because they know that their citizens can access care elsewhere, in keeping with the earlier discussion about accessing CBFC as an act of resistance, the United States can think of its open borders as a safe haven for those who would be denied fairness and equality in their countries of origin.").

Ana Lucia in this instance? The intuition here is quite different from the starting Murder Island case for two related reasons.

First, I have not asserted that Murder Island has no interest in the United States refraining from criminalizing U.S. citizen's actions in these cases; where the difference was between murder being lawful or not lawful, this interest was not enough to motivate the United States to refrain from protecting its citizen abroad. Where the difference is smaller, a detail in largely *sympatico* criminal schemes of the two jurisdictions, the home country is more likely, out of comity-like principles, to tolerate that difference. By "core" and "peripheral" here, I mean not just to invoke some notion of proportion but also of the type of divergence. Two countries may be committed to the same moral goals for their criminal law—to deter and punish the same acts—but differ in some of the details in how they think the criminal law should effectuate these goals.

Second, extending U.S. law to an assailant's actions might in this case put U.S. citizens traveling abroad in the difficult position of having to evaluate the citizenship of their assailants and trying to conform their self-defense behavior to conflicting rules. That was, of course, true in the initial Ben-John version of Murder Island as well, but because in that scenario the home country disapproved of the activity (murder simpliciter) without reservation, imposition of that potentially chilling obligation did not seem problematic, unlike in the self-defense case.

To amplify this last point, the initial Ben-John variant of Murder Island (and abortion and assisted suicide) differ from the more standard kinds of extraterritoriality issues, such as wage and hour laws. In these other cases, there is a claim (facetious or otherwise) that, when local law permits an activity that the home country's law prohibits, home country citizens will be put at a competitive disadvantage if they have to conform their behavior to the home country's laws while doing business abroad. For example, if I need to pay my workers U.S. minimum wages or hew to U.S. work hour restrictions for my factories abroad, I will not be able to compete in that textile market with the locals who can conform their behavior to their local law. This is a serious claim, even if we are not ultimately moved by it. By contrast, if a U.S. citizen says "I am put at a competitive disadvantage in committing murder of U.S. citizens on Murder Island compared to the islanders," that does not bother us because we believe it is wrong for the citizen to commit murder to begin with. The Ana Lucia–Shannon self-defense variant, by contrast, muddies the water and presents a case where, even as to murder, the "competitive disadvantage" argument has some teeth.

To close this discussion of the third exception, the more peripheral the divergence between the home and the destination country's criminal law on the issue, the more apt we should be to defer to the destination country and refrain from extraterritorial application. This is especially true when we view the destination country's interest as strong or where there are costs to our citizens of being governed by diverging laws that we think the citizens ought not to bear.

* * *

I have used Murder Island to show that a home country with a criminal prohibition on murder ought to criminalize the murders of its citizens by its citizens on the island, notwithstanding that the island's own law would render the murder entirely lawful, subject to some exceptions. Now I want to show how the philosophical analysis of Murder Island can help us better understand the real-world cases of travel abroad to circumvent prohibitions on access to abortion and assisted suicide.

B. Travel for Abortion

Having argued for extraterritorial criminalization in the case of Murder Island, my strategy in this section will be to examine in what ways travel for abortion is like and unlike the Murder Island hypothetical. Let us stipulate for the present (subject to some further nuances below) than Ireland prohibits abortion because it views fetuses as persons and abortion as akin to murder. Rather than Ben killing John, here we have a citizen mother terminating the life of a fetus, which Ireland views as murder against the fetus that Ireland views as another citizen person (more on that point in a moment). In abortion tourism, as in Murder Island, the "victim" has not gone abroad to consent to the activity performed on it; indeed, one might think the fetus's presence there is, if anything, less voluntary than in the prior cases. Moreover, just as the murder of a U.S. citizen abroad has effects within the United States, so too the termination of a fetus has effects within Ireland—at the very least, one fewer Irish person will exist.

One might respond that Ireland is mistaken, as a moral matter, about whether fetuses are persons and whether abortion is murder (in the sense that moral and legal condemnation is warranted for some killings). Once again, however, in this chapter I am not pressing that question but instead asking *if* the home country views its domestic prohibition as lawful and valid, then what should follow for its regulation of its citizens' conduct abroad? I discuss below the possibility that the home country's knowledge about the contestability of the norm within the home country should make a difference.

If the analogy Murder Island holds, then it seems that Ireland should extend its prohibition extraterritorially, to use one of the real-world examples discussed above. To defeat that claim one must argue that there is a morally relevant distinction between travel for abortion tourism and Murder Island. I will examine four such distinctions: motivations for criminalization other than protecting harm to fetuses, victim citizenship, the contestability of the underlying domestic prohibition, and timing. However, I ultimately find none of these distinctions persuasive.

i. Justifications Other than Harm to the Fetus

The most straightforward justification for abortion criminalization is that the fetus is a person (or at least merits harm-protection rights associated with personhood) and therefore abortion is equivalent (or at least close) to murder.[111] Alternatively, one could believe that fetuses are not actually persons but are sufficiently person-like that allowing their termination will cause our society to devalue life and put actual persons at risk.[112]

Although I think this is the most common form of justification for domestic prohibition of abortion, it is not the only possible one.

Some might try to justify antiabortion laws as "woman protective," a view that has gained more traction in U.S. jurisprudence after Justice Anthony Kennedy's opinion in *Gonzales v. Carhart*, which banned a particular abortion procedure because "[w]omen who have abortions come to regret their choices, and consequently suffer from [s]evere depression and loss of esteem."[113] This justification has, of course, been subject to significant criticism, but, as I said before and as to all the potential justifications I am canvassing in this chapter, we are assuming they are valid and lawful from the home country's perspective so as to examine what follows therefrom.

If woman-protective rationales underlie the home country's prohibition on abortion, then the prohibition is either best understood as being aimed at maintaining a particular view of women's roles and capacities in society or as protecting women notwithstanding their consent to the procedure. The latter tracks my discussion of the assisted suicide case later in this chapter, so I will postpone my discussion until then. The former tracks my discussion of one of the reasons to regulate reproductive technology use abroad by one's home country citizen, which is discussed in depth in the next chapter, as well as corruption arguments deployed in favor of prohibiting assisted suicide, which are discussed below.

Therefore, I will postpone my discussion of these kinds of reasons for outlawing abortion until those sections and, in this section focus exclusively on fetal-protective justifications. As it seems to me that the core of most arguments made for criminalizing abortion are made on these fetal-protective grounds, in the next several pages I will focus on analyzing the issue through this lens.

ii. Victim Citizenship

Another possible distinction from Murder Island pertains to victim citizenship, one which again echoes conflict-of-laws principles. As I noted above when discussing the international law question of passive personality jurisdiction based on fetus citizenship,

---

[111] *See, e.g.*, MICHAEL J. SANDEL, JUSTICE: WHAT'S THE RIGHT THING TO DO? 251 (2009) ("[I]f it's true that the developing fetus is morally equivalent to a child, then abortion is morally equivalent to infanticide. And few would maintain that government should let parents decide for themselves whether to kill their children.").

[112] Justice Kennedy's majority opinion in *Gonzales v. Carhart* makes this point as to the dilation and extraction, or so-called "partial birth abortion," procedure. 550 U.S. 124, 158 (2007) ("No one would dispute that, for many, D&E is a procedure itself laden with the power to devalue human life.").

[113] *Gonzales*, 550 U.S. at 183 (Ginsburg, J., dissenting) (internal quotation marks omitted).

one might argue that fetuses are not "citizens" of the home country for this purpose.[114] Although the State may often appear to be protecting the interests of its unborn citizens, these prohibitions might be overdetermined because they could also be justified in terms of territoriality—a desire to control the conduct of abortion within a State's territory rather than to protect its citizens per se.

The matter is still more complex because many of the usual trappings of citizenship—the bearing of reciprocal obligations, the potential to Exit, and others—are not yet actualized in the case of fetuses, although that is also true of young children and the severely mentally disabled. Baldly claiming an interest in the fetus as a *potential* citizen proves too much in that the eventual child might renounce citizenship, and many existing adults are potential citizens for whom we would not give the home country preference in terms of regulating.[115]

Lurking in the background here is whether, in declaring a pre-viability fetus a *citizen* for normative purposes, we also concede that it is a *person* in moral or legal terms. The fact that our hypothetical home country, with a criminal prohibition motivated by the view that abortion is murder, presumably does view the fetus at this stage as a person strongly indicates that the home country will also view the fetus as a citizen.

Further, the idea that a home country's citizenship-type interest could precede, rather than follow legal or moral personhood is not implausible, even if that initially seems a little awkward, as I have argued in depth elsewhere.[116]

Even if one decides the fetus is *not* a home country citizen for these purposes, there is still a strong argument that the home country should extend its prohibition extraterritorially, although the argument is admittedly somewhat weaker because there is no longer a double coincidence of citizenship.

If the fetus is not a home country citizen, we could think of it as a kind of stateless person—persons not considered to be citizens of any country, of which there are an estimated twelve million in the world today[117]—in terms of the home country's interests.

---

[114] One need not adopt the view that being a citizen for these purposes entails being a citizen for all purposes—for example, being counted in the census or paying taxes. *Cf.* Peter Singer, *All Animals Are Equal*, *in* Animal Liberation 1, 1–22 (2d ed. 1990) (making a similar point as to nonhuman animals).

[115] One might also try to make something of the fact that if the destination country recognizes *jus soli* citizenship conferral, then had the woman given birth to the baby in the destination country, that baby would have had destination country citizenship as well. On reflection, though, it is unclear that this claim has much argumentative purchase. Where recognized, such *jus soli* citizenship would add a second citizenship to the *jus sanguinis* citizenship from the home country. The home country's protection of its citizen is not reduced; rather, a conflicting citizenship claim is added. More important, given that the mother is traveling to the destination country to terminate her pregnancy, not to give birth, it is unclear what importance it has that the destination country would have a stronger interest claim had she given birth there. In any event, as I explain in the main text, even if the fetus is not considered a citizen of the home country, there is a strong argument for extraterritorial application.

[116] *See* Cohen, *supra* note 7, at 1366–69.

[117] *Stateless People: Searching for Citizenship*, UNHCR: The UN Refugee Agency, http://www.unhcr.org/pages/49c3646c155.html (last visited July 15, 2012).

To examine the question, let us return to Murder Island, but consider a different victim. Suppose Ben instead kills Richard Alpert, a stateless man not residing in and without any ties to the United States or any other country, after bringing him to Murder Island. Do we believe the United States should punish Ben for this action, knowing that if it does not prosecute its own citizen for the murder, neither will anyone else? I think most of us have the intuition "yes."

Why reach that conclusion? If Ben deserves punishment as retribution because he has done something we view as wrong, it seems immaterial that his victim is a stateless person. Our justification for punishing murder is that "absent a ground for excuse, murder (not only the murder of U.S. citizens) is wrong," and on that rationale, it is not relevant that the murder took place on Murder Island.

If deterrence, not retribution, is (at least partially) the motivation for punishment, we can ask whether our goal is to deter our citizens murdering others or merely to deter our citizens murdering other U.S. citizens? I think it is the former.

One way to get at this is through a thought experiment. Imagine the following facts are true: if U.S. citizens are allowed to murder stateless individuals but not U.S. citizens on Murder Island, forty U.S. citizens are murdered while fifty stateless individuals are murdered; if U.S. citizens are prohibited from murdering either group abroad fifty U.S. citizens are murdered and ten stateless individuals are murdered. If we cared only about deterring the murders of our own citizens, we should prefer the first because it is *pareto superior* as to our citizens, even though much worse in terms of the total number of murders, but our intuitions are to the contrary.[118]

Thus, on either retributivist or deterrence grounds, the home country that prohibits murder has a strong interest in punishing a citizen who commits murder against a stateless person on Murder Island. Under communitarian or liberal principles, the ties of U.S. citizenship seem strong enough to make Ben answerable to the United States for his crimes against a stateless person. It is the perpetrator's, not the victim's, ties to the home country that do much of the work, at least in cases where the victim is a stateless person (rather than, say, a member of the destination country).

Therefore, whether or not we view the fetus as a citizen, a State that views abortion as akin to murder should extend its domestic criminal prohibition of abortion to circumvention tourists. That said, I fully concede that the home country has a stronger reason to extraterritorialize its prohibition on abortion if it views the fetus as its citizen, in that the presence of the double coincidence of citizenship and preventing serious bodily harm is the strongest case for extraterritorial criminalization. But my point in this section has

---

[118] For some, I may need to increase the fifty murders of stateless individuals to one hundred, one thousand, or or ten thousand to pump the intuition. If the variable in that slot matters, it suggests that although we have an interest in deterring the murder of stateless individuals, it is not equal to the interest we have in deterring the murder of our citizens. That is consistent with my political theoretical claim that in the absence of the double coincidence of citizenship, our interest is weaker as to the stateless individual but still present.

been to show that the argument for extraterritorial criminalization remains quite strong even if the home country does not view the fetus as its citizen.

iii. Contestability of the Norm, Exit, and Exit-Light

Jurisdictions disagree on whether to criminally prohibit abortions at all, and if they do prohibit them, at what stage of fetal development, using what techniques, etc.[119] Moreover, even in a home country, the abortion prohibition may be controversial. Should the contestability of the norm distinguish abortion tourism? I have already afforded some role to the contestability of the norm in the home country through the safety valve exception, but is there a further role for contestability to play? As I suggested above, both Pennings and Huxtable have treated this kind of contestability of the norm as important in determining whether criminal prohibitions should be extended extra-territorially for abortion and assisted suicide. Pennings advocates for notion he calls "external tolerance," which he applies to abortion and assisted suicide, wherein "a certain norm is applicable and applied in society as wanted by the majority while simultaneously the members of the minority can still act according to their moral view by going abroad," and suggests that "[a]llowing people to look abroad demonstrates the absolute minimum of respect for their moral autonomy."[120]

As with travel abroad for the Female Genital Cutting (FGC) of minors, which I have written about elsewhere,[121] we can understand the demand made by those who seek to lawfully travel abroad to receive an abortion as a kind of accommodation claim. A State that has criminalized abortion domestically demands that "as a citizen, you are required to conform your behavior to our criminal prohibition by avoiding abortion and, if you are unwilling to do, so you may take up your Exit rights by renouncing your citizenship." The woman seeking an abortion counter demands: "accept that this is a personal and difficult decision and one which, despite the existence of a criminal prohibition, our society is deeply divided on, and honor my autonomy and that moral division by providing me an exemption to your otherwise applicable criminal prohibition." The State refuses. This is just to say that despite the existing moral disagreement, the home country in question has criminalized abortion.

We can conceive of circumvention tourism as representing an intermediate or second-best counter demand on the part of the cultural defender: "I will refrain from engaging in the prohibited activity on your soil, but allow me at least to undertake it in another State where it is permitted, for this is the bare minimum that freedom and self-actualization demands." Instead of imposing the huge cost of full Exit to undertake

---

[119] *See* Kreimer, *supra* note 26, at 907–13 (discussing some differences among domestic and international abortion regulations).

[120] Pennings, *supra* note 76, at 340.

[121] Cohen, *supra* note 7, at 1356–60.

this activity, the cultural defender must only incur the lesser cost of travel in order to be able to perform FGC on the child. I will call this "Exit-light."

This thinking would give *a* reason why the State could consistently prohibit the practice at home but not impose its criminalization extraterritorially. I do not, however, find it very persuasive. Although self-actualization, freedom, and the ability to have places of refuge from the home country's way of living are all good things that we should strive to give our citizens, we should not do so at the expense of allowing serious bodily harm to be done to our citizens.

In many ways "Exit-light" feels like a disingenuous and easy way out. For one thing, it would result in a kind of masking where what some might think of as an instance of child abuse or gender subordination continues to happen but we merely allow ourselves to avoid confronting it by making sure it happens outside our view.

Second, the accommodation privilege seems to be distributed in an at least partially morally arbitrary way that tracks whether the individual has the financial means to travel to the destination country at the right time.[122] If we were serious about accommodation, we in theory should instead lottery State support to travel abroad for abortion among those who cannot afford, or lottery an equivalent number of permits to do it within our territory. If this seems problematic, as I think it would to anyone who believes the domestic prohibition is justified, that might suggest that what lies behind the initial accommodation is an illusory State action/inaction distinction; in fact, the State is very much acting when it refuses to extend its domestic law extraterritorially.

Finally, when the interest is in preventing harm to a person who has in no way consented, and the State has decided that this interest outweighs the demand for accommodation within its territorial space, the claim for an Exit-light approach of allowing circumvention tourism seems hard to justify. From the point of view of the fetus that would suffer termination it seems irrelevant that the abortion took place in a destination country rather than the patient's home country. This is not to say it makes no difference that the action took place on the destination rather than the home country's soil, but that the comity-like interests that would ordinarily push for deferring to the destination country's laws in this regard seem inadequate when we are discussing serious bodily harm done by one of our citizens to another who has not meaningfully consented.

To buttress this, consider another common example taken from the debate between cultural defenders and liberals as to religious accommodation: suppose that a fourteen-year-old U.S. citizen girl who has lost her virginity is taken by her U.S. citizen

---

[122] Of course, this point has more force the more difficult or expensive it is to travel to the destination country. Compare flying from Bogotá to Switzerland to driving from Toronto to Buffalo in this regard. The fact that only some people can afford to use medical tourism extends beyond criminalized prohibitions as well.

father to a country where honor killings are treated as falling within a justification to murder, and she is killed there.[123] If the United States will not recognize the need to maintain this justification for killing at home, the United States should not, in the name of cultural accommodation, refuse to criminalize the act when it takes place abroad. This fourteen-year-old girl, by virtue of her membership in our society, deserves the protection of our laws against murder by her citizen relative whether she is at home or abroad. For a country that believes that abortion is murder, why should things be any different for abortion? Indeed, one might think the case for accommodation is *weaker* with abortion as there is no religious or cultural claim made by the person who wants to travel abroad, so no plausible claim to "dual citizenship" in a secular national and religious pan-national community.

Of course, one major disagreement between those countries that do and do not criminalize abortion is whether fetuses *are* persons. But once the home country has decided fetuses are persons and enforces its criminal law to that effect domestically despite contestation, it seems strange to think that accommodation requires a different result extraterritorially.[124] Just as it seems strange that we could believe that a citizen of African descent (or if one feels there is not enough contestability there, a several intellectually disabled child) could cease being a person (as to the protection afforded by our law against murder by his fellow citizens) by leaving our territory, the same should be true regarding fetuses. Indeed, one would need a kind of "just-so story" to sensibly ban abortions at home but not abroad to accommodate contestation: we are exactly sure enough of the personhood of fetuses to criminalize abortion at home but not quite sure enough to prevent the same act by our citizens abroad given the interests of the foreign State in being a haven for women who want to exercise this autonomy interest.

Does it matter if the home country's legislation is the result of an amalgam of views, where a portion of the population is sure fetuses are persons, a portion is sure they are not, and the determinative center is unsure but thinks it just possible enough that a criminal prohibition is warranted? With this uncertainty, the home country may be in no hurry to go off and proselytize destination countries to change their abortion law. It is less clear, though, why this divergence of opinion would prompt the home country to defer to the destination country's view on abortion as to abortion by home country citizens that take place abroad—and by deference here I mean in the form of the Exit-light solution. We would not expect deference with similar uncertainty about the moral status of other groups (say, the profoundly mentally disabled or one-day-old infants).[125]

---

[123] Until recently this was true in several Arab countries, with the details varying. *See* Lama Abu Odeh, *Honor Killings and the Construction of Gender in Arab Societies*, 58 AM. J. COMP. L. 911, 913–16 (2010).

[124] Again, no one would countenance a kind of abortion lottery through which those who "win" are exempted from territorial application of the law or, worse yet, receive payment from the State to travel abroad.

[125] *Cf.* Singer, *supra* note 114, at 17–20 (questioning the personhood of children in vegetative states).

To echo a point I made earlier, the international context differs from the U.S. intra-state context, where we view divergences in the law as Brandeisian experiments that will one day be resolved in favor of the "right" answer by a federal government.[126] At the horizontal level, there is no obvious policy learning. If the question is the personhood of the fetus or the balance of conflicting rights claims between mother and fetus, it is not clear what can be learned from the destination country's experience. Even in elements of the abortion debate where a home country could learn from other countries—for example, the risks of back-alley abortions when abortion is criminalized and the likelihood that women will seek them—it need not allow its citizens to travel abroad and circumvent our domestic laws in order to get that kind of learning. It can observe these lessons by looking at the destination country's experience with their policy choice as to their own citizenry, and, if anything, the travel of the home country's citizens into the destination country's legal culture muddies, rather than clarifies, the issue. If a home country learns from observing the destination country that they have the abortion issue "right," it should change its law domestically and extraterritorially; if not, it should prohibit both.

Again, this is not to say that the contestability argument is a nullity. When faced with conditions of uncertainty or pervasive disagreement, home countries often "split the difference" to some extent in their domestic criminal law, for example, by building in some exceptions or defenses or by maintaining a criminal law on the books but investing few resources into its enforcements. Exit-light can be thought of as consistent with these practices as an accommodation device. But compared to these kinds of attempts at Solomonic solutions, Exit-light is a particularly unappetizing one:

It benefits only select individuals based on wealth, expertise, and ability to travel. Unlike the use of prosecutorial discretion or built-in defenses and exceptions, Exit-light is not a flexible way of keying enforcement to the gravity of harm being done. Instead, it keys enforcement to where the harm is done, a facet that seems largely orthogonal to the wrongness of abortion. For those who hope that the confrontation with more liberal destination country norms will help educate those in the home country about why they are mistaken in their choices,[127] the secretive do-it-but-don't-tell-me nature of circum-vention tourism impedes that goal and likely forestalls deeper reconsideration through the safety valve dynamic I discussed above.

Although I reject the notion that contestability of the norm justifies Exit-light accommodations for abortion prohibitions premised on preventing harm to fetuses, I do not

---

[126] For cases in which both the home and destination countries share a supranational governance structure, such as travel from one EU Member State to another, the argument is weaker. Even here, though, we imagine Ireland acting (perhaps counterfactually) in the shadow of doctrinal discretion, not restriction. The supranational regulator may be free to step in to resolve policy divergences between Member States (that depends in part on the extent of its power), but, until it does so, it is not clear that this is really so different from the situation in which there is no supranational regulator.

[127] See Mutcherson, supra note 110, at 161.

mean to suggest this will be true for every kind of circumvention tourism. If one really understands abortion as the murder of a person, though, as many home countries that outlaw abortion do, even the attractive possibility of accommodation must give way.

Yet, even as to abortion, some of the exceptions discussed above may continue to apply. In particular, whether divergences between the home and destination country laws are core or peripheral may have some role to play. If the clash were between whether to permit abortions or not, the obligation to criminalize extraterritorially in spite of the destination country's claims would be at its zenith; the obligation seems weaker if the clash were regarding which abortion procedures would be available.

iv. Timing

A different argument for distinguishing abortion tourism from the Murder Island reasoning stems from the lead time in which one knows one will want to use the service. True Exit through renouncing citizenship may be impossible from the time pregnancy is detected to the time at which it is still possible to have an abortion under the law of the destination country. Thus, the home country may be offering a false choice in the trilemma: Exit, do not have the abortion, or have an abortion and face the penalty—but only the latter two of those options may be realistically available.

Even if true, it is not entirely clear what relevance the timing issue ought to have. Return for the moment to Murder Island. Imagine that U.S. citizen Charles Whitmore, a big-time financier, usually travels with a retinue of bodyguards but dismisses them from his service for one long weekend when he vacations on Murder Island. U.S. citizen Benjamin Linus, who has wanted to kill Whitmore for a long time, learns of this fact only two weeks before the vacation such that he lacks the requisite time to renounce his U.S. citizenship before committing the murder. It does not seem that the United States should fail to extend its prescriptive jurisdiction to his murder just because Ben lacked sufficient time to disclaim his citizenship. If that is right, it is not clear why things should be different with abortion.

Here is an argument for that same conclusion from the political theoretical vantage point: on social contract theories, it cannot be that the obligation one has undertaken is what contract law terms an "[i]llusory promise[]":[128] "I will refrain from legal access to abortion unless I find myself in need of it." A contract is meaningful precisely because it binds us in spite of our later preference.[129]

One might respond that abortion is different and the experience of pregnancy gives rise to a kind of changed-selves argument that alters its waiveability even for social

---

[128] *See, e.g.*, RESTATEMENT (SECOND) OF CONTRACTS § 77 & cmt. a (1981).

[129] The contract would not be illusory if the promise was to renounce one's citizenship after the fact if one undertook the act; that would be a contract of mutual consideration. It is for that reason that in this instance I am more open to the notion of just such a scheme in the form of Exile as I discuss.

contract theory purposes. I have explored this question in other work,[130] but, for present purposes, I note that accepting this changed-selves argument implies that the domestic prohibition on abortion is *also* itself improper, and thus it does not explain why one might accept a different course *only* extraterritorially. This is, in some sense, the difficulty faced by opponents of criminalizing circumvention tourism: they must offer us arguments against extraterritorial prohibition that do not also argue against domestic criminalization.

I am thus ultimately not persuaded by the timing argument. For those who remain unconvinced, I think the argument at most pushes us to a different kind of compromise: to escape the penalty associated with the unlawful act, the perpetrator is allowed to bindingly commit to Exit before the activity even if Exit will only actually occur after the fact. Thus, the individual who cannot accomplish Exit in a timely fashion before the abortion would be empowered to renounce citizenship after the abortion as a way of avoiding the criminal penalty. This regime would replace "Exit" with "Exile" in the choice set "Exit, refrain, or be punished."[131] Although theoretically pleasing, I am not sure this would work very well in practice.

In sum, most countries with abortion criminalization do not extend those prohibitions extraterritorially. My conclusion above is that international law would not prevent them from doing so. My conclusion in this section is that, as a normative matter, assuming these countries' domestic prohibitions are valid and lawful, there is a strong argument that these countries should alter their laws to criminalize abortions by their citizens abroad.

C. Travel for Assisted Suicide

Should the United Kingdom have extended its domestic prohibition on assisted suicide to its citizens who assisted their friends or family (also citizens) to die in Switzerland, where such assistance is lawful even for nonresidents? Note that this issue lies behind the *Purdy* and *Pretty* cases discussed above (even if those cases actually turned on far narrower and more doctrinal issues) and behind the policy decisions of the vast majority of home countries that do not criminalize assisted suicide extraterritorially.

As with abortion, my approach will be to examine in what ways this case is like and unlike Murder Island, though this section will be shorter as so much of the groundwork has been laid in the prior sections. I will once again begin by unpacking the possible justifications for the domestic prohibition to examine whether they justify extraterritorial

---

[130] *See* I. Glenn Cohen, *The Constitution and the Rights Not to Procreate*, 60 Stan. L. Rev. 1135, 1185–95 (2008); I. Glenn Cohen, *The Right Not to Be a Genetic Parent?*, 81 S. Cal. L. Rev. 1115, 1179–84 (2008).

[131] It is possible that a form of Exile is already indirectly accomplished in a system that affords extraterritorial prescriptive but not enforcement jurisdiction in that the individual who has committed the crime abroad may avoid punishment by never returning to the home country.

extension to circumvention tourists. I begin by dividing the arguments in two: those concerned with protecting the patient who seeks to end his or her life, and those concerned with changes in attitudes of society more generally.

i. Concerns about Protecting Patients and Consent

One prominent reason offered for outlawing assisted suicide domestically is the desire to protect vulnerable patients whose lives will be terminated. Hazel Biggs and Caroline Jones make this point explicitly about the UK prohibition, noting that it was "clearly designed to safeguard those who might be vulnerable to coercion from being persuaded to kill themselves at the behest of someone who could benefit from their death."[132] At first glance, that might seem quite analogous to Murder Island (and at least for those who believe in fetal personhood, the abortion case) in that the State's interest is in preventing the killing of one of its citizens by another of its citizens. However, at least in the cases of mentally competent adults, the presence of consent to the end of one's life might be thought to alter the analysis.

Should the possibility of consent lead us to a different conclusion?

Some, such as the Vatican, argue that in the domestic context, consent is irrelevant to negating the wrongfulness of the act of terminating the patient's life: "no one is permitted to ask for this act of killing, either for himself or herself or for another person entrusted to his or her care, nor can he or she consent to it, either explicitly or implicitly. [N]or can any authority legitimately recommend or permit such an action. For it is a question of the violation of the divine law, an offense against the dignity of the human person, a crime against life, and an attack on humanity."[133] Others argue that consent is meaningless because the patient is being manipulated or coerced into choosing death, subtly or grossly, benignly or maliciously.[134] Still others press a claim of false consciousness—the patient's desire to die results from temporary depression or cognitive narrowing, and the unavailability of assisted suicide helps the patient to clarify what he or she "really" wants.[135]

Once again, my aim is not to evaluate this dialectic but to ask what should follow about criminal prohibition of circumvention tourism on these patient-protective justifications.

Let me take each of these three variants in turn.

---

[132] Biggs & Jones, *supra* note 29, at 168.

[133] *See Declaration on Euthanasia*, Sacred Congregation for the Doctrine of the Faith (May 5, 1980), http://www.vatican.va/roman_curia/congregations/cfaith/documents/rc_con_cfaith_doc_19800505_euthanasia_en.html.

[134] *See, e.g.*, James L. Underwood, *The Supreme Court's Assisted Suicide Opinions in International Perspective: Avoiding a Bureaucracy of Death*, 73 N.D. L. Rev. 641, 669 (1997) ("The doctor can manipulate the determination that the patient's condition is hopeless by controlling the information presented to consultants.").

[135] *See, e.g.*, Erwin Chemerinsky, Washington v. Glucksberg *Was Tragically Wrong*, 106 Mich. L. Rev. 1501, 1510 (2008) ("There is a danger that people will use assisted death out of temporary depression.").

If the underlying reason for rejecting consent in the domestic context is that it is irrelevant in negating the wrongfulness of the act, then that reasoning would seem to hold irrespective of whether the assisted suicide occurs at home or abroad. The strongest argument to the contrary would incorporate what was said above in the abortion context about the contestability of the norm at home—the possibility of travel as Exit-light—but then press the way in which the assisted-suicide case is premised on paternalism and not the Harm Principle. If one thinks, as I do, that paternalism is a weaker basis for justifying criminal prohibition than the Harm Principle, then perhaps there is an argument for allowing Exit-light when paternalism underlies a contestable prohibition. Whether this argument would be persuasive, I think, will depend on (1) how attracted one is to paternalism as a moral basis for criminalization, and (2) how good the consent is. The second is a matter I discuss below whereas the first is more a general matter of criminal law theory. But if a home country believed that paternalism was as good a reason to criminalize conduct as a pure Harm Principle justification, it is unclear why it should make a difference that the act was committed abroad.

If the underlying reason for rejecting consent is fear of pressure or manipulation, then the home country has good reason to criminalize the act abroad. Indeed, it may seem that assisted-suicide tourism is *worse* in this regard because the State cannot use its existing laws relating to the supervision of its physicians (including licensure and disciplinary rules) as a bulwark against these undue influences. Because more of the assisted suicide takes place outside the gaze of the home country's regulatory authority, the case for prohibition is stronger with citizens abroad rather than at home.

In the opposite direction, if false consciousness is the concern, there is at least one way in which assisted-suicide tourism may be less problematic than assisted suicide in the home country. To use an analogy to contract theory, we can think of the criminalization of assisted suicide as a "default rule," and the relevant question is what the "altering rule" should be to make that conduct no longer criminal.[136]

In the domestic case, the person assisting suicide offers the patient's consent as the altering rule that should make his or her assistance lawful, but the State rejects the offer. In the tourism case, both the consent and the patient's travel are offered as altering rules. We might think of the time, expense, and preparation involved in traveling as somewhat analogous to the role played by formalities such as the writing requirement in Lon Fuller's classic treatment of the cautionary function of contract law—that it forces the parties to undertake a minimal amount of reflection before being bound by a contract.[137]

---

[136] *Cf.* Ian Ayres, *Menus Matter*, 73 U. CHI. L. REV. 3, 6 (2006) (exploring the altering rule idea); I. Glenn Cohen, *Protecting Patients with Passports: Medical Tourism, Medical Tourism and the Patient-Protective Argument*, 95 IOWA L. REV. 1467, 1532–33 (2010) (suggesting travel as a kind of altering rule for medical malpractice liability de facto waivers).

[137] *See* Lon L. Fuller, *Consideration and Form*, 41 COLUM. L. REV. 799, 800 (1941).

This is a valid distinction between the domestic and international case, but I think it is a fairly thin reed on which to hang such a strong difference in the treatment of the domestic and extraterritorial practice, especially when, domestically, the State could achieve far more of a cautionary function by building requirements such as psychological evaluations and waiting periods into its *domestic* regulation. Moreover, if the objection is false consciousness rather than mere lack of reflection, it is unclear that this "speed bump" is really responsive.

In sum, there are possible distinctions between the imperative to criminalize conduct domestically versus abroad in the assisted-suicide case on patient-protective grounds relating to consent, but they seem to be a fairly weak ground on which to justify differential treatment of the two cases; I think the better view is that, if patient protection is the motivation in the home country for criminalization, the home country has good reason to extend criminalization to the circumvention tourist as well.[138]

ii. Concerns about Changes in Attitudes: Corruption of the Profession, Slippery Slopes, and the Devaluation of Life

Aside from patient-protective arguments, there are a series of other arguments often raised in favor of criminalizing assisted suicide that focus on "victims" other than the patient who will receive the assistance. These arguments were nicely cataloged by the U.S. Supreme Court in its decision in *Washington v. Glucksberg*,[139] a case in which it rejected a constitutional right to assisted suicide: First, the State has an "interest in protecting the integrity and ethics of the medical profession" because "physician assisted suicide could, it is argued, undermine the trust that is essential to the doctor-patient relationship by blurring the time honored line between healing and harming." Second, the State has an interest in "protecting disabled and terminally ill people from prejudice, negative and inaccurate stereotypes, and 'societal indifference,'" with the prohibition on assisted suicide "reflect[ing] and reinforc[ing] its policy that the lives of terminally ill, disabled, and elderly people must be no less valued than the lives of the young and healthy, and that a seriously disabled person's suicidal impulses should be interpreted and treated the same way as anyone else's." Third, "the State may fear that permitting assisted suicide will start it down the path to voluntary and perhaps even involuntary

---

[138] I will note, though not fully resolve, an additional complication. Although the perpetrator citizen who assists in suicide will presumably be able to effect Exit and renounce citizenship, that may not be true of every "victim" citizen who wants assistance, in that patients with disabilities may be unable to renounce their citizenship. In such a case, if there was also meaningful consent to the Exit by the "victim" but the inability to execute it, perhaps the analysis should be different? I would be more inclined to argue that, in such a case, the State should assist the patient's Exit from citizenship, not render lawful assisting the patient's exit from life while treating the patient still as a citizen, but the question seems somewhat close.

[139] 521 U.S. 702 (1997).

euthanasia" such that "what is couched as a limited right to 'physician assisted suicide' is likely, in effect, a much broader license, which could prove extremely difficult to police and contain."[140]

Each of these is a type of what I have elsewhere called "corruption" or "attitude modification argument." Corruption arguments claim that allowing a practice to go forward will do violence or denigrate our views of how goods are properly valued.[141] As we will see in the next chapter, these arguments are frequently invoked as justifications for domestic reproductive technology prohibitions, especially for laws prohibiting compensation for selling sperm, egg, or surrogacy services. As I noted above, there is also a less prominent discourse arguing for abortion criminalization based on abortion's effect on our valuation of the lives of actual (undisputed) persons rather than its effect on the fetus itself. What I say here is also responsive to a case where *that* justification underlies the domestic prohibition on abortion.

1. Extraterritoriality and Corruption Justifications Generally

It is important to distinguish what I have called "consequentialist" and "intrinsic" corruption arguments. Consequentialist corruption justifies intervention to prevent changes to our attitudes or sensibilities that *will* occur if the practice is allowed,[142] for example, that we will "regard each other as objects with prices rather than as persons."[143] Margaret Radin's worry as to baby selling is representative of this strand:

> If a baby is the object of a market exchange, there may be an effect on that child's self conception when he or she grows up. You know your parents paid money for you, maybe enough to have bought a BMW, but not enough to have bought a house.... [K]ids talk to each other.... It's possible, in other words, that this way of thinking about children could spread.... The question to ask is: How bad is this risk? If the risk is not very bad, then we could buy and sell babies all the time, and we could still have a non-market conception at the same time with the market conception and neither one would drive each other out.[144]

This is a contingent critique: children may find out how much their parents paid for them and this knowledge may spread in society, undermining the nonmarket conception.

---

[140] *Id.* at 731–33.

[141] I. Glenn Cohen, Note, *The Price of Everything, the Value of Nothing: Reframing the Commodification Debate*, 117 HARV. L. REV. 689, 691–92 (2003).

[142] *Id.* at 692 n.13.

[143] Scott Altman, *(Com)modifying Experience*, 65 S. CAL. L. REV. 293, 294–97 (1991) (calling these "modified-experience arguments").

[144] Margaret Jane Radin, *What, if Anything, Is Wrong with Baby Selling?*, Address at the McGeorge School of Law (Mar. 4, 1994), *in* 26 PAC. L.J. 135, 144–45 (1995).

By contrast, the more intrinsic form of the objection focuses on the "inherent incompatibility between an object and a mode of valuation," where the wrongfulness of the action is completed at the moment of purchase irrespective of what follows; the intrinsic version of the objection obtains even if the act remains secret or has zero effect on anyone's attitudes.[145]

This distinction is important for extraterritoriality, and indeed I will return to it in the next chapter. If consequentialist corruption is the worry, then the home country has a stronger reason to prohibit the activity at home than abroad because there is likely a much stronger attitude-modifying effect. The domestic experience is "in your face" in a way that the extraterritorial circumvention is not, and one can ascribe the practice to "the Other."[146]

A contemporary example is offered by the Netherlands, which permits a regulated form of prostitution.[147] Home countries that prohibit prostitution domestically do not typically extend their criminal law extraterritorially to cover it. The degree of corruption that occurs by a home country's failure to criminalize its citizens engaging in prostitution in the Netherlands seems several orders of magnitude smaller than the degree of corruption that would occur if the home country made engaging the services of a prostitute legal domestically. Of course, there are many important differences between prostitution and the other medical practices I am discussing, but the comparison is meant simply to show that consequentialist corruption may be like a ripple on a pond—weakening as it radiates outward from its point of contact. Although the ripple analogy suggests geographic proximity, the extent of consequentialist corruption might instead turn on cultural (dis)similarities between the home and destination country. These are empirical questions, and hard ones to test, but, if validated, they may in principle give a reason that a home country should, on this justification, treat the domestic and extraterritorial cases differently.

However, there are at least two complications. First, if the home country sets a low enough threshold regarding how much attitude modification it is willing to risk, then even the lower amount stemming from circumvention tourism may be sufficient to justify extraterritorial criminalization. Second, to continue with the prostitution example for a moment, the United States may have an interest in the attitudes of *Dutch* individuals about women's sexuality, and it is possible that criminalizing the conduct of U.S. citizens while in the Netherlands might further that interest. Because such a justification switches the "victim" class to be members of the destination country, and thus disrupts

---

[145] Cohen, *supra* note 132, at 692 n.13.

[146] The same intuition may underlie many parents' attitude toward forbidding or punishing their children's behavior—the "not in my house, mister" sort of refrain under which parents will turn a blind eye to their children's activities off, but not in, their turf. Such a distinction might track the seriousness of the offense or its publicity.

[147] *See* Chi Mgbako & Laura A. Smith, *Sex Work and Human Rights in Africa*, 33 Fordham Int'l L.J. 1178, 1208 (2010).

the double coincidence of citizenship, we would be using the criminal law governing U.S. citizens to change the attitudes of the Netherlands' subjects in a way contrary to the attitude that the Netherlands wishes to foster within its citizenry.

That seems quite encroaching, but, if we transposed the example to attitudes toward women's rights to be part of the workforce in more repressive Middle Eastern countries, such attempts at attitude modification of those abroad might seem more palatable. Still, I think it safe to say that when the key concern is the corruption of the attitudes of *noncitizens*, the argument for extraterritorial criminalization is weakened.

What about intrinsic corruption? If we understand this as a more metaphysical objection—that something wrong has been done through the act of value denigration at the moment the act takes place irrespective of what follows thereafter—it seems that the home country has just as much of a reason to extend its criminal law to the actions of its citizen abroad as it does when the citizen acts at home. Wrong has been done at the moment the act is done (whatever its consequence), and the act of criminal condemnation is needed both to deter that act and, on retributivist or corrective justice—type grounds, to re-right the balance.

It would be a mistake to think that the home country has a greater interest in the intrinsic corruption of its citizens' bodies, sexuality, or reproductive labor than it does in protecting the intrinsic corruption of the destination country citizens in this way when the destination country does not view the activity as corrupting because the wrong is not done specifically to the person whose nature is corrupted—they are not alone in having standing. For those who believe that surrogacy is wrong because of intrinsic corruption, an issue I discuss in the next chapter, the surrogate's consent, for example, does not diminish that corruption. The consent of the home country sovereign should, in that circumstance, also make no difference. Intrinsic corruption conceives of the wrong as free-floating in a way that frustrates the attempt to territorialize it.

Does this mean that a home country such as Turkey ought to declare *universal* jurisdiction on commercial surrogacy and make it a crime under prescriptive Turkish jurisdiction for a citizen of any country to engage in commercial surrogacy anywhere? One might respond in several ways. First: Yes, but so what? This is not a *terrible* reductio ad absurdum. Second: yes, but that just shows why intrinsic corruption is not such a good justification for acting in the first place, domestically or universally. Third: yes as a normative matter, but perhaps as a doctrinal matter of international law universal jurisdiction will not extend so far—though, as discussed above, its scope has expanded in recent years.

Finally, the answer I am most attracted to: no. Even if the free-floating wrong is the same in all instances for intrinsic corruption, it is a mistake to think that every sovereign is equally morally obligated to punish every wrong done in the world under an intrinsic corruption framework. Rather, as discussed above, the citizenship tie of the perpetrator to the home country is important in helping to justify the home country's right to punish. By being a national and a member of the coercive structure of a country that both benefits and burdens a citizen, instead of choosing Exit, that citizen has accepted the sovereign's authority to punish in a way that the citizen has not accepted that of other sovereigns.

Consider an analogy to parenting. Perhaps it is your goal that your son not cuss, and you want to deter him through punishment. It does not follow that you welcome random individuals on the street punishing your child. Rather, there is something about your relationship that empowers you to punish to the exclusion of others. If your son were sleeping over at a friend's house and cussed, you might accept his being punished by the hosting parents as well (for example, by a half-hour time out). This shows that to accept both citizenship (roughly the parent-child relationship) and territoriality (roughly the sleeping over) as independent grounds for authorizing punishment does not imply that universal jurisdiction must follow (roughly the random stranger punishing your child).[148]

In sum, if the justification for the domestic prohibition is intrinsic corruption, I think the home country has good reason to punish the citizen who engages in the forbidden act abroad just as much as it does when the act takes place at home. By contrast, when the justification is consequentialist corruption, I think the home country may justifiably refuse to extend its prohibition to the extraterritorial conduct of its citizen. This conclusion seems appropriate for reproductive technology use, "devaluation" justifications for criminalizing abortions, and, as we will see in the next section, some reasons for outlawing assisted suicide.

2. Corruption and Assisted Suicide

With that primer on corruption arguments more generally, we can understand the three objections I have highlighted as to assisted suicide—corruption of the profession, slippery slopes leading to pressing those with intellectual disabilities or the elderly to end their lives, and the devaluation of life more generally—as each offering a form of the corruption argument.

---

[148] To be sure, that last answer depends in part on one's starting point in terms of deep theory about criminal law. I have already noted above my partiality to Duff's view of the matter, but there may be others for which the line between universal jurisdiction and nationality jurisdiction will be harder to draw. For example, Michael Moore has argued that "retributivism, when combined both with the principle of legality and the insight that law as law does not even prima facie obligate citizen obedience, yields the legal moralist theory of proper legislative aim: all and only moral wrongs should be prohibited by the criminal law, for the reason that such actions (or mental states) are wrongful (or culpable) and deserve punishment." Michael Moore, Placing Blame: A General Theory of Criminal Law 754 (1997). If there is a prima facie reason for a legislature to criminalize *all* wrongful conduct, then drawing a distinction between nationality and universal jurisdiction will turn on more second-order considerations, not the underlying obligation. In any event, even if one were more drawn to the Moore view, and there were not sufficient second-order reasons to distinguish the two types of jurisdictions, the other responses offered above to the universal jurisdiction *reductio* also apply.

Let us begin with the variant concerned with concerns about the way in which assisted suicide leads to a general devaluation of the value of life with spillovers in other domains that concern the home country. If this justification for prohibiting assisted suicide is understood as a form of consequentialist corruption and the home state believes attitude modification is sharply reduced when the activity occurs abroad, the State has good reason to treat the extraterritorial and domestic cases differently. Thus, this raises an empirical question (how much attitude modification is likely to occur of the home country's citizens' attitudes) and also a question of thresholds (even if the attitude modification will be much less compared to permitting the practice domestically, it may be that even a little attitude modification as to the value of life is more than the home country can bear). When the justification for criminalization is instead intrinsic corruption, it is irrelevant whether negative effects are likely or unlikely to occur, because the wrong has been done to the value of life at the moment of the suicide, regardless of whatever effects follow. Thus, intrinsic corruption more easily justifies extraterritorial criminalization than does consequentialist corruption.

A similar analysis of consequentialist and intrinsic corruption and extraterritoriality applies when the concern is the corruption of the profession, with a twist: if the home country permits circumvention tourism to the destination country for assisted suicide, the corruption effects on the profession may depend on whether we are discussing the medical profession writ large, or whether the right unit of analysis is the home country's versus the destination country's medical profession. I suggested above that home countries plausibly should care more about attitude modification among their citizens than among those abroad. It seems to me that the same is true when the attitude modification is of the medical profession. Therefore, home countries have a much stronger argument for extending extraterritorially a prohibition on assisted suicide when the corruption of the profession that will occur is that of *home country* health care providers as a profession rather than destination country ones. The same may be true as to intrinsic corruption, although here it seems somewhat less plausible to, as a metaphysical matter, distinguish (for example) the Swiss medical profession as being distinct from the British one.

The slippery slope version of the corruption argument introduces still further complexities. For example, how likely is it, in attitude-modification terms, that beginning down the slope *in Switzerland* will cause a slide *in Britain*? One might reply that by allowing British citizens to go abroad for assisted suicide, the slope will slip to circumvention tourism for involuntary euthanasia—that is, a version where the slip is entirely directed toward our own patients—but this is perhaps less plausible than the typical slippery-slope argument. The approach the British have ultimately taken, discussed above, of having the DPP spell out the factors favoring prosecution might be thought to be some evidence against this kind of concern. Indeed, here the safety valve dynamic may mean that the ability to travel to Switzerland makes the British ground less slippery, not more.

Finally, even if the possibility of a slippery slope in Switzerland is relevant, it may be that the destination country is more resistant to slippage than the home country because of the place of religious institutions in its society or political system, its form of government, or other factors. If the destination country is less prone to slippage than the home country, that may be a reason to maintain the prohibition domestically but not extraterritorially.

In sum, although I think the case is somewhat less strong than for abortion, when the rationale is protecting a vulnerable patient whose life will be ended I think there is a strong argument normative for countries that prohibit assisted suicide domestically to criminalize that assistance-providing conduct by their own citizens extraterritorially. The case for extraterritorial criminalization might be buttressed by "corruption" type concerns—as to the profession, the general devaluation of life, and/or slippery slopes to pressuring other groups to end their lives. When the concern is consequentialist corruption, criminalization is only justified to the extent fears about attitude-modification can be substantiated rather than asserted, and even then the imperative to criminalize extraterritorially is much stronger when the changes in attitude that are feared are of the home country (and not the domestic) citizens' attitudes. When the concern is intrinsic corruption, these same constraints do not apply. That said, many may find the intrinsic corruption argument, even as a justification for domestic criminalization, less persuasive (I will confess I am one of them) than the other possible arguments.

IV. CRIMINALIZING DOMESTIC SPEECH ON ABORTION AND ASSISTED SUICIDE

Extraterritorially criminalizing the activities of those who go abroad for abortion or to assist suicide represents the most direct way of attempting to prevent circumvention tourism. A less direct and complementary route is to criminalize the provision *within* the home country of information regarding the availability of prohibited services abroad. Although I will not attempt to offer a full analysis of the clash between freedom of expression and circumvention tourism, I do want to briefly discuss the existing case law on the subject and my views of it.

Ireland, again, has wrestled with this precise question. In a series of cases culminating in *Open Door Counselling Ltd. v. Ireland*, the European Court of Human Rights was asked to determine whether Ireland, which prohibited abortion at home, could lawfully prohibit Irish nonprofit organizations from "counselling pregnant women within the jurisdiction of the court to travel abroad to obtain an abortion."[149] The European Court of Human Rights ultimately determined that although the prohibition barring advising on overseas options "could be regarded as prescribed by law—that is, grounded in the

---

[149] Open Door Counselling Ltd. v. Ireland, 246 Eur. Ct. H.R. 1, ¶ 12 (1992).

Eighth Amendment to the Irish Constitution—and necessary to pursue the legitimate aim of the Irish State to protect the life of the unborn," that "the 'absolute nature' of the 'restraint imposed on the applicants from receiving or imparting information was disproportionate to the aims pursued' and was thus in violation of the right to freedom of information" as protected by the European Convention on Human Rights.[150]

Significantly, though, for our purposes, the court emphasized that "it is not a criminal offence under Irish law for a pregnant woman to travel abroad in order to have an abortion," that "the injunction limited the freedom to receive and impart information witrespect to services which are lawful in other Convention countries and may be crucial to a woman's health and well-being," and that "[l]imitations on information concerning activities which, notwithstanding their moral implications, have been and continue to be tolerated by national authorities, call for careful scrutiny by the Convention institutions as to their conformity with the tenets of a democratic society."[151] Thus, the case involved speech about circumvention tourism where the home country had not extraterritorially criminalized the same act it prohibited at home.

In finding the prohibition unlawful, the Court also noted many ways in which the prohibition was both overbroad and ineffective, including: that the prohibition on speech applied even to counseling the small number of women who *could* lawfully have abortions in Ireland; that "there can be little doubt that following such counselling there were women who decided against a termination of pregnancy" such that "the link between the provision of information and the destruction of unborn life is not as definite as contended"; that the government did not "seriously contest[]" that "information concerning abortion facilities abroad can be obtained from other sources in Ireland such as magazines and telephone directories... or by persons with contacts in Great Britain" such that the information in question was "already available elsewhere although in a manner which was not supervised by qualified personnel and thus less protective of women's health," and the prohibition was likely to have "had more adverse effects on women who were not sufficiently resourceful or had not the necessary level of education to have access to alternative sources of information."[152] Finally, and perhaps most damning, the court concluded that the prohibition appeared to "have been largely ineffective in protecting the right to life of the unborn since it did not prevent large numbers of Irish women from continuing to obtain abortions in Great Britain."[153]

Where circumvention tourism is *not* prohibited even though the activity is prohibited domestically, I think the *Open Door* largely gets it right as a normative and legal

---

[150] Federico Fabbrini, *The European Court of Human Rights, the EU Charter of Fundamental Rights, and the Right to Abortion:* Roe v. Wade *on the Other Side of the Atlantic?*, 18 COLUM. J. EUR. L. 1, 21 (2011) (quoting Open Door Counselling, 42 Eur. Ct. H.R. at ¶¶ 60–63, 73, 80).

[151] Open Door Counselling, 42 Eur. Ct. H.R. at ¶72.

[152] *Id.* at ¶¶ 72–73.

[153] *Id.*

matter—home countries that do not prohibit their citizens from going abroad for abortion or assisted suicide should also not prohibit domestic providers from apprising potential patients of those options. The harder, and I think, more interesting question is what to do about a case where the home country *has* criminalized circumvention tourism and rendered it a crime to go abroad for the service in question, an issue the *Open Door* court explicitly does not reach.

This is an issue that is still not definitively answered under U.S. law. A mere two years after *Roe v. Wade*, in a case called *Bigelow v. Virginia*, the U.S. Supreme Court held unconstitutional the conviction of a Virginia newspaper editor for printing an advertisement for an abortion referral service in New York, observing (in a passage that scholars continue to disagree on whether it was a holding or dictum) that Virginia "could not have regulated the advertiser's activity in New York, and obviously could not have proscribed the activity in that State" nor "could Virginia prevent its residents from traveling to New York to obtain those services, or, as the state conceded, prosecute them for going there."[154]

But *Bigelow* was a case where one U.S. state was attempting to regulate the activities of another U.S. state, and the Court noted its view (perhaps dictum) that one state could not prohibit its citizen from traveling to another state for an abortion. The question here is if a home country *has* lawfully made it a crime for a citizen to go abroad to get an abortion or assisted suicide, may it prosecute a citizen doctor for advising one of its citizens to do so?

This is not an issue that the U.S. Supreme Court has had the opportunity to weigh in on, though the lower courts have done so in somewhat analogous contexts. In 1997, the Fourth Circuit considered whether relatives and representatives of murder victims could bring a state law wrongful death action against a publisher who published a "hit man" manual that assisted murderers in soliciting, preparing for, and committing murders.[155] In summarizing its view of the case law to date, the court wrote that it had been "uniformly accepted" that "the provision of instructions that aid and abet another in the commission of a criminal offense is unprotected by the First Amendment."[156] In reaching that conclusion, it cited cases from other circuits upholding against a First Amendment challenge the charging of a publisher with "aiding and abetting a crime through the publication and distribution of instructions on how to make illegal drugs," and aiding and abetting evasion of tax laws by instructing individuals on how to fill in the requisite tax forms.[157] Importantly, these cases distinguish something such as "abstract criticism of income tax laws," or urging listeners "to seek congressional action to exempt wages from

---

[154] 421 U.S. 809, 822–24 (1975). *See also If Roe Were Overruled: Abortion and the Constitution in a Post-*Roe *World*, 51 ST. LOUIS U. L.J. 611, 628–33 (2007) (discussing the *Bigelow* case and its interpretation).

[155] Rice v. Paladin Enters., Inc., 128 F.3d 233 (4th Cir. 1997).

[156] *Id.* at 245.

[157] *Id.* at 244–46 (citing United States v. Barnett, 667 F.2d 835 (9th Cir. 1982); United States v. Kelley, 769 F.2d 215 (4th Cir. 1985); United States v. Rowlee, 899 F.2d 1275 (2d Cir. 1990); United States v. Moss, 604 F.2d 569 (8th Cir. 1979); United States v. Buttorff, 572 F.2d 619, 623–24 (8th Cir. 1978)).

income taxation" from urging listeners to "file false returns, with every expectation that the advice would be heeded"; that is, the "cloak of the First Amendment envelops critical, but abstract, discussions of existing laws, but lends no protection to speech which urges the listeners to commit violations of current law."[158]

Although some of these lines are fuzzy, under existing U.S. constitutional First Amendment case law, it appears to me that *if* abortion or assisted suicide were both constitutionally a crime domestically[159] *and* criminalized extraterritorially, the United States could *also* criminalize speech by physicians or others advising patients on how to procure an abortion or assisted suicide abroad. Drafting a prohibition that was not overbroad and reached protected speech would be challenging but not necessarily insurmountable. For example, it is likely unconstitutional to prohibit a physician from simply informing a patient that abortion/assisted suicide "was legal in country X that does not have a residency requirement," or even "the prohibition on abortion and assisted suicide in our jurisdiction is wrongheaded and should be unlawful, luckily patients can circumvent it by going to country X, which does not have a residency requirement," or even "in the past some of my patients have gone abroad to country X for abortions and assisted suicide." What it could criminalize, though, is speech much more directly tied to the circumvention tourism activity. The easy case would be when a home country physician phones a clinic abroad and arranges for that clinic to take the patient in question for the prohibited activity. Closer to the line, but I think still constitutional, would be prohibiting a physician from recommending a particular foreign abortion clinic for termination of the pregnancy of the patient. Whether criminalizing this type of speech (or even more extensive criminalization) would be permissible in other home countries will depend on that home country's case law relating to freedom of expression and the extent of the protection it offers.

Assume, though, for the moment that the home country *could*, as a matter of law criminalize this type of speech, *should* it do so? A full answer would require an in-depth analysis of the value of the criminalized speech. This includes the difficulties of enforcing such obligations and the difficult questions posed by "dual-use" speech—speech that is both promoting a crime but also serving advocacy or other core political speech goals. I do not purport to offer that in-depth analysis, which would take us a bit far afield from the topic of medical tourism that is our focus. Eugene Volokh, among others, has offered excellent work of this type on which I will draw.[160] Here I merely want to explain why even if one thinks that a home country should criminalize extraterritorially that which it criminalizes domestically—abortion and assisted suicide in our cases—and

---

[158] *Rice*, 128 F. 3d at 246, (quoting *Kelley*, 769 F.2d at 158–59).

[159] Again, as I noted above, in the U.S. context the current Supreme Court doctrine would make it unconstitutional to criminalize pre-viability abortions within the United States. What I say here still has application to circumvention tourism for any abortion that can be criminalized under U.S. law if it was hypothetically criminalized under federal law. It also has implications for a hypothetical but possible future where the abortion right in the United States is chipped away or eliminated.

[160] Eugene Volokh, *Crime-Facilitating Speech*, 57 STAN. L. REV. 1095 (2005).

presumably wants to reduce those activities as much as possible through the threat of criminal sanction, it does *not* necessarily follow that one should also want to criminalize the speech of doctors advising patients on the option of circumvention tourism.

First, the speech of physicians about options abroad has a series of positive uses that may balance the State's interest in deterring circumvention tourism. It can educate doctors about the questions and issues their patients are thinking about, and also give them an opportunity to help those patients make choices least likely to threaten the patient's health and safety. Allowing robust discussion of circumvention tourism options may also enable patients to engage in political debates at home regarding whether the domestic prohibition or the extraterritorial extension should be relaxed.[161] A State might be committed to enabling that robust debate even while it zealously pursues the criminalization of circumvention tourism, or it might more cynically want to use some of this speech to deplete pressure to relax the domestic prohibition. This is somewhat analogous to the safety valve exception discussed above, although in that case the idea was that rendering abortion or assisted suicide achieved abroad legal would reduce pressure to reverse the domestic prohibition, whereas on this logic the domestic and extraterritorial versions remain criminal but allowing physicians to advise patients about the illegal option is what has the pressure-reducing force.

Second, speech regarding medical tourism may in some ways be a form of dual-use material, akin to guns, knives, videocassette recorders, alcohol, and the like, that is, "materials [that] can be used both in harmful ways—instructions and chemicals can equally be precursors to illegal bombs—and in legitimate ways" and for which "it's usually impossible for the distributor to know whether a particular consumer will use the product harmfully or legally."[162] I think this is particularly likely as to fertility tourism, which is the subject of the next chapter; suppose the home country prohibits some forms of surrogacy agreements but not others? In this instance, the doctor's advice recommending a foreign clinic may be "dual use" in that she will be unable to determine if the patient will be using the lawful or unlawful variety. Even as to abortion, though, there could be dual-use cases. Suppose the home country only prohibits sex-selective or disability-selective abortions extraterritorially, but prohibits all forms of abortion at home, for example. Here it may be that the doctor advising the patient on using a foreign clinic will not know whether the patient will use it for the lawful or unlawful service.[163] That said, these fears relating to dual-use speech should not be exaggerated; one could

---

[161] *Cf.* Volokh, *supra* note 160, at 1112–26 (discussing the way crime-facilitating speech "can educate readers, or give them practical information that they can use lawfully… [and] help[s] people evaluate and participate in public debates").

[162] *Cf. id.* at 1127.

[163] To the extent that retaining the possibility of true "Exit" (or potentially "Exile" as discussed above) is also important—that individuals who want to engage in the prohibited conduct be able to do so by renouncing their citizenship—then one might also think that physician speech about the possibility of circumvention tourism is also a valuable dual use product in that it informs them that Exit may be worth considering.

try to accommodate these concerns by imposing on the doctor a duty of inquiry in giving the advice or a duty to not reference the unlawful services being offered while permitting a general description of the service. In theory statutes could be carefully tailored in that way, but in practice one may end up chilling more speech than one desires to.

This, however, leads into the final reason that I would be fairly cautious in criminalizing home country physician speech on circumvention tourism. This reason focuses on the kind of speech that is at issue here—speech between partners in a fiduciary relationship where trust and openness is essential. The same reasons that underlie the legal protection offered by the physician-patient privilege also mitigate against too much policing of physician speech. To be sure, that privilege protects the *patient*'s communication and not the physician's. Moreover, as I will discuss in greater depth in Chapter 10 on stem cell therapies, we do already have in place robust reporting requirements for child abuse that may serve as a relevant analogy here to medical tourism as well. Still, given that fixing the lines between appropriate and inappropriate physician speech regarding circumvention tourism will be difficult and that there is a real risk of chilling appropriate communication in this relationship, as well as the attendant concern that this chilling will itself undermine trust and have bad spillovers for the relationship, I think there is good reason to be cautious about criminalizing physician speech regarding circumvention tourism even where it is lawful. The closer the speech comes to actually facilitating travel abroad for circumvention tourism, which might be thought as a kind of conspiracy liability, the greater the normative justification for criminalizing the physician speech. Even here, though, I would argue for treading lightly on the offending physician.

V. CONCLUSION

Countries that prohibit abortion and assisted suicide face a policy question: Should they criminalize the same behavior by their citizens when done extraterritorially or should they permit circumvention tourism? I have argued that countries that have what they believe is a lawful and normatively justified prohibition on abortion or assisted suicide (1) may as a matter of international law extend the prohibition such that they assert prescriptive extraterritorial jurisdiction over their citizens in these cases, and (2) have strong normative and political theoretical reasons for doing so, especially as to abortion. On the other hand, I have suggested we should be far more cautious in concluding that countries that criminally prohibit circumvention tourism should also criminalize physician speech by home country physicians informing or advising patients on this option to go abroad for abortion or assisted suicide. The next chapter extends this discussion further by considering another area where patients use medical tourism to avoid home country rules (as well as for other reasons): fertility tourism.

9

Medical Tourism and the Creation of Life: A Study of Fertility Tourism

THE LAST CHAPTER examined the use of medical tourism to end life in the form of abortion and assisted suicide. In this chapter, I will discuss its use in creating life, the so-called "fertility tourism" industry, involving traveling abroad to use a variety of reproductive technologies such as artificial insemination, surrogacy, sex selection, etc.

In order to get a better handle on the industry, let me begin with some real-life cases:

In late 2010, Lee Shau-kee was an eighty-two-year-old chairman of property development at Henderson Land Development Ltd., living in Hong Kong, and one of the richest men in Asia. He was also about to become the grandfather of triplets.[1] In part because three is a particularly lucky number in Cantonese and sounds like the word for "birth," the triplets were seen as an auspicious sign celebrated with great fanfare, media attention, and gifts. A press release was issued, a donation was made to a local hospital, and each of Henderson Land's approximately 1300 employers were given a bonus of HK$10,000, or about $1,300. What was missing from all this celebration, was a mother.

---

[1] This account is drawn from Cathy Yan, *Maternal Mystery: Babies Bring Joy, and Questions, in Hong Kong*, WALL ST. J., Dec. 14, 2010, *available at* http://online.wsj.com/article/SB100014240527487034719045760 02913040745224.html.

While the children were born to Lee's forty-seven-year-old bachelor son, Peter Lee, no mother was named, and local newspapers reported that the triplets were born to a paid surrogate mother in California. Under Hong Kong's Reproductive Technology Ordinance, in effect since 2000, commercial surrogacy (among other practices) was rendered illegal. At a December 1, 2010, meeting of Hong Kong's legislature, shortly after Lee's announcement, lawmaker Cyd Ho—while refusing to name names—asked if authorities had looked into the case of a "male Hong Kong permanent resident" who "recently issued a press release on the triplets born to him." Ho later commented that "'Surrogacy with commercial interest is the same as the trade of organs[,] [i]t is still a trade, and women from poverty may be compelled into this transaction,'" and that she was wary that the press release "'gives the message that anybody can violate the law in Hong Kong without getting caught.'"

A quick reading of the law suggests Lee may have been in violation. The law states: "No person shall, whether in Hong Kong or elsewhere, make or receive any payment for initiating or taking part in any negotiations with a view to the making of a surrogacy arrangement," and the reference to "or elsewhere" seems to suggest extraterritorial reach of the prohibition. Despite the law, though, the business of connecting Hong Kong nationals with foreign surrogates appears to be booming.

The Surrogacy Center Hong Kong, based in Laguna Niguel, California, profits by serving Hong Kong prospective parents looking for surrogate mothers in the United States, particularly in U.S. states (such as California) where the practice is legal and facilitated by contract law. Roughly 40 percent of the center's clients are single men who pay between US$20,000 and $35,000 for a surrogate. The clinic does the entire process for international patients in the United States—sperm donation, birth, and everything in between. As Cathy Yan recites in her story on the case: "Lawyers are called in for both parties, contracts are drawn up and requests (for example, that the mother eat only organic food) are laid out." The story quotes Hilary Neiman, an attorney for the center, founded in 2004, as suggesting that they had yet to run into a legal problem (though one wonders whether this case ushered some!).

The Surrogacy Center Hong Kong clinic is not alone in catering to fertility tourists from outside the United States. Another U.S. surrogacy program, Surrogacy Source, based in Irvine, California, reported that one-third of its international clients are from Hong Kong. A third clinic, Fertility Miracles, in Beverly Hills, California, stated that 65 percent of its business came from international prospective parents, with many coming from Asia (including Hong Kong). And of course it is not just U.S. clinics seeing these patients. As discussed in Chapter 1, the Barbados Fertility Center is often regarded as a success story for medical tourism on the island.

What should we make of this trade? To ask a question that parallels that which was discussed in the last chapter, is Hong Kong justified in extending its prohibition on commercial surrogacy to its citizens when they pursue the practice abroad? Does it matter that the surrogates themselves in this case are U.S. and not Hong Kong citizens? Does it matter if our concern is exploitation of the surrogate, harm to the resulting children, or corruption of attitudes? Should the United States prohibit its own citizens from engaging in surrogacy with Hong Kong nationals out of respect for Hong Kong's sovereignty?

Although the United States is one major site for medical tourism for surrogacy, it is not the only one. In particular, as we will see below, India is a prime destination, with price being a major motivating factor. Should our analysis of surrogacy tourism change if instead of Californian clinics, surrogacy takes place in the developing world?

Consider the Akanksha Infertility Clinic, centered in the village of Anand, India, run by Doctor Nanya Patel, and featured on *The Oprah Winfrey Show*, which gives a good sense of travel for surrogacy in India today.[2]

The clinic employs only women who have been married and have had at least one child. In 2008, there were forty-five surrogates on the payroll who lived away from their families in a compound, which one author described as a "classroom-size space...dominated by a maze of iron cots that spills out into a hallway."[3] Surrogates receive $50 a month, plus $500 at the end of each trimester, and the balance upon delivery. A successful Akanksha surrogate makes between US$5,000 and $6,000 (slightly more if she bears twins), an amount that exceeds a typical salary for several years of ordinary labor in India. If a woman miscarries, she keeps what she has been paid up to that point. If she chooses to abort—an option the contract allows—she must reimburse the clinic and the client for all expenses. The clinic charges American medical tourists US$15,000 to $20,000 for the entire process, which includes in vitro fertilization, somewhere between a third and a fifth of what clients would pay for a similar service in the United States. Similar to U.S. pricing, the surrogate receives roughly a quarter of the total fees. There have been reports that the Ankanksha clinic routinely implants five or more embryos at a time, considerably more than the one or two implanted embryos recommended by the American Society for Reproductive Medicine. Under guidelines issued by the Indian Council of Medical Research, surrogate mothers sign away their rights to any children, and the surrogate's name is not even put on the birth certificate.

Writing in 2008, Smerdon gives more details about the origin of the clinic, its philosophy and the attitudes of some of the surrogates:

> Dr. Patel's first surrogacy effort was in 2003 when she assisted the surrogacy of a local forty-four year old woman who wished to bear a child for her daughter who was living in the United Kingdom. A snapshot of the company shows that in

---

[2] This account is drawn from Scott Carney, *Inside India's Rent-a-Womb Business*, MOTHER JONES, Mar.–Apr. 2010, *available at* http://motherjones.com/politics/2010/02/surrogacy-tourism-india-nayna-patel. *See also* Amelia Gentleman, *India Nurtures Business of Surrogate Motherhood*, N.Y. TIMES, Mar. 10, 2008, at A9, *available at* http://www.nytimes.com/2008/03/10/world/asia/10surrogate.html?pagewanted=all&_r=0; Glenn Cohen, *Circumvention Tourism*, 97 CORNELL L. REV. 1309 (2012).

[3] Carney, *supra* note 2.

August 2006, the clinic had nine IVF surrogates pregnant with babies for Indian and foreign couples. By 2007, the clinic had twenty surrogates contracted for couples abroad, a waiting list of 250 couples worldwide, and over forty total babies born to surrogates. In March of 2008, over fifty surrogates were carrying children for foreign clientele.

At Dr. Patel's clinic, babies are given up one to two days after birth. Dr. Patel claimed that no problems have arisen with surrogates bonding emotionally with the babies. She is quoted as saying, "[t]he first question is, '[i]s the baby OK?' The second is, '[i]s the couple happy?' And then they say, 'Thank God,' And then they don't think about it after that." As with other ART [Assisted Reproductive Technology] practitioners, Dr. Patel highlights the surrogate's altruistic motivations. She said, "If you say it's a business of emotions, I would say yes. It's not a business of economics and finances. There are a lot of emotions involved in this. And if a female is just doing this for business, I think this is not the right thing to do." Dr. Patel finds that convincing a woman to become a surrogate is the most difficult part: "[w]hen they come first to me they are really a desperate lot because this is the last thing they would want to try. It's not easy carrying a baby for 9 months for someone else."

Dr. Patel only provides services for couples who have a medical reason for turning to surrogacy. Citing her conservative cultural beliefs, she will not accept gay couples as clients. Dr. Patel permits commissioning couples to converse with the surrogates at the clinic; in fact, many commissioning couples shower the surrogate with attention and gifts. Some couples continue to stay in touch with the surrogate via the internet even after the birth.

Dr. Patel advertises, locates the surrogates, and matches them with commissioning couples herself. Most women live locally but some travel from far away places, lured by the money to be earned. Anand has a population of roughly 150,000, so it is not unusual for surrogacy for hire to be spread by word of mouth. There are instances of families in which several of the women have served as surrogates. For example, in one family, a mother and her three daughters served as surrogates, and in another, three sisters and a sister-in-law. Dr. Patel does acknowledge the difficulties faced by surrogates: "[y]ou see, Indian society is still quite conservative and questions get asked. So often these women will just move out of the local area to have the child." One surrogate mother recounted: "Madam told me I should become a surrogate and if I do, all my worries will go away." She told the women to "think of the pregnancy as 'someone's child comes to stay at your place for nine months.'"

In Dr. Patel's operation, several surrogates live together in a rented home near the clinic and some live on the third floor of the clinic itself, which has been converted into a dormitory. The surrogates' husbands and children may visit during the day, and some take classes such as English or computer skills.

Surrogates at Dr. Patel's clinic are paid on the upper end of the Indian surrogacy market scale...Many of the surrogates also donate eggs but are not allowed to serve as traditional surrogates. Dr. Patel herself retains control over the fee paid to surrogates, indicating that the clinic will hold the money for the surrogate if she wants to use it for a house purchase or that the clinic will accompany the surrogate to the bank to establish an account in her own name.[4]

Should our analysis of any of these questions change if the medical tourist is traveling to this clinic rather than one in the United States?

Consider a second case, the "Baby Manji" one:[5]

Two Japanese intended parents (i.e., parents seeking to produce a child through reproductive technology), Ikufumi and Yuki Yamada, went to the town of Anand in India to have a "traditional" surrogacy[6]: that is, the father's sperm was used, making him the genetic father, but his wife's eggs were not used; instead, the surrogate was both the genetic and gestational mother of the child. After insemination, but before birth, the intended parents divorced, with the father wishing to raise the child but his wife not wishing to do so. When, on July 25, 2008, the baby girl known as "Manji" was born, the wife "disowned the child."[7] When the father sought a passport from the Japanese embassy in Delhi to bring the child back to Japan, the Japanese embassy refused, claiming that because the child was born in India she needed an Indian passport and a "no-objection" certificate to enable the infant to leave the country. However, under Indian law, a passport may only be issued to an infant along with the passport of the mother because no female infant may leave India without the mother's consent, even if she is leaving with her genetic father. Both Yuki and the surrogate mother refused to take custody of baby Manji, so the child was left in legal limbo.

Ultimately, a solution was found after a number of court applications and the handling of further immigration issues, not completed until four months after Manji's birth. The Japanese grandmother of baby Manji, Emiko Yamada, arrived in India to claim the baby. She was eventually given custody of the baby, who was issued what is called a "certificate of identity," a document given to stateless individuals or those who cannot get a

---

[4] Usha Rengachary Smerdon, *Crossing Bodies, Crossing Borders: International Surrogacy between the United States and India*, 39 CUMB. L. REV. 15, 48–50 (2008) (citations omitted).

[5] This account of the case is drawn from Jennifer A. Parks, *Care Ethics and the Global Practice of Commercial Surrogacy*, 24 BIOETHICS 333, 333–35 (2010) and Erin Nelson, *Global Trade and Assisted Reproductive Technologies: Regulatory Challenges in International Surrogacy*, 41 J. L. MED. & ETHICS 240, 245 (2013).

[6] Nelson, *supra* note 5, at 241.

[7] Parks, *supra* note 5, at 333.

passport from their home country. The certificate issued to Manji was only valid for Japan and omitted any mention of the name or nationality of the mother of the child. Using the document, Emiko Yamada was able to bring the baby girl back to Japan. Japan then granted a visa to permit Manji to remain in Japan for one year, at which point the Japanese authorities signaled a willingness to allow the genetic father to adopt the child, as they would have formed a sufficient relationship.[8]

Although the four-month delay in bringing Baby Manji home was sad, other parents have waited longer still. In another infamous case, a German couple employed a gestational surrogate (i.e., the German man and woman were both the intended parents and the source of sperm and egg, making them genetic parents while the Indian surrogate carried the child). Though the birth certificate listed the Germans as mother and father, German law would not grant the children (twins) citizenship because they were conceived through a surrogacy agreement that was illegal in Germany. Indian law, in addition, would not recognize the twins as Indian citizens because Indian law requires that one of the parents must be an Indian citizen at the time of birth. After two years of litigation, the German couple was able to get the Indian Supreme Court to direct the Indian Central Adoption Resources Agency to allow the Germans to adopt the children and take them back to Germany.[9]

These problems have also occurred in destination countries other than India. Lin recounts the story of baby Samuel Ghilain, whom we first heard about in the Preface of this book, who was born in Ukraine to a surrogate commissioned by his intended parents, Laurent Ghilain and Peter Meurrens. The men were married in Belgium, which permits same-sex couples to adopt, but faced administrative difficulties that led them to surrogacy. They hired a gestational surrogate to carry a child created from Ghilain's sperm and the egg of an anonymous egg provider. Upon the birth of their son in November 2008, Samuel's parents went to the Belgian embassy in Kiev, Ukraine, which refused to recognize the child as a citizen of Belgium. Because Belgian law was silent on the legality of surrogacy, the Belgian government denied Samuel citizenship, reasoning that it had no legal basis to recognize the Ukrainian birth certificate, despite the fact that the child's genetic father was a Belgian citizen. In what will now, sadly, become a common refrain, Samuel also could not be a Ukrainian citizen because Ukrainian law recognizes the intended parents as the child's legal parents, so Samuel was neither a Ukrainian nor a Belgian citizen. Without citizenship Samuel could not get a passport and thus could not leave Ukraine. It took two years and three months to resolve the issue, with Samuel placed first with a foster family and then a Ukrainian orphanage, until a Belgian court

---

[8] Nelson, *supra* note 5, at 252 n.90.

[9] For articles detailing this case, *see* Nelson, *supra* note 5, at 245; Smerdon, *supra* note 4, at 62–65; Dhananjay Mahapatra, *German or Indian? Surrogate Twins in Legal No-Man's Land*, Times of India, Dec. 1, 2009, *available at* http://articles.timesofindia.indiatimes.com/2009-12-01/india/28087428_1_surrogate-twins-surrogacy-agreement-surrogate-mother.

ruled in favor of Samuel's parents, whereon the Belgian Foreign Ministry finally agreed to give him a passport. At that point, after a long odyssey, Samuel was finally brought to Belgium. At the same time, his case did not set a precedent for the future: following the resolution of Samuel's citizenship, the Belgian Foreign Ministry issued a press release advising against the hiring of foreign nationals because of difficulties in recognizing the citizenship of the children abroad, and, as of this writing, Belgium has still not passed a law on surrogacy.[10]

How should home countries treat children born through surrogacy or egg or sperm donation abroad when their citizens are the intended parents? If the home country prohibits the form of reproductive technology at use, for example, commercial surrogacy, it is appropriate for it to refuse to grant citizenship to the resulting child to try to deter its citizens from engaging in fertility tourism? Or does that approach unfairly penalize the child?

I seek to answer these and other questions relating to fertility tourism in this chapter, which proceeds as follows. Part I explains the major forms of reproductive technology used as part of fertility tourism, and also sketches what we know about the current flow of patients, doctors, surrogates, and egg and sperm donors in the trade. The next part of the chapter continues the discussion from the immediately prior chapter and examines under what circumstances home countries that prohibit particular reproductive technologies from being used by their citizens in the home country should extend that prohibition to those citizens who in order to pursue pregnancy go abroad to a country where the practice is legal. Among other things, I discuss the question of whether fertility tourism involving surrogacy is a morally problematic form of exploitation—a discussion that builds on a similar discussion in Chapter 7 as to organ sale—and, even if a home country concludes it is a morally problematic form of exploitation that justifies domestic criminal prohibition, whether that analysis also mandates extending the prohibition extraterritorially. The third part of this chapter examines the question of nationality and immigration for the children born through fertility tourism.

Fertility tourism is a large and complex phenomenon, and even merely as to its ethical and legal elements I cannot exhaustively deal in a chapter with all the issues it raises. Some of the additional issues that other authors identify—risk for home country patients of poor-quality treatment, risk of poor medical malpractice recovery should something go wrong, the effect on health care access for the destination country's poor[11]—are dealt with more comprehensively as to all forms of medical tourism in other chapters in this

---

[10] This account is taken from Tina Lin, Note, *Born Lost: Stateless Children in International Surrogacy Arrangements*, 21 CARDOZO J. INT'L & COMP. L. 545, 546–48 (2013).

[11] *See, e.g.*, Andrea Whittaker, *Cross-Border Assisted Reproductive Care: Global Quests for a Child, in* RISKS AND CHALLENGES IN MEDICAL TOURISM: UNDERSTANDING THE DYNAMICS OF THE GLOBAL MARKET FOR HEALTH SERVICES 167, 169, 174–80 (Jill Hodges et al. eds., 2012); Lin, *supra* note 10; Smerdon, *supra* note 4.

book, and readers interested in these aspects of fertility tourism can read my analysis there. In this chapter, I focus on issues more specific to fertility tourism.

I. WHAT IS KNOWN ABOUT FERTILITY TOURISM?

A. Types of Technology for Which Fertility Tourism Is Sought

Since the 1880s, modern medicine has added a number of methods for treating infertility.[12] Fertility tourism involves traveling abroad to use one of a series of different reproductive technologies. Let me review some of the main treatments in a nontechnical way as background for readers unfamiliar with these technologies.

In vitro fertilization, or "IVF," was first successfully used in Oldham, England, in 1978 to produce Louise Brown. IVF proceeds in four stages. First, the woman who will provide eggs is administered ovulation-stimulating hormones, which cause multiple egg-containing follicles to mature so that up to several dozen eggs can be harvested in a single treatment cycle. Second, just prior to ovulation, the eggs are removed by a minor surgical procedure; today, this is usually done by an ultrasound-guided needle inserted through the vaginal wall into a developed ovarian follicle through which, by suction, the egg is harvested. Third, sperm is introduced into individual culture dishes, each of which contains a culture medium and one egg, with the culture dish monitored after the first day to determine if fertilization occurs. Finally, if fertilization occurs, the preembryos are allowed to mature in the medium, usually for two to three days after egg retrieval, until the preembryos reach the four- or eight-cell stage when some or all of them are transferred into the woman's uterus to attempt implantation. Ten to fourteen days after embryo transfer, the woman will undergo a pregnancy test to determine if the transfer was successful. IVF can also be done using frozen eggs (i.e., those frozen between the second and third step), or frozen preembryos (i.e., preembryos frozen after the third step but before the fourth step). In the United States in 2010, the average cost per cycle of IVF was US$12,400, and it has been estimated that actually producing a live birth through IVF would cost an individual (on average) between US$66,667 and $114,286. Most individuals will not have these costs covered by their health insurance.[13]

Artificial insemination's history goes back much further still. Artificial insemination of dogs began in 1780 (in Italy by the priest Lazzaro Spallanzani) and then began in humans in 1785 (by the Scottish surgeon John Hunter). Artificial insemination using donor sperm occurred for the first time in 1884 by Doctor William Pancoast

---

[12] For a good guide through the history, see JUDITH F. DAAR, REPRODUCTIVE TECHNOLOGIES AND THE LAW 26–40 (2d ed. 2013).

[13] This description is taken from I. Glenn Cohen & Daniel L. Chen, Trading-Off Reproductive Technology and Adoption: Does Subsidizing IVF Decrease Adoption Rates and Should It Matter?, 95 MINN. L. REV. 485, 486, 490–91 (2010).

in Philadelphia.[14] In its modern form, semen is obtained from the male (usually through masturbation) and then injected into the woman's reproductive track in one of three ways: (1) intravaginal insemination, involving placing semen in the vagina near the cervical opening and then placing a device in the cervix to hold the semen there; (2) intra-cervical assisted insemination where a tube is inserted into the cervical opening to place a small amount of semen in the cervix; and (3) intrauterine insemination, in which the sperm is washed and bacteria removed and then injected through a narrow tube threaded through the cervix, vagina, and uterus.[15] When the insemination is done with donor sperm, it is referred to as artificial insemination by donor, or "AID." Artificial insemination can also be accomplished by Intracytoplasmic Sperm Injection (ICSI) in which a single sperm cell is injected directly into the egg. This is done by placing sperm in a solution that slows their movement, selecting and immobilizing a single sperm, and using a slim pipette to insert it directly into the cytoplasm of the egg, which is the material surrounding the nucleus.[16]

Surrogacy comes in two forms. The first is called "full" or "traditional" and involves artificial insemination of the surrogate with sperm, after which the surrogate carries the baby—her genetic child—to term as she would in a normal pregnancy. In "gestational" surrogacy, IVF is used to implant a fertilized embryo into the surrogate who carries it to term. Hence, the child is not the surrogate's genetic offspring; rather, it is the genetic offspring of the intended parents.[17]

Preimplantation Genetic Diagnosis (PGD), first introduced in the early 1990s as an experimental procedure, is used to screen embryos fertilized as part of IVF. The embryo (or "preembryo" as it is sometimes called—there are disputes about the nomenclature that are sometimes political) is allowed to grow to the eight-cell stage and then one cell (known as a blastomere) is removed using an injection pipette. This one cell is tested and, in the process, destroyed, because it is glued to a glass slide and repeatedly heated and cooled. Importantly, all current data indicates that removing the single cell causes no damage to the developing embryo (although it is hypothetically possible future science will prove this wrong) as the remaining seven fetal cells retain significant totipotency (the ability to divide and differentiate into different cell types) and can, unaffected, develop into a fully formed human being.

In current clinical practice, PGD has been used for so-called "medical selection," in which embryos that are aneuploidic (having particular genes or chromosomal regions

---

[14] *Id.* at 490.

[15] DAAR, *supra* note 12, at 39.

[16] *Id.* at 850. There are other technologies such as Gamete and Zygote Intrafallopian transfer ("GIFT" and "ZIFT") that I will not discuss here, but for more discussion, *see id.* at 850–52.

[17] Things can get more complicated, of course. Two parents can approach a surrogate to serve as a gestational surrogate, but get a separate sperm and egg provider, such that there are five parents involved in the reproduction: two intended parents, a sperm provider, an egg provider, and a gestational surrogate. For a legal case with facts like this, *see In re* Marriage of Buzzanca, 61 Cal. App. 4th 1410 (1998).

present in extra or fewer copies than in the normal type) or contain genetic muta-
tions likely to lead to serious diseases are discarded. It has also been used for "sex selection," discussed below, in which parents choose to implant embryos only of the desired
gender.[18] Less commonly, but in a few reported cases, it has been used to create children
with a particular "disability" shared by the parents such as deafness or achondroplasia
(being a "dwarf"), or to create so-called "savior siblings"—children capable, because of
matching tissue, of being stem cell or bone marrow donors to an ill, already-existing
child in a family.[19]

Sex selection is a practice that has been going on for centuries across the world, frequently through selective abortion. Diagnostic technologies such as amniocentesis and
chorionic villus sampling (CVS), and better ultrasound machines have facilitated the
practice by enabling detection of sex much earlier in pregnancy. In particular, they have
helped contribute to the practice of sex-selective abortions by making it easier for parents
to detect the sex of the fetus early in the pregnancy. Hence, the emerging technologies of
noninvasive prenatal diagnosis will mean much earlier detection of sex (as well as other
facts about the fetus) and earlier abortions.[20]

To the extent sex selection is accomplished by abortion, it is more in keeping with the
discussion of travel abroad for abortion discussed in the last chapter. There are, however,
two forms of sex selection that constitute fertility tourism. The first uses PGD to determine the sex of embryos being considered for implantation. The second is "sperm sorting," a technology originally developed for sorting the sperm of bulls, which in its human
commercial form is called "MicroSort," and "separates male and female sperm by using
flow cytometry (a process involving the use of a special fluorescent stain that attaches
temporarily to the DNA contained in the spermatozoa to determine the sex of the
sperm) and then injecting sperm with the chromosome of the desired sex" through artificial insemination or ICSI.[21] MicroSort improves the chances of having a female child
by approximately 90 percent and a male by approximately 75 to 85 percent. However,
due to difficulties MicroSort's parent company (the Genetics & IVF Institute) faced
when trying to get FDA approval for use in the United States, the company "decided

---

[18] This description of the process is drawn from Judith F. Daar, *ART and the Search for Perfectionism: On Selecting Gender, Genes, and Gametes*, 9 J. GENDER RACE & JUST. 241, 248–50 (2005).

[19] For descriptions of these uses and some of the ethical issues involved, *see generally* I. Glenn Cohen, *Intentional Diminishment, The Non-identity Problem, and Legal Liability*, 60 HASTINGS L.J. 347 (2008); Kirsten Rabe Smolensky, *Creating Children with Disabilities: Parental Tort Liability for Preimplantation Genetic Interventions*, 60 HASTINGS L.J. 299 (2008); Susan M. Wolf et al., *Using Preimplantation Genetic Diagnosis to Create a Stem Cell Donor: Issues, Guidelines & Limits*, 31 J.L. MED. & ETHICS 327 (2003).

[20] *See, e.g.*, Jaime S. King, *And Genetic Testing for All… The Coming Revolution in Non-invasive Prenatal Genetic Testing*, 42 RUTGERS L.J. 599 (2011); Annie Moskovian, *Bans on Sex-Selective Abortions: How Far Is Too Far?*, 40 HASTINGS CONST. L.Q. 423, 431 (2013).

[21] Kevin L. Boyd, Comment, *The Inevitable Collision of Sex-Determination by Cell-Free Fetal DNA in Non-invasive Prenatal Genetic Diagnosis and the Continual Statewide Expansion of Abortion Regulation Based on the Sex of the Child*, 81 UMKC L. REV. 417, 423–24 (2012) (internal quotation marks omitted).

not to further pursue FDA approval of MicroSort in the United States [although] the MicroSort technology is available for American patients through laboratories located in Mexico City, Guadalajara, and North Cyprus."[22] Although the United States, because of its lax regulatory structure over these services, is often a destination country for many of these forms of reproductive technology (as we will see below), MicroSort is the exception, requiring U.S. citizens to be the ones traveling abroad.

B. Data on Fertility Tourism
i. Shenfield et al.'s Study of Europe

In a 2010 study by the European Society of Human Reproduction and Embryology (ESHRE), Francoise Shenfield and colleagues collected information on female patients seeking reproductive technology services through medical tourism at forty-six clinics over a one-month period in six European countries thought of as prime destinations for fertility tourism—Belgium, Czech Republic, Denmark, Slovenia, Spain, and Switzerland—for a total of 1230 patients filling out their forms.[23] The researchers extrapolated, based on the schedules of the clinics, that the clinics would perform around twelve to fifteen thousand cycles of treatment for fertility tourists annually, yielding an estimate of eleven to fourteen thousand distinct patients per year.[24]

While the patients came from forty-nine different countries, there were four home countries that were heavy senders, collectively making up the country of origin for almost two-thirds of the medical tourists: Italy (31.8 percent), Germany (14.4 percent), the Netherlands (12.1 percent), and France (8.7 percent). In terms of where patients went, 29.7 percent of the patients went to clinics in Belgium, 20.5 percent to the Czech Republic, 12.5 percent to Denmark, 5.3 percent to Slovenia, 15.7 percent to Spain, and 16.3 percent to Switzerland. There were significant correlations between home and destination countries, suggesting the formation of reputational and referral pathways: the majority of Italians went to Switzerland and Spain, while the majority of Germans went to the Czech Republic. Most Dutch and French patients went to Belgium (with a smaller proportion going to Spain), and most Norwegians and Swedes went to Denmark.

In terms of the demographics of who uses fertility tourism, the authors found the mean age to be 37.3 years (with a range of 21–51 years), and that most prospective parents (69.9 percent) were married and the vast majority (90 percent) were heterosexuals,

---

[22] *Id.* at 423 (internal quotation marks omitted).

[23] All of the following data comes from F. Shenfield et al., *Cross Border Reproductive Care in Six European Countries*, 25 Hum. Reprod. 1361 (2010).

[24] One cannot immediately extrapolate to twelve to fifteen thousand *patients* annually, as some patients may have more than one cycle done, though it is unlikely that many would have had multiple cycles in the same month (i.e., over the period in which the data was collected).

although there was some variance by country of origin here—for example, 82 percent of Italians were married while 43.4 percent of the Swedish women who used fertility tourism were single, and the percentage of users who identified as bisexual or homosexual varied from a high of 39.2 percent of the French to a low of 1.5 percent of the Italians and zero percent for those who listed their home country as the United Kingdom.

In terms of what services they sought, 22.2 percent of patients were seeking only intra-uterine insemination, while the remainder wanted other reproductive technologies such as IVF. Significant proportions of fertility tourists were using gametes (sperm and egg) or embryos from third parties, with 18.3 percent of patients seeking sperm donation, 22.8 percent seeking egg donation, and 3.4 percent seeking embryo donation.[25] Again, there were considerable differences in the country of origin, with French, Norwegian, and Swedish women using sperm donation more often than others, whereas German and British women were more often seeking to use the eggs of third parties.

The motivations identified by respondents (and respondents were allowed to list more than one motivation, and many did) for using fertility tourism also varied substantially based on the patient's home country: "legal reasons were predominant for patients travelling from Italy (70.6%), Germany (80.2%), France (64.5%) and Norway (71.6%)," while "[d]ifficulties accessing treatment were more often noted by UK patients (34.0%) than by patients from other countries, and expected quality was an important factor for most patients," and "on average 17.9% patients indicated a 'wish for anonymous donation,' in particular the French (42.1%), British (26.4%), Germans (25.4%), Swedes (18.9%) and Norwegians (16.4%)."[26]

Delving a little deeper into these reasons, these authors—as I do in the book—divide the world of fertility tourism between those engaged in forms of circumvention tourism and those who travel for cost or quality reasons for services that are otherwise legal. Most of the patients in their study suggested "legal reasons," what I would call circumvention tourism. As they report:

Italian law banned all donor gametes and [Preimplantation Genetic Diagnosis] techniques in 2004, sending a wave of patients to neighbouring countries: Switzerland received 51% of the Italian patients, mostly for sperm donation and Spain received 31.7%, mostly for [egg donation]. German law bans [egg donation] and 44.6% of the German patients in this study were requesting [egg donation]…, although French law bans "private" advertising for recruiting, leading to a dearth of donors, and 20.6% of our French patients requested [egg donation]. Another legal barrier, which increases the number of movements across border for

---

[25] Although I use the term "donation" here to follow the authors' usage, in at least some jurisdictions, there is compensation of some form for sperm and eggs, such that "donation" may sometimes be a misnomer.

[26] Shenfield, *supra* note 23, at 1363.

donor insemination is the regulation regarding donor anonymity. Scandinavian patients often go to Denmark for donor insemination where anonymity is compulsory in the medical setting. In this study, 18.9% of Swedish and 16.4% of Norwegian patients stated they did not merely want donor insemination, but that they sought anonymous donation. Thus, for Sweden and Norway, this flow is most likely related to the legislation requiring nonanonymous donation. Another important legal reason is related to the civil status and sexual orientation of the patient.

In Sweden only couples have access, whether homosexual or heterosexual, which explains the high proportion of single Swedish women (43.4%) seeking treatment abroad. Also, until recently, donor insemination was unavailable to lesbian couples in Norway, where the reversal of this ban thanks to legislation on non-discrimination on the grounds of sexual orientation in early 2009 has not yet been followed by improved access, explaining why 20% of Norwegian participants were lesbians. In France, assisted conception for single women or same sex couples is illegal. Thus in our sample, almost 39.2% of the French women were lesbians and 16.4% were single. In contrast, none travelled from the UK for these reasons, as access to treatment for single or homosexual women has never been forbidden and the legislation is one of the most open and tolerant to differences in Europe (HFEAct, 2008). Indeed, for the patients originating from the UK, legal reasons were the lowest of our sample, with only 9.4%. Furthermore, lesbian couples going through ART have recently...been given equal parenting rights and responsibilities to heterosexual couples.

...

Thus, statutory limits concerning access to ART vary widely between European countries, and this may partially explain some of the movements. Additionally some countries have regulations that limit reimbursement of ART to a maximum age. For instance, in France state funding to reimburse costs if women are aged 43 years or over [is forbidden], and in the Netherlands treatment is forbidden after 41 years.

The lack of access to donor gametes may also be linked to the regulatory limits of compensation to donors. Examples of this are the UK allowing a very limited compensation and France where compensation is forbidden whereas in Spain (about 900 euros) and the Czech Republic (~500 euros) more compensation is allowed. The significance of this is supported by the observation that in our study 62.2% of foreign patients treated in Spain and 62.4% in Czech Republic requested OD. However, the degree of the compensation may not be the only cause of the high number of gamete recipients in these countries, since in Spain there is a strong tradition of donation reflected in the high rate of organ donation.[27]

---

[27] *Id.* at 1367.

For the smaller set of fertility tourists who were not traveling for circumvention tourism, insurance coverage in the home country was a major driver. The authors observe that for Germans, a recent decrease in the insurance funding of reproductive technology cycles may have prompted patients to go across the border to the Czech Republic where it was much cheaper. For the United Kingdom, they also detected intra-national differences in circumvention tourism stemming from the fact that individual regions have autonomy as to how much they fund IVF, "resulting in vastly different waiting lists and inequity of access, particularly in the number of cycles reimbursed."[28] By contrast, the authors conclude that the generous reimbursement for these services offered by Nordic countries helps explain why few patients identify these barriers to access as a prime motivation for fertility tourism. That said, as the authors recognize, because none of the study's sites were within Eastern Europe or India where prices for these services tend to be much cheaper, the study may underrepresent the number of Europeans traveling for cost reasons.

Though limited in the scope of countries it covered, the Shenfield and colleagues' study discussed above is by far the gold standard in measuring fertility tourism.

ii. Hughes and Dejean's Study of U.S. and Canadian Clinics

In a study published in 2010, Edward Hughes and Deirdre DeJean, mailed paper and online surveys of cross-border fertility care activity were sent to 34 Canadian and 392 U.S. fertility clinics and clinicians in cooperation with the Research Committee of the Society for Assisted Reproductive Technology (SART), a subsociety of the American Society for Reproductive Medicine (ASRM).[29]

First, they looked at travel to and from Canada for fertility services. They found that the most common service sought by Canadians out-of-country was IVF with an anonymous egg (363 out of 452 respondents, or 80 percent). When clinicians in Canada were asked if they recommended particular destination countries or providers to Canadian patients, 52 percent always recommended a destination country while only 21 percent always recommend a specific provider. When asked what factors they considered to be "very important" in making recommendations to Canadian patients regarding foreign treatment, the clinicians listed "confidence in effectiveness (88%), confidence in safety (80%), past experience of patients receiving care at the destination clinic (64%), strong regulatory control (40%), and language (40%)." In terms of what information clinics provided, only 29 percent of responding clinicians said that they felt that a referral letter was always necessary, and 88 percent said that they provided whatever information was requested by the destination country clinic. In terms of what information they would

---

[28] *Id.* at 1365.

[29] This description is taken from Edward G. Hughes & Deirdre DeJean, *Cross-Border Fertility Services in North America: A Survey of Canadian and American Providers*, 94 FERTILITY & STERILITY e16 (2010).

like to receive for patients who traveled abroad and returned to their care, they listed as most important complications of treatment, number of embryos transferred, and, as less important, the ongoing treatment recommendation. Looking at patients who chose Canada as their destination country, they found that standard IVF was the most commonly sought procedure (106 out of 146, or 73 percent). Fifty-four percent of these patients came from the United States.

Second, they looked at data from U.S. clinics. A review of the fertility tourists in their sample from across the world who came to U.S. clinics indicated that their clinics reported that a total of 1,399 women entered the United States to receive various types of IVF, representing 4 percent of the total number of IVF cycles provided by those clinics. They found that most out-of-country patients coming to the United States sought standard IVF (927 out of 1,809, 51 percent), with most of these patients coming from Europe (25 percent) and Latin America (39% percent). They also found that of U.S. patients who went abroad for IVF or donor-egg IVF treatment, most (41 percent and 52 percent respectfully) traveled to India or parts of Asia. When asked what factors they considered to be "very important" in prompting non-U.S. patients to come to them for care, they listed "confidence in treatment effectiveness (64%), safety (55%), and information from former patients (56%)."[30] When asked what information they would like to receive from home country clinics whose patients came to them for treatment, 84 percent of clinicians responded that track sheets from previous cycles should always be provided, as well as recent laboratory results (85 percent) and complete medical records (67 percent).

iii. Other Data

The other data that exists, although less complete, can help to somewhat flesh out the picture of what is going on with other destination countries and in regions not covered by these studies.

In 2008, Eric Blyth conducted an online patient survey targeting both patients and potential patients (whom he described as "individuals who have either experienced cross-border reproductive care, or have considered doing so").[31] He posted the survey on the websites of three patient organizations, one in Australia and two in Canada. There were ninety-five usable responses, of which twenty-eight were from individuals who had participated in fertility tourism. When asked why they had done so, the most common reason provided by respondents was lack of availability of eggs and sperm (75 percent)— of the twenty-eight, 54 percent reported they had gone abroad seeking eggs, while 7 percent had gone abroad to get both sperm and egg. Twenty-one of the twenty-eight

---

[30] *Id.* at e18.

[31] Eric Blyth, *Fertility Patients' Experiences of Cross-Border Reproductive Care*, 94 FERTILITY & STERILITY e11 (2010). For more Canadian data, *see also* Jocelyn Downie & Françoise Baylis, *Transnational Trade in Human Eggs: Law, Policy, and (In)Action in Canada*, 41 J.L. MED. & ETHICS 224, 226–27 (2013).

respondents provided their country of origin, with thirteen indicating that they were Canadian. The Canadians seeking eggs listed India, Mexico, and the United States as their destination countries, while the one Canadian seeking both sperm and egg listed the Czech Republic.

Writing on the Asian market for fertility tourism, Andrea Whittaker suggests that patients travel to Thailand for IVF in part because of its price advantage, with its leading hospitals charging between 80,000 baht (US$2,000) and 160,000 baht (US$4,000) per full cycle.[32] She suggests that Thailand has become a "popular destination for non-medical sex selection through preimplantation genetic diagnosis and microsorting," and that, although the industry had been relatively self-regulated until 2011, the "introduction of a new Reproductive Health Bill will affect the trade in Thailand, as it will include legal restrictions on clinical practices, such as the banning of nonmedical sex selection and commercial surrogacy," thus changing the market. In some parts of the market, the illegal nature of the trade resembles more closely trafficking and the organ trade discussed in Chapter 7. For example, a February 2011 media report suggested that Thai police were investigating allegations that fourteen Vietnamese women—seven of whom were pregnant at the time—had "been trafficked to act as surrogates for a Taiwanese company" and forced into the trade.[33]

Turning to India, Whittaker posits that the advent of legalized commercial surrogacy in 2002 led to the establishment of a number of clinics in India in Gujarat, Delhi, and Mumbai that specialized in providing commercial surrogacy or egg donation for foreign clients from the United States, the United Kingdom, and elsewhere, including some recipients who are themselves Indian expatriates. Under the guidelines put in place by the Indian Council for Medical Research, the surrogates could not also donate the eggs when donor eggs were required—they could serve only as gestational, not full surrogates—such that an egg donor was required in addition to the surrogate.[34]

Whittaker also reports on the results of a PhD thesis that studied forty-two surrogates in Anand, India, from 2006 to 2008, and found that the surrogates had a median family income of US$60 a month, with thirty-four of the forty-two women falling below the poverty level. For these women, surrogacy offered a significant financial incentive to participate—approximately 300,000 rupees (US$7500), which is roughly

---

[32] All of this is drawn from Andrea Whittaker, *Cross-Border Assisted Reproduction Care in Asia: Implications for Access, Equity and Regulations*, 19 REPROD. HEALTH MATTERS 107 (2011).

[33] *Id.* at 112 (citing *Thai Police Free Women from Surrogate Baby Ring*, AGENCE FRANCE-PRESSE (Feb. 24, 2011)), http://www.google.com/hostednews/afp/article/ALeqM5gXBt7gEuqdnil4KYH2zcvjZvsFpQ?do cId=CNG.e4206a773b164839c18a6b3802794fe5.6d1.

[34] *Id.* (citing INDIAN COUNCIL OF MEDICAL RESEARCH. NATIONAL GUIDELINES FOR ACCREDITATION, SUPERVISION AND REGULATION OF ART CLINICS IN INDIA. NEW DELHI: MINISTRY OF HEALTH AND FAMILY WELFARE, GOVERNMENT OF INDIA, NATIONAL ACADEMY OF MEDICAL SCIENCES. Chapter 3: Code of Practice, Ethical Considerations and Legal Issues. 2005, *available at* http://icmr.nic.in/art/Chapter_3.pdf).

one-third of what the prospective parents pay the agency or individuals who organize the surrogacy venture.[35] Whittaker suggests that "such commercial inducements may entice women to disregard the risks involved and face pressure from their family to be involved."[36] She also notes that "[a] number of surrogates report having no contracts and no third party legal representation," and that "[w]hile they receive medical care for the term of their surrogate pregnancies, this is not offered for any of their own subsequent pregnancies, despite the increased risks to their health."[37] Finally, she suggests that there are parallel concerns raised as to egg donation in "developing countries [as to] whether women donors are fully informed of the risks involved or whether financial inducements encourage them to overlook the risks, including the possible over-stimulation of their ovaries to maximise egg production."[38]

Other data from India estimates that the reproductive tourism sector is a US$500 million industry with approximately three thousand surrogacy clinics in India and two thousand children born to surrogates each year in India,[39] though, as I have said repeatedly throughout this book, we need to be somewhat skeptical about the accuracy of such estimates.

As with other parts of the industry, medical tourism to India for surrogacy is heavily marketed and coordinated by intermediaries. For example, in a 2008 article, Usha Rengachary Smerdon gives the following examples of marketing websites:

> The birth mother will deliver her baby at an excellent private hospital. If the surrogate is carrying twins, the mother will undergo caesarean delivery. The mother will not bond with the child but breast milk from the mother will be given to the baby (or babies).
>
> PlanetHospital takes a lot of the guess work, stress and confusion out of the equation. Based on your medical history and doctor recommendation we prepare everything you need to make your surrogacy journey stress-free—from ordering your tests to arranging passports and visas for your children.... When you arrive at the destination, a PlanetHospital concierge will be there to assist you every step of the way (for a small additional fee). So with PlanetHospital, all you have to do is show up.[40]

---

[35] *Id.* at 111 (citing A. Pande, *Commercial Surrogate Mothering in India: Nine Months of Labor?* PhD thesis, Amherst: University of Massachusetts (2009)).

[36] *Id.* at 112.

[37] *Id.* (citing Vora K. *Selling Potential: Surplus Fertility and Biocapital in the Production of Transnational Indian Surrogacy.* Paper presented at American Anthropological Association 107th Annual Meeting. San Francisco, CA (Nov. 2008), and A. Pande, *Commercial Surrogacy in India: Manufacturing a Perfect Mother-Worker,* 35 SIGNS 969 (2009)).

[38] Whittaker, *supra* note 32.

[39] Pamela Laufer-Ukeles, *Mothering for Money: Regulating Commercial Intimacy,* 88 INDIANA L.J. 1, 44 (2013).

[40] Smerdon, *supra* note 4, at 31.

In commenting on the number of children who find themselves denied citizenship in their parents' home country, Richard F. Storrow writes in 2012 that in "France alone, these refusals befall an estimated 400 French couples each year, leading lawyer Valérie Depadt-Sebag to designate the children 'a new category of pariahs' that reintroduces a distinction between legitimate and illegitimate long ago expunged from the law."[41]

Wannes Van Hoof and Guido Pennings note that because Sunni Islam forbids the use of donor gametes while Shia Islam permits it, and even where permitted the practice is controversial, many Muslims who want to use the gametes of third parties travel to Iran for reproductive technologies, whose Shia Islam domination leads to more care opportunities.[42] They also report that Dutch clinics are reluctant to treat women over forty years of age who seek treatment in Belgium, and that many French lesbians also seek care in Belgium because France prohibits access to donor insemination to homosexual couples.[43] Even where the use of "donated" gametes is permitted, the price paid for them varies dramatically across country: Van Hoof and Pennings note that UK egg providers receive 750 pounds, compared to 800 Euros in the Czech Republic, 900 Euros in Spain, US$200 in Romania, and a recommended amount of $US5000 in the United States (with sums over US$10,000 considered "inappropriate" by the American Society for Reproductive Medicine).[44]

These studies help paint a picture of what is going on with medical tourism for reproductive technology services, but we still have much to learn at the descriptive level. With this background, though, we are now ready to consider our two major legal and ethical issues, which relate to criminalization and citizenship.

II. EXTRATERRITORIAL CRIMINALIZATION: SHOULD HOME COUNTRIES CRIMINALIZE CIRCUMVENTION FERTILITY TOURISM?

As we have seen, many home countries prohibit domestically activities such as egg and sperm sales, commercial surrogacy, anonymous sperm donation, and sex selection. As the existing empirical data we have reviewed on the trade shows, these domestic prohibitions are a major motivator for fertility tourism in that home citizens are seeking to circumvent domestic prohibitions on certain reproductive technologies, much as the

---

[41] Richard F. Storrow, *"The Phantom Children of the Republic": International Surrogacy and the New Illegitimacy*, 20 AM. U. J. GENDER SOC. POL'Y & L. 561, 567 (2012) (citing Charlotte Rotman, *Gestation pour autrui: Les enfants fantômes de la République*, LA LIBÉRATION (2009) and quoting Charlotte Rotman, *"Filles fantôme" en mal de noms*, LA LIBÉRATION (2010)).

[42] Wannes van Hoof & Guido Pennings, *Cross Border–Reproductive Care around the World: Recent Controversies, in* MEDICAL TOURISM AND TRANSNATIONAL HEALTH CARE 98, 100 (David Boterrill et al. eds., 2013).

[43] *Id.* at 102.

[44] *Id.* at 105.

populations discussed in the last chapter traveled abroad to access abortion and assisted suicide procedures that were illegal at home.

Thus, we face the same policy question in this domain that we wrestled with in the previous chapter: Should home countries seek to criminalize circumvention fertility tourism by extending their domestic prohibitions extraterritorially?

At the current moment, few home countries do so, and it is the exceptions that prove the rule: Turkey makes it a crime punishable by one to three years in prison to use third-party donated eggs or sperm because it is illegal to "change or obscure a child's ancestry,"[45] and the Australian states of New South Wales and Queensland extend their prohibition on commercial surrogacy to citizens who travel abroad.[46] However, most countries do not make it a crime to use reproductive technologies on foreign soil, although the French have extended their criminal prohibition on commercial surrogacy to citizens who travel abroad to use surrogacy services.[47] In a recent article, Jocelyn Downie and Françoise Baylis have suggested that Canada's Assisted Human Reproduction (AHR) Act, which "prohibits purchasing, ordering to purchase, and advertising for the purchase of eggs and, arguably, also prohibits purchasing, offering to purchase, and advertising for the purchase of egg production services" has some extraterritorial application.[48] They argue that "[w]hen all of the prohibited activities associated with the transnational trade in eggs take place in Canada, then the AHR Act applies directly (e.g., the egg provider comes to Canada for the egg retrieval)," but go further and suggest that when "the activities take place in whole or in part outside Canada (e.g., the egg retrieval happens in India), the AHR Act may nonetheless apply through the 'qualified territorial application' of law."[49] But, as they admit, this theory of interpretation is as yet untested and would depend on the specific nexus between Canada and the form of fertility tourism in a particular case, and is even more uncertain at the present moment because many of the implementing regulations for the Act have not been promulgated and no prosecutions have been brought.[50]

---

[45] *See* Cohen, *supra* note 2, at 1325; Whittaker, *supra* note 32, at 113 (citing Gurtin-Broadbent Z. Banning *"Reproductive Tourism"—The Turkish Experience*. Paper presented at Cross Border Reproductive Care: Travelling for Conception and the Global ART Market. CRASSH, Cambridge University (Dec. 2010)).

[46] *New South Wales Surrogacy Act 2010* (No.102), *available at* www.legislation.nsw.gov.au/sessionalview/ sessional/act/2010-102.pdf; *Queensland Surrogacy Act 2010* (No.2), *available at* www.legislation.qld.gov. au/LEGISLTN/ACTS/2010/10AC002.pdf.

[47] Myriam Hunter-Henin, *Surrogacy: Is There Room for a New Liberty between the French Prohibitive Position and the English Ambivalence?*, *in* 11 LAW AND BIOETHICS: CURRENT LEGAL ISSUES 2008, at 329, 334 & n.29 (Michael Freeman ed., 2008).

[48] Downie & Baylis, *supra* note 31, at 227.

[49] *Id.*

[50] *See id.* at 230 (noting that "[w]ith respect to the trade in human eggs, it is not clear when the nexus between the conduct and Canada would be suffcient to trigger qualified territorial application of the AHR Act. Is ovarian stimulation in Canada (followed by travel to another country for egg retrieval) sufficient to trigger application of the law? Is e-mail or telephone communication from an intermediary in California to a woman in Canada seeking human eggs sufficient to trigger application of the law? Has the law been broken

But although the current modal regulatory approach is *not* to criminalize circumvention fertility tourism, as the doctrinal arguments I offered in the last chapter show (as well as the practice of the few outlier countries that have gone there), home countries *could* extend their criminal prohibitions in this regard. The real question is whether they *should* do so.

Both the doctrinal and normative questions were recently front and center in the European Court of Human Rights' 2011 decision in *S.H. v. Austria*. There, the court considered a challenge to Austria's 1992 Artificial Procreation Act, which prohibited entirely egg or sperm donation for the purpose of IVF.[51] After a thirteen-year litigation, the Grand Chamber of the European Court of Human Rights ultimately upheld the Austrian prohibition, finding it within the margin of appreciation granted to European legislatures.[52] For our purposes, the most important discussion in the opinion is its treatment of fertility tourism, on which the Grand Chamber majority and dissenting opinions disagreed. The majority thought the possibility of Austrians traveling abroad for services illegal in Austria helped *support* the rationality and justifiability of Austria's domestic reproductive technology restrictions (which applied domestically only and not extraterritorially). As the Grand Chamber's majority wrote, this policy "shows…the careful and cautious approach adopted by the Austrian legislature in seeking to reconcile social realities with its approach of principle in this field…that there is no prohibition under Austrian law on going abroad to seek treatment of infertility that uses artificial procreation techniques not allowed in Austria and that in the event of a successful treatment the Civil Code contains clear rules on paternity and maternity that respect the wishes of the parents."[53] By contrast, the dissent replied that "[t]he argument that couples can go abroad…does not address the real question, which is that of interference with the applicants' private life as a result of the absolute prohibition in Austria" and that "if the concern for the child's best interests—allegedly endangered by recourse to prohibited means of reproduction—disappear as a result of crossing the border, the same is true of the concerns relating to the mother's health referred to several times by the respondent Government to justify the prohibition."[54]

---

if a company in California arranges a contract between a couple in Canada, an egg provider in the Czech Republic, and a fertility clinic in India and the couple goes to India and receives IVF using the Czech woman's eggs? Is it legal for a Canadian company to advertise on the internet for women in India to become egg providers for reproductive purposes? Is a woman in Canada legally permitted to arrange to pay an egg bank in the U.S. to send frozen eggs to Canada for reproductive purposes?").

[51] S.H. and others v. Austria, App. No. 57813/00, Eur. Ct. H.R. (2011), *available at* http://cmiskp.echr.coe.int/tkp197/view.asp?action=html&documentId=894729&portal=hbkm&source=externalbydocnumber&table=F69A27FD8FB86142BF01C1166DEA398649; *see also* Wannes Van Hoof & Guido Pennings, *The Consequences of* S.H. and Others v. Austria *for Legislation on Gamete Donation in Europe: An Ethical Analysis of the European Court of Human Rights Judgments*, 25 Reproductive BioMedicine Online 665, 665–66 (2012).

[52] S.H. v. Austria, ¶¶ 115–16.

[53] *Id.* ¶ 114.

[54] *Id.*, Dissent, ¶ 13.

One way to frame the question of extraterritorial extension is whether the failure to criminalize these activities of one's citizen abroad shores up the justifiability of the domestic prohibition (by leaving a safety valve) or whether it instead should cause us to doubt the domestic prohibition's justification (by suggesting that the home country does not really mean it, is acting irrationally, or is actually victimizing the citizens of other countries by creating the conditions for the transnational market and allowing them to suffer the very harms that it seeks to shield its own citizens from).

The answer I will offer is "it is complicated." In particular, building on the analysis I offered in the last chapter, I want to suggest that whether home countries should assert prescriptive criminal jurisdiction extraterritorially as to the reproductive technology practices they criminalize at home depends on the justification for that domestic prohibition. The most illuminating analysis will not go practice-by-practice (distinguishing commercial surrogacy from egg sale from sex selection), but will instead recognize that many of these practices have multiple justifications, and whether extraterritorial criminalization is warranted will depend on which of the justifications one views as supporting the criminalization of the practice. In particular, I think it useful to divide potential justifications into three that I will discuss in the following order: harm to resulting children, corruption/commodification concerns, and exploitation of destination country citizens.

A. Child Welfare Concerns

Prohibitions on sperm donor anonymity, on commercial surrogacy, and on single parent or LGBT access to reproductive technologies are frequently premised on child-welfare or best-interests justifications—or Best Interests of the Resulting Child (BIRC) justifications as I have called them. I have cataloged this tendency in great depth elsewhere;[55] for now I will just mention a few examples:

Italy's Law 40/2004 confines use of reproductive technologies to infertile women of "potentially fertile age" who are married or part of a "stable" heterosexual couple, and, hence, indirectly burdens LGBT Assistive Reproductive Technology (ART) users by prohibiting the use of donated sperm or eggs.[56] The BIRC-roots of the legislation are evident in the Italian Parliamentary Commission for Social Affairs' review of the then-proposed legislation, which expressed concern for "avoiding psycho-social damage to the child, which can result from parenting models which are not socially consolidated,"[57] a view also espoused by more recent Italian governments.[58] The Australian

[55] I. Glenn Cohen, *Regulating Reproduction: The Problem with Best Interests*, 96 MINN. L. REV. 423, 447–71 (2011).

[56] *See* Rachel Anne Fenton, *Catholic Doctrine versus Women's Rights: The New Italian Law on Assisted Reproduction*, 14 MED. L. REV. 73, 73, (2006).

[57] *Id.* at 88.

[58] *Id.*

states of Western Australia, South Australia, and Victoria have all enacted similar legislation forbidding access to ART by LGBT and single individuals and permitting use
only where the reason for infertility is not age.[59] The statutes explicitly adopt BIRC
language: the Western Australian version requires "that the prospective welfare of any
child to be born consequent upon a procedure to which this Act relates is properly taken
into consideration."[60] Iceland's Act no. 55/1996 provides that "Artificial fertilisation may
only be carried out if…the child to be conceived by the procedure may be deemed to
be ensured good conditions in which to grow up."[61] Laws prohibiting sperm donor anonymity, which began in Sweden but have now spread more widely, stem from studies
of the welfare of adopted children, which the Swedes extrapolated to donor-conceived
children.[62] A number of jurisdictions followed suit, including, most recently, the United
Kingdom and New Zealand, both adopting similar policies in 2004 and, in both cases,
justifying the approach on BIRC grounds.[63] In the United Kingdom, the Human
Fertilisation and Embryology Act (HFEA) of 1990 specifies that "a woman shall not
be provided with treatment services unless account has been taken of the welfare of the
child who may be born as a result of the treatment (including the need of that child for
a father)."[64] The HFEA Act of 2008 recently liberalized that policy by substituting "supportive parenting" for "a father" in the parenthetical, after legislators decided that the

---

[59] See *Infertility Treatment Act 1995*, (Vict.) s 8 (Austl.), *available at* http://www.austlii.edu.au/au/legis/
vic/hist_act/ita1995264.pdf; *Human Reproductive Technology Act 1991*, (W. Austl.) ss 4, 23(c), *available at* http://www.austlii.edu.au/au/legis/wa/consol_act/hrta1991331/; *Reproductive Technology Act
1988*, (S. Austl.) ss 10(2), 13(3)(b), *available at* http://www.legislation.sa.gov.au/LZ/C/A/ASSISTED%20
REPRODUCTIVE%20TREATMENT%20ACT%201988/2010.08.31/1988.10.UN.PDF.

[60] *Human Reproductive Technology Act 1991*, (W. Austl.) s 4, *supra* note 59.

[61] Act No. 55/1996 On Artificial Impregnation and the Use of Hu-Man Sex Cells and
Embryos for Stem Cell Research (Iceland 1996), *available at* http://eng.velferdarraduneyti.is/
media/acrobat-enskar_sidur/Act_No_55_1996_on_Artificial_Fertilisation_etc_as_amended.pdf (translation courtesy of Sigridur Rut Juliusdottir).

[62] See Claes Gottlieb et al., *Disclosure of Donor Insemination to the Child: The Impact of Swedish Legislation on
Couples' Attitudes*, 15 Hum. Reprod. 2052, 2052 (2000); Michelle Dennison, *Revealing Your Sources: The
Case for Non-anonymous Gamete Donation*, 21 J.L. & Health 1, 8–10 (2008).

[63] Human Assisted Reproductive Technology Act 2004, § 4(a), (e) (N.Z.), *available at* http://www.legislation.
govt.nz/act/public/2004/0092/latest/whole.html#DLM319248 (stating that "the health and well-being of
children born as a result of the performance of an assisted reproductive procedure…should be an important
consideration in all decisions about that procedure," and more specifically, that "donor offspring should be
made aware of their genetic origins and be able to access information about those origins"); Ken Daniels
& Alison Douglass, *Access to Genetic Information by Donor Offspring and Donors: Medicine, Policy and
Law in New Zealand*, 27 Med& L. 131, 137 (2008) (noting how the New Zealand law reflects a principle
that "knowledge by donor-offspring of their genetic origins is central to the health and well-being of chil-
dren born as a result of assisted reproductive procedure"); *see also* Christopher De Jonge & Christopher
L.R. Barratt, *Gamete Donation: A Question of Anonymity*, 85 Fertility & Sterility 500 (2006); *Can
You Be Anonymous as a Sperm, Egg or Embryo Donor?*, Hum. Fertilisation & Embryology
Authority (Nov. 10, 2009), http://www.hfea.gov.uk/1973.html.

[64] Human Fertilisation & Embryology Act, (1990), c. 37, § 13(5) (Eng.), *available at* http://www.legislation.
gov.uk/ukpga/1990/37/section/13.

requirement discriminated against single mothers and lesbians; however, the "duty...to consider the welfare of any child who may be born as a result of the treatment..., and of any other child who may be affected" has been retained.[65] When it comes to surrogacy, child welfare concerns are often expressed in deciding whether to enforce such agreements. In the famous U.S. case of *Matter of Baby M*, the New Jersey Supreme Court famously held unenforceable a traditional surrogacy agreement between William and Elizabeth Stern and Mary-Beth Whitehead, relying on analogies to laws prohibiting baby selling and requiring a best interests of the child judgment before authorizing adoption, decrying that

> [w]orst of all, however, is the contract's total disregard of the best interests of the child. There is not the slightest suggestion that any inquiry will be made at any time to determine the fitness of the Sterns as custodial parents, of Mrs. Stern as an adoptive parent, their superiority to Mrs. Whitehead, or the effect on the child of not living with her natural mother.[66]

Other major U.S. court decisions on surrogacy arrangements have sounded similar child welfare themes.[67] Finally, in justifying prohibitions on sex selection, some have stressed the way in which parental control over traits such as sex will lead to bad rearing of children who show gender discordant behavior.[68]

I have argued elsewhere that, in many cases, justifications for regulating reproduction premised on the "best interests of the resulting child" are problematic, and attempts

---

[65] *Compare* Human Fertilisation & Embryology Act, (2008), c. 22, § 14(2) (Eng.), *available at* http://www. legislation.gov.uk/ukpga/2008/22/section/14 (Eng.), *with* Human Fertilisation & Embryology Act, 1990, c. 37, § 13(5) (Eng.), *supra* note 64; *see* Aidan Jones, *Rules Eased for Second Parent in IVF Births*, GUARDIAN, Mar. 2, 2009, http://www.guardian.co.uk/uk/2009/mar/02/law-family.

[66] *In re* Baby M, 537 A.2d 1227, 1248 (N.J. 1988).

[67] *See* Johnson v. Calvert, 851 P.2d 776, 783 (Cal. 1993); *id.* at 799–800 (Kennard, J., dissenting); J.R. M.R. & W.K.J. v. Utah, 261 F. Supp. 2d 1268 (D. Utah 2002).

[68] *E.g.*, MICHAEL SANDEL, THE CASE AGAINST PERFECTION 49 (2007) (worrying that parents who spend large sums to sex select and control that aspect of their offspring will "overreach"); Ethics Committee of the American Society for Reproductive Medicine, *Sex Selection and Preimplantation Genetic Diagnosis*, 72 FERTILITY & STERILITY 595, 596 (1999) (discussing the "risk of psychological harm to sex-selected offspring (i.e., by placing on them too high expectations)"); Daar, *supra* note 18, at 267 ("If parents elect to rig the gender of their child, they no doubt harbor expectations about the rearing experience a child of the selected sex will provide. A child of the 'preferred' sex may suffer psychological harms brought on by heightened and genderized parental expectations. If a child of a chosen gender fails to fulfill the gender stereotyping that propelled the parent to seek out PGD in the first place, the parent/child relationship could falter, and greatly aggrieve the child."); Inmaculada de Melo-Matin, *Sex Selection and the Procreatice Liberty Framework*, 23 KENNEDY INSTITUTE ETHICS J. 1, 11–12 (2013) (it is "plausible to believe that someone who has spent the amount of time, energy, money, and health risks that sex selection requires in order to have a child of a particular sex is not going to be particularly accepting if the child fails to fulfill his or her preconceived gender expectations").

at reformulating the claim carry with them problematic implications.[69] As in the last chapter, though, my method is not to judge the underlying justifications offered by home countries for criminalizing an activity domestically, but instead to assume this justification is valid and ask what follows about extraterritorial criminalization.

If child welfare concerns underlie restrictions, the case initially seems to parallel the assisted suicide and abortion cases we saw in the last chapter, as well as the initial starting hypothetical of Murder Island. There, we saw that if the home country's domestic prohibition on one citizen's action is premised on preventing serious harm to another citizen, the State has a strong justification for extending that prohibition extraterritorially to instances of circumvention tourism. I also argued, to the contrary of other bioethicists, that notions such as "external tolerance"—though laudable—are defeated when serious harm to unconsenting individuals is involved. Here, based on this justification for domestic prohibition, a child's welfare is endangered by the parental action, and the State has restricted that parental action for that reason. Moreover, to the extent that these reproductive technology usages produce children who impose some costs on the home country's health-care system later on when the children return home (or other forms of what I have elsewhere called "reproductive externalities"), the home country has a further interest in regulating circumvention tourism.

One might resist the analogy to the prior cases by suggesting that Murder Island and assisted suicide involved harm to a citizen child whereas the instant case involves harm to a child-to-be who is not yet a citizen. Even if we view the child as stateless rather than a citizen, an argument I also entertained as to abortion, there is, just as in the abortion case, a strong argument for extraterritoriality. This case differs from abortion in that, if an abortion succeeds, no child will come into existence who can be a citizen, whereas if this act of reproductive technology use is not prohibited, a child who will be a citizen will come into existence in the future. But, if anything, this distinction cuts in favor of extraterritoriality, as there are future costs to the State based on the health of this child that are not present in the abortion case if the activity goes forward.

The argument for extraterritorial criminalization of reproductive technology use based on child welfare concerns is somewhat weaker than the prior cases in two ways. First, in the prior cases, the purported harm to be prevented to the unconsenting child is a serious physical harm. In many of the reproductive technology cases, as I have noted elsewhere, the harms involved are more speculative and psychological in nature—though to be sure there are exceptions, such as low birthweight children with higher order multiple births. Whether criminal law (or law in general) is right to privilege physical harm as much as it does is an open question, but, to the extent the home country sees nonphysical harms as less serious, it ought to be more willing to defer to the destination country's

---

[69] See I. Glenn Cohen, *Response: Rethinking Sperm-Donor Anonymity: Of Changed Selves, Nonidentity, and One-Night Stands*, 100 GEO. L.J. 431, 435–36 (2012); I. Glenn Cohen, *Beyond Best Interests*, 96 MINN. L. REV. 1187, 1217–34 (2012).

norms, especially regarding the threshold for the retaliation and other exceptions. Still, the fact that the act remains criminal in the home country when this is the basis of harm should give us pause in thinking that this distinction should weaken the obligation to extraterritorialize. Second, given that reproductive technology is a multibillion-dollar industry, destination countries are likely to derive significant economic gains from this kind of circumvention tourism, and thus the strength of the home country's economic interest in maintaining access to these tourists is larger than in the other cases I have canvassed. From the point of view of the home country, though, this primarily inflects when the retaliation exception will kick in by amplifying the likelihood and size of the retaliation to be expected and not the actual obligation to criminalize. Further, the case is easier than assisted suicide because there is no possibility of consent playing a role.

Those inflections aside, the home country seems to have strong reasons to criminalize circumvention tourism in the reproductive technology arena when child welfare concerns are accepted as the justification for domestic prohibitions of those same reproductive technology practices. That many home countries have relied on this reasoning to justify prohibitions domestically but have not extended them extraterritorially suggests one of two things: either (1) despite their claims of fealty to this reasoning, it is not what primarily underlies the restriction; or (2) they have been wrong not to extend their laws to practices abroad and should follow the Australian and Turkish examples.

B. Corruption

As we saw in the last chapter, corruption arguments claim that allowing a practice to go forward will do violence or denigrate our views of how goods are properly valued. When it comes to reproductive technology domestic prohibitions, this justification has been particularly prominent for laws prohibiting compensation: the sale of sperm or egg or surrogacy services is sometimes said to do violence to the way we think the body, life, sexuality, or women's reproductive labor is properly valued, and thus instantiates an inappropriate mode of valuation.[70] For example, as Downie and Baylis note, the Canadian legislation barring payment for sperm and egg explicitly states that "Trade in the reproductive capabilities of women and men and the exploitation of children, women and men for commercial ends raises health and ethical concerns that justify their prohibition," a view that has also been endorsed by the Canadian Supreme Court in its case law on the Act.[71] Smerdon worries that "[c]ommodification extends to the

---

[70] *See, e.g.*, ELIZABETH ANDERSON, VALUE IN ETHICS AND ECONOMICS 144, 172 (1993) (describing ways in which contract pregnancy devalues children as "use-objects"); Margaret Jane Radin, *What, If Anything, Is Wrong with Baby Selling?*, Address at the McGeorge School of Law (Mar. 4, 1994), *in* 26 PAC. L.J. 135, 143–45 (1995) (discussing commodification of women's capacity to reproduce).

[71] Downie & Baylis, *supra* note 31, at 238, n.62 (quoting Assisted Human Reproduction Act S.C. 2004, c. 2, s. 2(f) (Can.) and citing Reference re Assisted Human Reproduction Act, 2010 S.C.C. 61, [2010] 3 S.C.R. 457 (Can.)).

children born of surrogacy as well," and that "[p]ersonhood is harmed when it is not adequately recognized that the product of a woman's reproductive labor is someone not something."[72] Some have suggested that sex selection leads to a devaluation of women ass they are often selected against.[73] More generally, Leon R. Kass has critiqued cloning and new reproductive technologies as ignoring the "[w]isdom of [r]epugnance," which "may be the only voice left that speaks up to defend the central core of our humanity."[74]

My approach to this kind of justification for a domestic prohibition on reproductive technology use echoes my treatment of corruption justifications for prohibiting assisted suicide and abortion discussed in the last chapter. As I suggested there, it is imperative to distinguish consequentialist from intrinsic corruption variants.

If consequentialist corruption is the worry, then the home country has a stronger reason to prohibit the activity at home than abroad because there is likely a much stronger attitude-modifying effect. This is partially an empirical question, and may in some instances track the mechanism by which corruption is thought to happen. For example, it may be that the effect of allowing home country citizens to buy the eggs of foreign women is unlikely to cause a devaluation of women's sexuality in the home country because the activity is "out of sight." By contrast, if sex selection's gender-devaluing role stems from the production of sex ratios imbalanced toward men, that result seems to obtain whether or not the act of sex selection occurs at home or abroad. However, because of the transaction costs associated with traveling abroad for the service, the *amount* of sex selection may be much less than if the practice is permitted only abroad and not domestically, in which case the gender devaluation effect may not obtain or may also be lessened.

By contrast, as I put it in the last chapter, the intrinsic corruption concern is more metaphysical and suggests that something wrong has been done through the act of value denigration at the moment the act takes place, irrespective of what follows thereafter. On this justification for criminalization, it seems that the home country has just as much of a reason to extend its criminal law to the actions of its citizen abroad as it does when the citizen acts at home. Wrong has been done at the moment the act is done (whatever its consequence), and the act of criminal condemnation is needed both to deter that act

---

[72] Smerdon, *supra* note 4, at 17.

[73] *E.g.*, Daar, *supra* note 18, at 267; Kristi Lemoine & John Tanagho, *Gender Discrimination Fuels Sex Selective Abortion: The Impact of the Indian Supreme Court on the Implementation and Enforcement of the PNDT Act*, 15 U. Miami Int'l & Comp. L. Rev. 203, 224–26 (2007) (discussing the effects of sex selection in India and observing that "[w]hile it might be assumed that a scarcity of women would lead to their increased value in society, as of yet nothing indicates that the worsening sex ratio over the past decades has enhanced the position of women in Indian society. In fact, the converse is likely true, for despite the lowest sex ratio in the past century, the status of women in India has arguably never been lower.... Instead of raising the value of women, skewed sex ratios only increase the frequency of rape, prostitution, and violence against women.").

[74] Leon R. Kass, *The Wisdom of Repugnance, in* The Ethics of Human Cloning 3, 19 (Leon R. Kass & James Q. Wilson eds., 1998).

and, on retributivist- or corrective justice–type grounds, to re-right the balance. That does not mean, as I stressed before, that the home country has reason to criminalize the act of reproductive technology use by noncitizens in foreign countries as well, as a kind of universal jurisdiction over the crime. Even if the free-floating wrong is the same in all instances for intrinsic corruption, it is a mistake to think that every sovereign is equally morally obligated to punish every wrong done in the world. Rather, the citizenship tie of the perpetrator to the home country is important in helping to justify the home country's right to punish. It is the fact that one is a national and a member of the coercive structure of a country that both benefits and burdens a citizen; instead of choosing Exit, that citizen has accepted the sovereign's authority to punish in a way that the citizen has not accepted of any other sovereign.

Indeed, some have claimed that the circumstances in which surrogacy as part of fertility tourism takes place is actually *more* corrupting than its domestic equivalent. Pamela Laufer-Ukeles, for example, picks out some contextual factors she suggests reflect a "greater dehumanization and medicalization of an intimate relationship that occurs in international surrogacy": the fact that "under the terms of most surrogacy contracts in India, the surrogate mother and her partner agree that if the childbearing woman is injured or diagnosed with a life-threatening disease during advanced pregnancy, she is to be sustained with life support equipment to protect the fetus viability and insure a healthy birth on the genetic parents' behalf," which Laufer-Ukeles claims reflects an understanding that the "fetus's health explicitly comes before the mother's"; the fact that Indian surrogates "often live in group homes during their pregnancy" with substantial control exerted over their daily activities, diet, prenatal medical care, and limitations on visitation by the surrogate's other children and conjugal activity with a spouse, which she claims are conditions imposed to "ensure fetal safety, but also to control the surrogates and ensure their docility and compliance with surrogate contracts"; and the practice of allowing surrogates to see the baby when born but then quickly separating the surrogate from the baby and commissioning couple, which she views as largely benefitting the intended parents couples, "as they do not need to deal with messy emotions and relationships." Each of these factors, Laufer-Ukeles suggests, "reflects a much narrower development of relationships and human attachment than in domestic surrogacy."[75] I read this as a claim that on corruption (as well as potentially other grounds) commercial surrogacy as practiced in India as part of medical tourism is worse than the domestic counterpart, though it is possible that someone such as Laufer-Ukeles might want to ban both.

Therefore, if the justification for the domestic prohibition on commercial surrogacy, egg sale, sex selection, etc., is intrinsic corruption, I think the home country has good reason to punish the citizen who engages in the forbidden act abroad just as much as

---

[75] Laufer-Ukeles, *supra* note 39, at 45–47 (internal quotation marks omitted).

it does when the act takes place at home. By contrast, when the justification is conse-quentialist corruption, I think the home country may justifiably refuse to extend its prohibition to the extraterritorial conduct of its citizen to the extent it believes that attitude-modification effects will be diminished.

C. Exploitation and Undue Inducement

An objection often raised to egg sale and commercial surrogacy is that the woman is being improperly exploited or unduly induced into participation. For example, Anne Donchin decries that the consent of destination country women in these practices "can't turn a morally unacceptable offer into a morally fair purchase," and that such "offers exploit their vulnerabilites, expand the reach of market forces, and subvert efforts by the purchasers' home countries to reign in unfair reproductive practices."[76] In a related vein, Casey Humbyrd argues that "the only valid objection to international surrogacy is that surrogate mothers may be exploited by being given too little compensation," although she ultimately concludes that "[i]nternational surrogacy is ethical provided it is practiced following the principles of Fair Trade," that is, fair wages and good working conditions.[77]

This justification differs from earlier cases we have considered in at least two ways: first, the "victim" whom the law seeks to protect is a citizen of the destination country (rather than the home country or a stateless person). Second, unlike abortion, assisted suicide, or murder, the harm is not loss of life or physical injury (core Harm Principle cases) but more a violation of relational or distributive justice, especially if the "victim" consents (in a formal sense) and is made better off by the victim's own current, subjective valuation.

Given what I have said in Chapter 7 regarding the moral force of exploitation argu-ments as applied to selling organs across borders, for many of the same reasons, I am skeptical that these arguments give a strong justification for criminalizing commercial surrogacy or egg provision. But, once again, for the purposes of the analysis in this chap-ter I am putting my own views about the moral cogency of a justification for a domestic prohibition to one side. Instead, I am taking the fact that the home country has pro-hibited the activity for this reason and asking what should follow for extraterritorial criminalization.

Here, I think there are good reasons a home country that criminalizes commer-cial surrogacy or egg sales domestically for exploitation reasons may not have good

---

[76] Anne Donchin, *Reproductive Tourism and the Quest for Global Gender Justice*, 24 BIOETHICS 323, 325 (2010); *see also* Whittaker, *supra* note 32, at 111 ("The degree of exploitation involved in such transactions depends upon whether there is undue inducement, given the unequal economic position of women donors/ surrogates, the level of control and coercion imposed upon them, their subordination within the arrange-ment, the degree of protection of their rights throughout the treatment process or pregnancy, and the extent of protection of their physical and mental health.").

[77] Casey Humbyrd, *Fair Trade International Surrogacy*, 9 DEVELOPING WORLD BIOETHICS 111, 112 (2009).

moral reasons to criminalize the same activity abroad. Put otherwise, it seems much more likely that my belief in the statement "X was paid $20,000 for surrogacy services by a U.S. citizen and has thus been wrongfully exploited" will vary based on the citizenship of X.

Why? It will be helpful to recall the philosophical account of exploitation that we discussed in our earlier chapter. To determine that A has wrongfully exploited B, three criteria must be met: (1) A benefits from the transaction, (2) the outcome of the transaction is harmful (harmful exploitation) or at least unfair (mutually advantageous exploitation) to B, and (3) A is able to induce B to agree to the transaction by taking advantage of a feature of B or his situation without which B would not ordinarily be willing to agree. Many elements of this definition and our analysis of whether to put in place legal interventions (and, if so, of what kind) will be different as between the domestic and medical tourism forms of these practices.

First, evaluation of whether these transactions are harmful exploitation depends on the harm or at least the risk to which egg providers and surrogates subject themselves. That will depend in turn on the prevailing standard of care for the procedures for egg retrieval, surrogacy, and post-operative care, as well as how these risks compare to the other risks of the women's day-to-day lives. Differences between the home and destination country on these factors might lead the home country to determine that the exchange should be banned at home but not abroad, though, on different country comparisons, the opposite conclusion might also obtain.

On the one hand, there is evidence that the physical and psychological risks of surrogacy in India, for example, are greater than in the United States. As Donchin notes (albeit without citation to medical or other literatures, for what it is worth):

> In more developed countries surrogates would have legal representation and independent counseling to explain the complexities of medical interventions. But in poor countries assistance to protect the decision-making authority of surrogates is seldom available.... The quality of medical treatment may be substandard. Infection rates are seldom available. Genetic tests may be unreliable. Donor sperm may not have been screened for viruses such as HIV. Reliable data on complication rates during pregnancy and pregnancy outcomes may not be available. Often more embryos are transferred than the home country would permit, risking higher rates of multiple pregnancy.[78]

Others have also reported that in Indian surrogacy, at least, "C-sections are performed as a matter of course," opining that they "may be more risky for the surrogates and their

---

[78] Donchin, *supra* note 76, at 326, 328.

nearly automatic use distinguishes the international system from the domestic system, where there is no evidence that C-Sections are regularly preferred."[79]

On the other hand, the kinds of risks faced by these women in everyday life in their home countries are also much worse than those faced by surrogates in developed home countries, such that these risks may actually seem more reasonable in relation to their day-to-day lives.[80]

Moreover, whether a surrogate is getting a "raw deal" will depend in part on whether the money involved is worth the risk; that, in turn, depends on how much the money offered is worth to her, which will in turn depend on her holdings, her alternatives, and where she is on the curve of diminishing marginal utility from income. In this regard, as Erin Nelson notes, in India, "women are in general less independent and have fewer opportunities for education or for employment that generates an income comparable to what they can earn as surrogate mothers."[81] Reporting the results of an unpublished study of forty-two surrogates in Anand in India from 2006 to 2008, Whittaker writes that "the median family income of the surrogates was US$60 per month," "meaning that 34 of the 42 women were below the poverty line" and that the "amounts of money involved for surrogates were significant in local terms—they were paid approximately 300,000 Rupees (US$7,500)—around one-third of the fees paid by contracting parents."[82] And as another author observes, "the fee paid for surrogacy in the international arena is quite high compared with other options afforded to women of the lower classes who engage in these contracts," and "[a]part from other problematic ways of earning money, such as drugs or prostitution, there is no comparable way for uneducated women in India to earn such large fees."[83]

Moreover, perhaps surprisingly, some work on Indian surrogates suggests that participation can elevate their sense of self-worth, a non-pecuniary form of benefit. One of Amrita Pande's interview subjects among Indian surrogates, a married, college-educated woman "proudly described her desirability as a surrogate in the eyes of clients, and

---

[79] Laufer-Ukeles, *supra* note 39, at 46. There are separate questions as to whether there are risks to the fetus/children who would be born that are different in India, such as concerns about low birthweight babies due to more multiple implantations and higher rates of triplets or other multiples being born. This would bring us back to the child welfare concerns discussed above, and the concern for the home country of externalities borne by its health care and other public systems upon the children

[80] That argument is not totally satisfying in that one might think the fact that these women face these risks in everyday life already is itself unjust and problematic, but as the hypocrisy argument I discussed in Chapter 7 reminds us: unless we are prepared to undertake a more full-scale reordering of these women's poverty, blocking this option may make them worse off.

[81] Nelson, *supra* note 5, at 248.

[82] Whittaker, *supra* note 32, at 111–12.

[83] Laufer-Ukeles, *supra* note 39, at 49. Laufer-Ukeles marshals these figures as arguments that surrogacy in India is problematic, that "[i]n this economic climate, these decisions seem much more coercive and pressured than in first world countries where women tend to have other choices to support themselves," *id.*, but I think the fact that the money is so valued by the surrogates actually improves the practice from a moral point of view.

emphasized that it was *she* who was doing the work, *she* who would decide what to do with the money, and *she* who would decide whether a couple who 'wanted [her]' was deserving of her services," and that "for some surrogates, the narrative of 'being special' did more than just counter the stigma of being disposable mothers; it also encouraged them to take care of their health and think of their own needs."[84] Pande writes that this "'I am special' narrative is particularly powerful when invoked by lower-class women in India, a country where sex-selective abortions, skewed sex ratios at birth, and high female infanticide and mortality present compelling evidence of the prevalence of son preference," and that the narrative then "increases the women's feelings of self-worth."[85]

Thus, even if the risks are greater than in domestic surrogacy, the rewards may in some cases bee greater too. If, as I suggested in Chapter 7, all exploitation arguments are such that there exists a price where an unfair exchange would be made fair, it may be that the value to these women of the money involved is at or exceeds that price.

Of course, as we observed in our earlier discussion of exploitation, even non-harmful exploitation can be wrongful; that is, there is a category of wrongful mutually advantageous exploitation. At the same time, as discussed before, the mere fact that a buyer takes advantage of a seller's unfortunate or unjust background situation is not enough to render the transaction unfair, or else many transactions we think of as perfectly fine and even desirable (previously, I used the example of the patient needing amputation) would be prohibited. What we need instead is a kind of moralized baseline, a sense of how much the person *ought* to receive, to which we can compare what the person actually is promised in the transaction. This is not an easy problem to resolve. We saw earlier that some have proposed using a hypothetical market approach to establish the relevant baseline, wherein we imagine what price would obtain in an unpressurized market. On this approach, there is reason to believe that the price at which it would be unfair in the developing world to pay a surrogate might be different from the price it would be unfair to pay a surrogate in the developed world, in part because the prices that we pay people in the developed world for all goods and services is so much lower.

Third, as we discussed in Chapter 7, some argue that it is problematically hypocritical to block an exchange by a poor person that would make the individual better off unless one is also committed to a redistributive program that would help that person regain the forgone welfare boost (or perhaps at least reach a certain welfare threshold). Smerdon worries that "[o]ne must question the notion of free choice and self-determination when

---

[84] Kristiana Brugger, *International Law in the Gestational Surrogacy Debate*, 35 FORDHAM INT'L L.J. 665, 677 (2012) (quoting Amrita Pande, *"At Least I Am Not Sleeping with Anyone": Resisting the Stigma of Commercial Surrogacy in India*, 36 FEMINIST STUD. 292, 304–06 (2010)).

[85] Pande, *supra* note 84, at 305. Of course, some will dismiss this feeling as false consciousness and suggest it is a further injury, not a benefit to these women. How to evaluate that concern depends in part on knowing more about the conditions under which this feeling of these women were formed as well as one's substantive theory of preference-laundering in welfare evaluation.

Indian women are agreeing to surrogacy to earn money to obtain urgent medical care for loved ones, win back lost children, raise children as a single parent or as the sole breadwinner, and pay for their children's dowries, particularly when the amount of money involved is so high in relation to the woman's standard of living."[86] Similarly, Laufer-Ukeles powerfully attests to the kind of need faced by these women who choose to be surrogates in India, suggesting that "[f]or many, surrogacy is their last resort for feeding and educating existing children."[87]

But I think these points actually cut the other way; they show us how banning the practice engaged in by these women means leaving their children to starve, a kind of "protection" we ought not to impose on the unwilling unless we are willing and able to be the ones to feed their children. Indeed, by way of the hypocrisy argument, one might conclude it is more justified to block the domestic exchange because one is committed to such a redistributive program but not the extraterritorial version because the home country is not inclined (or cannot) effect a redistribution to the destination country citizen, nor will the surrogate's country of citizenship.

There is also a related complication. On some theories of global justice, the individuals making the offer (the intended parents) owe the surrogate who is their fellow citizen something different than what they owe to a surrogate who is a citizen of another country; co-membership in the same nation-state is required to ground duties of distributive justice. We discussed in Chapter 6 the range of global justice theories and their views about when we owe duties to those in other countries. The more exploitation is thought of as an issue of *distributive* justice rather than obligations to avoid doing harm, the more this point seems to have bite in distinguishing wrongful exploitation, justifying legal intervention in the domestic and fertility tourism cases.

All this may mean that the reasons a home country gives for criminalizing commercial surrogacy or egg provision at home do not themselves necessarily justify its criminalizing the same activities as part of fertility tourism. To be fair, because many of these analyses turn on specific characteristics of the surrogates or egg donors, it may mean that the question of whether there is wrongful exploitation can only be judged on an individual-by-individual basis, but a home country might (for administrability or other reasons) take the country of origin of the individual as a proxy and determine extraterritorial application accordingly. This suggests that it might be too crude to focus on extraterritorial application simpliciter as a kind of on-off switch and that we should instead analyze extraterritorially as to a particular destination country.

It may also be that the prescriptive criminalization should treat all foreign countries the same but that we should use prosecutorial discretion to sort through these differences—although doing so would leave some deterrent effect in place due to fear of prosecution. Another possibility, one that parallels a suggestion I have made in

---

[86] Smerdon, *supra* note 4, at 54.
[87] Laufer-Ukeles, *supra* note 39, at 50.

Chapters 2 and 3 as to medical tourism for services legal in both the home and destination countries, would be to adopt a kind of certification regime through which penalties attach only to going to an unapproved fertility center.

III. SURROGACY AND THE CITIZENSHIP OF CHILDREN BORN ABROAD

As the Baby Manji case discussed and the introduction to this chapter suggested, countries with prohibitions on commercial and/or noncommercial surrogacy domestically have faced a persistent and repeated dilemma: What should they do when citizens travel abroad, use these services, successfully produce a child, and then seek to bring the child back to the home country? Should they grant the child citizenship or at least some form of permanent residency?

Before I discuss my own views of what policies home countries should adopt in this situation, let me briefly describe the landscape of possible approaches by reviewing the law on this subject that has developed in several home and destination countries.

To start at a somewhat more general level, there are two major principles that jurisdictions follow in determining nationality at birth. Some nations operate under the "*jus soli*" ("right of the soil") principle, in which any child born in that country's territorial space is a national of that territory, while others operate under the "*jus sanguinis*" ("right of the blood") principle, in which citizenship will pass based on the nationality of the child's parents or ancestors, and some countries adopt both principles.[88]

When the destination country where the child is born recognizes *jus soli* nationality, as the United States does, for example, the child will be able to take on the citizenship of that country and thus will at least not remain stateless, even if his or her parents' home country does not recognize the child as its citizen. By contrast, when the destination country recognizes only the *jus sanguinis* rule, there is a real possibility that the child will become stateless as no country will recognize the citizenship. This problem arises in particular, as with the case studies discussed above, when the home and destination countries adopt conflicting rules within a *jus sanguinis* framework as to how they define the parental relationship between gestational versus genetic parentage. To have a better grasp of this situation, let me explain how some countries have handled citizenship issues relating to surrogacy and egg donation abroad.

A. How Home Countries Have Handled These Cases

Unfortunately, several cases such as Baby Manji's have arisen in various home countries, such that we now have a broad pattern of case and statutory law on this subject. Although

---

[88] *E.g.*, Lin, *supra* note 10, at 556.

I cannot exhaustively review the law in every potential home country, I will review the cases and statutes that have received more attention due to controversies that have been litigated.

Under Canadian law, citizenship can be granted to a child born abroad via surrogacy and is granted automatically if the child is genetically related to at least one of the intended (Canadian parents).[89] As Nelson reports, though, there have been at least two known cases where the "fertility clinic errors meant that the requisite genetic connection did not exist," and, in one, the "Canadian intended parents returned home without the children they had hoped to raise" while, in the other, the "parents remained in India illegally and at great personal and financial cost until the immigration problems could be resolved."[90]

France has banned surrogacy since 1991. As Storrow explains, couples who travel abroad to engage a surrogate and return home are considered to have falsified their birth certificates, and the foreign birth certificate is not recognized by the French government, which will recognize only "the biological connection between the male partner and the child."[91] In one notable case, French consular officials in Los Angeles, suspicious that a surrogate had been used, refused to provide the French couple—the Mennessons—a passport or a visa for the children who were born. The children travelled on U.S. passports back to France with their parents, at which point French prosecutors attempted to charge the parents with fraud to set aside the parents' entry in the official register of parentage, which would deprive the children of French citizenship. A French judge determined that the criminal charges could not proceed because France had no extraterritorial jurisdiction in the case. When it came to citizenship and parentage, the court recognized the Mennessons's parentage, but refused to grant the children the French citizenship that would normally go with that recognition. French law further prohibits those who have resorted to international surrogacy from adopting the children because they have attempted to circumvent legal adoption procedures. After five court decisions in ten years, the Cour de Cassation (the highest court in France) ultimately ruled that the girls were not French citizens, though the couple apparently plans to take their case to the European Court of Human Rights.[92]

Spain has tussled with a similar case, in this instance involving a gay couple. Spanish officials in Los Angeles refused to recognize the parentage of two male Spanish nationals, married in Spain, who produced a child with the help of a U.S. surrogate mother who had twins. In keeping with California law, a pre-birth judgment was issued by a California

---

[89] Nelson, *supra* note 5, at 245–46 (citing Citizenship and Immigration Canada, *Operational Bulletin 381— March 8, 2012 Assessing Who Is a Parent for Citizenship Purposes Where Assisted Human Reproduction (AHR) and/or Surrogacy Arrangements Are Involved*, available at http://www.cic.gc.ca/english/resources/ manuals/bulletins/2012/ob381.asp).

[90] Nelson, *supra* note 5, at 246.

[91] Storrow, *supra* note 41, at 599.

[92] This account is drawn from *id.* at 599–600; *see also* Hunter-Henin, *supra* note 47, at 334; Gilles Cuniberti, *French Court Denies Recognition to American Surrogacy Judgement*, CONFLICT OF LAWS. NET: NEWS & VIEWS IN PRIVATE INT'L L. (June 30, 2009), http://conflictoflaws.net/2009/french-co urt-denies-recognition-to-american-surrogacy-judgement/.

court and the official birth certificate listed the men as parents with no reference to the twins' genetic or gestational mother. The men went to the consulate to register the twins in the Spanish civil registry, but the consulate refused, citing the Spanish law that prohibits surrogacy in Spain. The family returned to Spain and sought official recognition of the California birth certificate, for which they encountered resistance. The matter made its way to litigation, and the court hearing the matter declared that it was a violation of Spanish law not to include the gestational mother as a parent in the registry.

At this point, the Spanish Ministry of Justice intervened to establish guidelines for the entry into the civil registry of children born to surrogate mothers abroad, concluding that the proper balance between the interests of children and the Spanish government's interest in prohibiting surrogacy was achieved "by obtaining a judgment in a host country court recognizing the legal validity of the birth certificate and making factual findings to the effect that the contract for surrogacy was entered into without fraud, overreaching or exploitation of the surrogate mother."[93] Storrow views this approach with favor and connects it to the legal doctrine of comity under which "[f]inal judgments of courts of foreign nations, which concern the recovery of sums of money, the status of a person, or determine interests in property, are conclusive and entitled to recognition in the courts of other nations" if the judgment was "rendered under a judicial system providing impartial tribunals and procedures compatible with due process of law," and if the issuing court had jurisdiction to hear the case. Comity is refused "if the foreign judgment in question was obtained by fraud or if extending comity would undermine a strong public policy."[94] Of course, as my discussion below suggests, one key question will be whether recognizing the children born through circumvention tourism undermines public policy.

In Italy, Gruenbaum reports on a 2009 case raising similar issues. An Italian woman and a British man entered into an agreement with an English surrogate. After the children were born, the couple moved to Bari, Italy. The couple later divorced and the woman requested and was granted the recognition of the British Parental Orders. The Italian court concluded that "the prohibition of surrogacy under Italian law was not per se an indicator that the recognition would be against Italian (international) public policy," noting that "it was in the best interest of the children to be recognized as related to the couple because the children had lived in Bari with the commissioning parents as a normal family since early childhood, and that they had established a close bond with the commissioning mother and no one else in the past ten years."[95] In February 2014 the Civil Chamber of the Spanish Supreme Court also decided a similar case involving

---

[93] This account is drawn from Storrow, *supra* note 41, at 600–01.

[94] *Id.* at 602 (citing RESTATEMENT (THIRD) OF THE FOREIGN RELATIONS LAW OF THE UNITED STATES § 481(1), § 481 cmt. f (1987)).

[95] Daniel Gruenbaum, *Foreign Surrogate Motherhood:* Mater Semper Certa Erat, 60 AM. J. COMP. L. 475, 497–98 (2012) (discussing Corte di Appello di Bari 13.2.2009—I.M. c/ G.A.J.R., Riv. Dir. Int. Priv. Proc. 2009 (It.)).

a married gay couple who traveled to California to use a commercial surrogate and circumvent the Spanish domestic ban. The couple attempted to get their U.S. birth certificate recognized by the Spanish Consular Registry in Los Angeles, which was rejected on the ground that the foreign judgment was not entitled to recognition in Spain due to conflicting Spanish law, a position the Court upheld.[96]

In the United Kingdom, there have also been several high profile cases with similar facts. Under UK law, the intended parents who use a surrogate to produce a child are not given any legal rights or duties until a Parental Order is issued. To qualify for that order, the parents must meet several requirements. As Nelson describes them:

> the application must be made at least six weeks but less than six months after the child is born; the birth mother and her spouse or partner must consent to the Order; at least one intended parent must be domiciled in the U.K., the Channel Islands or the Isle of Man; the child must be in the care of and residing with the intended parents; at least one intended parent must be genetically related to the child (meaning that intended parents who are both unable to provide gametes are not candidates for a Parental Order); and the intended parents must be a couple (either married or civil partners)—single parents cannot obtain a Parental Order. Finally, and very significantly in the international surrogacy context, the court must be satisfied that "no money or other benefit (other than for expenses reasonably incurred) has been given or received by either of the applicants for or in consideration of" the agreement, handing over the child, or the making of the Order or making arrangements with a view to the making of the Order—unless the payment is authorized by the court. The purpose of this last requirement is to discourage intended parents from avoiding the prohibition on commercial surrogacy by participating in commercial surrogacy outside of the U.K.[97]

One case decided by the High Court of England and Wales, *Re X & Y (Foreign Surrogacy)*,[98] involved UK nationals who traveled to Ukraine to produce a child with a surrogate mother who lived there. Under Ukrainian surrogacy law, the surrogate mother and her partner or spouse are not treated as the parents of a child born through a surrogacy agreement and, instead, all duties and rights and the status of parent under the law are granted to the intended parents. By contrast, UK law adopts the exact opposite rule: that the birth mother is the legal mother of her child and that the birth mother's spouse or partner is the legal father, with the intended parents having no parental status until a Parental Order is

---

[96] *See* http://blogs.law.harvard.edu/billofhealth/2014/02/16/are-you-my-mother-the-spanish-supreme-court-and-surrogacy-tourism/

[97] Nelson, *supra* note 5, at 244 (citations omitted) (quoting Human Fertilisation and Embryology Act, 2008, c. 22, § 54(8) (U.K.)).

[98] Re X & Y (Foreign Surrogacy), [2008] E.W.H.C. 3030 (Fam.).

granted. The interplay of these two conflicting regimes led to a tragic result: the children were left stateless and parentless because the intended parents had no legal right to remain in Ukraine and, under UK law, the children were not UK citizens. Thus, the parents could not bring them back to England, although as I will discuss below the English courts ultimately interceded and found a way to grant a Parental Order.[99]

In a second case decided by the same court, *Re G (Surrogacy: Foreign Domicile)*,[100] the situation was reversed, with a UK citizen acting as the surrogate. The intended parents were Turkish nationals, domiciled in Turkey, who arranged for surrogacy services in England, and once the child was born they sought a Parental Order under British law. Because of the provision of that law discussed above, however, the parents had no entitlement to seek a Parental Order because neither was a domiciliary of the United Kingdom, the Channel Islands, or the Isle of Man. The case was ultimately resolved by allowing the intended parents to adopt the child (in Turkey) and granting them an order assigning them parental responsibility to facilitate the eventual adoption. In his opinion, McFarlane J. noted that, given the plain text of the statute, it should have been obvious to these intended parents before they began the surrogacy process that they would not have been able to get a Parental Order under UK law.[101]

While many individuals come to the United States to circumvent home country prohibitions on reproductive technology services, U.S. citizens also travel abroad for surrogacy, often for cost-saving reasons, as surrogacy is considerably cheaper in India, for example, than in the United States. The immigration rules relating to fertility tourism in the United States are complicated by the fact that a child born abroad to U.S. citizens has two separate routes to citizenship under the relevant statute, each of which leads to a different decision-maker: they can (1) apply while abroad, in which case the Secretary of State has jurisdiction and the application is governed by the interpretation of the statute in the Foreign Affairs Manual; or (2) return to the United States and raise citizenship as a defense in a removal proceeding, in which case the U.S. federal courts ultimately have jurisdiction over the case (on appeal after decision by an immigration judge and the Board of Immigration Appeals) and will decide based on their case law.[102] The two decision-makers have, however, adopted conflicting rules when it comes to the cases we are talking about, such that the route that is used (or usable) proves crucial.

The crucial section of the immigration statute these two decision-makers are interpreting provides, in relevant part, that "a child born abroad out of wedlock to a U.S. citizen mother will automatically receive U.S. citizenship," while "a child born abroad out of wedlock to a U.S. citizen father will receive citizenship only if certain conditions are met,

---

[99] This account is drawn from Nelson, *supra* note 5, at 246.

[100] Re G (Surrogacy: Foreign Domicile) [2007] E.W.H.C. 2814 (Fam.).

[101] This account is drawn from Nelson, *supra* note 5, at 246.

[102] Victoria Degtyareva, Note, *Defining Family in Immigration Law: Accounting for Nontraditional Families in Citizenship by Descent*, 120 YALE L.J. 862, 871–73 (2011).

one of which requires that 'a blood relationship between the person and the father is established by clear and convincing evidence.'"[103] Although ideas such as blood relationship and wedlock are easy to apply in traditional family formation, they are not self-evident in their meaning in reproductive technology usage. The Secretary of State and the only federal appellate court to have opined on the issue (the Ninth Circuit Court of Appeals) have reached diverging conclusions as to what these terms mean in our context.

The Ninth Circuit held that the immigration statute "does not require a blood relationship between a person born in wedlock and his parent who is a U.S. citizen" on the reasoning that "had Congress intended to require a blood relationship for children born in wedlock, it would have explicitly included it in the statute as it did in the provision concerning children born out of wedlock," while the Secretary of State has reached the opposite conclusion and interprets the statute to always require a blood relationship to transmit citizenship by descent, and has concluded that "the presumption that children born in wedlock are the product of that marriage is not determinative in citizenship cases because 'an actual blood relationship to a U.S. citizen parent is required.'"[104]

When it comes to the meaning of "born in wedlock," the Foreign Affairs Manual adopts a series of rules regarding surrogacy, namely:

> (1) a child born to a foreign surrogate mother who is also the biological mother and to a biological father who is a U.S. citizen is a child born out of wedlock to the U.S. citizen father (the identity of the intended, nonbiological mother is irrelevant); (2) a child born to a foreign surrogate mother who is not the biological mother and whose biological mother is a U.S. citizen and biological father is foreign is a child born out of wedlock to the U.S. citizen mother, even if the biological mother and father are married; and (3) a child born to a foreign surrogate mother who is not the biological mother and whose biological mother and father are both U.S. citizens is the child of two U.S. citizens.[105]

Although the Ninth Circuit has not addressed the meaning of "born in wedlock" for children born through reproductive technology, one commentator suggests that its existing jurisprudence as to naturally produced children suggests that "as long as the child's intended parents are married, the child will be considered born in wedlock."[106]

The result of all this is that whether the children born abroad of families formed through reproductive technology will be granted U.S. citizenship by descent will depend heavily on whether the matter is determined by an application while abroad (where, in many cases, the citizenship will not be granted) versus as a defense to a removal

---

[103] *Id.* at 874 (citing and quoting 8 U.S.C. § 1409 (2006).

[104] *Id.* at 875–76 (quoting and citing Scales v. INS, 232 F.3d 1159, 1166 (9th Cir. 2000) and 7 FOREIGN AFFAIRS MANUAL § 1131.4-1 (1998)).

[105] *Id.* at 878 (citing 7 FOREIGN AFFAIRS MANUAL § 1131.4-2 (1998)).

[106] *Id.*

proceeding for a child who has been brought to the United States (where the more permissive judge-made rule will apply).

This review of the case and statutory law pertaining to children born through reproductive technology outside the intended parents' home country suggests that, in many of these cases, intended parents face difficult, and, in some cases, insurmountable hurdles in trying to assert parentage over these children and bring them back to the home country. In the next section, I discuss what should be done.

B. Regulatory Options

There are a series of options available to regulate this space. It is useful to map these out in terms of the interplay between the extraterritorial criminalization issues discussed in the earlier part of this chapter and the immigration issues discussed in this part, as well as the possibility of restricting access.

One example of this last possibility comes from India: in 2008, India released the Assisted Reproductive Technologies ("Regulation") Bill and Rules ("Draft ART Bill"), and subsequently revised it in 2010, although at the time of this writing the Act continues to languish in India's parliament.[107] It has many provisions, but the one most relevant to us is Paragraph 34(19). providing that:

A foreigner or foreign couple not resident in India, or a non-resident Indian individual or couple, seeking surrogacy in India shall appoint a local guardian who will be legally responsible for taking care of the surrogate during and after the pregnancy as per clause 34.2, till the child / children are delivered to the foreigner or foreign couple or the local guardian. Further, the party seeking the surrogacy must ensure and establish to the assisted reproductive technology clinic through proper documentation (a letter from either the embassy of the Country in India or from the foreign ministry of the Country, clearly and unambiguously stating that (a) the country permits surrogacy, and (b) the child born through surrogacy in India, will be permitted entry in the Country as a biological child of the commissioning couple/individual) that the party would be able to take the child / children born through surrogacy, including where the embryo was a consequence of donation of an oocyte or sperm, outside of India to the country of the party's origin or residence as the case may be. If the foreign party seeking surrogacy fails to take delivery of the child born to the surrogate mother commissioned by the foreign party, the local guardian shall be legally obliged to take delivery of the child and be free to hand the child over to an adoption agency, if the commissioned party or their legal representative fails to claim the child within one months of the birth of the child. During the transition period, the local guardian shall be responsible

---

[107] Lin, *supra* note 10, at 561–62.

for the well-being of the child. In case of adoption or the legal guardian having to bring up the child, the child will be given Indian citizenship.[108]

The draft legislation would essentially prevent clinics in India from providing services to foreigners without written proof that the prospective parents' home country would be able to take the resulting child back to the home country. It also provides guardianship for the child, and, in the event the intended parents are unwilling or unable to take the child, the guardian may place the child for adoption within one month after the birth, and for Indian citizenship of the child in such cases. On the home country side, the Consul Generals of Belgium, France, Germany, Italy, the Netherlands, Poland, Spain, and the Czech Republic have in the interim sent letters to the reproductive technology clinics in India requesting that they no longer provide services to their citizens, and requiring that the citizens obtain pre-approval from their native government before proceeding with the treatments in India.[109]

With that background, let me outline a series of regulatory options and provide some analysis of their benefits and drawbacks:

(1) Do Not Criminalize, and Facilitate Immigration for the Child Back to the Genetic Parents' Home Country:

In this approach, essentially the home country would do nothing to obstruct the practice of fertility tourism, nor would the destination country. This approach would attempt to avoid some of the complicated legal battles involving citizenship discussed above by producing a clear and easy recognition-of-citizenship program for the home country. It would be enough for the home country to specify that if *either* genetic parent of the child born to a foreign surrogate is a citizen of the home country, then the child would receive citizenship through a *jus sanguinis* method. The integrity of the system could be ensured by requiring the filing with the application for citizenship in this instance of a genetic test showing relatedness. The destination country would in turn, to the extent necessary, amend its laws to allow the home country intended parents to remove the child from the destination country.[110] Thus, intended parents using egg or sperm provided by a third party and gestational or traditional surrogacy would be secured the ability to take their child back to the home country where the child would be given citizenship.

---

[108] Draft of The Assisted Reproductive Technologies (Regulation) Bill—2010, *available at* http://icmr.nic.in/guide/ART%20REGULATION%20Draft%20Bill1.pdf.

[109] Lin, *supra* note 10, at 562–63 (citing *Bar Our Nationals, European Countries Tell Surrogacy Clinics*, Times India (July 14, 2010, 3:00 AM), http://articles.timesofindia.indiatimes.com/2010-07-14/india/28305352_1_surrogacy-clinics-citizenship-rights).

[110] I will put to one side the question of what to do when a gestational or full surrogate herself tries to assert parentage rights over the child. How to resolve this kind of case, familiar in the domestic version in U.S. courts, would depend on how the destination country itself resolves cases where both genetic and gestational parents

This approach would prevent citizenship in one kind of case I discussed above, where *neither* intended parent is a genetic parent or a gestational surrogate to the resulting child.

In theory, one could expand the rule such that even in this case citizenship was provided to the child, by specifying that as long as one intended (if not genetic) parent is a citizen of the home country, then the home country will grant citizenship to the offspring. Some might object that such a case looks more like adoption than it does non-assisted reproduction, and the immigration rules of the home country pertaining to adoption of children abroad are the better way of regulating cases of this type. I will not take a strong position on this kind of case here, which occurs fairly rarely, except to say that one's attitude toward whether to extend citizenship directly to the child in this case will turn on (1) one's attitude as to the importance of genetic ties in family formation, and (2) in what ways reproductive technology is properly thought to be like adoption versus non-assisted reproduction, both issues that have preoccupied me in other work.[111]

But, let us put the case of genetically unrelated parents to the side once again. Under what circumstances would this policy option *not* be desirable? The answer comes from the earlier part of this chapter: cases of circumvention tourism. Where the justification for an equivalent domestic criminal prohibition in the home country is one that I have argued justifies extraterritorial prohibition as well—as I have argued that some but not all of the justifications do—then this approach to the problem would fail to effectuate the goal of deterring and punishing home country citizens who do abroad what they cannot do at home.

Thus, home and destination countries should adopt this permissive and facilitative approach where both countries permit the reproductive technology practice in question, or where the home country prohibits the activity but its justification for that prohibition does not also justify extending the prohibition extraterritorially. In cases where *neither* of those conditions are met, the system designer will have to choose among between two other possible approaches:

(2) Criminalize Parental Action but Facilitate Immigration for the Child Back to the Genetic Parents' Home Country:

---

assert parentage rights. There is also the opposite configuration, which sadly is also not unknown in U.S. circles; *see In re* Marriage of Buzzanca, 61 Cal. App. 4th 1410 (1998), of "hot potato," where no parent wants to assert parentage rights. Again, I suspect the right solution for such a case is to adopt whatever solution the destination country has put in place, to essentially make fertility tourism symmetrical with surrogacy usage within the destination country. A different approach, suggested by the Indian legislation discussed below, would be to enable guardianship and adoption of the child into a destination country family.

[111] *See generally* I. Glenn Cohen, *The Constitution and the Rights Not to Procreate*, 60 Stan. L. Rev. 1135 (2008); I. Glenn Cohen, *The Right Not to Be a Genetic Parent?*, 81 S. Cal. L. Rev. 1115 (2008); I. Glenn Cohen & Daniel L. Chen, *Trading-Off Reproductive Technology and Adoption: Does Subsidizing IVF Decrease Adoption Rates and Should It Matter?*, 95 Minn. L. Rev. 485 (2010); Cohen, *supra* note 55.

or

(3) Criminalize Parental Action and Deny Immigration for the Child Back to the Genetic Parents' Home Country:

The second approach attempts a kind of Solomonic solution. On the one hand, in cases of circumvention tourism where extraterritorial criminalization is justified, it honors that principle by giving symmetrical treatment of the parents' activity. If it is illegal to engage in artificial insemination by donor, procure a commercial surrogate,[112] purchase sperm or eggs, engage in sex selection, etc, in the home country, it should be symmetrically illegal to do it abroad (again assuming the justification is one that extends extraterritorially). However, to use the language of the Bible, this approach stops short of punishing the child for the sins of the father (and/or mother).[113] Justice Hedley, writing in the *Re X & Y (foreign surrogacy)* case, put his finger on the discomfort of using citizenship of the resulting child as a deterrent, writing:

> What the court is required to do is to balance two competing and potentially irreconcilably conflicting concepts. Parliament is clearly entitled to legislate against commercial surrogacy and is clearly entitled to expect that the courts should implement that policy consideration in its decisions. Yet it is also recognised that as the full rigour of that policy consideration will bear on one wholly unequipped to comprehend it let alone deal with its consequences (i.e. the child concerned) that rigour must be mitigated by the application of a consideration of that child's welfare. That approach is both humane and intellectually coherent. The difficulty is that it is almost impossible to imagine a set of circumstances in which by the time the case comes to court, the

---

[112] There remains a separate question of whether the home country ought to also seek to criminalize extraterritorially the activities of the destination country surrogate. Because it will be difficult to prosecute a foreign citizen whose activities take place abroad, as a practical matter this option does not seem all that appealing, although asserting prescriptive jurisdiction would at least give some expressive benefit. Whether that expressive benefit is worth it, I think, will depend again on the underlying justification. When the concern is exploitation of the destination country citizen, criminalizing her activity seems very strong medicine for a law meant ultimately to protect her from an exploitative action. When the concern is corruption of the consequentialist form, the key question seems to me what marginal reduction in corruption of the home country mores is achieved through adding this criminal penalty on to that established for the home country citizens. When the concern is child welfare, I think the case for criminalizing the activities of the destination country surrogate is the strongest, but like the abortion providers discussed in Chapter 8, I think that the concerns of comity as well as the difficulties of enforcement, coupled with the fact that we worry about the conditions that drove these women to participate in the first place, all mitigate against extending domestic criminal prohibitions to them.

[113] *Compare Ezekiel* 18:20 ("The person who sins will die. The son will not bear the punishment for the father's iniquity, nor will the father bear the punishment for the son's iniquity; the righteousness of the righteous will be upon himself, and the wickedness of the wicked will be upon himself."), *with Exodus* 20:5 ("You shall not worship them or serve them; for I, the Lord your God, am a jealous God, visiting the iniquity of the fathers on the children, on the third and the fourth generations of those who hate Me.").

welfare of any child (particularly a foreign child) would not be gravely compromised (at the very least) by a refusal to make an order.[114]

An editorial in the French newspaper *Le Monde* about the Mennesson case described above makes a similar claim: "How do you justify depriving these children, now strangers in their parents' country, of all the rights connected with citizenship, based solely on the way they were conceived and when there is no dispute over their parentage? What are they guilty of, besides their birth, to merit such sanctions?"[115] Justice Hedley's view in *Re X & Y* accords with those of most commentators, who have argued it is wrong to deny home country citizenship to these children.[116]

---

[114] Re X & Y (Foreign Surrogacy) [2008] E.W.H.C. 3030 (Fam.) ¶ 24.

[115] Najat Vallaud Belkacem, *Gestation pour autrui: Une question de responsabilité morale [Surrogacy: A Question of Moral Responsibility]*, Le Monde, Apr. 7, 2011, (Fr.), http://www.lemonde.fr/idees/article/2011/04/07/gestation-pour-autrui-une-question-de-responsabilite-morale_1504228_3232.html (translated by Storrow, *supra* note 41, at 600). To be clear here I am discussing whether the children, like the Menessons, should be given French citizenship, not whether the parents who commissioned surrogacy should be allowed to be their legal parents. One could imagine a version of Option 3 that went further still in its goal of deterrence and not only denied the child citizenship but denied the would-be parents parentage under that circumstance. That would produce a child who was not only potentially stateless but parentless as well. That poses at least two difficulties: first, it would require coordination of the parentage laws of several countries in this instance, for France would not only have to refuse to recognize the parentage status of these parents but insure that other countries would as well, a sort of judicial recognition of a non-parentage order. One might conclude that it is all fine and good under the usual principles of comity for France to make a decision as to whether to grant citizenship or recognize parenthood in France itself, but it oversteps its bounds to place a scarlet letter on this child's head and try to take steps to convince other countries to also render him or her an orphan. Second, the idea that the regime would end up producing children who were parentless and stateless in the face of parents who very much want the child seems a very hard result to take. Of course, as I will argue below, in resolving these conflicts we may be choosing between a number of bad options, and we have to consider not only the ex post perspective but the ex ante deterrence one as well. If the "extra" penalty were to have a major advantage in terms of deterring the behavior in question, then it might be worth considering on my view as discussed below—I am skeptical but it is an empirical question. In any event, even if this was the "right" answer, it is one that judges and legislatures would find a step too far.

[116] *E.g.*, Laufer-Ukeles, *supra* note 39, at 54 ("[I]t is very problematic not to allow those children to be raised by their intended parents. Refusal to let the child into the country seems particularly harsh when they were created at the behest of local citizens. The burden on the foreign country also seems unfair to that jurisdiction and overly punitive to the baby who may be a genetic relation to the intended parents. While this can be said of international adoption as well, children who are orphaned in foreign countries are still citizens of that country and clearly the responsibility of that country."); Lin, *supra* note 10, at 587 ("[B]y denying citizenship to the surrogate child, the 'sins' of the parents are visited upon the undeserving child. Therefore, domestic courts addressing this matter ought to look to the standard that has been adapted by the U.K. courts in resolving the dispute in the best interests of the child. Under this framework, the court must be mindful of the public policy considerations behind the prohibition of surrogacy, but maintain the child's welfare as its paramount consideration. This approach is in line with international norms on children's rights, which have recognized the child's right to a nationality and the right to stay with one's family where possible. The receiving country should make every effort to ensure that the child's rights are not violated, which may include issuing an emergency travel certificate where appropriate so that the child is not forcibly separated from his or her parents.").

These authors, though, subtly mix in ex ante and ex post perspectives in a way that may make their claims appear stronger than they are. More specifically, it seems reasonable to assume that a well-publicized rule applied non-retroactively denying immigration status to children born through circumvention tourism will alter how many parents seek to use circumvention tourism for reproductive technology. In the extreme case, imagine that a well-publicized rule along the lines of the second proposal I delineated reduced the incidence of circumvention tourism for reproductive technology to zero. In that case, there would be no child welfare argument available against the policy, for no children would be born who suffered that penalty. By contrast, at the other extreme, if the rule had no deterrent force, then every child born through circumvention tourism would be harmed by the rule. The key question is where on the spectrum between these two poles will the deterrent effect of preventing immigration status lie. To be more precise, if somewhat mathematical, we should actually ask for the "delta," the marginal deterrent effect of the rule beyond the other option of only criminalizing the behavior of the intended parents.

To use some fictitious numbers to illustrate how the analysis would go: in a regime where the home country does not criminalize parental behavior and facilitates immigration for the child (Option 1), four hundred pairs of home country parents each year employ a foreign surrogate through circumvention tourism, producing three hundred children. In a regime where the home country does criminalize the parental behavior and facilitates immigration for the child (Option 2), two hundred pairs of home country parents each year employ a foreign surrogate through circumvention tourism, producing 150 children. In a regime where the home country does criminalize parental behavior and denies immigration for the child (Option 3), twenty pairs of home country parents each year employ a foreign surrogate through circumvention tourism, producing fifteen children. The analysis I have suggested would ask, "Is the reduction of 180 acts of circumvention tourism for surrogacy (200 − 20) worth leaving fifteen children of intended parents without home country citizenship?"

That is an explicitly consequentialist approach to the problem, where the conceded welfare detriment to these children is weighed against the moral harm identified with surrogacy that we wish to deter. The alternative would be a more deontological approach, hinted at by some authors who have opposed Option 2. For example, Laufer-Ukeles writes that "[c]riminalization or refusing citizenship is extremely punitive and affects the children as much as the parents" and should be rejected because "[s]uch prohibitions or criminalization can serve to stigmatize children and punish innocent children in a manner that fails to protect children's civil rights."[117] Richard Storrow writes passionately that "[i]t is critical that any law reform efforts that lawyers choose to undertake forcefully articulate that rendering surrogate children 'illegitimate' harms them and furthers no proper public purpose" and "[b]estowing a subordinate status on any child

---

[117] Laufer-Ukeles, *supra* note 39, at 54.

born of surrogacy is every bit as invidious as was the stigma of 'illegitimacy' that historically attached to children born to families that did not fit the mold of one biological mother married to one biological father."[118]

My disagreement with these authors is twofold. First, as I suggested above, there is a potential "proper public purpose" in achieving deterrence and punishing wrongdoing by home country citizens, at least as understood through the lens of the home country's domestic prohibition.

Second, and more to the point, I think a rights-based conception of the need to avoid harm to the child's own welfare collapses under the weight of the principle. In home countries where the act of intended parents procuring a commercial surrogate is already criminalized, the only countries we are talking about in this section (as these are the only countries where circumvention tourism happens), the potential to send violating parents to jail *already* set back the welfare of the children who are born through this process. These countries have thus, to some extent, decided to trade off child welfare against the desire to deter and punish these practices that they find odious, for some of the reasons discussed above. Indeed, every time the State criminalizes *any* behavior by *any* parent, unrelated to reproduction, it also sets back the interests of that parent's children, and yet there is no "I have children" excuse for criminal behavior. This point, I think, readily answers objections to Option 2, which criminalizes parental behavior in circumvention tourism as it does in the patient's home country. Criminal liability against parents usually sets back the interest of their children, and yet we routinely permit it elsewhere in criminal law because we seek to vindicate deterrent and retributive aims.

Whether these objections provide a strong argument against Option 3, the use of immigration rules for children to deter bad parental conduct, strikes me as a closer question. One might be tempted to analogize to the way the law frequently provides tools to deprive those who commit crimes of their ill-gotten gains in financial and other kinds of crimes,[119] that depriving these parents of children achieved through illicit means is just another kind of "disgorgement," but that might be thought of as inappropriately treating these children as mere means to deterring parental behavior.

I think the better argument for Option 3 as against Option 2 is to put pressure on its opponents' underlying assumptions by asking the question why the injury to the child of not being given his or her intended parents citizenship and filiation is morally different from the harms to the child of the criminal incarceration of his or her intended parents. One could imagine that, in some instances, from a child welfare perspective, the flip of Option 2—no criminal liability for parents but also no immigration to the

---

[118] Storrow, *supra* note 41, at 608.

[119] *E.g.*, 2012 U.S. SENTENCING GUIDELINES MANUAL §§ 5E1.1, 5E1.4 (orders of restitution and forfeiture for individuals, respectively). I raised a similar analogy in Chapter 7 as an argument for refusing to pay for the immunosuppressive drugs of patients who bought kidneys through transplant tourism in violation of the law.

home country for the child outside of adoption proceedings—might be better for the child. And that last point is worth emphasizing: the question is not whether the child will forever be prohibited from becoming a home country citizen, but whether the child should be potentially available for adoption and thus on the same footing as other destination country children as opposed to enjoying the usual benefits of near automatic *jus sanguinis* citizenship.

The strongest argument for suggesting that the denial of immigration status is different in kind from the criminal sanction to parents is that it is a legal response applied directly to the resulting child, and not one that sets back his or her welfare indirectly through a sanction to parents. That is a distinction, but is it a morally relevant difference? The response presumes that the child is being *deprived* of something that is his or her due—citizenship status in the home country—but a deprivation assumes that the child has an *entitlement* to that status, and the grounds for that entitlement are not clear. As we have seen through the cases reviewed above, there is no firm agreement between nations that genetic parentage, rather than gestational parentage, rather than either/or should be the basis for *jus sanguinis* citizenship. It seems to fetishize an essential genetic connection over gestational connections to say that the mere fact that one of your genetic parents comes from a particular home country gives you an entitlement to that country as your citizenship as opposed to the country of the gestational or full surrogate, especially when your country has made the opposite decision in its own immigration law.

The importance of gestational versus genetic ties and their relationship to citizenship is deeply wedded into the culture and legality of the home country, and not something that comes from thin air. As Storrow summarizes the matter in regard to Europe:

[T]his approach to surrogacy arises from the intractable view of the legal implications of gestational motherhood. "[I]n traditional European-American thinking a mother's identity is understood as [an unwavering] natural fact:" "birth itself is conclusive proof of motherhood." In both the civil law and the common law, this tradition is embodied in the maxim "mater semper certa est, etiamsi vulgo conceperit, pater est quem nuptiae demonstrant," or "maternity is always certain even of illegitimate children, paternity follows marriage," which continues to carry considerable weight, having been enshrined in the Brussels Convention on the Establishment of Maternal Affiliation of Natural Children (1962) and the Convention on the Legal Status of Children Born out of Wedlock (1975). A Belgian newspaper explains: "The principle is simple: a child's legal mother is she who gives birth to it. Belgian law is extremely clear on this subject." Not only is the law perfectly clear, there simply is no legal way to "break the lines of filiation." This maxim holds even in the United Kingdom, where altruistic surrogacy is legal, but not in Greece, where the law recognizes the intending mother in surrogacy arrangements as the legal mother. Most countries in Europe reject surrogacy, however, so that in this area of assisted reproduction at least, the medical technologies of vitro fertilization and embryo transfer have not successfully eroded the force of the maxim.[120]

To draw an analogy outside of reproductive technology: suppose two parents from country X had forged the birth certificates of themselves and their genetic child to make them look like citizens of France, then transported them to France, and the day after the family was admitted and began enjoying the benefits of citizenship (welfare, for example) the forgery was discovered. If those who oppose Option 3 are right, it would be immoral to deny citizenship to the child at that moment because she is the victim of her parents' malfeasance. But that does not seem right. She has no entitlement to French citizenship, and although it is true that she does not deserve to be criminally punished—she was not the culpable actor—it also is the case that she has no entitlement under the law of France to the citizenship. What we are doing is discounting the criminal act, imagining it had not happened, and asking: Does she have an entitlement to French citizenship? She has no such entitlement, except to the extent she may become a citizen just as any other child seeking French citizenship should want to. Notice that in some ways this is the *harder* case than the surrogacy tourism in that she is already on French soil and we need to "send her home," whereas in the cases I am imagining the child is still in the destination country and has not traveled to or begun acculturation into French society. The way to define who is a member of a family (as well as who is a citizen) is traditionally at the center of state sovereign decisions, in part because family structure is so deeply enmeshed with cultural values and history. All the home country denying citizenship to these children born abroad is doing is applying its rules on these subjects to those children. There are many children across the world who would benefit by being conferred French, or U.S., or Canadian citizenship, but we certainly do not take all comers. It is unclear why these children born to surrogates have a superior claim when their claim arises out of a criminal prohibition that their parents have circumvented. They should not be punished for that activity, but neither should they be given priority because of it.

For these reasons, I think the strong case against Option 3, which relies on a deontological right of the child to the citizenship of his or her genetic parent(s), has not been adequately made. Instead, I think the right way to conceive of the problem is the one I set out above (now subject to some additional qualifications), that is, asking: "Is the reduction of X acts of circumvention tourism for surrogacy worth leaving Y children of intended parents without home country citizenship at birth through *jus sanguinis* routes?"

That analysis is further inflected by (1) the likelihood that citizenship for the resulting child might be achieved through adoption as with other potential destination country children (which should make us more comfortable with this approach), and (2) the

---

[120] Storrow, *supra* note 41, at 593–94 (citations omitted).

question whether these children (at least in the interim) will be given destination country citizenship as opposed to being rendered stateless (which should make us more comfortable with this approach).

That last point is worth amplifying. Recall that the draft Indian legislation discussed above provides guardianship for the child of intended parents, and, in the event the intended parents are unwilling or unable to take the child, allows the guardian to place the child for adoption within one month after the birth, and for Indian citizenship of the child in such cases. Where such measures are in place, such that the child born has a clear path to destination country citizenship and parentage if not home country citizenship or parentage by the intended parents, I think Option 3 becomes more appealing. Indeed, in such a case we think the child has been "injured" by not having home country citizenship only if we think he or she "deserves" that citizenship much more than destination country citizenship, but as I suggested above it is not clear whether that entitlement can be defended. To be sure, there is still a setback of welfare for the child if we assume that his life would go better with his intended parents and/or that he would fare better if raised in their home rather than the destination country (contestable assumptions to be sure), but it seems to me much more like the setbacks of welfare that resemble the general criminalization of parental behavior that violates the law.

Because the analysis I have offered as to whether facilitation or obstruction of immigration for resulting children trades off the setback of welfare to children as against the home country's anticipated marginal deterrence and retributive interests in preventing and punishing the acts it has criminalized, the analysis may once again vary based on the justification for the underlying criminal prohibition domestically and its extraterritorial extension. Where the justification for the prohibition is a powerful one, such as the Harm Principle, it seems to me less marginal deterrence may be tolerated in justifying the initial sanction.[121] Where the motivation is something like consequentialist corruption, which I (at least) find less powerful, it might demand significantly more deterrence to justify harm to the same number of children whose interests are set back.

IV. CONCLUSION

The emotional pull of children born abroad and unable to return home with their intended parents is undeniable, but I have suggested that we should resist giving in to our impulse to adopt rules giving the child automatically home country citizenship, in favor of a more subtle and nuanced analysis of these cases.

Where the home and destination country both permit the reproductive technology practice in question or where the home country prohibits the activity but its justification

---

[121] It is no contradiction to think that a justification focused on child welfare could justify the no-citizenship option that itself sets back child welfare.

for that prohibition does not also justify extending the prohibition extraterritorially, I have argued that the home country should grant *jus sanguinis* citizenship to the children born to foreign surrogates, at least in cases where a genetic parent of the child is also a home country citizen. Moreover, as the analysis in the first part of this chapter suggests, in such instances, the activities of the parents should not be subject to extraterritorial criminalization.

Where the home country prohibits the reproductive technology practice and its justification for that prohibition extends extraterritorially, I have suggested that the home country needs to engage in a complex analysis as to whether to only criminalize the extraterritorial actions of the home country parents or also deny *jus sanguinis* citizenship to the resulting child as a further deterrent of the activity. It must ask: "Is the reduction of X acts of circumvention tourism for surrogacy worth leaving Y children of intended parents without home country citizenship at birth through *jus sanguinis* routes?" Where the answer is no, the home country should only criminalize extraterritorially. Where the answer is yes, the home country should also deny citizenship to the children who result.

Although that seems like a neat-and-tidy analysis, the ability to clearly articulate a standard should not obscure the number of difficult judgment calls that must be made. First, how to fill in variables X and Y are never fully knowable in advance, so, like so much in the law, the home country must make decisions in the shadow of uncertainty based on its best information. Second, as I have suggested above, the "worth" evaluative part of the analysis is inflected by considerations such as (1) What is the justification for the home country criminal prohibition and its extraterritorial extension, and how powerful are those considerations?; (2) Can the child be easily adopted and receive home country citizenship that way, or are their great difficulties?; (3) Will the child remain stateless, or will the child be given destination country citizenship and a good possibility of adoption?

I have focused largely on what *home* countries should adopt as their rule in this section, but I want to recognize, like most authors, that international regulation would be very desirable, but, is also unlikely to occur in the short or medium term.[122] Nelson, I think, has the diagnosis exactly right: "In principle, the idea of international regulation seems to make sense; we are, after all seeking solutions," ideally through "a human-rights based instrument to regulate international surrogacy," but that "solution [of international regulations] is not realistically achievable." That is,

> One need only look at the wide variety of regulatory approaches taken to ARTs in general and surrogacy in particular to appreciate that international consensus will be impossible to achieve. In addition, surrogacy is a complex phenomenon that requires regulation through an array of legal and policy approaches. Because

---

[122] *See, e.g.,* Lin, *supra* note 10, at 586.

420 ~~ Medical Tourism for Services Illegal in the Patient's Home Country

regulation of international surrogacy potentially affects so many areas of domestic law (including family law, contract law, health law, and human rights law), international regulation would likely demand significant modifications to domestic law to eliminate conflicts with the international regime.[123]

Having now discussed four forms of medical tourism for services illegal in the patient's home country—travel abroad for organs, abortion, assisted suicide, and reproductive technology services—in the next chapter I discuss a form of medical tourism that is more in the gray zone based on most home country practices: stem cell tourism. As we shall see, this form of medical tourism also poses difficult questions relating to the interests of children, the State's interest in regulating, and parental prerogative.

---

[123] Nelson, *supra* note 5, at 248 (citing K. Brugger, *International Law in the Gestational Surrogacy Debate*, 35 FORDHAM INT'L L.J. 665, 680, 682–83 (2012)).

10

Medical Tourism for Experimental Therapies: An In-Depth
Exploration of Stem Cell Therapy Tourism

⌒ ——

THIS CHAPTER FOCUSES on patients who travel abroad to receive experimental
therapies unavailable in their home country, with a focus on stem cell therapies. This
form of medical tourism raises difficult issues about innovation, regulation, hope, and
paternalism. This chapter is different from the last few that preceeds it in that patients
are typically traveling for treatments that have *not yet but one day might* be approved, as
opposed to health care services that have explicitly been outlawed.

Before we can understand the phenomenon and the legal and ethical issues it poses, we
must understand why it occurs. Under the regulatory regimes currently in place in the
United States and other major research powerhouses, approval of new therapies can take a
long time.

In the United States, for example, the Food and Drug Administration (FDA) has a
rigorous multi-step process for approvals, wherein after filing an investigational new drug
application (IND), a drug must complete three phases of clinical trials. Phase I studies,
which typically are quite small in the number of patients involved, assess how the human
body metabolizes low doses of the drug and what side effects result. Phase II measures
the efficacy and safety of the drug in a small number of patients who suffer from the
targeted illness or condition. In Phase III, the drug sponsor has to provide the FDA
with substantial evidence confirming their successful Phase II results with a significantly

larger patient-base.[1] Similar oversight systems are in place in other developed countries; for example, the United Kingdom relies on the Medicines and Healthcare products Regulatory Agency; Japan has the Ministry of Health, Labor and Welfare; and the European Medicines Agency also provides oversight for EU Member States.[2]

It has been estimated that, from start to finish, the FDA approval process can take up to ten years for a successful drug.[3] Until a drug is approved, it is illegal to sell the drug to willing patients, unless the drug qualifies for one of FDA's narrow exceptions.[4]

In particular, under what is known as its "expanded access" program, FDA has made some experimental drugs available to patients before final approval. As part of the program, expanded access must "not interfere with the initiation, conduct, or completion of clinical investigations" required for market approval, and the FDA must determine that the drug is not available as part of a clinical trial. The program applies only to cases where the drug sponsor is actively "pursuing marketing approval of the drug for the expanded access use with due diligence." Under the program, the FDA must approve patient participation in an expanded access program, and the conditions of access are keyed to the level of severity of the patient's needs: where the patient seeks to use the drug for a "a serious disease or condition, there must be sufficient clinical evidence of safety and effectiveness to support the expanded access use," ordinarily consisting of "data from phase 3 trials, but could consist of compelling data from completed phase 2 trials." By contrast, where the drug is sought for an "immediately life-threatening disease or condition," for treatment to be authorized through this program the FDA must conclude that "the available scientific evidence, taken as a whole, provides a reasonable basis to conclude that the investigational drug may be effective for the expanded access use and would not expose patients to an unreasonable and significant risk of illness or injury," and suggests that this "evidence would ordinarily consist of clinical data from phase 3 or phase 2 trials, but could be based on more preliminary clinical evidence." In general, drug companies must seek FDA permission to charge for therapies and are prohibited from profiting from expanded access,

---

[1] 21 C.F.R. § 312.21(a)–(c) (2008); see, e.g., Vanessa Eng., Note, Drug Safety: It's a Learning Process, 24 ST. JOHN'S J. LEGAL COMMENT. 159 (2009).

[2] A.C. Regenberg & L.A. Hutchinson et al., Medicine on the Fringe: Stem Cell-Based Interventions in Advance of Evidence, 27 STEM CELLS 2312, 2312 (2009).

[3] See, e.g., Stacey L. Dogan & Mark A. Lemley, Antitrust Law and Regulatory Gaming, 87 TEX. L. REV. 685, 709 n.99 (2009); James O'Reilly & Amy Dalal, Off-Label or Out of Bounds? Prescriber and Marketer Liability for Unapproved Uses of FDA-Approved Drugs, 12 ANNALS HEALTH L. 295, 304 (2003); Holly Soehnge, The Drug Price Competition and Patent Term Restoration Act of 1984: Fine-Tuning the Balance between the Interests of Pioneer and Generic Drug Manufacturers, 58 FOOD & DRUG L.J. 51, 52 (2003).

[4] In a case that I handled at the rehearing stage when part of the U.S. Department of Justice, Abigail Alliance for Better Access to Dev. Drugs v. Eschenbach, 445 F.3d 470 (D.C. Cir. 2006), rev'd en banc, 495 F.3d 695 (D.C. Cir. 2007), the D.C. Circuit Court of Appeals reaffirmed the constitutionality of this scheme, denying terminally ill patients a constitutional right to access experimental drugs that had completed Phase 1 but not Phase 2 or 3 of clinical testing.

but in rare circumstances the programs allow a firm to charge for the clinical trial if it can show that the drug cannot be developed without charging patients.[5]

Many therapies sought by patients will not meet a number of the requirements of this program: the drug sponsor will not pursue marketing approval of the drug for the expanded access use with due diligence, nor will there be Phase II or III data, or its equivalent, proving safety or even effectiveness of the drug. The approval of the drug sponsor is also always required. Further, in some cases making the drug available to patients outside of formal clinical trials will interfere with the initiation or conduct of clinical trials. Medical tourism to countries with more permissive drug approval or access regimes will thus prove an enticing alternative for patients who want the drug or treatment in question.

Although the FDA does not regulate surgical interventions, and much of surgical innovation decisions are left in the hands of individual surgeons and hospitals, there are some legal barriers to patients getting experimental surgeries in the United States or other patient home countries. First, insurers in the United States typically do not reimburse for experimental or investigational surgeries whose clinical effectiveness is unproven. Second, medical malpractice liability may limit surgeons' willingness to provide experimental therapies, although patients have had some difficulties in establishing negligence on the part of surgeons even without any prior experimental evaluation of the surgery.[6] Third, if the innovative surgery is considered research it will be governed by the "Common Rule," and thus the Institutional Review Board system and other regulations of human subjects in the United States, which will essentially put in place the same ethical and regulatory restrictions as drug clinical trials.[7]

Because of these forms of regulation, experimental drug and surgical therapies are sometimes unavailable or prohibited in a patient's home country, but available in destination countries with different regulatory regimes.[8] By traveling abroad patients can

---

[5] Expanded Access to Investigational Drugs for Treatment Use, 71 Fed. Reg. 75,147, 75,150, 75,157 (Dec. 14, 2006) (to be codified at 21 C.F.R. pt. 312); Guidance for Industry—Expanded Access to Investigational Drugs for Treatment Use—Qs & As, 78 Fed. Reg. 27,115 (May 9, 2013) (to be codified at 21 C.F.R. pt. 312); *see* Anna B. Laakmann, *Collapsing the Distinction between Experimentation and Treatment in the Regulation of New Drugs*, 62 ALA. L. REV. 305, 322–24 (2011).

[6] *See* Anna C. Mastroianni, *Liability, Regulation and Policy in Surgical Innovation: The Cutting Edge of Research and Therapy*, 16 HEALTH MATRIX 351, 381 (2006) ("Case law supports that an innovative surgical approach may be used for the first time with no other performance standard to serve as a comparison, even with a bad outcome, at least under the following circumstances: the patient is suffering from a life-threatening condition, no alternative therapies are available, and the patient understood that the treatment was unproven and the risks unknown."); Karp v. Cooley, 493 F.2d 408 (5th Cir. 1974) (rejecting liability against surgeon performing first-ever use of a mechanical heart implant).

[7] *See generally* SUBPART A—BASIC HHS POLICY FOR PROTECTION OF HUMAN RESEARCH SUBJECTS, 45 C.F.R. pt. 46 (2010); *see also* Mastroianni, *supra* note 6, at 339–433 (discussing how surgery is governed when deemed research).

[8] There may also be other reasons that stem cell therapies are unavailable in a patient's home country, such as because the home country prohibits the destruction of embryos from which embryonic stem cells are derived,

engage in a form of circumvention tourism, or at least "regulatory arbitrage" to get experimental therapies they cannot get at home. As a historical matter, one of the most notable examples was U.S. patients traveling abroad for experimental cancer therapies. For example, in 1980 the American actor Steve McQueen died in a clinic in Rosarito, Mexico, where he was receiving the unapproved cancer treatment, Laetrile, which was later shown to be ineffective and unsafe.[9] In this chapter, I focus on the most notable current instance of medical tourism for experimental therapies: travel abroad for stem cell therapies, hereafter referred to as "stem cell tourism."[10]

To give but a few examples of this phenomenon: more than two hundred hospitals in China offer stem cell therapies that may be accessed by foreign patients.[11] One of the biggest operators is Beike Biotechnology, which claims to have treated more than nine hundred foreign patients in its twenty-six hospitals in China and Thailand, and usually charges US$30,000 for a treatment.[12] In one report involving that set of hospitals, a family from Detroit paid US$85,000 for treatment of their four-year-old daughter, who suffered from spastic quadriplegia. Although they failed to achieve the result they most sought (that she would be able to hold up her head) they credit the treatment with making her "more relaxed" and improving her "disposition."[13] In Russia, another hotbed for stem cell therapies, there are hundreds of unlicensed clinics, many employing practitioners without medical qualifications, and reports of skin and animal cells being used to replace the fetal cell injections patients were promised.[14] And yet patients who have used these treatments vocally defend the practices on personal blogs and clinic websites; for example, the family of a sixteen-year-old Norwegian boy with cerebral palsy who claim they have seen "remarkable" improvements in his language skills and temperament due to the treatment.[15] Moreover, the expectations of patients are being heavily shaped by

---

which is more similar to the abortion restrictions discussed in Chapter 8. Other patients may view travel abroad as a way of protecting their confidentiality from prying governmental eyes.

[9] *See* I. Glenn Cohen, *Patients with Passports: Medical Tourism and the Patient-Protective Argument*, 95 IOWA L. REV. 1467, 1471 (2010) (citing Anne Cearley & Penni Crabtree, *Alternative-Medicine Clinics in Baja Have History of Controversy*, SAN DIEGO UNION-TRIB., Feb. 1, 2006, at A8, *available at* 2006 WLNR 1918432); Allan J. Jacobs, *Is State Power to Protect Health Compatible with Substantive Due Process Rights?*, 20 ANNALS HEALTH L. 113 (2011).

[10] Although I will continue to use the term "experimental" to refer to stem cell therapies, there is a sense in which it may be too generous to the industry such that "unproven" would be better: many of the foreign clinics offering these therapies are not attempting to determine their efficacy in a rigorous way, and one of the main challenges this chapter addresses is how to shift them toward an innovation model. Still many other authors use "unproven," so in quotes of their work I will as well.

[11] Dominique Martin, *Perilous Voyages: Travel Abroad for Organ Transplants and Stem Cell Treatments. in* RISKS AND CHALLENGES IN MEDICAL TOURISM: UNDERSTANDING THE GLOBAL MARKET FOR HEALTH SERVICES 138, 152 (Jill Hodges et al. eds., 2012).

[12] *Id.* at 152–53.

[13] *Id.* at 153.

[14] *Id.* at 153.

[15] *Id.* at 157.

"science hype," the persistent focus of the media on the promise of stem cell technologies and the breakthroughs "just around the corner."

How to mediate this conflict between the desires of patients and the need for safe and effective medicine is the focus of this chapter. My analysis will show that based on what is known, we should be very skeptical of the therapies being offered to medical tourists today, which have no rigorous proof of effectiveness but in many cases significant health risks. How to communicate this reality to patients desperate for a chance at hope, and how to use regulation to shift funding and patients into stem cell treatments that are more promising and on innovation pathways while respecting patient autonomy, is the main regulatory challenge.

The first part of this chapter explains in a nontechnical manner what stem cell therapies are, how they work, and the potential risks. The second part of the chapter describes the available data on stem cell tourism and the facilities that offer these therapies. The third part examines a series of legal, ethical, and policy issues relating to stem cell tourism: how to design a pathway for innovation that protects patients without stifling the development of these therapies, how to provide effective professional self-regulation, what regulation (if any) home countries should attempt over patients seeking these therapies abroad, and the special difficulties involved when parents seek to take their children abroad for stem cell therapies.

I. THE SCIENCE OF STEM CELL THERAPIES[16]

A. What Are Stem Cells?

What are "stem cells?" Most "lay" readers who encounter the term will have a vague sense of a particular thing out there in the real world, but it is more helpful to think of "stem cells" as describing a category of cells that hold certain properties. Although the definition is not uncontestable, in nontechnical terms, stem cells are cells capable of both self-renewal and differentiation: a stem cell is any cell that has the ability not only to divide, but to create both new stem cells and daughter cells that have different characteristics. In this way, stem cells differ from other cells in the body that have more fixed characteristic and functions. Skin cells are different from blood cells are different from bone cells, etc.

---

[16] In writing this nontechnical introduction to the science of stem cell therapy, I drew on: Russell Korobkin, *Stem Cell Research and the Cloning Wars*, 18 STAN. L. & POL'Y REV. 161 (2007); Leeron Morad, Note, *Stemming the Tide: On the Patentability of Stem Cells and Differentiation Processes*, 87 N.Y.U. L. REV. 551 (2012); Daniele Lodi et al., *Stem Cell in Clinical Practice: Applications and Warnings*, 30 J. EXPERIMENTAL CANCER RES. 1 (2011); Jonathan Kahn, *Synthetic Hype: A Skeptical View of the Promise of Synthetic Biology*, 45 VAL. U. L. REV. 1343 (2011); John Robertson, *Embryo Stem Cell Research: Ten Years of Controversy*, 38 J.L. MED. & ETHICS 191 (2010); Rajesh C. Rao, *Alternatives to Embryonic Stem Cells and Cloning: A Brief Scientific Overview*, 9 YALE J. HEALTH POL'Y, L. & ETHICS 603 (2009); CYNTHIA B. COHEN, RENEWING THE STUFF OF LIFE: STEM CELLS, ETHICS, AND PUBLIC POLICY (2007).

To serve their different roles in our body, different genes are "expressed" (i.e., activated) in different types of cells, while other genes lie dormant. When specialized cells with fixed functions are created, biologists describe such cells as "fully differentiated." A stem cell, by contrast, is not fully differentiated and can divide not only into two identical copies of itself, but also into one copy of a different, more specialized cell, with a different gene expression pattern.

Stem cells come in different levels of differentiation, or plasticity, which determine just how many types of cells they can become. Embryonic stem cells (ESCs) are found in early stage embryos. Human Embryonic Stem Cells (HESCs) were first cultured in 1998 by James Thomson at the University of Wisconsin. They are typically derived from the inner cell mass of the pre-implantation blastocyst, a stage of human embryonic development occurring three to five days after fertilization, a process that involves the destruction of the early embryo. They are not totipotent (capable of forming a new embryo), but they are pluripotent (capable of forming all other cells in the body). They are also able to self-renew for extended periods of times in the laboratory, such that a single batch of stem cells can last quite a long time for laboratory research purposes.

More differentiated stem cells, often collectively called adult stem cells (ASCs), also exist, and are found in all of us. ASCs can be unipotent, developing into only one kind of specialized cell, or they can develop into multiple cells within the same type of tissue. For example, hematopoietic stem cells have the ability to develop into nine different types of blood cells. Even when they can develop into a range of different types of cells, adult stem cells are nowhere near as versatile as ESCs, and thus despite the ethical controversies surrounding their derivation (which involves embryo destruction), they have historically been the preferred choice of scientists for both research and the possibility of developing new therapies. That said, some scientists prefer adult stem cells because they are less likely to lead to adverse events. Moreover, as I discuss below, attempts to circumvent the regulatory authority of domestic regulators has also caused those developing therapeutics to move toward adult stem cells. Although, as I discuss, the FDA has recently successfully asserted its authority over autologous adult stem cell therapies, regulators in many other parts of the world have been less muscular in doing so.

Although we will not need to dwell on it too much for our purposes, it is worth noting that a number of scientists have been working on methods to create "induced pluripotent stem cells" (iPS cells), which are adult stem cells that are induced to have the same plasticity of embryonic stem cells. The results have been mixed, with some scientists suggesting that these "carry a memory of their past identities," and that whatever methods are used to reprogram the cells "still mutate the genes of the resulting cells," while others have been more enthusiastic about the results.[17]

---

[17] See Kahn, *supra* note 16, at 1348; K. Kim et al., *Epigenetic Memory of Induced Pluripotent Stem Cells*, 467 NATURE 285 (2010); Jose M. Polo et al., *Cell Type of Origin Influences the Molecular and Functional Properties of Mouse Induced Pluripotent Stem Cells*, 28 NATURE BIOTECH. 848 (2010).

B. What Might Stem Cell Therapies Look Like?

Now that we understand the basics of stem cells, let us turn to understanding how they might be used therapeutically on human patients. The International Society for Stem Cell Research (ISSCR) defines "stem cell therapy" broadly to include any "treatment that uses stem cells, or cells that come from stem cells, to replace or repair a patient's cells or tissues that are damaged," and notes that such "stem cells might be put into the blood, or transplanted into the damaged tissue directly, or even recruited from the patient's own tissues for self-repair."[18]

What might stem cell therapies look like? Steven Munzer has provided a useful list of some of the possibilities that I will draw from.[19] For our purposes, we ought to divide therapies that directly place stem cells or their derivatives into human bodies from therapies that are merely developed from stem cell models or information gleaned from stem cells. The first category is the focus of stem cell tourism at the moment, and what I will focus on. Among the possible therapies of this kind are: putting Type 1 diabetes into remission by injection of insulin-producing stem cells derived from hESCs; crafting an artificial pancreas from stem cells to replace a defective pancreas; using heart muscle cells (cardiomyocytes) derived from hESCs as replacement muscle tissue for heart cells destroyed by a myocardial infarction; treating spinal cord injuries with central nervous system cells derived from hESCs, such as oligodendroglial precursor cells, which could replace similar cells destroyed or compromised by physical trauma; weaving hESC cells into polymer threads to encapsulate and create replacement organs; using neural precursors derived from stem cells to produce various kinds of brain cells to treat Alzheimer's and Parkinson's diseases; and treating some forms of blindness with retinal cells derived from stem cells.

Today most of the stem cell therapies are using adult stem cell trials, for example:

> Human umbilical cord blood cells have been used in a large number of trials for paraplegia, ataxia, multiple sclerosis, amyotrophic lateral sclerosis, cerebrovascular disease, multiple system atrophy, motor neuron disease, among other indications, without severe immunological response.... Endothelial progenitor cells (CD34+/ CD133+/KDR+ or VEGFRII+) may be sourced from several sources including bone marrow, umbilical cord blood and adipose tissue. They are effective in the stimulation of angiogenesis and in clinical studies requiring revascularization and remodeling of collaterals in atherosclerotic cardiovascular disease.... Corneal

---

[18] INTERNATIONAL SOCIETY FOR STEM CELL RESEARCH (ISSCR), PATIENT HANDBOOK ON STEM CELL THERAPIES 3 (2008).

[19] Stephen R. Munzer, *Risk and Reward in Stem Cell Products: A New Model for Stem Cell Product Liability*, 18 B.U. J. SCI. & TECH. L. 102, 107–08 (2012).

epithelial stem cells are located at the basal layer of the limbus epithelium and provide for replacement of corneal epithelial cells that are lost or damaged.[20]

More systematically, Lindvall and Hyun has suggested we divide possible future therapies by (1) cell type—adult (somatic) stem cells used in novel ways, derivatives of hES cells and/or iPS cells; (2) cell source—"the patient's own cells (autologous transplantation), a donor's cells (allogeneic transplantation), genetically modified cells, cells used in their site of origin (homologous transfer), or cells used outside of their site of origin (non-homologous transfer)"; and (3) method of delivery or transplantation, as well as cell dosage, frequency of cell transfer, and the stage of disease in which the therapy is used.[21]

Currently, however, with the exception of hematopoietic stem cell transplantation for blood disorders, all other stem cell therapies are "unproven."[22] As we will see momentarily when we review the data on what is being offered, this means that the vast majority of stem cell tourism currently undertaken is for unproven therapies.

C. Current FDA Regulation of Stem Cell Therapies

In order to understand why stem cell therapies are flourishing abroad, it is useful to briefly explain the regulatory limitations on stem cell therapies currently in place in the United States.

As Steven Munzer has noted, stem cell therapies do "not fit nicely into a single FDA product classification," of which there are four primary ones: (1) drugs, (2) biologics, (3) devices, and (4) combination products.[23] Although technically potentially meeting the definition of "drug," the FDA is unlikely to categorize stem cells as such because it "rarely uses that category for living cells or tissues that have continuing biological action." Although the implements used by physicians to deliver and direct stem cells to the right parts of the body might be classified as devices, the stem cells themselves are unlikely to be treated as such by the FDA.[24] It is more likely that the FDA will classify stem cell products as "biological products" (also called "biologics"), such as vaccines and blood products, as some treatments can be conceptualized like vaccines for use in reconstituting or strengthening the immune system of a patient, and hematopoietic stem cells seem to qualify as blood components already.[25] Many more such therapies will fall in the "combination products" category, which

---

[20] Id.

[21] Olle Lindvall & Insoo Hyun, *Medical Innovation versus Stem Cell Tourism*, 324 SCI. 1664, 1665 (2009); Dominique Martin, *Perilous Voyages: Travel Abroad for Organ Transplants and Stem Cell Treatments, in* RISKS AND CHALLENGES IN MEDICAL TOURISM: UNDERSTANDING THE GLOBAL MARKET FOR HEALTH SERVICES 138 (Jill Hodges et al. eds., 2012) 138.

[22] Lindvall & Hyun, *supra* note 21, at 1665. Some patients will use medical tourism to get this therapy as well because, although well-established, it is unavailable in their home country.

[23] Munzer, *supra* note 19, at 109–11.

[24] Id.

[25] Id. at 109–10.

involves combinations of the other three categories such as transdermal patches for drug delivery and cardiac stents.[26] Some stem cell therapies seem plausibly analogous, for example administering "hematopoietic stem cells through catheters into the coronary arteries, or into the myocardium, during a coronary artery bypass graft" and "having a scaffold seeded with autologous stem cells for organ transplantation."[27]

In general, FDA review of stem cell therapies in the United States proceeds as follows: "to determine whether it is reasonable to grant permission for a clinical trial to proceed, FDA evaluates potential risk based on results derived from analytical assessment of product characteristics as well as preclinical proof-of-concept and safety testing, which, collectively, are considered within the context of a proposed clinical study."[28]

More technically (and some readers will want to skip the rest of this paragraph) as FDA reviewer Donald Fink noted in 2009, this starts with extensive preclinical animal studies, for which the FDA looks for "(i) selection of relevant disease/injury models, (ii) testing of the product intended for clinical administration, (iii) using a route and method of delivery comparable to what is planned clinically, (iv) optimal timing of product administration with respect to disease/injury onset, and (v) an appropriate study duration that permits simultaneous assessment of potential adverse safety events and provides evidence of durable biological activity."[29] However, there are also significant hurdles in translating the results of these animal tests into predictions of safety as to human testing. In its worries about risks, FDA puts particular importance in evaluating "teratoma-forming potential of differentiated cellular products derived from ES cells, because the appearance of a teratoma in an anatomically sensitive location such as the central nervous system, joint capsule, or myocardium could pose a considerable safety concern."[30] It is also quite concerned about "the potential for spontaneous malignant transformation due to protracted, ex vivo culture expansion, a propensity for cells to migrate from the original site of administration, development of immunogenicity resulting from eventual expression of the cell/tissue donor human leukocyte antigen molecules, and the biologic impact of nontarget cellular impurities within the differentiated cell product," and considers all these risks in its approval processes.[31] Because of "the biological complexity exemplified by cellular composition heterogeneity, FDA suggests a multiparametric testing approach for characterization of stem cell–based products," involving the "development of quantitative analytical techniques for conducting a panel of tests such as morphologic evaluation, detection of phenotype-specific cell surface antigens, assessment of unique biochemical markers, and genomic/proteomic analysis."[32]

---

[26] *Id.*

[27] *Id.*

[28] Donald W. Fink Jr., *FDA Regulation of Stem Cell-Based Products*, 324 Sci. 1662 (2009).

[29] *Id.*

[30] *Id.*

[31] *Id.*

[32] *Id.*

Some stem cell therapy companies had tried to do an end run around FDA approval by limiting themselves to the use of adult stem cells and claiming they were not "drugs" or "biological products" within the meaning of the FDA's jurisdiction. The matter came to a head in the July 2012 decision in *United States v. Regenerative Sciences*, in which the FDA asserted that the "Regenexx™ Procedure constitutes the manufacturing, holding for sale, and distribution of an unapproved biological drug product" and that the company had violated statutory prohibitions on "adulteration and misbranding a drug with their Regenexx Procedure," while the company claimed that it was merely "the practice of medicine as defined by Colorado law and that the FDA lacks jurisdiction to regulate it."[33] The court sided with the FDA and found the procedure to be either a drug or biological product subject to the FDA's regulation and granted the FDA the power to shut down the production of the therapy. The decision was upheld by the U.S. Court of Appeals for the D.C. Circuit,[34] and subject to a potential course change from the U.S. Supreme Court, it seems clear that whether embryonic or adult stem cells are used, those producing the therapies in the United States must comply with the FDA's extensive regulatory rules.

To comply with the FDA's approach and ultimately receive approval to develop stem cell therapies that could ultimately (if everything checks out) be marketed in the United States is expensive and complex. Many foreign providers are happy offering therapies outside of these regulatory requirements in their local markets and having American and other patients come to them, rather than trying to meet the requirements set by the FDA.

II. THE SCOPE OF STEM CELL TOURISM: LESSONS FROM THE AVAILABLE DATA

As has become something of a refrain in this book, when it comes to data on the extent of this form of medical tourism, we are still in our infancy. I will begin by setting out what we do currently know, divided into studies of stem cell clinics and studies of the patients who use them, and adverse event reports.

A. Studies of Clinics

It is hard to systematically measure how many clinics are offering experimental stem cell therapies to how many patients, but a few authors have attempted this difficult task. In 2006, writing in *Science*, Martin Enserink identified nine active clinics and estimated that they had treated in excess of 4,800 patients.[35] By 2007, two groups

---

[33] 878 F. Supp. 2d 248, 254 (D.D.C. 2012).

[34] United States v. Regenerative Scis., 741 F.3d 1314 (2014).

[35] Martin Enserink, *Selling the Stem Cell Dream*, Sci., July 14, 2006, at 160–63, *available at* http://www.sciencemag.org/content/313/5784/160; *see* Aaron D. Levine & Leslie E. Wolf, *The Roles and Responsibilities*

working independently suggested that there were twenty clinics offering unproven stem cell therapies.[36] A report from mid-2010 by Kristen A. Ryan and A.N. Sanders in *Regenerative Medicine* suggested the number is growing considerably, with more than two hundred clinics offering these therapies worldwide.[37]

If we turn to the content of these providers' offerings, the best data comes from two studies.

i. Regenberg et al.'s study of Stem Cell Therapy Websites

The first is a 2009 study, in which Alan Regenberg and colleagues examined the websites offering stem cell therapies between April and August of 2007. They performed Google searches using the keywords "stem cell treatment" and "stem cell therapy," and Google news alerts and LexisNexis searches were programmed with these same search terms to monitor media accounts of patients receiving these therapies; they also examined disease advocacy bulletin boards. They found twenty-four clinics offering stem cell therapies, of which twenty-three had an accessible website; they admit this list was not exhaustive but included the clinics most easily accessible by potential patients. E-mails were sent to the clinics asking for more information, although only ten responded. They evaluated the information available (website or website plus additional e-mail responses) for the websites on a few axes: provider location, therapy costs in U.S. dollars, conditions for which therapies were offered, cell sources, cell product "dosages," SCBI delivery methods, cell quality assurance procedures, provider credentials, risks, and benefits.

Let me summarize their key findings:

> In terms of location, thirty-seven SCBI delivery locations were identified across providers, with nineteen delivery sites (51%) in Asia, nine delivery sites (24%) in Europe, eight delivery sites (22%) in Central America/Caribbean, and one (3%) in Africa. In terms of credentials, only nineteen of the providers listed staff with a scientific or academic credential: Four (21%) of these referred to those involved as "Dr." with no further information, fifteen clinics listed some combination of specific credentials, primarily MDs and PhDs, and of these provided more information on professional distinctions such as fellowships in professional societies and board certifications. Of the four sites that listed no credentials, two made allusions to the providers having some grounding in science or medicine.

---

of Physicians in Patients' Decisions about Unproven Stem Cell Therapies, 40 J.L. MED. & ETHICS 122, 122 (2012).

[36] D. Lau et al., *Stem Cell Clinics Online: The Direct-to-Consumer Portrayal of Stem Cell Medicine*, 3 CELL STEM CELL 591, 591–94 (2008); Regenberg, *supra* note 2, at 2312–19; *see* Levine & Wolf, *supra* note 35, at 122.

[37] K.A. Ryan et al., *Tracking the Rise of Stem Cell Tourism*, 5 REGENERATIVE MED. 27, 27–33 (2010); *see* Levine & Wolf, *supra* note 35, at 122.

In terms of costs, twelve clinics provided cost estimates, which ranged from US$5,000 to $39,500. Four providers indicated payment was due in advance, and two specifically noted that "boosters" may be required after the initial treatment at additional costs.

In terms of stem cell delivery methods, only fifteen (65 percent) clinics listed the method used to deliver stem cells. Among the methods they listed were invasive surgical procedures; intravenous, intra-arterial, or subcutaneous injections; and direct injection into the cerebrospinal fluid through a lumbar puncture. Only 13 percent of the clinics described the dose of cells delivered, and the dosages varied significantly. Only thirteen clinics (57 percent) gave quality assurances for the cell products they used to do the therapies. Of these, thirteen clinics claimed their cell producers were tested to be free of infectious agents, seven noted their products were manufactured in accordance with some form of international protocol or standards such as current Good Manufacturing Practice or Good Laboratory Practice, six claimed their cell products were tested to ensure that they contain only the intended cells, and three noted testing by independent laboratories to verify quality assurances.

Clinics offered stem cell treatments for a very wide range of disorders, including "aging, impotence/fading potency, spinal muscular atrophy, dementia, osteoarthritis, rheumatoid arthritis, cancers, depression, Down syndrome, autism, Huntington's disease, epilepsy, hepatitis B/C, cirrhosis, lupus, macular degeneration, male/female infertility, skin conditions (scars/burns/ulcers), bone damage, early menopause, blindness, glaucoma, pain, shingles, allergies, gangrene, spina bifida, and B12 and folic acid deficiencies."

Some clinics were more tempered in their description of benefits than others. Five clinics (22 percent) claimed that, in the words of the study authors, the treatment would result in "a clinically significant benefit to a majority of their clients," making statements such as: the treatment "generated an estimated 80% incidence of significant clinical benefit," the treatment "can substantially improve the flow of blood in a large majority of the patients treated, thus reducing chest pains and sharply increasing physical capacity," and that the clinic could "assure you that the first round of treatment will give close to 100% success rate" for "so-called incurable diseases" such as AIDS and diabetes. A second group of eight clinics (35 percent) were more careful in suggesting that, in the words of the study authors, "client outcomes are variable and that a range of beneficial outcomes is possible," with statements such as "results range from very minor to very significant improvements" and "[i]t is a process of repair that occurs at varying levels in different patients and disease states." The largest group of clinics, 48 percent of the sample, were in the words of the study authors "less direct in their assessment of benefits," with statements such as: "embryonic cells can potentially repair and if needed rebuild practically all organs," "[s]ubstantial patient improvement from stem cell therapy has been documented," and "[a]dult stem cell therapies have produced life changing outcomes for individuals located all over the world." In a slightly different grouping of clinic websites, the study authors note that four clinics specifically noted that the benefits offered by the therapies exceeded the standard treatment for targeted conditions, including "previously incurable" diseases such as multiple sclerosis, cerebral palsy, and Down syndrome, and three clinics "while claiming benefits for a majority of their clients, also offer the caveat that these interventions are not a cure. An additional three providers specifically note that benefits cannot be guaranteed."

On the flip side, clinics tended to downplay discussion of the risks involved. Six of the clinics (26 percent) provided no information about risks. Of the remaining seventeen clinic (74 percent) providers, fifteen described the therapies as having, in the words of the study authors, "no risks or only minimal risks, which are attributed to the delivery method (e.g., surgery or injections)." Two of the websites described greater than minimal risks, one of which says that stem cell differentiation in the laboratory remained "beyond our control" and that undesired cell types may be included in therapy and subsequently grow in harmful locations.

Only one clinic mentioned clinical trials, stating without any additional information: "Stem cell therapy for the treatment of damaged myocardium. Safety and efficacy study. Stem cell therapy for the treatment of Spinal cord injury: safety and efficacy study. Therapeutic Angiogenesis for Patients with Limb Ischemia by Autologous Transplantation of Bone Marrow Stem Cells: safety and efficacy study."

The study authors also surveyed the 533 "case studies" provided by eleven (48 percent) of the clinics. Twenty (4 percent) of the cast studies were only digital videos, and the rest were presented in text. The ages in the case studies varied widely from a one-year-old patient to an eighty-four-year-old one, but about 50 percent of the case studies (254) involved individuals between forty and sixty-four years of age. Among 480 cases that report the client's country of origin, the largest group of 181 (38 percent) cases came from the United States. For the 338 cases where the date of last follow-up was available, the average number of days between first treatment and the final follow-up was 256 days (SD: 255), with a range of 1–533 days. Not a single one of the 533 case studies described a significant adverse event, such as tumor formation. Interestingly, no case study claimed that a previously incurable disease was irrefutably cured. Instead, what was typical, in the words of the study authors, was "a description of a range of outcomes from the client receiving little or no benefit to significant symptomatic improvements," with some case studies describing "initial improvements that then recede over time, often resulting in suggestions that 'booster' doses of" stem cells were required. Most case studies presented as evidence for improvements were anecdotal reports from third-party observers or client self-reports, but some cases did present pre- versus post-intervention results from standardized testing instruments such as the American Spinal Injury Association assessment scale scores.

To give a flavor of what these case reports sounded like, the study authors presented a series of excerpts. Here are three of them: for a traumatic brain injury patient, "[h]is mother stated that '[h]e could control his saliva, with no drooling and he can eat well, with mouth closed and drink water by himself. His eyes move faster and see clearly so as to help him walk better'"; for a stroke patient, "[a]t discharge, the patient gained some neurological functional improvements. The patient was able to move his right upper and lower extremities more freely, and his gait became much stable. His muscular tone ameliorated. The pain in the right released remarkably by 90% approximately compared with before"; and one more mixed report from a multiple sclerosis patient, "[I] have been feeling about the same as before having stem cell treatment with no real changes to report. I have gone through periods of feeling better, but then it goes back to normal. I am interested in going for retreatment in spring."

As the authors concluded regarding these findings, although "[t]he vast majority of the reviewed providers present themselves, by virtue of their credentials, as members of the medical/scientific community" and use the medical and scientific credentials to suggest that they are bringing this expertise, and that claims about the safety and efficacy of the therapies are empirically based, "apart from a brief mention of clinical trials by a single provider, there is no information within the available content to suggest that the providers are making serious efforts to draw on or expand the body of scientific knowledge as they deliver therapies." Although most of these websites tout the benefits and suggest minimal or no risks, in fact the risks and benefits of these therapies is largely unknown. That is, "[t]he benefits and risks are presented in a manner that seems to be inconsistent with the current state of the science," which suggests that "the field is far away from demonstrating the effectiveness of [stem cell therapies] for the conditions claimed by these providers."

ii. Lau et al.'s Website Study

In 2008 Darren Lau and coauthors also published a systematic website analysis performed in August 2007 of nineteen websites offering stem cell therapies found using a Google search for "stem cell therapy" or "stem cell treatment." Let me summarize their findings.

In terms of therapies being offered, the most common was autologous stem cells (nine sites) followed by fetal stem cells (six), cord blood stem cells (four), and embryonic stem cells (two).

Six listed the method of administration as infusion into cerebrospinal fluid, six listed peripheral intravenous administration, and four sites listed insertion by access to deep body cavities, and there were even sites that advertised stem cell transplant into the brain via craniotomy or by injection into the spinal cord parenchyma via laminectomy. In terms of disorders treated, the most common were neurological (sixteen sites or 84 percent of the sample)—most commonly multiple sclerosis (MS), stroke, Parkinson's disease, spinal cord injury, and Alzheimer's disease—and cardiovascular (twelve sites or 63 percent of the sample)—especially ischemic heart disease–related disorders. Seven sites (37 percent) treated congenital diseases—primarily cerebral palsy, autism, and Duchenne muscular dystrophy.

Similar to the Regenberg et al. study, there was a skewed representation of risks and benefits, in that all websites advertised improvement in the disease state as a benefit, while most of the websites (fourteen sites or 74 percent of the sample) did not mention any particular risks, and a few sites mentioned "procedural risks or other risks," such as nonspecific fever or tingling.

The authors also scored each site's "portrayal of the indications, risks, benefits, and readiness of the therapy offered." They found that 68 percent of the websites were "somewhat unclear or indeterminate," which was described as a measure of the "extent to which indications were well bounded and specific, as opposed to open ended or vague," which they ascribe to "the presence of catch-all categories like aging, 'increased feelings of energy,' and by long lists of diseases spanning numerous clinical categories." Turning to risk and benefit, while 79 percent of the sites portrayed the potential benefits of these therapies as "somewhat or very relevant," 74 percent of the sites portrayed the risks as "very irrelevant." Finally, they rated the websites based on how ready they portrayed the therapies as being for public access, and found that 53 percent of the sites portrayed the therapies as "very positive" in terms of their readiness. Overall, despite a couple of sites that gave more appropriate descriptions of the therapies, the authors concluded these sites demonstrated a "general portrayal of therapy as safe and effective for a broad range of diseases in the context of routine clinical use," which were largely at variance with the existing medical literature.

Comparing the claims on these websites to the peer-reviewed literature on stem cell therapies for these ailments, the authors concluded that "the published clinical evidence is unable to support the use of these therapies for the routine treatment of disease," and that the "direct-to-consumer portrayal of stem cell medicine is optimistic and unsupported by published evidence." While noting a few cautions as to their analysis—that they are analyzing websites and there may be different information shared with patients during clinical encounters, that they do not test the accuracy of the websites' claims directly by evaluating actual outcome data but instead show "that there is a lack of high quality evidence supporting stem cell clinics' claims"—the authors interpret their results as showing that patients may not be receiving "sufficient and appropriate information and may be shouldering inordinate risks," and that the clinics "may also be contributing to public expectations that exceed what the field can reasonably achieve." Moreover, given the high price tag assigned to these therapies (an average of US$21,500 for a course of therapy excluding travel and accommodations for the patient and family, based on the four websites that provided cost data), patients may be paying a lot to get ineffective treatments that put them at serious risks.

B. Studies of Patients

i. A Patient Blog Study[38]

Because stem cell therapies are typically accessed and paid for outside the usual health care channels, Ryan, Sanders, Wang, and Levine looked to "an alternative data source—blogs

---

[38] All materials are drawn from Ryan et al., *supra* note 37.

written by patients (or their caretakers) about their experiences with these unproven therapies," and studied 161 of these blogs (discussing 162 patients) written in English over a three-week period in 2008. They found the blogs through Google searches and blog-specific search engines as well as following links from one patient blog to another, and then repeated the process iteratively. As they noted, "[a]lthough we likely missed a small number of blogs that existed at the time of our search, we believe this saturation search strategy identified the vast majority of relevant blogs."

In terms of results, they found that the number of patients seeking these therapies abroad increased over the study period (twice as many in 2008 as 2007, and ten times as many in 2008 as in 2006), although they note this may be in part a function of an increase in the popularity of blogging. Fifty-eight percent of the patients were male, and 45 percent of the 157 whose age they could classify were less than eighteen years old, pointing to the importance for regulation of considering pediatric populations, a matter the chapter takes up below.

They found that patients traveled to eleven different clinics in eight different countries (China, India, the Dominican Republic, Costa Rica, Russia, Mexico, Germany, and Turkey). China was by far the largest destination, with 86 percent of patients going there, and one Chinese company—Bieke Biotechnology—offering services to 115 (71 percent) of the patients studied. Beike encourages patients to blog, so as the researchers note it is possible that this overstates its importance in the market. After grouping together similar medical conditions leading patients to seek these therapies, the study found that there were thirteen conditions for which at least three patients sought therapies: spinal cord injury (20 percent of patients), optic nerve hypoplasia (14 percent), ataxia (10 percent), brain injury (10 percent), multiple sclerosis (10 percent), ALS (4 percent), batten disease (4 percent), septo-optic dysplasia (4 percent), autism (2 percent), encephalitis (2 percent), infantile spasms (2 percent), and Parkinson's disease (2 percent) as well as a residual category of "other" (9 percent).

The treatment regimes varied by clinic. At Beike-affiliated clinics in China the patients typically received a series of injections that were described as "umbilical cord blood stem cells" usually in combination with acupuncture and physical/occupational therapies. The stem cells were injected either intravenously or in the cerebrospinal fluid. In some cases patients also were given autologous bone marrow stem cells. These injections were used for a wide variety of quite different conditions, prompting the researchers to note that "[t]his sort of generic treatment has been previously highlighted as a concern." Other clinics claimed to be injecting patients with umbilical cord blood stem cells, bone marrow stem cells, fetal stem cells, neural stem cells derived from fetal cells, and partially differentiated embryonic stem cells. Treatment length varied from a day or two to a month.

The authors observe that their "preliminary readings of patient blogs revealed that many patients were aware of the skepticism of these treatments by physicians in their home country and chose to pursue these unproven treatments despite warnings about potential health risks." The main reasons patients gave for dismissing these warnings was that they were outweighed by testimonials posted on clinic websites, on patient blogs, and heard in conversation. This prompts the study authors to suggest that strategies such as patient guidelines and handbooks, discussed below, are an important step but unlikely to succeed on their own. They instead urge that a forum to provide information on these treatments, risks, and benefits be provided by a "neutral third party, not an agency or organization perceived by patients to be an advocate for the status quo, as some patients expressed distrust of the western medical establishment."

ii. A Study of Thirteen Stem Cell Tourists at Beike Clinics in China[39]

In addition to studying websites and blogs, a study by Haidin Chen and Herbert Gottweis intensively examined the experience of patients who had received stem cell therapies at the Bieke group's clinic in China.

By typing in "stem cell treatment China" into Facebook they identified sixty-two patients who had links with Beike, contacted the fifty-two who had e-mail addresses they could find, and received thirteen responses: three from potential patients who were still raising money for the treatments, three from patients undergoing stem cell treatments in China, and seven from patients who had already received stem cell treatments and had returned home. They then conducted e-mail interviews in which the patients were asked why they had consulted Beike initially, their involvement with the clinics, what effect the stem cell treatments had, how their current condition was affected by the treatment, if Chinese doctors had told them about uncertainties regarding outcomes, if there had been ethics counseling before the treatment, if there had been an informed consent document, and whether they though other patients they had met in China seemed well-informed about the various aspects of the therapies. Separately they also studied the "Web 2.0 world of Beike Biotech" (its websites, Facebook pages, blogs, and forums), did fourteen face-to-face interviews with "policy makers, bioethicists, scientists, clinicians, patients, the staff working in Beike Biotech, and the company's collaborative partners," and joined two patients' discussion groups for observation.

Let me highlight a few of their findings centered on the patient experience.

One of Beike's collaborative stem cell treatment centers provided the study authors a two-page bilingual (Chinese and English) informed consent form, which contained:

> basic information about patients such as name, gender, age, diagnosis before operation; stem cell treatment indication, notice, preventive measures, the patient's statement that he/she has read the consent form and knows the advantages and disadvantages of stem cell treatment, and so on. In the notice, patients are

---

[39] Unless otherwise noted, all references in this subsection are to Haidan Chen & Herbert Gottweis, *Stem Cell Treatments in China: Rethinking the Patient Role in the Global Bio-Economy*, 27 BIOETHICS 194 (2013).

reminded that "stem cell treatment is a new clinical treatment technique. As is the case with other clinical treatment techniques, there may be significant risks due to individual variation, condition abnormalities, or other unpredictable factors," and that "there remains the possibility of unforeseen consequences."

There was some inconsistency among their thirteen patients as to whether they has signed an informed consent document, with at least one indicating not remembering doing so and one indicating having done so and feeling well-informed. That said, there were reasons to suspect that the information was not completely internalized. As the study authors note, "[i]t seemed that, except for those with scientific and biomedical backgrounds, the majority of the patients we interviewed just had a general sense that there were risks in undergoing unapproved, untested medical procedures, but they didn't have a concrete understanding of specific risks," and that because of a lack of "credible options, they were ready to accept those risks weighed against the possible benefits, regardless of warnings."

In terms of patient reports on their outcome, the authors noted that "[j]ust as in the numerous blog statements and exchanges, the patients that responded to our interview request were full of praise about their experience with Beike."

One patient, an adolescent Canadian girl who had been wheelchair bound most of her life said "that she felt good after the stem cell treatments, which were combined with Chinese acupuncture" and her mother expressed her views still more strongly, stating

> The Chinese doctors are better than Canadian doctors, Canadian doctors are greedy, they work for the rich, but the Chinese doctors are happy to help, they are more responsible to their patients, and more professional. Our doctors in Canada said Chinese medicine was 30 years ahead of Canada. We think highly of Chinese doctors, we receive very good care and have positive experience here to know that you've done and that you've tried every-thing. Even if that means going offshore and trying something experimental.

This quote references three themes that I will return to later: (1) suspicion about the motives of home country physicians who do not offer these treatments, (2) the fact that there appeared to be some consultation with a home country physician about using Chinese medicine, and (3) the portrayal of Chinese medicine as more advanced.

Another threw a party to thank his Chinese doctors, where he told them he was "in a bad condition after he had had a car accident, with a head injury and weakened eyesight, and he said that he had lost hope in his life," but that after the treatment "he felt that stem cells were a miracle—his eyesight had improved and he had recovered some body function, which brought him and his family new hope."

Another patient, though reporting a positive experience, did not get as much as he hoped, stating that his "overall experience was excellent…no problems with booking the trip and no problems with our stay in China," and although the treatment produced "wonderful effects, however they weren't as long lasting as we had hoped," but this had "more to do with my disease than the stem cells," and although his current "condition is about the same as it was two years ago[,] I am planning on returning this summer for more treatments." Reflecting on this and other patients, the study authors observe that

> as long as there were discernible positive effects after stem cell treatment, even if the effects later disappeared, patients would be willing to undertake untried therapies again.

A number of the interviews were with parents who took their children abroad, a focus of the legal and bioethical discussion later in this chapter. The mother of a three-year-old child with cerebral palsy who took her child for stem cell treatments in China emphasized the way in which seeking the treatment fit in with her conception of good parenting, noting that "[l]ike any parent, you want to do the best you possibly can with your child and at the end of the day you want to know that you've done and that you've tried every-thing[;] even if that means going offshore and trying something experimental."

Another parent sounded a similar note regarding her child's (referred to as "C") treatment for seroptic dysplasia, albeit with more of a tone of desperation:

> C was only 18 months old, his health was deteriorating, we had been told numerous times when C was admitted to the hospital, "All we can do for C is to try to stabalize [*sic*] him and try to level out his blood sugars because there is no treatments available for his disorders." For us as a family the reality was do we continually risk C dieing [*sic*] in a hospital in the United States where there is no treatment or do we risk an unproven, experimental treatment in China that may give him a better Quality of Life! We are extremely thankful that C was accepted for umbilical stem cell treatments in China.

Others evinced a mix of disappointment and hopefulness, such as "Patient N's" parents who reported:

> In China during treatment, N crawled into her wheel- chair on her own. Now this could have been possible because of Physiotherapy, Occupational Therapy and Acupuncture everyday. Back home in South Africa she cannot do it anymore. As a parent I always want to look at the positive side of the treatment. To put it simply, N does not have any life-altering improvements but improvements nonetheless…she has very minute improvements. With further research that I have done, Stem Cell supposed to show effects after three to six months of administering so we still have a few months left to wait for us to see definite visible differences.

Reflecting more generally on their data, the study authors noted the "emergence of risk-taking patients as 'consumers' of medical options, as well as the drive of patients to seek treatment options in the global arena, rather than being hindered by the ethical and regulatory constraints applicable in their home countries," as well as "evidence of patients seeking treatments abroad as motivated by what they perceive as an undue politicization of stem cell research in their home countries, and, more generally, the dominance of red-tape regulations hindering medical progress within reasonable time-frames." Rather than "lonely individuals traveling the globe for treatment options; instead," they found that patients "tend to operate in more or less stable networks and groups, in which they interact and cooperate closely and develop opinions and assessments of available treatment options for their ailments." But they were careful to emphasize that this was not a purely organic development, rather "Beike's Web 2.0 architecture has been a key element in bringing thousands of patients from Western countries and China to its treatment centers," and noted the symbiotic relationship of Beike and its patients, in the way they "fulfill important strategic functions in funding the company, in enabling its research agenda, and in particular the Western patients as legitimizing Beike as a health-care provider," and suggest "de facto also adopt important roles as research subjects, and funders of research, a role combination that is uniquely fitted to the regulatory setting of China."

Important for the discussion of innovation pathways below, in understanding Beike's stem cell treatments in the ecology of innovation, the authors note that the "scale of these treatments at Beike clearly surpasses medical innovation models not involving clinical trials that would typically operate with a few seriously ill patients, rather than with thousands of patients," and that because of their role in funding the treatments that are experimentally used on them—something the U.S. human subjects research regulation attempts to prevent—patients have "created a circle in which, driven by economic necessity, the scale of Beike's treatments by far surpasses any possibly existing scientific or medical rationales."

All this has taken place because, since 2005, "Beike has operated in a political-regulatory void in China," until the March 2009 Regulations on Clinical Application of Medical Technology that defined stem cell therapies as medical technologies for the first time. Under the new regulations, providers of "autologous stem cell and immunocyte treatment technology, gene therapy technology, and allogeneic stem cell transplantation technology" such as Beike are listed in a category denoting treatments presenting "major ethical issues and high risk, so their safety and efficacy need to be tested in further clinical research and study." If a clinic was providing such therapies *before* the regulation went into effect on May 1, 2009, as were the Beike clinics, it was required to apply for review within six months. But due to delays in formulating review criteria, the authors claim that such reviews have been delayed (with business proceeding on as before), and the authors suggest the regulations have thus far not become effective due to lack of implementation, and conclude that at least until the time their article went to press in 2011, "[w]hile clinics in the main Western health care markets operated within a tight regulatory environment, Beike basically was creating its own codes of conduct in dealing with ethical issues concerning its patients," free from governmental oversight.[40]

iii. Focus Groups of Potential Patients[41]

Edna F. Einsiedel and Hannah Adamson conducted five focus groups with a diverse group of thirty-six healthy Canadian men and women in groups of six to ten participants at each session, with each session lasting 1.5 hours. The first part of their study examined awareness of stem cell research, therapies, and their risks. They found that all participants were familiar with stem cell research, and some specifically mentioned the actors Michael J. Fox and Christopher Reeve. No one was familiar with any specific findings from that research, but there was a "general perception that the outcomes of this research could only be beneficial." Close to two-thirds of the participants said they were unaware of any risk relating to stem cell therapies, and those who did think about risks suggested the risk was similar to organ transplants and would consist largely of the intervention being unsuccessful. "When informed that very few clinical trials had been performed, some participants suggested that the Canadian government should focus on performing such trials to develop stem cell therapies."

The researchers also provided participants a "new story hand-out detailing the experience of two patients who had obtained [stem cell] treatment in a Costa Rican clinic" in order to specifically discuss stem cell tourism. The focus group participants recognized the desperation of the patients described in the story, and although they acknowledged the risks were augmented by that desperation, "[i]n the end, most participants sympathized with" the patients' situation, or as one participant put it "[y]ou're terminally ill and there's so much going on in your life and this seems like a last resort. I'd probably encourage anybody to go if they can." As the authors put it "[m]ost participants saw the positive aspects of the decision to undergo stem cell treatments," emphasizing, among other things, "[t]he right of individuals to make a choice about their own health," and other autonomy themes even in the face of "limited evidence of [the therapy's] therapeutic value." That said, "participants also consistently expressed the need for more research into these stem cell therapies and pointed to the opportunities in the clinics themselves" for understanding effectiveness. In what will surely dishearten anyone who believes in rigorous scientific testing, "[t]he fact that both individuals [in the news story] had beneficial results from their treatment led a few [participants] to believe that stem

---

[40] Doug Sipp's blogging has suggested that as of late Beike has done more to conform to the new Chinese laws, but I am aware of no audit on the subject. Doug Sipp, *Beike Biotech under New Ownership?*, STEM CELL MONITOR (Jan. 23, 2011), http://sctmonitor.blogspot.com/2011/01/beike-biotech-under-new ownership.html?q=beike.

[41] Unless otherwise noted, all references in this subsection are to Edna F. Einsiedel & Hannah Adamson, *Stem Cell Tourism and Future Stem Cell Tourists: Policy and Ethical Implications*, 12 DEVELOPING WORLD BIOETHICS, 34 (2012).

cell treatments were proven in the countries offering them, like Costa Rica," with one observing "[i]f it's proven that it works, why not do it? They don't just lure you in for some pie in the sky."

On the negative side "[t]here were also a number of concerns raised with stem cell tourism, although these were, for the most part, less emphatic than the benefits noted." The main topics of concern were "a foreign country's standard of care, possible fraud involved, lax or non-existent regulatory oversight, and language barriers." There were some discussions of placebo effects, but "not all participants saw this as a bad thing." Those who did oppose stem cell tourism in the focus groups "commented on the financial gain of these clinics, the lack of information regarding treatment effectiveness, and doubts over another country's health care standards and practices, particularly those in developing countries."

In a subsequent stage of the focus group the participants were provided with a "handout explaining what stem cells were, what a stem cell therapy was and a set of questions that encouraged the patient or family members to pose to service providers" as well as "[p]recautionary advice...including warning signs to watch out for when assessing such services," drawn from the *International Society for Stem Cell Research Patient Handbook*. Although the authors found that after exposure to these materials participants noted "that these were helpful guidelines that could be useful for any unproven procedure, [however,] only one participant made the observation that the questions 'scared' her away from accessing this type of treatment." The authors also tried to determine how many of the participants would consider undergoing stem cell therapies based on various "illness severity," and found that, for the most severe illness, almost two-thirds of patients either "definitely would consider" or "would consider with conditions," with more in the former group than the latter.

C. Adverse Outcome Reports

A number of authors have reported on stem cell therapies being offered to medical tourists that have led to adverse outcomes. One should be cautious about the probity of these more anecdotal accounts, but given the general lack of data they may be the best that we can do at the present moment. Let me give a flavor of these accounts.

In an observational study in China discussed in the journal *Cell Stem Cell* in 2008, more than four hundred patients with spinal cord injuries received fetal brain tissue transplants at Beijing's Chaoyang and West Hills (Xishan) hospitals. They found no evidence of clinical improvement in any of the patients, and several of the patients developed meningitis from the stem cell injections.[42]

---

[42] Lau et al., *supra* note 36, at 591; *see* Lesley N. DeRenzo, Note, *Stem Cell Tourism: The Challenge and Promise of International Regulation of Embryonic Stem Cell-Based Therapies*, 43 CASE W. RES. J. INT'L L. 877, 889 (2011).

An Israeli child and his family traveled to Russia to receive an unconventional stem cell therapy to treat the rare and severely disabling neurological disorder called ataxia telangiectasia. The treatment did not improve the child's symptoms and instead caused recurring headaches, which researchers in Sheba Medical Center in Tel Aviv determined was the result of abnormal growths (i.e., tumors) in the child's brain and spinal cord that developed from the stem cell–based injections.[43]

In Hungary, police arrested four people in a raid on a clinic that was allegedly charging US$25,000 per treatment and injecting patients with illegally obtained embryonic and fetal stem cells, derived without authorization or safety testing, presenting significant safety concerns.[44]

In other reports, the stem cell therapies are merely the modern day equivalent of snake oil. After seeing online advertising, one family brought their blind, seven-month-old daughter to Hangzho, China, and paid Beike Biotechnology US$23,000 to infuse stem cells in her eyes. While the Chinese doctors advised the parents that the therapy worked, Dr. Bruce Dobkin, Director of the Neurologic Rehabilitation and Research Program at the University of California, Los Angeles, stated that "it is extreme nonsense to think that cells can be incorporated into the complex nervous system and do so much, when we cannot even get cells in mice and rats to do very much."[45]

III. THE LEGAL AND BIOETHICAL ISSUES RAISED BY STEM CELL TOURISM

Stem cell tourism already raises a large number of legal, bioethical, and regulatory design questions. Because the phenomenon is in its infancy, we are also likely to be merely at the tip of the iceberg. In this chapter, I want to focus on two main clusters of issues. The first cluster concerns how to design a pathway for innovation that protects patients without stifling the development of these therapies, how to provide effective professional self-regulation, and what regulation (if any) home countries should attempt for patients seeking these therapies abroad. I will argue that while there *is* a justifiable place for innovative stem cell therapies apart from the clinical trial regime, a second pathway to innovation that more closely resembles surgical innovation, this pathway must be substantially reined in compared to the existing "Wild West" that the empirical evidence suggests now exists. In particular, I recommend transforming the professional self-regulation proposals of the International Society for Stem Cell Research (ISSCR)

---

[43] Ninette Amariglio et al., *Donor-Derived Brain Tumor following Neural Stem Cell Transplantation in an Ataxia Telangiectasia Patient*, 6 PLOS MED. 221(2009); DeRenzo, *supra* note 42, at 889.

[44] DeRenzo, *supra* note 42, at 890 (citing *Stem Cell Tourism on the Rise*, CELL MED. (Aug. 13, 2009), http://www.cellmedicine.com/tourism-caveat-emptor.asp (discussing the risks associated with stem cell tourism)).

[45] Louisa Lim, *Stem-Cell Therapy in China Draws Foreign Patients*, NPR (Mar. 18, 2008), http://www.npr.org/templates/story/story.php?storyId=88123868; *see* DeRenzo, *supra* note 42, at 890–91.

into a soft law approach that incorporates channeling of patients and a private/public enforcement mechanism against fraud. The second set of issues concerns the duties of the State and physicians in the difficult case of parents who seek to take their children abroad for stem cell therapies.

A. Developing a Responsible Innovation Pathway for Stem Cell Therapies, Self-Regulation, and Channeling

After understanding the huge gap between the panaceas these patients are promised and the risky and unproven therapies they are actually receiving, one's first reaction might be that whatever we can do to shut down this industry is desperately needed. However, as Insoo Hyun has suggested, "the distance between problematic stem cell tourism and acceptable pursuits of innovative therapies may be far less than we might expect, with fewer markers in between."[46]

In particular, the existing regulatory structure for drug approval may be a bad fit for some portion of possible stem cell therapies. Stem cell therapies have none of the stability and predictability of the small molecules that make up pills. Instead they are living biological products that are susceptible to genetic instability, that may behave differently when "transplanted into injured sites as opposed to healthy bodies (since they are influenced by biochemical variations in their niche environments), and they may continue to act until they are surgically or chemically removed from their host."[47] As Hyun notes, although "some stem cell-based interventions may prove to be amenable to a multi-stage clinical trials approach," a surgical or transplantation approach may be more appropriate for others, and in those fields clinical trials are the exception rather than the norm because they are so hard to do properly; "in the last 40 years less than 20% of all surgical interventions were developed through a clinical trials process, with some specialties such as cardiac transplant and laparoscopic surgery arising entirely without clinical trials."[48]

Using stem cell therapies for Parkinson's disease provides a good example: in the past the need to rely on fetal cells from multiple heterogeneous sources was a problem, which we may now be able to overcome with the transplantation of standardized stem cells. However, if such therapies "are to become 'clinically competitive' with other accepted treatment options, such as neurotransmitter drugs and deep brain stimulation, then the transplantation procedure will have to be tailor-made as much as possible with each patient's brain," and the therapy is likely to have to be combined with the other existing therapies in a patient-by-patient way, requiring experience gleaned from innovative

---

[46] Insoo Hyun, *Allowing Innovative Stem Cell-Based Therapies Outside of Clinical Trials: Ethical and Policy Challenges*, 38 J.L. Med. & Ethics 277, 279 (2010).

[47] *Id.* at 280.

[48] *Id.* at 280–81.

care *before* one can initiate clinical trials for stem cell–based therapies for Parkinson's disease.[49]

In the United States and countries with similarly rigorous clinical trial regimes, requiring all those who want to develop stem cell therapies to fit their research into this one box is a nonstarter and essentially an invitation to go offshore toward more permissive countries.[50] This is problematic from the point of view of funding and developing this research, including scientific brain drain, but also in terms of assisting patients: if the therapy providers who are selling snake oil and those who are developing promising therapies are both forced to go offshore and operate in a legal and ethical gray zone, it is very hard for individual patients—especially those with chronic or terminal conditions who are desperate for hope—to tell the difference. Our goal should be instead to develop a regulatory framework that helps patients and funders sort the wheat from the chaff (or in some cases, poison).

i. Professional Self-Regulation and Its Limits

To try to do exactly that, a number of professional organizations have promulgated guidelines related to stem cell therapies. I will focus on the guideline put forth by the International Society for Stem Cell Research (ISSCR), which has been a leading voice in stem cell research regulation.

The ISSCR is a professional organization founded in 2002 whose membership consists primarily of stem cell scientists. After creating a task force in February 2008 to examine the "scientific, clinical, regulatory, ethical and societal issues that must be addressed to ensure that basic stem cell research is responsibly transitioned into appropriate clinical applications," the group developed the 2008 "Guidelines for the Clinical Translation of Stem Cells."[51, 52]

The tone of the Guidelines is largely condemnatory of existing stem cell therapies being offered, stating that "The ISSCR is deeply concerned about the potential physical, psychological, and financial harm to patients who pursue unproven stem cell–based 'therapies' and the general lack of scientific transparency and professional accountability

---

[49] *See id.* at 281.

[50] Although they take the point further than I would, as Murdoch and Scott observe, "[t]here are many reasons for not conducting clinical trials beyond merely avoiding broader scientific scrutiny," such as the fact that "several of these clinics operate in countries that lack the economic and scientific infrastructure of, for instance, the United States, and in some cases it may not be financially or logistically viable to conduct trials." Charles E. Murdoch & Christopher Thomas Scott, *Stem Cell Tourism and the Power of Hope*, 10 Am. J. Bioethics 16, 18 (2010). The key question for me, however, is how to get these centers to both evaluate the work they are doing and move into an innovation pathway where clinical trials will take place, perhaps with the aid of U.S. or other developed country investment and infrastructure.

[51] *See* Levine & Wolf, *supra* note 35, at 125–26.

[52] ISSCR, Guidelines for the Clinical Translation of Stem Cells, *available at* http://www.isscr. org/clinical_trans/pdfs/ISSCRGLClinicalTrans.pdf [hereinafter "ISSCR Guidelines"].

of those engaged in these activities," and that the "marketing of unproven stem cell interventions is especially worrisome in cases where patients with severe diseases or injuries travel across borders to seek treatments purported to be stem cell–based 'therapies' or 'cures' that fall outside the realm of standard medical practice," further noting that these patients engaging in stem cell–therapy tourism "may be especially vulnerable because of insufficient local regulation and oversight of host clinics" and the lack of medical negligence claims in some jurisdictions.[53]

The Guidelines contain a number of important recommendations, but I will just pick out a few that are particularly relevant for our purposes. Perhaps most important is the way the ISSCR draws a distinction between "the commercial purveyance of unproven stem cell interventions and legitimate attempts at medical innovation outside the context of a formal clinical trial." Although "responsible clinician-scientists may have an interest in providing medically innovative care to a few patients using stem cells or their derivatives prior to proceeding," the Guideline recommends that in doing so they follow a series of recommended steps, encapsulated in Recommendation 34 of the Guidelines:

> Clinician-scientists may provide unproven stem cell–based interventions to at most a very small number of patients outside the context of a formal clinical trial, provided that:
> (a) there is a written plan for the procedure that includes:
>   i. scientific rationale and justification explaining why the procedure has a reasonable chance of success, including any preclinical evidence of proof-of-principle for efficacy and safety;
>   ii. explanation of why the proposed stem cell–based intervention should be attempted compared to existing treatments;
>   iii. full characterization of the types of cells being transplanted and their characteristics as discussed in Section 4, Cell Processing and Manufacture;
>   iv. description of how the cells will be administered, including adjuvant drugs, agents, and surgical procedures; and
>   v. plan for clinical follow-up and data collection to assess the effectiveness and adverse effects of the cell therapy;
> (b) the written plan is approved through a peer review process by appropriate experts who have no vested interest in the proposed procedure; to a formal clinical trial regulations and put them into practice.
> (c) the clinical and administrative leadership supports the decision to attempt the medical innovation and the institution is held accountable for the innovative procedure;

---

[53] *Id.* at 4.

(d) all personnel have appropriate qualifications and the institution where the procedure will be carried out has appropriate facilities and processes of peer review and clinical quality control monitoring;

(e) voluntary informed consent is provided by patients who appreciate that the intervention is unproven and who demonstrate their understanding of the risks and benefits of the procedure;

(f) there is an action plan for adverse events that includes timely and adequate medical care and if necessary psychological support services;

(g) insurance coverage or other appropriate financial or medical resources are available to patients to cover any complications arising from the procedure; and

(h) there is a commitment by clinician-scientists to use their experience with individual patients to contribute to generalizable knowledge. This includes:

   i. ascertaining outcomes in a systematic and objective manner;

   ii. a plan for communicating outcomes, including negative outcomes and adverse events, to the scientific community to enable critical review (for example, as abstracts to professional meetings or publications in peer-reviewed journals); and

   iii. moving to a formal clinical trial in a timely manner after experience with at most a few patients.[54]

This set of recommendations tries to find a place for innovative stem cell therapies in the shadow lands of research and treatment, combining centralized review and obligations to generate useful knowledge with patient-focused concern and informed consent. It contemplates that these therapeutic interventions outside of clinical trials will be done on only a few patients as a way station toward more formalized research models, rather than therapies pursued indefinitely on their own.

The Guidelines also make a series of specific recommendations for the clinical trials themselves, some of which are worth highlighting here.

First, there are recommendations aimed at risk reduction and informing the patients. In terms of stem cells used, the Guidelines recommend development of uniform standards along the lines of those proposed by the Alliance for Harmonisation of Cellular Therapy Accreditation (AHCTA), which sets forth "a minimum set of standards for the collection of hematopoietic stem and progenitor cells, including cord blood, that include minimal required testing of the donor, a donor identification number, and an identification of the process of obtaining tissue, along with tracking and tracing requirements and product labeling nomenclature including information on split number and clinical expiry date."[55] Furthermore, the Guidelines declare that "[s]ufficient preclinical

---

[54] *Id.* at 15–16.
[55] *Id.* at 8.

studies in relevant animal models—whenever possible for the clinical condition and the tissue physiology to be studied—are necessary to make proposed stem cell–based clinical research ethical, unless approved, controlled, and conclusive humans studies are already available with the same cell source."[56] For efficacy testing, the Guidelines also recommend moving from small to large animal models including, possibly, primate studies, before using these therapies on humans.[57]

Turning to specific risks, the Guidelines recognize that even "local transplantation into organs like the heart or the brain may lead to life-threatening adverse events related to the transplantation itself or to the damage that transplanted cells may cause to vital structures," and recommends that "[r]isks for tumorigenicity must be assessed for any stem cell–based product, especially when extensively manipulated in culture or when genetically modified" and a "clear plan to assess the risks of tumorigenicity for any cell product must be implemented under the direction of an independent review body prior to approval for human clinical use."[58] It recommends that "[r]isks should be identified and reduced, and potential benefits to subjects must be realistically delineated but not overemphasized. Subject selection can affect the risks and benefits of the study and subjects should be selected to minimize risks, maximize the ability to analyze results, and enhance the benefits to individual subjects and society."[59] It also suggests that as "a general principle, a stem cell–based approach must aim at being clinically competitive or superior to existing therapies," and if

> an efficacious therapy already exists, the risks associated with a stem cell–based approach must be low and the stem cell–based approach must offer a potential advantage (for example, better functional outcome; single procedure (cell administration) versus life-long drug therapy with associated side effects; reduction in long-term cost). If an efficacious therapy is not available, then the severity of the disease, especially if the disease to be treated is severely disabling and life-threatening, might justify the risks of a stem cell–based experimental intervention in patients. Maximum effort should be made to minimize the risks for all possible adverse events associated with stem cell–based approaches. Care must also be taken to not take advantage of the hopes of patients with poor short-term prognoses.[60]

In terms of informed consent, the Guidelines delineate that

(a) Patients need to be informed when novel stem cell–derived products have never been tested before in humans and that researchers do not know whether they will work as hoped.

---

[56] *Id.* at 8.
[57] *Id.* at 9.
[58] *Id.* at 9.
[59] *Id.* at 12.
[60] *Id.* at 12–13.

(b) Cell-based interventions, unlike many pharmacological products or even many implantable medical devices, may not leave the body and may continue to generate adverse effects for the lifetime of the patient. The possible irreversibility of a cellular transplant should be explained clearly.

(c) Subjects should be informed about the source of the cells so that their values are respected.

(d) Ensuring subject comprehension must be done at each phase of the clinical trials process. Ideally, the subject's comprehension of information should be assessed through a written test or an oral quiz during the time of obtaining consent.

(e) Human subjects research committees should ensure that informed consent documents accurately portray these uncertainties and potential risks, and clearly explain the experimental nature of the clinical study. Monitoring, and additional safeguards for ongoing patient privacy should be provided.[61]

In terms of oversight of research using stem cell therapies, the Guidelines recommend that all studies, publicly or privately funded, should be "subject to independent review, approval, and ongoing monitoring by human subjects research oversight bodies with supplemental appropriate expertise to evaluate the unique aspects of stem cell research and its application in a variety of clinical disciplines" and that "[t]his review oversight process must be independent of the investigators regardless of whether it occurs at the institutional, regional, or national level, and regardless of whether investigators employ the services of a contract research organization."[62] As to adverse events, it recommends that a "data monitoring plan, which may involve an independent data safety and monitoring process, is required for all clinical studies, and aggregate updates should be provided to peer review committees on demand, complete with adverse event reporting and ongoing statistical analysis."[63]

These Guidelines are an excellent starting point for a pragmatic regulatory structure for stem cell therapies and stem cell tourism. The core elements are: oversight modeled on the IRB and surgical review systems, peer review, risk reduction techniques, transparent communication of risk and benefit to patients, limitation of nonclinical trial therapies to a few patients, and the requirement of a move to formal clinical trials relatively soon thereafter.

Although professional self-regulation is desirable, given the magnitude of the problems identified above and the fact that many of these unscrupulous clinics are providing

---

[61] *Id.* at 13.
[62] *Id.* at 12.
[63] *Id.* at 14.

high-cost, unproven, and dangerous therapies to individuals who are vulnerable, there is good reason to suspect it will not be sufficient.

In 2010, the ISSCR proposed going one step further and developing a Web-based resource wherein individuals can "submit an entity to the ISSCR for formal inquiry," and that in turn, the ISSCR would perform an evaluation of each clinic for each of the diseases for which it advertises a therapy.[64] To simplify somewhat (the full system of proposed review is provided in Figure 10.1), if the clinic is advertising a therapeutic intervention that uses stem cells or their derivatives, and it advertises clinical applications *other than* "blood stem cells used to treat conditions of the blood-forming or immune systems, epidermal stem cell therapies for burns or limbal stem cell transplantation" for which there is existing documented evidence of effectiveness, then the ISSCR will request that the clinic provide two things: "[e]vidence of review and approval for human subject protection by an independent committee or agency such as" an IRB "established under internationally acceptable guidelines," and "[r] eview and authorization or approval by relevant supranational or national regulatory authorities such as the European Medicines Agency (EMA) or the US Food and Drug Administration (FDA) for clinical trial or, where applicable, reimbursed therapies/commercial use based on data provided by the clinic or others under supervised trials; or evidence of exemption from review."[65] If the clinic adequately documents *both* of those things, the ISSCR proposes to list it on its website as "documented," while if it fails to list both ISSCR proposes to list it as "undocumented."[66] The ISSCR very deliberately contends that "the listing of an entity does not imply either ISSCR approval or disapproval, [but] rather that specific elements of inquiry have not been adequately addressed," and that if an entity is not listed it may mean "one of three very different things: no inquiry has been made; the inquiry is still in process; or the clinic has not addressed each of the elements of the inquiry."[67] ISSCR emphasizes the way in which the review is for documentation, not its accuracy or the underlying science.[68] Where a clinic claims it no longer offers the treatment for that disease, "its name will be removed from this listing but a footnote will be included that the clinic no longer treats this disease."[69]

---

[64] ISSCR, *Patients Beware: Commercialized Stem Cell Treatments on the Web*, 7 CELL STEM CELL 43, 46 (2010).

[65] *Id.* at 46–47.

[66] *Id.* at 47.

[67] *Id.*

[68] *Id.*

[69] *Id.*

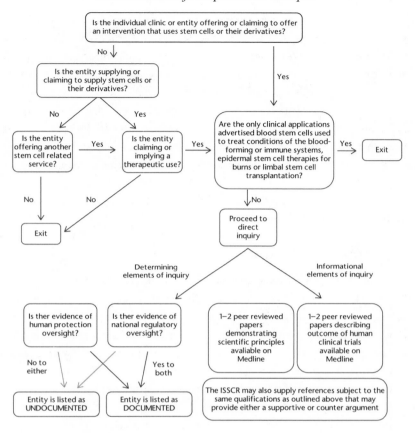

FIGURE 10.1[70] Schematic of Inquiry and Review Process for Listing Stem Cell

ISSCR also proposes to "invite[]" clinics to submit "examples of preclinical and clinical research published in the peer-reviewed literature," and that it will provide references to this literature alongside the individual clinics listing.[71]

ISSCR's proposed system is innovative and thoughtful, and could prove very useful. Unfortunately due to lawyers' letters from individual clinics threatening it with legal action, the ISSCR decided to suspend the program.[72] Although in most jurisdictions truth is a defense to defamation charges, the costs of having to defend such claims in

---

[70] Permission to use this figure has been granted. This figure was published in ISSCR Report, Treatment Providers, Cell Stem Cell 7, 43–49, July 2, 2010. Copyright Elsevier (2010).

[71] *Id.* at 46–48.

[72] *See* Heidi Ledford, *Stem-Cell Scientists Grapple with Clinics Offering Unproved Therapies*, 474 NATURE 550 (2011).

many different jurisdictions across the world is quite threatening to a nonprofit organization whose primary role is bringing together scientists. The ISSCR has tried to explicitly disclaim the notion that its listing counts as an endorsement or caution against any particular clinic offering any particular therapy, and has carefully chosen the terms "documented" and "undocumented," but in reality it seems beyond cavil that the hope of the organization is that its listing will cause prospective patients to shy away from "undocumented" clinics. It would be better to understand the ISSCR proposal as a soft accreditation process, albeit one that focuses on process not substance, similar in spirit (but not at all in scope) to that offered by JCI for other forms of medical tourism, as discussed in Chapter 3.

I will argue that ISSCR is on the right track, but that this approach needs some assistance from governments to be more effective.

ii. Criminalizing and Channeling

As we saw, the ISSCR's attempt to create a soft accreditation system for stem cell therapies appears to be stalled by threats of defamation liability. As a small institution primarily designed to bring scientists together, it lacks the manpower to put in place a robust review process. Moreover, although there is no particular evidence that this is true with ISSCR, one might also worry that given its dues-paying members are scientists in some of the very clinics it regulates, asking it to be the one to engage in this form of accreditation would invite conflicts of interests, or at least the appearance of impropriety.[73]

Just as we discussed for other kinds of medical tourism earlier in this book, an approach I call "channeling" might also be useful here. I propose that we adapt ISSCR's approach but make it governmental or intergovernmental. Specifically a national (such as FDA), or supranational (such as the European Medicines Agency), or international (such as WHO) body could be tasked with implementing an accreditation system building off the ISSCR's model. Like the ISSCR's proposal, the agency would collect information on the two key procedural issues that ISSCR identified: IRB (or its equivalent) approval, and review by a national or supranational regulatory agency. In my ideal world, though, the review process would go further. Not only would it offer the clinics the opportunity to provide supporting peer-reviewed journal articles, but it would *require* that they do so. It could also incorporate several of the safeguards proposed in ISSCR's separate 2008 Guidelines for the Clinical Translation of Stem Cells.

Specifically, it would review the quality of information both on the website and in informed consent documents relating to risks and benefits, the qualifications of the personnel involved in administering and developing the therapies (perhaps based on volume

---

[73] These concerns are, if anything, more manifest with other organizations that have a large number of providers as part of their membership, such as the International Cellular Medicine Society (ICMS), http://www.cellmedicinesociety.org/.

and proficiency), the quality of the data monitoring plan and adverse event reporting system, the quality of stem cells being used and the transparency of the descriptions being offered, the prior preclinical animal modeling of the therapy, and the issue of whether there exists other established therapies for the problem in question. Somewhat similar to the approach taken in human research subjects regulation (I will say more about this below), I propose that the various therapies be grouped into relative risk categories ranging from minimal to significant risk, and that the intensity of the review and the amount demanded on each of these criteria would be proportional to the anticipated risk posed by the procedure (including what is known about tumorgenecity) but also the stage of decline of the patient and possible benefit (i.e., more risks would be tolerable for clinics catering to terminally ill patients who face imminent death). Moreover, my proposed regulator would not wait for patients to initiate a review request the way the ISSCR has, but would instead actively seek out those who advertise these therapies and ask them for supporting documents.

The result would be a kind of regulatory "seal of approval," like the accreditation that JCI currently offers medical tourism facilities not engaged in the experimental side. One existing governmental analog is the American Centers for Disease Control and Prevention (CDC) reporting on assisted reproductive technologies.[74] For each clinic in the United States, the CDC provides a searchable database including the various types of reproductive technology assistance provided, the patient diagnosis, and the success rates.[75]

What I am envisioning is something halfway between the detailed database CDC creates and the binary "documented/undocumented" distinction ISSCR proposed. While trying to avoid information overload for patients,[76] the approval system would at the very least provide a measure of three separate things. At the threshold it would indicate whether the clinic has met the regulatory compliance requirements (or perhaps some subset of them) such as IRB (or other oversight committee) approval, adverse event reporting, adequate informed consent, etc. This compliance could be ensured through relatively nonexpert individuals of the kind that populate many of the potential agencies I have in mind, and focuses more (though not exclusively) on the process elements. For clinics that comply and provide the relevant information, the regulator would then "rate" the therapy being offered into one of three risk categories (minimal, medium, and high,

---

[74] The data is available at http://www.cdc.gov/art/ARTReports.htm. For the statute requiring clinics to provide the information, *see* 42 U.S.C. § 263a-5(1)(A) (2006). For an in-depth discussion of the information contained in this database, *see* I. Glenn Cohen & Daniel L. Chen, *Trading-Off Reproductive Technology and Adoption: Does Subsidizing IVF Decrease Adoption Rates and Should It Matter?*, 95 Minn. L. Rev. 485, 540–41 (2010).

[75] Cohen & Chen, *supra* note 74, Although a small number of clinics do not comply, the non-reporting clinics are also reported as such with attendant reputational consequences. *See id.*

[76] For a discussion of this concern and the behavioral economics evidence behind it, *see* Cohen, *supra* note 9, at 1506–11, 1550–53.

recognizing that few of the potential therapies we are discussing will fall in the minimal risk category) and also one of three levels of scientific validation (well-established, some evidence, poorly validated). This type of assessment would require more stem cell scientific expertise, but an institution such as the FDA could draw on the same mix of internal and external talent it currently does in reviewing drug protocols. Importantly, I would apply this proposed framework to all forms of stem cell therapies, and thus consider it orthogonal to the question of whether autologous stem cell therapies are medical services versus falling under the traditional jurisdiction of agencies such as the FDA. Here, I am more interested in the functional reasons for this kind of review, which apply to all forms of stem cell therapies, than traditional agency divisions of labor.

Although for the sake of uniformity it would be desirable to have one agency involved in these assessments, for the sake of getting it off the ground and comity, it may be that the ultimate reviewing agency should also be willing to defer to national research bodies that have approved individual clinics and "piggyback" on that approval. My own sense is that this trade-off between uniformity and comity would depend on how harmonized the underlying approaches of national bodies were to the list I have suggested; it would be all right to tolerate some divergence in review approach but not too much. Although in their patient blog study Ryan and her colleagues expressed legitimate concern that a "neutral third party, not an agency or organization perceived by patients to be an advocate for the status quo, as some patients expressed distrust of the western medical establishment,"[77] the experience with the ISSCR-proposed website's failure to deploy due to litigation threats suggests to me that an entity large and well-heeled enough to fend off litigation threats and intimidation might be needed. Although this does not necessarily have to be an existing agency or set of agencies, and could be a governmentally created entity with representation from various stakeholders, I do think that something with State-support is necessary rather than an NGO. To be sure, this will be no easy task. In particular, clinics that are doing well financially may not have the incentive to participate in a process that will expose their practices to negative reviews. The best way to achieve compliance, as I discuss in more depth below, is a combination of carrot and stick. The carrot is access to a pool of patients whose care is covered by domestic private or public insurers conditional on accreditation; the stick is fraud prosecutions and increasing domestic regulation by destination country authorities. This will require a long-drawn-out process of stakeholder consensus building, but seems to me the best way forward.

The bigger question is whether this informational intervention would go far enough. As we saw in Chapter 2, patients frequently ignore other informational interventions in the health care arena.[78] Indeed, for stem cell therapies specifically, as Einsendel and

---

[77] Ryan et al., *supra* note 37, at 32.
[78] *See also id.*

Adamson's focus group study above concluded, even when individuals were exposed to "cautionary information…most remained receptive to obtaining (unproven) treatments under desperate circumstances," the patient blog study had similar conclusions,[79] and Chen and Gottweis's patient study showed that many patients were deeply skeptical of the motives or attitudes of home country authorities that were naysayers.[80] On the one hand, there is something quite different between being provided a general guideline and being told that a regulatory agency has *not* "approved" a given therapy as being grounded in clinical evidence and of acceptable risks. On the other hand, the participants in Einsendel and Adamson's study were healthy, but asked to imagine themselves as having various illnesses, and if anything the vulnerability and desperation of patients actually facing terminal or highly debilitating diseases is likely to be greater still.

The real question is what it would mean to go further as a regulatory matter. On one extreme, one could theoretically imagine seeking to subject these foreign clinics to the same rules regarding promoting and providing experimental therapies outside of established clinical trials that apply in the United States (or other home countries). This would essentially criminalize the activity of these foreign clinics as an extraterritorial extension of the law of the home country similar to what we discussed in prior chapters. As a matter of international law, it may be possible to defend such a move as consistent with passive personality prescriptive jurisdiction, as discussed in Chapter 8, in which jurisdiction is asserted based on the fact that the victim (rather than perpetrator) is a national of one's State, although as one leading treatise suggests, this principle's increased acceptance as a basis for prescriptive jurisdiction is category-specific, that although it is "widely tolerated when used to prosecute terrorists," it is far from clear that it would be found "acceptable if used to prosecute, for example, adulterers and defamers."[81] It might also be possible to ground jurisdiction in "subjective territorial jurisdiction," which involves crimes that are initiated in one's home territory but completed in another territory, such as loading a bomb in the United States on to a plane that will explode in Israel.[82] The argument would be that the advertising and recruitment of patients from abroad by websites in the United States constitutes the beginning of a crime within the United States, though whether that assertion would hold up in court is far from certain, as I discuss in regards to fraud below. Moreover, even if it were possible to assert prescriptive jurisdiction over these foreign facilities, actually prosecuting them in the United States is a different matter; unlike some of the other forms of circumvention tourism discussed in the last few chapters (abortion, assisted suicide, reproductive technology), here we are targeting the behavior of the foreign corporation rather than the home country citizen, and it may be difficult to enforce a civil or criminal judgment against a foreign corporation from the home country's court.

---

[79] Einsendel & Adamson, *supra* note 41, at 42; Ryan et al., *supra* note 37, at 31–32.

[80] *See* Chen & Gottweis, *supra* note 39, at 11, 13.

[81] Vaughn Lowe, *Jurisdiction, in* MALCOLM D. EVANS, INTERNATIONAL LAW 335, 351–52 (2d ed. 2006).

[82] *Id.*

Moreover, even if it were possible to effectuate an extension of the U.S. domestic criminal prohibition to foreign providers, the argument for doing so seems less compelling to
me than in other instances of circumvention tourism I have discussed, particularly abortion, when we understand the true motivation for the *domestic* prohibition on accessing
therapies that have not been through the clinical trial regime. To illustrate, consider a
recent landmark U.S. case where terminally ill patients sought a right to access drugs
outside of the clinical trial regime that had made it through Phase I clinical testing but
had gone no further, *Abigail Alliance v. Eschenbach*.[83] As an argument for the constitutionality of the statute, the FDA articulated its interest in protecting patients from
harm, which included even terminally ill patients for whom unapproved therapies could
hasten death, which the court ultimately accepted.[84] That is an explicitly paternalistic
argument for State regulation.

Although we do not want to tread too deeply into these waters, there is a long libertarian tradition rejecting the use of criminal law sanctions to protect individuals from
their own bad decisions, and the experimental drug case for terminally ill patients seems
a particularly hard one because there is (at least in the patient's own mind) some chance
of benefit for which he or she may be prepared to accept the risk.[85] Indeed at least one
author has analogized the right involved to be one of "medical self-defense," an analogy
the *Abigail Alliance* court ultimately rejected.[86] There is also the complicated fact that
in their own welfare assessments, some patients might prefer hope (even if false) with
risks, to no hope and no risks.[87] To the extent criminalizing patient use of experimental
drugs or therapies is already a close issue, and to the extent one believes that paternalism is a weaker justification for criminal law than preventing harm to others, there is a

---

[83] Abigail Alliance for Better Access to Developmental Drugs v. von Eschenbach, 495 F.3d 695 (D.C. Cir.
2007) (en banc). In the interests of full disclosure, I represented the government in the *En Banc* petition in
this case.

[84] *Id.* at 712–13.

[85] *See, e.g.*, JOEL FEINBERG III, THE MORAL LIMITS OF THE CRIMINAL LAW: HARM TO SELF (1986);
Mark S. Stein & Julian Savulescu, *Welfare versus Autonomy in Human Subjects Research*, 38 FLA. ST. U. L.
REV. 303 (2011); Eugene Volokh, *Medical Self-Defense, Prohibited Experimental Therapies, and Payment for
Organs*, 120 HARV. L. REV. 1813 (2007).

[86] *Compare* Volokh, *supra* note 85, *with Abigail Alliance*, 495 F.3d at 708–10.

[87] *See, e.g.*, Murdoch & Scott, *supra* note 50, at 20. Hope is valuable, and where placebo effects may result
in beneficial gains, that is something that needs to be factored in, although I think Murdock and Scott
again take things further than I would when they observe that "[i]f we remove alternative options for these
individuals, there may be an argument we rob them of hope, hope that itself could produce a net beneficial
outcome." *Id.* I would also disagree with their argument that it is "too strong" to say that "social systems
operating without peer review and preclinical evidence of efficacy be condemned," *id.* and am much closer
to the ISSCR's position on this, especially where safety risks are involved. Where I would agree with them
is not so much about whether "condemnation" is justified in such circumstances (I think it is), but the
permissible scope of state intervention to prevent individuals from using these services, where I am more
libertarian when it comes to adult users and more paternalistic when it comes to pediatric ones.

stronger argument for permitting "Exit-light" (as I have termed it earlier in this book) and permitting circumvention tourism, especially for patients facing terminal illnesses.

One might object that the domestic prohibitions are not wholly paternalistic, that, as some authors (but not the *Abigail Alliance* court majority) have argued, there is a second justification that focuses on the success of the research process. Because in most clinical trials for life-saving therapies patients are randomly assigned to either the standard treatment or an experimental treatment (in this setting there are few placebos), the "[f]ear is that if those seeking experimental drugs have free access, they will not volunteer to be subjects in a clinical trial, where they will likely have no more than a fifty percent chance of receiving the experimental drugs they seek."[88]

That fear is not purely speculative: there are claims that this is what occurred with autologous bone marrow transplantation as part of the therapy for metastatic breast cancer in the United States; the widespread availability of the therapy outside of clinical trials made it difficult to recruit subjects and thereby delayed the completion of clinical trials, such that it took far longer for the scientific establishment to determine that high-dose chemotherapy with bone marrow transplant was inferior to standard chemotherapy.[89] Some have claimed that denying patients access to experimental drugs outside of clinical trials is unacceptably coercive, while others have responded that patients have no rights claim to an experimental drug, especially one with no proven effectiveness, and any loss of their autonomy can be justified by increased welfare to those who benefit from speedier drug trials.[90]

We need not resolve this debate fully. Instead, I think it is enough to say that the effects of failing to criminalize the travel abroad for stem cell therapies is less likely to delay clinical trials of those therapies domestically, for several reasons. First, fewer patients have the wherewithal to go abroad compared to those who would use the experimental therapy domestically were it available, so the effect on clinical trials at home will be muted. This is especially true when we consider the high prices charged for these therapies (as discussed above) and the fact that insurance will not cover them. Second, there are few if any stem cell therapies for which clinical trials are being done in the United States (or other home countries) to delay, which is not true as to other areas of medical innovation. This last point cuts both ways—the paucity of clinical trials for the types of stem cell therapies being offered abroad is at least in part a reflection of the fact that those with the resources to conduct such trials have not found them promising, but that goes more to the paternalism problem discussed above.

Thus, some combination of administrative (the difficulty in implementing a prohibition on going abroad for these therapies) and normative (the weaker justification for

---

[88] Stein & Savulescu, *supra* note 85, at 318.

[89] *See* Ezekiel J. Emanuel, *Drug Addiction*, New Republic, July 3, 2006, at 9; Stein & Savulescu, *supra* note 85, at 318.

[90] *See* Stein & Savulescu, *supra* note 85, at 322 (summarizing this debate).

acting on paternalistic motives) reasons lead me to think that criminalizing the activities of these stem cell clinics abroad outright would be wrongheaded.

Is there a happy medium between criminalization and purely informational/accreditation approaches? Channeling, an approach I have championed elsewhere in this book, may again offer a promising alternative especially on the reimbursement side. If home country public and private insurers undertook only to reimburse patients for services sought by "approved" stem cell clinics, that would have two effects: first, a communicative effect, whereby the quality of the public or private insurer's endorsement amplifies and draws attention to the accreditation, both for patients examining the marketplace and for clinics that want access to that reimbursement revenue. Second, it has a revenue-directing effect whereby the hope is that the approved clinics can use the extra revenue to thrive and the clinics selling modern-day snake oil get pushed out of the market.

That would be a happy end to our story. How realistic is it? It is hard to know. One problem with channeling in this domain is that insurers may be unable/unwilling to reimburse for stem cell therapies that have not achieved the *highest* echelon of acceptance into clinical practice already, such that we will find it difficult to use channeling to draw distinctions between "snake-oil" therapies and very promising therapies that have considerable scientific backing but are not yet approved. One possibility would be for governments to "put their money where their mouth is" and agree to fund therapies receiving high marks in the approval/accreditation system I have proposed above, essentially creating a kind of prize system for safe, ethical, and effective innovation in this domain, but it is unclear how realistic a proposal that is. Until and unless enough money is flowing in the stem cell therapy world to providers of "approved" therapies, it may be hard to get a channeling regime off the ground. There may be additional complications from the translational medical nature of stem cell therapies. Unlike pharmaceuticals, where industry is involved during the development process, the same may not be true for stem cell therapies.

Moreover, and this is worth emphasizing, if the standards are set as high as one might all things being equal want to set them, it is possible that few (if any) foreign clinics will qualify. The most promising middle-term strategy is to attempt to partially co-opt the lobbying force of patient advocacy groups, so that when they press for increased funding for disease-specific therapies and research, governments can condition that funding on going to approved centers of excellence rather than being more generally available. Paradoxically, it may also be desirable to lower the standards for approval at first (for example by focusing in safety and stem cell provenance more than effectiveness) to try and exclude the bad apples, and then slowly increase the requirements in a way that keeps pace with innovation.

Alongside these initiatives, authorities should where possible pursue common law fraud or consumer fraud actions against clinics making false claims.[91] I say "where

---

[91] In the United States common law fraud requires establishing five basic elements: "(1) a false representation or concealment of fact; (2) knowledge of its falsity; (3) the intent to induce reliance; (4) justifiable reliance;

possible," because at least in the United States there will be difficulties in asserting personal jurisdiction against some clinics if their websites are largely passive and provide information and advertising, rather than interactively enabling prospective patients to request a quote from the clinic or specifically reaching out to U.S. patients, because of the doctrinal developments discussed in Chapter 3.[92]

Criminal actions are also a possibility. In 2006, two American citizens were prosecuted for "providing false and misleading information to individuals suffering from incurable diseases" such as ALS and multiple sclerosis, by promising stem cell therapies that were not scientifically grounded, in violation of various provisions of the Public Health Service Act and the Food Drug and Cosmetic Act.[93] The charges stemmed both out of their website, www.biomark-intl.com, and their activities injecting patients with purported stem cell treatments, and were jurisdictionally possible in part due to the fact that the website claimed business addresses in Georgia and identified its local address as residential condominium addresses in Georgia and Florida.[94] In exposing their website activities to the jurisdiction of the U.S. courts in this way, these purveyors were careless, and there is no reason to think that most of the stem cell clinics abroad are likely to have similar jurisdictional ties to the United States. The couple fled to South Africa, where they are still fighting extradition, although one of the alleged perpetratorshas since passed away.[95]

In sum, I have argued that stem cell therapies need a distinctive innovation pathway somewhere between the one we use for drugs and the one we use for surgeries in the United States, and that policies on stem cell therapy tourism need to reflect that liminal

and (5) damages." *E.g.*, 37 AM. JUR. 2D FRAUD AND DECEIT § 23 (2014). Most states also have a separate consumer fraud statute that tends to relax some of these requirements in the context of commercial transactions. For example, the Illinois Consumer Fraud Act requires a plaintiff to show only that "(1) a deceptive act or practice, (2) intent on the defendant's part that plaintiff rely on the deception, and (3) that the deception occurred in the course of conduct involving trade or commerce," thus omitting any requirement of to show "actual reliance, an untrue statement regarding a material fact, or knowledge or belief by the party making the statement that the statement was untrue." *See, e.g.*, Martin v. Heinold Commodities, Inc., 643 N.E.2d 734, 754 (1994).

92 In some instances, of course, the defendants may themselves be based in the United States making personal jurisdiction easy. *See, e.g.*, Lee v. Human Biostar Inc, Notice of Removal of Action, CV12 05668 (W.D. Cal. May 21, 2012) (suit against a Korean corporation with offices in California relating to stem cell treatments performed in Korea, claiming for intentional misrepresentation of fact, negligent misrepresentation of fact, false advertising in violation of California Business and Professions Code, unfair competition in violation of California Business and Professions Code, financial elder abuse, negligence, and breach of implied covenant of good faith and fair dealing).

93 *See* Indictment at 1–5, United States of America v. Laura Brown and Steven Mark Van Rooyen, No. 1:06CR1534 (N.D. Ga. Mar. 29, 2006).

94 *Id*. at 2.

95 *See, e.g.*, Katie Hodge, *Doctor "Exploited Vulnerable MS Patients,"* GUARDIAN, Apr. 12, 2010, *available at* http://www.independent.co.uk/life-style/health-and-families/health-news/doctor-exploited-vulnerable-ms-patients-1942713.html; Laura Brown Died, INTERNATIONAL EXTRADITION BLOG, Sept. 6, 2011, *available at* internationalextraditionblog.com/tag/laura-brown-died/.

position. I have applauded the efforts of the ISSCR and others to engage in professional self-regulation, but have discussed why such self-regulation is likely to be insufficient. Instead I have proposed developing an accreditation/approval system based on many of the thoughtful recommendations offered by the ISSCR that could be administered either by a single home country agency (such as the FDA) or by a supranational or international body that would evaluate the therapies being offered by particular clinics, and give patients information on risk, clinical evidence, and oversight and governance. Although, as throughout this book, I recognize the limitations of informational interventions such as the one I have proposed, I also think that for administrative and normative reasons it would be undesirable to try to criminally sanction foreign providers or patients who seek stem cell therapies, especially for patients with terminal illnesses. I have examined whether a form of channeling, akin to what I have proposed elsewhere in this book, might offer us an intermediate position, although I have expressed some concerns about the way the background realities of insurance reimbursement for these kinds of therapies may make channeling more difficult to implement. I have also suggested that civil fraud actions and criminal fraud prosecutions should be used against rogue clinics whose information is false and misleading, while recognizing that jurisdictional limitations will hamper the effectiveness of this method of achieving compliance.

In the remainder of this chapter I consider issues relating to a common subtype of stem cell tourism: parents who want to use stem cell therapies on their minor children.

IV. STEM CELL TOURISM WITH CHILDREN AS PATIENTS

As the review of clinic offerings and patient blogs discussed above reflect, parents are increasingly pursuing stem cell treatments for their children,[96] often going abroad in desperation for cases where there are no accepted alternative treatments available at home.[97] Many of these treatments lack any clinical evidence for effectiveness, and as discussed above, there have been documented cases where children have died or suffered other serious injuries from these stem cell therapies offered abroad. The interplay of children, stem cell therapies, and medical tourism raises two questions: First, can and should the State try to prevent parents from taking their children abroad for these therapies? Second, what is the role of home country pediatricians in advising parents on these

---

[96] In this section I am explicitly focused on stem cell treatments used on children rather than older adolescents. For bioethical purposes, the space between adolescence and adulthood presents much more nuanced and complex bioethical issues. *See, e.g.,* Insoo Hyun, *When Adolescents "Mismanage" Their Chronic Conditions: An Ethical Exploration,* 10 KENNEDY INST. ETHICS J. 147 (2000). Furthermore, bioethical and legal thinking about the capacity and rights of adolescents may diverge in complex ways. In what follows I focus on children.

[97] Amy Zarzeczny & Timothy Caulfield, *Stem Cell Tourism and Doctors' Duties to Minors—A View from Canada,* 10 AM. J. BIOETHICS 3, 5 (2010).

therapies, and potentially reporting them to the authorities if the pediatricians fear for the child's health and safety because of the parent's desire to seek one of these therapies offered in the destination country?

A. Parents, the State, and the Best Interests of Children in Stem Cell Therapies

The law governing parental decision-making over treatment for children varies by nation, and even within a nation sometimes by jurisdiction. I cannot offer a comprehensive analysis based on every nation's laws but in this chapter will instead discuss the way existing U.S. and Canadian law is likely to govern these issues, as well as discuss desirable changes to that jurisprudence as adapted to this context.

i. Existing Canadian and U.S. Law

The United States has largely adopted a balancing approach to parental rights and the protection of children that waxes and wanes based on the area of law involved. Under a doctrine known as family privacy or familial autonomy, the U.S. Supreme Court has begun with the view that the family is a "unit with broad parental authority over minor children," enabling parents to raise children as they see fit and make most decisions about care for children, without government interference.[98] At the same time, even these broad rights are subject to some limitations. Thus as the Supreme Court noted, although "custody, care, and nurture of the child reside first in the parents," the State too has an interest in protecting children's health and safety.[99] The Court has ruled, among other things, that this permits the State to require students to engage in compulsory schooling in tension with parental religious beliefs, be vaccinated, forbid sending their children to work in hazardous occupations, and intervene to protect abused or neglected children.[100]

When it comes to health care though, the courts have been somewhat more deferential of parental prerogative. As Alicia Ouellette has noted, in the United States parents are given "extraordinary power over their children's bodies," which they have used to lawfully do everything from "westernize the eyes of their adoptive Asian children, to modify the facial features of children with Down Syndrome, to inject human growth hormone (HGH) into healthy children, to enlarge the breasts of or suck the fat from teenagers, to attenuate the

---

[98] Parham v. J.R., 442 U.S. 584, 602–03 (1979); *See also* M.L.B. v. S.L.J., 519 U.S. 102, 116 (1996) ("Choices about marriage, family life, and the upbringing of children are among associational rights this Court has ranked as 'of basic importance in our society,' rights sheltered by the Fourteenth Amendment against the State's unwarranted usurpation, disregard, or disrespect." (citations omitted) (quoting Boddie v. Connecticut, 401 U.S. 371, 376 (1971))).

[99] Prince v. Massachusetts, 321 U.S. 158, 166 (1944).

[100] *See, e.g.*, Sturges & Burn Mfg. Co. v. Beauchamp, 231 U.S. 320, 325–26 (1913); Wisconsin v. Yoder, 406 U.S. 205, 226–29 (1972); Vernonia Sch. Dist. 47J v. Acton, 515 U.S. 646, 656 (1995); Zucht v. King, 260 U.S. 174, 176–77 (1922); Hollingsworth v. Hill, 110 F.3d 733, 739 (10th Cir. 1997); *see also* Ouellette, *infra* note 100, at 967–68.

growth and remove the reproductive organs of a child with disabilities, and to remove bone marrow from a nine-year-old girl for use by a brother who sexually abused her."[101]

The leading U.S. Supreme Court case on parental decision-making over children's health care is *Parham v. J.R.* That case involved a challenge to a Georgia law allowing parents to institutionalize children with psychiatric illness, brought on behalf of a six-year-old child whose mother resorted to forced institutionalization after she found herself unable to manage the child at home.[102] The lawsuit alleged that the child's *procedural* due process rights were violated by institutionalizing him without a full adversarial hearing. What is relevant for our purposes is the way the Court framed the scope of parental prerogative. The Court began by noting that "our constitutional system long ago rejected any notion that a child is 'the mere creature of the State' and, on the contrary, asserted that parents generally 'have the right, coupled with the high duty, to recognize and prepare [their children] for additional obligations,'" and then went on to note that "[s]urely, this includes a 'high duty' to recognize symptoms of illness and to seek and follow medical advice."[103] That is, "[t]he law's concept of the family rests on a presumption that parents possess what a child lacks in maturity, experience, and capacity for judgment required for making life's difficult decisions," and that since Blackstone the law has recognized that natural bonds of affection lead parents to act in the best interests of their children."[104] At the same time the Court recognized that this presumption is a rebuttable one and that "a state is not without constitutional control over parental discretion in dealing with children when their physical or mental health is jeopardized."[105] Still the Court made clear that deference to parental views on health care, even in the face of child opposition, would be the constitutional norm:

> Simply because the decision of a parent is not agreeable to a child or because it involves risks does not automatically transfer the power to make that decision from the parents to some agency or officer of the state. The same characterizations can be made for a tonsillectomy, appendectomy, or other medical procedure. Most children, even in adolescence, simply are not able to make sound judgments concerning many decisions, including their need for medical care or treatment. Parents can and must make those judgments. Here, there is no finding by the District Court of even a single instance of bad faith by any parent of any member of appellees' class.... The fact that a child may balk at hospitalization or complain about a parental refusal to provide cosmetic surgery does not diminish the parents' authority to decide what is best for the child....

---

[101] Alicia Ouellette, *Shaping Parental Authority over Children's Bodies*, 85 IND. L.J. 955, 959–60 (2010) (citations omitted).

[102] 442 U.S. 584, 587–97 (1979).

[103] *Id.* at 602–03 (citations omitted).

[104] *Id.* at 602 (citations omitted).

[105] *Id.* at 603.

In defining the respective rights and prerogatives of the child and parent in the voluntary commitment setting, we conclude that our precedents permit the parents to retain a substantial, if not the dominant, role in the decision, absent a finding of neglect or abuse, and that the traditional presumption that the parents act in the best interests of their child should apply. We also conclude, however, that the child's rights and the nature of the commitment decision are such that parents cannot always have absolute and unreviewable discretion to decide whether to have a child institutionalized. They, of course, retain plenary authority to seek such care for their children, subject to a physician's independent examination and medical judgment.[106]

In the wake of *Parham*, there have been some carve-outs where parental authority has been curbed: limitations on or requirements of procedural safeguards before parental decisions bind in cases of refusal of life-sustaining treatment for children, minors' abortions, sterilization, and an outright prohibition at the federal level on female genital cutting of minors.[107]

Most important for our purposes are cases involving parents who opt for experimental or alternative therapies over conventional and clinically established ones. These cases often turn on fact-bound assessments of the evidence presented as to effectiveness and risk of the treatment.

Although it has been more than three decades since its heyday, the key cases in the jurisprudence concern the use of Laetrile instead of other treatments for cancer.[108] Let me discuss two leading precedents from two separate U.S. states to give a sense of the state of the law.

In 1979 the New York Court of Appeals refused to allow the state to intervene (based on a claim of child neglect) when parents opted to treat their seven-year-old who suffered from Hodgkin's disease with nutritional and metabolic therapy, including injections of Laetrile, instead of the standard therapy of radiation and chemotherapy.[109] The court held that "the most significant factor in determining whether a child is being deprived of adequate medical care, and, thus, a neglected child within the meaning of the statute, is whether the parents have provided an acceptable course of medical treatment for their child in light of all the surrounding circumstances."[110] The court rejected the

---

[106] *Id.* at 603–05.

[107] *See* Ouellette, *supra* note 101, at 968–69 (citing Custody of a Minor, 379 N.E.2d 1053 (Mass. 1978); Planned Parenthood of Cent. Missouri v. Danforth, 428 U.S. 52 (1976); 18 U.S.C. § 116 (2006); Wash. Rev. Code § 11.92.043(5) (West 2007); *In re* Guardianship of Hayes, 608 P.2d 635, 641 (Wash. 1980)).

[108] For a comprehensive survey of all published cases from 1912 to 2001 involving conflicts between parents and physicians over appropriate pediatric care, *see generally* Derry Ridgway, *Innocent of Empirical Rigor*, 14 St. Thomas L. Rev. 165 (2001). A review of the cases listed shows that the vast majority involve conflicts with Jehovah's Witnesses or other religious parents rather than the use of experimental therapies that is the focus of our inquiry.

[109] *In re* Hofbauer, 393 N.E.2d 1009, 1011–12 (N.Y. 1979).

[110] *Id.* at 1014.

notion that it could resolve the matter by deciding "whether the parent has made a 'right' or a 'wrong' decision, for the present state of the practice of medicine, despite its vast advances, very seldom permits such definitive conclusions," as well as the idea that the court could "assume the role of a surrogate parent and establish as the objective criteria with which to evaluate a parent's decision its own judgment as to the exact method or degree of medical treatment which should be provided, for such standard is fraught with subjectivity."[111]

Instead the standard it announced was whether "the parents, once having sought accredited medical assistance and having been made aware of the seriousness of their child's affliction and the possibility of cure if a certain mode of treatment is undertaken, have provided for their child a treatment which is recommended by their physician and which has not been totally rejected by all responsible medical authority."[112] On the particular facts of the case, the court found that standard met, noting that the lower courts found "that these findings are supported by the record that numerous qualified doctors have been consulted by Dr. Schachter [who would provide the Laetrile] and have contributed to the child's care; that the parents have both serious and justifiable concerns about the deleterious effects of radiation treatments and chemotherapy; that there is medical proof that the nutritional treatment being administered Joseph was controlling his condition and that such treatment is not as toxic as is the conventional treatment; and that conventional treatments will be administered to the child if his condition so warrants."[113] In emphasizing how much deference it was willing to give the parents in this case, the court took pains to "stress that a parent, in making the sensitive decision as to how the child should be treated, may rely upon the recommendations and competency of the attending physician if he or she is duly licensed to practice medicine in this State, for '[i]f a physician is licensed by the State, he is recognized by the State as capable of exercising acceptable clinical judgment.'"[114] This may be important in the stem cell therapy tourism context where the foreign provider is typically *not* licensed to practice in the home country physician's jurisdiction, and suggests that parents will be more likely to avoid claims of neglect or abuse if a home country physician has been consulted and supports the travel. The court's noting that "conventional treatments will be administered to the child if his condition so warrants" suggests the court was viewing the Laetrile more as a "first attempt," with chemotherapy available to use if it failed, with the chief threat to the patient's health being the forgoing of conventional treatment in the interim until after Laetrile was tried. Understood in these terms, the concerns about stem cell therapies strike me as quite different; their threat is not only their lack of efficacy and delay in using conventional therapy but the independent risks to the patient's health they impose.

---

[111] *Id.*

[112] *Id.*

[113] *Id.*

[114] *Id.* (citation omitted).

A nearly contemporaneous case from Massachusetts went the other way and demonstrates how fact-bound these determinations are: in that case, the Massachusetts Supreme Judicial Court ordered that a three-year-old be given chemotherapy treatment for leukemia over parental objection (and removed the child from parental custody), because it held that evidence supported the findings that the condition was fatal if untreated, that chemotherapy was the only available medical treatment offering a hope for a cure, and "that the risks of the treatment are minimal when compared to the consequences of allowing the disease to go untreated."[115] After that decision, on remand before the trial court the parents indicated that "they now accept the necessity of having their child receive chemotherapy treatment" but sought the "legal authority to supplement the chemotherapy with a program of 'metabolic therapy' involving the daily administration of enzymes, large doses of vitamins, and the drug amygdalin, more popularly known as laetrile."[116] The lower court judge, after reviewing expert testimony from both sides, found that "each major element of the proposed metabolic regimen poses a serious risk of harm to the child," and focusing on Laetrile specifically found that it was

> potentially harmful to the child in three respects: First, the quality of the laetrile that is generally available in this country is poor. The drug is not routinely subjected to testing for quality and purity by the Food and Drug Administration, and as a result, much of it is contaminated by bacteria and fungi and is of varying and uncertain strength. Second, there is a possibility that laetrile might compromise the effectiveness of the chemotherapy treatments. Although there are no studies confirming this fear, neither are there any dispelling it. Third, and of greatest significance, is the possibility of acute or chronic cyanide poisoning arising from the daily ingestion of laetrile.[117]

The case once again came before the Massachusetts Supreme Judicial Court, which concluded that "[f]aced with the facts that metabolic therapy was not only medically ineffective but was poisoning the child, the judge inescapably concluded that the treatment was not consistent with good medical practice, and, most important, was contrary to the best interests of the child," and that this in turn led to the conclusion "that the child is without necessary and proper physical care and that the parents are unwilling to provide that care within the meaning of" the neglect and abuse statute.[118] It distinguished the New York Court of Appeals decision discussed above by noting that "[t]he medical evidence in that case was sharply conflicting," with testimony by two sets of physicians for and against the metabolic therapy, and this was a "far cry from the unsupported stance

---

[115] Custody of a Minor, 379 N.E.2d 1053, 1055–58, 1063 (Mass. 1978).
[116] Custody of a Minor, 393 N.E.2d 836, 838–39 (Mass. 1979).
[117] *Id*. at 841.
[118] *Id*. at 845.

of the parents in the instant case, and the compelling evidence that for this child meta-bolic therapy, including the use of laetrile, is useless and dangerous."[119]

Although one cannot make sweeping conclusions about all stem cell therapies, as the survey of the available data discussed above suggests, many of these therapies lack good (or any) evidence for clinical effectiveness, and pose serious risks of producing tumors and other negative health effects in those subjected to them. My reading of the existing U.S. case law is that parents who would expose their children to many of these therapies are engaging in child neglect or child abuse, for which the State could pursue the removal of custody, guardianship, or an injunction prohibiting the parents from taking their chil-dren abroad for stem cell therapies. That conclusion would be particularly likely, I believe, in a case where the risks of therapy are clear and the patient has not yet exhausted con-ventional therapies, and perhaps less assured where the disorder is life-threatening and there is no conventional therapy available or it has been tried and failed. That said, given that we have no existing U.S. case law on stem cell therapies sought abroad, we will have to wait to see whether future case law bears out this projected path.

Canadian law has reached similar conclusions. In *K v. British Columbia (Public Trustee)*, involving parents who sought a hysterectomy performed on their mentally handicapped child when she began menstruating, due to the child's phobic reaction to the sight of blood. The British Columbia Court of Appeals held that when a "court is reasonably satisfied that the decisions would not be in the best interests of the child, it may and should interfere" but cautioned that courts should "proceed on the premise, also, that wise and caring parents should have the right to make the decision with regard to their child and that generally they are in a better position than a court is to make the decision."[120] In practice, when Canadian courts face these kinds of conflicts—usually due to a clash of views between parents and physicians over the course of treatment—courts have the power to either order treatment the parents opposed or prevent the parents from imposing treatment they desire, when the court determines the best interests of the child are served by the opposite course.[121] In particular, as one academic commentator notes, "courts have consistently refused to order treatment which is desired by the parents but rejected by the treating physician on clinical grounds."[122]

Jurisprudence from several Canadian provinces has also used the equivalent of child abuse and neglect law to appoint guardians in cases of parental and physician disagreement over appropriate pediatric treatment. In *Re M.M.*, the Provincial Court of Alberta made an order for permanent guardianship of a minor pursuant to Alberta's Child, Youth, and Family Enhancement Act, whose touchstone is substantial risk of physical injury to the

---

[119] *Id.* at 846.

[120] K v. British Columbia (Public Trustee), [1985] B.C.W.L.D. 2170 (BCCA), ¶ 3; *see* Zarzeczny & Caulfield, *supra* note 97, at 6.

[121] *See* Zarzeczny & Caulfield, *supra* note 97, at 6.

[122] *Id.* (quoting Sabine Michalowski, *Reversal of Fortune—Re A (Conjoined Twins) and Beyond: Who Should Make Treatment Decisions on Behalf of Young Children?*, 9 HEALTH L.J. 149, ¶ 32 (2001)); Zarzeczny & Caulfield, *supra* note 97, at 6.

child.[123] The court sided with the doctors who wanted to continue providing psychiatric care to a schizophrenic minor, to which the child was responding well, and without which the child would suffer significant ill effects, over the mother who wished to employ naturopathic remedies that had no evidence of effectiveness.[124] To give another example from Canadian law, in *Children's Society of Peel Region v. B. (C.)*, the Ontario Provincial Court ordered that a child diagnosed with cystic fibrosis be provided with a gastronomy tube to provide nourishment over the object of her mother who wanted to instead use nutritional approaches.[125] Although accepting that the mother loved and was committed to her child, the court nonetheless determined that there was "overwhelming uncontradicted, highly reputable medical evidence" regarding the alternative therapies that showed the child was in need of protection "since she requires medical treatment to cure, prevent, or alleviate physical harm or suffering."[126]

As Amy Zarczeny and Timothy Caulfield note, these cases are not a perfect analogue to stem cell tourism because "clear and unconverted expert medical evidence recommended the course of treatment and the consequences of not following it," while in stem cell therapies there are many more unknowns as to both risks and benefits.[127] Still, the analogy is much stronger when there is reason to believe the stem cell therapy poses physical risks (including infection risks for cells produced under poor manufacturing conditions), and in such cases I believe that guardianship or other intervention to prevent that treatment would be authorized by Canadian law, but the matter is admittedly somewhat fact specific.

ii. Where Should the Law Be Going?

Although the existing law on experimental therapies is somewhat unsettled, and we have no existing case law on these child protective issues relating to stem cell therapies, let me use some of the ideas in that case law to formulate an approach courts should take to stem cell therapy cases involving minors.

As is the case more generally, parents seeking stem cell therapies for their children should be afforded a presumption that they are acting in the best interests of their children. However, given that there is no existing scientific literature establishing the effectiveness of stem cell therapies except in a few very specific applications, and given that there are significant documented risks (as discussed above), I think we should understand this presumption as very weak in this context. Guardianship or other State intervention to protect children is appropriate in any case where there is existing evidence that the stem cell therapy in question poses moderate to substantial risk of death or

---

[123] Re M.M., 2007 ABPC 6; Zarzeczny & Caulfield, *supra* note 97, at 7.
[124] Re M.M., 2007 ABPC 6, ¶¶ 6, 13, 21; Zarzeczny & Caulfield, *supra* note 97, at 7.
[125] Children's Society of Peel Region v. B. (C.), [1988] W.D.F.L. 794 (Ont. Prov. Ct. Fm. Ct. Div.).
[126] *Id.* at ¶¶ 32, 51, 70; Zarzeczny & Caulfield, *supra* note 97, at 10.
[127] Zarzczny & Caulfied, *supra* note 97, at 8.

other injury to the child and there is not strong scientific evidence of countervailing benefit to the therapy. Intervention is also appropriate in any case where the risks posed by the therapy are unknown but there is a chance of significant injury.

Thus, to restate the rule somewhat differently, the State should seek to intervene unless there is strong scientific evidence that the risks to the child involved are minor and/or that they are outweighed by the promise of therapeutic benefit, as demonstrated through appropriate preclinical testing. To be clear, this may mean that the State should intervene in most cases of stem cell tourism for pediatric populations currently available today. To be sure, this will require training workers in child and protective services regarding stem cell therapies, who may lack sufficient background or experience to make judgments in these cases.

The case of children with terminal or otherwise extremely debilitating illnesses for which there is no established treatments represents a harder situation. Although I argued for a more libertarian approach to stem cell therapies for adults in general, and in particular as to those facing such illnesses, I think the State is much more justified in restricting parents' ability to use stem cell therapies *on their children*. While I am sympathetic to an individual who says "I would rather take the gamble, to take on some of these risks for a chance of benefit, it is my life to live," I think the situation is quite different for children. Simply put, it is one thing to bet your own life and quite a different thing to bet your child's life.

With that general approach set out, let me add some nuance.

First, the channeling/approval system I proposed above could be usefully adapted for the case of children, and we could (by separate legislation or by developing the case law) as a safe harbor from child abuse or neglect charges the use of a therapy that had received the requisite level of approval, or at least create a rebuttable presumption to that effect.

Second, as I have stressed above, stem cell therapies fall in the shadowland between research and treatment. The United States has a well-established set of rules that govern participation of minors in *experimental* research, including therapeutic research. If run as a clinical research aimed at regulatory approval, stem cell therapies would have to meet the requirements of these rules, often referred to as Subpart D of the Common Rule.[128] I have discussed these rules in great depth elsewhere,[129] but for our purposes a passing glance will be enough. Under the review and supervision of an IRB, the rules recognize four types of ethically permissible research on children:

First, section 46.404 pertains to research not involving greater than minimal risk. This is permissible with the child's assent and the permission of one parent.

---

[128] *See, e.g.*, I. Glenn Cohen, *Therapeutic Orphans, Pediatric Victims? The Best Pharmaceuticals for Children Act and Existing Human Subject Protections*, 58 Food & Drug L.J. 661, 678–79 (2003).

[129] *See generally id.*

Second, section 46.405 addresses research involving greater than minimal risk but presenting the prospect of direct benefit to the individual subjects, sometimes referred to as "therapeutic research" or "beneficial research." This means that if the hypothesis of the research is correct, the subjects who participate should receive direct benefit from their participation. The IRB is required to find that: 1) the risk is justified by the "anticipated benefit to the subjects"; 2) the child assents; and 3) at least one parent gives permission.

Third, section 46.406 allows research involving greater than minimal risk and no prospect of direct benefit to individual subjects, but likely to yield generalizable knowledge about the subject's disorder or condition. This class of research is permitted: 1) if the risk represents a "minor increase over minimal risk"; 2) the interventions are "reasonably commensurate" with those inherent in their actual medical, dental, social, or educational situations; 3) the intervention is "likely" to yield generalizable knowledge "about the subject's disorder or condition" that is of "vital importance" for the understanding or amelioration of the disorder or condition; 4) the child assents; and 5) both parents (if they are available) give their permission....

Fourth, section 46.407 discusses research not otherwise approvable that presents an opportunity to understand, prevent, or alleviate a serious problem affecting the health or welfare of children. This section presents a procedure whereby the secretary of [DHHS] can have the opportunity to approve research that is not approvable under the other three sections.[130]

If a destination country's stem cell clinic meets the requirements of these rules, or perhaps the rules governing pediatric research in other countries with well-regarded research infrastructures, there should be a rebuttable presumption that the parents have not engaged in child neglect or abuse and can pursue the stem cell therapy. We can see these requirements as representing two separate aims—the protection of pediatric human subjects and the production of usable and useful research—that are often intertwined but need not be. One possible way to expand this safe harbor would be to grant the rebuttable presumption to therapies that have many of the safeguards of true experimental research (as to unbiased review, risk-to-benefit ratio, and appropriate child assent or consent) even if the therapy is being pursued as therapy with no intention of systematic study to produce generalizable knowledge. There would be some downsides to such an expansion—it would reduce the incentive to publish findings or have them rigorously evaluated such that ineffective or dangerous therapies might be offered indefinitely—but this may also be a more appropriate way to enable parents to get access to innovative therapies that have some promise. I have mixed feelings about whether such an expansion of the safe harbor is wise, but at the very least I would want to also build

---

[130] Leonard H. Glantz, *Research with Children*, 24 AM. J.L. & MED. 213, 230–31 (1998).

in some time limit, such that parents using such therapies would only be within the safe harbor when the therapy had been used by the clinic offering it without pursuing clinical trials for under two years. This would create a timeline of brief nonclinical trial therapeutic innovation followed as a pathway to proper research geared toward approval.

Third, it is worth emphasizing the way in which the typical State mechanisms for detecting child abuse and neglect, with admittedly limited effectiveness already, are further hampered in the stem cell tourism context. With ill children hospitalized or at least seen by home physicians, there is an infrastructure in place for detecting and notifying child and family protective services when parents refuse conventional treatment for a seriously ill child. When a parent, for example, transports the child abroad for stem cell therapy promising a cure for blindness or Crohn's disease, it is less likely that there will be formal mechanisms in place to detect and report it such that the State can intervene before the travel takes place. The best "informant" regarding parental intention to use stem cell therapies is the treating physician, who will often be most aware of parental dissatisfaction as to existing therapies and of when parents are considering experimental therapies, including stem cell treatments sought abroad.[131] Thus, the treating physician is the one who can most usefully be enlisted to set in motion the State's ability to intervene in these cases. Doing so, however, puts physicians in a difficult position: the doctor as double agent. How to manage that complex reality is the matter I turn to next.

B. Doctors' Obligations

Suppose that a patient approaches a doctor indicating the patient has heard about a promising treatment for Crohn's disease being offered at a stem cell clinic in China, and is thinking of taking his or her nine-year-old child to that clinic for treatment. How should the physician proceed?

There are no existing codes of conduct for physicians specifically governing stem cell tourism, but as Zarczeny and Caulfield have suggested, existing guidance on patients seeking Complimentary and Alternative Medicines (CAM) can help us find a path forward.[132] When a patient indicates an interest in pursuing CAM, "[t]he consensus in Canada appears to be that while there has not been substantive consideration of the issue, physicians may be required to discuss with the patient both the known and unknown risks associated with the CAM," and the Australian Medical Association has suggested a similar rule.[133]

---

[131] Of course, given parental suspicion of the home country medical establishment, as noted above, many parents are likely not to disclose their stem cell tourism plans to their physicians such that this will not be a perfect safeguard. Instead it should be seen for what it is: the best we can do.

[132] Zarzeczny & Caulfield, *supra* note 97, at 8.

[133] *Id.* at 9.

In the United States, the American Academy of Pediatrics has provided a guidance document on CAM aimed at physicians treating children with disabilities, that, among other things, urges pediatricians to "seek information for yourself and be prepared to share it with families," to "[e]valuate the scientific merit of specific therapeutic approaches," to identify both "direct" harms (e.g., toxic effects, compromising nutrition, interrupting effective therapies the child is already using, postponing use of therapies with proven effectiveness) and "indirect" harms (e.g., costs to the family, time investment in getting the therapy, and guilt associated with inability to adhere to a rigorous treatment regime).[134] The Guidance also encourages doctors to provide families with information on a range of treatment options, to avoid feelings of powerlessness, to advise patients to be "vigilant for exaggerated claims of cure, especially if such claims are for treatments requiring intense commitments of time, energy, and money," and to avoid "dismissal of CAM in ways that communicate lack of sensitivity or concern for the family's perspective."[135]

In principle, all of the Guidance advice stated thus far is equally applicable to the case of stem cell therapy. With sensitivity to the desperation that is driving some parents to take their children halfway across the world for injections of stem cells, home country pediatricians should give an honest appraisal of the risks and benefits as well as alternative treatment possibilities. Understanding the science behind CAM and its claims, where there is some, is well within the competency of the average pediatrician. The science behind stem cell therapies is much more complex and moving much quicker such that the duties of inquiry suggested by this Guidance may be less realistic for pediatricians.

In any event, the governmentally organized approval/channeling system I have outlined above can helpfully fill gaps here. It would enable pediatricians to much more quickly and easily understand just what the foreign clinic proposes to do, the rigors of the review process it has undergone, and the dangers involved, and to find whatever peer-reviewed data supports the claims. Of course, this will not be available for clinics whose therapies are unapproved, but this too can give pediatricians a useful tool by allowing them to explain to patients that a clinic they are eyeing is unapproved, the ramifications of that lack of approval for whether the clinic is offering promising and safe therapies, and the ability to channel patients to other clinics that have been approved.

What about parents who nonetheless want to pursue a treatment that the pediatrician finds too risky? Again the CAM Guidance is useful. As it suggests, "[i]f a child receiving alternative therapy is at direct or indirect risk of harm, the pediatrician should advise against the therapy. In some circumstances, it may be necessary for the pediatrician to

---

[134] American Academy of Pediatrics' Committee on Children With Disabilities (AAPCCD), *Counseling Families Who Choose Complementary and Alternative Medicine for Their Child with Chronic Illness or Disability*, 107 PEDIATRICS 598–601, 600 (2001).

[135] *Id.*

seek an ethics consult or to refer to child welfare agencies. If there is no risk of direct or indirect harm, a pediatrician should be neutral."[136]

Focusing on the Canadian context, Zarceczny and Caulfield have reached a similar conclusion suggesting that the possible cases can be divided into three: (1) those where, contrary to physician recommendation, parents pursue stem cell therapies with clear risks, where reporting duties are likely to be triggered; (2) those where a child is stable and parents want to pursue a treatment to improve his condition, where they think that reporting duties will be triggered only in the "rare circumstance" where there is "evidence of significant risk"; (3) those where a child has a serious degenerative condition with no recommended alternative therapy, where they think obligations to report would be "unlikely."[137]

I am generally in agreement with their conclusions but would go a little bit further than they do. In the United States, every state requires physicians to report instances of child abuse; a majority of states require the reporting of instances of suspected child abuse.[138] Where the doctor thinks the stem cell therapy poses risks, I agree with the American Academy of Pediatrics and with Zarceczny and Caulfield that the right sequence is for physicians to attempt to dissuade by first providing information and an assessment of the risks, then seek to actively dissuade parents from choosing stem cell tourism, and only then consider reporting the parents to child and protective services.

I would, however, advocate for a lower threshold for when such reporting is appropriate that mirrors my claim above as to when State intervention is appropriate. I proposed that the State should seek to intervene unless there is strong scientific evidence that the risks to the child involved are minor and/or that they are outweighed by the promise of therapeutic benefit, as demonstrated through appropriate preclinical testing. This differs from Zarceczny and Caulfield in that in cases involving unknown safety risks to children from stem cell therapies, I would trigger reporting requirements, while they would limit it to cases where there are known substantial risks.[139] Moreover, for cases involving terminal or degenerative conditions with no recommended alternative therapies, I would be less quick to assume that there will not be reporting requirements triggered; merely because one can say "she will die if we do not act" does not justify authorizing parents to take any course available, whatever the risk. The key question is "are the anticipated pain

---

[136] *Id.* at 601.

[137] Zarceczny & Caulfield, *supra* note 97, at 10.

[138] *See, e.g.*, Hadley Hamilton & Samuel D. Hodge, Jr., *A Look behind the Closed Doors of the Emergency Room—A Medical/Legal Perspective*, 16 MICH. ST. U. J. MED. & L. 1, 16 (2011) (citing Malkeet Gupta, *Mandatory Reporting Laws and the Emergency Physician*, 49 ANNALS EMERGENCY MED. 369, 371 (2007)); Levine & Wolf, *supra* note 35, at 129.

[139] Like Zarceczny and Caulfied, Levine and Wolf would allow for more discretion in this zone than I would, observing that "the more challenging situation is also the more common one for SCBIs where harms are uncertain, but plausible. In such cases, a physician must evaluate on which end of the spectrum the SCBI falls based on available (but uncertain) information and her own medical judgment." *Id.* at 129.

and suffering of the child and/or hastening of death, possible further degeneration, justified by the promise of therapeutic benefit?" For many existing stem cell therapies being offered abroad, I think the answer is likely no, such that reporting and State intervention will be more often appropriate than Zarczeny and Caulfield seem to endorse.

The cases of children with terminal or otherwise extremely debilitating illnesses without established treatments represent a harder judgment. Although I argued for a more libertarian approach to stem cell therapies for adults in general, and in particular as to those facing such illnesses, I think the State is much more justified in restricting parents' ability to use stem cell therapies *on their children*. To be sure, there are major difficulties here to which one cannot turn a blind eye: in some cases medical guardianship/custody will not be enough to prevent parents from taking their children abroad, and instead full State guardianship or custody will be required. We do not always do well for children in such custody, and the worry is more serious for a child who is already quite ill. My hope is the threat of State intervention will in many cases cause parents to back down and obviate the need for actually taking the children into State custody. Still in cases where that is the only way forward, though tragic, I think the State has a responsibility to act.

What about the opposite situation? Can a physician face liability for *failing* to inform a parent about a possible stem cell therapy abroad for his or her child? As a legal matter, this is best thought of as an issue of whether the physician has obtained adequate informed consent for the non–stem cell therapy the physician would otherwise perform.[140] As part of this obligation, in the United States, as in most countries, the physician must disclose "material information to the patient about the patient's diagnosis and prognosis, the risks, benefits and consequences of the proposed treatment, as well as any alternative treatments, which includes the option of no treatment."[141] In the United States there are currently two competing disclosure rules, one focused on what a reasonable *physician* would disclose and the other as to what a reasonable *patient* would want disclosed, with U.S. jurisdictions differing on the matter.[142] Even within the patient standard for disclosure, there is some variation in the way courts handle the matter, with most courts using an objective test, asking whether a reasonable person would regard the information as important, with a minority of courts using a subjective test that looks to the prior knowledge and preferences of the particular patient.[143]

As Aaron D. Levine and Leslie E. Wolf argue, under either standard, there should currently be no legal obligation for the physician to disclose the possibility of alternative stem cell therapies that have not yet received regulatory approval.[144]

---

[140] *See* Levine & Wolf, *supra* note 35, at 126.

[141] *Id.* (citing Canterbury v. Spence, 464 F.2d 772 (D.C. Cir. 1972)).

[142] *Id.; see also* MARK HALL ET AL., HEALTH CARE LAW AND ETHICS 213–15 (7th ed. 2007).

[143] Lars Noah, *Informed Consent and the Elusive Dichotomy between Standard and Experimental Therapy*, 28 AM. J.L. & MED. 361, 367–68 (2002).

[144] Levine & Wolf, *supra* note 35, at 126.

They note one California Appellate Court decision, *Schiff v. Pardos*,[145] that seems very much on point. The case was brought by the parents of a child who died from a malignant brain tumor against the neurosurgeon and others who treated the child, claiming their consent to treatment (surgery followed by aggressive radiation and chemotherapy) was not informed, because the physicians did not tell them about an experimental treatment offered by a Texas physician, even though they specifically asked about available alternative treatments.[146] They discovered the experimental treatment after the treatment offered by their neurosurgeon failed to completely remove the child's tumor, and then spoke to the neurosurgeon about the experimental operation, who told them he was "adamantly opposed" to it.[147] The treatment in question was not FDA approved and criminal and licensing actions were pending against the Texas doctor who offered it.[148]

The California Court of Appeals affirmed the trial court and found that the duty of informed consent extended only to "available choices," and any non–FDA approved treatment was not "available" in California within the meaning of informed consent law.[149] Indeed, the court went further and suggested there is no duty to inform patients about treatment alternatives not available in California but available in other states, and that this would be "beyond what the law expects from physicians."[150] Moreover, the court held that there "there is no general duty of disclosure with respect to non-recommended procedures," although whether an alternative treatment should be "recommended" will be determined based on what a reasonable physician would recommend.[151]

Although it is only the decision of an appellate court in one jurisdiction of the United States, and thus must be taken with a grain of salt, under *Schiff* it does not seem there is a duty to disclose to patients the possibility of foreign stem cell therapies, even if asked about them, because they are both unapproved by FDA and unavailable in the particular U.S. state of the patient, who must travel abroad for them. Interestingly, although the

---

[145] 92 Cal. App. 4th 692 (2001). The only other comparable case I have uncovered is Moore v. Baker, 989 F.2d 1129, 1133 (11th Cir. 1993), which held that summary judgment was appropriate in a case where the doctor contended he had "no duty to inform Moore about [an alternative therapy] because it is not generally recognized and accepted among the medical community as an alternative treatment for" the patient's condition. *Id.* The court noted that the "evidence overwhelmingly suggests that the mainstream medical community does not recognize or accept" that therapy as an alternative treatment for the disease in question, and that opposition to the therapy was premised not only "upon the lack of objective evidence that the treatment is effective, but also upon evidence that the treatment may be dangerous." *Id.* Although the court seems to endorse a general rule similar to the *Schiff* court of no duty to disclose experimental therapies, it also puts a lot of weight on the summary judgment posture of the case, such that it speaks less clearly in support of that conclusion than *Schiff* does. *Id.*

[146] *Id.* at 694–99.

[147] *Id.*

[148] *Id.*

[149] *Id.* at 701–94.

[150] *Id.* at 707.

[151] *Id.* at 701.

case sounds very much like it was decided on the reasonable physician standard, as a formal matter California has adopted the reasonable patient standard, suggesting that the result obtains even on the standard favoring more disclosure.[152]

Although I think the rule in *Schiff* comports with the best understanding of the obligations under a *reasonable physician* standard of disclosure, I have more doubts about its capturing the law as to jurisdictions that adopt a *reasonable patient* standard. In particular, the *Schiff* court seems to have implicitly assumed that a "reasonable patient" would want to know only about approved stem cell therapies available in that state. Given the deep interest in stem cell tourism we are seeing by U.S. patients and/or parents of patients, as a factual matter many U.S. patients *are* interested in these options. This puts a lot of pressure on the concept of reasonableness. Although it is reasonable as a general matter to limit a physician's obligation to know about alternative therapies to approved ones in his or her jurisdiction, in a case such as *Schiff* where the parents explicitly asked about an alternative therapy, it seems harder to justify a failure to inform them of the doctor's assessment of those alternatives to treatment.

All that said, although I do think the decision in *Schiff* is in tension with the existing doctrine on reasonable patient disclosure standards, because in the pediatric (outside of clinical trials) case I believe that we should be discouraging parents from seeking unapproved therapies that carry certain risks, I find the blanket exclusion of all unapproved therapies from informed consent disclosure requirements desirable as a policy matter even if not entirely consistent with existing doctrine.

Although I have discussed these disclosure requirements in the context of pediatric populations, the same standards apply when it is adults rather than children who are being treated. Although I conclude that doctors have discretion not to inform patients about possible experimental stem cell treatments available abroad, in some instances they might nonetheless choose to do so. When they refer patients to foreign clinics they may face potential referral liability and obligations relating to follow-up care, as discussed in Chapter 3.

V. CONCLUSION

There are many reasons the typical path for innovation in the United States and other home countries may not be a good fit for developments in stem cells. At the same time, as the empirical studies described at the beginning of this chapter suggest, currently patients (and in the case of children, their parents) are going abroad to access treatments with serious or unknown health risks and little prospect of therapeutic benefit, given

---

[152] James A. Bulen, Jr., *Complementary and Alternative Medicine: Ethical and Legal Aspects of Informed Consent to Treatment*, 24 J. LEGAL MED. 331, 345 (2003) (citing Cobbs v. Grant, 502 P.2d 1 (Cal. 1972)). The *Schiff* court acknowledged this as well. *Schiff*, 92 Cal. App. 4th at 702.

what we know about current stem cell therapeutic science. I do not mean to downplay the importance of hope and placebo benefits, but there is a line between the experimental ethos and fraud, and my own view of the existing literature is that many (though not all) of the stem cell clinics offering therapeutics today are engaging in fraud or at least taking advantage of patients.

The harder question is what to do about it. The ISSCR has spearheaded a form of professional self-regulation that I applaud and would like to see continued. Its attempt to have a public web-based review system of existing therapies, though, never got off the ground, in part because of liability concerns. I have suggested building on the system they had intended to implement and transforming it into an accreditation/approval system that could be administered either by a single home country agency (such as the FDA) or by a supranational or international body that would evaluate the therapies being offered by particular clinics, and give patients information on risk, clinical evidence, and oversight and governance.

The existing literature on information provision in stem cell therapies suggests that it may be difficult by providing this information to shake loose the pull of hope that motivates many of these patients. Although in theory we could go further and seek to actually try to criminalize the behaviors of patients going abroad for their own stem cell treatments, for administrative and normative reasons, I have argued against this more forceful approach, while suggesting increased pursuit of fraud charges against offending clinics themselves where possible. Instead I have championed a channeling approach in parallel to that I have recommended elsewhere in this book, with the hope that by steering public and private insurers by law toward "approved" stem cell clinics we send not only a signal of quality that draws attention but also direct more revenue toward "good" clinics and help them to thrive. A regulatory attempt to segment "approved" clinics from "bad apples" is also important in managing the public's expectation and confidence, in that it may help promising stem cell therapies escape the "junk science" or "dangerous science" moniker when exposes are done on "bad apples." It may also serve as an important signal to investors and help direct more venture capital and other funding to those whose behavior comports with the best legal, ethical, and scientific processes, and thus incentivize adoption of those standards.

There are some signs of enthusiasm for this kind of a model among the funder community. Alan Trounson and his coauthors, at the California Institute for Regenerative Medicine (CIRM), one of the major U.S. funders of stem cell work, has recently proposed a model they call "Alpha Stem Cell Clinics." As they describe it:

> The Alpha Stem Cell Clinics will have the capability to address the three fundamental functions critical for advancing stem cell–based science into safe, effective, and accessible therapies for patients by: 1) fostering clinical trials; 2) evaluating investigational cell therapies through carefully controlled clinical studies to obtain the evidence needed for establishing safe and effective therapies, and 3) providing

access and delivery of proven therapies to patients. Patients accessing Alpha Stem Cells Clinics will comprise three categories, according to the maturity of the cell therapy they seek (Fig. 1), ranging from patients with no therapeutic options seeking experimental treatment to patients seeking standard of care treatment that will be paid for by their insurance. Clinical trials will require a source of funding, and effective access and delivery will require that the therapy is valued by physicians, patients, and those who pay the bill. In many circumstances, this will, by necessity, require that the therapy have a market advantage over other available therapeutic options and require the appropriate levels of coverage and reimbursement....

The financing of the "Alpha Clinic" will require public support in the beginning, and CIRM sees this as a potential role for this agency in California, which has, through a public initiative, Proposition 71, committed substantial resources toward the goal of advancing stem cell basic research and emerging therapies towards the clinics. Through providing funding, CIRM and analogous funding bodies can also provide a review structure, whereby clinics applying for Alpha Clinic funding and designation would be vetted by clinicians and scientists engaged in translational research, clinical trials, cell therapies, and cell manufacturing (when appropriate). In parallel, the business model will have to develop as the cell therapies move through clinical trials to proven patient availability. Insurance reimbursements will need to accompany these developments to constrain the costs to individual patients. The business model developed for IVF clinics may be useful in this regard. This is a mixture of patient fees and reimbursement in the U.S., but, in other countries, a variety of public and private funding is used successfully.[153]

The Alpha Stem Cell Clinic model is one possible way of implementing the kind of channeling regimes I have championed here and elsewhere in my work. The optimal mix of public and private, state and national, funding and regulation is still very much in the air, and I am hopeful the coming years will enable us to engage in significant experimentation in regulatory design.

When it comes to pediatric patients and their parents, a large swath of the existing patient base for stem cell therapies, I have argued for a considerably more muscular intervention. I have argued that the State should seek to intervene through guardianship or other child and protective services methods to prevent stem cell tourism unless there is strong scientific evidence that the risks to the child involved are minor and/or that they are outweighed by the promise of therapeutic benefit, as demonstrated through appropriate preclinical testing. I would extend this approach even to children facing terminal illnesses or degenerative conditions with no effective treatment. Although sensitive to

---

[153] Alan Trounson et al., *The Alpha Stem Cell Clinic: A Model for Evaluating and Delivering Stem Cell Based Therapies*, 1 STEM CELL TRANSLATIONAL MED. 9, 10 (2012).

the difficult position in which this puts physicians and their desire not to act as a double agent, I have argued that home country physicians bear significant reporting obligations in these cases, as even though parents are acting with the best of intentions, in many instances the result is child abuse. Physicians should seek to dissuade by first providing information and an assessment of the risks, then seek to actively dissuade parents from choosing stem cell tourism, and only then consider reporting the parents to child and protective services. I have also shown that in the United States, physicians do not face liability for breach of informed consent for failing to recommend or even discuss stem cell therapies, and thus can adopt a skeptical eye toward these therapies without the prospect of being sued.

Although my focus has been on stem cells, the most prominent current example, much of what I have said in this chapter is also applicable to other forms of experimental therapy tourism, such as CCSVI ("liberation") therapy for Multiple Sclerosis.

INDEX